CELEBRATING THE MOVING IMAGE

BFI FILM AND TELEVISION HANDBOOK 1994

Supported by

Editors: David Leafe, Terry Ilott
Deputy Editor: Gill Crawford
Consultant Editor: Wayne Drew
Research: Sue George
Statistics research: Phil Wickham
Picture research: Yvonne Salmon
Additional research/editorial assistance: Allen Eyles, Lira Fernandes, Gillian Hartnoll, Jane Ivey, Geraldine Jeffers, Vanessa Maddox, Linda Wood, Andrew Youdell
Cover: Calvin McKenzie Graphic Design, London
Design: Stone Design Associates, London; Florencetype, Kewstoke, Avon
Advertisement Manager: Robert Winter

With special thanks to BFI staff for their assistance and advice

With thanks also to all those who assisted with photographs:
Anglia Television, Matthew Antrobus, Artificial Eye Film Co, The Associates, BBC Photographic Library, BBC Picture Publicity, BFI Production, BFI Stills, Posters & Designs, Blue Dolphin Films, Brook Productions, British Sky Broadcasting, Buena Vista, Carlton Television, Central Television, Channel Four Television, Charles McDonald, Hanya Chlala, Cine Electra, Columbia Pictures, Columbia TriStar Films (UK), Contemporary Films, Corbett & Keene, Darwell Smith Associates, Dennis Davidson Associates, The Walt Disney Company, Carlos Dominguez, Andrew Dunsmore, Electric Pictures, Entertainment Group of Companies, Feature Film Company, Film Four International, First Independent, Gala Film Distributors, Samuel Goldwyn, Granada Television, Guild Film Distribution, IAC Film Sales, ICA Projects, Island Pictures, ITC Entertainment Group, J & M Entertainment, Carolyn Jardine Publicity, Lambeth Productions, Lay & Partners, London Weekend Television, Mainline Pictures, Majestic Films, Manifesto Film Sales, Mathieu Thomas, Mayfair Entertainment UK, Mayfair Palace, Meridian Television, Metro Goldwyn Mayer, Metro Pictures, MCEG Virgin Vision, Oasis Film Productions, Optimum Communications, Orion Pictures International, Paramount Pictures, Jörg Pohl, Portman Entertainment, Rank Film Distributors, Rogers & Cowan/PSA, S4C, The Sales Company, Sovereign Pictures, Stone Hallinan McDonald, Thames Television, Jack Tolley, TriStar Pictures, Twentieth Century Fox, United International Pictures (UK), The Video Collection, Warner Bros Distributors, Winsor Beck PR, World Films, Yorkshire Television, Zenith Productions

21 Stephen Street, London W1P 1PL
Tel: 071 255 1444
Fax: 071 436 7950

Made and printed in Great Britain by:
Garden House Press, Perivale, Middlesex

British Library
Cataloguing in Publication Data.
A catalogue record for this book is available from the British Library

ISBN 0 85170 411 5

Price: £14.95

Cover pictures
(Clockwise from top left): Kenneth Branagh's *Much Ado About Nothing* and Mike Leigh's *Naked*, two very different British productions started in 1992 (courtesy of Entertainment Film Distributors/First Independent Films); Moslem refugees at a Bosnian Serb detention camp, the continuing news story of recent months (courtesy of ITN); *Have I Got News for You*, a highly successful independently-commissioned BBC series (courtesy of Hat Trick Productions/BBC); *Lady Chatterley*, controversy surrounding which began even before its transmission (courtesy of London Films/Global Arts); *Jurassic Park*, breaking box-office records across the world in the summer of 1993 (courtesy of UIP); *Wittgenstein* (Channel 4 and BFI in association with Uplink present a Bandung Production, photograph Howard Sooley), a film co-produced by the BFI; *Football Italia*, an example of a new type of sports coverage on television (courtesy of Chrysalis Television Production)

Nicholson Graham & Jones is an award winner under the Business Sponsorship Incentive Scheme for its support of the BFI Film and Television Handbook. The BSIS is a Government Scheme administered by the Association for Business Sponsorship of the Arts

CONTENTS

FOREWORD

The 'BFI Film and Television Handbook' plays an important role in highlighting both the opportunities and obstacles confronting the British film industry. There is no doubt that Britain has the writing, directing and acting talent to produce films which are both culturally and commercially successful.

As our expanded section of statistics demonstrates, British films such as the Oscar-winners *Howards End* and *The Crying Game* can earn not just critical acclaim but significant box-office overseas. Yet, as our statistics also show, British talent is increasingly being denied the investment it needs to prove itself. Even when British films do get made, they are often denied an audience, as evidenced by the new table in our statistical section which highlights the distribution problems facing our filmmakers. In the exciting work of succeeding Lord Attenborough as Chairman of the BFI, one of my priorities is that the BFI should continue to work with Government to tackle such problems.

The Handbook's statistical section provides an important focus on these issues and we are grateful to Nicholson Graham & Jones, whose support has enabled us to maintain both this section and the Directory of facts, contacts and addresses which combine to make up this invaluable reference guide.

Jeremy Thomas
Chairman of the British Film Institute

Richard Blanshard

INTRODUCTION

Film-making is a unique creative process. John Boorman eloquently describes it as a means of turning money into light. For Sam Goldwyn the process represented the collision of money with art. The film-making process involves the skills and talents of a wide range of people and, like any task connected with money, the services of lawyers and other professionals are required.

Few people outside the industry are aware of the enormity of the task undertaken to create a film. The production process creates a vast sea of paperwork full of hidden perils, and it is the role of the film industry lawyer to ensure that the producer's creative endeavours are protected and to negotiate favourable terms for distribution and exploitation.

Nicholson Graham & Jones is actively involved across a broad spectrum of media and intellectual property industries. Whilst we pursue a policy of obtaining information to advise our clients, we also actively share and disseminate knowledge and know-how among the legal profession and the industry generally. We lobby on the commercial and legal aspects of the industry to change the law, both at UK and EC level. We regard this as part of our support to the industry, by being involved and working towards common objectives.

The BFI Handbook is the single most useful reference guide for anyone working in the film or television industries in the UK. Copies of it are to be found close to the desk of anyone who is actively working in these areas. Since the Department of Trade and Industry stopped collating and publishing statistical information on the film industry, it has been almost impossible to obtain reliable statistical information. The BFI has taken the initiative and the expanded Handbook now represents a vital contribution to industry know-how. The BFI continues to make a major contribution to the promotion of audio-visual culture in the UK and European Community.

We are proud to be associated with the BFI and to be supporting the Handbook as a tangible display of our support and commitment to the UK film industry. The BFI's role and contribution to the industry both as a cultural organisation and as a charity which supports a wide range of activities, is crucial to the development of film and television in the UK.

Michael Henry
Partner, Nicholson Graham & Jones

At a Glance

The BFI's varied activities include......

- *preservation and conservation of the national moving image heritage at the National Film and Television Archive*
- *making classics of world cinema available via screenings of the 'Treasures from the National Film and Television Archive' collection at BFI on the South Bank and through the 'Classic Film Collection' sponsored by Champagne Piper-Heidsieck*
- *exhibition, nationally and regionally at the National Film Theatre, the Museum of the Moving Image and at BFI-supported regional film theatres and media centres around the country*
- *distribution of both film and video including the Connoisseur Video label*
- *film production and the fostering of new talent through BFI Production*
- *publishing of books, 'Sight and Sound' magazine, and one-off monographs*
- *the world's largest computerised database of information about film and television in Library and Information Services*
- *education at all levels, from infant school to post-doctoral research in media by BFI Media Education and Research*
- *the presentation of the best in world cinema at festivals including the annual London Film Festival*
- *conferences, debates, publications and TV documentaries produced by the Research and Education Division*
- *the co-ordination of regional and other pan-Institute policies, the funding of Regional Arts Boards and the running of the MEDIA desk by the Funding Department of BFI Cinema Services and Development*
- *the recognition of achievement in all areas of the moving image via the annual BFI Awards organised by the Central Press and Promotions Office*

By Wilf Stevenson

Director of the British Film Institute

Like the moving image, the 20th century's major art form, the BFI has grown and developed since it was first established in 1933. But our remit today is essentially the same as it was when we were founded: to promote and develop knowledge and enjoyment of the culture of the moving image.

The BFI is a unique body – it is both a cultural organisation and an integral part of the industry itself. Unlike any other body of its kind, it combines in a single organisation activities and expertise across all aspects of film, video and television.

BFI on the South Bank

Museum of the Moving Image (MOMI)

This award-winning museum tells the story of moving images from the earliest pre-cinema experiments to the technical wizardry of a modern television studio. Beginning in 2,000 BC with Javanese shadow puppets, the displays move on through early Victorian pre-cinema toys, the silent era, the golden age of Hollywood, the birth of television and the recent history of satellite and cable TV. There are lots of interactive displays and hundreds of film stills, posters and treasures such as Chaplin's hat and cane. MOMI's resident company of actor-guides entertain and inform. MOMI has a busy education department and every year enables resident animators to work in public view, in the museum. MOMI shows a repertory collection of 360 classic films in the 'Treasures from the National Film and Television Archive' series and presents special one-off exhibitions which have recently examined subjects ranging from the history of the pop video to the work of trick filmmaker Georges Méliès.

The newly refurbished NFT foyer

National Film Theatre (NFT)

More than 1,000 films are shown annually at the NFT in three cinemas to audiences of almost 200,000. One of the world's leading cinémathèques, the NFT's programme of films is screened using the best available prints, in seasons themed by director, star, country, period, genre or issue. Great care is taken in presentation and the NFT is equipped to screen film formats from Super 8mm to 70mm. Silent films often have piano accompaniment and foreign films are shown in original versions, subtitled or with earphone commentary. The NFT also hosts debates and lectures including 'The Guardian' series of events.

London Film Festival (LFF)

The annual LFF, established in 1956, is regarded as Europe's leading non-competitive film festival. Each year in November, it presents the best new films from the spectrum of world cinema, with over 300 screenings from more than 40 countries to audiences of over 70,000. Directors and actors visit the festival to introduce and discuss their work and the LFF uses the NFT as its base as well as venues across the capital.

Top: A 'Film on the Square' venue at the 1992 LFF
Above: George Méliès' *Deux cent milles lieues sous les mers* (1906), from MOMI's 'Méliès: Father of Film Fantasy' exhibition

Top: An original *Ossessione* poster, newly acquired by BFI Stills, Posters and Designs. Middle: Peter Brooke CH MP, Secretary of State for National Heritage, plants a tree at the J Paul Getty Jnr Conservation Centre on a visit to open the new Paper Store

Above: The NFTVA's latest restoration, *Under Capricorn*

A variety of Rank's distinctive British comedy posters, held in the BFI Library's Special Materials Unit

National Film and Television Archive

The NFTVA acquires, preserves and makes permanently available a national collection of moving images: valuable and lasting examples of the art and history of cinema and television, and a documentary record of the twentieth century. It now holds over 200,000 titles from 1895 to the present and an extensive collection of photographs, posters and costume and set designs.

The J Paul Getty Jnr Conservation Centre in Berkhamsted houses the Archive's preservation work: a constant race against time. Some 140 million feet of flammable, fragile nitrate film is being copied onto modern safety film stock. The Archive also carries out major restoration projects and is building the 'Treasures from the National Film and Television Archive' collection of international film classics, in their original versions, for year-round repertory screening at MOMI.

The NFTVA also preserves and makes accessible the BFI's collection of stills, posters and designs from more than 60,000 films and television programmes. Its six million images are used in publishing and exhibition projects and the collection also includes 15,000 posters and 2,500 set and costume designs.

BFI Library and Information Services

The world's largest collection of information on film and television, this national research collection includes books, periodicals, more than a million newspaper cuttings, 16,000 published and unpublished scripts, campaign books, festival catalogues and personal papers from major figures going back to the beginnings of cinema. SIFT, the BFI's computer database holds references on 400,000 films, 280,000 personalities, 115,000 organisations and 5,000 events. Each year, information on a further 11,000 titles is added.

BFI Cinema Services and Development

Distribution and Exhibition Departments

Working to maintain and increase the range of films and work on video available to cinema audiences, the Division releases both new and classic films, from *Daughters of the Dust* and a touring package of gay and lesbian films to Syberberg's controversial seven-hour epic *Hitler, ein Film aus Deutschland* (1977). The Exhibition Department provides programming and publicity support and advice for a 46-strong network of regional film theatres which have more than 1.4 million admissions annually. In addition this Division supports the British Federation of Film Societies, whose 280 societies screen films to more than 50,000 members annually.

Connoisseur Video, the BFI's video arm, has brought more than 130 titles on to the UK sell-through market. The 'Champagne Piper-Heidsieck Classic Film Collection' will include up to 200 new prints and restorations from world cinema, made available in seasons for screenings around the world.

Above: UK MEDIA Desk Eurimages Information Seminar at the NFT, March 1993. Right: Belfast's Cinemagic Festival, part-funded by the Funding Unit

Above: Julie Dash's *Daughters of the Dust*, released by the Distribution Department

Funding Unit

From funding the building of a new art-house cinema in Exeter to supporting the Wales Film Archive, the Unit plays a key part in making film and video more accessible across the UK. Working together with other arts bodies to determine regional strategies for funding, the Funding Unit funds film and video activity in the regions via block grants to the Regional Arts Boards and other projects through its development budget. The Department is responsible for direct grant funding to exhibition clients and also administers the Regional Exhibition Project Fund.

The unit is active in establishing facilities for disabled groups, coordinates general BFI policy and runs the MEDIA Desk – the UK base for information about the audiovisual industries in Europe.

BFI Research and Education

The Research and Education Division co-ordinates research projects and high-profile events such as 'One Day in the Life of World Cinema', which invited filmmakers across the world to contribute diaries about their day's work to provide a fascinating kaleidoscopic picture. The results of these projects are published in various forms – for example, a major 5-year study into representations of black people on British TV resulted in two BFI-produced documentaries, shown on BBC2, and an accompanying book. The Group also organises events such as the BFI/BAFTA Commission of Inquiry into the future of the BBC and the International Television Studies Conference. The regular 'Television on BFI South Bank' evenings at the Museum of the Moving Image include screenings, debates and other events, with personal appearances by John Thaw, Jack Rosenthal, Fay Weldon and many others.

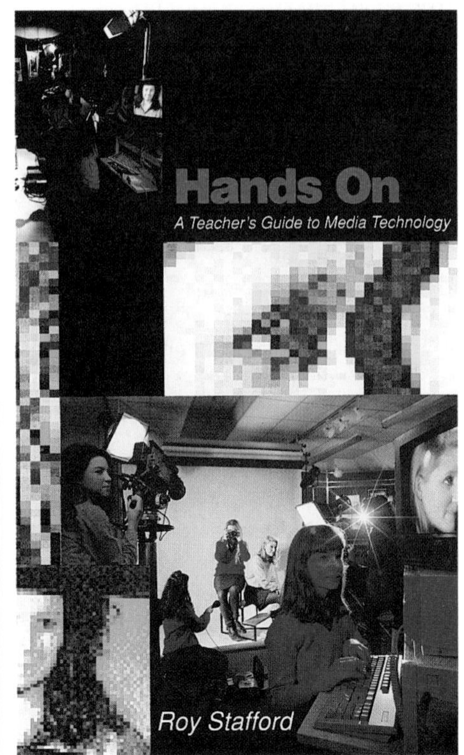

Above: A teaching aid from the Research and Education division

Above: German stuntman Jörg Pohl at work on 10 June 1993, and a participant in 'One Day in the Life of World Cinema'

BFI Media Education and Research

Learning about the media is a fast-growing part of the school curriculum. Young people now study the media as part of their English lessons; an estimated 20,000 students each year opt for Media Studies as a GCSE subject; and new courses are also springing up in Higher Education. BFI Media Education and Research is at the forefront of these developments. It lobbied for the inclusion of media education in the National Curriculum and helps to develop knowledge, ideas and understanding about cinema, television, video, cable and satellite, working with colleagues in education and training. It works at all levels, from infant school to post-doctoral research and including adult education. The BFI recently welcomed the second group of students onto its new MA course, run in conjunction with Birkbeck College, London.

BFI Book Publishing

BFI Publishing's expanding list of titles ranges from examinations of the work of Sergei Eisenstein to popular books such as 'The BFI Companion to the Western'. Most recently the 'BFI Film Classics' series invites distinguished writers to discuss a film of their choice from the 'Treasures from the National Film and Television Archive' collection. The BFI also publishes one-off monographs on industry issues such as the future of the UK film industry.

'Sight and Sound'

'Sight and Sound', the monthly magazine, provides in-depth reviews, detailed synopsis and full credits for every feature film released in the UK and articles by leading writers on cinema and television.

BFI Production

The Production division develops new talent and new ideas in UK film and television. It has provided filmmakers such as Karel Reisz, Lindsay Anderson, Stephen Frears, Bill Douglas, Peter Greenaway, Terence Davies and Derek Jarman with the finance to make their first films.

BFI Production produces short films and videos alongside feature-length films, acting as producer and co-investor. Focusing on work which is innovative both in theme and style, it aims to encourage challenging and different approaches to cinema in the UK. Recent productions include Terence Davies' *The Long Day Closes* (British Competition Entry, Cannes 1992) and *Anchoress* (selected for the Un Certain Regard section at Cannes in 1993). Its New Directors films are shown on Channel Four and festivals and cinemas internationally. BFI Production also organises events which aim to stimulate debate about the film and television industries, for example a recent series of seminars, in conjunction with British Screen, aimed at getting more Black and Asian British cinema into development and production.

Above: Craig K McCall's *Notes from Underground*, supported by BFI Production Projects

Above: Natalie Morse in Chris Newby's *Anchoress*, shown in Un Certain Regard at Cannes in 1993

Central Press and Promotions Office

The Press and Promotions office handles all corporate press and publicity and produces corporate publications including the Annual Report. It also organises the annual BFI Awards and represents the BFI at the major European Film Festivals.

Above: Wilf Stevenson (left) and Jeremy Thomas (second right) with BFI Fellows Maureen O'Hara, Sir Denis Forman and Clint Eastwood at the 1993 BFI Awards

CONTACTS AT THE BFI

British Film Institute

21 Stephen Street
London W1P 1PL
Tel: 071 255 1444
Telex: 27624 BFILDNG
Fax: 071 436 7950
Director: Wilf Stevenson
Assistant Director: Michael Prescott

Corporate Press Contacts

Head of Press and Promotions: Wayne Drew
Press Officer: Gill Harrison

National Film and Television Archive

(At Stephen Street)
Curator: Clyde Jeavons
Deputy Curator: Anne Fleming
Head of BFI Stills, Posters and Designs: Bridget Kinally
(At the J Paul Getty Jnr Conservation Centre, Kings Hill Way, Berkhamsted, Hertfordshire HP4 3TP. Tel: 04428 76301 Fax: 04428 75607)
Head of Conservation: Henning Schou

BFI Cinema Services & Development

Head: Irene Whitehead
Deputy Head: Stephen Bell
Head of Distribution Department: Heather Stewart
Marketing Officer, Distribution Department: Karen Alexander
Head of Funding Unit: Marion Doyen
Head of Film Society Unit: Tom Brownlie
Film Society Unit Information Officer: Peter Cargin

BFI Library and Information Services

Head: Gillian Hartnoll
Deputy Head: David Sharp

BFI Research and Education

Head of Research and Education: Colin MacCabe
Deputy Head of Division/Head of Media Education and Research: Richard Paterson
Head of Book Publishing: Ed Buscombe
(Sales enquiries 29 Rathbone Street, London W1P 1AG. Tel: 071 636 3289)
Principal Education Officer: Cary Bazalgette
Senior Projects Officer: Tana Wollen
Editor 'Sight and Sound': Philip Dodd
Publishing Director, 'Sight and Sound': Caroline Moore

BFI Production

29 Rathbone Street
London WlP lAG
Tel: 071 636 5587/4736
Fax: 071 580 9456
Head: Ben Gibson
Deputy Head: Angela Topping
Sales: Sue Bruce-Smith
Press and Publicity: Liz Reddish

BFI on the South Bank

National Film Theatre and Museum of the Moving Image,
South Bank
London SE1 8XT
Tel: 071 928 3535
Telex: 929229 NATFIL G
Fax: 071 633 9323
Head of BFI on the South Bank: Adrian Wootton
Head of Programme Planning: Mark Adams
London Film Festival Director: Sheila Whitaker
Head of Marketing: Penny Owens
Deputy Head of Marketing: Brian Robinson
Curator of MOMI: Leslie Hardcastle

FACILITIES FOR THE DISABLED

The British Film Institute is working to improve access to its buildings for disabled visitors. Facilities include:

21 Stephen Street: unisex toilet for disabled on ground floor; car parking at rear of building (please contact security staff beforehand to check availability, and on arrival to gain access via ramp into rear ground floor corridor); ramps to basement viewing theatres; induction loop in the Boardroom. Access to all areas (except nitrate viewing area on roof) via lifts situated in rear ground floor corridor and main reception (no steps into main reception from street). Assistance may be necessary for unaccompanied wheelchair users as there are several heavy fire doors.

Museum of the Moving Image: (a leaflet outlining facilities for people with disabilities is available on request from NFT reception). Reduced admission charge, and group rate, for registered disabled people. There are several heavy fire doors in MOMI which may be difficult to use, but there is always assistance available.

There are three parking spaces for the disabled on the Royal Festival Hall access road and two on the access road leading to MOMI. Visitors may also use Euro car parks at the Hayward Gallery and National Theatre. There is a ramp from the Hayward Gallery car park to MOMI. There are no steps into the main foyer of the building where a central telephone call point can be used to gain help with buying tickets and entry to MOMI.

Most areas of the museum are accessible to wheelchair users although in a slightly different order from the usual route. Two scissor lifts and one stair lift operate between the ground and first floor and there is one stair lift between the first and second floor. There are help points placed at each of these lifts to enable disabled visitors to call for assistance.

MOMI's cinema has three wheelchair positions at the front of the auditorium and an induction loop system for those wearing hearing aids incorporating a T switch. There are disabled toilet facilities in the toilets in the first exhibition area.

National Film Theatre: NFT1 has 6 wheelchair positions at the rear of the auditorium which must be booked in advance. A disabled person may occupy seat N1 in NFT2 if accompanied by an able-bodied person who will occupy the adjacent seat. A wheelchair may only be used when the general lighting is on and it must be stored out of the way at the rear of NFT2. There is a unisex disabled toilet situated in the new foyer at the back of NFT1 and in the passageway off the main NFT/MOMI foyer. NFT1 and NFT2 both have an induction loop system for those with hearing aids incorporating a T switch, and also certain seats with a special earphone facility. Please ask for this service when booking.

29 Rathbone Street: lift access to the first floor offices and ramp access to the technical facilities. Three parking spaces; please contact reception (071 636 5587) before arrival to check availability.

National Film and Television Archive, Berkhamsted: ramps into J Paul Getty Jnr Conservation centre, electronically operated doors, unisex disabled toilet, lift access to all areas.

Above: Jeremy Isaacs interviewing BBC Director-General John Birt at the NFT, with signer

Overview of Film, Television and Video in the UK

Contents

Left: NFT 1

INTRODUCTION

Above: *Damage*, a bold attempt at a fully-fledged English-language European movie

Last year's Handbook included the first BFI statistical overview of British film, television and video. Despite some presentational errors, it was very well received. We hope that this edition not only improves on that first effort but will enable the reader to make useful comparisons between one year and the next. It is expected that the Handbook will eventually become the standard reference tool for workers on both the cultural and commercial sides of the screen entertainment industries.

Statistics were compiled by Phil Wickham of the BFI information service, BFI Library and Information Services, whose task would not have been possible without the help of the monthly industry journal 'Screen Digest'. We are also grateful to the sources listed opposite for their advice and contributions.

We have followed as closely as possible the format that we used last year, although improvements have been made in the choice and presentation of data. Also, we have dropped the separate section of the commentary that last year was devoted to independent television producers. This is now included in the TV section.

As before, the commentary attempts to illuminate the data and put it into a general context. Inevitably, it is not clinically objective; others examining the figures might draw different conclusions.

A warning given last year has to be repeated. The statistics here are the best we could compile. But they are still far from complete and they are not always convincing. While film and television data is mostly reliable, the video industry is ill-served by its statisticians; many figures are extrapolated from market research conducted from samples of the trade and public that may be unrepresentative. Where we have doubts, we have expressed them in footnotes.

Terry Ilott
Editor

First, a question of definition. According to the Films Act 1985, a film is British when its maker was, at the time of filming, an EC resident; it was made in the EC or a Commonwealth country; and not less than 75% of its labour costs, with certain exemptions, was paid in the EC or the Commonwealth. While this is the basis for all attempts to define British films, it isn't much of a starting point. We therefore have to come up with a definition of our own.

Last year, we included co-productions where the impetus, subject matter, location, cast and/or crew were not British. Thus, Jean Jacques Annaud's *The Lover* was included by virtue of producer Tim Burrill's association. On reflection, we think this was a mistake.

This year, we have opted to include feature-length films which are expected by their makers to receive theatrical distribution and for which either the financial or the creative impulse came from Britain. The guiding principle is to identify films which directly contribute to British film culture or to the culture of the British film industry.

Thus, we include Working Title's *Posse*, which is an important venture for the British company, even though the film was shot in the US with an American cast and crew.

That our definition is not without problems is demonstrated in the text that follows, where, on occasion, films are taken in or out of the "British" list to accommodate certain important observations.

The British film-making community can take some satisfaction from the fact that 47 films went before the cameras in 1992. This is down on the previous year, when 59 films were made, but it is just above the 13-year average of 46 **(table 1)**.

The level of British film production has fluctuated since 1980, with a low of 24

We would like to express our gratitude to the following organisations and individuals for their help in supplying and commenting upon the data. (Addresses for the media organisations listed below can be found in the relavant sections of the Directory.)

The Advertising Association (AA)
British Audience Research Bureau (BARB)
British Broadcasting Corporation (BBC)
British Screen Finance
British Videogram Association (BVA)
Central Statistical Office
Chart Information Network (CIN)
Cinema Advertising Association (CAA)
Entertainment Data Inc. (EDI)
Independent Television Commission (ITC)
MRIB
Screen Digest
Screen Finance

Special thanks to Norman Abbott, Kim Ballard, Peter Compton, John Chittock OBE, Jonathan Davis, Phil Matcham, Steve Perrin, Cheryl Wilson

Above: It was financed by Polygram, but *Posse* was shot in the US with an American cast and crew

films in 1981 and a high of 60 films in 1990. Over the years, the UK has been roughly on a par with Spain and behind Germany, Italy and France in the league table of European producers. The pattern was repeated again in 1992, when Spain produced 52 films, Germany 63, Italy 127 and France 155 **(table 5)**.

But investment in British films continues to fall. In 1992, the total production cost of our films was £185 million, which was about £58 million less than the year before. In fact, at 1993 prices our movie investment in 1992 was less than half (43%) the amount we spent in 1984, the high-point of film investment in recent years **(table 1)**.

By contrast, French investment in films has steadily increased, from £350 million in 1989, to £404 million in 1990, £449 million in 1991 and £504 million in 1992. In Italy, the equivalent figures are £152 million, £161 million, £223 million and £235 million **(table 6)**.

The decline in investment means that, once again, the average budget of British movies has fallen, to £3.94 million. This is a mere 44% of the inflation-adjusted £8.97 million average recorded in 1980. If the seven US-backed productions, whose average cost was £9.69 million, are taken out of 1992's equation, the average British budget falls to £2.99 million **(tables 2 and 3)**.

Even this overstates the case in some ways, for the biggest "British" film of 1992 was the £18 million *Little Buddha*, which was wholly financed by a French company, Ciby 2000. Removing *Little Buddha* from the lists would reduce the average British budget to below £2 million.

In France, the average budget in 1992 was £3.25 million, up from £2.88 million in 1991. In Italy, the average was £1.85 million, up from the previous year's £1.72 million. It should be noted that, unlike the UK, neither France nor Italy is fishing in the same talent pool as Hollywood.

There is no rule that says the greater the cost of a movie the the more likely it is to be a success. But it is at least arguable that the greater the average cost, whether of a company's or a country's output, the better the average box-office performance. Low-budget films, by definition, do not include major stars, special effects, lavish sets, props or costumes, top-flight directors or 'A' list writers. These are substantial competitive disadvantages.

In recent years, production costs in the English-speaking world have risen much faster than inflation, reflecting both the higher fees commanded by a stubbornly small talent pool (the three major Hollywood talent agencies, ICM, William Morris and CAA, have about 5,000 clients between them) and the increased costs associated with enhanced production values, notably in special effects

The biggest budgets, of course, are incurred in Hollywood, whose output provides British films with their strongest competition, even among British audiences **(table 15)**. With studio pictures now each costing on average $28.8 million - more than nine times the average British budget - the competition is heavily one-sided.

Indeed, the continued fall in film budgets suggests that the British production sector has given up competing with Hollywood and is now concentrating on specialist niches that can be filled by low-budget exploitation or art films.

This trend was noted in the BFI Handbook last year, when an admittedly subjective content-analysis showed that of 1991's output, only seven films were aimed at the mass audience, eight seemed to be hoping for crossover business (one of which, *The Crying Game*, achieved this triumphantly) and 17 were destined from the outset for the arthouse circuit.

1 Number, Value and Average Budget of UK films, 1981- 1992

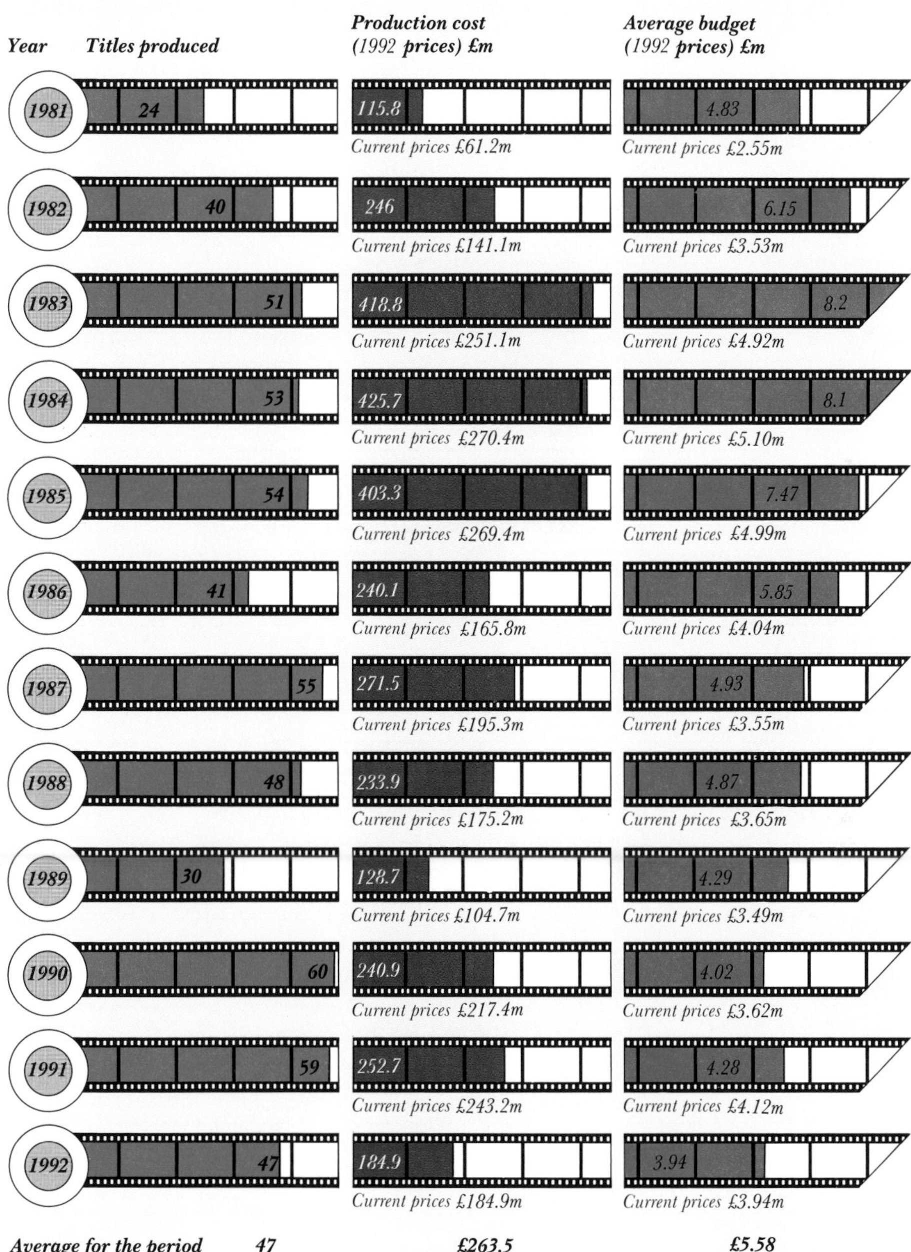

***Notes:** In defining a UK film here, we include all films produced/ co- produced by a UK production company or made in the UK by an overseas producer. It should be stressed that these are estimates. Price adjustments according to CSO RPI figures.*
Source: Knowledge Research/ Screen Finance/ CSO

2 UK Feature Film Production, 1992

A feature film is defined here as being made on celluloid, over 72 minutes long and with the intention of theatrical release.

Title	***Producer***	***Production cost (£m)***
Anchoress	*BFI/Corsan*	*1.0*
The Baby of Mâcon	*Allarts/UGC/Cine Electra/Channel 4 Schlemmer Films/North Rhine Westphalian Film Fund*	*2.0*
Bad Behaviour	*Parallax Pictures for Film Four International and British Screen*	*1.05*
Bhaji on the Beach	*Umbi Films/Film Four International*	*1.0*
Blue Black Permanent	*BFI/Viz Film/Channel 4/Scottish Film Production Fund*	*0.5*
Blue Ice	*Blue Ice Productions*	*5.0*
Carry on Columbus	*Island World/Comedy House Productions*	*2.5*
The Cement Garden	*Neue Constantin/Laurentic Films/ Toni Productions*	*1.9*
Century	*BBC/Beambright International Sales/ The Sales Company*	*1.8*
Damage	*NEF/Skreba Films/Studio Canal Plus in association with Channel 4, Canal Plus and the European Co-production Fund.*	*6.6*
Death Train	*British Lion/Jadran (Croatia)*	*2.3*
Dirty Weekend	*Scimitar Films*	*2.3*
Friends	*Friends Prod/British Screen/ European Co-production Fund*	*1.45*
Great Moments in Aviation	*BBC*	*2.5*
The Hawk	*BBC/Initial Films and TV*	*1.8*
High Boot Benny	*First City*	*1.5*
The Hour of the Pig	*BBC/CiBy 2000/British Screen/ European Co-production Fund*	*3.0*
The Innocent	*Lakehart/Norma Heyman/Chris Sievernich Wieland Schults-Keil Production*	*8.25*
Leon the Pig Farmer	*Leon the Pig Farmer plc.*	*0.5*
Little Buddha	*Recorded Picture Company/CiBy 2000*	*18.0*
Lost in Africa	*Hotspur Productions*	*2.5*
Much Ado About Nothing	*Renaissance Films/Samuel Goldwyn Co.*	*5.6*
Mystery of Edwin Drood	*Bevanfield Films*	*2.0*
Naked	*Thin Man Films/Film Four International/ British Screen*	*2.5*
No Worries	*Film on Four International/British Screen/ Palm Beach/Initial Film and TV in association with Southern Star*	*2.7*

Title	Producer	Production cost (£m)
Orlando	*British Screen/Rio SA/Mikado Films/ Sigma Films/Lenfilm*	*6.6*
Peter's Friends	*Renaissance Films*	*2.0*
Posse	*Working Title*	*6.0*
Psychotherapy	*BFI/TiMe/Skyline/Mervyn Film NRW film foundation/WDR*	*1.3*
Raining Stones	*Parallax Pictures/Film Four International*	*0.75*
Romeo is Bleeding	*Working Title/Hilary Henkin*	*6.0*
The Secret Rapture	*Greenpoint Films/Channel Four/British Screen*	*1.5*
Soft Top, Hard Shoulder	*Guber Brothers Productions*	*0.2*
Splitting Heirs	*Prominent Features*	*4.5*
Tale of a Vampire	*State Screen Productions*	*0.6*
The Trial	*BBC/Santa Ana*	*4.0*
The Turn of the Screw	*Michael White Productions/Lakedell Ltd/Cinemax*	*2.0*
White Angel	*Living Spirit Productions*	*0.25*
Wittgenstein	*Bandung Films/BFI/Channel Four*	*0.23*
The Young Americans	*Working Title/Trybits Worrell Associates*	*3.0*
Total of 40 Films.	***Average Budget £ 2.99m***	***Total Production Cost £ 119.18m***

Source: Screen Finance/BFI

3 Films with a British involvement but where the financial and/or creative impetus was from major studios in the USA

Title	Producer	Production cost (£m)
Being Human	*Enigma Films/Warner Brothers*	*13.0*
Foreign Affairs	*Stagescreen/Interscope/Turner Entertainments*	*3.0*
The Hudsucker Proxy	*Working Title/Silver Productions*	*16.8*
The Muppet Christmas Carol	*Jim Henson Productions/Walt Disney*	*8.0*
The Remains of the Day	*Columbia/Merchant Ivory*	*6.0*
The Secret Garden	*Warner Brothers/Zoetrope*	*8.0*
Son of the Pink Panther	*MGM*	*13.0*
Total of 7 Films.	***Average Budget £9.69m***	***Total cost £67.8m***

Source: Screen Finance/BFI

Above: *Peter's Friends* - aspired to crossover business

In 1992, the focus on the art market intensified. Only five mass-market films can be identified (*Carry On Columbus*, *Death Train*, *Dirty Weekend*, *Posse* and *Splitting Heirs*), two films aspire to crossover business (*Peter's Friends* and *Little Buddha*) and 24 movies are identifiably aimed at the art circuit **(table 2)**.

Two observations arise from this. The first is that Britain produces a wealth of big-budget talent that cannot find work at home. Anthony Hopkins, Daniel Day Lewis, Gary Oldman, Alan Parker and Ridley Scott are just the best-known members of the substantial British colony in Hollywood.

In recent years, our exiled actors and directors have been joined by a host of senior technicians and even by production companies, notably affiliates of Polygram Filmed Entertainment, whose European resources are now put to the service of making American films. Thus, one of the stalwart British production houses of the 1980s, Working Title, made two Hollywood movies in 1992, *Romeo Is Bleeding* and *Posse*.

As mentioned above, the latter film in particular, a black Western, underlines the difficulty of identifying films by nationality. In terms of British culture, the only interesting thing to say about *Posse* is that it was made by a British company in Hollywood. In terms of its tone and content, the film is purely American.

It should be said that Polygram, which last year acquired a controlling stake in Hollywood's Interscope Pictures, is not the only European company plunging into the American mainstream. Canal Plus, Penta, RCS Video, Regency and Lumiere have done the same.

The second observation is that, as the big talent and the big money drifts to Hollywood, the British film industry doesn't need, and can't afford, the level of production services that was built up in the 1950s and 1960s. As if in recognition of this, the threatened closure of Elstree Studios in the summer of 1993 brought only a muted response from the industry.

The fate of Elstree illustrates another key aspect of Britain's film-making decline: the withdrawal of American investment. Elstree always depended very heavily on Hollywood productions; most famously, the studio was home to the *Indiana Jones* and *Star Wars* series.

American investment in British production has steadily declined from its 1984 peak of £142 million, when films such as *Legend*, *King David* and *Lifeforce* went before the cameras. In 1991, Hollywood invested only £83.5 million in British production. In 1992, the figure was down to £67.8 million **(table 3)**. Adjusted for inflation, Hollywood's investment in British production has fallen to less than one-third of its 1984 total.

Even that figure overstates the position in some ways, since it includes *The Hudsucker Proxy*, which was made in America at a cost of £16.8 million, and MGM's £13 million *Son Of The Pink Panther*, which was made on locations in Europe. Neither production drew significantly on British skills or services.

Another way of looking at British film investment is to compare it with domestic consumer expenditure on feature films. While consumer spending has grown from £473 million in 1985, the year in which the historic decline of cinema was halted, to £1.5 billion in 1992, our investment in films in the same period has fallen from £269 million to £185 million. Adjusted for inflation, our film investment has fallen to less than half its 1985 level while our spending has more than trebled **(table 4)**. It is little wonder that we find it increasingly difficult to compete.

Why has investment in British-made films collapsed in so spectacular a fashion when we not only manifestly have the talent but are in midst of a market in which consumer demand for films has continued to grow despite the recession?

The usual, and partly correct, answer is to point to the changed regulatory and fiscal climate for film investment. The Eady Levy (which took money from the box-office and distributed it among producers) was abolished in 1985, capital allowances (which permitted 100% of the cost of a movie to be set against tax in the first year) were phased out between 1984 and 1986 and the dollar went into such a nose-dive in the late 1980s that it gave British production the reputation of being a very expensive option (a reputation which, even though the dollar has since recovered, it has been impossible to shake off).

But declining competitiveness is a feature even in those countries where a high level of incentives and subsidies has been maintained. There is reason to believe that European cinema suffers from the decadence of the commercial culture from which it arises. Britain's contribution to that decay can be measured in the loss of major film companies, the diminution of budgets and the disengagement from the mass audience.

Below: The BBC's *Enchanted April*, underlining the importance of TV finance

4 Investment in UK film production vs UK Consumer Expenditure on Feature Films

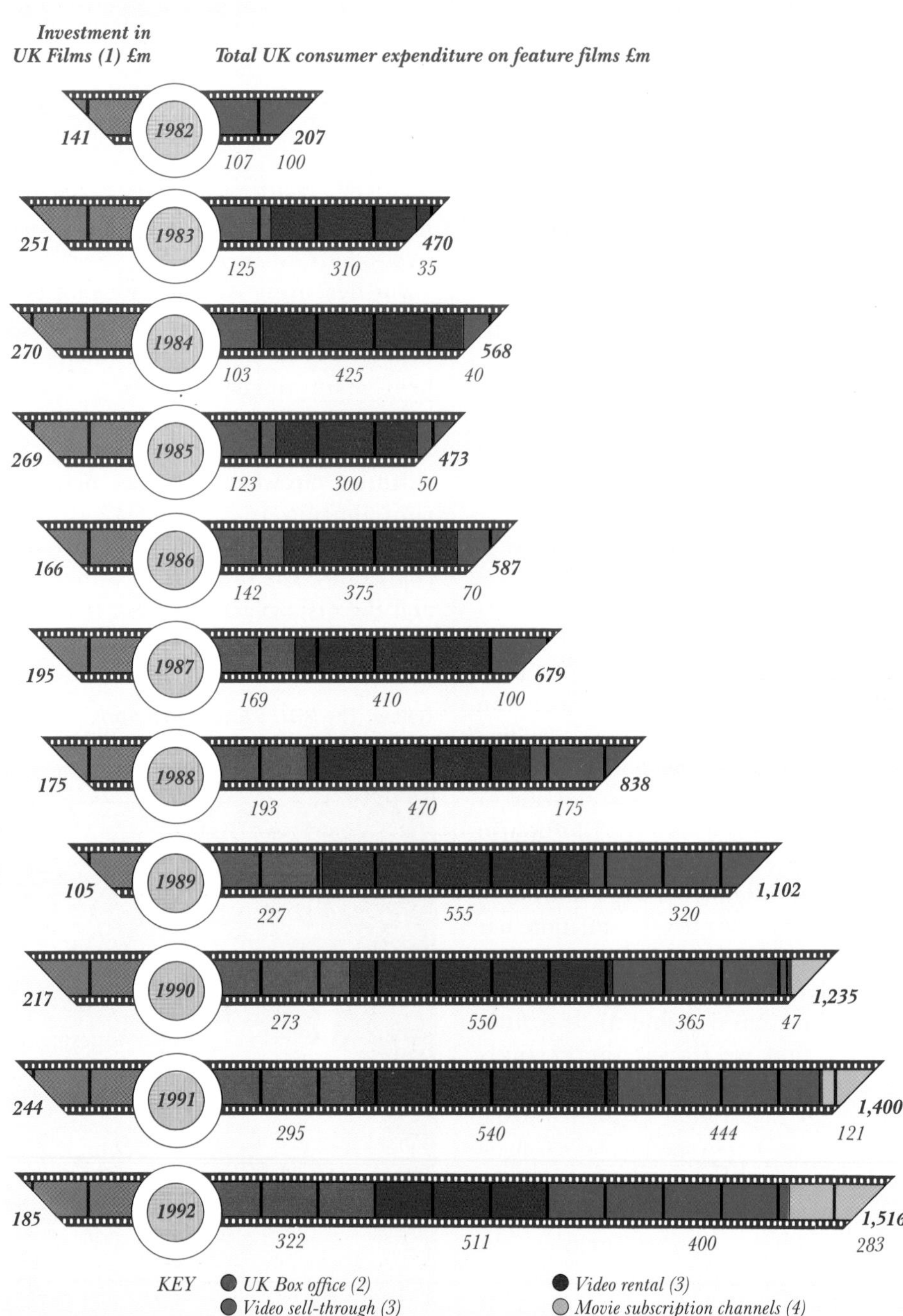

Sources: (1) BFI/Screen International/BFTPA/Screen Finance/Knowledge Research. (2) Screen Digest/Entertainment Data Inc. (3) Mintel (1981-1984);BVA/Dodona Research (1985-1990); BVA (1992). (4) BSkyB/Knowledge Research.

5 Number of Films produced by EC Countries 1990-1992 (£m)

	1990	1991	1992
Belgium	20	3	12
Denmark	13	11	16
France	146	156	155
Germany	48	72	63
Greece	n.a.	15	10
Ireland	3	1	4
Italy	119	129	127
Luxembourg	1	1	5
Netherlands	13	14	13
Portugal	9	9	8
Spain	47	64	52
UK*	54	48	7*

Notes: **Screen Digest have used different definitions of a UK film to those in table 1 in order to make international comparisons. They quote a figure of 42. (n.a.= not available)*

6 Total EC feature film production investment 1990-1992 (£m)

	1990	1991	1992
Belgium	21.9	7.6	18.4
Denmark	12.3	14.0	n.a.
France	404.3	449.4	504.1
Germany	83.0	99.6	n.a.
Greece	n.a.	n.a.	n.a.
Ireland	16.1	1.6	n.a.
Italy	161.5	222.9	235.4
Luxembourg	n.a.	1.7	1.1
Netherlands	n.a.	n.a.	n.a.
Portugal	2.4	4.0	4.1
Spain	n.a.	n.a.	1.08
UK*	258.7	244.5	185*

Notes: **Screen Digest have used different definitions of a UK film to those in table 1 in order to make valid international comparisons. They quote a figure of £136.7m. If just the films described in table 1 as being 'British or European in financial and conceptual impetus' are included the cost is £119.2m.*

7 Source of funding for British Screen Films 1990-1992

	1990 £000s	Percentage	1991 £000s	Percentage	1992 £000s	Percentage
British Screen	4,865	19.6%	4,559	19.5%	2,700	10.5%
European Co-production Fund	n.a.	n.a.	250	1.1%	2,043	8.0%
Channel Four	5,524	22.2%	3,933	16.8%	4,709	18.4%
Other UK Investors	7,497	30.2%	4,057	17.3%	2,546	9.9%
EC Investors	3,384	13.6%	5,948	25.4%	7,878	30.7%
US Investors	1,822	7.3%	4,223	18.1%	3,697	14.4%
Other	1,756	7.1%	421	1.8%	2,069	8.1%
Total	**24,848**	**100%**	**23,391**	**100%**	**25,642**	**100.0%**

Source: British Screen

This is too big a subject to deal with here. What we can do is look at the figures and add to the well-worn observations about the negative fiscal and regulatory environment in Britain. First, the uncertainty created by the Broadcasting Act of 1990 virtually eliminated film investment by ITV companies, a number of which, including Granada (*My Left Foot*, *The Field*) and LWT (*A Handful Of Dust*, *Wilt*) had already enjoyed some movie success. Others, such as Yorkshire, had plans to enter the film-making arena which had to be shelved.

The ITV companies were further dissuaded from making film investments by changes in the composition of their levy payments to the Treasury. In the 12 years from 1974, ITV companies paid a 66.7% levy on profits made in the UK but paid no tax on earnings overseas. Since films are inherently exportable (much more so than most TV programmes), there was an in-built incentive to invest.

But the taxation differential between home and overseas profits was narrowed to 22.5% in 1986. Then, in 1990, the

8 Distribution of 1991 UK Films

Received Theatrical Distribution in 1991/2
Ama
As You Like It
Bitter Moon
Blame it on the Bellboy
Blonde Fist
Bob Roberts
Chaplin
City of Joy
The Crying Game
Double X
Dream On
Edward II
Elenya
Enchanted April
Howards End
Into the West
Just Like A Woman
The Lawnmower Man
London Kills Me
The Long Day Closes
The Lover
Naked Lunch
The Playboys
Prague
Rebecca's Daughters
Secret Friends
Simple Men
Split Second
Truly, Madly, Deeply
Under Suspicion
Waterland
Release Date in 1993
Map of the Human Heart
The Silent Touch
Wild West
UK Distributor but no release Date
The Boy From Lucky Village
How's Business
The Punk
Sweet Killing
Limited short run in repertory cinemas
Paper Marriage
Dust Devil
No Distribution Deal
Canvas
A Cry in the Night
Double Vision
For Better or for Worse
The Perfect Husband
The Plague
Weep No More My Lady
Straight to Television
Hostage
The Railway Station Man
Utz
Production Abandoned
Freddie goes to Washington

qv 1993 BFI Film and Television Handbook p22-23
Screen Finance/ BFI

rules were changed so that part of the Treasury levy was raised from ITV advertising sales. Under the regulations governing the new ITV network, which was launched on 1 January 1993, differential treatment was abandoned altogether and ITV companies now pay the Treasury fixed sums plus a share of their net advertising revenues **(table 29)**.

Not surprisingly, the ITV companies, which are operating in a much more competitive broadcast market, in which Channel Four, satellite and cable are making inroads into their audiences and advertising sales, have virtually dropped out of films altogether. There was not a single ITV investor in 1992's crop of British productions **(table 1)**.

Does this matter? Taking the long view, it matters very much, for the second observation about the decline of investment is that there is a dearth of large commercial companies involved in British film production.

Apart from Polygram (which is officially Dutch) and Rank (which doesn't have a production division and tends to invest mostly in American movies), the only British corporates of any size that have shown an interest in films are the bigger ITV companies. Under a different fiscal regime, we might have expected them to become the flagships of British film production. That role falls instead to Channel Four and the BBC, both of which have public-service remits and neither of which can be counted properly commercial.

The third observation is that, without the reassurance provided by big commercial companies, the City is reluctant to participate in film production. In the 1970s and 1980s, a number of production funds were raised without corporate sponsors within the entertainment industry; all of them failed. It is not an experience that City institutions are keen to repeat.

One could go further and say, as many City insiders do, that the financial community in the UK is constitutionally averse to entertainment investments. It is an aversion, moreover, that is fuelled by the industry's naivete in all things financial. It is arguable that the distrust between the two sides is at least as damaging to the cause of British cinema as the oft-bemoaned absence of fiscal or other incentives for investment.

For one thing, it is self-fulfilling. As the City shies away from entertainment (the aversion is visceral rather than rational, as anyone who has touted a film prospectus around the City will testify), so it leaves the door open for Hollywood to take an increasing grip on all aspects of the UK market.

In exhibition, the effective duopoly that long existed between Rank and EMI, both British companies, has been broken by United Cinemas International, MGM Cinemas, Warner Theatres and National Amusements – all of them American. Between them, these companies have added more than 500 multiplex screens to the UK and, with Rank, now control about 77% of the market.

In cable television, all the major investors are American, among them Nynex, US West, Bell Canada and Southwestern Bell. In video retailing, our leading company is Florida-based Blockbuster.

As Hollywood's grip becomes stronger, the City is able to point to British firms' inability to compete as a reason to stay away.

But there is some good news on the film front. In 1992, British Screen, which, with Channel Four, is our most reliable source of investment funds — they invested in eight and 10 films respectively — was able to kick-start productions worth £25.6 million, an improvement on the previous year's £23.4 million **(table 7)**.

Its own contribution to those productions declined, from 23.1% of the total in 1989 to 10.5%, which probably indicates that British Screen is taking an increasingly commercial view of its investment responsibilities. Anyone, after all, if they have the money, can put up 100% of the finance for a film; it takes impressive powers of persuasion, or a compelling commercial case, to raise 90% from other partners.

Of special interest is British Screen's growing alignment with other European investors. In 1989, only 3.4% of British Screen's production costs was provided by non-UK EC companies. In 1990, the proportion was 13.2%. In 1991, it had reached 25.4%, with a further 1.1% provided under the auspices of the European Co-production Fund. In 1992, EC investors provided 30.7% and the Co-production Fund 8% of the aggregate production spend.

Channel Four's investment in British Screen films has remained relatively steady, at about 18%. But other UK investment has fallen, from 39.2% of the total in 1989 to 9.9% in 1992.

The shift from the UK to continental Europe reflects both necessity and the inclinations of the present management of British Screen, which can play a role in

Above: *Howards End* was one of a handful of British successes in 1992

broadening the outlook of British film-makers and bringing European film-making talent into the English-speaking world.

But it has two enormous in-built dangers. The first is of producing "Euro puddings": films that, in their desire to please everyone, end up pleasing no-one. As yet, there is no sign of British Screen falling into this trap.

The second, which is harder to resist, is of making films that are of interest only to the tiny British audience that exists for European movies. As we have noted, the output of British film-makers is becoming increasingly elitist and this is surely a tendency to be reversed rather than encouraged.

One indicator of commercial viability is distribution. If a film fails to find a distributor it can reasonably be deemed unviable. Of 1991's British output of 52 films (that is, excluding American-financed movies made in the UK), 40 have or will receive theatrical distribution, three have already gone straight to television and one, *Freddie Goes To Washington*, was abandoned **(table 8)**.

Leaving aside the last, that means that 11 films out of 51, nearly one-quarter of the total, have so far failed to find a theatrical distributor in the UK. Each of these productions has its own story to tell, but that there should be so many British films without British distribution is surely alarming.

Indeed, it is hard to reconcile the producers' constant lament that they lack finance with their apparent penchant for making unreleasable films.

On the other hand, 1992's crop of British releases included some outstanding successes, including *The Crying Game*, *Howards End*, *Truly, Madly, Deeply* and *Enchanted April*. *The Long Day Closes* and *The Naked Lunch* provoked strong, and mostly approving, critical reactions, while, at the other end of the scale, *Split Second* and *The Lawnmower Man* demonstrated that Britain can still produce profitable action-thrillers.

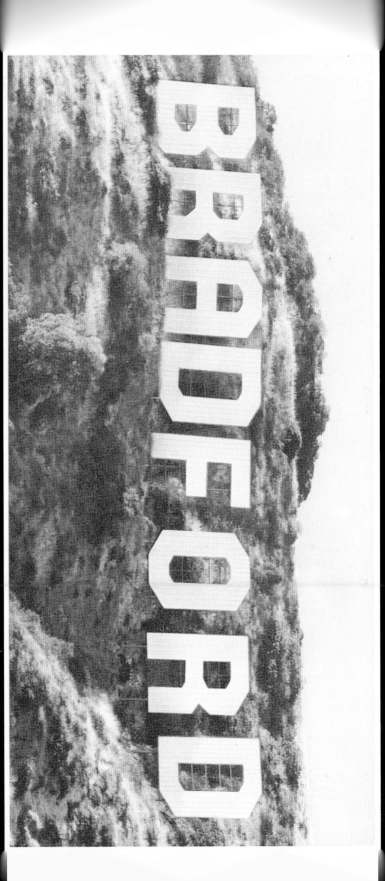

Above: Big Budget *Chaplin* missed the big audiences

Total UK cinema admissions increased by two percent in 1992, to reach 103.6 million **(table 9)**. This is the eighth year in a row that admissions have grown.

The increase has been steady rather than spectacular and it has been achieved at a price. Since American Multi Cinema opened Britain's first multiplex, The Point in Milton Keynes, in 1985, thereby reversing the decades-long decline in British cinema admissions, an estimated £500 million has been spent on building multiplexes and refurbishing existing cinemas. That's a hefty investment for an addition to the gross box-office over the period that can't have exceeded £700 million.

Even so, independent analysis by Dodona Research recently concluded that the new multiplexes are starting to move into profit. This may explain why ticket prices have been reduced, relative to inflation, to the level they were in 1980 **(table 9)**. Cheaper tickets have long been urged by major distributors anxious to defend cinema's hard-won gains from rival entertainment and leisure activities.

Beckoning profitability and the decline in recession-hit building costs and land values would also help to explain the continued growth of the exhibition sector. By the end of 1992, there were 1,848 screens in the UK, compared with 1,777 the year before and 1,284 in 1985. The number of multiplex screens increased last year to 556, from 510 in 1991, while the number of single screens increased to 338, from 328 **(table 9)**.

To put matters into one kind of perspective, today's cinema audience, despite the growth of the last eight years, is only about 6% the size of the audience in 1946 **(table 10)**. Average visits per head today stand at 1.8, compared to more than 30 then.

But another kind of perspective tells us that, on average, people today watch about 1.8 films a week on television and one film every three weeks on video, giving a per-person viewing habit of between 75 and 100 films a year. The golden age of cinema may be over, but films themselves seem to have lost none

9 UK Cinema Screens, Admissions, box-office gross and average ticket prices

	1989	1990	1991	1992
Box Office Grosses (£ millions)	2,260	2,610	2,955	3,223
Average UK admission prices (£)	2.35	2.66	2.90	3.11
Index at Constant Price (1980 = 100)	97	100	103	100
Screens taking advertising	1,432	1,552	1,642	1,805
Regional Film Theatres	33	36	38	43
Multiplexes (5 plus screens)	29	41	57	63
Number of multiplex screens	285	387	510	556
Number of single screens	341	349	328	338
Total Screens	1,550	1,673	1,777	1,848
Average US admission prices (US$)	4.44	4.75	4.90	5.06
Index at Constant Prices	112	115	115	115

Source: Screen Digest /CAA/BFI

10 Comparative Admissions

Total admissions (millions)

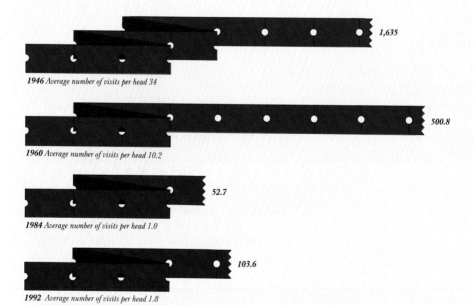

Source: Policy Studies Institute, Cultural Trends 1992:13/Business Monitor MA2; Central Statistics Office, CSO Bulletin Issue 3/92 GB Cinema Exhibitors (Quarter 3 1991); Variety, 27/1/92; Cinema Advertising Association/Screen Digest/BFI/Entertainment Data Inc.

11a Frequency of cinema-going 1992

Age group *Number of people*	*7 -14* *5.46m*	*15 - 24* *8.11m*	*25 - 34* *8.56m*	*35+* *28.52m*	*ABC1*	*C2DE*
Twice a month or more	6	15	6	1	5	4
Once a month	10	16	8	3	9	5
Once every 2-3 months	16	21	12	5	12	8
2-3 times a year	28	20	19	8	15	14
Once a year	13	9	13	8	10	9
Less often	13	8	15	21	18	16

11b Age of Multiplex and Non-Multiplex Visits %

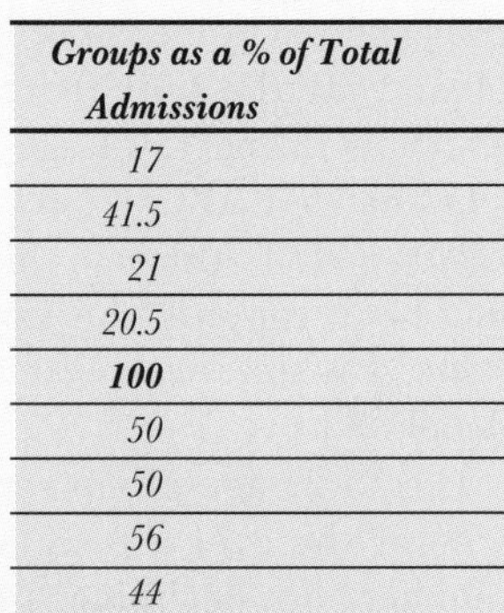

Age group	*Multiplex Visits*		*Non-Multiplex Visits*		*Groups as a % of Total Admissions*
	1991%	*1992%*	*1991%*	*1992%*	
7 - 14	13	14	17	20	17
15 - 24	44	45	33	38	41.5
25 - 34	24	24	25	18	21
35+	19	17	25	24	20.5
Total	**100**	**100**	**100**	**100**	**100**
Male	53	50	53	50	50
Female	47	50	47	50	50
ABC1	54	55	56	57	56
C2DE	46	45	44	43	44

Percentage of the population aged 7 and over who "Ever Go" to the cinema

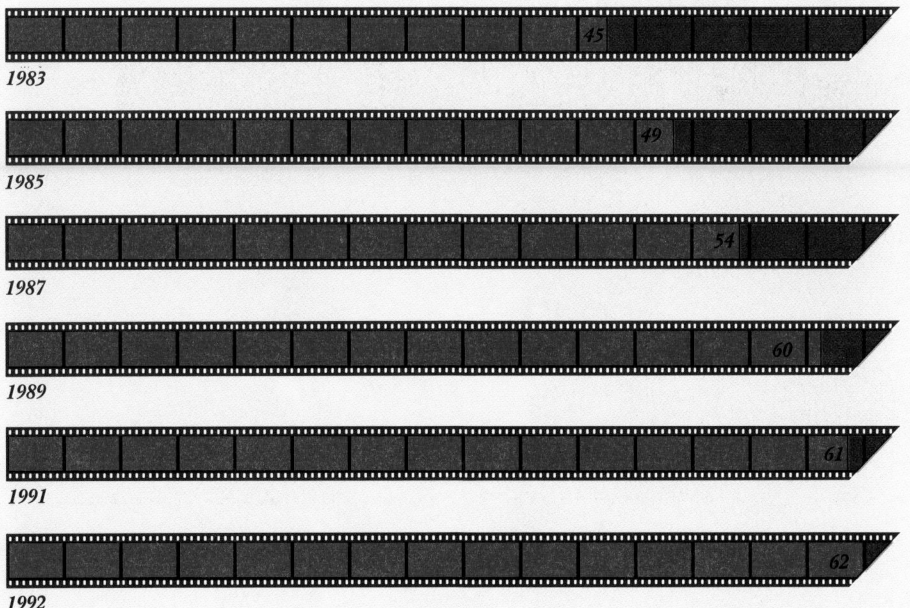

Source: Cinema and Video Industry Audience Research (CAVIAR).

of their appeal, even if many of them, outside the cinema environment, are watched with less concentration than before.

In 1991, it was observed that all age-groups except one had increased the frequency of their cinema-going. The exception was the 7-14 group. In 1992, the trend continued, with a 7% decline in the proportion of young children "ever going" to the cinema. That's a loss of at least 380,000 ticket sales.

But the loss has been more than compensated by increases elsewhere. It is clear that the bulk of the audience, 41.5%, is in the 15-24 age group **(table 11)** and that ABC1s (56%) outnumber C2DEs (44%). Although this composition has been roughly the same for some years, it is still worth examining in more detail.

The 15-24 age group represents only 16% of the over-7 population and its numbers are declining. In 1985, there were 9.3 million in that group. By 1992, the figure was down to 8.1 million.

Of the 15-24s, just under one-third go to the cinema once a month or more. That's 2. 5 million people. To them can be added the 870,000 frequent cinema-goers in the 7-14 group, the 1.2 million enthusiasts among the 25-34s and the 1.1 million among the middle-aged and elderly. That makes a core cinema audience in the UK of 5.7 million people, which is just over 10% of the over-7 total.

It can be assumed that these 5.7 million, who between them account for at least two-thirds of all tickets sold in the UK, are the arbiters of taste for the rest. They should be the target of all cinema marketing, which, in addition, should be skewed slightly towards the upmarket ABC1s.

Yet we know from other research that cinema marketing typically reaches more than 90% of the cachement population, regardless of age or socio-economic group. This is true of art movies (albeit perhaps to a lesser degree) as well as blockbusters.

Below: Made in the UK and a big hit with British audiences - *Alien*[3]

12 Top 20 Non-English Language Films at the UK Box-Office 1992

Title	Country	Distributor	Box-Office
Delicatessen	France	Electric	1,267,000
High Heels	Spain	Rank	409,160
Les Amants Du Pont Neuf	France	Artificial Eye	181,253
Merci La Vie	France	Artificial Eye	173,541
Until the End of the World	Fr/Ger/Aus	Entertainment	125,557
Raise the Red Lantern	China/Hong Kong	Mayfair	101,633
Betty Blue (Version Intégrale)	France	20th Century Fox	88,257
Van Gogh	France	Artificial Eye	86,187
La Belle Noiseuse	France	Artificial Eye	79,549
Europa Europa	Fr/Ger	Arrow	76,566
My Night With Maud	France	BFI	74,294
Belle De Jour	France	Electric	67,418
The Double Life of Véronique	France	Gala	36,187
The Best Intentions	Sweden	Artificial Eye	37,151
Aux Yeux Du Monde	France	Artificial Eye	32,293
Jacquot De Nantes	France	Gala	26,294
Mon Pere ce Héros	France	Gala	25,461
Pepi, Luci, Bom...	Spain	Metro	23,759
Urga	France/USSR	Mayfair	20,981
Europa	Denmark	Electric	18,409

(Source EDI)

Thus, film distributors are expending significant resources on marketing films in the sure knowledge that most of that effort — on the face of it, as much as 80% per film — is wasted.

It is a situation that exercises the minds of distributors around the world, but, as yet, none has come up with a solution. Meanwhile, the apparent inefficiency of cinema marketing is half-heartedly justified on the grounds that it has a beneficial effect on sales in video and pay-TV.

The distributors' dilemma is exacerbated by the polarisation of the theatrical market, whereby a handful of mega-hits takes all the money and most of the rest fail to cover the costs of marketing. This has been a bugbear for distributors for many years and anecdotal evidence suggests that the problem is getting worse, as the audience becomes less discriminating and more swayed by hype. But while the long-term trend may be towards greater polarisation, there is reason to believe it has an ebb and flow, depending on the quality of films on release.

In 1992, the top 20 films, representing 8.6% of all releases, took £162.3 million at the box-office. This was 50.4% of the total **(table 17)**. The previous year, the top 20 took £169.5 million, or 57.5% of the total. Indeed, the polarisation in 1991 was even more marked if we look at just the top five films, representing 1.85% of all releases, which took £78.9 million, or 46% of the entire box-office that year.

In 1992, the top five took 38% (£61.8 million) of the total. Last year's top films, *Basic Instinct*, *Hook* and *Lethal Weapon 3*, sold roughly three million tickets fewer than 1991's *Robin Hood: Prince Of Thieves*, *Terminator 2* and *The Silence Of The Lambs*.

Polarisation is not just a phenomenon affecting the mass market. In 1991, the top foreign-language film, *Cyrano De Bergerac*, took 62% of the box-office for the entire foreign-language top 20. The top five films took 96%. In 1992, the

 1992 UK Box Office for UK Feature Films

Title	Year	Country	Production Company	Distributor	Production Costs(£m)	Box Office(£m)
Afraid of the Dark	*1991*	*UK/France*	*Ariane/Telescope/ Cine Cinq*	*Rank*	*n.a.-*	*0.049*
As You Like It	*1991*	*UK*	*Sands/Aim/ Reinhart*	*Squirrel*	*1.0*	*0.012*
Bitter Moon	*1991*	*UK/France*	*Burrill Prods/ RP Prods*	*Columbia*	*7.0*	*0.5*
Blame it on the Bellboy	*1991*	*UK/US*	*Prominent Features/ Disney*	*Warner Bros*	*5.0*	*2.6*
Blue Ice	*1992*		*Blue Ice Prods*	*Guild*	*5.0*	*0.2*
Bob Roberts	*1991*	*US/UK*	*Working Title*	*Rank*	*2.2*	*0.4*
The Bridge	*1990*	*UK*	*Moonlight (Bridge) Prods*	*Eclectic*	*n.a.*	*0.016*
Carry On Columbus	*1991*		*Comedy House/ Peter Rogers Prods*	*UIP*	*2.5*	*1.6*
*Chaplin**	*1991*	*US/UK*	*Caroloco/Lambeth*	*Guild*	*16.6*	*1.8*
City of Joy	*1991*	*UK/France*	*Lightmotive/Pricel/ Majestic*	*Warner Bros.*	*13.0*	*0.8*
*The Crying Game**	*1991*	*UK*	*Palace/ British Screen*	*Mayfair*	*2.1*	*2.02*
Dakota Road	*1990*	*UK*	*Film Four International/ British Screen/ Working Title*	*Mayfair*	*1.0*	*0.029*
Double X	*1991*	*UK*	*String of Pearls*	*Feature Film Co.*	*0.35*	*0.002*
Dream On	*1991*	*UK*	*Amber/ British Screen/ Channel 4*	*Amber*	*0.43*	*0.002*
Electric Moon	*1991*	*UK*	*Grapevine Media/ Channel 4*	*Goldwyn/ Winstone*	*n.a.*	*0.002*
Elenya	*1991*	*UK/Germany*	*BFI/S4C/ Frankfurter/ZDF*	*BFI*	*0.75*	*0.005*
The Favour, the Watch & the Very Big Fish	*1990*	*UK/France*	*Fildebroc/ Films Ariane/ Umbrella Films*	*Rank*	*n.a.*	*0.031*
Enchanted April	*1991*	*UK*	*BBC/Greenpoint*	*Mayfair*	*1.1*	*0.063*
Freddie as F.R.O.7	*1990*	*UK*	*Hollywood Road*	*Rank*	*9.9*	*0.39*
Hear My Song	*1991*	*UK*	*Film Four International/ Limelight/British Screen*	*Mayfair*	*n.a.*	*0.73*
*Howards End**	*1991*	*UK*	*Merchant Ivory*	*Mayfair*	*4.0*	*3.7*

UK Box Office for UK Feature Films.

Title	Year	Country	Production Company	Distributor	Production Costs(£m)	Box Office(£m)
Immaculate Conception	*1991*	*UK/Pak*	*Dehlavi Films/ Film Four*	*Feature Film Co.*	*n.a*	*0.012*
Into The West	*1991**	*UK/Eire*	*Little Bird/ Channel 4/ British Screen/ Miramax*	*Entertainment*	*3.5*	*0.056*
Just Like A Woman	*1991*	*UK*	*Zenith/LWT Rank/ British Screen.*	*Rank*	*2.3*	*0.31*
The Lawnmower Man	*1991*	*US/UK*	*Allied Vision*	*First Independent*	*4.5*	*3.6*
Life on a String	*1991*	*China/ Germany/UK*	*Pandora Film/ Film Four International*	*ICA*	*n.a.*	*0.026*
The Long Day Closes	*1991*	*UK*	*BFI/ Film Four International*	*Mayfair*	*1.7*	*0.20*
Lost In Siberia	*1991*	*CIS/UK*	*Spectator/ Mosfilm*	*Winstone*	*n.a.*	*0.003*
The Lover	*1991*	*France/UK*	*Burrill Prods./ Renn*	*Guild*	*10.0*	*1.3*
The Monk	*1990*	*UK/Spain*	*Celtic Films/ Mediterreano Cine TV*	*Arrow*	*n.a.*	*n.a.*
The Naked Lunch	*1991*	*Canada/UK*	*Recorded Pictures/ Telefilm/ Ontario.*	*First Independent*	*10.0*	*0.54*
Peter's Friends	*1992*	*UK*	*Renaissance*	*Entertainment*	*2.0*	*3.07*
The Playboys	*1991*	*UK*	*Green Umbrella*	*Goldwyn/ Winstone*	*2.0*	*0.54*
The Pleasure Principle	*1991*	*UK*	*Psychology News/ Palace*	*Mayfair*	*n.a.*	*0.031*
Prague	*1991*	*UK/France*	*Constellation/ British Screen/ UGC/ BBC*	*Goldwyn/ Winstone*	*1.8*	*0.015*
The Princess and the Goblin	*1992*	*UK/Hungary*	*Siriol/ Pannonia/S4C*	*Entertainment*	*n.a.*	*0.025*
Rebecca's Daughters	*1991*	*UK*	*RDL/British Screen/BBC*	*Mayfair*	*2.86*	*0.007*
Secret Friends	*1991*	*UK*	*Whistling Gypsy/ Film on Four.*	*Feature Film Co*	*1.5*	*0.002*
Simple Men	*1991*	*US/UK*	*Zenith/ True Fiction*	*Metro*	*1.2*	*0.005*
Split Second	*1991*	*UK*	*Challenge/Muse*	*Entertainment*	*2.5*	*0.37*
Strip Jack Naked	*1991*	*UK*	*BFI/ Channel 4*	*BFI*	*-*	*0.006*

Title	Year	Production Country	Company	Production Distributor	Costs*	Box Office*
Time Will Tell	*1991*	*UK*	*Initial/ Island*	*Theatrical Experience*	*n.a.*	*0.003*
Waterland		*UK/US*	*Palace/British Screen/Fine Line/Channel 4*	*Mayfair*	*3.6*	*0.2*

**These figures are cumulative and include money made in 1993*

Hollywood's British Productions						
Alien 3	*1991*		*20th Century Fox*	*20th Century Fox*	*24.0*	*6.5*
The Muppet Christmas Carol	*1992*		*Jim Henson Prods*	*Buena Vista*	*8.0*	*2.5*
Patriot Games	*1991*		*Paramount*	*UIP*	*20.0*	*6.5*
The Power Of One	*1991*		*Warner/Regency*	*Warner Bros*	*8.5*	*0.25*
Wuthering Heights	*1991*		*Paramount*	*UIP*	*6.0*	*0.2*

Source: EDI

14 Box-Office Revenues of British Films Released in the US in 1992-3

Title	Country	Distribution Company	Box-Office
The Crying Game	UK	Miramax	62,539,006
The Lawnmower Man	US/UK	New Line	32,071,997
Howards End	UK	Sony Classics	17,982,985
Enchanted April	UK	Miramax	12,562,372
Chaplin	US/UK	Tristar	8,576,068
Split Second	UK	Paramount	5,742,781
Damage	UK/France	New Line	5,340,451
The Playboys	UK/Eire	Samuel Goldwyn	4,906,900
Bob Roberts	US/UK	Paramount	4,233,302
The Lover	France/UK	MGM	4,170,000
Hear My Song	UK	Miramax	3,519,704
Peter's Friends	UK	Samuel Goldwyn	3,200,000
Blame it on the Bellboy	UK/US	Buena Vista	2,891,055
Naked Lunch	UK/Canada	Fox	2,278,178
Where Angels Fear to Tread	UK	Fine Line	1,394,566
Freddie as FRO7	UK	Miramax	1,200,000
Waterland	UK	Fine line	1,093,599
Antonia and Jane	UK	Miramax	880,774
Edward II	UK	Fine Line	684,834
Under Suspicion	UK	Columbia	183,701
London Kills Me	UK	Fine Line	165,370
The Favour, the Watch & the Very Big Fish	UK/France	Tri Mark	149,204
Close My Eyes	UK	Castle Hill	135,893
Simple Men	US/UK	Fine Line	133,706
Afraid of the Dark	UK/France	Fine Line	46,570

Source: Screen Finance/ BFI

Left: *London Kills Me* died in the US

15 Breakdown of 1992 UK Box Office by Country of Origin*

Country	Number of titles	% of the 267 titles released	Box office (£)	% of the total box office
United States	*136*	*56.4%*	*249,758,323*	*85.8%*
UK - Hollywood films	*4*	*1.7%*	*13,501,103*	*4.6%*
UK - UK films	*25*	*10.8%*	*10,407,363*	*3.6%*
UK Co-productios	*18*	*7.5%*	*9,335,114*	*3.2%*
Other EC (inc. Co-productions between Non-UK EC Nations)	*31*	*12.9%*	*2,430,191*	*0.8%*
Other Europe	*3*	*1.2%*	*41,360*	*0.1%*
Other Co-Productions.	*6*	*2.5%*	*1,527,240*	*0.5%*
Rest of the World English-speaking	*12*	*4.9%*	*3,852,267*	*1.3%*
Rest of the World, other	*6*	*2.5%*	*120,433*	*0.1%*
Total	***241***	***100%***	***290,973,394***	***100%***

Source: EDI/ BFI

pattern was repeated, albeit not in quite so spectacular a fashion, with the top film, *Delicatessen*, taking 43% of the top 20 takings and the top five taking 73% **(table 12)**.

(Non top-20 foreign-language films can be discounted since in 1991 the best of them would have taken less than £13,000 and in 1992 less than £18,000.)

In 1992, the UK top 20 was again wholly American **(table 17)**. In fact, although there were fewer American films released in the year (136 compared with 166 the year before), Hollywood maintained its overall 84% market-share **(table 15)**.

Thus, far from the long-awaited fightback by British movies getting underway, British films are actually doing worse than before at the British box-office.

In 1992, there were only three British films that can be said to have had a successful British release: *The Lawnmower Man* (£3.6 million), *Peter's Friends* (£3 million) and *Howards End* (£2.7 million) **(table 13)**.

Only two other British films took over £2 million, *Blame It On The Bellboy* (£2.6 million), which was a considerable disappointment to Buena Vista and Warner Bros, and *The Crying Game* (£2.02 million).

Three other films, *Chaplin* (£1.7 million), *Carry On Columbus* (£1.6 million) and *The Lover* (£1.4 million) took over £1 million. All were box-office disappointments.

In total, 1992's crop of 25 British films accounted for 10.8% of all releases but captured just 3.6% of the box-office. The 18 co-productions involving British partners accounted for a further 7.5% of releases but captured only 3.2% of the box-office **(table 15)**.

Taken together, films with British content accounted for 18.3% of releases and 6.8% of the box-office. (In 1991, the comparable figures were 16.5% and 5.9%.) That means that, on average, British films took about one-third of the average box-office of all films released in the year.

European films did even worse. There

were 34 European films distributed in the UK in 1992, accounting for 14.1% of all releases. But they took less than 1% of the total box-office **(table 15)**.

There is a strongly-held view that the real problem lies in distribution, the theory being that the major studios monopolise the best screens. If only we could get access to playdates, the argument goes, we would be able to reach our audience. But it is always hard to find which films exactly have been harmed. The performance of most British films on television, where there is no distribution problem, does not suggest that the cinema audience is being misled by theatrical distributors **(table 24)**.

What is harder to explain is that a clutch of British films did better in the US, where, perhaps, they benefit from the cachet of being exotic, than they did at home. *The Lawnmower Man* took $32 million, *Howards End* took $18 million and *Enchanted April*, which, at the BBC's insistence, got only a token theatrical release in the UK, took $12.6 million.

Above: *The Crying Game*, a smash hit in the US, but a modest success at home

Best of all, *The Crying Game* took $14.5 million in 1992 and a further $48 million in 1993, making it the most successful British film in the US since *Chariots Of Fire* **(table 14)**.

In the absence of strong British competition, the American dominance at the UK box-office was repeated in distribution. All but one of 1992's top 20 films in the UK were distributed by the major studios, whereas in 1991 six films were independent releases. This enabled the majors to increase their market share from 66% in 1991 to 77.7% in 1992 **(table 18)**.

This was achieved by 92 films, accounting for 38.2% of all releases. On average, major studio releases took 189.9% of the average box-office of all films released in the UK.

The only relief from American hegemony in distribution was again provided by Guild, now part of France's Chargeurs group. Guild achieved the fourth-highest average box-office per title, £2.6 million, behind Buena Vista (£3.5 million), UIP (£2.8 million) and Warner Bros (£2.7 million). Guild's 12 releases achieved a market-share of 10.3% **(table 18)**.

But satisfaction at this result is constrained by the knowledge that Guild's successful releases were all American, most notably *Basic Instinct*. Also, Guild's performance was well down on the previous year, when its 11 releases achieved a 13.4% market-share and averaged £3.6 million at the box-office.

Unfortunately, the story in the rest of Europe is not much better. Belgium's share of its own market fell from 3% in 1991 to 2.2% in 1992. Italy's remained stable at around 24%. Germany's fell to 10.5% and Spain's fell to 9.2%. Only France seems to have stiffened its resistance to American power, increasing its share of the domestic market to 35% from 1991's 30.1% **(table 16)**.

16 Indigenous and US Films' shares of National Markets %

	Indigenous	US Films	Others
Belgium	2.2	78.6	19.2
Denmark	15.3	n.a.	n.a.
France	35	58.3	6.7
Germany	10.5	80+	8.5
Greece	n.a.	n.a.	n.a.
Ireland	n.a.	n.a.	n.a.
Italy	24	68	8.0
Luxembourg	2.6	80	17.4
Netherlands	13.7	n.a.	n.a.
Portugal	n.a.	68.4	n.a.
Spain	9.2	75.8	15.0
UK	3.7	92.5	3.8

Source: Screen Digest

17 Top 20 Films at UK Box Office 1992

Title	Country	Distributor	Box Office(£)
1. Basic Instinct	US	Guild	15,480,560
2. Hook	US	Columbia TriStar	13,099,578
3. Lethal Weapon 3	US	Warner Bros	11,878,179
4. Batman Returns	US	Warner Bros	10,979,599
5. Cape Fear	US	UIP	10,360,215
6. Beauty and the Beast	US	Warner Bros	9,717,735
7. Wayne's World	US	UIP	9,133,551
8. Home Alone 2: Lost in New York	US	20th Century Fox	8,263,681
9. My Girl	US	Columbia TriStar	7,629,917
10. The Hand that Rocks the Cradle	US	Warner Bros	7,306,665
11. JFK	US	Warner Bros	7,017,004
12. Beethoven	US	UIP	6,757,980
13. Father of the Bride	US	Warner Bros	6,649,715
14. Alien^3	US	20th Century Fox	6,552,103
15. Patriot Games	US	UIP	6,542,299
16. Bill and Ted's Bogus Journey	US	Columbia TriStar	5,412,724
17. Sister Act	US	Buena Vista	5,354,853
18. Far and Away	US	UIP	4,815,223
19. Unforgiven	US	Warner Bros	4,689,237
20. Snow White & the Seven Dwarfs	US	Warner Bros	4,657,649

Source: EDI/ Moving Pictures/ Screen International

18 Breakdown of 1992 UK Box-Office by Distributor

Distributor	Number of titles	As a % of total no. of titles	Box-office (£)	As a % of total box-office	Average box-office per title (£)	As a % of average box-office/title
Majors						
Warner Bros	33	13.7	90,094,791	30.9	2,730,145	226.1
UIP	23	9.5	65,168,906	22.3	2,833,430	234.7
Columbia TriStar	19	7.9	45,899,753	15.7	2,415,776	200.0
20th Century Fox	15	6.2	23,735,186	8.1	1,582,346	131.0
Buena Vista	2	0.8	6,983,409	2.4	3,491,705	289.2
Total, majors	**92**	**38.2**	**231,882,045**	**79.5**	**2,520,457**	**208.7**
Others						
Guild	12	5.0	30,846,086	10.5	2,570,507	212.9
Rank	18	7.5	6,975,472	2.4	387,526	32.1
Entertainment	12	5.0	4,836,420	1.7	403,035	33.4
First Independent	6	2.5	5,760,044	2.0	960,007	79.5
Mayfair	14	5.8	4,271,735	1.5	305,124	25.3
Electric	11	4.6	3,223,652	1.1	293,059	24.2
Goldwyn/Winstone	6	2.5	1,311,271	0.4	218,545	18.1
Artificial Eye	10	4.1	684,262	0.2	68,426	5.6
Metro	10	4.1	290,500	0.1	29,050	2.4
Mainline	3	1.3	257,439	0.1	85,813	7.1
Blue Dolphin	5	2.2	139,388	0.05	27,878	2.3
Gala	5	2.2	115,273	0.04	23,055	1.9
BFI	6	2.5	114,181	0.04	19,030	1.5
Arrow	3	1.3	85,776	0.03	28,592	2.4
Feature Film Company	9	3.7	70,384	0.02	7,820	0.6
ICA Projects	7	3	60,332	0.02	8,617	0.7
Squirrel	2	0.9	13,700	0.001	6,860	0.5
Central TV	1	0.4	10,882	0.001	10,882	0.8
Out on a Limb	2	0.9	9,419	0.001	4,710	0.4
Contemporary	4	1.6	8,250	0.001	2,338	0.2
Theatrical Experience	1	0.4	3,000	0.001	3,000	0.2
Oasis	1	0.4	2,432	0.001	2,432	0.2
Amber	1	0.4	2,000	0.001	2,000	0.2
Total	**149**	**61.8**	**659,091,898**	**20.5**	**396,598**	**32.8**
Grand Total	**241**	**100**	**290,973,394**	**100**	**1,207,358**	**100**
of which Integrated Distrib.*	**136**	**56**	**171,143,670**	**59**	**1,258,409**	**104.2**
Non- Integrated Distributors	**105**	**44**	**119,829,720**	**41**	**1,141,235**	**94.5**

*Distributors who own cinemas i.e Warner, UIP, Rank, BFI, ICA, Artificial Eye, Mainline, Mayfair, Oasis, Electric and Metro

Source: EDI/ BFI

Overleaf: ***Home Alone 2***

19 Television homes (December 1992)

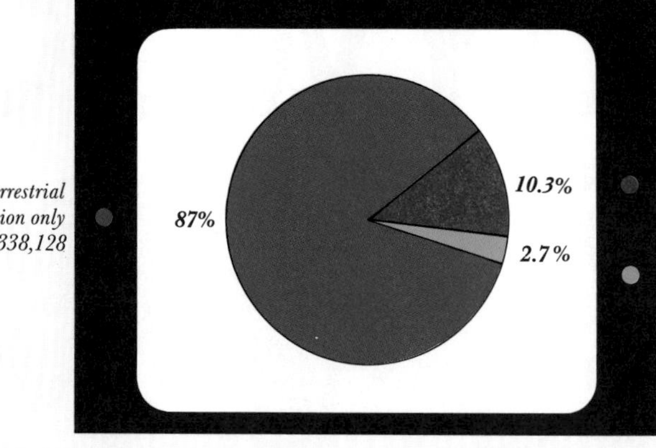

* *This is the figure calculated by BARB. The figure calculated by Continental Research for the FT Satellite Monitor is significantly higher at 2,644,000.*

Source: Screen Digest/BARB

20 Viewing of the cable and satellite channels

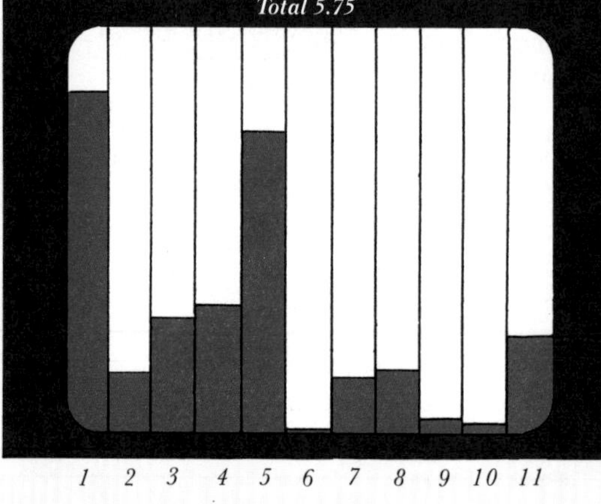

Source: *Screen Digest average figures for 4th quarter of 1992*

Over the past three years, British television has had to deal with a host of problems. Unlike those of the film industry, however, these have been more to do with upheavals in the regulatory environment than failure to meet the expectations of audiences.

The dust had no sooner settled after the award of the new ITV franchises, than major questions arose concerning the workings of the Network Centre and mooted changes to the takeover rules. The ITV network had to pay £211 million in levy payments to the Treasury in 1993 **(table 29)**, to which were added percentages of net advertising revenues, making a total contribution of more than £330 million. This compares with payments of £69 million in 1992 and £126 million in 1991.

The additional funds have to be found from within the resources of the network itself, which took the lion's share of the marginally improved £1.7 billion net advertising revenues earned by British broadcasters in 1992 **(table 30)**. But the burden is very unevenly distributed and this has given rise to considerable tension between the ITV companies.

On the one hand, Yorkshire-Tyne Tees has to find £52.7 million every year just to meet the fixed cost of its franchise; Carlton has to find £43 million and Meridian has to find £36.5 million. On the other, Granada has to cough up £9 million, LWT £7.5 million and Scottish TV and Central a mere £2,000 each **(table 29)**.

That the ITV companies would be unable to walk in step was not envisaged by Parliament and sits awkwardly with the network's federal structure.

The BBC, which in 1992 was losing the ratings war with ITV **(table 23)**, continued with its internal review in preparation for the renewal of its charter in 1996, in the process generating a mountain of paper and sending further shivers of anxiety down the spines of long-serving staffers.

Cable television, which former Home Secretary Kenneth Baker had once predicted would be in every home by the end of the 1980s, was still on the starting

21 Programme Transmission on ITV and Channel 4 1992 (Weekly Average)

	ITV Hours: Mins	*%*	*CHANNEL 4 Hours: Mins*	*%*
News & News Related	*18:45*	*13*	*10:16*	*7.2*
Factual Material inc. Documentaries	*21:61*	*15.3*	*20:47*	*14.6*
Education	*2:09*	*1.5*	*14:11*	*10.0*
Religion	*2:11*	*1.5*	*1:02*	*0.7*
Arts	*1:20*	*0.9*	*4:07*	*2.9*
Informative	***46:26***	***32.2***	***50:23***	***35.4***
Plays, Series & Serials	*31:00*	*21.5*	*12:08*	*8.5*
Feature Films & TV Movies	*20:31*	*14.2*	*28:06*	*19.8*
Narrative	***51:31***	***35.7***	***40:14***	***28.3***
Entertainment	*26:33*	*18.4*	*26:30*	*18.6*
Sport	*8:10*	*5.7*	*11:08*	*7.8*
Children's Programmes	*11:22*	*7.9*	*13:57*	*9.8*
Total	***144:02***	***100***	***142:12***	***100***

Source: ITC Annual Report 1992

Top 25 Programmes for all Channels

(Excluding multiple occurrences)

	Title	Programme Type	Channel	Date	TV Rating	Audience (millions)	Channel Share
1.	EastEnders	UK soap opera	BBC1	2/1/92	46	24.3	64%
2.	Coronation Street	UK soap opera	ITV	8/1/92	41	21.6	74%
3.	EastEnders	UK soap opera	BBC1	27/10/92	40	21.3	69%
4.	Coronation Street	UK soap opera	ITV	10/1/92	40	21.3	77%
5.	Coronation Street	UK soap opera	ITV	3/2/92	38	20.3	77%
6.	Only Fools & Horses	Sitcom	BBC1	25/12/92	38	20.1	67%
7.	Worst of Alright on the Night	Light Entertainment	ITV	1/2/92	37	19.9	74%
8.	You've been Framed	Access TV	ITV	19/1/92	36	19.3	65%
9.	The Trouble with Mr. Bean	Comedy	ITV	1/1/92	35	18.3	62%
10.	The Darling Buds of May	Drama series	ITV	26/1/92	35	18.1	58%
11.	Merry Xmas Mr. Bean	Comedy	ITV	29/12/92	35	18.5	60%
12.	More Auntie's Bloomers	Light Entertainment	BBC1	27/12/92	35	18.4	66%
13.	Taggart	TV Film	ITV	1/1/92	34	18.3	67%
14.	Three Men and a Baby	Feature Film	ITV	15/2/92	34	18.3	68%
15.	Neighbours	Australian Soap	BBC1	21/12/92	34	18.1	55%
16.	Elizabeth R	Documentary	BBC1	6/2/92	34	17.9	60%
17.	Mr. Bean Rides Again	Comedy	ITV	17/2/92	32	17.1	56%
18.	Birds of a Feather	Sitcom	BBC1	25/12/92	32	16.9	62%
19.	The Bill	Drama Series	ITV	28/1/92	32	16.9	67%
20.	A Touch of Frost	Drama Series	ITV	6/12/92	32	16.8	65%
21.	Inspector Morse	Drama Series	ITV	15/4/92	32	16.8	62%
22.	It'll be Alright on the Night	Light Entertainment	ITV	19/1/92	31	16.7	62%
23.	Casualty	Drama Series	BBC1	14/11/92	31	16.6	58%
24.	Wish You Were Here	Lifestyle	ITV	3/2/92	31	16.3	71%
25.	One Foot in the Grave	Sitcom	BBC1	8/3/92	31	16.2	57%

Source: BARB

23 Average Hours of TV Viewing per Person Per Week by Channel 1987-1992, All Homes.

Year	BBC 1	BBC2	ITV	Channel 4	Other	Total
1987	9:32	2:52	11:11	2:16	n.a.	25:51
1988	9:23	2:58	10:32	2:11	n.a.	25:04
1989	9:45	2:42	10:40	2:12	n.a.	25:19
1990	9:01	2:25	10:24	2:08	n.a.	23:58
1991	9:05	2:30	11:03	2:28	n.a.	25:06
1992	9:00	2:47	10:54	2:45	1:18	26:44

Source: AGB/ BARB

 UK TV Films Premiered in 1992

*All but two of the 1992 Film on Four season have had a previous theatrical release but this is their first UK TV transmission

Title	Transmission Date	BARB Rating
Film on Four		
Life is Sweet	15/9/92	3.66m
Riff Raff	22/9/92	2.65m
Paris by Night	29/9/92	3.18m
Venus Peter	6/10/92	1.81m
Queen of Hearts	13/10/92	1.78m
December Bride	20/10/92	2.57m
Stormy Monday	27/10/92	4.29m
Bye Bye Baby*	3/11/92	2.34m
Resurrected	10/11/92	3.00m
I Hired A Contract Killer	17/11/92	2.53m
Diamond Skulls	24/11/92	3.28m
The Deceivers	1/12/92	3.23m
Sour Sweet	8/12/92	2.44m
Strapless	15/12/92	1.84m
Fools of Fortune	22/12/92	1.19m
God on the Rocks*	19/12/92	1.35m

Films marked * have received no theatrical release prior to transmission

Title	Transmission Date	BARB Rating
BBC TV Films		
An Ungentlemanly Act	13/6/92	3.00m
Adam Bede	1/1/92	6.28m
Ghostwatch	31/10/92	11.07m
Screen One		
A Very Polish Practice	6/9/92	5.42m
Disaster at Valdez	13/9/92	6.14m
Born Kicking	20/9/92	7.05m
Black and Blue	27/9/92	7.18m
Seconds Out	4/10/92	4.22m
Running Late	11/10/92	6.60m
Losing Track	15/10/92	4.56m
Trust Me	25/10/92	6.43m
The Humming Bird Tree	20/12/92	4.76m
Screen Two		
The Grass Arena	19/1/92	2.58m
Flea Bites	26/1/92	2.13m
The Count of Solar	2/2/92	2.36m
The Lost Language of Cranes	9/2/92	3.39m
The Object of Beauty*	16/2/92	2.91m
My Sister-Wife	23/2/92	3.52m
Truly, Madly, Deeply*	1/3/93	5.67m
The Common Pursuit	8/3/92	1.97m
Utz	15/3/92	2.29m
The Law Lord	22/3/92	2.91m
The Last Romantics	29/3/92	1.55m
Enchanted April*	5/4/92	4.64m
Memento Mori	19/4/92	2.86m

* These films were given a theatrical release prior to transmission
Source: BARB

25 Top Audiences for Feature Films on Television, 1992

Rank	Title	Origin	Year	Channel	Viewing figures
1.	*Three Men and a Baby*	US	1987	ITV	18,272,000
2.	*Indiana Jones & the Last Crusade*	US	1989	BBC1	15,779,000
3.	*Turner and Hooch*	US	1989	ITV	15,452,000
4.	*Who Framed Roger Rabbit*	US	1988	ITV	15,104,000
5.	*Twins*	US	1988	BBC1	15,038,000
6.	*Die Hard*	US	1988	ITV	14,768,000
7.	*Naked Gun*	US	1988	BBC1	14,206,000
8.	*Romancing the Stone*	US	1984	ITV	14,117,000
9.	*K9*	US	1988	BBC1	13,890,000
10.	*Shirley Valentine*	UK/US	1989	BBC1	13,861,000
11.	*Flight of the Navigator*	US	1986	BBC1	13,805,000
12.	*Batteries Not Included*	US	1987	BBC1	13,395,000
13.	*Tremors*	US	1989	BBC1	13,366,000
14.	*Working Girl*	US	1988	ITV	13,337,000
15.	*Vice Versa*	US	1988	ITV	13,304,000
16.	*Heartbreak Ridge*	US	1986	ITV	13,174,000
17.	*Coming To America*	US	1988	BBC1	13,169,000
18.	*Crocodile Dundee II*	US	1986	ITV	12,661,000
19.	*The Living Daylights*	UK/US	1987	ITV	12,440,000
20.	*Beverly Hills Cop*	US	1984	BBC1	12,410,000

Source: Screen Finance

26 Where Feature Films shown on Terrestrial* TV Come From; Transmission in 1992 by Country of Origin

United States	*1,503*
United Kingdom	*571*
Australia	*55*
France	*86*
Germany	*16*
Italy	*27*
Others	*151*
Co- Productions	*83*
Total	***2,480***
Of Which, Made for TV Movies	*243*

** BSkyB do not record the country of origin of films transmitted but estimate that well over 80% of their films come from the USA*

Source: Screen Digest

blocks and looking desperately for new capital at the start of the new decade. By mid-1993, sufficient new funds had been procured, mostly from the US, for the industry to look as if it meant business.

More positively, satellite broadcaster BSkyB moved into operating profitability and Channel Four, arguably the most fortunate as well as the most enterprising broadcaster in the UK, proved enormously successful in selling its own airtime. How long before the minority broadcaster is privatised?

Viewers have taken all this in their stride. In 1992, the average hours of viewing per person increased by one hour 38 minutes, to reach 26 hours 44 minutes a week **(table 23)**. This followed a

27 The Programmes the BBC transmits and Where They come From, Year To 31st March 1992

	hrs	New hrs made by independents	New in-house production
Features, Documentaries & Current Affairs	*2,409*	*252*	*2,157*
Sport	*1,189*	*88*	*1,101*
Light Entertainment	*861*	*148*	*713*
Children's Entertainment	*587*	*47*	*540*
Schools	*624*	*n.a.*	*n.a.*
Drama	*398*	*35*	*363*
Continuing Education	*257*	*25*	*232*
Religion	*100*	*11*	*89*
Music and Art	*75*	*27*	*48*
Weather	*82*	*n.a.*	*n.a.*
Regional	*866*	*82*	*784*
Total Qualifying hrs*	***7,448 (100%)***	***715 (10%)***	***6,027 (81%)***
News and Daily News Related	*4,215*		
Parliamentary Broadcasting	*322*		
Acquired Programmes	*1,440*		
Total First Transmissions	***13,425***		
Total Repeats	*4,444*		
Open University	*719*		
Continuity	*647*		
Total Hours of Broadcasting	***19,235***		

** Broadcast output of which 25% has to be commissioned from independent production companies*

Source: BBC Facts and Figures 1992/ BBC Annual Report 1991-2

similar increase in average viewing in 1991. It is beginning to look as if the fall in viewing noted in the late 1980s was not, after all, of great significance.

The number of TV homes increased to 22.2 million, from 21.8 million in 1991, and satellite services were received in another 800,000 households, making a total of 2.3 million (although Continental Research puts the figure higher, at 2.6 million). Cable systems, meanwhile, linked about 600,000 subscribers, although only about 440,000 of these were attached to a broadband (multi-channel) network **(table 19)**.

What were we watching? The top shows of 1992 included six soap operas, four drama series, three variety shows and two sitcoms **(table 22)**. This is much the same mix as before.

1992 also confirmed the well-established trend away from imports, which have vanished entirely from the prime-time schedules of the major broadcasters. There was only one import in the top 20 *(Neighbours)* and one feature film *(Three Men And A Baby)*. With those exceptions in mind, we can observe that our viewing habits incline heavily towards home-produced drama.

One particularly interesting feature of the 1992 top 20 is that six shows starred either David Jason or Rowan Atkinson. In the increasingly competitive, multichannel environment of the 1990s, it is likely that the star system in television will become even more pronounced. And the stars, like most of the programmes, will be home-grown.

Perversely, despite the television audience's proven appetite for locally-produced drama, British films performed only modestly on the small screen.

Only two of last year's top-rated films on television were British, *Shirley Valentine*, which was watched by 13.8 million people, and *The Living Daylights*, which was watched by 12.4 million **(table 25)**.

The rest, led by *Three Men And A Baby* (18.3 million), *Indiana Jones And The Last Crusade* (15.8 million), *Turner And Hooch* (15.4 million) and *Who Framed Roger Rabbit* (15.1 million), were American. All the films in the top 20 achieved audiences of more than 12 million.

For comparison, 1992's number-one film at the box-office, *Basic Instinct*, was seen by about 4.95 million people **(table 17)**.

This comparatively modest figure makes the performance of Channel Four's most popular home-produced feature film, *Stormy Monday*, which was watched by 4.29 million viewers, look good. But only three Channel Four

28 The Programmes Channel Four Transmits and Where they come from Year to 31st December 1991.

Where they Come From	*Hrs*	*Cost (£m)*	*Cost/Hr (£)*
New - Independent Commissions	*1,671*	*£126.9m*	*54,277*
Repeats - Independents	*667*		
New - ITVA	*1,551*	*£37.6m*	*21,017*
Repeats - ITVA	*238*		
US Programmes	*800*	*£6.9m*	*6,256*
US Repeats	*303*		
Other Purchased Programmes	*569*	*£6m*	*6,536*
Other Purchased Repeats	*349*		
Feature Films (1st Transmission)	*475*	*£7m*	*7,238*
Feature Films Previously Transmitted	*492*		
Total	***7,115***	***184.4***	***25,917***

Types of Programmes	*Hrs*	*Cost (£m)*	*Cost/Hr (£)*
Drama/Film on Four	*719*	*35.9*	*49,930*
Entertainment	*1,190*	*33.3*	*27,983*
News	*638*	*21.1*	*33,072*
Documentaries	*494*	*18.9*	*38,259*
Current Affairs	*613*	*15.3*	*24,959*
Education/Schools	*779*	*14.6*	*18,741*
Arts/Music	*364*	*13.9*	*38,187*
Feature Films	*1,427*	*9.5*	*6,657*
Sport	*569*	*8.7*	*15,290*
Quiz	*148*	*5.2*	*34,459*
Multicultural	*98*	*4.8*	*48,979*
Religion	*76*	*3.2*	*42,105*
Total	***7,115***	***184.4***	***25,917***

Source: Channel Four Annual Report to 31st December 1991

29 Channel 3 Licences Payments to ITC/Exchequer 1993

Station	% Annual Qualifying Revenue	Cash Bid
Border TV	0	£ 52,000
Scottish TV	2	£ 2,000
Channel TV	0	£ 1,000
Central Independent TV	11	£ 2,000
Anglia TV	7	£ 17,804,000
Carlton TV	11	£ 43,170,000
London Weekend TV	11	£ 7,585,000
Grampian TV	0	£ 720,000
Granada TV	11	£ 9,000,000
Ulster TV	0	£ 1,027,000
Meridian Broadcasting	11	£ 36,523,000
Westcountry TV	0	£ 7,815,000
HTV Group	2	£ 20,530,000
Yorkshire	7	£ 37,700,000
Tyne Tees	2	£ 15,057,000
GMTV	15	£ 34,610,000

Source: ITC

30 Television Advertising

	1985	1989	1990	1991	1992
Television advertising in £ millions:					
Gross TV advertising revenue	1,374	2,286	2,325	2,313	2,478
Deduct production costs	188	296	321	335	364
Deduct agency commission	176	297	301	304	362
TV companies net advertising revenue	1,010	1,693	1,703	1,674	1,732

Source: ITC

movies attracted more than three million viewers and the average audience for Film On Four in 1992 was a mere 2.57 million **(table 24)**.

On BBC2, the story was much the same. *Truly, Madly, Deeply* did well with 5.67 million viewers and Oscar-winner *Enchanted April* attracted 4.64 million, but the average audience for movies in the Screen Two strand was only 2.99 million.

Mainstream channel BBC1 did better, with three home-produced films gaining audiences of more than seven million. The average audience for the Screen One strand was 5.8 million **(table 24)**.

But the ratings overall are poor, given the high cost of films and the audience's proven taste for home-produced drama in other formats. BBC2 and Channel Four have the excuse that catering for minority audiences is an important part of their remits. But BBC1 is supposed to have broad appeal. Either the TV film/single play format doesn't work with audiences who prefer to get to know on-screen characters over a period of time, or the BBC drama department, like its film industry counterparts, has been making the wrong choices.

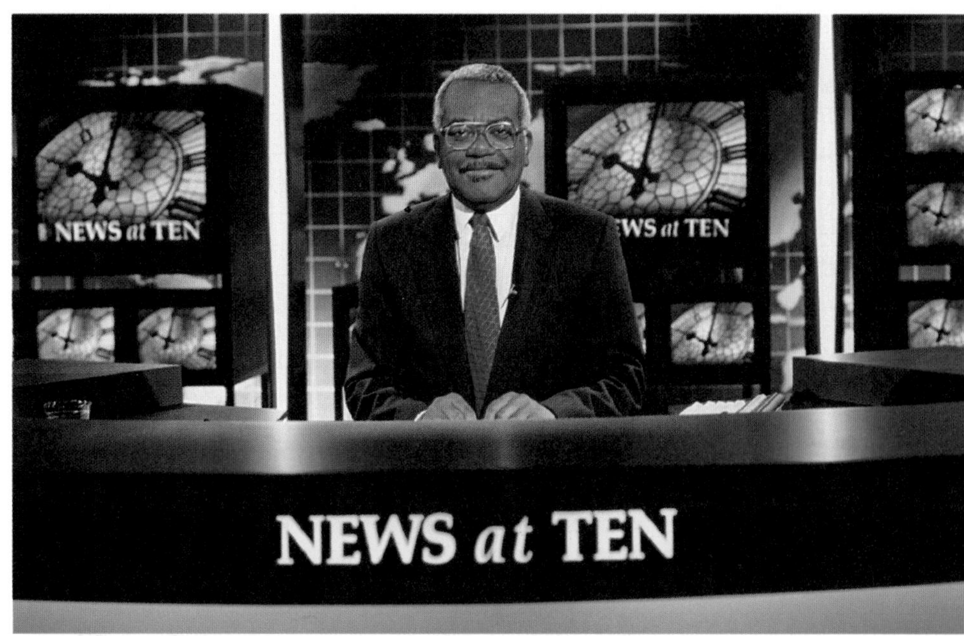

Above: In 1993 the ITV network moved to relocate its main evening news bulletin to an earlier time-slot, to make way for movies

31 *Independent Commissions by ITV Hours and Cost 1989- 1992*

	1989	1990	1991	1992
Total Hours commissioned	1,169	1,335	1,323	1,104.3
Change on previous year	+79%	+14%	-1%	-16%
Cost per hour (£000)	99	79	69	78
Change on previous year	-18%	-20%	-13%	+13%

Interestingly, the average amount of time in multi-channel homes spent watching movie channels declined dramatically in 1992, from four hours and two minutes to two hours and 49 minutes **(table 20)**.

These figures are drawn from the fourth quarter of 1992 only and there may be some seasonal explanation, although this would be hard to reconcile with the fact that all other forms of satellite and cable viewing increased in that period, from a per person average of four hours 34 minutes to five hours 26 minutes.

A more likely explanation is that the major terrestrial broadcasters, ITV in particular, alarmed by the performance and forecasts of BSkyB, adopted a much more competitive programming strategy. This will continue: ITV still doesn't have a branded movie slot, but the move to shift *News At Ten* to an earlier period was prompted by the desire to clear the peak-time schedule for more feature films and TV movies.

Out of approximately 135 broadcast hours a week, the leading ITV companies expect to screen about 18 hours of feature films, which, together with light entertainment, make up the biggest single category of programmes. In recent years, ITV companies have typically screened 400-500 movies a year.

32 Value of Overseas Television sales Versus Programme Expenditure, BBC and Channel Four

Company	Overseas programme sales (£m)	Overseas sales as % of cost of programmes
Channel 4	10	5%
BBC	47.9	10.1%

33 UK Overseas Trade in respect of Film and Television material (£m)

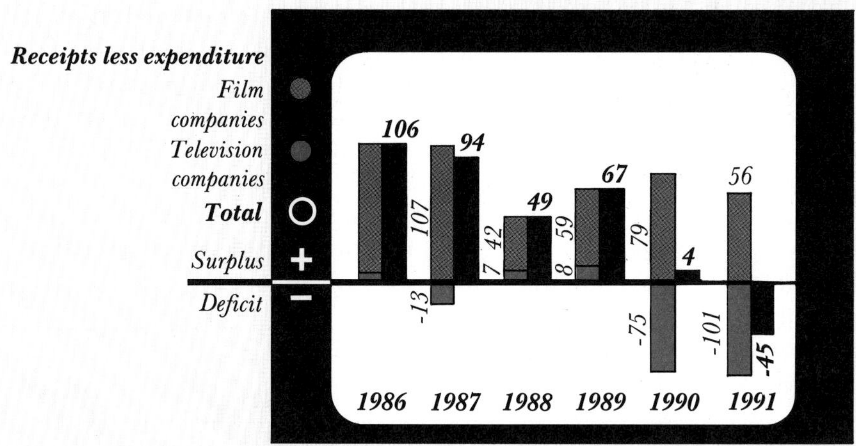

	1986	1987	1988	1989	1990	1991
Receipts (1)						
Film companies (2)	210	264	230	263	329	313
Television companies (3)	101	117	128	194	138	132
Total	**311**	**381**	**358**	**457**	**467**	**445**
Expenditure (4)						
Film companies (2)	106	157	188	204	250	257
Television companies (3)	99	130	121	186	213	233
Total	**205**	**387**	**309**	**390**	**463**	**490**
Receipts less expenditure						
Film companies (2)	104	107	42	59	79	56
Television companies (3)	2	-13	7	8	-75	-101
Total	**106**	**94**	**49**	**67**	**4**	**-45**

Notes: (1) Sums receivable from overseas residents (2) Includes transactions by film companies in respect of TV rights (3) Includes transactions in respect of BBC sound broadcasting and Independent Television News (4) Sums payable to overseas residents (CSO Bulletin 26/10/92)

BBC and Channel Four have much bigger appetites **(table 21)** and the overall output of films on terrestrial television last year was 2,480 titles, of which 1,503 were American and 571 were British. In addition, there were 243 TV movies **(table 26)**.

Television's vast appetite for feature films, in the context of added channels and the extension of the broadcasting day, may explain why, despite the public's increasing preference for home-produced shows, our programme import-bill continues to grow. In 1992, British broadcasters spent £233 million on foreign product, compared with £213 million the year before and a mere £99 million back in 1986 **(table 33)**.

Exports, on the other hand, fell, to £132 million in 1992 from £138 million in 1991. The net effect was that we spent £101 million more than we earned in foreign trade, the biggest deficit ever.

It is hard to know where this will lead. When Britain had only three channels and a thriving production community whose work was acknowledged to be superior to almost anything else available in the world, our balance of trade was always in surplus. But now we have a multitude of channels to fill at home and a financially hard-pressed creative community, in both the private and public sectors, that many believe couldn't now create an export-winning epic like *The Jewel In The Crown*.

The film industry has always been a good exporter and in 1992 it achieved a balance-of-trade surplus of £56 million. But this was not enough to prevent our combined film and television account from falling into deficit for the first time in recent years **(table 33)**.

The news for independent television producers is mixed. BBC commissions were up 18% in 1992, but only to 744 hours out of a total output of 17,200 hours **(table 27)**. Even when repeats, news and current affairs, Open University, continuity and Parliamentary broadcasts are taken out of the equation, the BBC's independent commissions only amounted to 11% of its programmes.

Channel Four commissions were also up, by three percent, to 1,723 hours. That represents 24% of Channel Four's total broadcast output of 7,020 hours. But the average price per hour paid by Channel Four fell by 5%, to £72,320 **(table 28)**.

As for ITV, its independent commissions actually fell, from 1,323 hours in 1991 to 1,104 hours in 1992. That 16% decline means that, in 1992, new independent programmes accounted for 16% of ITV's broadcast output. The good news for independent producers is that ITV prices rose by 13%, to £78,000 an hour **(table 31)**.

Above: Rowan Atkinson, one of TV's superstars

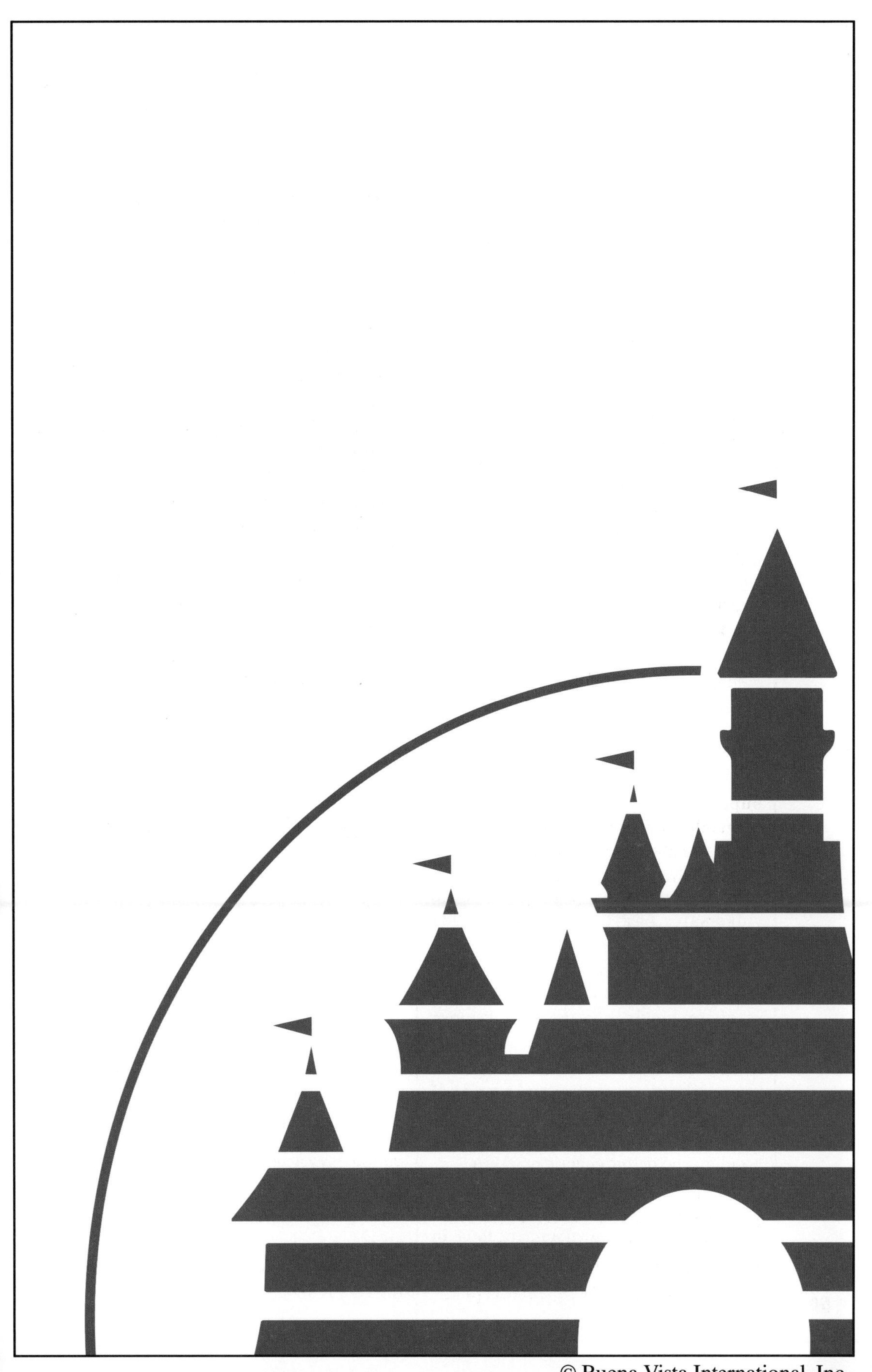

The signs are that the UK video market is beginning to contract. This is said with some caution since video statistics are notoriously unreliable, especially at the retail level. There are three main sources: distributor sales figures as collated by the British Videogram Association; specialist market research, mostly conducted by MRIB, whereby global figures are extrapolated from population or trade samples; and general surveys of household expenditure and consumer trends carried out by government agencies. Figures produced from these three sources rarely match.

The rental side of the business has been in decline since its 1989 peak, when 385 million transactions (6.7 per head of population) generated revenues of about £555 million. By 1992, transactions were down to 317 million, generating about £511 million at the retail level **(table 34)**.

The sell-through side of the business, which has enjoyed much stronger growth than rental in recent years, now also seems to be in decline. After hitting peak sales of 51 million units worth £444 million in 1991, sell-through fell back in 1992, selling 48 million units worth about £400 million.

This means that for the first time, the combined value of rental and sell-through video sales has declined, from £984 million in 1991 to £911 million in 1992.

Recession has probably played its part, as have greater competition from satellite movie channels and more aggressive scheduling and marketing of films on terrestrial television. But the video industry must itself take some of the blame, especially in the rental sector, which cries out for more efficient retailing and better generic marketing.

These shortcomings may be resolved as Blockbuster, the highly successful US chain which is now the dominant force in UK video rental, increasingly sets the standard for specialist retailing.

Above: *Terminator 2,* video rental champ

Also, it has to be borne in mind that Britain has by far the most developed video market in the EC. 1992's £911 million rental and sell-through revenues accounted for about one-third of the Community's entire video turnover. This is way out of line with all other indicators of Britain's relative economic importance.

The explanation lies mostly in the VCR penetration rate, which, at 70% of television households **(table 43)**, is on a par with Australia, Japan and the US. The second-largest European video market is Germany, with a 19.6% share, which is way below what could be expected of Europe's richest economy. But VCR penetration in Germany is only 59%. Third-placed France, with 16.8% of the market, has a VCR penetration rate of 52%, while fourth-placed Italy, with 12.8% of the market, has a VCR penetration rate of 32%.

These four markets account for 83% of all video business in the EC, where the average VCR penetration rate (including the UK) is about 52%.

In the UK, the average video household spent £32.97 on rental and £25.80 on sell-through cassettes in 1992, making a total of £58.77 **(table 34)**. That's £1.13 a week, compared with a total average household expenditure on TV, video and audio products of £6.30 **(table 43)**.

In 1992, none of the top ten rental titles was British, whereas in the previous year one title, *Memphis Belle*, could at least claim British authorship even if it was financed by Warner Bros. 1992's top ten accounted for 27.4 million transactions and generated revenues of £68.5 million **(table 37)**. This compares with 24.9 million transactions and £50 million revenues in 1991, which would suggest that the concentration at the top of the market has become more intense.

But MRIB's research suggests the opposite: that whereas the top ten titles accounted for 19.4% of transactions in 1991, in 1992 they accounted for just 14.5% **(table 36)**. According to MRIB, the greatest growth, from 21.9% of the total to 43.4%, has been outside the top

Above: *The Commitments,* the top European rental title in the UK
Below: *Lawnmower Man* is one of a spate of relatively cheap British genre movies

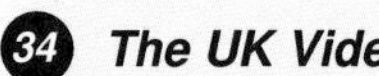

34 The UK Video Market, 1986-1992

Total retail £m

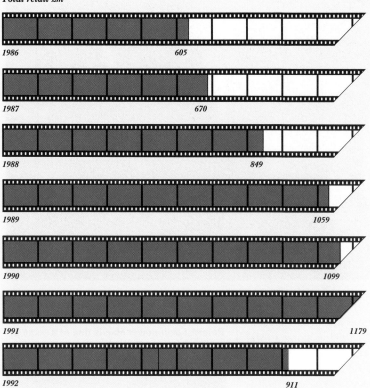

	Video Rental Units sold By Distributors	*Value(£m)*	*Retail Transactions*	*Value(£m)*	*Video Sell-Through Units Sold*	*Value (£m)*	*Blank Cassettes Units Sold*	*Value (£m)*
1986	*4.2m*	*125*	*300m*	*375*	*6m*	*70*	*35m*	*160*
1987	*4.5m*	*135*	*320m*	*410*	*10m*	*100*	*37m*	*160*
1988	*5.2m*	*155*	*350m*	*470*	*18m*	*175*	*55m*	*204*
1989	*6.2m*	*185*	*385m*	*555*	*37m*	*320*	*56m*	*184*
1990	*7.4m*	*185*	*365m*	*550*	*41m*	*365*	*59m*	*184*
1991	*6.7m*	*170*	*330m*	*540*	*51m*	*444*	*65m*	*195*
1992	*48m*	*400*	*317m*	*511*	*48m*	*400*	*n.a.*	*n.a.*

	Rental	**Purchase**	**Total**
Average Video Software Spending per head of population 1992 (£)	*8.88*	*6.95*	*15.83*
Average Software Spending per Video household 1992	*32.97*	*25.80*	*58.77*
Video Distributor Revenue 1992	*139.27*	*258.40*	*397.67*

35 UK Video Rentals by Country of Origin 1992

36 UK Video Rentals, 1992: the Top 100 and the Rest

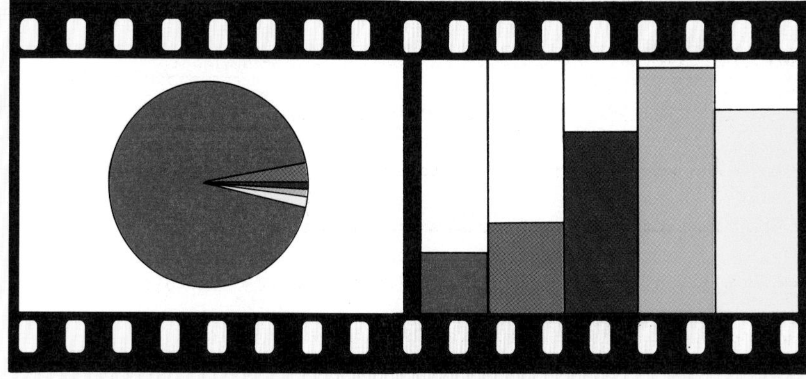

USA 92.5%
UK 5.8%
Australia 0.6%
Rest of EC 0.8%
Rest of world 0.8%

*
Top ten 14.5%
Top twenty 23.1%
Top fifty 40.9%
Top one hundred 56.6%
The rest 43.4%

* *These figures are based on MRIB's research which estimates the total number of rental transactions among the top 100 titles to be 189,420,000. This is considerably lower than the British Videogram Association estimate, based on all releases, of 317,000,000 quoted in Table 34.*
Source : MRIB

37 Top 10 Video Rental Titles, 1992

Title	No. Rentals	Est. Value (£)	Distributor
Terminator 2: Judgment Day	3,579,422	8,948,555	Guild
Basic Instinct	3,400,164	8,500,410	Guild
Robin Hood: Prince of Thieves	3,152,153	7,880,382	Warner
Point Break	3,067,853	7,669,632	Fox Video
Backdraft	2,656,948	6,642,370	CIC
The Silence of the Lambs	2,645,204	6,613,100	20:20 Vision
City Slickers	2,298,964	5,747,410	First Independent
Naked Gun 2 1/2	2,235,216	5,588,040	CIC
Hot Shots!	2,200,079	5,500,197	Fox Video
Father of the Bride	2,179,089	5,447,722	Touchstone
Total	**27,415,092**	**68,537,730**	

Source: BVA/MRIB Value is calculated on a basis of an average £2.50 rental charge per transaction for a top title.

38 Distributors' shares of UK Video Rentals 1992

Number of titles in top 495		
Distributor	**No.**	**%**
Columbia TriStar/20:20 Vision	96	19.4
Warner Home Video	60	12.1
CIC	59	11.9
Fox Video	43	8.7
Entertainment	35	7.1
Buena Vista/Touchstone	29	5.8
Guild	27	5.5
First Independent	24	4.8
Odyssey	19	3.8
Medusa	16	3.2
Vision	13	2.6
High Fliers	9	1.8
Hollywood	9	1.8
American Imperial/VPD	8	1.6
MGM/Pathé	7	1.4
Others (20 Companies)	41	8.3
Total	**495**	**100**

Source: MRIB

39 UK Video Rental: Top European titles 1992

Title	Country	Distributor	Est. No. of Rentals
The Commitments	UK/US/Eire	Fox Video	2,176,422
The Lawnmower Man	UK	First Independent	1,101,307
Split Second	UK	Entertainment	1,096,027
Blame it on the Bellboy	UK/US	Hollywood	683,756
Under Suspicion	UK	20:20 Vision	569,900
The Pope Must Die	UK	RCA/Columbia	481,274
Let Him Have It	UK	First Independent	463,527
The Naked Lunch	UK/Canada	First Independent	245,579
A Rage In Harlem	UK/US	Palace	239,565
Twenty One	UK	Entertainment	165,692
Hear My Song	UK	CIC	143,931
Truly, Madly, Deeply	UK	Buena Vista	93,296
Blonde Fist	UK	Hollywood	76,557
Revenge of Billy the Kid	UK	Medusa	68,607
Memphis Belle	UK	Warner	62,341
Nuns on the Run	UK	Fox Video	62,155
The Krays	UK	RCA/Columbia	61,479
The Pleasure Principle	UK	Palace	60,746
Until the End of the World	Ger/Fr/Aus	Entertainment	57,581
Young Soul Rebels	UK	Braveworld	57,309

Source: MRIB

100. This would be hard to explain other than by changes in the sample or method of calculation.

As ever, the rental sector is completely dominated by Hollywood movies. Of the top 495 releases in 1992, 92.5% were American. This is a two percent increase on the previous year. The British share remained steady at about 5.8% **(table 35)**.

Inevitably, American dominance was also evident among video distributors, whose revenues in 1992 probably totalled about £346 million **(table 34)**. The majors accounted for 72.7% of all rentals in 1992, compared with 69. 5% in 1991. The share taken by British distributors fell from 30.5% to 27.3% **(table 38)**.

Only three European titles released in the UK exceeded one million rentals, *The Commitments, The Lawnmower Man* and *Split Second*. There were no foreign-language films among the top European rentals, whereas in 1991 there were four **(table 39)**.

In the sell-through sector, which is much less dependent on feature films, there were only four British titles in the 1992 top 20, compared with eight the year before. Eight titles were aimed at the children's market (seven in 1991) and five were distributed by Buena Vista, which handles Disney films **(table 40)**.

Buena Vista is believed to have the biggest share of the sell-through market although the available figures don't exactly bear this out.

For example, taking just the top ten sell-through titles by value (excluding music videos), in 1992 the BBC appeared to have 10.5% of the market, Warner had 10.3% and Buena Vista 9.9% **(table 41)**. But there is reason to doubt that the sample, which is skewed towards music retailers, accurately reflects the industry as a whole.

Above: *Split Second,* one of three British films to exceed one million rentals

40 Top 20 Selling UK Video Sell-through titles, 1992

Rank	Title	Year	Country	Company
1	Cinderella	1950	US	Buena Vista
2	Robin Hood: Prince of Thieves	1991	US	Warner Home Video
3	Terminator 2: Judgment Day	1991	US	Guild
4	Hook	1992	US	Columbia Tristar
5	Batman Returns	1992	US	Warner Home Video
6	Fantasia	1940	US	Buena Vista
7	The Rescuers Down Under	1991	US	Buena Vista
8	Dances with Wolves	1990	US	Guild
9	The Silence of the Lambs	1991	US	Columbia Tristar
10	Cherfitness: A New Attitude	1992	US	Fox Video
11	25BC - The best of 25 years	1992	UK	VVL
12	Home Alone	1991	US	Fox Video
13	The Little Mermaid	1990	US	Buena Vista
14	Aliens	1986	US	Fox Video
15	Ghost	1990	US	CIC
16	Basil the Great Mouse Detective	1989	US	Buena Vista
17	Tale of Peter Rabbit & Benjamin Bunny	1992	UK	Pickwick
18	Amazing Adventures of Mr Bean	1992	UK	Video Collection
19	JFK	1991	US	Warner Home Video
20	The Commitments	1991	UK/US	Fox Video

Source: CIN/ Gallup

41 Video sell-through: Non-music videos, market share by company

Company	Market Share
BBC	10.5%
Warner Home Video	10.3%
Buena Vista	9.9%
Polygram	7.7%
Video Collection	7.7%
Fox Video	6.6%
CIC	6.5%
VVL	4.9%
Columbia Tri-Star	4%
Guild	3%

Source: Gallup/CIN

Although these are the main published figures they are not believed to wholly reflect the market. The CIN survey is based primarily on stores engaged in record retailing and sales from these outlets are not necessarily representative of the industry as a whole. The survey does not include supermarkets and other non-media based stores nor mail order operations.

42 Video Sell-Through: Distributors' Share of Top 100

Buena Vista	*12*	*Guild*	*4*
BBC	*11*	*BMG Video*	*4*
Polygram	*10*	*Columbia Tristar*	*3*
FoxVideo	*9*	*Ritz*	*1*
Warner Home Video	*8*	*EUK*	*1*
VVL	*7*	*MGM/UA*	*1*
CIC	*7*	*First Independent*	*1*
Pickwick	*5*	*Braveworld*	*1*
Video Collection	*5*	*Watershed*	*1*
PMI	*5*	*Silvervision*	*1*

Produced by TV Cartoons for F Warne & Co

Above: *The Tale of Peter Rabbit and Benjamin Bunny*. The sell-through market has created a significant new revenue stream for children's titles, especially animation

CONCLUSION

Above: *The Young Americans*, a new type of British film

Surveying the film production and cinema statistics, it is hard to avoid the conclusion, reached some years ago by many commentators, that the British film industry is dead. While individual producers show great resourcefulness and our pool of talented writers, directors, actors and technicians continues to be restocked (mostly thanks to television, commercials and Hollywood), there is nothing here on which to build. Budgets get inexorably smaller and the performance of our films continues to diminish even among our own audiences.

Crucially, the British film community lacks a centre of gravity, such as was last provided in the mid-80s by the combination of Thorn EMI Screen Entertainment, Goldcrest and Rank. The one candidate for the role is Polygram, but Britain is too small a territory to contain the Dutch music giant's global ambitions. Other large corporates on the edge of the industry, such as Pearson, Carlton and Granada, have the resources to succeed in films but, so far, don't feel the need to get involved.

One school of thought believes we should look towards mainland Europe, with whom we may not share a common language or culture but with whom we do share a common bondage to Hollywood. For such an initiative to bear worthwhile fruit, however, we would all have to learn to put audiences, not film-makers, first.

Even those who do not share the view that cinema is essentially a popular medium can see that, as the contrasting fortunes of Hollywood and Europe over the last three decades demonstrate, good work cannot exist in a vacuum. There has to be quantity for there to be quality. Quantity means audiences.

An alternative to the European route is to work more closely with commercial television. There are compelling business reasons for farsighted ITV companies to get involved in film and the biggest of them pledged commitment to film-making in their franchise applications. It could yet happen.

At all events, British films will continue to get made, because producers, writers, directors, actors and technicians want to make them. There is proof enough of this in the recent spate of "no-budget" films, notably *Leon The Pig Farmer,* in which all the participants worked for deferred fees and points.

Meanwhile, we should be looking for stirrings of interest among the telecom companies and major retailers like Kingfisher. They know that interactive, digital media, driven by entertainment, is going to change everything. They don't want to miss out. When they come knocking, let's hope there's enough of a film community left to open the door.

43 General Statistics

	1986	1991	1992
Annual rate of inflation (%)	3.4	6.7	3.7
Gross domestic product, Current Prices (£m)	380,623	596,631	595,209
Population (000s)	56,763	57,494	57,561
Number of households (000s)	21,248	22,178	22,800
TV households (000s)	20,614	21,792	22,237
VCR households (000s)	9,149	15,429	15,565
Satellite dish households (000s)	0	2,040	2,667
Cable: Homes passed (000s)	1,176	2,105	2,718
Cable: Subscribers (000s)	188	535	602
TV and video software - total expenditure	**1,659**	**2,854**	**2,680**
BBC licence fee (£m)	1,026	1,409	1,486
VCR software (£m)	615	1,183	911
Premium cable (£m)	18	47	50
Satellite subscriptions (£m)	0	215	233
Expenditure on cinema (£m)	**142**	**295**	**322**

Above: *Leon the Pig Farmer*, a "no-budget" success story
Over: *The Secret Rapture*

DIRECTORY

ARCHIVES AND FILM LIBRARIES

FIAF (International Federation of Film Archives)
rue Franz Merjay 190
1180 Brussels
Belgium
Tel: (32) 2 343 06 91
Fax: (32) 2 343 76 22
FIAF, which has over 50 member archives and many Provisional members and Associates from 59 countries, exists to develop and maintain the highest standards of film preservation and access. It also publishes handbooks on film archiving practice which can be obtained from the above address

FIAT (International Federation of Television Archives)
Sveriges Television SVT
105 10 Stockholm
Sweden
Tel: (46) 87845760
Fax: (46) 86631232
Sten Frykholm
FIAT membership is made up mainly of the archive services of broadcasting organisations but also encompasses national archives and other television-related bodies. It meets annually and publishes its proceedings and other recommendations concerning television archiving

NATIONAL ARCHIVES

Imperial War Museum
Department of Film
Lambeth Road
London SE1 6HZ
Tel: 071 416 5000
Fax: 071 416 5379
The national museum of twentieth century conflict, illustrating and recording all aspects of modern war. The Department of Film reflects these terms of reference with an extensive archive of film and video material, which is widely used by historians and by film and television companies

bfi National Film and Television Archive (NFTVA)
21 Stephen Street
London W1P 1PL
Tel: 071 255 1444
Fax: 071 580 7503
The NFTVA preserves and makes permanently available a national collection of moving images which have value as examples of the art and history of cinema and television, or as a documentary record of the twentieth century. The collection now stands at over 200,000 titles dating from 1895 to the present. The Archive also preserves and makes accessible the BFI's collection of stills, posters and designs

Scottish Film Archive
Dowanhill
74 Victoria Crescent Road
Glasgow G12 9JN
Tel: 041 334 4445
Fax: 041 334 8132
Janet McBain, Archivist
Almost exclusively non-fiction film, the collection dates from 1897 to the present day and concerns aspects of Scottish social, cultural and industrial history. Access charges and conditions available on request

Wales Film and Television Archive
Unit 1, Aberystwyth Science Park
Cefn Llan
Aberystwyth
Dyfed SY23 3AH
Tel/Fax: 0970 626007
Iola Baines
Gwenan Owen
The Archive locates, preserves and catalogues film and video material relating to Wales. The collection is made accessible where possible for research, viewing and exploitation by the Archive's Education and Outreach Officer

REGIONAL COLLECTIONS

East Anglian Film Archive
Centre of East Anglian Studies
University of East Anglia
Norwich
Norfolk NR4 7TJ
Tel: 0603 592664
Fax: 0603 58553
David Cleveland
Cathryn Terry
Jane Alvey
Preserving documentary films, both amateur and professionally made, showing life and work in Norfolk, Suffolk, Essex and Cambridgeshire. Collection includes farming, rural life, the Fens, Norfolk Broads, fishing industry, and the seaside

North West Film Archive
The Manchester Metropolitan University
Minshull House
47-49 Chorlton Street
Manchester M1 3EU
Tel: 061 247 3097
Fax: 061 247 3098
Maryann Gomes, Curator
Marion Hewitt, Librarian
The North West Film Archive preserves moving images showing life in the North West and operates as a public regional archive. Urban and industrial material is particularly well illustrated

Northern Film and Television Archive
36 Bottle Bank
Gateshead
Tyne and Wear NE8 2AR
Tel: 091 477 3601/5532
Fax: 091 478 3681
Bob Davis
A Northern Regional collection with an emphasis on industry, especially coalmining, and the mining community

Wessex Film and Sound Archive
Hampshire Record Office
Sussex Street
Winchester SO23 8TH
Tel: 0962 847742
Fax: 0962 878681
David Lee
Preserves and makes publicly accessible for research, films, video and sound recordings of local interest to central southern England

NEWSREEL, PRODUCTION AND STOCK

SHOT LIBRARIES

These are film and television libraries which specialise in locating material on a particular subject. For other, sometimes more specialised, film libraries consult the 'Researcher's Guide to British Film and Television Collections' and the 'Researcher's Guide to British Newsreels', published by the BUFVC

Archive Film Agency
21 Lidgett Park Avenue
Roundhay
Leeds LS8 1EU
Tel: 0532 662454
Fax: 0532 664703
Agnèse Geoghegan
Film from 1898 to present day and video – comedy, documentary, newsreel and feature film, silent and sound. Specialists in music hall, Birmingham, Yorkshire. 1930s stills. Cassette service

Archive Films
4th Floor
184 Drummond Street
London NW1 3HP
Tel: 071 383 0033
Fax: 071 383 2333
Angela Saward
Stock film footage collection covering silent comedies, feature films, documentaries, TV programmes, rare music footage, industrial films and newsreels. Same day service of a research cassette for almost any request

Boulton-Hawker Films
Hadleigh
Ipswich
Suffolk IP7 5BG
Tel: 0473 822235
Fax: 0473 824519
Peter Boulton
Educational films produced over 46 years. Subjects include: health, biology, botany, geography, history, archaeology, and the arts

British Movietone News Film Library
North Orbital Road
Denham, Uxbridge
Middx UB9 5HQ
Tel: 0895 833071
Fax: 0895 834893
London Office:
76 Old Compton Street
London W1V 5PA
Tel: 071 437 7766 x262
Newsreel (1929-1979), b/w, some colour, 35mm

British Pathé News
Pinewood Studios
Iver Heath
Bucks SL0 0NH
Tel: 0753 630361
Fax: 0753 655365
Ron Saunders
London Research Office
Balfour House
46/54 Great Titchfield St
London W1P 7AE
Tel: 071 323 0407
Fax: 071 436 3232
Larry McKinna
50 million feet of newsreel and social documentary from 1896 to 1970. Rapid research and sourcing through computerised catalogue

Chameleon Film & Stockshot Library
The Magistretti Building
Harcourt Place
Leeds LS1 4RB
Tel: 0532 434017
Fax: 0532 431267
David Wright
16mm material includes travel, mountaineering, caving footage, plus wide range of general footage from all over the world. Also handles Channel Four programme out-takes

Channel Four Clip Library
60 Charlotte Street
London W1P 2AX
Tel: 071 927 8490/8754
Fax: 071 580 2622
Claire Austin
An ever growing portfolio of programmes and a diverse collection of library material

Educational and Television Films (ETV)
247a Upper Street
London N1 1RU
Tel: 071 226 2298
Fax: 071 226 8016
Documentaries on Eastern Europe, USSR, China, British Labour movement, b/w and colour, 16mm and 35mm, 1896 to present day

Film Archive Management and Entertainment (FAME)
18-20 St Dunstan's Road
London SE25 6EU
Tel: 081 771 6522
Fax: 081 653 9773
Barry Coward
British Railways, British Waterways and London Transport film archives covering over sixty years of industrial, agricultural, transport and social history are held along with other transport and travel material

Film Research & Production Services
25 Heddon Street
London W1R 7LG
Tel: 071 734 1525
Fax: 071 734 8017
Amanda Dunne
James Clarkson Webb
Sharon Bainbridge
Film holding of space footage, also film research and copyright clearance facilities

GB Associates
80 Montalt Road
Woodford Green
Essex IG8 9SS
Tel/Fax: 081 505 1850
Malcolm Billingsley
An extensive collection, mostly on 35mm, of fact and fiction film from the turn of the century, including many adverts and numerous vintage trailers

Fred Goodland Film, Video and Sound Collections
81 Farmilo Road
Leyton
London E17 8JN
Tel: 081 539 4412
Actuality and entertainment material from the 1890s through to the 1960s. Specialist collections include the early sound period and a wide range of musical material. Extensive film research facilities available on tape

Ronald Grant Archive
The Cinema Museum
The Old Fire Station
46 Renfrew Road
London SE11 4NA
Tel: 071 820 9991/4
Fax: 071 793 0849
Martin Humphries
10 million feet of fact and fiction film, mainly 35mm, from 1896 on. Also 300,000 film stills, posters, programmes, scripts and information. The museum is affiliated to FIAF

Huntley Film Archives
22 Islington Green
The Angel
London N1 8DU
Tel: 071 226 9260
Fax: 071 704 0847
John Huntley
Amanda Huntley
Documentary and newsreel film, 16mm/35mm specialist collections in transport, street scenes, industrial history, music etc from 1895

ITN Film Library Sales
200 Gray's Inn Road
London WC1X 8XZ
Tel: 071 430 4480
Fax: 071 430 4453
Malcolm Smith
Worldwide TV news coverage on film and video tape, from 1956 to the present day. Complete library archive on site including multi format transfer suite. Also a stills collection and information service

Index Stock Shots
12 Charlotte Mews
London W1P 1LN
Tel: 071 631 0134
Fax: 071 436 8737
Stock footage on film and video, including international locations, aircraft, and wildlife

LWT Images
London Television Centre
Upper Ground
London SE1 9LT
Tel: 071 261 3690/3771
Fax: 071 261 3456
Lynne Giddens
Clips, stockshots and cassettes available from London Weekend Television's programme library. Drama, entertainment, music, arts and international current affairs. Plus London's news, housing, transport, politics, history, wildlife etc

London Video Access (LVA)
5-7 Buck Street

London NW1 8NJ
Tel: 071 284 4588
Fax: 071 267 6078
Britain's national centre for video and new media art, housing the most extensive collection of video art in the country. Artists' work dating from the 1970s to the present

Lumiere Pictures
Pinewood Studios
Pinewood Road
Iver, Bucks SL0 0NH
Tel: 0753 631111
Fax: 0753 655813
John Herron
Feature films, TV series and stock shot, b/w and colour, 35mm, 1925 to present day

Medi Scene
32-38 Osnaburgh Street
London NW1 3ND
Tel: 071 387 3606
Fax: 071 387 9693
Carol Naylor
Wide range of accurately catalogued medical and scientific shots available on film and video. Part of the Medi Cine Group

Moving Image Research and Library Services
21-25 Goldhawk Road
London W12 8QQ
Tel: 081 740 4606
Fax: 081 749 6142
Michael Maloney
Wide range of quality footage. Collections include: Britain 1930 to present day, American Newsreels, Natural History – Africa, 1950s travelogue classics, Medical Technology. External research undertaken. Copyright clearance for all media

Oxford Scientific Films
Long Hanborough
Oxford OX8 8LL
Tel: 0993 881881
Fax: 0993 882808
Stock footage and stills libraries; 16mm, 35mm film and transparencies covering wide range of wildlife and special effects subjects

Post Office Film and Video Library
PO Box 145
Sittingbourne
Kent ME10 1NH
Tel: 0795 426465
Fax: 0795 474871
Barry Wiles, Linda Gates
Holds a representative selection of documentary programmes made under the GPO Film Unit, including the classic *Night Mail* etc. Catalogue available

RSPB Film and Video Unit
The Lodge
Sandy
Beds SG19 2DL
Tel: 0767 680551
Fax: 0767 692365
Pauline Miller
Over one million feet of 16mm film covering a wide variety of wildlife subjects and their habitats, particularly European birds. Viewing facilities and tape duplication are available on request

Reuters Television – Visnews Library
40 Cumberland Avenue
London NW10 7EH
Tel: 081 453 4338
Fax: 081 965 0620
Pam Turner
Newsreel, TV news, special collections. Colour and b/w, 16mm, 35mm, 1896 to present day and all material pre 1951 and post July 1981 on 1" video

TWI Sports Video Library
TWI House
23 Eyot Gardens
London W6 9TR
Tel: 081 846 8070
Fax: 081 746 5334
Archive footage of major and minor sports plus worldwide stockshot catalogue available

Timescape Image Library
4th Floor
184 Drummond Street
London NW1 3HP
Tel: 071 383 2777
Fax: 071 383 2333
Ann Williams
Original specially shot production quality colour 35mm footage library covering cityscapes, people, landscapes, seascapes, skyscapes and timelapse. Same day service of a research cassette for almost any request

World Backgrounds Film Production Library
Imperial Studios
Maxwell Road
Borehamwood
Herts
Tel: 081 207 4747
Fax: 081 207 4276
Ralph Rogers
Locations around the world. Fully computerised. All 35mm including 3000 back projection process plates. Numerous video masters held. Suppliers to TV commercials, features, pop promos, TV series, corporate videos etc

Worldwide Television News Archives
The Interchange
Oval Road
London NW1 7EP
Tel: 071 410 5270
Fax: 071 413 8327
David Simmons
David Muddyman
WTN libraries in London and New York form the largest collection of news archives in the world. Stories from most countries, many hours added every week

PHOTOGRAPHIC LIBRARIES

The following companies specialise in supplying still photographic images

BBC Photograph Library
Photograph Sales
Unit 1
29 North Acton Road
London NW10 6PE
Tel: 081 743 8000 x63314
Fax: 081 965 2485
The BBC's unique archive of radio and television programme stills, equipment, premises and personalities dating from 1922. B/w and colour. Visits by appointment

bfi BFI Stills, Posters and Designs
21 Stephen Street
London W1P 1PL
Tel: 071 255 1444
Fax: 071 323 9260
A visual resource of over 6 million images, illustrating every aspect of the development of world cinema and television

see also
Ronald Grant Archive

see also
ITN Film Library Sales

Image Diggers Picture and Tape Library
618b Finchley Road
London NW11 7RR
Tel: 081 455 4564
Fax: 071 431 7636
Neil Hornick
35mm slides, stills, postcards, sheet music, magazine and book material for hire. Audio/visual tape resources in performing arts and other areas, plus theme research

Imperial War Museum
Dept of Photographs
Lambeth Road
London SE1 6HZ
Tel: 071 416 5000
Fax: 071 416 5379
Within an overall photographic collection of some 5 million images, the Department has several thousand film stills, mainly from material in the Museum's own film archive

Kobal Collection
Fourth Floor
184 Drummond Street
London NW1 3HP
Tel: 071 383 0011
Fax: 071 383 0044
Dave Kent
One of the world's leading film photo archives in private ownership. Film stills and portraits, lobby cards and posters, from the earliest days of the cinema to modern times

Retrograph Archive
164 Kensington Park Rd
London W11 2ER
Tel: 071 727 9378
Fax: 071 229 3395
Jilliana Ranicar-Breese
Hiring out of transparencies from original packaging, advertising, commercial and fine art material from 1860-1960, including a high percentage of unique items. Supply to publishers, film and TV producers, record companies and manufacturers. In-house picture research and photography

THE DAILY
MIRROR
NEWS

AWARDS

The following awards were presented between January and December 1992

BAFTA AWARDS – BRITISH ACADEMY OF FILM AND TELEVISION ARTS

Awarded 22 March 1992 for 1991 films/programmes

BAFTA special award 1992: Audrey Hepburn
Academy fellowships: Sir John Gielgud and David Plowright
Michael Balcon award for outstanding British contribution to cinema: Derek Jarman
Alan Clarke award for outstanding creative contribution to television: Robert Young
Writers award: G F Newman
Richard Dimbleby award for the year's most important personal contribution on the screen in factual television: John Simpson
Television award for originality: *Vic Reeves Big Night Out* (Channel Four Television)
Best foreign television programme: *The Civil War* (USA) (PBS)

Film

Best film: *The Commitments* (USA) Dir Alan Parker
David Lean award for best achievement in direction: Alan Parker for *The Commitments*
Best original screenplay: Anthony Minghella for *Truly, Madly, Deeply* (UK) Dir Anthony Minghella
Best adapted screenplay: Dick Clement, Ian La Frenais and Roddy Doyle for *The Commitments*
Best actress: Jodie Foster for *The Silence of the Lambs* (USA) Dir Jonathan Demme
Best actor: Anthony Hopkins for *The Silence of the Lambs*
Best supporting actress: Kate Nelligan for *Frankie & Johnny* (USA) Dir Garry Marshall
Best supporting actor: Alan Rickman for *Robin Hood: Prince of Thieves* (USA) Dir Kevin Reynolds
Best original film music: Jean-Claude Petit for *Cyrano de Bergerac* (France) Dir Jean-Paul Rappeneau
Best film not in the English language: *Das Schreckliche Mädchen (The Nasty Girl)* (Germany) Dir Michael Verhoeven
Best short film: *The Harmfulness of Tobacco* (UK) Dir Nick Hamm
Best short animated film: *Balloon* (UK) Dir Ken Lidster

Television

Best single drama: *A Question of Attribution* (Screen One) (BBC Television)
Best drama serial: *Prime Suspect* (Granada TV)
Best drama series: *Inspector Morse* (Zenith Production for Central Independent TV)
Best factual series: *Naked Hollywood* (BBC Television)
Best light entertainment programme/series: *Have I Got News for You* (Hat Trick Productions for BBC Television)
Best comedy programme/series: *One Foot in the Grave* (BBC Television)
Best actuality coverage: The ITN coverage of the Gulf War (The Brent Sadler production team)
Best actress: Helen Mirren for *Prime Suspect*
Best actor: Robert Lindsay for *G.B.H.* (Channel Four)
Best light entertainment performance: Richard Wilson for *One Foot in the Grave*
Best original television

■ The Commitments

■ **HRH The Princess of Wales and BFI Fellow Sir Richard Attenborough**

music: Richard Harvey and Elvis Costello for*G.B.H.*
Best children's programme (entertainment/drama): *Jim Henson's Greek Myths* (Channel Four)
Best children's programme (documentary/ educational): *Blue Peter* (BBC Television)
Flaherty documentary award: *35 Up* (Granada Television)
Huw Wheldon award (best arts programme): *J'accuse – Citizen Kane (Without Walls)* (Channel Four)

BAFTA CRAFT AWARDS

Awarded 15 March 1992

Film

Cinematography: Pierre Lhomme for *Cyrano de Bergerac*
Production design: Bo Welsh for *Edward Scissorhands* (USA) Dir Tim Burton
Editing: Gerry Hambling for *The Commitments*
Sound: Lee Orloff, Tom Johnson, Gary Rydstrom and Gary Summers for *Terminator 2: Judgment Day* (USA) Dir James Cameron
Achievement in special effects: Stan Winston, Dennis Muren, Gene Warren Jr and Robert Skotak for *Terminator 2: Judgment Day*
Make-up: Jean-Pierre Eychenne and Michele Burke for *Cyrano de Bergerac*
Costume design: Franca Squarciapino for *Cyrano de Bergerac*

Television

Video lighting: Robert Byde for *Royal Gala: The Prince of Wales's Symphony for the Spire* (TVS)
Film or video photography (factual): Dianne Tammes for *Casualties* (Cutting Edge) (Channel Four)
[Jury commendation for the ITN coverage of the Gulf War especially Phil Bye's work]
Film or video photography (fiction): Ken Morgan for *Prime Suspect*
Sound (factual): Robert Edwards for *Royal Gala: The Prince of Wales's Symphony for the Spire*
Sound (fiction): Tony Dawe, Brian Saunders, Nigel Galt and Paul Conway for *Inspector Morse*
Film or video editor (factual): Barry Spink for *Children of Chernobyl (True Stories)* (Yorkshire Television)
Film or video editor (fiction): Edward Mansell for *Prime Suspect*
Graphics: Martin Lambie Nairn and Daniel Barber for BBC2 Network Identities
Make-up: Sue Kneebone for *Casualty* (Episodes 2, 5, 6, 8) (BBC Television)
Best design: Eileen Diss for *Jeeves and Wooster* (Granada Television)
Costume design: Joan Wadge for *The House of Eliott* (BBC Television)

bfi BFI AWARDS 1992

Awarded 20 September 1992 in association with Ernst & Young

BFI Fellowships: Sir Richard Attenborough, Dame Maggie Smith
BFI Award for Innovation: Chris Newby
Archival Achievement Award: *Selling Murder: The Killing Films of the Third Reich* (Director Joanna Mack, written and researched by Michael Burleigh, Domino Films)

■ **BFI Fellow Dame Maggie Smith**

Mari Kuttna Award for best British animated film: *A is for Autism* Dir Tim Webb (Finetake for Channel Four Television)
Michael Powell Book Award: John Boorman and Walter Donohue for 'Projections: A Forum for Filmmakers' (Faber & Faber)
Anthony Asquith film music Award: John Altman for *Hear My Song* (Film Four International)
Grierson Award (for best documentary): *Children of Chernobyl* (Yorkshire Television for Channel Four Television)
Sutherland Trophy (for best first feature shown at the National Film Theatre during the year): *Proof* Dir Jocelyn Moorhouse (House and Moorhouse Films)
Career in the Industry: Douglas Slocombe, director of photography

41st BERLIN FESTIVAL

Held 13-24 February 1992

GOLDEN BEAR
Grand prix: *Grand Canyon* (USA) Dir Lawrence Kasdan
SILVER BEARS
Special jury prize: *Édes Emma, Drága Böbe – Vazlatok, Aktok (Sweet Emma, Dear Böbe – Sketches, Nudes)* (Hungary/Germany) Dir István Szabó

■ Have I Got News For You

■ Howards End

Best director: Jan Troell for *Il Capitano* (Sweden/Finland/Denmark)
Best actor: Armin Mueller-Stahl for *Utz* (UK/Germany/Italy) Dir George Sluizer
Best actress: Maggie Cheung for *Ruan Ling Yu (Centre Stage)* (Hong Kong/Taiwan) Dir Stanley Kwan
Best cinematography: *Beltenebros (Prince of Shadows)* (Spain) Dir Pilar Miró
Alfred Bauer prize: *Infinitas* (Russia) Dir Marlen Chutsiev
[Special mention: Barbara Tummet for *Gudrun* (Germany) Dir Hans W Geissendorfer]
Children's Jury prize: *Huo Yan Shan Lei de Gu Shou (The Drummer from the Huoyan Mountains)* (China) Dir Guang Chunlan
[Second prize: *Shimantogawa (The Shimanto River)* (Japan) Dir Hideo Onchi]
OCIC (Catholic) prize: *Infinitas*
Interfilm (Protestant) prize: *Infinitas*
GDF (German Art Film Theatre Association) prize: *Utz*
Berliner Morgenpost (audience): *Utz*
CIAE (International Confederation of Arts Cinemas) prize: *Together Alone* (USA) Dir P J Castellaneta
UNICEF prize: *Mov und Funder (The Hideaway)* (Denmark) Dir Niels Grabol
[Special mention: *Shimantogawa*]
UNICEF best short film: *Manipulation* (UK) Dir Daniel Greaves
CIFEJ (International Centre of Films for Children and Young People): *Mov und Funder*
Teddy Bear Special Jury prize: *Edward II* (UK) Dir Derek Jarman
Gay Teddy Bear best short film: *Caught Looking* (UK) Dir Constantine Giannaris
Gay Teddy Bear best documentary: *Voices from the Front* (USA) Dir Robyn Hutt, David Meieran and Sandra Elgear from Testing The Limits Video Collective
Peace prize: *Rodina Heisst Heimat (Rodina Means Home)* (Germany) Dir Helga Reidemeister
Caligari prize: *Swoon* (USA) Dir Tom Kalin
Wolfgang Staudte prize: *The Hours and Times* (USA) Dir Christopher Munch

BROADCASTING PRESS GUILD AWARDS

Awarded 19 March 1992

Best single drama: *Prime Suspect*
Best drama series: *G.B.H.*
Best single documentary: *Panorama: The Max Factor* (BBC)
Best documentary series: *The Second Russian Revolution* (Brian Lapping Associates with The Discovery Channel for BBC)
Best entertainment programme: *Have I Got News for You* (Hat Trick Productions for BBC)
Best actor: Robert Lindsay for *G.B.H.*
Best actress: Helen Mirren for *Prime Suspect*
TV performance (non-acting role): Angus Deayton, presenter, for *Have I Got News for You*
Writers award: Alan Bennett for *A Question of Attribution* (BBC)
Harvey Lee award for outstanding contribution to broadcasting: John Tusa (BBC World Service)

45th CANNES FESTIVAL

Held 7-18 May 1992

"Perspectives du Cinéma Français" category replaced by "Cinémas en France" this year.
45th Anniversary special jury prize: *Howards End* (UK) Dir James Ivory
Palme d'Or (Golden Palm): *Den Goda Viljan (The Best Intentions)* (Sweden) Dir Bille August
Grand jury prize: *Il ladro di bambini (Stolen Children)* (Italy/France) Dir Gianni Amelio
Jury prize [joint]: *El sol del membrillo (The Quince Tree Sun)* (Spain) Dir Victor Erice & *Samostoiatelnaia Jizn (An Independent Life)* (Russia/France) Dir Vitali Kanievski
International Critics prize [joint]: *El sol del membrillo* & *C'est arrivé près de chez vous (Man Bites Dog)* (Belgium) Dir Rémy Belvaux
Best director: Robert Altman for *The Player* (USA)
Best actor: Tim Robbins for *The Player*
Best actress: Pernilla August for *Den Goda Viljan*
Caméra d'Or (Golden Camera for best first film): *Mac* (USA) Dir John Turturro

■ I'll Fly Away

■ Tous les matins du monde

Grand prize for superior technical achievement: *El viaje (The Voyage)* (Argentina) Dir Fernando Solanas
Palme d'Or (Golden Palm) for best short film: *Omnibus* (France) Dir Sam Karmann
Special jury prize for a short film: *La Sensation* (Belgium) Dir Manuel Poutte
Ecumenical prize: *Il ladro di bambini*
Prix de la jeunesse: *Strictly Ballroom* (Australia) Dir Baz Luhrmann
SACD prize (Critics week): *C'est arrivé près de chez vous*
FIPRESCI prize: *El sol del membrillo*
Critics week Canal Plus award: *Floating* (UK) Dir Richard Heslop
Cinémas en France: *Versailles Rive Gauche* (France) Dir Bruno Podalydès

CESARS 1992

Awarded 22 Feb 1992 for 1991 films

This year's Césars were dedicated to Yves Montand who died in November 1991
Best actor: Jacques Dutronc for *Van Gogh* (France) Dir Maurice Pialat
Best actress: Jeanne Moreau for *La Vieille qui marchait dans la mer (The Old Lady Who Wades in the Sea)* (France) Dir Laurent Heynemann
Best supporting actor: Jean Carmet for *Merci la vie* (France) Dir Bertrand Blier
Best supporting actress: Anne Brochet for *Tous les matins du monde (All the World's Mornings)* (France) Dir Alain Corneau
Most promising young actor: Manuel Blanc for *J'embrasse pas (I Don't Kiss)* (France) Dir André Téchiné
Most promising young actress: Geraldine Pailhas for *La neige et le feu (Snow and Fire)* (France) Dir Claude Pinoteau
Best director: Alain Corneau for *Tous les matins du monde*
Best French film: *Tous les matins du monde*
Best foreign film: *Toto le héros* (France/Belgium/ Germany) Dir Jaco van Dormael
Best first feature: *Delicatessen* (France) Dir Jean-Pierre Jeunet and Marc Caro
Best original script: Jean-Pierre Jeunet, Marc Caro and Giles Adrien for *Delicatessen*
Best music: Jordi Savall for *Tous les matins du monde*
Best short feature: *25 Decembre 58, 10h.38* (France) Dir Diane Bertrand
Best cinematography: Yves Angelo for *Tous les matins du monde*
Best set design: Jean-Philippe Carp and Kreka Kljakovic for *Delicatessen*
Best sound: Pierre Gamet, Gerard Lamps and Anne Lecampion for *Tous les matins du monde*
Best editing: Hervé Schneid for *Delicatessen*
Best costumes: Corinne Jorry for *Tous les matins du monde*
Honorary Césars: Michèle Morgan and Sylvester Stallone

EMMY AWARDS - NATIONAL ACADEMY FOR TELEVISION ARTS AND SCIENCES (44th Annual Prime-Time Awards)

Awarded 30 August 1992

DRAMA
Outstanding series: *Northern Exposure* (CBS)
Director: Eric Laneuville for *I'll Fly Away (All God's Children)* (NBC)
Lead actor: Christopher Lloyd for *Avonlea* (Disney Channel)
Lead actress: Dana Delany for *China Beach* (ABC)
Supporting actor: Richard Dysart for *L.A. Law* (NBC)
Supporting actress: Valerie Mahaffey for *Northern Exposure*
Writing: Andrew Schneider & Diane Frolov for *Northern Exposure: Seoul Mates*
COMEDY
Outstanding series: *Murphy Brown* (CBS)
Director: Barnet Kellman for *Murphy Brown: Birth 101*
Lead actor: Craig T Nelson for *Coach* (ABC)
Lead actress: Candice Bergen for *Murphy Brown*
Supporting actor: Michael Jeter for *Evening Shade* (CBS)
Supporting actress: Laurie Metcalf for *Roseanne* (ABC)
Writing: Elaine Pope and Larry Charles for *Seinfeld: The Fix Up* (NBC)

■ The Player

Lighting direction (Electronic): Donald A Morgan for *Home Improvement: Luck be a Taylor Tonight* (ABC)
MINI-SERIES/SPECIAL
Outstanding miniseries: *A Woman Named Jackie* (NBC)
Director: Joseph Sargent for *Hallmark Hall of Fame: Miss Rose White* (NBC)
Lead actor: Beau Bridges for *Without Warning: The James Brady Story* (HBO)
Lead actress: Gena Rowlands for *Face of a Stranger* (CBS)
Supporting actor: Hume Cronyn for *Neil Simon's "Broadway Bound"* (ABC)
Supporting actress: Amanda Plummer for *Hallmark Hall of Fame: Miss Rose White*
Writing: Joshua Brand & John Falsey for *I'll Fly Away* (Pilot Episode)
Music composition (Dramatic underscore): Bruce Broughton for *Hallmark Hall of Fame: O Pioneers!* (CBS)
VARIETY/MUSIC PROGRAM
Outstanding Variety/Music or Comedy Program: *The Tonight Show Starring Johnny Carson* (NBC)
Individual performance: Bette Midler for *The Tonight Show Starring Johnny Carson*
Directing: Patricia Birch for *Unforgettable, With Love: Natalie Cole Sings The Songs Of Nat King Cole* (PBS)
Writing: Hal Kanter, Buz Kohan, Billy Crystal, Marc Shaiman, David Steinberg, Robert Wuhl and Bruce Villanch for *The 64th Annual Academy Awards* (ABC)

Outstanding made-for-television movie: *Hallmark Hall of Fame: Miss Rose White*
Outstanding Informational Series: *MGM: When The Lion Roars* (TNT)
Outstanding Informational Special: *Abortion: Desperate Choices* (HBO)
Outstanding Children's Program: *Mark Twain and Me* (Disney)
Outstanding Animated Program: *A Claymation Easter* (CBS)
Outstanding achievement in choreography: Paul Taylor for *Dance in America: Paul Taylor's "Speaking in Tongues"* (PBS)
Outstanding achievement in animation: John Ashlee Pratt for *A Claymation Easter*
Outstanding achievement in music and lyrics: Curt Sobel (composer) and Dennis Spiegel (lyricist) for *Cast A Deadly Spell (Why Do I Lie)* (HBO)
Outstanding achievement in music direction: Bill Conti (music director) & Jack Eskew, Julie Giroux, Ashley Irwin and Hummie Mann (arrangers) for *The 64th Annual Academy Awards*
Governor's Award: R.E. "Ted" Turner
Syd Cassyd Founders' Award (for long and distinguished service to the Academy): Robert F. Lewine

20th INTERNATIONAL EMMYS 1992

Awarded 24 November 1992

Best drama: *A Dangerous Man: Lawrence of Arabia* (UK) Enigma Film & Television/Sands Films/WNET for Anglia Films. Dir Chris Menau
Best documentary: *The Fifth Estate: To Sell a War* (Canada) (Canadian Broadcasting Corporation)
Best Arts Documentary: *The South Bank Show: José Carreras – A Life Story* (UK) (Iambic Prods/ Primetime) Dir Chris Hunt
Best performing arts programme: *Pictures on the Edge* (Canada/USA) (Rhombus Media/CBC/ WNET)
Best popular arts programme: *Drop the Dead Donkey* (UK) (Hat Trick Productions for Channel Four Television)
Children's and young people's award [joint]: *Beat That: Hairdressing* (UK) (Tiny Epic Video Productions for Channel Four Television) and *Sorrow: The Nazi Legacy* (Sweden) (Lidingo Filmpoint Sweden)
International Council's Directorate Award: Silvio Berlusconi
Founder's Award: Bill Cosby

5th EUROPEAN [FELIX] FILM AWARDS

Awarded 12 December 1992

European Film of the Year: *Il ladro di bambini (Stolen Children)* (Italy/France) Dir Gianni Amelio
Young European Film of the Year: De *Noorderlingen (The Northeners)* (Netherlands) Dir Alan van Warmerdam
European Documentary Film of the Year: *Negegeu*

■ **Il ladro di bambini (Stolen Children)**

■ **La vie de Bohème (Bohemian Life)**

Zeme (Earth of the Blind) (Lithuania) Dir Audrius Stonys
[Special mentions: *Dostoevsky's Travels* (UK) Dir Paul Pawlikowski & *Lovers on Trial* (Belgium) Dir Manu Bonmariage]
European Actor of the Year: Matti Pellonpää for *La vie de Bohème (Bohemian Life)* (Finland/France/Sweden) Dir Aki Kaurismäki
European Actress of the Year: Juliette Binoche for *Les Amants du Pont Neuf* (France) Dir Léos Carax
European Supporting Actor of the Year: André Wilms for *La vie de Bohème*
European Supporting Actress of the Year: Ghita Nørby for *Freud Flyttar Hemifran (Freud Leaving Home)* (Sweden/Denmark) Dir Susanne Bier

■ Beauty and the Beast

European Screenwriter of the Year: István Szabó for *Édes Emma, Drága Böbe – Vazlatok, Aktok (Sweet Emma, Dear Böbe – Sketches, Nudes)* (Hungary/Germany) Dir István Szabó
European Cinematographer of the Year: Jean-Yves Escoffier for *Les Amants du Pont Neuf*
European Film Composer of the Year: Vincent van Warmerdam for *De Noorderlingen*
European Film Editor of the Year: Nelly Quettier for *Les Amants du Pont Neuf*
European Production Designer of the Year: Rikke Jelier for *De Noorderlingen*
European Film Academy Lifetime Achievement Award: Billy Wilder
European Academy Award of Merit: The Museum of the Moving Image, London

49th GOLDEN GLOBE AWARDS

Awarded 18 January 1992

Film

Best drama: *Bugsy* (USA) Dir Barry Levinson
Best comedy/musical: *Beauty and the Beast* (USA) Dir Kirk Wise
Best foreign language film: *Europa, Europa* (Germany/France) Dir Agnieszka Holland
Best actor (drama): Nick Nolte for *The Prince of Tides* (USA) Dir Barbra Streisand
Best actor (comedy/musical): Robin Williams for *The Fisher King* (USA) Dir Terry Gilliam
Best supporting actor: Jack Palance for *City Slickers* (USA) Dir Ron Underwood
Best actress (drama): Jodie Foster for *The Silence of the Lambs*
Best actress (comedy/musical): Bette Midler for *For the Boys* (USA) Dir Mark Rydell
Best supporting actress: Mercedes Ruehl for *The Fisher King*
Best director: Oliver Stone for *JFK* (USA)
Best screenplay: Callie Khouri for *Thelma & Louise* (USA) Dir Ridley Scott
Best original score: Alan Menken for *Beauty and the Beast*
Best original song: Alan Menken (song) and Howard Ashman (lyrics) for 'Beauty and the Beast' from *Beauty and the Beast*

■ Quantum Leap

■ Les Amants du Pont Neuf

Television

DRAMA
Best series: *Northern Exposure* (CBS)
Best actress: Angela Lansbury for *Murder She Wrote* (CBS)
Best actor: Scott Bakula for *Quantum Leap* (NBC)
COMEDY/MUSICAL
Best series: *Brooklyn Bridge* (CBS)
Best actress: Candice Bergen for *Murphy Brown* (CBS)
Best actor: Burt Reynolds for *Evening Shade* (CBS)
MINI-SERIES OR FILMS MADE FOR TV
Best series: *One Against the Wind* (CBS)
Best actress: Judy Davis for *One Against the Wind*
Best actor: Beau Bridges for *Without Warning: the James Brody Story* (HBO)
Best supporting actress: Amanda Donohoe for *L.A. Law* (NBC)

Best supporting actor: Louis Gossett Jr for *The Josephine Baker Story* (HBO)

28th KARLOVY VARY FESTIVAL

Held 9-18 July 1992

Crystal Globe: *Krapatchouk* (Spain/France/Belgium) Dir Enrique Gabriel Lipschutz
Best actor: Guy Pion for *Krapatchouk*
Best actress: Evdokija Germanova for *Kiks (Cracked)* (Russia) Dir Sergei Livnev
Special jury prize: *Ruzi, Ruzagari, Cinema (Once Upon a Time, Cinema)* (Iran) Dir Mohsen Makhmalbaf
FIPRESCI (International Critics' prize) [joint]: *Krapatchouk & Ruzi, Ruzagari, Cinema*
City of Karlovy Vary prize: *Cholod (The Cold)* (Russia) Dir Husein Erkenov

45th LOCARNO FESTIVAL

Held 5-15 August 1992

Golden Leopard: *Qiuyue (Autumn Moon)* (Hong Kong) Dir Clara Law
Silver Leopard: *Kairat* (Kazakhstan) Dir Darezhahn Omirbaev
Bronze Leopard [Third prize]: *Die Terroristen! (Terrorists)* (Germany) Dir Philip Gröning
Bronze Leopard [Fourth prize]: *Eddie King* (Israel) Dir Giddi Dar
Special Jury Prize: *Holozan* (Switzerland) Dir Heinz Butler & Manfred Eicher
Public vote for the best film: *Il ladro di bambini (The Stolen Children)*

LONDON FILM CRITICS' CIRCLE AWARDS

Awarded 24 February 1992

Film of the year: *Thelma & Louise* (USA) Dir Ridley Scott
Director of the year: Ridley Scott
Screenwriter of the year: David Mamet
Actor of the year: Gérard Depardieu
Actress of the year: Susan Sarandon
Newcomer of the year: Annette Bening
British film of the year: *Life is Sweet* (UK) Dir Mike Leigh
British producer of the year: Lynda Myles & Roger Randall-Cutler for *The Commitments* (USA) Dir Alan Parker
British screenwriter of the year: Dick Clement, Ian La Frenais & Roddy Doyle for *The Commitments*
British actor of the year: Alan Rickman
British actress of the year: Juliet Stevenson
British technical achievement of the year: Peter Greenaway for *Prospero's Books* (Netherlands/France/Italy)
Foreign language film of the year: *Cyrano de Bergerac* (France) Dir Jean-Paul Rappeneau
Special award: Kevin Brownlow, "for reviving public interest in the silent cinema, and achievements in editing and direction"
Special award: John Sayles, "for services to the American independent cinema"

■ **Prospero's Books**

■ **Man Bites Dog**

The Dilys Powell award: Sir Dirk Bogarde, "for lifetime achievement as an actor"

32nd MONTE CARLO TV FESTIVAL

Held 9-14 February 1992

NEWS (DOCUMENTARY)
Gold nymph: *Dubrovnik – Diary of a Siege* (UK) (ITV)
Silver nymph: *Albaneze Vluchtelingen in Bari, Italie (Albanian refugees in Bari, Italy)* (Netherlands) (KRO)
Special jury mention: *Skotten i Vilnius (The Shots in Vilnius)* (Sweden) (SVT)
NEWS (MAGAZINE)
Gold nymph: *Flugten til Europa (Europe Besieged)* (Denmark) (DR)
Silver nymph: *Koerden in de Kou (Kurds in the Cold)* (Belgium) (BRTN)
Special jury mention: *Viet-Kun, Duc-Kun Monogatari (Innocents of War: The Story of Viet and Duc, Siamese twins)* (Japan) (NTV)
Special critics prize: *Koerden in de Kou*
FICTION Mini-Series
Gold nymph: *The Wall Climber* (Sweden) (SVT)
Silver nymph (best actress): Sara Paavolainen for *House of Cards* (Finland) (YLE/Finnish Broadcasting Company)
Silver nymph (best actor): John Hurt for *Red Fox* (UK) (LWT)
Special jury mention: *Strauss Dynasty* (Austria) (ORF)
FILMS FOR TV
Gold nymph: *Alive and Kicking* (UK) (BBC)
Silver nymph (best director): Paul Wendkos for *Presumed Guilty* (USA) (World International Network)
Silver nymph (best script): Christian Gorlitz for *Der Deal* (Germany) (ZDF)
Silver nymph (best actor): Rentaro Mikuni for *Fuyo No Tabi (The Winter Journey)* (Japan) (NHK)
Silver nymph (best actress): Hannelore Elsner for *Elsa* (Germany) (ARD-SR)
Special critics prize: *Der Vergessene Tal (The Forgotten Valley)* (Switzerland) (DRS)
PRIX UNDA
Documentary: *A Coeur, A Corps, A Cris* (France) (FR)
Fiction: *Fuyo No Tabi*
Prix de Croix Rouge Monegasque: *Alive and Kicking*
Prix du Public: *Presumed Guilty*
Prix special de SAS le prince Rainier III: *Envoyé Spécial, Biosphère 2* (France) (A2)

32nd GOLDEN ROSE OF MONTREUX TV FESTIVAL

Held 28 April-2 May 1992

Golden Rose: *Night Moves* (Canada) Canadian Broadcasting Corporation
Silver Rose: *KYTV – Good Morning Calais* (UK) (BBC Television)
Bronze Rose: *Everybody Dance Now (Great Performances)* (US) (PBS)
Special mention: *Victor Borge in Tivoli* (Denmark) (TV2); *S&M* (UK) (Channel Four Television); *The Loves of Emma Bardac* (Germany) (ZDF)
Special prize for funniest programme: *KYTV – Good Morning Calais*
PRODUCERS' JURY PRIZES:
Golden Rose: *TV Masque* (Netherlands) (Fun Channel/TROS)
Silver Rose: *HBO Comedy Hour: Mambo Mouth* (US) (HBO)
Bronze Rose: *Whose Line Is It Anyway?* (UK) (Hat Trick Productions for Channel Four Television)
Special prize for funniest programme: *HBO Comedy Hour: Mambo Mouth*
Special mentions: *Medusa: Dare to be Truthful* (US) (Showtime Networks); *Cirque du Soleil: Nouvelle Expérience* (FR) (Les Productions Telemagik); *Eric Clapton: 24 Nights* (UK) (Hadrian Television)

■ **Red Fox**

64th OSCARS – ACADEMY OF MOTION PICTURE ARTS AND SCIENCES

Awarded 31 March 1992 for 1991 films

Best film: *The Silence of the Lambs* (USA) Dir Jonathan Demme
Best foreign language film: *Mediterraneo* (Italy) Dir Gabriele Salvatores
Best director: Jonathan Demme for *The Silence of the Lambs*
Best actor: Anthony Hopkins for *The Silence of the Lambs*
Best actress: Jodie Foster for *The Silence of the Lambs*
Best supporting actor: Jack Palance for *City Slickers* (USA) Dir Ron Underwood
Best supporting actress: Mercedes Ruehl for *The Fisher King* (USA) Dir Terry Gilliam
Best original screenplay: Callie Khouri for *Thelma and Louise* (USA) Dir Ridley Scott
Best screenplay adaptation: Ted Tally for *The Silence of the Lambs*
Best cinematography: Robert Richardson for *JFK* (USA) Dir Oliver Stone
Best editing: Joe Hutshing and Pietro Scalia for *JFK*
Best original music score: Alan Menken for *Beauty and the Beast* (USA) Dir Kirk Wise
Best original song: Alan Menken (music) and Howard Ashman (lyrics) for 'Beauty and the Beast' from *Beauty and the Beast*
Best art direction: Dennis

■ **City Slickers**

Gassner (art direction) and Nancy Haigh (set decoration) for *Bugsy* (USA) Dir Barry Levinson
Best costume design: Albert Wolsky for *Bugsy*
Best make-up: Stan Winston and Jeff Dawn for *Terminator 2: Judgment Day* (USA) Dir James Cameron
Best visual effects: Dennis Muren, Stan Winston, Gene Warren Jr and Robert Skotak for *Terminator 2: Judgment Day*
Best sound: Tom Johnson, Gary Rydstrom, Gary Summers, and Lee Orloff for *Terminator 2: Judgment Day*
Best sound effects editing: Gary Rydstrom and Gloria S Borders for *Terminator 2: Judgment Day*
Best short film (animated): *Manipulation* (UK) Dir Daniel Greaves
Best short film (live action): *Session Man* (USA) Prod Seth Winston and Rob Fried
Best documentary feature: *In the Shadow of the Stars* (USA) Prod Allie Light and Irving Saraf
Best documentary short: *Deadly Deception: General Electric, Nuclear Weapons and Our Environment* (USA) Prod Debra Chasnoff
Academy honorary award: Satyajit Ray for "his rare mastery of the art of motion pictures and for his profound humanitarian outlook, which has had an indelible influence on filmmakers and audiences throughout the world"
Gordon E Sayer award: Ray Harryhausen "whose technical contributions have brought credit to the motion picture industry"
Irving G Thalberg Memorial Award: George Lucas

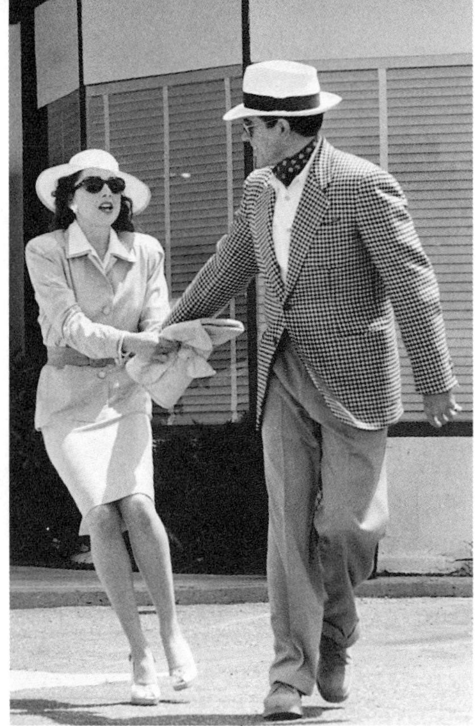

ROYAL TELEVISION SOCIETY AWARDS

PROGRAMME AND TECHNOLOGY AWARDS FOR 1991

Awarded 28 May 1992

PROGRAMME AWARDS
Single drama: *Prime Suspect* (Granada Television)
Drama series: *Casualty* (BBC Television)
Drama serial: *Children of the North* (BBC Television)
Single documentary: *The Leader, His Driver & The Driver's Wife (True Stories)* (Lafayette Films for Channel Four Television)
Documentary series: *Secret History* (Channel Four Television)
Situation Comedy: *One Foot in the Grave: The Man in the Long Black Coat* (BBC Television)
Entertainment: *Vic Reeves Big Night Out II* (Channel X for Channel Four Television)
Arts: *Bookmark: Dostoevsky's Travels* (BBC Television)
Outside broadcasts: *As It Happens: Moscow New Year* (Barraclough Carey Productions for Channel Four Television)
Regional Programme: *Scotch & Wry 1991* (BBC Scotland)
Regional Documentary: *Summer on the Estate: Episode 1* (Wild & Fresh Productions for London Weekend Television)
Technique award (highlighting the substantial contribution of the camera person Alison Chapman): *The Bill: They Also Serve* (Thames Television)
Children's award (Factual): *Mozart is Alive and Well in Milton Keynes* (BBC Television)
Children's award (Drama & Light Entertainment): *Dodgem* (BBC Television)
Performance awards: Helen Mirren for *Prime Suspect* & Robert Lindsay for *G.B.H.* (Channel Four Television)
Writer's award: Lynda La Plante
Cyril Bennett award: Liz Forgan
Judges' award: David Croft
Gold Medal: Sir Paul Fox CBE
TECHNOLOGY AWARDS
Research and development: Vistek VMC Television Converter
Communications innovation: Continental Microwave Technology for the Ka Band satellite news gathering terminal Judges' award: Don Kershaw

■ Bugsy

TELEVISION JOURNALISM AWARDS

Awarded 25 February 1992

Regional daily news magazine: *Coast to Coast – South* (TVS)
Regional current affairs: *Week In Week Out, Asbestos* (BBC Wales)
News, home: *Orkney Satanic Abuse* (Channel Four News)
Current affairs, home: *Panorama: The Max Factor* (BBC)
[Special commendation: *The Shooting of Planning Officer – Harry Collinson* (Tony Belmont, BBC)]
News, topical feature:

■ Glengarry Glen Ross

■ **Prime Suspect**

The Secret City (Channel Four News)
[Special commendation: *Newsnight: Forgotten Prisoners in Kuwait* (Charles Wheeler, BBC)]
Current affairs, international: *The Second Russian Revolution – Coup* (Brian Lapping Associates with The Discovery Channel for BBC)
News, international: *Flight from Saddam Hussein* (News at Ten, ITN)
[Special commendation: *Albania – The Children's Tragedy* (Bill Hamilton and Bhasker Solanki, BBC)]
Television news cameraman of the year: Nigel Thompson, ITN
Television journalist of the year: Michael Nicholson OBE, ITN
Judges' award: Mohamed Amin MBE

49th VENICE FESTIVAL

Held 1-12 September 1992

Golden Lion: *Qiu Ju Da Guansi (The Story of Qiu Ju)* (China/Hong Kong) Dir Zhang Yimou
Special Jury prize: *Morte di un Matematico Napoletano (Death of a Neapolitan Mathematician)* (Italy) Dir Mario Martone
Silver Lion [joint]: *Jamón Jamón* (Spain) Dir Bigas Luna & *Un Coeur en Hiver* (A Heart in Winter) (France) Dir Claude Sautet & *Hotel de Lux* (Romania) Dir Dan Pita
Volpi Cup for best actor: Jack Lemmon for *Glengarry Glen Ross* (US) Dir James Foley
Volpi Cup for best actress: Gong Li for *Qiu Ju Da Guansi (The Story of Qiu Ju)*
FIPRESCI (International critics') prize [joint]: *Un Coeur en Hiver (A Heart in Winter)* & *Leon the Pig Farmer* (UK) Dir Vadim Jean and Gary Sinyor
Golden Lions for career achievement: Jeanne Moreau, Paolo Villaggio and Francis Ford Coppola
International Catholic Film Bureau prize: *Orlando* (UK/Russia/France/Italy/Netherlands) Dir Sally Potter
Senate Medal: *Guelwaar* (Senegal/France) Dir Ousmane Sembene

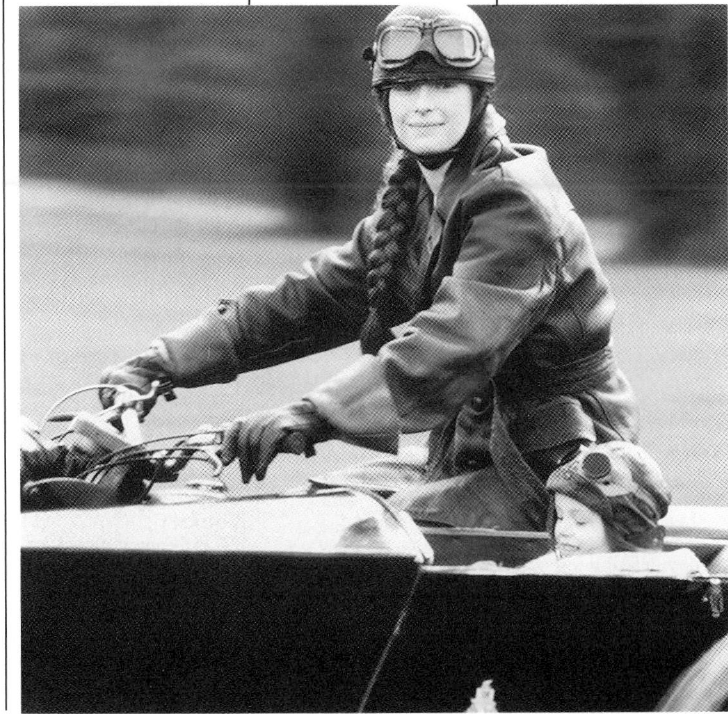

■ **Orlando**

BOOKSHOPS

Most bookshops stock film and cinema books and, if they don't have the book you want, they will usually order it direct from the publisher. However, if the book you are looking for proves elusive or if you are looking for magazines, posters or memorabilia, most of the following companies offer specialist mail order services

Arnolfini Bookshop
Ground Floor
16 Narrow Quay
Bristol BS1 4QA
Tel: 0272 299191
Fax: 0272 253876
Stock: A, B, C, F
Open: 10.00-19.00 Mon-Sat, 12.30-18.30 Sun
Based in the Arnolfini Gallery, concentrating on the visual arts. No catalogues are issued. Send requests for specific material with SAE

B H Blackwell
48-51 Broad Street
Oxford OX1 3BQ
Tel: 0865 792792
Fax: 0865 794143
Stock: A
Open: 9.00-18.00 Mon, Wed-Sat, 9.30-18.00 Tue
Literature department has sections on cinema, media studies and performing arts. An international charge and send service is available

Blackwell's Art & Poster Shop
27 Broad Street
Oxford OX1 2AS
Tel: 0865 792792
Stock: A, B, C, F
Open: 9.00-18.00 Mon, Wed-Sat, 9.30-18.00 Tue
A wide selection of books, posters, cards, calendars and gift items, all available by mail order

The Cinema Bookshop
13-14 Great Russell St
London WC1B 3NH
Tel: 071 637 0206
Stock: A, B, C, D
Open: 10.30-17.30 Mon-Sat
Comprehensive stock of new, out-of-print and rare books. No catalogues are issued. Send requests for specific material with SAE

The Cinema Store
46 Monmouth Street
London WC2H 9EP
Tel: 071 379 7838
Stock: A, B, C, D, E, F
Open: 10.00-18.00 Mon-Wed, 10.00-19.00 Thu-Sat, 12.00-17.00 Sun
Mail order available. Latest and vintage posters and stills, magazines, models and lazer discs

Geoffrey Clifton's Performing Arts Bookshop
44 Brazennose Street
Manchester M2 5EA
Tel: 061 831 7118
Stock: A, B, F
Open: 9.00-17.30 Mon-Sat
Stocks new books

Cornerhouse Books
70 Oxford Street
Manchester M1 5NH
Tel: 061 228 7621
Fax: 061 236 7323
Stock: A, B, C, E, F
Open: 12.00-20.30 daily
No catalogues are issued. Send requests for specific material with SAE

A E Cox
21 Cecil Road
Itchen
Southampton SO2 7HX
Tel: 0703 447989
Stock: A, B, C, D
Telephone enquiries and orders accepted at any time. Mail order only. A catalogue, including scarce items, is published at least six times yearly. Send two first-class stamps or three international reply vouchers overseas to receive the current issue

Culture Vultures Books
329 St Leonard's Road
Windsor SL4 3DS
Tel: 0753 851693
Stock: A
Mail order only. Periodic catalogues issued (Separate catalogues for cinema, theatre, music). SAE appreciated. Comprehensive stock of out-of-print titles

Dress Circle
57-59 Monmouth Street
Upper St Martin's Lane
London WC2H 9DG
Tel: 071 240 2227
Stock: A, B, C, D, E, F
Open: 10.00-19.00 Mon-Sat
Specialists in stage music and musicals. A catalogue of the entire stock is issued annually with updates twice yearly. Send SAE for details

Sylvia Edwards
23 Marchmont Road
Edinburgh EH9 1HY
Tel: 031 229 5165
Stock: C, D
Mail order only. Visitors by appointment. Fully illustrated catalogues of rare film posters and select ephemera issued quarterly at £3. Fully illustrated catalogue of over 3,000 star portraits at £2

58 Dean Street Records
58 Dean Street
London W1V 5HH
Tel: 071 437 4500/734 8777
Stock: E
Open: 10.00-18.30 Mon-Sat
Retail shop with recorded mail order service. Over 7,000 titles including soundtracks, original cast shows, musicals and nostalgia. Telephone for information

Film Magic
The Business Centre
Colne Way
Watford
Stock: A, B, C, D, E, F
Mail order only. Comprehensive catalogue costing £1.00 available on request

STOCK

A – Books
B – Magazines
C – Posters
D – Memorabilia (eg stills)
E – Cassettes, compact discs, records and videos
F – Postcards and greetings cards

Anne FitzSimons
62 Scotby Road
Scotby
Carlisle
Cumbria CA4 8BD
Tel: 0228 513815
Stock: A, B, C, D, F
Mail order only.
Antiquarian and out-of-print titles on cinema, broadcasting and performing arts. A catalogue is issued three times a year. Send three first-class postage stamps for current issue

Flashbacks
6 Silver Place
Beak Street
London W1R 3LJ
Tel: 071 437 8562
Stock: C, D
Open: 10.30-19.00 Mon-Sat
Shop and mail order service. Send SAE and 'wanted' list for stock details

Forbidden Planet
71 New Oxford Street
London WC1A 1DG
Tel: 071 836 4179/379 6042
Fax: 071 497 2632
Stock: A, B, C, D, E, F
Open: 10.00-18.00 Mon-Wed, Sat
10.00-19.00 Thur, Fri
Science fiction, horror, fantasy and comics specialists. Mail order service available on 071 497 2150

Heffers Booksellers
20 Trinity Street
Cambridge CB2 3NG
Tel: 0223 358351
Stock: A, E
Open: 9.00-17.30 Mon-Sat
Catalogues of videocassettes and spoken word recordings are issued. Copies are available free on request

David Henry
36 Meon Road
London W3 8AN
Tel: 081 993 2859
Stock: A, B
Mail order only. A catalogue of out-of-print and secondhand books is issued two or three times a year and is available on request. There is a search service for titles not in stock. New books can also be obtained to order, including those published in the USA

L V Kelly Books
75/77 Chapel Street
Tiverton
Devon EX16 6BU
Tel: 0884 256170
Stock: A, B, E
Principally mail order but visitors welcome by appointment. Catalogue issues regularly on broadcasting and mass communications.
Occasional lists on cinema, music, theatre

Legends
406 Cranbrook Road
Gants Hill
Essex IG2 6HW
Tel/Fax: 081 554 5788
Stock: B, C, D, F
Open: 9.30-18.30 Mon-Sat
A gallery dealing in memorabilia ranging from limited edition prints to custom made T-shirts.
Prints of the famous from film, TV, music (jazz and blues a speciality), sport, world figures. Framing service. Mail order available

MOMI Bookshop
South Bank
London SE1 8XT
Tel: 071 815 1343
Stock: A, B, C, D, E, F
Open: 10.30-18.30 daily
Based in the Museum of the Moving Image. Mail order available with special orders on request

Ed Mason
Shop 5
Chelsea Antiques Market
253 Kings Road
London SW3
Tel: 071 352 6338
Stock: A, B, C, D
Open: 10.00-18.00 Mon-Sat. Closed all public holidays.
Mainly shop service. No catalogue or lists. Will serve through the post.
Specialist in original film memorabilia from the earliest onwards

NFT Bookshop
South Bank
London SE1 8XT
Tel: 071 815 1343
Stock: A, B, C, E, F
Open: 12.30-21.00 daily
Based in the main foyer.
Mail order available on request. Book/Video orders taken.
Comprehensive range of film/media magazines

National Museum of Photography, Film and Television
Pictureville
Bradford BD1 1NQ
Tel: 0274 727488
Fax: 0274 723155
Stock: A, C, D, F
Open: 10.30-18.00 Tue-Sun
Mail order available.
Send SAE with requests for information

Offstage Theatre & Cinema Bookshop
37 Chalk Farm Road
London NW1 8AJ
Tel: 071 485 4996
Stock: A, B, E, F
Open: 10.00-18.00 daily
Free cinema and media catalogues available.
Send SAE

C D Paramor
25 St. Mary's Square
Newmarket
Suffolk CB8 0HZ
Tel: 0638 664416
Stock: A, B, C, D, E, F
Mail order only. Visitors welcome strictly by appointment. Catalogues on most of the performing arts issued regularly free of charge

Pleasures of Past Times
11 Cecil Court
Charing Cross Road
London WC2N 4EZ
Tel: 071 836 1142
Stock: A, D, F
Open: 11.00-14.30, 15.30-17.45 Mon-Fri. First Sat in month 11.00-14.30.
No catalogue

Roxie the Shop
84 Wardour Street
London W1V 4BX
Tel: 071 437 2233
Fax: 071 434 9990
Stock: A, D, E
Open: 9.30-18.00 Mon-Fri
Film memorabilia. Mail order available. Full catalogue of Electric, Tartan, Curzon, Aikman, Connoisseur and Artificial Eye videos. BFI books

Spread Eagle Bookshop
(incorporates the Greenwich Gallery)
9 Nevada Street
London SE10 9JL
Tel/Fax: 081 305 1666
Stock: A, B, C, D
Open: 10.00-17.30 daily
All second-hand stock.
Memorabilia, ephemera.
Also old cameras and equipment

Tyneside Cinema Shop
10 Pilgrim Street
Newcastle upon Tyne
NE1 6QG
Tel: 091 232 5592
Fax: 091 221 0535
Stock: A, B, C, D, F
Open: 10.30-18.00 Mon-Sat
Based in Tyneside Cinema. Send requests for specific material with SAE

Vintage Magazine Co
39-41 Brewer Street
London W1R 3FD
Tel: 071 439 8525
Stock: B, C, D, F
Open: 10.00-20.00 Mon-Sat, 12.00-19.00 Sun
247 Camden High Street
London NW1
Tel: 071 482 0587
Stock: B, C, D, F
Open: 10.00-18.00 Mon-Fri, 10.00-19.00 Sat, Sun
For details of catalogues, picture library and research services available, call 081 533 7588. Mail order service available. Send requests for specific material with SAE to:
203/213 Mare Street
London E8 3QE

Peter Wood
20 Stonehill Road
Great Shelford
Cambridge CB2 5JL
Tel: 0223 842419
Stock: A, D, F
Mail order. Visitors are welcome by appointment.
A free catalogue is available of all books in stock

A Zwemmer
80 Charing Cross Road
London WC2H 9NJ
Tel: 071 379 7886
Stock: A, B
Open: 9.30-18.00 Mon-Fri, 10.00-18.00 Sat
A catalogue of new and in-print titles on every aspect of cinema is available on request. Mail order service for all books available through Mail Order Dept.
A Zwemmer Ltd
24 Litchfield Street
London WC2H 9NJ

CABLE AND SATELLITE

All broadband cable franchises to date were granted by the Cable Authority (apart from 11 previously granted by the Department of Trade and Industry), the role of which was taken over by the Independent Television Commission in January 1991. Since that date no further franchises have been awarded

The franchises are arranged in alphabetical order of area. Where appropriate the principal towns in the area are identified under the area name; cross references are provided for these and other principal towns at the appropriate alphabetical point.

'Homes passed' is the number of homes to which a cable service is available and has been offered by the operator.

'Subscribers' are those taking at least the basic service, with the percentage this represents of homes passed. Unless stated, services have not yet begun.

Addresses are given where the operator has only one franchise or where a local address serves the area. Where no address is given, see the appropriate reference in the Group ownership (abbreviated to GO) section which follows.

In some towns an older cable system still exists. These are not franchised but are licensed by the Independent Television Commission to provide limited services. They are gradually being superseded by new broadband networks

Aberdeen
Franchise holder: Aberdeen Cable Services
Ownership: Devanha Group (see GO)
Awarded: 29 Nov 83
Homes passed: 93,622 (build complete)
Service start: 1 May 85
Subscribers: 15,019 = 16.0% (1 Apr 93)

Abingdon see ***Oxford***
Accrington see ***Lancashire, East***
Airdrie see ***Cumbernauld***
Aldershot see ***Guildford***

Andover
Franchise holder: Andover Cablevision = IVS Cable Holdings (see GO)
Homes in area: 11,500 (build complete)
Awarded: Apr 89
Service start: Mar 90

Ashford see ***Kent, South East***

Avon
Bristol, Bath, Weston-super-Mare, Frome, Melksham etc
Franchise holder: United Artists Communications (Avon) = TeleWest (see GO)
Homes in area: 300,000
Awarded: 16 Nov 88
Homes passed: 80,543 (1 Apr 93)
Service start: 14 Sep 90
Subscribers: 16,901 = 21.0% (1 Apr 93)
Separate upgrade system in Bristol operated by Metro Cable

Aylesbury/ Amersham/ Chesham
Franchise holder: Jones Cable Group (see GO)
Homes in area: 62,000
Awarded: 31 May 90

Baldock see ***Hertfordshire, Central***
Barking and Dagenham, London Borough of see ***Greater London East***
Barnet, London Borough of see ***London, North West***

Barnsley
Franchise holder: General Cable (see GO)
Homes in area: 82,000
Awarded: 14 Jun 90; acquired Apr 93

Basildon see ***Thames Estuary North***
Basingstoke see ***Thames Valley***
Bath see ***Avon***

Bearsden/ Milngavie
Franchise holder: Clyde Cablevision = Insight Communications (see GO)
Homes in area: 16,000
Awarded: 7 Jun 90

Bedford
Franchise holder: Cablevision North Bedfordshire = English Cable Enterprises (see GO)
Homes in area: 55,000
Awarded: 14 Jun 90

Bedworth see ***Nuneaton***

Belfast
Franchise revoked from Ulster Cablevision
Homes in area: 136,000
Awarded: 29 Nov 83

Berkhamsted see ***Hertfordshire, West***
Bexley, London Borough of see ***Greater London East***

Birmingham/ Solihull
Franchise holder: Birmingham Cable
Cablephone House
Small Heath Business Park

Data for this section has been kindly provided by Screen Digest from its data base, and compiled and presented for the Handbook by David Fisher, Editor of Screen Digest. We gratefully acknowledge the continuing support of Screen Digest in providing this information

Small Heath
Birmingham B10 0HJ
Tel: 021 628 1234
Ownership: TeleWest, Comcast, Compagnie Générale des Eaux (see GO for all three), Standard Life Assurance
Homes in area: 465,000
Awarded: 19 Oct 88
Homes passed: 109,443 (1 Apr 93)
Subscribers: 39,628 = 36.2% (1 Apr 93)
Service start: Dec 1989

Bishops Stortford see ***Harlow***

Black Country

Dudley, Sandwell, Walsall, Wolverhampton, urban parts of Bromsgrove, Cannock, Kidderminster
Franchise holder: Midlands Cable Communications = SBC Cablecomms UK (see GO)
Homes in area: 470,000
Awarded: 14 Jul 89
Homes passed: 63,374 (1 Apr 1993)
Service start: Sep 91
Subscribers: 11,917 = 18.8% (1 Apr 1993)

Blackburn see ***Lancashire, East***

Bolton

Franchise holder: Nynex CableComms Bolton (see GO)
25-30 Queensbrook
Bolton Technology Exchange
Spa Road
Bolton BL1 4AY
Tel: 0204 365440
Fax: 0204 365417
Homes in area: 135,000
Awarded: 13 Aug 85; acquired 22 Mar 93
Homes passed: 32,545 (1 Apr 93)
Service start: Jul 90
Subscribers: 5,894 = 18.1% (1 Apr 93)

Bootle see ***Liverpool, North***
Borehamwood see ***Hertfordshire, South***

Bournemouth/Poole/Christchurch

Franchise holder: Nynex Cablecomms Wessex (see GO)
Suite 314, Premier House
Hinton Road
Bournemouth
Dorset BH1 2EF
Tel: 0202 294346
Fax: 0202 299569
Homes in area: 143,000
Awarded: 6 Apr 90

Bracknell see ***Thames Valley***

Bradford

Franchise holder: Bradford Cable Communications = General Cable (see GO)
Communications House
Mayfair Business Park
Broad Lane
Bradford BD4 8PW
Tel: 0274 848484
Ownership: Compagnie Générale des Eaux (see GO), Yorkshire Water
Homes in area: 175,000
Awarded: 14 Jun 90
Homes passed: 11,942 (1 Apr 93)
Service started: Jul 92
Subscribers: 3,702 = 31.0% (1 Apr 93)

Brent, London Borough of see ***London, North West***
Brentwood see ***Thames Estuary North***
Brighouse see ***Calderdale***

Brighton/Hove/Worthing

Franchise holder: Nynex Cablecomms Sussex (see GO)
Rayford School
School Road
Brighton BN3 5HZ
Tel: 0273 208308
Homes in area: 160,000
Awarded: 20 Oct 89; acquired 22 Mar 93
Homes passed: 35,527 (1 Apr 93)
Service start: Apr 1992
Subscribers: 35,527 = 18.0% (1 Apr 93)
Separate upgrade system in Brighton operated by Multichannel Television = Devanha Group (see GO)

Bristol see ***Avon***
Broadstairs see ***Thanet, Isle of***

Bromley, London Borough of

Franchise holder: Nynex Cablecomms Bromley (see GO)
Beeline House
51-67 Farwig Lane
Bromley
Kent BR1 2WD
Tel: 081 466 9966
Fax: 081 313 9613
Homes in area: 117,000
Awarded: 16 Mar 90

Burgess Hill see ***Haywards Heath***

Burton-on-Trent/Swadlincote/Ashby

Franchise revoked from N-Com Cablevision of Burton
Homes in area: 40,000
Awarded: 21 Jun 90

Bury/Rochdale

Franchise holder: Nynex CableComms (see GO)
Homes in area: 143,000
Awarded: 17 May 90; acquired 4 May 93
Separate upgrade system in Rochdale operated by Metro Cable

Bushey see ***Hertfordshire, South***

Calderdale

Halifax, Brighouse
Franchise holder: General Cable (see GO)
Homes in area: 75,000
Awarded: 14 Jun 90

Camberley see ***Guildford***

Cambridge and district

Cambridge, Newmarket, Ely, Saffron Walden, Huntingdon, St Ives, St Neots, Royston etc
Franchise holder: Cambridge Cable
Ainsworth Place
72a Ainsworth Street
Cambridge CB1 2PD
Tel: 0223 464201
Fax: 0223 467347
Ownership: Comcast Corporation, 41.25% (see GO), Singapore Telecom 41.25%, Kingston Communications 17.5%
Homes in area: 132,000
Awarded: 4 Jun 89
Homes passed: 37,005 (1 Apr 93)
Service start: Jul 91
Subscribers: 7,788 = 21.2% (1 Apr 93)

Camden, London Borough of

Franchise holder: Cable London (see GO)
Homes in area: 70,000
Awarded: 1 Feb 86
Homes passed: 41,724 (1 Apr 93)
Service start: Dec 89
Subscribers: 9,233 = 22.1% (1 Apr 93)

Cardiff/Penarth

Franchise holder: Insight Communications Cardiff (see GO)
Homes in area: 103,000
Awarded: 5 Feb 86

Carlisle

Franchise surrendered by Carlisle Cablevision
Homes in area: 30,000
Awarded: 21 Jun 90

Castleford see ***Wakefield***
Chatham see ***Thames Estuary South***
Chelmsford see ***Thames Estuary North***

Cheltenham/Gloucester

Franchise holder: United Artists Communications (Cotswolds) = TeleWest (see GO)
Homes in area: 90,000
Awarded: 13 Aug 85

Cheshire, North

Chester, Ellesmere Port, Warrington, Widnes, Runcorn
Franchise holder: Nynex CableComms (see GO)
Homes in area: 175,000
Awarded: 12 Jan 90; acquired 21 Apr 93

Cheshunt see ***Hertford***
Chigwell see ***Epping Forest***
Chorley see ***Lancashire, Central***
Chorleywood see ***Hertfordshire, South***
Christchurch see ***Bournemouth***
Cleethorpes see ***Grimsby***
Clydebank see ***Glasgow, North West***
Coatbridge see ***Cumbernauld***

Colchester/Ipswich/Felixstowe/Harwich/Woodbridge

Franchise holder: East Coast Cable
Ownership: Maclean Hunter (see GO), Kingston Communications
Homes in area: 126,000
Awarded: 21 Jul 89

Colne see ***Lancashire, East***

Corby/Kettering/Wellingborough/Market Harborough

Franchise holder: Northampton Cable Television = CUC Cablevision (see GO)
Homes in area: 90,000
Awarded: 21 Jun 90
Separate upgrade system in Wellingborough operated by Cablevision Wellingborough (homes passed: 20,000)

Coventry
Franchise holder:
Coventry Cable
Blackburn House
Whitley Village
London Road
Coventry CV3 4HL
Tel: 0203 505345
Fax: 0203 505445
Ownership: Devanha Group (see GO)
Awarded: 29 Nov 83; acquired 92
Homes passed: 117,038 (build complete)
Service start: 1 Sep 85
Subscribers: 11,645 = 10.0% (1 Apr 93)

Crawley/Horley/ Gatwick
Franchise holder:
Eurobell
Block C, Lloyds Court
Manor Royal
Crawley
West Sussex RH10 2PT
Tel: 0293 518070
Fax: 0293 517400
Ownership: Orbis Trust/ Broadband Systems 54%; Detecon, Oy Extel, Transon
Homes in area: 44,000
Awarded: 27 Apr 89
Service start: Jan 93

Crosby see **Liverpool, North**

Croydon, London Borough of
Franchise holder: United Artists Communications (London South) = TeleWest (see GO)
Awarded: 1 Nov 83
Homes passed 108,111 (build complete)
Service start: 1 Sep 85
Subscribers: 25,904 = 24.0% (1 Apr 93)

Cumbernauld/ Kilsyth/Airdrie/ Coatbridge
Franchise holder:
Scotcable (Cumbernauld) = Post-Newsweek UK Cable (see GO)
Homes in area: 55,000
Awarded: 27 Apr 89

Cwmbran see **Newport**
Dagenham see **Greater London East**

Darlington
Franchise holder: Nynex Cablecomms Darlington (see GO)
Homes in area: 34,000
Awarded: 21 Jun 90

Dartford/Swanley
Franchise holder: Encom Cable TV and Telecommunications (see GO)
Homes in area: 35,000
Awarded: 16 Mar 90

Deal see **Kent, South East**

Derby/Spondon
Franchise holder: Nynex CableComms (see GO)
Unit A, Chequers Business Park, Chequers Lane
Derby
Tel: 0332 200002
Homes in area: 83,000
Awarded: 16 Feb 90; acquired 22 Mar 93
Homes passed: 12,509 (1 Apr 93)
Service start: Oct 91
Subscribers: 2,724 = 21.8% (1 Apr 93)

Devon, South
Exeter, Plymouth, Torbay
Franchise holder: Devon Cablevision = Maclean Hunter (see GO)
Homes in area: 236,000
Awarded: 15 Dec 89
Separate upgrade systems in Plymouth operated by Cablecom Investments, in Exeter operated by Multi Channel Television = Devanha Group (see GO)

Dewsbury see **Huddersfield**

Doncaster/ Rotherham
Franchise holder: South Yorkshire Cablevision = Pactel Cable UK (see GO)
Tel: 0302 329596
Homes in area: 192,000
Awarded: 10 May 90
Franchise for sale

Dorset, West
Dorchester, Weymouth, Portland
Franchise revoked from Coastal Cablevision = Leonard Communication (US)
Homes in area: 35,000
Awarded: 10 Feb 90

Dover see **Kent, South East**
Droitwich see **Worcester**
Dudley see **Black Country**

Dumbarton/Vale of Leven
Franchise holder:
Scotcable (Dumbarton) = Post-Newsweek UK Cable (see GO)
Homes in area: 17,000
Awarded: 27 Apr 89

Dundee/Monifieth/ Carnoustie
Franchise holder: Tayside Cable Systems = Post-Newsweek UK Cable (see GO)
Homes in area: 95,000
Awarded: 19 Jan 90
Homes passed: 35,177 (1 Apr 93)
Service start: Jan 91
Subscribers: 9,984 = 28.4% (1 Apr 93)

Dunstable see **Luton**
Durham see **Wearside**

Ealing, London Borough of
Franchise holder:
Videotron Corporation (see GO)
Homes in area: 105,000
Awarded: 8 Nov 83
Homes passed 58,171 (1 Apr 93)
Service start: 1 Nov 86
Subscribers: 12,170 = 21.0% (1 Apr 93)

East Kilbride see **Motherwell**
Eastleigh see **Southampton**

Edinburgh
Franchise holder: United Artists Communications (Scotland) = TeleWest (see GO)
Homes in area: 183,000
Awarded: 5 Feb 86
Homes passed: 17,623 (1 Apr 93)
Service start: May 92
Subscribers: 4,844 = 27.5% (1 Apr 93)

Ellesmere Port see **Cheshire, North**
Elmbridge see **Surrey, North**
Elstree see **Hertfordshire, South**

Enfield
Franchise holder: Cable London (see GO)
Homes in area: 105,000
Awarded: 31 May 90
Homes passed: 27,908 (1 Apr 93)
Service start: Oct 91
Subscribers: 8,780 = 31.5% (1 Apr 93)

Epping Forest/ Chigwell/ Loughton/Ongar
Franchise holder: Encom Cable TV and Telecommunications (see GO)
Homes in area: 45,000
Awarded: 3 May 90

Epsom see **Surrey, North East**
Exeter see **Devon, South**

Falkirk/West Lothian
Franchise holder:
Scotcable (Forth Towns) = Post-Newsweek UK Cable (see GO)
Homes in area: 30,000
Awarded: 21 Jun 90

Fareham see **Portsmouth**
Farnborough see **Guildford**
Felixstowe see **Colchester**

Fenland
Wisbech, March, Whittlesey
Franchise holder:
Fenland Cablevision = Pactel Cable UK (see GO)
Homes in area: 21,000
Awarded: 5 Jul 90

Folkestone see **Kent, South East**
Gateshead see **Tyneside**
Gatwick see **Crawley**
Gillingham see **Thames Estuary South**

Glamorgan, West
Swansea, Neath, Port Talbot
Franchise holder:
Starvision Network = Starstream Europe (see GO)
Network House
Baglan Industrial Estate
Baglan, Port Talbot
West Glam SA12 7DJ
Tel: 0639 899999
Fax: 0639 891110
Homes in area: 110,000
Awarded: 16 Nov 89
Homes passed: 26,000 (1 Apr 93)
Service start: Dec 90
Subscribers: 3,519 = 13.5% (1 Apr 93)
Separate upgrade systems in Neath/Port Talbot operated by Cable and Satellite TV Holdings, in Swansea by Metro Cable

Glasgow, Greater
Franchise holder: Clyde Cablevision = Insight Communications (see GO)
Homes in area: 274,000
Awarded: 7 Jun 90

Glasgow, North West/Clydebank
Franchise holder: Clyde Cablevision = Insight Communications (see GO)
Homes in area: 112,000; 16,000 business premises

Awarded: 26 Nov 83
Homes passed: 54,863 (1 Apr 93)
Service start: 1 Oct 85
Subscribers: 5,195 = 9.5% (1 Apr 93)

Glenrothes/ Kirkcaldy/Leven
Franchise holder: Kingdom Cablevision = Post-Newsweek UK Cable (see GO)
Homes in area: 60,000
Awarded: 21 Jun 90
Homes passed: 12,500 (1 Apr 93)
Service start: Oct 91
Subscribers: 5,035 = 40.2% (1 Apr 93)

Gloucester see ***Cheltenham***
Godalming see ***Guildford***
Gosport see ***Portsmouth***
Gourock see ***Inverclyde***

Grantham
Franchise holder: Diamond Cable (Grantham) (see GO)
Homes in area: 14,000
Awarded: 26 Apr 90

Gravesend see ***Thames Estuary South***

Great Yarmouth/ Lowestoft/Caister
Franchise holder: Broadland Cablevision = Pactel Cable UK (see GO)
Homes in area: 64,000
Awarded: 5 Jul 90

Greater London East
Boroughs of Barking/ Dagenham, Bexley, Redbridge
Franchise holder: Encom Cable TV and Telecommunications (see GO)
Homes in area: 229,000
Awarded: 15 Dec 88
Homes passed: 6,000
Service start: Dec 90

Greenock see ***Inverclyde***

Greenwich/ Lewisham, London Boroughs of
Franchise holder: Videotron London (see GO)
Homes in area: 175,000
Awarded: 7 Apr 89
Homes passed: 73,690 (1 Apr 93)
Service start: Jan 91
Subscribers: 17,586 = 23.9% (1 Apr 93)
Separate upgrade system

Grimsby/ Cleethorpes
Franchise holder: Diamond Cable (see GO)
Homes in area: 63,000
Awarded: 5 Jul 90

Guildford/West Surrey/East Hampshire
Guildford, Aldershot, Farnborough, Camberley, Woking, Godalming
Franchise holder: Insight UK Management Co (see GO)
170 Walnut Tree Close
Guildford
Surrey GU1 4TP
Homes in area: 22,000 + 115,000
Awarded: 29 Nov 83 + Aug 85
Service start: 1 Jul 87

Hackney/Islington, London Boroughs of
Franchise holder: Cable London (see GO)
Homes in area: 150,000
Awarded: 13 Apr 90
Service start: Jun 91

Halifax see ***Calderdale***
Hamilton see ***Motherwell***
Hammersmith and Fulham, London Borough of see ***London, North West***

Haringey, London Borough of
Franchise holder: Cable London (see GO)
Homes in area: 85,000
Awarded: Sep 89
Homes passed: 17,036 (1 Apr 93)
Subscribers: 3,290 = 19.3% (1 Apr 93)

Harlow/Bishops Stortford/Stansted Airport
Franchise holder: Anglia Cable Communications
123 The Stow
Harlow
Essex CM20 3AW
Tel: 0279 411059
Fax: 0279 416047
Homes in area: 43,000
Awarded: 23 Mar 90

Harpenden see ***Hertfordshire, West***
Harrogate see ***York***

Harrow
Franchise holder: Videotron Corporation (see GO)
Homes in area: 79,000
Awarded: 24 May 90
Service start: Dec 91

Hartlepool see ***Teesside***
Harwich see ***Colchester***
Hatfield see ***Hertfordshire, Central***
Havant see ***Portsmouth***

Havering, London Borough of
Franchise holder: Encom Cable TV and Telecommunications (see GO)
Homes in area: 90,000
Awarded: 6 Apr 90

Haywards Heath/ Burgess Hill
Franchise revoked from N-Com Cablevision
Homes in area: 25,000
Awarded: 5 Jul 90

Heathrow see ***Windsor***
Hemel Hempstead see ***Hertfordshire, West***
Henley-on-Thames see ***Thames Valley***

Hertford/ Cheshunt/Ware/ Lea Valley/ Hoddesdon
Franchise holder: Lea Valley Cablevision Communications Company = English Cable Enterprises (see GO)
Homes in area: 60,000
Awarded: 31 May 90

Hertfordshire, Central
Stevenage, Welwyn, Hatfield, Hitchin, Baldock, Letchworth
Franchise holder: Cablevision Communications Company = English Cable Enterprises (see GO)
Homes in area: 100,000
Awarded: 3 Nov 89
Separate upgrade systems in Hatfield, Stevenage, Welwyn operated by Metro Cable

Hertfordshire, South
Watford, Chorleywood, Rickmansworth, Bushey, Radlett, Elstree, Borehamwood, Potters Bar
Franchise holder: Jones Cable Group (see GO)
Homes in area: 95,000
Awarded: 3 Nov 89
Service start: Apr 92

Hertfordshire, West
Harpenden, Hemel Hempstead, St Albans, Berkhamsted, Tring, Redbourne
Franchise holder: County Cable Telecommunications = CUC Cablevision (see GO)
Knoll House
Maylands Avenue
Hemel Hempstead
Hertfordshire HP2 7DE
Tel: 0442 231311
Fax: 0442 234892
Homes in area: 100,000
Awarded: 3 Nov 89
Homes passed: 6,000
Service start: Mar 91

High Wycombe see ***Thames Valley***

Hillingdon
Franchise holder: Middlesex Cable Communications = General Cable (see GO)
Homes in area: 92,000
Awarded: 24 May 90
Service start: Nov 91

Hinckley
Franchise revoked from N-Com Cablevision
Homes in area: 20,000
Awarded: 6 Apr 90

Hitchin see ***Hertfordshire, Central***
Hoddesdon see ***Hertford***
Horley see ***Crawley***

Hounslow
Franchise holder: Middlesex Cable Communications = General Cable (see GO)
Homes in area: 79,000
Awarded: 24 May 90
Homes passed: 17,107 (1 Apr 93)
Subscribers: 3,104 = 18.1% (1 Apr 93)

Hove see ***Brighton***

Huddersfield/ Dewsbury
Franchise holder: Kirklees Communications = Insight Communications (see GO)
Homes in area: 148,000
Awarded: 14 Jun 90

Inverclyde
Greenock/Port Glasgow/ Gourock
Franchise holder: Clyde Cablevision = Insight Communications (see GO)
Homes in area: 32,000
Awarded: 5 Jul 90

Isle of Thanet see ***Thanet, Isle of***
Islington see ***Hackney***
Ipswich see ***Colchester***

Jersey
Franchise holder: Jersey

Cable = IVS Cable Services (see GO)
PO Box 233
St Helier
Jersey JE4 8SZ
Channel Islands
Homes in area: 23,000
Homes passed: 12,000
Subscribers: 7,230 (end 1990)
Service start: 1987

Kenilworth see ***Warwick***

Kensington/ Chelsea, London Borough of
Franchise holder: Videotron Cable Communications (see GO)
Homes in area: 82,000
Awarded: 4 Feb 88
Homes passed: 36,621 (1 Apr 93)
Subscribers: 7,731 = 20.6% (1 Apr 93)
Service start: Sep 89

Kent, South East
Dover, Deal, Folkestone, Ashford
Franchise holder: Starside Network = Starstream Europe (see GO)
The Old Pumping Station
Pluckley Road
Charing
near Ashford
Kent TN27 0AH
Tel: 023371 3939
Fax: 023371 3933
Homes in area; 77,000
Awarded: 3 May 90
Separate upgrade systems operated by Metro Cable

Kettering see ***Colby***
Kidderminster see ***Black Country***
Kilsyth see ***Cumbernauld***

Kingston and Richmond, London Boroughs of
Franchise holder: United Artists Communications (London South) = TeleWest (see GO)
Homes in areas: 124,000
Awarded: 6 May 89
Service start: Jan 91

Kirkcaldy see ***Glenrothes***
Kirkby-in-Ashfield see ***Mansfield***
Knaresborough see ***York***
Knowsley see ***St Helens***

Lambeth/Southwark, London Boroughs of
Franchise holder: Videotron Corporation (see GO)
Homes in area: 191,000
Awarded: 6 Jul 89
Homes passed: 33,446 (1 Apr 93)
Service start: Jul 91
Subscribers: 7,734 = 23.1% (1 Apr 93)

Lanark see ***Motherwell***

Lancashire, Central
Preston, Chorley, Leyland
Franchise holder: North West Cable Communications = SBC Cablecomms UK (see GO)
Homes in area: 114,000
Awarded: 5 Feb 86
Homes passed: 54,755 (1 Apr 93)
Subscribers: 10,110 = 18.5% (1 Apr 93)

Lancashire, East
Blackburn, Accrington, Nelson, Colne, Rossendale Valley
Franchise holder: Nynex CableComms
Homes in area: 168,000
Awarded: 9 May 88; acquired 21 Apr 93
Homes passed: 42,000 (1 Apr 93)
Service start: 30 Nov 89
Subscribers: 4,567 = 10.9% (1 Apr 93)

Lancaster/ Morecambe
No applications
Homes in area: 40,000

Leamington Spa see ***Warwick***
Lea Valley see ***Hertford***

Leeds
Franchise holder: Jones Cable Group (see GO)
Homes in area: 289,000
Awarded: Mar 90

Leicester
Franchise holder: Leicester Communications (see GO)
Homes in area: 147,000
Awarded: 22 Sep 89
Homes passed: 25,439 (1 Apr 93)
Service start: 1 Mar 91
Subscribers: 6,887 = 27.1% (1 Apr 93)
Separate upgrade system operated by Metro Cable

Leighton Buzzard see ***Luton***
Letchworth see ***Hertfordshire, Central***
Leyland see ***Lancashire, Central***

Lincoln
Franchise holder: Diamond Cable (see GO)
Homes in area: 42,000
Awarded: 5 Jul 90

Liverpool, North/ Bootle/Crosby
Franchise holder: North West Cable Communications = SBC Cablecomms UK (see GO)
Homes in area: 119,000
Awarded: 5 Jul 90
Homes passed: 27,646 (1 Apr 93)
Subscribers: 7,781 = 28.2% (1 Apr 93)

Liverpool, South
Franchise holder: North West Cable Communications (Liverpool) = SBC Cablecomms UK (see GO)
Century Building
Atlantic Way
Brunswick Business Park
Liverpool L3 4BL
Tel: 051 708 0280
Fax: 051 708 0263
Homes in area: 125,000
Awarded: 29 Nov 83
Homes passed: 54,498 (1 Apr 93)
Service start: Oct 90
Subscribers: 14,236 = 26.2% (1 Apr 93)

London, North West
Boroughs of Barnet, Brent, Hammersmith and Fulham
Franchise holder: Videotron Corporation (see GO)
Homes in area: 280,000
Awarded: 19 Jan 89
Homes passed: 27,204 (1 Apr 93)
Service start: Jul 91
Subscribers: 5,625 = 20.7% (1 Apr 1992)

London see also ***Greater London East*** and individual boroughs

Loughborough/ Shepshed
Franchise holder: Leicester Communications (see GO)
Homes in area: 30,000
Awarded: 9 Mar 90

Loughton see ***Epping Forest***
Lowestoft see ***Great Yarmouth***

Luton/Dunstable/ Leighton Buzzard
Franchise holder: Cablevision Bedfordshire = English Cable Enterprises (see GO)
Homes in area: 97,000
Awarded: Jul 86
Homes passed: 10,000
Service start: Nov 86 on upgrade system, Mar 90 on new build network

Macclesfield/ Wilmslow
Franchise holder: Nynex CableComms (see GO)
Homes in area: 45,000
Awarded: 11 Jul 90; acquired 4 May 93

Maidenhead see ***Windsor***
Maidstone see ***Thames Estuary South***

Manchester/ Salford
Franchise holder: Nynex CableComms (Greater Manchester) (see GO)
28 Magnetic House
Waterfront Quay
Salford Quays
Manchester M5 2XW
Tel: 061 876 5537
Homes in area: 363,000
Awarded: 17 May 90; acquired 22 Mar 93

Mansfield/Sutton/ Kirkby-in-Ashfield
Franchise holder: Diamond Cable (Mansfield) (see GO)
Homes in area: 58,000
Awarded: 3 Mar 90
Separate upgrade system operated by Kinshine

March see ***Fenland***
Margate see ***Thanet, Isle of***
Market Harborough see ***Colby***
Marlow see ***Thames Valley***

Melton Mowbray
Franchise holder: Diamond Cable (Melton Mowbray) (see GO)
Homes in area: 30,000
Awarded: 26 Apr 90

Merton and Sutton, London Boroughs of
Franchise holder: United Artists Communications (London South) = TeleWest (see GO)
Homes in area: 135,000
Awarded: 6 May 89
Homes passed: 76,700 (1 Apr 93)
Service start: Mar 90
Subscribers: 18,859 = 24.6% (1 Apr 93)

Middlesbrough see ***Teesside***
Mole Valley see ***Surrey, North East***

Monifieth see ***Dundee***
Morecambe see ***Lancaster***

Motherwell/East Kilbride/Hamilton/Wishaw/Lanark
Franchise holder: Scotcable Motherwell = Post-Newsweek UK Cable (see GO)
Homes in area: 125,000
Awarded: 27 Apr 89
Homes passed: 13,707 (1 Apr 93)
Subscribers: 4,441 = 32.4% (1 Apr 93)

Neath see ***Glamorgan, West***
Nelson see ***Lancashire, East***

Newark on Trent
Franchise holder: Diamond Cable (Newark) (see GO)
Homes in area: 18,000
Awarded: 26 Apr 90

Newbury see ***Thames Valley***
Newcastle-under-Lyne see ***Stoke-on-Trent***
Newcastle-upon-Tyne see ***Tyneside***

Newham and Tower Hamlets, London Boroughs of
Franchise holder: Encom Cable TV and Telecommunications (see GO)
Homes in area: 127,000
Awarded: 13 Aug 85
Homes passed: 54,250 (1 Apr 93)
Service start: May 87
Subscribers: 9,255 = 17.1% (1 Apr 93)

Newport/Cwmbran/Pontypool
Franchise holder: Newport Cablevision = Insight Communications (see GO)
Homes in area: 85,000
Awarded: 11 Jul 90

Northampton
Franchise holder: County Cable Telecommunications (Northants) = CUC Cablevision (see GO)
Homes in area: 72,000
Awarded: 19 Jan 89
Homes passed: 23,631 (1 Apr 93)
Service start: 1988 on narrowband network, Mar 91 on new-build network
Subscribers: 13,221 = 56.0% (1 Apr 93)

Norwich
Franchise holder: Norwich Cablevision = Pactel Cable UK (see GO)
Homes in area: 83,000
Awarded: 21 Jul 89
Homes passed: 30,678 (1 Apr 93)
Service start: Jun 90
Subscribers: 3,118 = 15.1% (1 Apr 93)
Separate upgrade system operated by Cablecom Investments

Nottingham
Franchise holder: Diamond Cable (Nottingham) (see GO)
Homes in area: 160,000
Awarded: 22 Sep 89
Homes passed: 10,500 (1 Apr 93)
Service start: 10 Sep 90
Subscribers: 2,825 = 27.0% (1 Apr 93)
Separate upgrade system operated by Kinshine

Nuneaton/Bedworth/Rugby
Franchise holder: County Cable Telecommunications = CUC Cablevision (see GO)
Homes in area: 67,000
Awarded: 6 Apr 90

Oldham/Tameside
Franchise holder: Nynex CableComms (see GO)
Homes in area: 172,000
Awarded: 17 May 90; acquired 4 May 93

Ongar see ***Epping Forest***

Oxford/Abingdon
Franchise holder: Oxford Cable = IVS Cable Services (see GO)
Homes in area: 72,000
Awarded: 14 Jun 90
Separate upgrade system in Oxford operated by Metro Cable

Paisley/Renfrew
Franchise holder: Clyde Cablevision = Post-Newsweek UK Cable (see GO)
Homes in area: 67,000
Awarded: 7 Jun 90

Penarth see ***Cardiff***

Perth/Scone
Franchise holder: Tayside Cable Systems = Post-Newsweek UK Cable (see GO)
Homes in area: 18,000
Awarded: 19 Jan 90

Peterborough
Franchise holder: Peterborough Cablevision = Pactel Cable UK (see GO)
Homes in area: 58,000
Awarded: 21 Jul 89
Homes passed: 23,687 (1 Apr 93)
Service start: May 90
Subscribers: 4,815 = 20.3% (1 Apr 93)

Plymouth see ***Devon, South***
Pontefract see ***Wakefield***
Pontypool see ***Newport***
Poole see ***Bournemouth***
Port Glasgow see ***Inverclyde***
Port Talbot see ***Glamorgan, West***

Portsmouth/Fareham/Gosport/Havant
Franchise holder: Nynex Cablecomms (Solent) (see GO)
Homes in area: 150,000
Awarded: 2 Feb 90
Homes passed: 74,949 (1 Apr 93)
Subscribers: 3,406 = 14.7% (1 Apr 93)
Service start: Sep 91
Subscribers: 15,220 = 20.3% (1 Apr 93)

Potters Bar see ***Hertfordshire, South***
Preston see ***Lancashire, Central***
Radlett see ***Hertfordshire, South***
Ramsgate see ***Thanet, Isle of***
Reading see ***Thames Valley***
Redbourne see ***Hertfordshire, West***
Redbridge, London Borough of see ***Greater London East***
Redditch see ***Worcester***
Redhill see ***Surrey, North East***
Reigate see ***Surrey, North East***
Renfrew see ***Paisley***
Richmond, London Borough of see ***Kingston***
Rickmansworth see ***Hertfordshire, South***
Rochdale see ***Bury***
Rochester see ***Thames Estuary South***
Rossendale Valley see ***Lancashire, East***
Rotherham see ***Doncaster***
Rugby see ***Nuneaton***
Runcorn see ***Cheshire, North***
Runnymede see ***Surrey, North***
St Albans see ***Hertfordshire, West***

St Helens/Knowsley
Franchise holder: North West Cable Communications = SBC Cablecomms UK (see GO)
Homes in area: 121,000
Awarded: 5 Jul 90
Service start: Jun 92

Salford see ***Manchester***

Salisbury
Franchise holder: Wessex Cable
Ownership: IVS Cable Services 90% (see GO); Southern Newspapers 10%
Homes in area: 15,000
Awarded: 6 Apr 90

Sandwell see ***Black Country***
Scone see ***Perth***

Sheffield
Franchise holder: Sheffield Cable Media = General Cable (see GO)
Provincial House
Solly Street
Sheffield S1 4AB
Tel: 0742 701700
Fax: 0742 701274
Homes in area: 210,000
Awarded: 31 May 90

Sittingbourne see ***Thames Estuary South***
Slough see ***Windsor***
Solihull see ***Birmingham***

Southampton/Eastleigh
Franchise holder: Videotron Corporation (see GO)
Homes in area: 97,000
Awarded: 12 Sep 86
Homes passed: 74,154 (1 Apr 93)
Service start: 1 Dec 90
Subscribers: 12,910 = 17.4% (1 Apr 93)

Southend see ***Thames Estuary North***
Southwark, London Borough of see ***Lambeth***

Stafford/Stone
Franchise holder: Stafford Communications = IVS Cable Services (see GO)
Homes in area: 24,000
Awarded: 1 Dec 89

Staines see ***Windsor***
Stanwell see ***Windsor***
Stevenage see ***Hertfordshire, Central***

Stockport
Franchise holder: Nynex CableComms (see GO)
Homes in area: 113,000
Awarded: 17 May 90; acquired 4 May 93

Stockton see ***Teesside***

Stoke-on-Trent/Newcastle-under-Lyne
Franchise holder: Nynex CableComms (see GO)
Homes in area: 156,000
Awarded: 1 Dec 89; acquired 21 Apr 93
Separate upgrade system in Stoke operated by Kinshine

Stone see ***Stafford***
Stratford-upon-Avon see ***Warwick***
Sunderland see ***Wearside***

Surrey, North
Elmbridge, Runnymede
Franchise holder: Nynex Cablecomms Surrey (see GO)
Homes in area: 71,000
Awarded: 21 Jun 90

Surrey, North East
Epsom, Mole Valley, Reigate, Redhill
Franchise holder: Nynex Cablecomms Surrey (see GO)
Homes in area: 98,000
Awarded: 21 Jun 90

Sutton see ***Mansfield***
Sutton, London Borough of see ***Merton***
Swansea see ***Glamorgan, West***

Swindon
Franchise holder: Swindon Cable = CUC Cablevision (see GO)
Homes in area: 75,000
Awarded: 29 Nov 83
Homes passed: 60,342 (build complete)
Service start: 1 Sep 84
Subscribers: 19,755 = 32.7% (1 Apr 93)

Tameside see ***Oldham***

Tamworth
Franchise revoked from N-Com Cablevision
Homes in area: 25,000
Awarded: 6 Apr 90

Teesside
Middlesbrough, Stockton, Hartlepool
Franchise holder: Nynex Cablecomms Teesside (see GO)
Homes in area: 195,000
Awarded: 5 Jul 90
Option to purchase held by US Cable
Separate upgrade systems in each town operated by Cablecom Investments

Telford
Franchise holder: Midlands Cable Communications = SBC Cablecomms UK (see GO)
2 Hawksworth Road
Central Park
Telford TF2 9TU
Homes in area: 55,000
Awarded: 26 Apr 90
Homes passed: 17,512 (1 Apr 93)
Service start: May 92
Subscribers: 4,004 = 22.9% (1 Apr 93)

Thames Estuary North
Southend, Basildon, Brentwood, Chelmsford etc
Franchise holder: North Estuary Cable = TeleWest (see GO)
Homes in area: 300,000
Awarded: 16 Nov 88
Separate upgrade system in Basildon operated by Metro Cable

Thames Estuary South
Gravesend, Chatham, Rochester, Gillingham, Maidstone, Sittingbourne
Franchise holder: United Artists Communications (South Thames Estuary) = TeleWest (see GO)
Homes in area: 145,000
Awarded: 16 Nov 88
Separate upgrade systems in Maidstone operated by Metro Cable, in Chatham operated by MultiChannel Television

Thames Valley
Reading, Twyford, Henley-on-Thames, Wokingham, High Wycombe, Marlow, Bracknell, Basingstoke, Newbury, Thatcham
Franchise holder: County Cable Telecommunications = CUC Cablevision (see GO)
Homes in area: 215,000
Awarded: 2 Dec 88
Homes passed: 16,288 (1 Apr 93)
Service start: Dec 91
Subscribers: 3,865 = 23.7% (1 Apr 93)
Separate upgrade system in Reading operated by Metro Cable

Thamesmead
Franchise holder: Videotron Thamesmead (see GO)
Homes in area: 11,000 (build complete)
Awarded: 31 May 90
Service start: Jul 91

Thanet, Isle of
Margate, Ramsgate, Broadstairs
Franchise revoked from Coastal Cablevision = Leonard Communications
Homes in area: 51,000
Awarded: 16 Feb 90
Separate upgrade system operated by MultiChannel Television

Torbay see ***Devon, South***
Tower Hamlets, London Borough of see ***Newham***
Tring see ***Hertfordshire, West***
Twyford see ***Thames Valley***

Tyneside
Newcastle-upon-Tyne, Gateshead, North and South Tyneside
Franchise holder: United Artists Communications (North East) = TeleWest (see GO)
Homes in area: 325,000
Awarded: 14 Dec 89
Separate upgrade systems operated by Cablecom Investments

Wakefield/Pontefract/Castleford
Franchise holder: Wakefield Cable = General Cable (see GO)
Homes in area: 94,000
Awarded: 2 Mar 90; acquired Apr 93

Walsall see ***Black Country***

Waltham Forest, London Borough of
Franchise holder: Encom Cable TV and Telecommunications (see GO)
Homes in area: 83,000
Awarded: 28 Sep 89

Wandsworth, London Borough of
Franchise holder: Videotron Cable Communications (see GO)
Homes in area: 100,000
Awarded: 13 Aug 85
Service start: autumn 1991

Ware see ***Hertford***
Warrington see ***Cheshire, North***

Warwick/Stratford-upon-Avon/Kenilworth/Leamington Spa
Franchise holder: County Cable Telecommunications = CUC Cablevision (see GO)
Homes in area: 50,000
Awarded: 30 Mar 90

Watford see ***Hertfordshire, South***

Wearside
Sunderland/Durham/Washington
Franchise holder: Comment Cablevision Wearside = US Cable (see GO)
Gibson House
Holly Hill
Felling
Gateshead
Tyne & Wear WE10 9NQ
Tel: 091 469 8800
Fax: 091 469 1491
Homes in area: 200,000
Awarded: 14 Jun 90

Wellingborough see ***Colby***
Welwyn see ***Hertfordshire, Central***
West Lothian see ***Falkirk***

Westminster, London Borough of
Franchise holder: Westminster Cable Television = British Telecom (see GO)
87-89 Baker Street
London W1M 1AG
Tel: 071 935 6699
Fax: 071 486 9447
Homes in area: 120,000
Awarded: 29 Nov 83
Homes passed: 56,176 (1 Apr 93)
Service start: Sep 85
Subscribers: 11,198 = 19.9% (1 Apr 93)

Weymouth see ***Dorset, West***
Whittlesey see ***Wisbech***
Widnes see ***Cheshire, North***

Wigan
Franchise holder: North West Cable Communications = SBS Cablecomms UK (see GO)
Homes in area: 110,000
Awarded: 17 May 90

Homes passed: 32,771 (1 Apr 93)
Subscribers: 6,746 = 20.6% (1 Apr 93)

Wilmslow see ***Macclesfield***

Winchester
Franchise holder: Videotron Cable Communications (see GO)
Homes in area: 33,000
Awarded: 6 Apr 90

Windsor/Slough/ Maidenhead/ Ashford/Staines/ Stanwell/Heathrow
Franchise holder: Windsor Cable Communications = General Cable (see GO)
Homes in area: 110,000
Awarded: 1 Nov 83
Homes passed: 91,546 (1 Apr 93)
Service start: 1 Dec 85
Subscribers: 15,834 = 17.3% (1 Apr 93)

Wirral, The
Franchise holder: Nynex Cablecoms Wirral (see GO)
Homes in area: 120,000
Awarded: 11 Jul 90

Wisbech see ***Fenland***
Wishaw see ***Motherwell***
Woking see ***Guildford***
Wokingham see ***Thames Valley***
Wolverhampton see ***Black Country***

Worcester/ Redditch/Droitwich
Franchise holder: Comment Cablevision = US Cable (see GO)
Homes in area: 70,000
Awarded: 14 Jun 90

Worthing see ***Brighton***

York/Harrogate/ Knaresborough
Franchise holder: Yorcan Communications
Great Givendale
Pocklington
York YO4 2TT
Tel: 0759 6316
Homes in area: 78,000
Homes passed: 3,925
Awarded: 30 Mar 90

GO (GROUP OWNERSHIP)

Almost all franchises are held as part of groups of holdings. Such groups are called multiple system operators. In some cases precise composition of share ownership may vary slightly between franchises in a group, especially where local and/or founding directors and managers have retained equity stakes after major groups have taken over the franchise

HiA = homes in area

Total HiA aggregates number of homes in broadband franchise areas (ie, excluding upgrades), including proportional percentage only where franchise is not wholly owned

Bell Canada Enterprises (BCE)
Limeharbour Court
Limeharbour
London E14 9TY
Tel: 071 895 9910
Fax: 071 895 9755
74.5% stake in Encom Cable TV and Telecommunications (qv)
30% stake in partnership with Videotron in Videotron Corporation (qv)
Total HiA: 799,605

British Telecom Visual and Broadcast Services
Room 26/20
Euston Tower
286 Euston Road
London NW1 3DG
Tel: 071 728 3405
Fax: 071 380 2635
Areas:
Westminster LB (HiA 107,000)
Total HiA: 107,000

Bruncor
(Canadian telecom operator of New Brunswick)
Areas:
with US Cable Corporation 49%:
Worcester (HiA 70,000)
Wearside (HiA 200,000)
Total HiA: 121,500

CUC Cablevision (UK)
Link 2
Beaconsfield Plaza
Gillette Way
Reading RG2 0BS
Tel: 0734 756475
Ownership: CUC (Canadian multiple systems cable operator) 50%, Telus Corporation 50%
Areas:
as County Cable Communications:
Hertfordshire, West 90% (HiA 100,000)
Nuneaton/etc (HiA 43,000)
Thames Valley (HiA 215,000)
Warwick/etc (HiA 50,000)
as Swindon Cable:
Swindon (HiA 75,000)
13.5% stake in Coventry Cable

11 Duncan Close
Moulton Park
Northampton NN3 1WL
Tel: 0604 494949
Areas:
as County Cable Telecommunications:
Corby/etc 80% (HiA 90,000)
Northampton (HiA 72,000)
Total HiA: 632,800

The Cable Corporation
Cable House
Waterside Drive
Langley
Berkshire SL3 6EZ
Tel: 0753 810810
Fax: 0753 810808
Ownership: Compagnie Générale des Eaux (44.77%), Standard Life Assurance (19.52%), TeleWest (16.39%), CIN Industrial Investments
Areas:
as Middlesex Cable:
Hillingdon (HiA 92,000)
Hounslow (HiA 79,000)
as Windsor TV: Windsor/etc (HiA 110,000)
Total HiA: 281,000

Cable London
Centro House
20-23 Mandela Street
London NW1 0DU
Tel: 071 922 0555
Fax: 071 922 0111
Ownership: Comcast UK (44%) (qv), TeleWest (44%) (qv)
Areas:
Camden LB (HiA 70,000)
Enfield (HiA 105,000)
Hackney & Islington LBs (HiA 150,000)
Haringey LB(HiA 85,000)
Total HiA: 410,000

Comcast UK
Centro House
Mandela Street
London NW1 0DU
Tel: 071 528 0555
Ownership: Comcast Corporation (US)
Areas:
with Singapore Telecom:
Harlow/etc 50% (HIA 53,000)
with Singapore Telecom and others:
Cambridge/etc 41.25% (HiA 134,000)
with TeleWest (qv):
Birmingham/etc 40% (HIA 465,000)
with TeleWest and others: Cable London 44% (qv)
Total HiA: 448,175

Compagnie Générale des Eaux
(French water utilities company)
100% ownership of General Cable (qv)
44.77% stake in The Cable Corporation (qv)
Total HiA: 660,526

Devanha Group
303 King Street
Aberdeen AB2 3AP
Tel: 0224 649444
Areas:
Aberdeen 100% (HiA 93,000)
Coventry 87.75% (HiA 119,000)
5% stake in Tayside Cable Systems, 3.5% in Kingdom Cablevision see Post-Newsweek UK Cable
Total HiA: 212,000

Diamond Cable
Regency House
2a Sherwood Rise
Nottingham NG7 6JN
Tel: 0602 503021
Fax: 0602 605111
Areas:
Grantham (HiA 14,000)
Grimsby/etc (HiA 63,000)
Lincoln (HiA 30,000)
Mansfield/etc (HiA 58,000)
Melton Mowbray (HiA 30,000)
Newark-on-Trent (HiA 18,000)
Nottingham (HiA 160,000)
Total HiA: 373,000

Encom Cable TV and Telecommunications
2 Millharbour
London E14 9TE
Tel: 071 895 9910
Fax: 071 895 9755
Ownership: BCE Telecom International (qv) 74.5%,

Jones Cable Group (qv) (15%), Mercury Communications, GEC, Prudential Assurance, Robert Fleming Mercantile Investment Trust, Electricity Council Pension Fund, Ferranti International
Areas:
Dartford/etc (HiA 35,000)
Epping Forest LB/etc (HiA 45,000)
Greater London East (HiA 229,000)
Havering LB (HiA 90,000)
Newham LB/etc (HiA 127,000)
Waltham Forest LB (HiA 83,000)
Total HiA: 609,000

English Cable Enterprises
Cablevision House
20 Cosgrove Way
Luton
Bedfordshire LU1 1XL
Tel: 0582 401044
Areas:
as Cablevision Bedfordshire: Luton/etc (HiA 10,000)
as Cablevision Communications Company: Hertfordshire, Central (HiA 100,000)
as Cablevision North Bedfordshire: Bedford (HiA 55,000)
as Lea Valley Cablevision Communications: Hertford/etc (HiA 60,000)
Total HiA: 225,000

General Cable
22 Headfort Place
London SW1X 7DH
Tel: 071 235 9555
Fax: 071 235 1775
Ownership: Compagnie Générale des Eaux (qv)
Areas:
Barnsley (HiA 82,000)
as Bradford Cable Communications: Bradford 80% (HiA 75,000)
as Middlesex Cable Communications 58.85%:
Hillingdon (HiA 93,000)
Hounslow (HiA 79,000)
as Sheffield Cable Communications: Sheffield 95% (HiA 210,000)
as Wakefield Cable: Wakefield/etc (HiA 94,000)
Total HiA: 534,722

Insight Communications
PO Box 9
Lambourn
Newbury
Berkshire RG16 7NB
Tel: 0488 73189
Fax: 0488 71232
Areas:
as Insight Communications Cardiff: Cardiff/etc 95% (HiA 103,000)
as Insight UK Management Co: Guildford/etc (HiA 137,000)
as Kirklees Cable: Huddersfield/etc (HiA 148,000)
as Newport Cablevision: Newport/etc (HiA 85,000)
40 Anderston Quay
Glasgow G3 8DA
Tel: 041 221 7040
Fax: 041 248 2921
Areas:
as Clyde Cablevision 95%: Bearsden/etc (HiA 16,000)
Glasgow Greater (HiA 274,000)
Glasgow North West/etc (HiA 112,000)
Inverclyde (HiA 32,000)
Paisley/etc (HiA 67,000)
Total HiA: 948,950

IVS Cable Holdings
284 Weyhill Road
Andover
Hampshire SP10 3LS
Tel: 0264 334607
Fax: 0264 332071
Ownership: Flextech 49.5%
Areas:
as Andover Cablevision: Andover (HiA 11,500)
as Oxford Cable: Oxford (HiA 55,000)
as Wessex Cable: Salisbury 90% (HiA 15,000)
also as Jersey Cable: Jersey (HiA 23,000 not ITC licensed)
Total HiA: 103,000

Jones Cable Group
Jones House
9 Greycaine Road
Watford WD2 4JP
Tel: 0923 211440
Fax: 0923 210006
Ownership: Jones Intercable (US)
Areas:
Aylesbury/etc (HiA 62,000)
Hertfordshire, South (HiA 95,000)
Leeds (HiA 289,000)
15% partner in Encom Cable TV and Telecommunications (qv)
Total HiA: 537,350

Leicester Communications
12 Elstree Way
Borehamwood
Hertfordshire WD6 1NF
Tel: 081 207 5232
Ownership: Fundy Cable 35.7%, John Laing 31%, Sasktel International 31%, other 2.73%
Areas:
Leicester (HiA 147,000)
Loughborough/etc (HiA 30,000)
Total HiA: 177,000

Maclean Hunter Cablevision
Glenfield Park Site 2
Blakewater Road
Blackburn
Lancashire BB1 5QF
Tel: 0254 680094
Fax: 0254 679236
Ownership: Maclean Hunter Cable TV (Canada)
Areas:
as Devon Cablevision: Devon, South (HiA 236,000)
as East Coast Cable: Colchester/etc (HiA 126,000)
Total HiA: 362,000

Nynex UK
Wimbledon Bridge House
1 Hartfield Road
Wimbledon
London SW19 3RU
Tel: 081 540 8833
Fax: 081 544 0811
Ownership: Nynex Corporation (US)
Areas:
Bolton (HiA 135,000)
Bournemouth/etc (HiA 143,000)
Brighton/etc (HiA 160,000)
Bromley LB (HiA 117,000)
Bury/etc (HiA 145,000)
Cheshire North (HiA 175,000)
Darlington (HiA 34,000)
Derby/etc (HiA 96,000)
Lancashire East (HiA 168,000)
Macclesfield/etc (HiA 45,000)
Manchester/etc (HiA 363,000)
Oldham/etc (HiA 172,000)
Portsmouth/etc (HiA 213,000)
Stafford/etc (HiA 24,000)
Stockport (HiA 113,000)
Stoke-on-Trent/etc (HiA 156,000)
Surrey, North (HiA 71,000)
Surrey, North East (HiA 98,000)
*Teesside (HiA 195,000)
The Wirral (HiA 120,000)
Total HiA: 2,738,000
* Optioned to US Cable (qv)

Pactel Cable UK
Ownership: Pacific Telesis Group (California telecom operator)
Areas:
as South Yorkshire Cablevision: Doncaster/etc (HiA 192,000)
29 Metro Centre
Shrewsbury Avenue
Peterborough PE4 0BX
Tel: 0733 230303
Fax: 0733 238405
Areas:
as Fenland Cablevision: Wisbech/etc (HiA 21,000)
as Peterborough Cablevision: Peterborough (HiA 58,000)
32a Whiffler Road
Norwich NR3 2AZ
Tel: 0603 787892
Fax: 0603 787851
Areas:
as Broadland Cablevision: Great Yarmouth/etc (HiA 64,000)
as Norwich Cablevision: Norwich (HiA 83,000)
Total HiA: 226,000

Post-Newsweek UK Cable
Tay Works
Brown Street
Dundee DD1 5EF
Tel: 0382 22220
Fax: 0382 22225
Areas:
as Kingdom Cablevision: Glenrothes/etc (HiA 60,000)
as Scotcable 90%: Cumbernauld/etc (HiA 55,000)
Dumbarton/etc (HiA 18,000)
Falkirk/etc (HiA 30,000)
Motherwell/etc (HiA 125,000)
as Tayside Cable Systems 80%: Dundee/etc (HiA 99,000)
Perth/etc (HiA 18,000)
Total HiA: 351,000

SBC Cablecomms UK
Hollywood House
Church Street East
Woking
Surrey GU21 1HJ
Tel: 0483 751756
Fax: 0483 740922

Ownership: Southwestern Bell (75% (US telecom operator), Cox Cable Communications 25% (US cable operator)
Areas:
as North West Cable Communications: Liverpool South (HiA 125,000)
Ribble View
Frenchwood Avenue
Preston
Lancashire PR1 4QF
Tel: 0772 202888
Areas:
as North West Cable Communications:
Lancashire Central (HiA 114,000)
Liverpool North/etc (HiA 119,000)
St Helens/etc (HiA 121,000)
Wigan (HiA 110,000)
Cable House
Waterfront
Merry Hill
Dudley
W Midlands DY5 1XJ
Tel: 0384 482448
Areas:
as Midlands Cable Communications: Black Country (HiA 470,000)
Telford (HiA 55,000)
Total HiA: 1,114,000

Starstream Europe

Ownership: Cable & Satellite Television Holdings (CAST)
Areas:
as Starside Network (North Downs): Kent, South East (HiA 77,000)
as Starvision Network (West Glamorgan): Glamorgan, West (HiA 110,000)
Total HiA: 187,000

TeleWest Communications

Unit 1
Genesis Business Park
Albert Drive
Woking
Surrey GU21 5RW
Tel: 0483 750900
Fax: 0483 750901
Ownership: TeleCommunications Inc (TCI) 76.25% and US West (qv) 23.75%
Areas:
as United Artists Communications:
Avon (HiA 300,000)
Cheltenham/etc (HiA 90,000)
Croydon LB 95% (HiA 120,000)
Edinburgh (HiA 183,000)
Kingston LB/etc 95% (HiA 124,000)
Merton LB/etc 95% (HiA 135,000)
Thames Estuary North (HiA 300,000)
Thames Estuary South (HiA 159,000)
Tyneside (HiA 340,000)
with Comcast Corporation (qv):
Birmingham/etc 45%
44% stake in Cable London (qv)
16.39% stake in The Cable Corporation (qv)
Total HiA: 1,889,340

US Cable Corporation

PO Box 319
Dunstable
Bedfordshire LU6 3NA
Tel: 0582 60138
Fax: 0582 471530
Areas:
as Comment Cablevision 51%: Wearside (HiA 200,000)
Worcester (HiA 70,000)
Total HiA: 137,700

Vento Cable Management

Tay Works
Brown Street
Dundee DD1 5FF
Tel: 0382 22220
Fax: 0382 22225
Small stakes in Tayside Cable Systems and Scotcable see Post-Newsweek Cable

Videotron Corporation

Ownership: Le Groupe Vidéotron (Canada) 64%, Bell Canada Enterprises 30% (qv)
West London division:
Parkways
179-181 The Vale
London W3 7QS
Tel: 081 740 4848
Fax: 081 740 4583
Areas:
Ealing LB (HiA 105,000)
Harrow (HiA 79,000)
Kensington LB/etc (HiA 82,000)
London, North West (HiA 280,000)
South London division:
Belmont House
11-29 Belmont Hill
London SE13 5AU
Tel: 081 852 0123
Fax: 081 852 2232
Areas:
Greenwich LB/etc (HiA 175,000)
Lambeth LB/etc (HiA 191,000)
Thamesmead (HiA 11,000)
Wandsworth LB (HiA 100,000)
Southern division:
Ocean House
West Quay Road
Southampton SO1 0XL
Tel: 0703 333020
Fax: 0703 335237
Areas:
Southampton/etc (HiA 97,000)
Winchester (HiA 33,000)
Total HiA: 1,153,000

ENGLISH-LANGUAGE SATELLITE AND CABLE TELEVISION CHANNELS

All channels transmitting via satellite from or to the UK, wholly or partly in the English language. A full list of all services licensed to date by the Independent Television Commission follows. Not all channels are intended for reception in the UK. The television standard and encrypting system used are indicated after the name of the satellite. Services for which a separate charge is made are marked (premium) after the programming type

MULTIPLE SERVICE PROVIDERS (MSP)

BBC Enterprises

Woodlands
80 Wood Lane
London W12 0TT
Tel: 081 576 2000
Fax: 081 746 1922
Ownership: British Broadcasting Corporation
Services: BBC World Service Television, UK Gold 20%

British Sky Broadcasting (BSkyB)

6 Centaurs Business Park
Grant Way
Syon Lane
Isleworth
Middx TW7 5QD
Tel: 071 705 3000
Fax: 071 705 3030
Ownership: News International 50%, Pearson 17.5%, Chargeurs 17.5%, Granada Group 13.9%
Services: The Movie Channel, Nickelodeon, Sky Movies Gold, Sky Movies Plus, Sky News, Sky One, Sky Sports

Home Video Channel

Unit 111
Canalot Production Studios
222 Kensal Road
London W10 5BN
Tel: 081 964 1141
Fax: 081 964 5934
Ownership: Graff Per-Per-View 35%, R Christopher Yates, Andrew Wren
Services: The Adult Channel, Home Video Channel

Turner Broadcasting System (TBS)

CNN House
19-22 Rathbone Place
London W1P 1DF
Tel: 071 637 6700
Fax: 071 637 6768
Services: Cartoon Network, CNN International, Turner Network Television

United Artists Programming

Twyman House
16 Bonny Street
London NW1 9PG
Tel: 071 482 4824
Ownership: United Artists International = TeleCommunications Inc
Services (including managed services): Bravo, CMT Europe, The Children's Channel 25%, The Discovery Channel Europe, The Learning Channel, The Parliamentary Channel, Wire TV: The Cable Network

CHANNELS

The Adult Channel

Ownership: Home Video Channel (see Multiple service providers (MSP above))
Service start: Feb 1992
Satellite: Astra 1B (PAL/Videocrypt)
Programming: 'adult' entertainment *(premium)*

AsiaVision
3 Emperors Gate
London SW7 4HH
Tel: 071 370 2668
Fax: 071 370 2656
Service start: May 1986 as Indra Dhnush; relaunched July 1992
Cable only from videotape
Programming: movies and entertainment in Hindi and other languages

BBC World Service Television
Ownership: BBC Enterprises (see MSP)
Service start: Apr 1991
Satellite: Intelsat 601 (D2-MAC/Eurocrypt M)
Programming: news, information, entertainment, international coverage outside UK

The Box
Camberley House
Portesbery Road
Camberley
Surrey GU15 3SZ
Tel: 0276 691410
Fax: 0276 691460
Service start: Mar 1992
Cable only from videotape
Programming: interactive pop music

Bravo
Ownership: United Artists Programming (see MSP)
Service start: Sep 1985
Satellite: Intelsat 601 (PAL/Save); Astra 1C (PAL/Videocrypt)
Programming: old movies and TV programmes

CMT Europe
Ownership: Gaylord Entertainment 67%, Group W Satellite Communications 43%; management: United Artists Programming (see MSP)
Satellite: Intelsat 601 (PAL/clear)
Programming: country music

CNN International
CNN House
19-22 Rathbone Place
London W1P 1DF
Tel: 071 434 9323
Fax: 071 637 6768
Ownership: Turner Broadcasting System (see MSP)
Service start: Oct 1985
Satellite: Astra 1B/ Intelsat 601 (PAL/clear)
Programming: news

The Cartoon Network
Ownership: Turner Broadcasting System (see MSP)
Service start: Sep 1993
Satellite: Astra 1C (PAL/ clear)
Programming: children's

The Channel Guide
1a French's Yard
Amwell End
Ware
Herts SG12 9HP
Tel: 0920 469238
Fax: 0920 468372
Ownership: Picture Applications
Service start: May 1990
Cable only (text)
Programming: programme listings

The Children's Channel
9-13 Grape Street
London WC2H 8DR
Tel: 071 240 3422
Fax: 071 497 9113
Ownership: Starstream = Flextech Communications 75%, D C Thomson 18%, Thames TV 7%. Flextech Communications is 67:33 partnership between Flextech and TeleCommunications Inc
Service start: Sep 1984
Satellite: Intelsat 601, Astra 1A, Astra 1B (PAL/ clear), Astra 1C (PAL/ Videocrypt)
Programming: children's

The Discovery Channel Europe
Ownership: Discovery Communications = TeleCommunications 49%, Cox Communications, Newhouse, John Hendricks; management: United Artists Programming (see MSP)
Service start: Apr 1989
Satellite: Intelsat 601, Astra 1C (PAL/clear)
Programming: documentaries

Euronews
60 chemin des Mouilles
69130 Ecully
France
Tel: (33) 72 18 80 00
Fax: (33) 73 18 93 71
Ownership: RTBF (Belgium), Cyprus Broadcasting Corporation, ERTU (Greece), YLE (Finland), France 2, France 3, Radio Televisione Italiana, TéléMonteCarlo, Radio Televisão Portuguesa, Radio Television Española
Service start: Jan 93
Satellite: Eutelsat II-F1 (PAL/clear)
Programming: news in English, French, Spanish, German and Italian

Eurosport
1 quai du Point du Jour
Boulogne
France
Tel: (33) 41 41 22 42
Fax: (33) 41 41 28 90
Ownership: ESO Ltd = TF1 34%, Canal Plus 33%, ESPN 33%
Service start: Feb 1989
Satellite: Astra 1A, Eutelsat II-F1 (PAL/clear)
Programming: sport

Eurostep
PO Box 11 112
Rapenburg 63
2311 GJ Leiden
Netherlands
Tel: (31) 71 12 06 63
Ownership: educational institutions in several countries
Service start: 1990
Satellite: Eutelsat II-F3 (D2-MAC/Eurocrypt M)

Home Video Channel
Ownership: Home Video Channel (see MSP)
Service start: Sep 1985
Cable only from videotape
Programming: movies *(premium)*

Landscape Channel
Landscape Studios
Hye House
Crowhurst
East Sussex TN33 9BX
Tel: 0424 83688
Fax: 0424 83680
Service start: Nov 1988 (on videotape); Apr 1993 (on satellite)
Satellite: Intelsat 601 (PAL/clear)
Programming: music and visual wallpaper

The Learning Channel
Ownership: Discovery Communications = TeleCommunications 49%, Cox Communications, Newhouse, John Hendricks; management: United Artists Programming (see MSP)
Service start: Mar 1992
Satellite: Intelsat 601 (PAL/clear)
Programming: popular educational documentaries, family, leisure

MBC: Middle East Broadcasting Centre
10 Heathman's Road
London SW6 4TJ
Tel: 071 371 9597
Fax: 071 371 9601
Service start: Sep 1991
Satellite: Eutelsat II-F1 (PAL/clear)
Programming: general and news in Arabic

MTV Europe
Hawley Crescent
London NW1 8TT
Tel: 071 284 7777
Fax: 071 284 7788
Ownership: MTV Networks = Viacom (100)
Service start: Aug 1987
Satellite: Astra 1A, Astra 1B (PAL/clear)
Programming: pop music

The Movie Channel
Ownership: British Sky Broadcasting (see MSP)
Service start: Apr 1991
Satellite: Astra 1B (PAL/ Videocrypt)
Programming: movies *(premium)*

Namaste
Kingfisher 3
Trinity Park, Trinity Way
Chingford
London E4 8TD
Tel: 081 523 1442
Fax: 081 523 1455
Service start: Sep 1992
Cable only from videotape
Programming: Asian entertainment

Nickelodeon
Ownership: British Sky Broadcasting 50% (see MSP), Viacom 50%
Service start: Third quarter 1993
Satellite: Astra 1C (PAL/ Videocrypt)
Programming: children's

The Parliamentary Channel
Ownership: consortium of nine cable operators, management: United Artists Programming (see MSP)
Service start: Jan 1992
Satellite: Intelsat 601 (PAL/clear)
Programming: coverage of British parliamentary debates

Performance: The Arts Channel
Symal House
Edgware Road
London NW9 0HU
Tel: 071 905 9191
Fax: 071 205 8619
Service start: Oct 1992
Cable only from videotape
Programming: opera, jazz and classical concerts, drama

Quantum TV/Sell-a-Vision
Minor House
21 Soho Square
London W1V 5FD
Tel: 071 465 1234
Ownership: National Media Corporation Inc
Service start: 1992
Satellite: Astra 1A (PAL/clear)
Programming: home shopping in English, Dutch and German

Sky Movies Gold
Ownership: British Sky Broadcasting (see MSP)
Service start: Oct 1992
Satellite Astra 1B (PAL/Videocrypt)
Programming: movies *(premium)*

Sky Movies Plus
Ownership: British Sky Broadcasting (see MSP)
Service start: Feb 1989
Satellite: Astra 1A (PAL/Videocrypt)
Programming: movies *(premium)*

Sky News
Ownership: British Sky Broadcasting (see MSP)
Service start: Feb 1989
Satellite: Astra 1A (PAL/clear)
Programming: news

Sky One
Ownership: British Sky Broadcasting (see MSP)
Service start: Feb 1989
Satellite: Astra 1A (PAL/clear)
Programming: entertainment

Sky Sports
Ownership: British Sky Broadcasting (see MSP)
Service start: Apr 1991
Satellite: Astra 1B (PAL/Videocrypt)
Programming: sport *(premium)*

Super Channel
Melrose House
14 Lanark Square
Limeharbour
London E14 9QD
Tel: 071 637 3700
Fax: 071 637 6768
Ownership: Beta Television/Marcucci Group 66%, Virgin 31%
Service start: Jan 1987
Satellite: Eutelsat II-F1 (PAL/clear)
Programming: entertainment in English, Dutch and German

TV Asia
7 Belvue Business Centre
Belvue Road
Northolt
Middx UB5 5QQ
Tel: 081 845 2266
Ownership: Asia TV Ltd = Ajitabh Bachchan (majority)
Service start: Jan 1992
Satellite: Astra 1A, Astra 1B (PAL/Videocrypt)
Programming: entertainment and news in Hindi, Urdu and English *(premium)*

Turner Network Television
Ownership: Turner Broadcasting System (see MSP)
Service start: Sep 1993
Satellite: Astra 1C (PAL/clear)
Programming: movies, entertainment

UK Gold
306 Euston Road
London NW1 3BB
Tel: 071 387 9494
Ownership: Cox Communications 38%, TeleCommunications Inc 27%, Thames Television 15%, BBC Enterprises 20%
Service start: Nov 1992
Satellite: Astra 1B (PAL/clear)
Programming: entertainment

Vision
Shaftesbury Centre
Percy Street
Swindon
Wilts SN2 2AZ
Tel: 0793 511244
Fax: 0793 512477
Cable only from videotape
Programming: non-denominational religious

Wire TV: The Cable Network
Ownership: Comcast, Nynex, Southwestern Bell, TCI, US West; management: United Artists Programming (see MSP)
Satellite: Intelsat 601 (PAL/clear)
Programming: general

Worldnet
US Information Agency
American Embassy
24 Grosvenor Square
London W1A 1AE
Tel: 071 499 9000
Fax: 071 499 2485
Ownership: US Government
Service start: 1985
Satellite: Eutelsat II-F1 (PAL/clear) from USA
Programming: news

ITC LICENSED PROGRAMME SERVICES

Not all of the following channels are currently active, some have never passed the planning stage. Those in the main listing are highlighted. All, however, have been granted Programme Service or Non-Domestic Satellite licences by the Independent Television Commission

English language services
The Ability Channel, **The Adult Channel**, The Afro Caribbean Channel, BVTV, **Bravo**, **British Sky Broadcasting (BSkyB) (The Movie Channel, Sky Movies Gold, Sky Movies Plus, Sky One, Sky Sports)**, **Cable Jukebox**, CBP Sport, Channel e, **The Channel Guide**, **The Children's Channel**, **CNN International**, **Discovery Channel Europe**, Education & Training Channel (University of Sunderland), The Education Channel (Blackburn), The European Family Christian Network, GNB TV Network, **Home Video Channel**, The Ideas Factory, Identity Television, International Shopping Network, Intershop, Jukebox Network, **The Landscape Channel**, **Lifestyle**, London Live Television, Mind Extension University, **MTV Europe**, **The Movie Channel**, Multi Screen Channel, Olympus/Greensat, **The Parliamentary Channel**, **Performance: The Arts Channel**, **Quantum Home Shopping**, Quest Television, Regal Shop, Royal Opera House Channel, Satellite Information Services Sporting Facts, Sell-a-vision Shopping, Star Television: The Black Entertainment Channel, **Superchannel**, Supersell, The UK Channel, **UK Gold**, **Vision**, Visual Arts

Foreign-language UK services
ART: Anadolu Radio Television, Ahmadiya Muslim Presentations, The Arabic Channel, Asian Television Network, **AsiaVision**, British Greek Community Channel, China News Europe, The Egyptian Channel, Hellenic Television, Japansat, **MBC: Middle East Broadcasting**, **Namaste**, PTV: The Persian Channel, Middle East Broadcasting (Arabic), TV Asia, Uzay Television

Local services
Aberdeen Channel, Arcade (United Artists Cable TV), Arcade (Windsor Television), Cable 7 (East Lancashire), Cable 10 (Port Talbot), Channel A (Star Promotions, Leicestershire), Channel 15 (United Artists Cable TV), Channel Seven (Midlands Cable Communications), Clyde Cablevision, Colt TV (Coventry Cable), Leicester Community Channel, Local 8 (Norwich Cablevision), Redbridge Community Channel, The Skelmersdale Local Channel, Swindon Local, Tower Hamlets/Newham Community Channel, Videotron Channel, Westscan

Overseas-based services
Kanal 6, Kindernet, TV1000, TV3 Denmark

CINEMAS

Key to symbols

bfi – Supported by the BFI through finance, programming assistance or occasional programming/publicity services

* – Part-time or occasional screenings

• – Cinema open seasonally

Key to Disability codes

West End/Outer London

E – Hearing aid system installed. Always check with venue whether in operation

W – Venue with unstepped access (via main or side door), wheelchair space and adapted lavatory

X – Venue with flat or one step access to auditorium

A – Venue with 2-5 steps to auditorium

G – Provision for Guide Dogs

England/Channel Islands/Scotland/Wales/ Northern Ireland

X – Accessible to people with disabilities (advance arrangements sometimes necessary – please phone cinemas to check)

E – Hearing aid system installed. Always check with venue whether in operation

Listed below are the companies who control the major chains of cinemas and multiplexes in the UK, followed by the cinemas themselves listed by area, with seating capacities. The listing includes disabled access information where this is available (see the key below left for details)

CINEMA CIRCUITS

Apollo Cinemas UK

16 Arkwright Office Suite
Mill Lane
Coppull
Lancs PR7 5AN
Tel: 0257 471012
Fax: 0257 794109
Operates 55 screens on 19 sites in the North West, Wales, Yorkshire and the Midlands. Apollo's Theatre Division operates the Apollo, Ardwick, and Futurist, Scarborough, which occasionally show films

Artificial Eye Film Co

211 Camden High Street
London NW1 7BT
Tel: 071 267 6036/482 3981
Fax: 071 267 6499
Film distributors operating the Lumiere, Camden Plaza, Chelsea Cinema and Renoir in London's West End

CAC Leisure

PO Box 21
23-25 Huntly Street
Inverness IV1 1LA
Tel: 0463 237611
Operates 18 screens on 8 sites, all in Scotland

Mainline Pictures

37 Museum Street
London WC1A 1LP
Tel: 071 242 5523
Fax: 071 430 0170
Operates Screen cinemas at Baker Street, Haverstock Hill, Islington Green, Reigate and Walton-on-Thames

Metro Goldwyn Mayer Cinemas

84-86 Regent Street
London W1R 5PF
Tel: 071 915 1717
Operated 421 screens on 129 sites at June 1993, including Cannon cinemas

National Amusements (UK)

200 Elm Street
Dedham
Massachusetts
02026-9126, USA
Tel: 0101 617 461 1600
Fax: 0101 617 326 1306
Operators of ten Showcase Cinemas with 127 screens in Nottingham, Derby, Peterborough, Leeds, Liverpool, Walsall, Birmingham, Coventry, Manchester and Stockton

Odeon Cinemas

439-445 Godstone Road
Whyteleafe
Surrey CR3 0YG
Tel: 0883 623355
The Odeon chain totalled over 319 screens on 73 sites at summer 1993, with additional screens under construction

Panton Films

Coronet Cinema
Notting Hill Gate
London W11 3LB
Tel: 071 221 0123
Fax: 071 221 6312
Operates the Coronet circuit of 11 screens on 5 sites, comprising former circuit cinemas of Rank and MGM-Cannon

Recorded Cinemas

3rd Floor
155-157 Oxford Street
London W1R 1TB
Tel: 071 734 7477
Fax: 071 734 7470
Owns the Gate Notting Hill and Cameo Edinburgh, and is redeveloping Ritzy Brixton into a five-screen multiplex

Robins Cinemas

13 New Row
London WC2N 4LF
Tel: 071 497 3320
Operates 13 buildings with 25 screens, with recent additions at Dunfermline, Leeds and Worthing

Charles Scott Cinemas

Alexandra
Newton Abbot
Devon
Tel: 0626 65368
West Country circuit with cinemas at Bridgwater, Exmouth, Lyme Regis, Newton Abbot, Sidmouth and Teignmouth

UCI (UK)

Parkside House
51-53 Brick Street
London W1Y 7DU
Tel: 071 409 1346
Operators of 23 purpose-built multiplexes plus Empire and Plaza in London's West End in summer 1993, with 2 more multiplexes in progress

Warner Bros Theatres (UK)

135 Wardour Street
London W1V 4AP
Tel: 071 437 5600
Total re-building of Warner West End Theatre in Leicester Square. Currently operating 8 regional multiplexes with 75 screens at Bury, Newcastle, York, Basingstoke, Thurrock Lakeside Shopping Centre, Preston, Doncaster and Sheffield

The help of Artsline, London's Information and Advice Service for Disabled People on Arts & Entertainment, in producing this section, including the use of their coding system for venues in the Greater London area, is gratefully acknowledged. Please let us know if you have any further information on disability access, as we are keen to extend the information contained in this section of the Handbook

LONDON WEST END – PREMIERE RUN

Astral
Brewer Street, W1
Tel: 071 734 6387
Seats: 1:89, 2:159

Barbican
Silk Street, EC2 **WE**
Tel: 071 638 8891/638 4141
Seats: 1:288, 2:255

Camden Parkway
Parkway, NW1
Tel: 071 267 7034
Seats: Kings: 946, Regency: 90

Camden Plaza
Camden High Street, NW1 **A**
Tel: 071 485 2443
Seats: 340

Centre Charles Peguy
Leicester Square, WC2 ***X**
Tel: 071 437 8339
Seats: 100

Chelsea Cinema
Kings Road, SW3
Tel: 071 351 3742
Seats: 713

Coronet
Notting Hill Gate, W11 **A**
Tel: 071 727 6705
Seats: 396

Curzon Mayfair
Curzon Street, W1
Tel: 071 465 8865
Seats: 542

Curzon Phoenix
Phoenix Street, WC2
Tel: 071 867 1044
Seats: 212

Curzon West End
Shaftesbury Avenue, W1
Tel: 071 439 4805
Seats: 624

Design Museum
Butler's Wharf, Shad Thames, SE1 ***X**
Tel: 071 403 6933
Seats: 70

Electric
Portobello Road, W11 **X**
Tel: 071 792 2020/0328
Seats: 437

Empire
Leicester Square, WC2
Tel: 071 497 9999/437 1234
Seats: 1:1,330 **X**, 2:353, 3:80

French Institute
Queensberry Place, SW7 *
Tel: 071 589 6211
Seats: 350

Gate
Notting Hill Gate, W11 **X**
Tel: 071 727 4043
Seats: 241

Goethe Institute
Princes Gate, Exhibition Road, SW7 *
Tel: 071 411 3400
Seats: 170

bfi ICA Cinema
The Mall, SW1 **AG**
Tel: 071 930 3647
Seats: 208, C'thèque: 50

Imperial War Museum
Lambeth Road, SE1 ***X**
Tel: 071 735 8922
Seats: 216

bfi London Film Makers' Co-op
Gloucester Avenue, NW1 ***EG**
Tel: 071 586 8516
Seats: 100

Lumiere
St Martin's Lane, WC2 **X**
Tel: 071 836 0691/379 3014
Seats: 737

MGM Baker St
Marylebone Road, NW1 **A**
Tel: 071 935 9772
Seats: 1:171, 2:169

MGM Chelsea
King's Road, SW3
Tel: 071 352 5096/351 1026
Seats: 1:233, 2:264, 3:151, 4:119

MGM Fulham Rd
Fulham Road, SW10
Tel: 071 370 0265/2636/ 2110
Seats: 1:416 **X**, 2:374 **X**, 3:223 **X**, 4:223 **X**, 5:222

MGM Haymarket
Haymarket, SW1
Tel: 071 839 1527/1528
Seats: 1:448, 2:200, 3:201

MGM Oxford St
Oxford Street, W1
Tel: 071 636 0310/3851
Seats: 1:334, 2:227, 3:195, 4:225, 5:47

MGM Panton St
Panton Street, SW1
Tel: 071 930 0631/2
Seats: 1:127 **X**, 2:144 **X**, 3:138, 4:136

MGM Piccadilly
Piccadilly, W1
Tel: 071 437 3561
Seats: 1:124, 2:118

MGM Swiss Centre
Swiss Centre, W1
Tel: 071 439 4470/437 2096
Seats: 1:97, 2:101, 3:93, 4:108

MGM Shaftesbury Avenue
Shaftesbury Avenue, WC2
Tel: 071 836 6279/379 7025
Seats: 1:616, 2:581

MGM Tottenham Court Road
Tottenham Court Road, W1
Tel: 071 636 6148/6749
Seats: 1:328, 2:145, 3:137

MGM Trocadero
Trocadero Centre Piccadilly Circus, W1 **XE**
Tel: 071 434 0031
Seats: 1:548, 2:249, 3:145, 4:154, 5:122, 6:94, 7:89

Metro
Rupert Street, W1 **W**
Tel: 071 437 0757
Seats: 1:195, 2:85

Minema
Knightsbridge, SW1
Tel: 071 235 4225
Seats: 68

Museum of London
London Wall, EC2 ***X**
Tel: 071 600 3699/1058
Seats: 270

bfi National Film Theatre/ Museum of the Moving Image
South Bank, Waterloo, SE1 **WE**
Tel: 071 928 3232
Seats: 1:466, 2:162; MOMI:130

Odeon Haymarket
Haymarket, SW1 **A**
Tel: 071 839 7697/0426 915353
Seats: 600

Odeon Kensington
Kensington High Street, W8
Tel: 071 602 6644/5/0426 914666
Seats: 1:645, 2:73, 3:110, 4:297 **X**, 5:190 **X**, 6:234 **X**

Odeon Leicester Sq
Leicester Square, WC2
Tel: 071 930 6111/4250/ 4259/0426 915683
Seats: 1,965 **X**; Mezzanine: 291 (5 screens)

Odeon Marble Arch
Marble Arch, W1 **E**
Tel: 0426 914501/071 723 2011
Seats: 1,360

Odeon Swiss Cottage
Finchley Road, NW3
Tel: 0426 914098
Seats: 1:752, 2:112, 3:250, 4:200, 5:150, 6:153

Odeon West End
Leicester Square, WC2
Tel: 0426 915574/071 930 7615
Seats: 1:503, 2:838

Plaza Piccadilly Circus
Lower Regent Street, W1
Tel: 071 497 9999/437 1234
Seats: 1:732, 2:367 **X**, 3:161, 4:187

Prince Charles
Leicester Place, WC2 **X**
Tel: 071 437 8181
Seats: 487

Queen Elizabeth Hall
South Bank, Waterloo, SE1 ***X**
Tel: 071 928 3002
Seats: 906

Renoir
Brunswick Square, WC1
Tel: 071 837 8402
Seats: 1:251, 2:251

Royal Festival Hall
South Bank, Waterloo, SE1 ***X**
Tel: 071 928 3002
Seats: 2,419

Screen on Baker Street
Baker Street, NW1
Tel: 071 935 2772
Seats: 1:95, 2:100

Screen on the Green
Upper Street Islington, N1 **A**
Tel: 071 226 3520
Seats: 300

Screen on the Hill
Haverstock Hill, NW3 **A**
Tel: 071 435 3366/9787
Seats: 339

UCI Whiteleys
Queensway, Bayswater, W2 **WG**
Tel: 071 792 3332/3303
Seats: 1:333, 2:281, 3:196, 4:178, 5:154, 6:138, 7:147, 8:125

Warner West End
Leicester Square, WC2
9 screens

OUTER LONDON

Barking
Odeon
Longbridge Road
Tel: 0426 910596
Seats: 1:806, 2:83, 3:131 **X**, 4:130, 5:132, 6:162

Barnet
Odeon
Great North Road
Tel: 0426 911167
Seats: 1:528, 2: 140, 3:150, 4:193, 5:158

Battersea
Arts Centre
Old Town Hall
Lavender Hill, SW11 *X
Tel: 071 223 2223
Seats: 180

Beckenham
Cannon High Street
Tel: 081 650 1171/658 7114
Seats: 1:478, 2:228 **A**, 3:127 **A**

Borehamwood
Hertsmere Hall
Elstree Way *WG
Tel: 081 953 9872
Seats: 664

Brentford
Watermans Arts Centre
High Street WEG
Tel: 081 568 1176
Seats: 240

Brixton
Ritzy
Brixton Oval, SW2 A
Closed for restoration and addition of 4 new screens – reopens spring 1994

Bromley
Odeon High Street
Tel: 0426 910468
Seats: 1:402, 2:125 **X**, 3:98 **X**, 4:273

Catford
Cannon Central
Parade, SE6 EG
Tel: 081 698 3306/697 6579
Seats: 1:519 **X**, 2:259

Clapham
Picture House,
Venn Street, SW4
Tel: 071 498 2242
Seats: 1:202, 2:127 **X**, 3:110 **X**

Croydon
Cannon London Road
Tel: 081 688 0486/5775
Seats: 1:650, 2:399 **X**, 3:187 **X**
Fairfield Hall/Ashcroft Theatre Park Lane *
Tel: 081 688 9291
Seats: Fairfield: 1,552 **WEG**; Ashcroft: 750

Dalston
Rio Kingsland High Street, E8 WEG
Tel: 071 254 6677/249 2722
Seats: 400

Ealing
Cannon Northfields Avenue, W13
Tel: 081 567 1075
Seats: 1:155, 2:149
MGM
Uxbridge Road, W5
Tel: 081 567 1333/579 4851
Seats: 1:764, 2:414 **X**, 3:210 **X**

East Finchley
Phoenix
High Road, N2 XG
Tel: 081 883 2233
Seats: 300

Elephant & Castle
Coronet Film Centre
New Kent Road, SE1
Tel: 071 703 4968/708 0066
Seats: 1:546, 2:271 **X**, 3:211 **X**

Enfield
Cannon
Southbury Road
Tel: 081 363 4411/367 4909
Seats: 1:700, 2:356, 3:217 **X**, 4:140 **X**

Ewell
MGM Kingston Road
Tel: 081 393 2211
Seats: 1:606, 2:152 **X**

Golders Green
Ionic
Finchley Road, NW11
Tel: 081 455 1724/4134
Seats: 518

Greenwich
Greenwich Cinema
High Road, SE10 WEG
Tel: 081 853 0053
Seats: 1:350, 2:288, 3:144

Hammersmith
Cannon
King Street, W6
Tel: 081 748 0557/2388
Seats: 1:955, 2:455 **A**, 3:326 **A**
Riverside Studios
Crisp Road, W6 E
Tel: 081 748 3354
Seats: 200

Hampstead
MGM Pond Street, NW3
Tel: 071 794 4000/435 3168
Seats: 1:474, 2:197 **X**, 3:191 **X**
Everyman
Holly Bush Vale, NW3 X
Tel: 071 435 1525
Seats: 285

Harrow
Cannon Station Road
Tel: 081 427 1743/863 4137
Seats: 1:612, 2:133
Cannon
Sheepcote Road
Tel: 081 863 7261/427 1946
Seats: 1:628, 2:207 **X**, 3:204 **X**

Hayes
Beck Theatre
Grange Road *XE
Tel: 081 561 8371
Seats: 536

Hendon
MGM
Central Circus, NW4
Tel: 081 202 7137/4644
Seats: 1:572, 2:346 **X**, 3:320 **X**

Holloway
Odeon
Holloway Road, N7
Tel: 0426 914042
Seats: 1:388, 2:198 **X**, 3:270 **X**, 4:391, 5:361

Ilford
Odeon Gants Hill
Tel: 0426 939518
Seats: 1:768, 2:255 **X**, 3:290 **X**, 4:190, 5:62

Kilburn
Sentinel
Willesden Lane, NW6
Seats: 265

Kingston
Cannon Options
Richmond Road
Tel: 081 546 0404
Seats: 1:303 **X**, 2:287 **X**, 3:208

Muswell Hill
Odeon
Fortis Green Road, N10
Tel: 0426 911885
Seats: 1:610, 2:134 **X**, 3:130 **X**

Purley
MGM High Street
Tel: 081 660 1212/668 5592
Seats: 1:438, 2:135 **X**, 3:120 **X**

Putney
MGM
High Street, SW15
Tel: 081 788 2263/3003
Seats: 1:434, 2:312 **AWG**, 3:147

Richmond
Filmhouse
Water Lane WG
Tel: 081 332 0030
Seats: 150
Odeon Hill Street
Tel: 081 940 5759/948 8143
Seats: 1:478, 2:201 **X**, 3:201 **X**
Odeon Studio
Red Lion Street
Tel: 0426 915474
Seats: 1:81, 2:78, 3:78, 4:92

Romford
Cannon South Street
Tel: 0708 743848/747671
Seats: 1:652, 2:494 **A**, 3:246 **X**
Odeon
Mercury Gardens
Tel: 0426 910609
Seats: 1:410, 2:255, 3:150, 4:181, 5:181, 6:150, 7:335, 8:253

Sidcup
Cannon High Street
Tel: 081 300 2539/309 0770
Seats: 1:516 **A**, 2:303

Staples Corner
MGM Geron Way WE
Tel: 081 208 2277
Seats: 1:455, 2:362, 3:214, 4:210, 5:166, 6:166

Streatham
Cannon
High Road, SW16
Tel: 081 769 1928/6262
Seats: 1:630, 2:432 **X**, 3:231 **X**

Odeon
High Road, SW16
Tel: 0426 912977
Seats: 1:1,091, 2:220 **X**, 3:168 **X**, 4:240, 5:196

Sutton
Secombe Centre
Cheam Road *XE
Tel: 081 661 0416
Seats: 330
UCI St Nicholas Centre
St Nicholas Way
Tel: 081 395 4400/4477
Seats: 1:305, 2:297, 3:234, 4:327, 5:261, 6:327

Turnpike Lane
Coronet
Turnpike Parade, N15
Tel: 081 888 2519/3734
Seats: 1:624, 2:417 **X**, 3:269 **X**

Walthamstow
Cannon
Hoe Street, E17
Tel: 081 520 7092
Seats: 1:960, 2:181 **A**, 3:181 **A**

Well Hall
Coronet
Well Hall Road, SE9
Tel: 081 850 3351
Seats: 1:450, 2:131 **XG**

Willesden
Picture House
Willesden Green
Library Centre, NW10
Tel: 081 830 0822
Seats: 200

Wimbledon
Odeon
The Broadway, SW19
Tel: 0426 919227/081 542 2277
Seats: 1:702, 2:90, 3:190 **X**, 4:175, 5:218 **X**

Woodford
Cannon
High Road, E18
Tel: 081 989 3463/4066
Seats: 1:562, 2:199 **X**, 3:131 **X**

Woolwich
Coronet
John Wilson Street
Tel: 081 854 2255
Seats: 1:678, 2:370 **X**

ENGLAND

Aldeburgh Suffolk
Aldeburgh Cinema
High Street X
Tel: 072 885 2996
Seats: 286

Aldershot Hants
Cannon High Street
Tel: 0252 317223/20355
Seats: 1:313, 2:187, 3:150
West End Centre
Queens Road X
Tel: 0252 330040
Seats: 98

Alnwick
Northumberland
Playhouse Bondgate Without *
Tel: 0665 510785
Seats: 272

Alton Hants
Palace Normandy Street
Tel: 0420 82303
Seats: 111

Ambleside Cumbria
Zeffirelli's
Compston Road
Tel: 0966 33845
Seats: 180

Andover Hants
Savoy London Street
Tel: 0264 354337
Seats: 350

Ardwick
Greater Manchester
Apollo
Ardwick Green *X
Tel: 061 273 6921
Seats: 2,641

Ashington
Northumberland
Picture House
Station Road *
Tel: 0670 520237
Seats: 102

Ashton-under-Lyne
Greater Manchester
Metro Old Street
Tel: 061 330 1993
Seats: 987

Aylesbury Bucks
Odeon
Cambridge Street
Tel: 0296 82660
Seats: 1:450, 2:108, 3:113

Banbury Oxon
Cannon The Horsefair
Tel: 0295 262071
Seats: 1:432, 2:225

Barnsley South Yorks
Odeon Eldon Street
Tel: 0226 205494
Seats: 1:419, 2:636

Barnstaple Devon
Astor Boutport Street
Tel: 0271 42550
Seats: 360

Barrow Cumbria
Astra Abbey Road
Tel: 0229 825354
Seats: 1:640, 2:260, 3:260

Basildon Essex
Cannon Great Oaks
Tel: 0268 527421/527431
Seats: 1:644, 2:435, 3:101
Towngate *
Tel: 0268 23953
Seats: 459

Basingstoke Hants
Warner Basingstoke Leisure Park
Churchill Way West XE
Tel: 0256 818739/818448
Seats: 1:427, 2:238, 3:223, 4:154, 5:157, 6:157, 7:154, 8:223, 9:238, 10:427

Bath Avon
Cannon Beau Nash
Westgate Street X
Tel: 0225 461730/462959
Seats: 733
Robins St John's Place
Tel: 0225 461506
Seats: 1:126, 2:151 **X**, 3:49
Little Theatre
St Michael's Place
Tel: 0225 466822
Seats: 1:222, 2:78

Bedford Beds
Civic Theatre
Horne Lane *
Tel: 0234 44813
Seats: 266
MGM Aspect Leisure Park Barkers Lane XE
Tel: 0234 212844
Seats: 1:340, 2:300, 3:300, 4:300, 5:200, 6:200

Berwick
Northumberland
Playhouse Sandgate
Tel: 0289 307769
Seats: 650

Beverley East Yorks
Playhouse
Market Place
Tel: 0482 881315
Seats: 310

Bexhill-on-Sea
East Sussex
Curzon Western Road
Tel: 0424 210078
Seats: 215

Billingham Cleveland
Forum Theatre
Town Centre *
Tel: 0642 552663
Seats: 494

Birmingham
West Mids
Capitol
Alum Rock Road
Ward End
Tel: 021 327 0528
Seats: 1:340, 2:250, 3:130
MGM
Arcadian Centre XE
Tel: 021 622 3323/5551
Seats: 1:419, 2:299, 3:275, 4:240, 5:192, 6:222, 7:210, 8:196, 9:168
Midlands Arts Centre
Cannon Hill Park
Tel: 021 440 3838
Seats: 1:202, 2:144
Odeon New Street
Tel: 0426 855103
Seats: 1:238, 2:387, 3:308, 4:239, 5:204, 6:190, 7:126, 8:80
Showcase Cinemas
Kingsbury Road, Erdington
Tel: 021 382 9779
Seats: 3,400 (12 screens)
Tivoli Station Street
Tel: 021 643 1556
Two screens
bfi **Triangle**
Gosta Green X
Tel: 021 359 4192/2403
Seats: 180

Blackburn Lancs
Unit Four
King William Street
Tel: 0254 51779
Seats: 1:315, 2:256, 3:186

Blackpool Lancs
MGM Church Street
Tel: 0253 27207/24233
Seats: 1:717, 2:330, 3:231
Odeon Dickson Road
Tel: 0253 26211
Seats: 1:1,404, 2:190, 3:190

Blyth Northumberland
Wallaw Union Street
Tel: 0670 352504
Seats: 1:850, 2:150, 3:80

Bognor Regis
West Sussex
Cannon Canada Grove
Tel: 0243 823138
Seats: 1:391, 2:96

Bolton
Greater Manchester
Cannon Bradshawgate
Tel: 0204 25597
Seats: 1:275, 2:329, 3:100

Boston Lincs
Regal West Street
Tel: 0205 50553
Seats: 182

Bournemouth Dorset
MGM Westover Road
Tel: 0202 558433/290345
Seats: 1:652, 2:585, 3:223
Odeon Westover Road

Tel: 0426 915625
Seats: 1:757, 2:359, 3:267, 4:119, 5:121

Bowness-on-Windermere Cumbria
Royalty Lake Road
Tel: 09662 3364
Seats: 399

Bracknell Berks
South Hill Park Arts Centre X
Tel: 0344 427272/484123
Seats: 1:60, 2:200 *
UCI The Point
Tel: 0344 868181/868100
Seats: 1:177, 2:205, 3:205, 4:177, 5:316, 6:316, 7:177, 8:205, 9:205, 10:177

Bradford West Yorks
bfi **National Museum of Photography, Film and Television Prince's View X**
Tel: 0274 732277/727488
Seats: 340 (IMAX)
Odeon Prince's Way
Tel: 0274 726716/722442
Seats: 1:467, 2:1,190, 3:244
bfi **Pictureville Cinema Pictureville**
Tel: 0274 727488
Seats: 306
bfi **Film Theatre Chapel Street Little Germany XE**
Tel: 0274 729053
Seats: 1:286, 2:50

Braintree Essex
Embassy Arena Fairfield Road
Tel: 0376 326026
Seats: 333

Brentwood Essex
Cannon Chapel High
Tel: 0277 212931/227574
Seats: 1:300, 2:196

Bridgnorth Shropshire
Majestic Whitburn Street
Tel: 0746 761815/761866
Seats: 1:500, 2:86, 3:86

Bridgwater Somerset
Film Centre Penel Orlieu
Tel: 0278 422383
Seats: 1:246, 2:245

Bridport Dorset
Palace South Street
Tel: 0308 22167
Seats: 420

Brierfield Lancs
Unit Four Burnley Road
Tel: 0282 698030
Seats: 1:70, 2:70, 3:61, 4:66

Brierley Hill
West Mids
UCI Merry Hill 10
Tel: 0384 78244/78282
Seats: 1:175, 2:254, 3:226, 4:254, 5:350, 6:350, 7:254, 8:226, 9:254, 10:175

Brighton East Sussex
Cannon East Street
Tel: 0273 327010/202095
Seats: 1:345, 2:271, 3:194
Duke of York's Preston Circus
Tel: 0273 602503
Seats: 359
MGM Marina Village
Tel: 0273 818114/818094/818180
Seats: 1:351, 2:351, 3:251, 4:251, 5:223, 6:223, 7:202, 8:203
Odeon Kingswest, West Street
Tel: 0426 941661/0273 323317
Seats: 1:388, 2:883, 3:504, 4:275, 5:242, 6:103

Bristol Avon
Arnolfini Narrow Quay XE
Tel: 0272 299191
Seats: 176
Arts Centre Cinema King Square X
Tel: 0272 422110
Seats: 124
Cannon Frogmore Street
Tel: 0272 262848/9
Seats: 1:411, 2:301
Cannon Northumbria Drive Henleaze
Tel: 0272 621644
Seats: 1:186, 2:124, 3:129
Gaiety Wells Road
Tel: 0272 776224
Seats: 650
MGM Whiteladies Road
Tel: 0272 730679/733640
Seats: 1:372, 2:253 **X**, 3:135 **X**
Odeon Union Street
Tel: 0272 290882
Seats: 1:399, 2:224, 3:215
bfi **Watershed XE**
Tel: 0272 276444
Seats: 1:200, 2:50

Broadstairs Kent
Windsor Harbour Street •
Tel: 0843 65726
Seats: 100

Bromborough
Merseyside
Odeon Wirral Retail Park X
Tel: 051 334 5998/0777
Seats: 1:465 **E**, 2:360, 3:211 **E**, 4:206, 5:310 **E**, 6:169, 7:169 **E**

Burgess Hill
West Sussex
Robins Cyprus Road
Tel: 0444 232137/243300
Seats: 1:150, 2:121

Burnham-on-Crouch Essex
Rio Station Road
Tel: 0621 782027
Seats: 1:220, 2:60

Burnham-on-Sea
Somerset
Ritz Victoria Street
Tel: 0278 782871
Seats: 260

Burton-on-Trent
Staffs
Odeon Guild Street
Tel: 0283 63200
Seats: 1:502, 2:110, 3:110

Bury
Greater Manchester
Warner 12
Tel: 061 766 2440/1121
Seats: 1:559, 2:322, 3:278, 4:434, 5:208, 6:166, 7:166, 8:208, 9:434, 10:278, 11:322, 12:573

Bury St Edmunds
Suffolk
MGM Halter Street
Tel: 0284 754477
Seats: 1:196, 2:117

Buxton Derbyshire
The Movie-House
Seats: 78

Camberley Surrey
Cannon London Road
Tel: 0276 63909/26768
Seats: 1:441, 2:114, 3:94
Globe Hawley *
Tel: 0252 876769
Seats: 200

Cambridge Cambs
bfi **Arts Market Passage XE**
Tel: 0223 352001/462666
Seats: 275
Corn Exchange Wheeler Street *
Tel: 0223 357851
Seats: 453

Cannock Staffs
Cannon Walsall Road
Tel: 05435 2226
Seats: 1:363, 2:178
MGM St Andrews Street
Tel: 0223 354572/645378
Seats: 1:736, 2:452

Canterbury Kent
bfi **Cinema 3 University of Kent**
Tel: 0227 769075
Seats: 300
MGM St Georges Place
Tel: 0227 462022/453577
Seats: 1:536, 2:404

Carlisle Cumbria
Lonsdale Warwick Road
Tel: 0228 25586
Seats: 1:375, 2:216, 3:54
City Cinemas 4 & 5 Mary Street
Seats: 4:122, 5:96

Chatham Kent
Cannon High Street
Tel: 0634 846756
Seats: 1:520, 2:360, 3:170

Chelmsford Essex
Cramphorn Theatre Fairfield Road *
Tel: 0245 495028
Seats: 190
Odeon
4 screens, scheduled to open October 1993

Cheltenham Glos
Odeon Winchcombe Street
Tel: 0426 914551
Seats: 1:756, 2:129, 3:104, 4:90, 5:204

Chesham Bucks
Elgiva Theatre Elgiva Lane *XE
Tel: 0494 774759
Seats: 328

Chester Cheshire
MGM Greyhound Park Sealand Road XE
Tel: 0224 380459/380301/380155
Seats: 1:366, 2:366, 3:265, 4:232, 5:211, 6:211
Odeon Northgate Street
Tel: 0244 324930
Seats: 1:406, 2:151, 3:151, 4:122, 5:122

Chesterfield
Derbyshire
Regal Cavendish Street
Tel: 0246 73333
Seats: 484

Chichester
East Sussex
Minerva Studio Theatre Oaklands Park •X
Tel: 0243 781312

Seats: 214
New Park Film Centre
New Park Road X
Tel: 0243 786650
Seats: 120

Chippenham Wilts
Cannon
Marshfield Road
Tel: 0249 652498
Seats: 1:215, 2:215

Chipping Norton
Oxon
The Theatre
Spring Street *
Tel: 0608 2349/2350
Seats: 195

Christchurch Hants
Regent Centre
High Street *
Tel: 0202 479819
Seats: 370

Cirencester Glos
Regal Lewis Lane
Tel: 0285 658755
Seats: 1:100, 2:100

Clacton Essex
Coronet Century
Pier Avenue
Tel: 0255 429627
Seats: 1:600, 2:187

Clevedon Avon
Curzon
Old Church Road
Tel: 0272 872158
Seats: 425

Clitheroe Lancs
Civic Hall York Street
Tel: 0200 23278
Seats: 400

Colchester Essex
Odeon Crouch Street
Tel: 0426 932407/0206 44869
Seats: 1:480, 2:235, 3:118, 4:133, 5:126, 6:177

Coleford Glos
Studio High Street
Tel: 0594 833331
Seats: 1:200, 2:80

Consett Co Durham
Empire
Front Street XE
Tel: 0207 506751
Seats: 535

Corby Northants
Talkies Market Square
Tel: 0536 401026
Seats: 1:100, 2:80

Cosford Staffs
Astra RAF Cosford *
Tel: 090 722 2393
Seats: 460

Coventry West Mids
bfi **Arts Centre University of Warwick X**
Tel: 0203 417417/417314
Seats: 1:250
Odeon Jordan Well
Tel: 0203 222042
Seats: 1:712, 2:155, 3:172, 4:390, 5:121
Showcase Cinemas
Gielgud Way Walsgrave
Tel: 0203 602111
Seats: 3,400 (12 screens)
Theatre One
Ford Street
Tel: 0203 224301
Seats: 1:230, 2:140, 3:135

Cranleigh Surrey
Regal High Street
Tel: 0483 272373
Seats: 268

Crawley West Sussex
Hawth
Hawth Avenue *XE
Tel: 0293 553636
Seats: 800
MGM High Street
Tel: 0293 527497/541296
Seats: 1:297, 2:214, 3:110

Crewe Cheshire
Apollo High Street
Tel: 0270 255708
Seats: 1:110, 2:110, 3:95
Lyceum Theatre
Heath Street *
Tel: 0270 215523
Seats: 750
Victoria Film Theatre
West Street •
Tel: 0270 211422
Seats: 180

Cromer Norfolk
Regal Hans Place
Tel: 0263 513311
Seats: 1:129, 2:136, 3:66

Crookham Hants
Globe Queen Elizabeth Barracks
Tel: 0252 876769
Seats: 340

Crosby Merseyside
Apollo
Crosby Road North
Tel: 051 928 2108
Seats: 1:671, 2:103, 3:103

Darlington Co Durham
Arts Centre
Vane Terrace *XE
Tel: 0325 483168/483271
Seats: 100
Cannon Northgate
Tel: 0325 62745/484994
Seats: 1:590, 2:218, 3:148

Dartford Kent
Orchard Theatre
Home Gardens *XE
Tel: 0322 343333
Seats: 930

Dartington Devon
bfi **Barn Theatre *X**
Tel: 0803 862224
Seats: 203

Daventry Northants
Regal Bowen Square
Tel: 0327 702674
Seats: 180

Deal Kent
Flicks Queen Street
Tel: 0304 361165
Seats: 173

Derby Derbyshire
Assembly Rooms
Market Place *XE
Tel: 0332 255800
Seats: 998
Guildhall Theatre
Market Place *
Tel: 0332 255447
Seats: 186
bfi **Metro**
Green Lane XE
Tel: 0332 40170
Seats: 126
Showcase Cinemas
Outer Ring Road
Osmarton Park Road at Sinfin Lane X
Tel: 0332 270300
Seats: 2,600 (11 screens)
UCI Meteor Centre 10
Mansfield Road X
Tel: 0332 295010/296000
Seats: 1:192, 2:189, 3:189, 4:192, 5:278, 6:278, 7:192, 8:189, 9:189, 10:192

Dereham Norfolk
Hollywood Dereham Entertainment Centre
Market Place
Tel: 0362 3261
Seats: 210

Devizes Wilts
Palace Market Place
Tel: 0380 722971
Seats: 253

Didcot Oxon
New Coronet
The Broadway *
Tel: 0235 812038
Seats: 490

Doncaster
South Yorks
Civic Theatre
Waterdale *
Tel: 0302 62349
Seats: 547
Odeon Hallgate
Tel: 0302 344626
Seats: 1:1,003, 2:155, 3:155
Warner Doncaster
Leisure Park
Bawtry Road
Tel: 0302 371313
Seats: 1:224, 2:212, 3:252, 4:386, 5:252, 6:212, 7:224

Dorchester Dorset
Plaza Trinity Street
Tel: 0305 262488
Seats: 1:100, 2:320

Dorking Surrey
Grand Hall
Dorking Halls *
Tel: 0306 889694
Seats: 851

Dover Kent
Silver Screen
White Cliffs
Experience Gaol Lane
Tel: 0304 228000
Seats: 110

Durham Co Durham
Robins North Road
Tel: 091 384 3434
Seats: 1:316 **X**, 2:96, 3:96, 4:66

Eastbourne
East Sussex
Curzon Langney Road
Tel: 0323 731441
Seats: 1:530, 2:236, 3:236
MGM The Crumbles
Pevensey Bay Road XE
Tel: 0323 470070/470071
Seats: 1:322, 2:312, 3:271, 4:254, 5:221, 6:221

Elland Yorks
Rex
Tel: 0422 372140

Ellesmere Cheshire
Arts Centre *
Tel: 0691 622828
Seats: 220

Ely Cambs
The Maltings *
Tel: 0353 666388
Seats: 212

Epsom Surrey
Playhouse
Ashley Avenue *XE
Tel: 0372 742555/6
Seats: 300

Erith Kent
Academy Sports Centre Avenue Road *
Tel: 0322 350271
Seats: 160

Esher Surrey
Cannon High Street
Tel: 0372 465639/463362
Seats: 1:918 **A**, 2:117

Evesham
Hereford & Worcs
Regal Port Street

Tel: 0386 6002
Seats: 540

Exeter Devon
Northcott Theatre
Stocker Road *
Tel: 0392 54853
Seats: 433
Odeon Sidwell Street
Tel: 0392 54057
Seats: 1:744, 2:119, 3:105, 4:344

Exmouth Devon
Savoy Market Street
Tel: 0395 268220
Seats: 1:230, 2:110

Fawley Hants
Waterside Long Lane
Tel: 0703 891335
Seats: 355

Felixstowe Suffolk
Top Rank
Crescent Road
Tel: 0394 282787
Seats: 1:150, 2:90

Filey Yorks
Grand Union Street •
Tel: 0723 512129
Seats: 576

Folkestone Kent
Silver Screen
Guildhall Street
Tel: 0303 221230
Seats: 1:423, 2:114

Frome Somerset
Westway Cork Street
Tel: 0373 465685
Seats: 304

Gainsborough Lincs
Trinity Arts Centre
Trinity Street *
Tel: 0427 617 242
Seats: 210

Gateshead
Tyne & Wear
UCI Metro 10
Metro Centre
Tel: 091 493 2022/3
Seats: 1:196, 2:196, 3:227, 4:252, 5:364, 6:364, 7:252, 8:227, 9:196, 10:196

Gatley
Greater Manchester
Tatton Gatley Road
Tel: 061 491 0711
Seats: 1:648, 2:247, 3:111

Gerrards Cross
Bucks
Cannon
Ethorpe Crescent
Tel: 0753 882516/883024
Seats: 1:350, 2:212

Gloucester Glos
Guildhall Arts Centre
Eastgate Street *
Tel: 0452 505086/9
Seats: 120
MGM Peel Centre
Bristol Road XE
Tel: 0452 331181/35
Seats: 1:354, 2:354, 3:238, 4:238, 5:219, 6:219

Godalming Surrey
Borough Hall *
Tel: 0483 861111
Seats: 250

Gosport Hants
Ritz Walpole Road
Tel: 0705 501231
Seats: 1,136

Grantham Lincs
Paragon
St Catherine's Road
Tel: 0476 70046
Seats: 1:270, 2:160

Gravesend Kent
Cannon King Street
Tel: 0474 356947/352470
Seats: 1:576, 2:320, 3:107

Grays Essex
Thameside
Orsett Road *
Tel: 0375 382555
Seats: 303

Great Yarmouth
Norfolk
Royalty
Tel: 0493 842043/842707
Seats: 1:1,342, 2:296
Windmill
Marine Parade •
Tel: 0493 843504
Seats: 140

Grimsby Humberside
Cannon
Freeman Street
Tel: 0472 342878/349368
Seats: 1:419, 2:251, 3:130
bfi **Whitgift**
Crosland Road *X
Tel: 0472 887117
Seats: 206

Guildford Surrey
Odeon Epsom Road
Tel: 0426 941049
Seats: 1:452, 2:135, 3:144, 4:250

Halifax West Yorks
Cannon Ward's End
Tel: 0422 352000/346429
Seats: 1:670, 2:199, 3:172

Halstead Essex
Empire Butler Road
Tel: 0787 477001
Seats: 320

Halton Bucks
Astra RAF Halton
Tel: 0296 623535
Seats: 570

Hanley Staffs
Cannon Broad Street
Tel: 0782 22320/268970
Seats: 1:573, 2:233, 3:162

Harlow Essex
MGM Queensgate Centre
Edinburgh Way XE
Tel: 0279 433333/436014/424242
Seats: 1:356, 2:260, 3:240, 4:234, 5:233, 6:230
Odeon The High
Tel: 0426 916802
Seats: 1:450, 2:243, 3:201
Playhouse
The High *XE
Tel: 0279 424391
Seats: 435

Harrogate
North Yorks
Odeon East Parade
Tel: 0423 503626
Seats: 1:532, 2:108, 3:75, 4:259

Harwich Essex
Electric Palace
King's Quay Street *
Tel: 0255 553333
Seats: 204

Haslemere Surrey
Haslemere Hall
Bridge Road *
Tel: 0428 2161
Seats: 350

Hastings East Sussex
Cannon Queens Road
Tel: 0424 420517
Seats: 1:376, 2:176, 3:128

Hatfield Herts
Forum *
Tel: 0707 271217
Seats: 210
UCI The Galleria
Tel: 0707 270222/272734
Seats: 1:172, 2:235, 3:263, 4:167, 5:183, 6:183, 7:260, 8:378, 9:172

Haywards Heath
West Sussex
Clair Hall
Perrymount Road *
Tel: 0444 455440/454394
Seats: 350

Heaton Moor
Greater Manchester
Savoy
Heaton Manor Road
Tel: 061 432 2114
Seats: 496

Hebden Bridge
West Yorks
Picture House
New Road XE
Tel: 0422 842807
Seats: 498

Hemel Hempstead
Herts
Odeon Marlowes *
Tel: 0442 64013
Seats: 785

Henley-on-Thames
Oxon
Kenton Theatre
New Street *X
Tel: 0491 575698
Seats: 240

Hereford
Hereford & Worcs
Cannon
Commercial Road
Tel: 0432 272554
Seats: 378

Hexham
Northumberland
Forum Market Place
Tel: 0434 602896
Seats: 207

High Wycombe
Bucks
UCI Wycombe 6
Crest Road
Cressex
Tel: 0494 463333/464309/465565
Seats: 1:390, 2:390, 3:285, 4:285, 5:200, 6:200

Hoddesdon Herts
Broxbourne Civic Hall
High Road *
Tel: 0992 441946/31
Seats: 564

Holbury Hants
Waterside Long Lane
Tel: 0703 891335
Seats: 355

Hollinwood
Greater Manchester
Roxy Hollins Road
Tel: 061 681 1441
Seats: 1:470, 2:130, 3:260, 4:260, 5:320, 6:96

Hordern Co Durham
WMR Film Centre
Sunderland Road
Tel: 0783 864344
Seats: 1:156, 2:96

Horsham Sussex
Arts Centre (Ritz Cinema and Capitol Theatre) North Street
Tel: 0403 268689
Seats: 1:126, 2:450 *

Horwich Lancs
Leisure Centre

Victoria Road *
Tel: 0204 692211
Seats: 400

Hoylake Merseyside
Cinema
Alderley Road X
Tel: 051 632 1345
Seats: 382

Hucknall Notts
Byron High Street
Tel: 0602 636377
Seats: 430

Huddersfield
West Yorks
Cannon Queensgate
Zetland Street
Tel: 0484 530874
Seats: 495

Hull Humberside
bfi **Film Theatre**
Central Library
Albion Street XE
Tel: 0482 224040 x30
Seats: 247
Odeon
Kingston Street XE
Tel: 0482 586420
Seats: 1:170, 2:170, 3:150, 4:172, 5:418, 6:206, 7:132, 8:150
UCI St Andrew's Quay
Clive Sullivan Way X
Tel: 0482 587525
Seats: 1:166, 2:152, 3:236, 4:292, 5:292, 6:236, 7:152, 8:166

Hunstanton Norfolk
Princess Theatre
The Green *
Tel: 0485 532252
Seats: 467

Huntingdon Cambs
Cromwell Cinema
Centre Princes Street
Tel: 0480 411575
Seats: 264

Hyde
Greater Manchester
Royal
Corporation Street
Tel: 061 368 2206
Seats: 224

Ilfracombe Devon
Pendle Stairway
High Street
Tel: 0271 63484
Seats: 460

Ilkeston Derbyshire
Scala Market Place
Tel: 0602 324612
Seats: 500

Ipswich Suffolk
bfi **Film Theatre**
Corn Exchange XE
Tel: 0473 55851
Seats: 1:221, 2:40
Odeon Majors Corner
Tel: 0426 915622
Seats: 1:506, 2:318, 3:290, 4:218, 5:218

Kendal Cumbria
bfi **Brewery Arts**
Centre
Highgate •XE
Tel: 0539 725133
Seats: 246

Keswick Cumbria
Alhambra
St John Street •
Tel: 0596 72195
Seats: 313

Kettering Northants
Ohio Russell Street
Tel: 0536 515130
Seats: 1:145, 2:206

King's Lynn Norfolk
Arts Centre
King Street
Tel: 0553 774725/773578
Seats: 359
Majestic Tower Street
Tel: 0553 772603
Seats: 1:450, 2:130, 3:400

Kirkby-in-Ashfield
Notts
Regent
Tel: 0623 753866
Seats: 180

Knutsford Cheshire
Civic Centre Toft Road
Tel: 0565 3005
Seats: 400

Lake Isle of Wight
Screen De Luxe
Sandown Road
Tel: 0983 404050
Seats: 150

Lancaster Lancs
Cannon King Street
Tel: 0524 64141/841149
Seats: 1:250, 2:250
bfi **Duke's Playhouse**
Moor Lane *XE
Tel: 0524 66645/67461
Seats: 307

Leamington Spa
Warwicks
Regal Apollo
Portland Place
Tel: 0926 26106/27448
Seats: 904
Robins Spa Centre
Newbold Terrace
Tel: 0926 887726/888997
Seats: 208

Leatherhead Surrey
Thorndike Theatre
Church Street *
Tel: 0372 376211/377677
Seats: 526

Leeds West Yorks
Cottage Road Cinema
Headingley
Tel: 0532 751606
Seats: 468
Hyde Park
Brudenell Road
Tel: 0532 752045
Seats: 360
Lounge North Lane
Headingley
Tel: 0532 751061/58932
Seats: 691
MGM Vicar Lane
Tel: 0532 451013/452665
Seats: 1:670, 2:483, 3:227
Odeon The Headrow
Tel: 0532 430031/2
Seats: 1:982, 2:441, 3:200, 4:174, 5:126
Showcase Gelderd
Road Birstall X
Tel: 0924 420071
Seats: 3,700 (14 screens)

Leicester Leics
Cannon Belgrave Gate
Tel: 0533 24346/24903
Seats: 1:616, 2:408, 3:232
Cannon Cutting Room
Abbey Street
Tel: 0533 519699/620005
Seats: 1:254, 2:187
Odeon Queen Street
Tel: 0533 622892
Seats: 1:872, 2:401, 3:111, 4:142
bfi **Phoenix Arts**
Newarke
Street *XE
Tel: 0533 559711/555627
Seats: 270

Leiston Suffolk
Film Theatre
High Street
Tel: 0728 830549
Seats: 350

Letchworth Herts
Broadway Eastcheap
Tel: 0462 684721
Seats: 1,410

Lichfield Staffs
Civic Hall Castle Dyke
Tel: 0543 254021
Seats: 278

Lincoln Lincs
Ritz High Street
Tel: 0522 546313
Seats: 1,400

Littlehampton
West Sussex
Windmill Theatre
Church Street *
Tel: 0903 724929
Seats: 252

Liverpool Merseyside
Cannon Allerton Road
Tel: 051 709 6277/708 7629
Seats: 493
Cannon Lime Street
Tel: 051 709 6277/708 7629
Seats: 1:697, 2:274, 3:217
Cinema 051 Mount
Pleasant Media Centre
Tel: 051 707 0257
Seats: 1:122, 2:116, 3:108
MGM Edge Lane Retail
Park Binns Road XE
Tel: 051 252 0550/0551/0544
Seats: 1:356, 2:354, 3:264, 4:264, 5:220, 6:220, 7:198, 8:200
Odeon London Road
Tel: 0426 950072
Seats: 1:976, 2:597, 3:167, 4:148, 5:148
Philharmonic Hall
Hope Street *X
Tel: 051 709 2895/3789
Seats: 1,627
Showcase West Derby
Tel: 051 549 2021
Seats: 3,400 (12 screens)
Woolton Mason Street
Tel: 051 428 1919
Seats: 256

Long Eaton Notts
Screen Market Place
Tel: 0602 732185
Seats: 253

Looe East Cornwall
Cinema
Higher Market Street
Tel: 05036 2709
Seats: 95

Loughborough Leics
Curzon Cattle Market
Tel: 0509 212261
Seats: 1:420, 2:303, 3:199, 4:186, 5:140, 6:80

Louth Lincs
Playhouse
Cannon Street
Tel: 0507 603333
Seats: 218

Lowestoft Suffolk
Hollywood
London Road South
Tel: 0502 564567
Seats: 1:200, 2:175, 3:40
Marina Theatre
The Marina *
Tel: 0502 573318/514274
Seats: 751

Ludlow Shropshire
Picture House
Castle Square *
Tel: 0584 875363

Luton Beds
Cannon George Street
Tel: 0582 27311/22537

Seats: 1:615, 2:458, 3:272
St George's Theatre Central Library *
Tel: 0582 21628
Seats: 238

Lyme Regis Dorset
Regent Broad Street
Tel: 0297 442053
Seats: 400

Lymington Hants
Community Centre New Street *
Tel: 05907 2337
Seats: 110

Mablethorpe Lincs
Bijou Quebec Road
Tel: 0521 77040
Seats: 264

Macclesfield Cheshire
Majestic Mill Street
Tel: 0625 22412
Seats: 687

Maghull Merseyside
Astra Northway
Tel: 051 526 1943
Seats: 1:200, 2:200, 3:300, 4:300

Maidenhead Berks
Studio 3
Opens late autumn 1993

Maidstone Kent
MGM
Lower Stone Street
Tel: 0622 752628/758838
Seats: 1:260, 2:90, 3:260

Malton North Yorks
Palace The Lanes E
Tel: 0653 600008
Seats: 142

Malvern
Hereford & Worcs
Cinema Grange Road
Tel: 0684 892279/892710
Seats: 407

Manchester
Greater Manchester
bfi **Cornerhouse Oxford Street XE**
Tel: 061 228 7621
Seats: 1:300, 2:170, 3:58
Odeon Oxford Street
Tel: 061 236 8264
Seats: 1:629 **E**, 2:326 **E**, 3:145 **X**, 4:97, 5:203 **E**, 6:142 **X**, 7:97
Showcase Hyde Road Belle Vue
Tel: 061 220 8765
Seats: 3,400 (14 screens)

Mansfield Notts
Cannon
Leeming Street
Tel: 0623 23138/652236
Seats: 1:367, 2:359, 3:171

March Cambs
Hippodrome
Dartford Road *
Tel: 0354 53178
Seats: 150

Margate Kent
Dreamland
Marine Parade
Tel: 0843 227822
Seats: 1:378, 2:376

Market Drayton
Shropshire
Royal Festival Centre *
Seats: 165

Marple
Greater Manchester
Regent
Stockport Road
Tel: 061 427 5951
Seats: 285

Matlock Derbyshire
Ritz Causeway Lane
Tel: 0629 2121
Seats: 1:176, 2:100

Melton Mowbray
Leics
Regal King Street
Tel: 0664 62251
Seats: 226

Middlesbrough
Cleveland
Odeon
Corporation Road
Tel: 0642 242888
Seats: 1:616, 2:98, 3:122, 4:246

Middleton
Greater Manchester
Palace Manchester Middleton Gardens
Tel: 061 643 2852
Seats: 234

Millom Cumbria
Palladium Horn Hill •
Tel: 0657 2441
Seats: 400

Milton Keynes Bucks
UCI The Point 10
Midsummer Boulevard
Tel: 0908 661662
Seats: 1:156, 2:169, 3:248, 4:220, 5:220, 6:220, 7:220, 8:248, 9:169, 10:156

Minehead Somerset
Regal The Avenue
Tel: 0643 702439
Seats: 1:406, 2:89

Mirfield West Yorks
Vale Centre
Huddersfield Road
Tel: 0924 493240
Seats: 1:98, 2:96

Monkseaton
Tyne & Wear
Cannon Caldwell Lane
Tel: 091 252 5540
Seats: 1:351, 2:116

Monton
Greater Manchester
Princess Monton Road
Tel: 061 789 3426
Seats: 580

Morpeth
Northumberland
New Coliseum
New Market
Tel: 0670 516834
Seats: 1:132, 2:132

Nantwich Cheshire
Civic Hall
Market Street *
Tel: 0270 628633
Seats: 300

Nelson Lancs
Grand Market Street
Tel: 0282 692860
Seats: 388

Newark Notts
Palace Theatre
Appleton Gate *
Tel: 0636 71636
Seats: 351

Newbury Berks
Cannon Park Way
Tel: 0635 41291/49913
Seats: 484

Newcastle upon Tyne Tyne & Wear
Jesmond Cinema
Lyndhurst Avenue
Tel: 091 281 0526/2248
Seats: 608
Odeon Pilgrim Street
Tel: 091 232 3248
Seats: 1:1,228, 2:159, 3:250, 4:361
bfi **Tyneside Pilgrim Street XE**
Tel: 091 232 8289/5592
Seats: 1:400, 2:155
Warner Manors
Tel: 091 221 0202/0545
Seats: 1:404, 2:398, 3:236, 4:244, 5:290, 6:657, 7:509, 8:398, 9:248

Newport Isle of Wight
Cannon High Street
Tel: 0983 527169
Seats: 377
Medina Theatre
Fairlee Road *XE
Tel: 0983 527 020
Seats: 419

Newquay Cornwall
Camelot The Crescent
Tel: 0637 874222
Seats: 812

Newton Abbot
Devon
Alexandra
Market Street X
Tel: 0626 65368
Seats: 370

Northallerton
North Yorks
Lyric Northend
Tel: 0609 2019
Seats: 305

Northampton
Northants
Cannon
Abingdon Square
Tel: 0604 35839/32862
Seats: 1:1,018, 2:275, 3:210
bfi **Forum, Weston Favell Centre** *
Tel: 0604 401006/407544
Seats: 250

Northwich Cheshire
Regal London Road
Tel: 0606 3130
Seats: 1:797, 2:200

Norwich Norfolk
Cannon Prince of Wales Road
Tel: 0603 624677/623312
Seats: 1:524, 2:343, 3:186, 4:105
bfi **Cinema City St Andrews Street X**
Tel: 0603 625145
Seats: 230
Odeon
Anglia Square E
Tel: 0603 621903
Seats: 1:442, 2:197, 3:195 **X**

Nottingham Notts
bfi **Broadway Nottingham Media Centre**
Broad Street
Tel: 0602 410053
Seats: 1:450 **E**, 2:155 **XE**
MGM Chapel Bar
Tel: 0602 45260/418483
Seats: 1:764, 2:437, 3:280
Odeon Angel Row
Tel: 0602 417766
Seats: 1:924, 2:581, 3:141, 4:153, 5:114, 6:96
Savoy Derby Road
Tel: 0602 472580
Seats: 1:386, 2:128, 3:168
Showcase
Redfield Way
Lenton
Tel: 0602 866766
Seats: 3,200 (13 screens)

Nuneaton Warwicks
Abbey Arts Centre
Abbey Theatre Pool
Bank Street *
Tel: 0203 382706

Okehampton Devon
Carlton St James Street
Tel: 0822 2425
Seats: 380

Oswestry Shropshire
Regal Salop Road *
Tel: 0691 654043
Seats: 261

Oxford Oxon
MGM George Street
Tel: 0865 244607/723911
Seats: 1:626, 2:326, 3:140
MGM Magdalen Street
Tel: 0865 243067
Seats: 866
Penultimate Picture Palace Jeune Street
Tel: 0865 723837
Seats: 185
Phoenix Walton Street
Tel: 0865 54909/512526
Seats: 1:200, 2:95
Playhouse Beaumont Street *
Tel: 0865 247134/798600
Seats: 638

Oxted Surrey
Plaza Station Road West
Tel: 0883 712567
Seats: 442

Padstow Cornwall
Capitol Lanadwell Street •
Tel: 0841 532344
Seats: 210

Paignton Devon
Torbay, Torbay Road
Tel: 0803 559544
Seats: 484

Penistone South Yorks
Metro Town Hall
Tel: 0226 767532/205128
Seats: 450

Penrith Cumbria
Alhambra Middlegate
Tel: 0768 62400
Seats: 202

Penzance Cornwall
Savoy Causeway Head
Tel: 0736 3330
Seats: 1:200, 2:50, 3:50

Peterborough Cambs
Showcase Mallory Road Boongate X
Tel: 0733 558498
Seats: 2,900 (13 screens)

Pickering North Yorks
Castle Burgate
Tel: 0751 72622
Seats: 250

Plymouth Devon
Arts Centre Looe Street X
Tel: 0752 660060
Seats: 73
Drake Odeon
Tel: 0752 668825/227074
Seats: 1:420, 2:166, 3:166, 4:220, 5:120
MGM Derry's Cross
Tel: 0752 63300/225553
Seats: 1:583, 2:340, 3:115

Pontefract West Yorks
Crescent Ropergate
Tel: 0977 703788
Seats: 412

Poole Dorset
Ashley Arts Centre Kingsland Road *
Tel: 0202 670521
Seats: 143
UCI Tower Park 10
Tel: 0202 715010
Seats: 1:192, 2:186, 3:186, 4:192, 5:270, 6:270, 7:192, 8:186, 9:186, 10:192

Portsmouth Hants
Cannon Commercial Road
Tel: 0705 823538/839719
Seats: 1:542, 2:255, 3:203
Cannon High Street Cosham
Tel: 0705 376635
Seats: 1:441, 2:118, 3:107
Odeon London Road
Tel: 426 915490
Seats: 1:524, 2:225, 3:173, 4:259
Rendezvous The Hornpipe Kingston Road •
Tel: 0705 833854
Seats: 90
UCI Port Solent Portway, Cosham
Tel: 0705 649999
Seats: 1,534 (6 screens)

Potters Bar Herts
Wyllyotts Centre Dark Lane *X
Tel: 0707 45005
Seats: 345

Preston Lancs
UCI Riversway 10
Tel: 0772 728888/722322
Seats: 290 (2 screens), 180 (8 screens)
Warner The Capitol London Way Walton-Le-Dale
Tel: 0772 881313
Seats: 1:180, 2:180, 3:412, 4:236, 5:236, 6:412, 7:192

Quinton West Mids
Cannon Hagley Road West
Tel: 021 422 2562/2252
Seats: 1:300, 2:236, 3:232, 4:121

Ramsey Cambs
Grand Great Whyte *
Tel: 0487 813777
Seats: 173

Ramsgate Kent
Granville Victoria Parade *
Tel: 0843 591750
Seats: 861

Reading Berks
Film Theatre Whiteknights *
Tel: 0734 868497/875123
Seats: 409
MGM Friar Street
Tel: 0734 573931
Seats: 1:532, 2:226, 3:118
Odeon Cheapside
Tel: 0426 915484
Seats: 1:410, 2:221, 3:221

Redcar Cleveland
Regent
Tel: 0642 482094
Seats: 350

Redditch Hereford & Worcs
Cannon Unicorn Hill
Tel: 0527 62572
Seats: 1:208, 2:155, 3:155

Redhill Surrey
The Harlequin Warwick Quadrant *X
Tel: 0737 765547
Seats: 494

Redruth Cornwall
Regal Film Centre Fore Street
Tel: 0209 216278
Seats: 1:200, 2:128, 3:600, 4:95

Reigate Surrey
Screen Bancroft Road
Tel: 0737 223213
Seats: 1:139, 2:142

Rickmansworth Herts
Watersmeet Theatre High Street *
Tel: 0923 771542
Seats: 390

Royston Herts
Priory, Priory Lane
Tel: 0763 43133
Seats: 305

Rugeley Staffs
Plaza Horse Fair
Tel: 0889 574856
Seats: 1:210, 2:104 X, 3:104 X

Rushden Northants
Ritz College Street
Tel: 0933 312468
Seats: 822

St Albans Herts
Alban Arena Civic Centre *XE
Tel: 0727 44488
Seats: 800
Odeon London Road
Tel: 0426 911842
Seats: 1:452, 2:115 X, 3:128 X, 4:145

St Austell Cornwall
Film Centre Chandos Place
Tel: 0726 73750
Seats: 1:276, 2:134, 3:133, 4:70, 5:70

St Helens Merseyside
Cannon Bridge Street
Tel: 0744 51947/23392
Seats: 1:494, 2:284, 3:179

St Ives Cornwall
Royal, Royal Square
Tel: 0736 796843
Seats: 682

Salford Quays Lancs
MGM Quebec Drive Trafford Road
Tel: 061 873 7155/7279
Seats: 1:265, 2:265, 3:249, 4:249, 5:213, 6:213, 7:177, 8:177

Salisbury Wilts
Odeon New Canal
Tel: 0426 915564
Seats: 1:471, 2:120, 3:120, 4:70

Scarborough North Yorks
Futurist Forshaw Road *
Tel: 0723 365789
Seats: 2,155
Hollywood Plaza North Marine Road •
Tel: 0723 365119
Seats: 275
Opera House St Thomas Street *
Tel: 0723 369999
Seats: 225

Scunthorpe Humberside
Majestic Oswald Road
Tel: 0724 842352
Seats: 1:176, 2:155 X, 3:76 X, 4:55 X, 5:38
bfi **Film Theatre Central Library Carlton Street *X**
Tel: 0724 860161 x30
Seats: 249

Sevenoaks Kent
Stag Theatre and Majestic 1 & 2 London Road

Tel: 0732 450175/451548
Seats: 1:455 *, 2:102, 3:102

Shaftesbury Dorset
Arts Centre *
Tel: 0747 54321

Sheffield South Yorks
Odeon Barker's Pool
Tel: 0742 767962
Seats: 1:500, 2:324
Odeon Seven Arundel Gate
Tel: 0742 723981
Seats: 1:254 **XE**, 2:254 **X**, 3:251 **XE**, 4:117 **XE**, 5:115 **XE**, 6:186, 7:139
UCI Crystal Peaks 10 Eckington Way Sothall
Tel: 0742 480064/470095
Seats: 1:200, 2:200, 3:228, 4:224, 5:312, 6:312, 7:224, 8:228, 9:200, 10:200
Warner Meadowhall Shopping Centre
Tel: 0742 569523
Seats: 1:199, 2:198, 3:98, 4:233, 5:198, 6:362, 7:192, 8:192, 9:80, 10:190, 11:329

Sheringham Norfolk
Little Theatre Station Road •
Tel: 0263 822347
Seats: 198

Shipley West Yorks
Unit Four Bradford Road
Tel: 0274 583429
Seats: 1:89, 2:72, 3:121, 4:94

Shrewsbury Shropshire
Cannon Empire Mardal
Tel: 0743 62257/233527
Seats: 573
bfi **The Cinema in the Square Music Hall**
Tel: 0743 50763
Seats: 100

Sidmouth Devon
Radway Radway Place
Tel: 039 55 3085
Seats: 400

Sittingbourne Kent
Cannon High Street
Tel: 0795 423984
Seats: 1:300, 2:110

Skegness Lincs
Tower Lumley Road
Tel: 0754 3938
Seats: 401

Skelmersdale Lancs
Premiere Film Centre
Tel: 0695 25041
Seats: 1:230, 2:248

Skipton North Yorks
Plaza Sackville Street
Tel: 0756 3417
Seats: 320

Sleaford Lincs
Sleaford Cinema Southgate
Tel: 0529 303187
Seats: 60

Slough Berks
MGM High Street
Tel: 0753 692233/692244
Seats: 1:192 **X**, 2:147 **X**, 3:134 **X**, 4:166 **X**, 5:411 **X**, 6:487 **X**, 7:217, 8:113, 9:150, 10:96

Solihull West Mids
UCI 8 Stratford Road
Tel: 021 733 3696
Seats: 286 (2 screens), 250 (2 screens), 210 (2 screens), 180 (2 screens)

South Woodham Ferrers Essex
Flix Market Street
Tel: 0245 329777
Seats: 249

Southampton Hants
bfi **The Gantry Off Blechynden Terrace X**
Tel: 0703 229319/330729
Seats: 194
MGM Ocean Village
Tel: 0703 330666
Seats: 1:421, 2:346, 3:346, 4:258, 5:258
Mountbatten Theatre East Park Terrace *
Tel: 0703 221991
Seats: 515
bfi **Northguild Lecture Theatre Guildhall *XE**
Tel: 0703 632601
Seats: 118
Odeon Above Bar Street
Tel: 0703 229188/0426 920330
Seats: 1:468, 2:748, 3:98

Southend Essex
Cannon Alexandra Street
Tel: 0702 344580
Seats: 1:665, 2:498
Odeon Elmer Approach
Tel: 0426 916782
Seats: 1:455, 2:1,235

Southport Merseyside
Arts Centre Lord Street *
Tel: 0704 40004/40011
Seats: 400
Cannon Lord Street
Tel: 0704 530627
Seats: 1:494, 2:385

Spilsby Lincs
Phoenix Reynard Street
Tel: 0790 53675/53621
Seats: 264

Stafford Staffs
Apollo New Port Road
Tel: 0785 51277
Seats: 1:305, 2:170, 3:168
Picture House Bridge Street
Tel: 0785 58291
Seats: 483

Staines Middlesex
MGM Clarence Street
Tel: 0784 453316/459140
Seats: 1:586, 2:361 **X**, 3:173 **X**

Stalybridge Greater Manchester
New Palace Market Street
Tel: 061 338 2156
Seats: 414

Stanley Co Durham
Civic Hall *
Tel: 0207 32164
Seats: 632

Stevenage Herts
Cannon St Georges Way
Tel: 0438 313267/316396
Seats: 1:340, 2:182
Gordon Craig Theatre Lytton Way *
Tel: 0438 354568/316291
Seats: 507

Stockport Greater Manchester
Davenport Buxton Road
Tel: 061 483 3801/2
Seats: 1:1,794 •, 2:170
MGM Grand Central Wellington Road South XE
Tel: 061 476 4797/1798/5996
Tel: 1: 303, 2:255, 3:243, 4:243, 5:122, 6:116, 7:96, 8:120, 9:84, 10:90

Stockton Cleveland
Cannon Dovecot Street X
Tel: 0642 676048
Seats: 1:242, 2:110, 3:125
Dovecot Arts Centre Dovecot Street
Tel: 0642 611625/611659
Seats: 100
Showcase Cinemas Teeside Leisure Park
Tel: 0642 633222
Seats: 3,400 (14 screens)

Stoke-on-Trent Staffs
bfi **Film Theatre College Road**
Tel: 0782 411188
Seats: 212
Odeon 10 Etruria Road
Tel: 0782 215311
Seats: 1:177, 2:177, 3:309, 4:150, 5:160, 6:160, 7:521, 8:150, 9:80, 10:80

Stowmarket Suffolk
Regal Ipswich Street *
Tel: 0449 612825
Seats: 234

Stratford-upon-Avon Warwicks
Waterside
Tel: 0789 69285
Seats: 140

Street Somerset
bfi **Strode Theatre Church Road *XE**
Tel: 0458 42846
Seats: 400

Sudbury Suffolk
Quay Theatre Quay Lane
Tel: 0787 74745
Seats: 129

Sunderland Tyne & Wear
Cannon Holmeside
Tel: 091 567 4148
Seats: 1:550, 2:209
Empire High Street West *
Tel: 0783 42517
Seats: 1,000
Studio High Street West
Tel: 0783 42517
Seats: 150

Sunninghill Berks
Novello Theatre High Street *
Tel: 0990 20881
Seats: 160

Sutton Coldfield West Mids
Odeon Birmingham Road
Tel: 021 354 2714
Seats: 1:598, 2:132, 3:118, 4:307

Swanage Dorset
Mowlem Shore Road
Tel: 0929 422239
Seats: 400

Swindon Wilts
MGM Multiplex Shaw Ridge Leisure Park XE
Tel: 0793 877727/881118
Seats: 1:349, 2:349, 3:297, 4:297, 5:272, 6:166, 7:144
Wyvern Theatre Square *

Tel: 0793 24481
Seats: 617

Tadley Hants
Cinema Royal
Boundary Road *
Tel: 0734 814617

Tamworth Staffs
Palace
Lower Gungate *
Tel: 0827 57100
Seats: 325
UCI Bolebridge Street
Tel: 0827 66702
Seats: 203 (8 screens), 327 (2 screens)

Taunton Somerset
Plaza Station Road
Tel: 0823 351226
Seats: 1:502, 2:71

Teignmouth Devon
Riviera Den Crescent
Tel: 0626 774624
Seats: 417

Telford Shropshire
UCI Telford Centre 10
Forgegate
Tel: 0952 290606/290126
Seats: 1:192, 2:189, 3:189, 4:192, 5:278, 6:278, 7:192, 8:189, 9:189, 10:192

Tenbury Wells
Hereford & Worcs
Regal Teme Street
Tel: 0584 810235
Seats: 260

Tewkesbury Glos
Roses Theatre *
Tel: 0684 295074
Seats: 375

Thirsk North Yorks
Studio One
Tel: 0845 524751
Seats: 238

Tiverton Devon
Tivoli Fore Street
Tel: 0884 252157
Seats: 364

Toftwood Norfolk
CBA Shipham Road
Tel: 0362 3261
Seats: 30

Tonbridge Kent
Angel Centre
Angel Lane *
Tel: 0732 359588
Seats: 306

Torquay Devon
English Riviera Centre
Chestnut Avenue *XE
Tel: 0803 295676
Seats: 800
Odeon Abbey Road
Tel: 0803 292324
Seats: 1:309, 2:346

Torrington Devon
Plough Fore Street
Tel: 0805 22552/3
Seats: 108

Truro Cornwall
Plaza Lemon Street
Tel: 0872 72894
Seats: 1:849, 2:102, 3:160

Tunbridge Wells
Kent
MGM Mount Pleasant
Tel: 0892 541141/523135
Seats: 1:450 **X**, 2:402, 3:124

Uckfield East Sussex
Picture House
High Street
Tel: 0825 763822
Seats: 1:150, 2:100

Ulverston Cumbria
Laurel & Hardy Museum
Upper Brook Street *•
Tel: 0229 52292/86614
Seats: 50
Roxy Brogden Street
Tel: 0229 53797/56211
Seats: 310

Urmston
Greater Manchester
Curzon Princess Road
Tel: 061 748 2929
Seats: 1:400, 2:134

Uttoxeter Staffs
Elite High Street
Tel: 08893 3348
Seats: 120

Uxbridge Middx
Odeon High Street
Tel: 0426 931395/0895 813139
Seats: 1:230, 2:439

Wadebridge Cornwall
Regal The Platt
Tel: 020 881 2791
Seats: 1:250, 2:120

Wakefield West Yorks
Cannon Kirkgate
Tel: 0924 373400/365236
Seats: 1:532, 2:233, 3:181

Walkden
Greater Manchester
Unit Four Bolton Road
Tel: 061 790 9432
Seats: 1:118, 2:108, 3:86, 4:94

Wallasey Merseyside
Apollo 6 Egremont
Tel: 051 639 2833
Seats: 1:181, 2:127, 3:177, 4:105, 5:91, 6:92

Wallingford Oxon
Corn Exchange *
Tel: 0491 39336
Seats: 187

Walsall West Mids
Cannon
Townend Bank
Tel: 0922 22444/644330
Seats: 1:506, 2:247, 3:143
Showcase
Bentley Mill Lane
Darlaston
Tel: 0922 22123
Seats: 2,800 (12 screens)

Waltham Cross
Herts
Cannon High Street
Tel: 0992 761160/761044
Seats: 1:460, 2:284 **X**, 3:103 **X**, 4:83

Walton on Thames
Surrey
Screen High Street
Tel: 0932 252825
Seats: 1:200, 2:140

Wantage Oxon
Regent
Newbury Street
Tel: 02357 71155/67878
Seats: 1:109, 2:90

Wareham Dorset
Rex West Street
Tel: 0929 552778
Seats: 239

Warrington Cheshire
Odeon
Buttermarket Street
Tel: 0426 950170
Seats: 1:576, 2:291, 3:196
UCI Westbrook 10
Westbrook Centre
Cromwell Avenue
Tel: 0925 416677
Seats: 1:192, 2:189, 3:189, 4:192, 5:278, 6:278, 7:192, 8:189, 9:189, 10:192

Washington
Tyne & Wear
Fairworld
Victoria Road
Tel: 091 416 2711
Seats: 1:227, 2:177

Watford Herts
Cannon Merton Road
Tel: 0923 24088/33259
Seats: 1:356, 2:195

Wellingborough
Northants
Palace
Gloucester Place
Tel: 0933 222184
Two screens

Wellington Somerset
Wellesley Mantle Street
Tel: 0823 666668/666880
Seats: 400

Wells Somerset
Wells Film Centre
Princes Road
Tel: 0749 672036/672195
Seats: 150

Welwyn Garden City Herts
bfi **Campus West**
The Campus *
Tel: 0707 332880
Seats: 365

West Bromwich
West Mids
Kings Paradise Street
Tel: 021 553 7605/0030
Seats: 1:326, 2:287, 3:462

Westgate-on-Sea
Kent
Carlton
St Mildreds Road
Tel: 0843 832019
Seats: 303

Weston-super-Mare Avon
Odeon The Centre
Tel: 0426 950499
Seats: 1:590, 2:109, 3:130, 4:264
Playhouse
High Street *
Tel: 0934 23521/31701
Seats: 658

West Thurrock Essex
UCI Lakeside 10
Lakeside Retail Park X
Tel: 0708 869547/869920
Seats: 270 (2 screens), 192 (4 screens), 186 (4 screens)
Warner Lakeside Shopping Centre
Tel: 0708 891010/890567
Seats: 1:382, 2:184, 3:177, 4:237, 5:498, 6:338, 7:208

Weymouth Dorset
Cannon
Gloucester Street
Tel: 0305 785847
Seats: 412

Whitby North Yorks
Coliseum
Victoria Square •
Tel: 0947 604641
Seats: 226

Whitefield Lancs
Mayfair Bury Old Road
Tel: 061 766 2369
Seats: 1:578, 2:232

Whitehaven Cumbria
Gaiety Tangier Street
Tel: 0946 3012
Seats: 330

Whitley Bay
Tyne & Wear
Playhouse
Marine Avenue
Tel: 091 252 3505
Seats: 860

Wigan
Greater Manchester
Ritz Station Road
Tel: 0942 323632
Seats: 1:485, 2:321, 3:106
Unit Four
Ormskirk Road
Tel: 0942 214336
Seats: 1:99, 2:117, 3:88

Wilmslow Cheshire
Rex Alderley Road *
Tel: 0625 522145
Seats: 838

Winchester Hants
Theatre Royal
Jewry Street *
Tel: 0962 842122
Seats: 405

Windsor Berks
Old Trout
River Street *
Tel: 0753 869897

Winsford Somerset
Civic Hall *

Withington
Greater Manchester
Cine-City
Wilmslow Road
Tel: 061 445 3301
Seats: 1:150, 2:150, 3:150

Witney Oxon
Corn Exchange *

Woking Surrey
Peacock Cinemas
Peacock Arts &
Entertainment Centre
Tel: 0483 761144
Seats: 1:434, 2:447, 3:190

Wolverhampton
West Mids
Light House
Chubb Buildings
Fryer Street XE
Tel: 0902 312033
Seats: 1:242, 2:80

Woodbridge Suffolk
Riverside Theatre
Quay Street
Tel: 039 43 2174
Seats: 280

Woodhall Spa Lincs
Kinema in the Woods
Coronation Road
Tel: 0526 52166
Seats: 365

Worcester
Hereford & Worcs
Odeon Foregate Street
Tel: 0905 24733
Seats: 1:650, 2:205, 3:109, 4:109, 5:66

Worksop Notts
Regal Carlton Road
Tel: 0909 482896
Seats: 1:326 *, 2:154

Worthing West Sussex
Connaught Theatre
Union Place *
Tel: 0903 31799/35333
Seats: 400
Dome Marine Parade
Tel: 0903 200461
Seats: 650

Wotton Under Edge Glos
Town Cinema
Tel: 0453 521666
Seats: 200

Wymondham
Norfolk
Regal Friarscroft Lane
Tel: 0953 602025
Seats: 300

Yeovil Somerset
MGM Court
Ash Terrace
Tel: 0935 23663
Seats: 1:575, 2:239, 3:247

York North Yorks
bfi **City Screen**
Tempest
Anderson Hall *X
Yorkshire Museum
Tel: 0904 612940
Seats: 300
bfi **Film Theatre**
Central Hall York
University *X
Tel: 0904 612940
Seats: 750
Odeon Blossom Street
Tel: 0904 623040
Seats: 1:834, 2:111, 3:111
Warner Clifton Moor X
Tel: 0904 691199/691094
Seats: 1:128, 2:212, 3:316, 4:441, 5:185, 6:251, 7:251, 8:185, 9:441, 10:316, 11:212, 12:128

ISLE OF MAN AND CHANNEL ISLANDS

Douglas Isle of Man
Palace Cinema
Tel: 0624 76814
Seats: 1:319, 2:120
Summerland Cinema
Tel: 0624 25511
Seats: 200

St Helier Jersey
Odeon Bath Street
Tel: 0534 24166
Seats: 1:409, 2:244, 3:213, 4:171

St Peter Port Guernsey
Beau Sejour Centre
Tel: 0481 26964
Seats: 398

St Saviour Jersey
Cine de France
St Saviour's Road
Tel: 0534 71611
Seats: 291

SCOTLAND

A number of BFI-supported cinemas in Scotland also receive substantial central funding and programming/management support via the Scottish Film Council

Aberdeen Grampian
Cannon Union Street
Tel: 0224 591477/587458
Seats: 1:566, 2:153, 3:146
Capitol Union Street
Tel: 0224 583141
Seats: 2,010
Odeon
Justice Mill Lane
Tel: 0224 587160
Seats: 1:400, 2:123, 3:123, 4:216, 5:216

Annan Dumfries & Gall
Ladystreet
Lady Street •
Tel: 0461 22796
Seats: 450

Aviemore Highland
Speyside
Aviemore Centre
Tel: 0479 810627
Seats: 721

Ayr Strathclyde
Odeon
Burns Statue Square
Tel: 0292 264048
Seats: 1:388, 2:166, 3:135, 4:366

Bathgate Lothian
Regal
Northbridge Street X
Tel: 0506 634152
Seats: 467

Campbeltown Strathclyde
Picture House
Hall Street *
Tel: 0586 2264
Seats: 265

Castle Douglas Dumfries & Gall
Palace
St Andrews Street •
Tel: 0556 2141
Seats: 400

Clydebank Strathclyde
Mercat Theatre
Drumchapel *
UCI Clydebank 10
Clyde Regional Centre
Britannia Way
Tel: 041 951 1949/2022
Seats: 1:200, 2:200, 3:228, 4:252, 5:385, 6:385, 7:252, 8:228, 9:200, 10:200

Dumfries Dumfries & Gall
Cannon
Shakespeare Street
Tel: 0387 53578
Seats: 532
Robert Burns Centre
Film Theatre
Mill Road *
Tel: 0387 64808
Seats: 67

Dundee Tayside
Cannon Seagate
Tel: 0382 26865/25247
Seats: 1:618, 2:319
Odeon The Stack
Leisure Park Harefield Road X
Tel: 0382 400855
Seats: 1:574, 2:210, 3:216, 4:233, 5:192, 6:221
bfi **Steps Theatre**
The Wellgate *X
Tel: 0382 24938/23141
Seats: 250

Dunfermline Fife
Robins East Port
Tel: 0383 721934
Seats: 1:217, 2:175, 3:100

Dunoon Strathclyde
Studio John Street
Tel: 0369 4545
Seats: 1:188, 2:70

East Kilbride Strathclyde
UCI Olympia Mall 9
Town Centre
Tel: 03552 49022
Seats: 319, 217 (3 screens), 209, 206 (4 screens)

Edinburgh Lothian
Cameo Home Street
Tollcross X
Tel: 031 228 4141
Seats: 1:398, 2:78, 3:68
Dominion
Newbattle Terrace
Tel: 031 447 2660
Seats: 1:584, 2:296, 3:47
bfi **Filmhouse**
Lothian Road XE
Tel: 031 228 2688/6382
Seats: 1:285, 2:101
MGM Lothian Road
Tel: 031 228 1638/229 3030
Seats: 1:868, 2:738 **X**, 3:318 **X**
Odeon Clerk Street
Tel: 031 667 7331/2
Seats: 1:695, 2:293 **X**, 3:201 **X**, 4:259, 5:182
Playhouse
Leith Walk *
Tel: 031 557 2692
Seats: 3,131
UCI Craig Park
Newcraighall Road
Tel: 031 669 0777
Seats: 168 (6 screens), 208 (4 screens), 308 (2 screens)

Elgin Grampian
Moray Playhouse
High Street
Tel: 0343 542680
Seats: 1:330, 2:220

Eyemouth Berwicks
Cinema Church Street
Tel: 0390 50490
Seats: 220

Falkirk Central
Cannon
Princess Street
Tel: 0324 31713/23805
Seats: 1:704, 2:128 **X**, 3:128

Fort William Highlands
Studios 1 and 2
Tel: 0397 705095

Galashiels Borders
Kingsway
Market Street
Tel: 0896 2767
Seats: 395

Girvan Strathclyde
Vogue
Dalrymple Street •
Tel: 0465 2101
Seats: 500

Glasgow Strathclyde
Cannon Clarkston
Road Muirend X
Tel: 041 637 2641
Seats: 1:482, 2:208
bfi **Film Theatre**
Rose Street XE
Tel: 041 332 6535
Seats: 1:404, 2:144
Grosvenor Ashton
Lane Hillhead
Tel: 041 339 4298
Seats: 1:277, 2:253
MGM The Forge
Parkhead XE
Tel: 041 554 1483
Seats: 1:434, 2:434, 3:322, 4:262, 5:208, 6:144, 7:132
MGM Sauchiehall
Street
Tel: 041 332 1592/9513
Seats: 1:970, 2:872 **E** (rear), 3:384, 4:206 **E**, 5:194 **E**
Odeon
Renfield Street X
Tel: 041 332 8701/3413
Seats: 1:1,138, 2:208, 3:227, 4:240, 5:288, 6:222

Glenrothes Fife
Kingsway
Church Street
Tel: 0592 750980
Seats: 1:294, 2:223

Hamilton Strathclyde
Odeon
Townhead Street
Tel: 0698 283802/422384
Seats: 1:466, 2:224, 3:310

Inverness Highland
Eden Court
Bishops Road
Tel: 0463 221718/239841
Seats: 1:797, 2:70
La Scala
Strothers Lane
Tel: 0463 233302
Seats: 1:438, 2:255

Inverurie Grampian
Victoria
West High Street
Tel: 0467 21436
Seats: 473

Irvine Strathclyde
Magnum
Harbour Street
Tel: 0294 78381
Seats: 323
WMR Film Centre
Bank Street
Tel: 0294 79900/76817
Seats: 252

Kelso Borders
Roxy
Tel: 0573 24609
Seats: 260

Kilmarnock
Strathclyde
Cannon
Titchfield Street
Tel: 0563 25234/37288
Seats: 1:602, 2:193, 3:149

Kirkcaldy Fife
bfi **Adam Smith Theatre**
Bennochy Road *XE
Tel: 0592 260498/202855
Seats: 475
MGM High Street
Tel: 0592 260143/201520
Seats: 1:547, 2:287 X, 3:235 X

Kirkwall Orkney
Phoenix
Junction Road
Tel: 0856 4407
Seats: 500

Livingston Lothian
Caledonian
Almondvale Centre X
Tel: 0506 33163
Seats: 1:168, 2:165

Lockerbie
Dumfries & Gall
Rex Bridge Street •
Tel: 05762 2547
Seats: 195

Millport Strathclyde
The Cinema (Town Hall) Clifton Street •
Tel: 0475 530741
Seats: 250

Motherwell
Lanarkshire
Civic Theatre
Civic Centre *
Tel: 0698 66166
Seats: 395

Newton Stewart
Dumfries & Gall
Cinema Victoria Street
Tel: 0671 2058
Seats: 412

Oban Strathclyde
Highland Theatre
George Street *
Tel: 0631 62444
Seats: 420

Paisley Strathclyde
Kelburnie
Glasgow Road
Tel: 041 889 3612
Seats: 1:249, 2:248

Perth Tayside
Playhouse
Murray Street
Tel: 0738 23126
Seats: 1:590, 2:227, 3:196

Peterhead Grampian
Playhouse
Queen Street
Tel: 0779 71052
Seats: 731

Pitlochry Tayside
Regal Athal Road •
Tel: 0796 2560
Seats: 400

St Andrews Fife
New Picture House
North Street
Tel: 0334 73509
Seats: 1:739, 2:94

Saltcoats Strathclyde
La Scala
Hamilton Street
Tel: 0294 63345/68999
Seats: 1:301, 2:142

Stirling Central
Allanpark
Allanpark Road
Tel: 0786 74137
Seats: 1:321, 2:287
bfi **MacRobert Arts Centre University of Stirling** *XE
Tel: 0786 73171
Seats: 500

WALES

Aberaman Aberdare
Grand Theatre
Cardiff Road *
Tel: 0685 872310
Seats: 950

Aberdare Mid Glam
bfi **Coliseum Mount Pleasant Street** *X
Tel: 0685 882380
Seats: 621

Aberystwyth Dyfed
Commodore
Bath Street
Tel: 0970 612421
Seats: 410

Bagillt Clwyd
Focus High Street
Tel: 0352 715670
Seats: 160

Bala Gwynedd
Neuadd Buddig *
Tel: 0678 520 800
Seats: 372

Bangor Gwynedd
Plaza High Street
Tel: 0248 362059
Seats: 1:306, 2:163
Theatr Gwynedd
Deiniol Road
Tel: 0248 351707/351708
Seats: 343

Bargoed Mid Glam
Cameo High Street
Tel: 0443 831172
Seats: 302

Barry South Glam
Theatre Royal
Broad Street
Tel: 0446 735019
Seats: 496

Blackwood Gwent
bfi **Miners' Institute High Street** *X
Tel: 0495 227206
Seats: 409

Blaengarw Mid Glam
bfi **Workman's Hall Blaengarw Rd** *X
Tel: 0656 871142
Seats: 250

Brecon Powys
Coliseum Film Centre
Wheat Street
Tel: 0874 622501
Seats: 1:164, 2:164

Brynamman Dyfed
Public Hall
Station Road
Tel: 0269 823232
Seats: 838

Brynmawr Gwent
Market Hall
Market Square
Tel: 0495 310576
Seats: 320

Builth Wells Powys
Wyeside Arts Centre
Castle Street
Tel: 0982 552555
Seats: 210

Cardiff South Glam
bfi **Chapter Market Road** X
Tel: 0222 396061
Seats: 1:195, 2:78
MGM Queen Street
Tel: 0222 31715
Seats: 1:616, 2:313, 3:152
Monico Pantbach Road
Tel: 0222 691505
Seats: 1:500, 2:156
Monroe Globe Centre
Albany Road
Seats: 216
Odeon Queen Street
Tel: 0222 227058
Seats: 1:448, 2:643
Odeon Capitol Shopping Centre
Queen Street
Tel: 0222 377410
Seats: 1:435, 2:261, 3:223, 4:186, 5:161
St David's Hall
The Hayes *
Tel: 0222 371236/42611
Seats: 1,600
bfi **Sherman Theatre Senghennydd Road** *XE
Tel: 0222 30451/396844
Seats: 474

Cardigan Dyfed
Theatr Mwldan
Bath House Road *X
Tel: 0239 612687
Seats: 210

Carmarthen Dyfed
Lyric King's Street *
Tel: 0267 612200
Seats: 800

Cwmbran Gwent
Scene The Mall
Tel: 063 33 66621
Seats: 1:115, 2:78, 3:130

Denbigh Powys
Futura
Tel: 0745 715210
Seats: 112

Ferndale Mid Glam
Cinema *
The Hall High Street

Fishguard Dyfed
Studio West Street
Tel: 0348 873421/874051
Seats: 252

Gilfach Goch
Mid Glam
Workmen's Hall
Glenarvon Terrace
Tel: 044 386 231
Seats: 400

Haverfordwest
Dyfed
Palace
Upper Market Street
Tel: 0437 2426
Seats: 538

Holyhead Gwynedd
Empire Stanley Street
Tel: 0407 2093
Seats: 159

Llandudno Gwynedd
Palladium
Gloddaeth Street
Tel: 0492 76244
Seats: 355

Llanelli Dyfed
Entertainment Centre
Station Road
Tel: 0554 774057/752659
Seats: 1:516, 2:310, 3:122

Merthyr Tydfil
Mid Glam
Flicks High Street

Tel: 0685 723877
Seats: 1:98, 2:198

Milford Haven Dyfed
Torch Theatre
St Peters Road
Tel: 064 62 4192/5267
Seats: 297

Mold Clwyd
bfi **Theatr Clwyd**
Civic Centre X
Tel: 0352 56331
Seats: 1:530, 2:129

Monmouth Gwent
Magic Lantern
Church Street
Tel: 0600 3146
Seats: 124

Newport Gwent
Cannon Bridge Street
Tel: 0633 54326
Seats: 1:572, 2:190, 3:126

Newtown Powys
Regent Broad Street
Tel: 0686 625917
Seats: 210

Pontypool Gwent
Scala Osborne Road
Tel: 049 55 56038
Seats: 197

Pontypridd Mid Glam
Muni Screen
Municipal Hall
Gelliwastad Road *XE
Tel: 0443 485934
Seats: 400

Porthcawl Mid Glam
Regent Trecco Bay •
Tel: 065 671 2103
Seats: 168

Portmadoc Gwynedd
Coliseum Avenue Road
Tel: 0766 512108
Seats: 582

Port Talbot
West Glam
Plaza Theatre
Talbot Road
Tel: 0639 882856
Seats: 1:846, 2:196, 3:111

Prestatyn Clwyd
Scala High Street
Tel: 0745 854365
Seats: 314

Pwllheli Gwynedd
Odeon Butlin's
Starcoast World
Seats: 200
Town Hall Cinema
Tel: 0758 613371
Seats: 450

Resolven West Glam
Welfare Hall Cinema
Tel: 0269 592395
Seats: 541

Rhyl Clwyd
Apollo High Street
Tel: 0745 353856
Seats: 1:250, 2:225

St Athan South Glam
Astra Llantwit Major
RAF St Athan
Tel: 04465 3131 x4124
Seats: 350

Swansea West Glam
Odeon Kingsway
Tel: 0792 652351
Seats: 1:708, 2:241, 3:170
bfi **Taliesin Arts**
Centre XE
University College
Singleton Park
Tel: 0792 296883
Seats: 328
UCI Parc Tawe 10
Tel: 0792 644980
Seats: 277 (2 screens), 174 (4 screens), 156 (4 screens)

Taibach West Glam
Entertainment
Taibach
Seats: 200

Tenby Dyfed
Royal Playhouse
White Lion Street
Tel: 0834 4809
Seats: 479

Treorchy Mid Glam
Parc and Dare Theatre
Station Road
Tel: 0443 773112
Seats: 794

Tywyn Gwynedd
The Cinema
Corbett Square X
Tel: 0654 710260
Seats: 368

Welshpool Powys
Pola Berriew Street
Tel: 0938 555715
Seats: 500

Wrexham Clwyd
Hippodrome
Henblas Street
Tel: 0978 364479
Seats: 613

Ystradgynlais Powys
bfi **Miners' Welfare**
and Community
Hall Brecon Road *X
Tel: 0639 843163
Seats: 345

NORTHERN IRELAND

Antrim Antrim
Coltworthy House
Arts Centre Louth
Road

Ballymena Antrim
State Ballymoney Road
Tel: 0266 652306
Seats: 1:215, 2:166

Banbridge Down
Iveagh Huntley Road
Tel: 082 06 22423
Seats: 930

Bangor Down
Cineplex
Valentine's Road
Tel: 0247 271360
Seats: 1:287, 2:196, 3:163, 4:112

Belfast Antrim
Cineworld
Kennedy Centre
Falls Road E
Tel: 0232 600988
Seats: 1:296, 2:190, 3:182, 4:178, 5:165
Curzon 300
Ormeau Road
Tel: 0232 491071/641373
Seats: 1:453, 2:360, 3:200, 4:104, 5:90
MGM Dublin Road
Tel: 0232 245700
Seats: 1:436, 2:354, 3:262 **X**, 4:264 **X**, 5:252, 6:272, 7:187 **X**, 8:187 **X**, 9:169, 10:118 **X**
The Movie House
York Gate Shopping
Centre X
Tel: 0232 741404
Seats: 1:340, 2:230, 3:220, 4:160, 5:120, 6:90, 7:90, 8:90
bfi **Queen's Film**
Theatre
University Square
Mews X
Tel: 0232 244857/667687
Seats: 1:250, 2:150
The Strand
Hollywood Road
Tel: 0232 673500
Seats: 1:276, 2:196, 3:90, 4:80

Coleraine Londonderry
Jet Centre
Dunhill Road
Tel: 0265 58011
Seats: 1:286, 2:193, 3:152, 4:124

Cookstown Tyrone
Ritz Studio Burn Road
Tel: 06487 65182
Seats: 1:192, 2:128

Dungiven
Londonderry
St Canice Hall
Main Street

Enniskillen
Fermanagh
Castle Centre Race
View Factory Road
Tel: 0365 324172
Seats: 1:302, 2:193, 3:130

Glengormley Antrim
Movie House
Glenville Road
Tel: 0232 833424
Seats: 1:309, 2:243, 3:117, 4:110, 5:76, 6:51

Kilkeel Down
Vogue Newry Street
Seats: 413

Larne Antrim
Regal Curran Road
Tel: 0574 277711
Seats: 1:300, 2:220, 3:120, 4:120

Limavady
Londonderry
Regal
Tel: 05047 66518
Seats: 368

Lurgan Armagh
Centre Point Cinemas
Multi-Leisure Complex
Portadown Road
Seats: 1:304, 2:254, 3:160, 4:110

Magherafelt
Londonderry
Cinema Queen Street
Tel: 0648 33172
Seats: 230

Newry Down
Savoy 2
Merchant's Quay
Tel: 0693 67549
Seats: 1:197, 2:58

Omagh Tyrone
Studio Drum
Quin Road
Seats: 1:800, 2:144, 3:300, 4:119

Portrush Antrim
Playhouse Main Street
Tel: 0265 823917
Seats: 299

COURSES

Film and TV study courses generally fall into two categories: academic and practical. Listed here are a number of educational establishments which offer film and television as part of a course or courses. Where a course is mainly practical, this is indicated with a P next to the course title. In the remaining courses, the emphasis is usually on theoretical study; some of these courses include a minor practical component as described. More information about the courses listed can be found in two BFI Education booklets, 'Film and television training: A guide to courses' and 'Studying film and tv: A list of courses in higher education', along with information on certain further education courses not included here

A.F.E.C.T (Advancement of Film Education Charitable Trust)

4 Stanley Buildings
Pancras Road
London NW1 2TD
Tel: 071 837 5473
The purpose of this organisation is to make professional-level, practical film education available on a part-time basis to those who may have neither the means nor the time to attend a full-time film course

P The Practical Part-time 16mm Film-making Course
Two-year course integrating learning with production. Bias is traditional narrative; despite limitations of scale, students are enabled to realise personal, artistic, social and cultural expression in this medium. Term 1: 35mm stills exercise. Instruction/practicals camera. Interior lit sequence. Editing. Term 2: Script/shoot/edit group mute film with individual sequences, rotating crewing jobs. Term 3: Individual mute 2-minute films. Term 4: Obtaining and adding sound. Dubbing. Sync-sound intro. Term 5: Individual 5-minute sync-sound film each. Term 6: Completing these. Year 3: Advanced projects

The American College in London

Department of Video Production
110 Marylebone High Street
London W1M 3DB
Tel: 071 486 1772
Fax: 071 935 8144

P BA Video Production
Associate degree in Video Production
BA four years, associate degree two years. Four-year course has option to concentrate on commercial, documentary or music video

Barking College

General and Visual Studies
Dagenham Road
Romford RM7 0XU
Tel: 0708 766841
Fax: 0708 731067

P B/TEC National Diploma in Media
Two-year full-time course in video, radio and print

University of Bath

School of Modern Languages and International Studies
Claverton Down
Bath BA2 7AY
Tel: 0225 826482
Fax: 0225 826099

BA (Hons) Modern Languages and European Studies
First year lectures and seminars on the language and theory of film, whilst the second and fourth years offer a wide range of options on French films between the wars, the films of the Nouvelle Vague, film and television in German speaking countries and film in Italy and Russia under 'glasnost'. There is a final year option in European cinema in the 70s and 80s

MPhil and PhD
Part-time or full-time research degrees in French and Russian cinema

Bedford College of Higher Education

Polhill Avenue
Bedford MK41 9EA
Tel: 0234 351671
Fax: 0234 217738

Modular BA/BSc Programme (Arts Pathway) Film Studies
Second and third level modules studying film as a cultural product and a social practice through lectures, screenings, seminars. Level 2: double module – early to contemporary mainstream cinema; level 3: single module – European and World

Cinema plus optional research module
Television and Drama
Two third level modules. 1: forms of television drama and study of key practitioners; 2: television as a cultural practice

University of Birmingham

Department of French
Birmingham B15 2TT
Tel: 021 414 5965
Fax: 021 414 5966

BA (Hons) French Studies
Four-year course which includes options on French cinema (Year 1); documentary film (Year 2); the practice of transposing works of fiction to the screen and Auteur Theory and the Star as Sign (Year 4). Also options on French television: Reading television (Year 1), packaging television programmes (Year 2), and television genres (Year 4). Year 3 is spent at a French university. Students are encouraged to follow courses in Cinema and/or TV as preparation for Year 4 studies

Bournemouth and Poole College of Art and Design

School of Film, Television and Audio Visual Production
Wallisdown Road
Poole
Dorset BH12 5HH
Tel: 0202 538204
Fax: 0202 537729

P **B/TEC National Diploma in Audio Visual Design**
A course offering tape-slide, video production and audio recording at a practical level. Supported by design studies, creative writing, music and word processing

P **B/TEC HND in Design (Film and Television)**
An extensive and intensively practical two-year course based on the production process. All areas of film and television production are covered, with an emphasis on drama and documentary. The majority of work is student originated, with an equal emphasis on film and tape processes. The course has a substantial input from, and contact with, working professionals within the industry. The course has full BECTU accreditation

P **Advanced Diploma in Media Production**
Film/television option. One-year production opportunity for post B/TEC, postgraduate and mid-career students. Application through personal statement of intent and interview. Runs in tandem with HND course, as above

Bournemouth University

Media Production Department
Talbot Campus
Fern Barrow
Poole
Dorset BH12 5BB
Tel: 0202 595351
Fax: 0202 595530

P **BA (Hons) Media Production**
A three-year course covering the academic, practical, aesthetic, technical and professional aspects of work in the media. The course is equally divided between practical and theoretical studies. After Year 1 students can specialise in audio, video or computer graphics, leading to a major production project in Year 3. In addition students complete a piece of individual written research

P **BA (Hons) Scriptwriting for Film and Television**
This course, staffed by professionals, provides a comprehensive three-year programme of theoretical and practical work specifically designed to meet the needs of new writers in the industry. All graduates will have a thorough knowledge of the industry and a portfolio of work developed to a very high standard. Applications from mature students are encouraged

P **Postgraduate Diploma/MA in Video Production**
A one-year full-time course for graduates wishing to acquire the skills of producing and directing television and video. It is based on practical project work in the studio and on location, using Betacam SP

University of Bristol

Department of Drama
Cantocks Close
Woodland Road
Bristol BS8 1UP
Tel: 0272 303030
Fax: 0272 288251

BA Drama
Three-year course, includes introduction to critical and theoretical approaches to film and television in year 1; core seminar courses in film history, with additional academic and practical options in year 2; specialised critical, theoretical and practical options in film and television in year 3. Practical courses extend the critical and practical work using multi-camera studio and single camera OB video resulting in the production of original works in the most appropriate format

P **Postgraduate Diploma in Film and Television Studies**
One-year practical course. It offers a grounding in practical skills and conceptual skills in film and TV production, culminating in location and studio film and TV projects, fiction and non-fiction for public exhibition and/or broadcast. The course is BECTU accredited

bfi British Film Institute and Birkbeck College, University of London

The MA Course Director
British Film Institute
21 Stephen Street
London W1P 1PL
Tel: 071 255 1444 x 375

MA in Cinema and Television
A one-year full-time course in moving image theory and history. In addition to the taught course, work/study placements within the BFI and the submission of a dissertation are required

Brunel University

Department of Human Sciences
Uxbridge
Middx UB8 3PH
Tel: 0895 274000
Fax: 0895 32806

BSc Communication and Information Studies
Four-year interdisciplinary course which aims to give an understanding of the social, intellectual and practical dimensions of the communications media, with particular reference to the new information technologies. Includes practical courses in computing and in video production and technology. All students undertake two periods of work placement of five months each

MA in Communications and Technology
This course offers detailed study of the new communications and information technologies; in particular it looks at the social impact of these technologies, with special reference to issues of communications and cultural policy, and questions of social and cultural change. Students take a core course in Communications and Technology, a research course leading to a dissertation, and two optional courses. The course is completed in one year (full-time) or two years (part-time)

Canterbury Christ Church College

Department of Radio, Film and Television
North Holmes Road
Canterbury
Kent CT1 1QU
Tel: 0227 767700
Fax: 0227 470442

P **BA or BSc (Hons) in Radio, Film and**

Television with one other subject
RFTV is one-half of a three-year joint honours degree and may be combined with Art, English, Geography, History, Mathematics, Movement Studies, Music, Religious Studies and Science. The course introduces students to an understanding and appreciation of radio, film and TV as media of communication and creative expression, stressing their relevance to the individual and to society. It also offers an opportunity to develop and practice production skills in each of the three media

P MA in Media Production
A one-year taught MA which concentrates on production in radio, film and TV. Part I of the course introduces relevant production skills; in Part II members will fulfil a measurable major role in a production project in either radio, film or TV. Course members with practical experience can update their skills and concentrate on one medium in Part I. All course members will attend theory seminars through the course. Assessment will be based on the major piece of practical work and an extended essay

Coventry University
Coventry School of Art and Design
Priory Street
Coventry CV1 5FB
Tel: 0203 838690
Fax: 0203 838667

BA (Hons) Communication Studies
Three-year course which includes specialisms in Cultural and Media Studies, and in Communication Management, built around a core of studies in communication, culture and media, with a range of other options from which students select. European exchange and work placement programmes are included; also options in journalism, photography and video. Projects enable students to combine theoretical and practical work according to their particular interests

Postgraduate Programme in Communication, Culture and Media MA or PgC/PgD
One-year full-time, two-year part-time. The programme is a modular scheme with core theory and research elements, specialist options, and a selection of electives which include film theory and psychoanalysis, journalism, media policy, television culture and politics. Students may specialise in communication management, or cultural policy, or media and culture for the MA qualification

De Montfort University Leicester
School of Arts
The Gateway
Leicester LE1 9BH
Tel: 0533 551551

BA (Hons) Media Studies (Single, Joint or Combined Honours Degrees)
As a Single Honours degree, Media Studies offers a range of courses which focus specifically on Film, Television/Video, Photography and Media institutions. It offers courses in both theoretical and practical work which provide students with the opportunity to develop their skills and learning through detailed analysis of media texts, through understanding the social and political processes of media industries and institutions and through practical work in video, photography, radio and journalism. As Joint Honours, it is possible to take Media Studies in conjunction with one other arts discipline; for Combined Honours, with two other disciplines

University of Derby
Faculty of Art and Design
Film & Video
Green Lane
Derby DE1 1RX
Tel: 0332 622222
Fax: 0332 294861

P BA (Hons) Photographic Studies (Film & Video)
A full-time three-year visual arts course with 70% practical work and 30% academic studies. Creative and inventive use of the media is encouraged through all stages from conception to projection: the development of ideas and the practical experience gained in carrying them out being the essential ingredients of the course

BA/BSc Modular Scheme
Film and Television Studies may be taken as a Major (75%), Joint (50%) or Minor (25%) option. Students may complete a dissertation of 5,000 words in film and/or television studies

Film and Television Studies
Green Lane
Derby DE1 1RX
Tel: 0332 622222
Fax: 0332 294861

MA/Diploma/ Certificate in Film and Television Studies
One-year full-time or two- to three-year part time modular programme concerned with theoretical and historical issues in the study of film and television. Core modules are taken in classical and post-classical narration in film and television and critical approaches to the analysis of mainstream film and television. Optional modules include: audiences and prime-time TV, early cinema, other voices, other visions and television drama, series and serials

MPhil and PhD
Students are accepted for MPhil or PhD by thesis. Particular expertise is offered in the areas of early film, European TV, popular culture and cultural identity

Dewsbury College
Batley Art & Design Centre
Providence Street
Batley
West Yorkshire
WF17 5JB
Tel: 0924 474401
Fax: 0924 457047

P B/TEC National Diploma in Design (Audio-Visual)
Two-year full-time course developing creative and technical skills in graphics, photography, reprographics, sound recording, audio-visual and video production, together with business and complementary studies

P B/TEC HND Design (Communications) Media Production option
Full-time two-year course covering video production, tape slide, computer graphics and animation. Professional video production company on site provides students with a realistic environment to create and produce a variety of productions. The course features visiting specialists, a modular structure, work placements, European exchange schemes and a strong emphasis on practical production skills, with opportunities to explore negotiated and experimental projects

University of East Anglia
School of English and American Studies
Norwich NR4 7TJ
Tel: 0603 56161

BA (Hons) Film and English Studies
A Joint Major programme which integrates Film and Television study with English Literature, History and Cultural Studies. Course includes formal instruction in use of 8mm film and VHS video equipment, and either a practical project on film or video or an independent dissertation on a film or television topic

BA (Hons) Film and American Studies

A four-year joint major programme which integrates the study of cinema and television with work on American literature, history, politics and cultural studies. Course includes a year at university in the USA, and formal instruction in use of VHS video and 8mm film equipment

BA (Hons) in Literature, History, Linguistics, Drama or American Studies

Film can be taken as a substantial Minor programme (up to 40% of degree work) in combination with any of these Major subjects. There is no formal practical element in these programmes, but students have access to instruction in the use of 8mm film and VHS video equipment

MA Film Studies

One-year full-time taught programme. MA is awarded 50% on coursework, 50% on individual dissertation. Courses include: Early Cinema: British cinema to 1930; contemporary film theory and narrative space; and film history and research: Anglo-American relations. There is scope for work on television as well as on other aspects of cinema

P MA Film Archiving

One-year full-time taught programme, run in conjunction with the East Anglian Film Archive. Involves two seminars from the MA film offerings (Early Cinema: British Cinema to 1930 and Research: Anglo-American Relations), and training in film handling, film and video production, and film archive administration and policy. Includes a placement. Assessment includes two essays, a video, placement report and dissertation (50%)

MPhil and PhD

Students are accepted for research degrees

University of East London

Faculty of Design, Built Environment
Greengate Street
London E14 0BG
Tel: 081 590 7722
Fax: 081 849 3694

P BA (Hons) Fine Art, Time Based Art

During the first year students can experiment with each of the disciplines that are available but can also specialise in film, video and video animation throughout the three years

BA Visual Theories: Film Studies

A specialist pathway within the university's modular structure and the range of options is generally extensive with theoretical work on the history of cinema and avant-garde film. Complementary options would include art and psychoanalysis, semiotics, and the history and theory of photography

Department of Cultural Studies
Longbridge Road
Dagenham
Essex RM8 2AS
Tel: 081 590 7722 x2741
Fax: 081 849 3598

BA (Hons) Cultural Studies

Three-year course offering options on media, film and photography in Years 2 and 3. Also includes a practical component (20%) in video, tape-slide and photography over all three years

BA (Hons) Media Studies

The degree includes theory, history and production units at all levels. Approximately one-third is practical. Students specialise in either video, sound/radio or computer-based print/graphics. Additional units can be selected from a wide range of options in the Media Studies, Cultural Studies, Third World Studies, Innovation Studies, Women's Studies 'programmes' and from others available in the University's modular scheme

Department of Innovation Studies
Maryland House
Manbey Park Road
London E15 1EY
Tel: 081 590 7722 x4216
Fax: 081 849 3677

BSc (Hons) New Technology: Media & Communication

This degree examines the media industries in the context of a study of technological change in society. Covers the social relations of technology, the film, recording, newspaper, TV, cable and satellite industries. Students opt for a practical path in either computer graphics or video production. The degree builds a combination of analytical, critical, writing, research and production skills

Edinburgh College of Art

Visual Communications Department
School of Design and Crafts
Lauriston Place
Edinburgh EH3 9DF
Tel: 031 229 9311

P BA (Hons) Film and Television

The course runs for three years and most applicants have done either a foundation course in art and design or a further education course in video/audio-visual. A second subject – usually animation, illustration, photography, or graphic design – must be taken for the first year and may be continued up to final degree level. Film/TV students will generally combine individual projects with participation in group projects. All kinds of work can be tackled – drama, documentary and experimental

P Postgraduate Diploma/Masters Degree in Design

A small number of postgraduates can be accepted, studying either for a diploma (three terms) or a masters degree (four terms). In both cases there is no formal taught course – the programme is tailored to the practical production proposals of the individual student. Postgraduates must already have appropriate skills and experience to use the resources available. The diploma/masters degree are awarded on the strength of the practical work produced

University of Exeter

American and Commonwealth Arts
School of English
Queen's Building
The Queen's Drive
Exeter EX4 4QH
Tel: 0392 264263
Fax: 0392 264377

BA (Hons) American and Commonwealth Arts

BA (Combined Hons) American and Commonwealth Arts and English

BA (Combined Hons) American and Commonwealth Arts and Music

BA (Combined Hons) American and Commonwealth Arts and Italian

Students can take up to a third of their degree in Film Studies, with the emphasis on American film. Combined Hons with Italian also include a course on Italian cinema and culture. No practical component

MA, MPhil and PhD

Students wishing to take an MA degree by coursework and dissertation or an MPhil or PhD by thesis alone can be accommodated and candidates with proposals in any aspect of American or Commonwealth cinema will be considered. Applications for postgraduate study in American Film History will be particularly welcome

School of Education
Media and Resources Centre
St Luke's
Exeter EX1 2LU
Tel: 0392 264866
Fax: 0392 264736
Includes subsidiary courses in Media Education at undergraduate, post-graduate, Inset and research level. The courses are both academic

(award bearing) and practical (video/ programme production) 40% practical, 60% theory. The Centre houses the Robert Barr Archive of TV scripts, including the first *Z Cars*. Independent TV production unit specialising in media and corporate video

School of Modern Languages
Tel: 0392 264231
Fax: 0392 264377

BA (Single and Combined Hons) Italian
Italian either on its own or combined with another subject. One of the six courses that students take is Italian cinema and culture. In general, Neo-realism to the present day

BA (Single and Combined Hons) Spanish
Option in Spanish cinema. Spanish films 1963 to 1990. Selection covering social, literary and war themes. Film censorship and its circumvention

Farnborough College of Technology

Education and Media Studies
Boundary Road
Farnborough
Hampshire GU14 6SB
Tel: 0252 515511

P HND Media Production and Business Studies
Two-year full-time course to study media production techniques with business studies. Course includes TV and video production, video and audio systems, radio, journalism and finance in the media

P HND in Design (Media Production, Video Graphics and Animation)
This course has been designed to provide training in TV and video production, animation and computerised video graphics. In the first and second years, all students will undertake the following modules: Visual Studies, TV and Video Production, Animation and Graphics, Historical and Contextual Studies and Business Management. In the second year students will select three options from the following: Video Systems, Documentary and Drama Production, Advertising Copywriting, Photography, Marketing and the Media, Journalism, Desktop Publishing and Radio Production

University of Glasgow

Department of Theatre, Film and TV Studies
Glasgow G12 8QQ
Tel: 041 330 5162
Fax: 041 330 4142

MA Joint Honours in Film and Television Studies
Four-year undergraduate course. Film/TV Studies represents 50% of an Honours degree or 30% of an Ordinary degree. Year 1 is concerned with Film and TV as 'languages', the institutional structures of British TV, and the implications of recent developments in technology and programming. Year 2 is structured under two headings: Genre in Film and Television and Film, Television and British National Culture. Years 3 and 4 consist of a range of Honours courses, four to be taken in each year. There is also a compulsory practical course, involving the production of a video

Department of French
Glasgow G12 8QQ
Tel: 041 339 8855

MA (Hons) French
Study of French Cinema is a one-year special subject comprising one two-hour seminar per fortnight and weekly screenings. No practical component

Glasgow Caledonian University

Department of Language and Media
Cowcaddens Road
Glasgow G4 0BA
Tel: 041 331 3000
Fax: 041 331 3005

BA Communication and Mass Media
Four-year course (unclassified and honours) examining the place of mass communication in contemporary society. Includes practical studies in print, television, advertising and public relations

Goldsmiths' College, University of London

Lewisham Way
London SE14 6NW
Tel: 081 692 7171

P BA Communications
This course brings together theoretical analyses in social sciences and cultural studies with practical work in creative writing (fiction), electronic graphics and animation, photography, print journalism, radio, script writing and TV (video and film) production. The practical element constitutes 50% of the total degree course. The theoretical element includes media history and sociology, textual and cultural studies, personal and interpersonal contexts of communication and media management

BA Anthropology and Communication Studies
Half of this course constitutes Communication Studies. The course is mainly theoretical but does include a short practical course of ten weeks in length in one of the practice areas. These include TV, videographics and animation, radio, print journalism, photography, creative writing and script writing. The theory component is concerned with media history, sociology, psychology, textual and cultural studies

BA Communication Studies/Sociology
Communication Studies constitutes half this course and is split into theoretical studies and a ten week practical course. Practical options include TV, videographics and animation, radio, print journalism, photography, creative writing and script writing. The theory component is concerned with psychology, media sociology, cultural studies, semiotics and media history

P MA in Image and Communication (Photography or Electronic Graphics)
One-year full-time course combines theory and practice, specialising in either photography or electronic graphics. Practical workshops cover medium and large format cameras, flash, colour printing, lighting, computer and video graphics, design, desktop publishing, animation, animatics, two and three dimensional computer animation. Assessment by coursework and practical production

P MA in Television (TV Drama or Documentary)
One-year full-time course specialising in either documentary or drama modes, taught by practical and theoretical sessions. Course covers script writing, programme planning, camera work, studio and location work, interviewing, sound and post production. Assessment is by coursework and practical production and viva voce

MA in Media and Communication Studies
This course offers an interdisciplinary approach as well as the opportunity to specialise in media and communications. The course is based around a series of compulsory courses and options drawing on theoretical frameworks from cultural studies, political economy, sociology, anthropology, and psychology to develop a critical understanding of the role of the media and communications industries in

contemporary culture. Assessment is by coursework, written examinations and dissertation

Gwent College of Higher Education

Newport School of Art and Design
Clarence Place
Newport
Gwent NP9 0UW
Tel: 0633 430088
Fax: 0633 432006

P BA (Hons) Film and Photography (Animation)
This course is intended for students who want to become professional animators, working in the broadcasting, advertising or independent sectors of the animation industry. It is also available to those who wish to use animation as part of a wider personal or professional practice. The course is practical and designed to stimulate and develop students' imagination and ideas and extend their animation technique. Therefore it is presented in a cultural and intellectual context which promotes critical debate and analysis

P BA (Hons) Film and Photography (Film and Video)
This course is for students who want to explore the moving image as an expressive, communicative medium. It combines technical tuition with an understanding of film language and culture. Students are encouraged to be analytical and critical. Final examination is by submission of a complete film or several smaller productions

P BA (Hons) Film and Photography (Biovisual Studies)
For students who want to link their interest in the visual arts with an understanding of aspects of biological sciences and current environmental issues. The course is particularly for those wishing to pursue careers as wildlife film makers, photographers or illustrators. It provides a rigorous approach to biological, anthropological and cultural studies, combined with practical work to a professional level in wildlife and anthropological film and video making

Harrogate College

Faculty of Creative Arts
Hornbeam Park
Hookstone Road
Harrogate HG2 8QT
Tel: 0423 879466
Fax: 0423 879829

P B/TEC Diploma in Media Production
Two-year diploma, vocationally based, providing practical experience of TV studio, ENG, computer graphics, animation, DTP, tapeslide work, plus research script editing and related design. The course provides the student with a realistic appreciation of all aspects of the media, with a chance to specialise in TV, video, radio, animation or A/V

Harrow School of Design and Media

University of Westminster
Northwick Park
Harrow
Middlesex HA1 3TP
Tel: 071 911 5000
Fax: 081 864 6664

P BA (Hons) in Contemporary Media Practice
This is a modular three-year full-time course which offers an integrated approach to photography, film, video and digital-imaging. Students are encouraged to use a range of photographic and electronic media and theoretical studies are considered crucial to the development of ideas. In years 1 and 2 the taught programme covers basic and applied skills on a project basis; these are complemented by a range of options. In year 3 students are given the opportunity to develop their own programme of study resulting in the production of major works in practice and theory

Havering College of Further and Higher Education

Department of Art & Design
Ardleigh Green Road
Hornchurch
Essex RM11 2LL
Tel: 04024 55011

P B/TEC National Diploma Media
Full-time two-year course. Options include Film and Video, Radio, Audio-visual and Print Production

University of Hertfordshire

Wall Hall Campus
Aldenham
Watford
Herts WD2 8AT
Tel: 0707 284000

BA (Hons) Contemporary Studies
Full-time and part-time degree for mature students. Media Studies is a component on the first year introductory course and an option for second year students. Study includes popular media, audiences and institutions. There is also the option to submit a final year dissertation/ project in media. No practical component

BA (Hons) Humanities
Full- or part-time degree. Within the Historical Studies major/minor and single honours there is a second year option, Film and History, which examines the inter-war period through film and focuses on the historian's use of film. No practical component

University of Hull

Department of Drama
Cottingham Road
Hull HU6 7RX
Tel: 0482 46311

P BA Joint and Special Honours
Introduction to film and TV studies in Year 1. Honours students may opt for practical courses in radio (sound engineering, radio drama and advanced radio drama) and filmmaking in subsequent years

University of Humberside

School of Social and Professional Studies, Division of Humanities and IT
Inglemire Avenue
Hull HU6 7LU
Tel: 0482 440550
Fax: 0482 449624

BA (Hons) Communication Processes
This course is designed to prepare students for entry into the communications industry and to provide fluency in different communication processes. Various academic subjects (Psychology, Literature, Sociology, History, Information Technology, Media and Cultural Studies) are combined with practical skills development in areas such as video and sound production, creative writing and Information Technology. The course is one fifth practical. Year 1: ENG video production and editing, sound production, presentation skills, computer graphics. Year 2: TV studio, multi-track recording, computer based hypertext programming, multi-media. Year 3: independent study

School of Art, Architecture and Design
Queens Gardens
Hull HU1 3DQ
Tel: 0482 440550
Fax: 0482 586721

P BA (Hons) Graphic Design
Students may specialise in animation/film/video or graphic design or illustration. After an introductory period, animation and film primers are located in Terms 1 and 2. Full specialisation begins at the start of term 3. The course is essentially practical, with a strong theoretical/critical element and a programme of visiting animators and filmmakers. The course has strong components in scriptwriting, cinematography, direction, animation and production competence. Films are initiated by students in narrative fiction, animation, and include sponsored public-information film and videotape productions, computer animation and much experimental work

P BA (Hons) Fine Art
Time-based media: 8mm and 16mm film; SVHS and U-Matic video; sound photography; and related live work. Course is essentially practical (80%), projects being student-initiated. Work frequently crosses disciplines including photography, printmaking, painting and sculpture. Supported by a programme of visiting tutors, artists, film/videomakers, screenings and critical/theoretical studies (20%)

P BA (Hons) Documentary Communication
This is a mixed mode honours degree, 70% practical, 30% theoretical, with three production pathways: still photography/text; sound/radio; and video. Students follow a multi-disciplinary first year and then specialise in one pathway for the following two years. The course provides the context within which individuals acquire the knowledge and skills pertinent to communicating in documentary forms. It seeks to produce graduates who are able to operate professionally in a variety of contexts producing a range of work within a strong conceptual base

P BA (Hons) European Audio-Visual Production
The degree will equip graduates with producers skills for the developing European market, including language skills. There will be stress on generating creative and successful ideas and having the expertise required to get them on screen. 80% practice, 20% theory. Teaching is largely project based. The third year is spent abroad at a university in France or Spain. Graduates emerge with a showreel and business plan suitable for the European market place. Studio and single camera video operation is supported by projects focusing on research and development, programme proposals, sound, scripting and storyboarding

P BA (Hons) Media Production
This course offers its students technical pathways in combinations of sound, video, photography, graphic design and typography and is 80% practical. It has three major strands in fiction, journalism and alternative practices and concentrates on 'writing the image'. It will give students experience of working in multi-disciplinary teams. Integrated with the practical work is an analysis of cultural industries

Institute of Education, University of London

Department of English, Media and Drama
20 Bedford Way
London WC1H 0AL
Tel: 071 612 6511/3
Fax: 071 612 6330

MA Media Education
One-year full-time or two-year part-time. Three elements: 1) Mandatory module in The Theory and Practice of Media Education, assessed by final examination; 2) Optional module, assessed by course work, from Ideology and the Media; Childhood, Youth and Popular Culture; Media Race and Gender; Principles of Production for Media Education; British Media: the European Dimension; Hollywood Cinema: Text and Context; Television and its Audiences; Text in a Social Semiotic Perspective; 3) Dissertation

MA Media Studies
One-year full-time, two-year part-time, with three elements: 1) Mandatory Module in Ideology and the Media (assessed by final examination); 2) Optional module, assessed by coursework, as for the MA Media Education with The Theory and Practice of Media Education replacing Ideology and the Media; 3) Dissertation

MPhil and PhD
Supervision of research theses in the area of Film Studies, TV Studies, Media Studies and Media Education

Institute Associateship
Individualised one-year courses for mature educationalists wishing to study pedagogic and intellectual developments in the field of Media Education and Media Studies

Kent Institute of Art and Design

School of Visual Communication
Rochester upon Medway College
Fort Pitt
Rochester
Kent ME1 1DZ
Tel: 0634 830022
Fax: 0634 829461

P B/TEC HND in Advertising and Editorial Photography
Two-year course. It aims to provide a route into professional photography and work is carried out using a wide range of formats, mainly large, medium and small format still photography, complemented by audio visual, 16mm film and video, and is aimed at publication in forms including print, exhibition display, tape-slide presentation, broadcast television and video

School of Visual Communication
Oakwood Park
Maidstone
Kent ME16 8AG
Tel: 0622 757286
Fax: 0622 692003

P BA (Hons) Communication Media
Three-year course with pathways in graphic design, illustration, photography, time-based

media (film/video) and combined studies. The course encourages a broad view of visual and audio-visual communication

University of Kent

Rutherford College
Canterbury
Kent CT2 7NX
Tel: 0227 764000

BA Combined Hons
A Part 1 course on Narrative Cinema is available to all Humanities students in Year 1. The Part 2 component in Film Studies in Years 2 and 3 can vary from 25% to 75% of a student's programme. Courses include Film Theory, British Cinema, Non-narrative cinema, Comedy and Sexual Difference and Cinema. The rest of a student's programme consists of courses from any other Humanities subject. No practical component

BA Single Hons
Available 1994/95. This will include a practical film production option

MA, MPhil and PhD
An MA course in Film and Art History will be available in 1993/94. Students are also accepted for MA, MPhil and PhD by thesis

King Alfred's College Winchester

(Affiliated to Southampton University)
Department of Drama and Television
Sparkford Road
Winchester SO22 4NR
Tel: 0962 841515
Fax: 0962 842280

BA (Hons) Drama, Theatre and TV
Three-year course that relates theories of contemporary television and drama to practical work in both media. The course looks at both the institutions and the practices of the two media from the perspectives of the psychology and critical ideologies, including women's studies, of the twentieth century. It includes 3 major TV projects in which students work together to produce documentaries or drama documentaries

Postgraduate Diploma/ MA Degree in Television for Development
This one-year course aims to be of value to students who wish to work or are working in development agencies in the UK and overseas as well as the staff of broadcasting institutions in developing countries. The rationale of the course is to produce an interface between development and the media, both in the north and in the south

Kingston University

School of Three Dimensional Design
Knights Park
Kingston-upon-Thames
Surrey KT1 2QJ
Tel: 081 547 2000

P CNAA Post-graduate Diploma in Design for Film and Television
One-year course in scenic design tailored to the needs of those who wish to enter the industry with the eventual aim of becoming production designers or art directors. The course is constructed as a series of design projects to cover different types of film and television production

School of Art and Design History
Tel: 081 547 7112

BA/BA (Hons) Combined Studies: History of Art, Architecture and Design
Five- to six-year part-time or three-year full-time. Three Film Studies modules, each representing one sixth of a full-time student's yearly programme, one third of a part-time student's. Foundation level: concepts of "Art" cinema. Intermediate level: photographic issues. Advanced level: the study of a selected artist

School of Graphic Design

P BA (Hons) Graphic Design
The course aims to give students a technical and practical understanding of animation and moving image on film and video. Students learn to research, script and storyboard ideas, prepare sound tracks and take their projects through to shooting and post-production

School of Languages
Penrhyn Road
Kingston-upon-Thames
Surrey KT1 2EE
Tel: 081 547 2000
Fax: 081 547 7292

BA (Hons) Modern Arts/BA Combined Studies
Two-term option course in Year 2 on French Cinema since 1930. No practical component. Modular part-time degree

BA (Hons) French Studies
As combined studies, plus two term year 4 special subject on French New Wave Cinema

Kingsway College

Media and Photography Unit
Sidmouth Street
Grays Inn Road
London WC1H 8JB
Tel: 071 278 0541
Fax: 071 833 8964

P B/TEC National Diploma in Design Communications (Media Studies)
Two-year full-time course for those interested in pursuing a career in the media industry. The course covers an integrated programme of practical training in photography, video, film and computer technology, and theoretical studies relating to the analysis of media texts

LSU College of Higher Education

The Avenue
Southampton SO9 5HB
Tel: 0703 228761
Fax: 0703 230944

BEd (Hons) and BA (Hons) in Combined Studies
Both courses contain options in Film Study for those students for whom English is a significant component of their degree

Leicester Polytechnic see *De Montfort University Leicester*

University of Leicester

Centre for Mass Communication Research
104 Regent Road
Leicester LE1 7LT
Tel: 0533 523863
Fax: 0533 523874

BSc Communications and Society
A three-year social science based undergraduate course. The modules taught cover a wide range of areas including media institutions, research methods in mass communications, film and TV forms. Students are assessed by a combination of continuous assessment and examination

MA Mass Communications
One-year taught course studying the organisation and impact of the mass media both nationally and internationally and providing practical training in research methods

University of Liverpool

School of Politics and Communication Studies
Roxby Building
PO Box 147
Liverpool L69 3BX
Tel: 051 794 2890

BA Combined Hons (Social and Environ-mental Studies)
BA Joint Hons (English and Communication Studies)
BA Joint Hons (Politics and Communication Studies)
In all these programmes, students combine work in the Communication Studies Department with largely non media-related work in other Departments; Communication Studies forms up to 50% of their programme. Year 1: Communication: a programme of introductory work on communication and cultural analysis. Year 2: courses on Broadcasting,

Film Studies and Drama. Year 3: courses available include 'Documentary', exploring a range of work in literature, photography, film and TV. No practical component

Liverpool John Moores University

68 Hope Street
Liverpool L1 9EB
Tel: 051 231 2121
Fax: 051 709 0172
School of Design and Visual Arts

P BA (Hons) Graphic Design (modular)
Film/Animation is a specialised option within the Graphic Design degree. After a general first year a number of students may specialise in Film/Animation in their second and third years

School of Media, Critical and Creative Arts

BA/BA (Hons) Media and Cultural Studies
Some practical components within this degree are integrated into a theoretical study of television, film, video and radio. First year courses in reading and producing the media lead to specialist options in film studies, video, photography and newspaper and broadcast journalism

London College of Printing

The Media School
School of Film and Video
6 Back Hill
Clerkenwell Road
London EC1R 5EN
Tel: 071 278 7445
Fax: 071 833 8842

P BA (Hons) Film Video and Animation
An autonomous course in Film and Video, part of a degree scheme in Communication Media courses, leading to the award of BA (Hons) degree. Main concerns are Women's Cinema, Third World Cinema, Popular Culture and Film. Stress on experimentation and innovation, education, independent filmmakers. Practice/Theory ratio is 70:30. Course stresses integration of theory and practice. Since 1988 the course has included an option in Animation. This course is accredited by BECTU

London Guildhall University

Department of Communications and Music Technology
41 Commercial Road
London E1 1LA
Tel: 071 320 1000
Fax: 071 320 3134

BA (Hons) Communication Studies
This degree includes both practical and theoretical studies. Practical units include film TV and video production, photojournalism, radio journalism and writing for the media. Theoretical units include cultural history and cultural studies. The degree may be studied full-time or part-time. Communication Studies may also be studied as half of a joint degree or as a minor component of a degree

P BA (Hons) Audio Visual Production
This new degree will start in 1994. Please contact the Admissions Office for details

The London Institute

Central St Martins College of Art and Design
Southampton Row
London WC1B 4AP
Tel: 071 753 9090
Fax: 071 379 8105

P BA (Hons) Fine Art, Film and Video
Three-year full-time. Students are recruited directly into the Film and Video subject of the Fine Art course. The first four terms are designed to develop technical and conceptual skills with a series of projects which explore image, sound, animation, video and 16mm film production. During the first year of the course there will be opportunities to spend some time in another area of Fine Art and a placement during the second year. The Fine Art context strongly encourages experimental enquiry, and the course is 80% practical and 20% theoretical

P Advanced Diploma in Film and Video
Aone-year full-time course which is taught as a practical subject. Students design and submit an outline of a year's programme of study which they will be encouraged to realise through tutorial guidance and technical assistance. Students will be expected to participate in a weekly critical seminar with third year BA undergraduates, and to present work at the final Degree shows. They will have full access to the equipment and facilities which are outlined in the text for the BA (Hons) Fine Art Film and Video course. Application to the Advanced Course in Film and Video is made directly to the: Registrar, School of Art, Central St Martins College of Art and Design. Details of the BA (Hons) Fine Art Film and Video course are obtainable from the same office, although applications are made through the: Art and Design Registry, Penn House, 9 Broad Street, Hereford HR4 9AP

London International Film School

Department F16
24 Shelton Street
London WC2H 9HP
Tel: 071 836 9642

P Diploma in Film Making
A two-year full-time practical course teaching skills to professional levels. All students work on one or more films each term and are encouraged to interchange unit roles termly to experience different skill areas. Approximately half each term is spent in film making, half in practical instruction, seminars, workshops, tutorials, and script writing. Established for over 35 years, the school is constituted as an independent, non profit-making, educational charity and is a member of NAHEFV and CILECT – respectively the national and international federations of film schools. Graduates include Bill Douglas, Danny Huston, John Irwin, Mike Leigh, Michael Mann and Franc Roddam. The course is accredited by BECTU and widely recognised by local education authorities for grants. New courses commence each January, April and September

University of Manchester

Department of Drama
Oxford Road
Manchester M13 9PL
Tel: 061 275 3347
Fax: 061 275 3349

BA Single and Joint Honours in Drama
Normally an optional course in film studies in Year 3 with a compulsory course for Single Honours in Year 2 (optional for Joint). No practical component

MPhil/PhD
Possibility for research theses on aspects of film and TV drama

Department of Education
Oxford Road
Manchester M13 9PL
Tel: 061 275 3463

MEd in Education and the Mass Media
This full- or part-time course enables teachers and others involved in education and the mass media to explore effective communication techniques within their fields of work. Some practical work; emphasis on experiential learning and interpersonal communications. Visits to media organisations and contributions from media specialists are arranged

Diploma in Advanced Study in Education and the Mass Media
Designed for educators from the UK and overseas, this full- or part-time course provides an introduction to the study of mass media systems and the use of audiovisual material for teaching and learning

Manchester Metropolitan University

Department of Communication Media
Television Area
Capitol Building
School Lane, Didsbury
Manchester M20 0HT
Tel: 061 247 2000 x7123
Fax: 061 448 0135

P **BA (Hons) Television Production or Design**
A three-year full-time course offering options in production (research, scripting, directing, camerawork, editing etc) and design (sets, costumes etc). Normal intake 16 for production and 8 for design. Course is organised around practical, group-based projects. These include dramas, documentaries and music programmes. There is collaboration between options and with other areas including theatre school

Department of English and History
Lower Ormond Street
Manchester M15 6BX
Tel: 061 247 1730

BA (Hons) Modern Studies
Film/TV small component. A mixed course of English, Film and Current TV News. Mass Media: a multi-disciplinary course which applies the methodologies of the social sciences and the humanities to the mass media. May run as one-year course for students with Dip HE, or as three-year BA

BA Humanities & Social Sciences/BA English Studies
Film and film theory third year optional course. No practical component

Department of Interdisciplinary Studies
Cavendish Building
Cavendish Street
Manchester M15 6BG
Tel: 061 247 3026

Dip HE
Two-year course which includes an introduction to film and film theory in Year 1 and a course on film as propaganda in Year 2. Also a second year course on Gender and the Gothic and third year on Hollywood Text into film

Middlesex University

Faculty of Humanities
White Hart Lane
Tottenham
London N17 8HR
Tel: 081 362 5000

BA (Hons) Contemporary Cultural Studies
One-year course (or two- to three-years part-time) designed for students who possess a Dip HE or equivalent (two years full-time degree-level work). Film and television are studied as aspects of cultural practice. No practical component

Faculty of Art and Design
Cat Hill
Barnet
Herts EN4 8HT
Tel: 081 362 5000

BA (Hons) History of Art, Design and Film
Modular system degree. Film studies set as part of multidisciplinary programme, together with subjects from another discipline. First two years as multi-disciplinary programme. Third year allows greater specialisation and includes dissertation which could be in film or TV studies. No practical component

P **MA in Video**
A one-year full-time course (48 weeks) emphasising the creative aspects of professional video production in the independent sector. Intended for graduate students with considerable lo-band video experience. The course covers all aspects of the production cycle, with an emphasis on scriptwriting. 50% practical; 50% theoretical

Napier University

Department of Photography, Film and Television
61 Marchmont Road
Edinburgh EH9 1HU
Tel: 031 444 2266
Fax: 031 228 3828

P **BA/BA Hons Photography, Film and TV**
With option of specialising in Film and TV production from middle of second year

P **MSc Film and TV Production**
Post graduate/experience one-year full-time course in Film and TV production

National Film and Television School

Beaconsfield Studios
Station Road
Beaconsfield
Bucks HP9 1LG
Tel: 0494 671234
Fax: 0494 674042

P The School offers full-time professional training leading to an NFTS Associateship (ANFTS) in the specialisations of producer, director, director of photography, editor, animator, art director, sound recordist, documentary and film composers. A one-month writing workshop is available for Screen Writers with the possibility of a further year for some participants. Previous experience in film or a related field is expected. The school is funded by a partnership of Government and industry (film, TV and video). Its graduates occupy leading roles in all aspects of film and TV production. It is a full member of CILECT and actively co-operates with professional bodies in the UK and abroad

University of Newcastle upon Tyne

School of English
Newcastle upon Tyne
NE1 7RU
Tel: 091 222 7787

BA (Hons) English/BA Combined Honours
Modules in classical and contemporary Hollywood. No practical component

MA in Twentieth Century Studies: English and American Literature and Film
Modules in film and television are available in one year full-time, two-year part-time course

MA in Film
Two-year part-time course with modules in British, American and European cinema, plus dissertation. Commencing either 1993-4 or 1994-5

MLitt, PhD
Applicants for study in English and American film welcome

Combined Honours Centre
Newcastle upon Tyne
NE1 7RU
Tel: 091 222 6000

BA (Hons) Combined Studies
Two-year course, available in the second year of the degree. Year 1 covers American film, and Theory and History of Film; Year 2 includes studies in European film, British cinema from 1940 and the option of a dissertation

School of Modern Languages
Newcastle upon Tyne
NE1 7RU
Tel: 091 232 8511

BA (Hons) Modern Languages
Optional final year course: studies in European film. Optional final year course in French: French Film in the 1980s

Department of Spanish, Portuguese and Latin-American Studies
Old Library Building
Newcastle upon Tyne
NE1 7RU
Tel: 091 222 6000

BA (Hons) Spanish
Undergraduate special subject Hispanic Literature and Film. Option in European Film Studies

MA Spanish Literature and Film Since 1939
MA in film is in two parts: Buñuel and post-50s Spanish Film. No practical component

Northbrook College

Littlehampton Road
Goring-by-Sea
Worthing
West Sussex BN12 6NU
Tel: 0903 830057

P **B/TEC HND Design (Audio Visual Production)**
Two-year full-time creative video production course with computer graphics and access to film and animation. The course includes supporting studies (business studies, visual studies, technical matters, cultural background) and work experience

North Cheshire College
Media & Theatre Studies
Padgate Campus
Fearnhead Lane
Fearnhead
Warrington WA2 0DB
Tel: 0925 814343
Fax: 0925 816077

P **BA (Joint Hons) Media with Business Management and Information Technology**
A modular system degree. The media component offers practical production work in video, sound recording, photography, graphics or print media, with academic analysis of the media through modules on Forms, Representations, Institutions and Audiences. The course structure enables students to relate their business and information technology studies to their work in media. Students are asked to specialise in one medium of production, and choose from a number of options in the theory course. The programme includes one term in Year 2 devoted to work experience in the media industry and institutions

BA (Hons) Mature Student Programme
A modular system degree, designed specifically for mature student entry. A broad range of modules is available, and students can choose some or all of the media modules, theoretical and practical

Diploma in Media Education
A part-time postgraduate Diploma designed for serving teachers in the primary, secondary and further education sectors. The course calls for analysis of key theoretical issues, consideration of issues of curriculum and pedagogy, together with practical work in video, sound and photography. Attendance is either one evening a week over two years or day release over one year

The following MAs are validated by the University of Manchester and are subject to final approval

MA in Media and Cultural Studies
This course is offered on a one-year full-time basis or a two-year part-time basis. The course consists of 3 core modules: IT and research methods; classical and post-classical narrative; contemporary theory and critique and 3 optional modules. A dissertation is also required

MA in Screen Studies
One-year full-time, or two-year part-time. The course consists of 3 core modules: IT and research methods; classical and post-classical narrative; contemporary theory and critique. 3 optional modules. A dissertation is also required

P **MA in Video Production**
This course is designed to extend practical production skills and techniques in video to a professional standard. It includes production work in studio practices, documentary production and corporate video, as well as contextualising courses in professional and organisational studies, broadcasting policy, structures and audiences. Students also need to complete a dissertation, which can be a conventional academic study, an industrial study or an original script

Northern School of Film and Television
This is run by Leeds Metropolitan University with the support of Yorkshire Television providing postgraduate level professional training in practical film production. At present two courses are offered

NSFTV
Leeds Metropolitan University
2-8 Merrion Way
Leeds LS2 8BT
Tel: 0532 832600
Fax: 0532 833194

P **MA/Postgraduate Diploma in Scriptwriting for Film and Television (Fiction)**
An intensive one-year practical course running from January to January, based at Leeds Metropolitan University. Staffed largely by working professional writers, it covers the various forms of fiction scriptwriting for film and TV – short film, feature film, TV drama, soap opera, series etc. The course has a strong emphasis on professional presentation, and aims to help graduates to set up a credible freelance practice. After an initial module in screen storytelling, the course proceeds to work on a short film and TV projects. The major project, in the third term and over the summer, is a 20,000 word script, either feature film or TV drama

P **MA/Postgraduate Diploma in Film Production (Fiction)**
An intensive one-year practical course running from October to October. Students are admitted into specialist areas: Direction (6 students per year), Production (3), Camera (3), Art-Direction (3), Editing (3) and Sound (3). Students work in teams to produce six short films, in two batches of three. The resulting films may be broadcast on Yorkshire Television, who provide the base production funding and some facilities. Scripts are normally drawn from the product of the Script-writing Course at NSFTV and the emphasis is on team working and joint creativity under pressure. It is not a course for 'author' film makers. There is also a theoretical studies component

University of North London
School of Literary and Media Studies
Prince of Wales Road
London NW5 3LB
Tel: 071 607 2789
Fax: 071 753 5078

Humanities Scheme
Three-year full-time course. Six-year part-time course by day or evening study. Film Studies is one of 14 subject components and may be taken as a Major, Joint or Minor. One practical component

MA Modern Drama Studies
Two-year part-time evening modular course with optional Film Studies. No practical component

MA Theories of Representation
Two-year part-time evening modular course. Core courses in Mimesis/Anti-mimesis and Signification and the subject. Optional unit in Film Studies

University of Northumbria at Newcastle
Faculty of Arts and Design
Squires Building
Sandyford Road
Newcastle upon Tyne
NE1 8ST
Tel: 091 227 4935
Fax: 091 227 3632

P **BA (Hons) Media Production**
Practical three-year course with fully integrated theoretical and critical components in which students are offered the opportunity to specialise in individual programmes of work. Organised into three stages with the Media Theory programme continuing throughout

BA (Hons) History of Modern Art, Design and Film
Offered as a three-year full-time course. Film Studies is given equal weighting with painting and design in the first year. In the second year up to 60% of a student's

time can be devoted to Film Studies, with this rising to nearly 100% in the third year

MPhil
There are possibilities for research degrees in either film theory or practice

Nottingham University

School of Education
Nottingham NR7 2RD
Tel: 0602 515151

MEd/Diploma module in Mass Media Communication
Particular emphasis on TV and media studies in schools. Opportunities are provided for a good deal of practical work, though the major emphasis is upon analysis and criticism

MPhil and PhD
Research can be supervised for higher degrees by thesis

Nottingham Trent University

Faculty of Art & Design
Department of Visual and Performing Arts
Burton Street
Nottingham NG1 4BU
Tel: 0602 486405
Fax: 0602 486403

P BA (Hons) Fine Art
Film and video is available as either an option or a main field of study on this broad based fine art course. Students can develop their work across a range of media including painting, print, sculpture and photography. The moving image caters for 8 and 16mm film, video, installation and multi-media work, computer imaging, sound and animation. The course is 80% practical under-pinned by a framework of contextual studies

P BA (Hons) Creative Arts
This modular course comprises 3 main subject areas: music, performance, visual arts, with a strong interdisciplinary, critical and experimental emphasis in both practice (70%) and theory (30%). For two years students take two of three subjects and several faculty modules, developing their special interests in third year practical and theoretical projects. Video installation, video, film, photography, computer imaging, animation are amongst potential vehicles for realising ideas, but not as independent studies outside the visual arts component

Plymouth College of Art and Design

Department of Photography, Film and Television
Tavistock Place
Plymouth
Devon PL4 8AT
Tel: 0752 385987
Fax: 0752 385972

P B/TEC HND in Media Production
(in partnership with the University of Plymouth)
A two-year modular course with pathways in film, video animation and computer graphics. All areas of film, video and television production are covered and the course is well supported by visiting lecturers and workshops. Strong links with the industry have been developed and work based experience forms an important part of the course. The course has BKSTS accreditation. Opportunities exist through the ERASMUS programme to undertake a programme of exchange with European universities or polytechnics during the course

P Advanced Diploma in Photography, Film and Television leading to the BIPP Professional Qualifying Exam
A one-year course post HND and post graduate. The film and television option allows students to plan their own line of study, including practical work, dissertation and an extended period of work based experience. Students from both courses have had considerable success in film and video scholarships and competitions. Students on both courses have the opportunity for three-month work placements in the media industry in Spain

University of Portsmouth

School of Social and Historical Studies
Milldam
Barnaby Road
Portsmouth PO1 3AS
Tel: 0705 827681

BA (Hons) Cultural Studies
Year 1: 10 one-hour introductory lectures, five seminars. Year 2 options: 10 lectures – the Studio system. Options on Popular Texts, including Melodrama. Year 3: options on British Cinema 1933-70, British TV Drama, Avant-Garde Films and Feminism

Department of Design
Lion Gate Building
Lion Terrace
Portsmouth PO1 3HF
Tel: 0705 842293
Fax: 0705 842077

BA (Hons) Art, Design and Media
Three-year unitised programme has nine specialist pathways. All are structured around historical, cultural and theoretical analysis which form an important part of the degree. Student placements in Europe and the UK and outside funded projects maintain the degree's links with industry

P Video and Film Pathway
In the first and second years students undertake issue based briefs around cultural identity, gender etc. In the third year students work on self directed projects

P Graphic Design Pathway
Design for TV and video graphics are central areas of concern

Historical and Theoretical Studies Pathway
Aim is to produce graduates with particular skills in research and communication. Projects include scriptwriting for factual and fiction and production management

P Computer Illustration Pathway
Offers the opportunity to develop computer animation, computer-based illustration for print and interactive multimedia

Ravensbourne College of Design and Communication

School of Television
Walden Road
Chislehurst
Kent BR7 5SN
Tel: 081 468 7171
Fax: 081 295 1070

P B/TEC HND in Engineering Communications (Television Studio Systems Engineering)
Two-year full-time vocational course designed in consultation with the TV broadcasting industry leading to employment opportunities as technician-engineers

P B/TEC HND in Design Communication (Television Programme Operations)
Two-year full-time vocational course designed in consultation with the TV broadcasting industry leading to employment opportunities in television and video production as members of programme making teams in lighting, camera operators, sound, video recording and editing, vision-mixing, telecine, and audio-recording

University of Reading

Faculty of Letters and Social Sciences
Whiteknights
Reading RG6 2AA
Tel: 0734 875123

BA Film and Drama (Single Subject)
After the first two terms in which three subjects are studied (two being in film and drama), students work wholly in film and drama. The course is critical but with significant practical elements which are

designed to extend critical understanding. It does not provide professional training

BA Film and Drama with English, French, German, Italian or Sociology

Students in general share the same teaching as Single Subject students but the course does not include practical work

MA Film and Drama

One-year course. Three taught elements: Text and Performance Analysis (Term 1, covering both film and drama), Critical Case Studies (Terms 2 and 3, one case study each for film), Critical Practice (Terms 2 and 3, group practical assignments in drama and video). Plus 15,000 word dissertation

MPhil and PhD

Research applications for MPhil and PhD degrees are also invited in areas of cinema, television and twentieth century theatre

Department of English

BA (Hons) English

Second year optional course on literature, film and television. Third year optional course in media semiotics

PhD

Research can be supervised on the history of the BBC and other mass media topics

Department of French Studies

BA (Hons) French

First year introductory course: detailed study of one film (one half-term). Final year: Two-term option: French cinema, with special emphasis on the 30s, 40s and the 'Nouvelle Vague'. Includes introductory work on the principle of film study. Available also to students combining French with certain other subjects. No practical component

Department of German

BA (Hons) German

Two-term Finals option: The German Cinema. Course covers German cinema from the 1920s to the present, with special emphasis on the Weimar Republic, the Third Reich, and the 'New German Cinema'. No practical component

Department of Italian Studies

BA (Hons) Italian/ French and Italian with Film Studies

First year introductory course: Post-War Italian Cinema (one half-term). Second year course: Italian Cinema (three terms). Final year course: European Cinema (two terms). Dissertation on an aspect of Italian cinema. These courses available to students reading other subjects in the Faculty. No practical component

MA Italian Cinema

One-year full-time or two-year part-time course on Italian Cinema: compulsory theory course, options on film and literature, Bertolucci, Italian industry and genre – the Spaghetti Western. No practical component

MPhil and PhD

Research can be supervised on Italian cinema for degree by thesis

Richmond upon Thames College

Media Workshop
Visual Communications
Egerton Road
Twickenham TW2 7SJ
Tel: 081 892 6656

P B/TEC National Diploma in Design Communications

This course combines the study of the media with practical training in video, desk top publishing, radio, photography and journalism. The course includes regular input from practising media professionals. Assessed by coursework portfolio

College of Ripon and York St John

York Campus
Lord Mayor's Walk
York YO3 7EX
Tel: 0904 656771

BA Combined Hons

Honours degree students take 17 courses in three years. Of these, seven are drama/TV courses. The practical component includes some off-campus work and can include experience in related industries

Roehampton Institute

Department of Drama and Theatre Studies
Digby Stuart College
Roehampton Lane
London SW15 5PU
Tel: 081 392 3000
Fax: 081 392 3231

BA Drama and Theatre Studies

The Drama and Theatre Studies modular programme is combined with one other subject. Year One includes a one term module in Film Analysis with some practical work in portable video. A double module in Contemporary Television Drama and a practical double module in Television Drama Production are offered in Year Three. Other modules, such as Representing Women and Shakespeare in Contemporary Performance, contain substantial study of film and television production. Students may also specialise in areas of film and television for research dissertations

Royal College of Art

School of Film and Television
Kensington Gore
London SW7 2EU
Tel: 071 584 5020
Fax: 071 589 0178

P MA in Film and Television Direction

Two-years practical craft course including production of narrative fiction and documentary film. Emphasis is placed on pre-production development, scripting and planning. Professional workshops, accompanied by seminars covering development and history of cinema and television. Inter-related with film and television production and design for film and television courses. Assessment by submission of practical work and interview

P MA Film and Television Production

Inter-related with film and television direction and design for film and television courses. Students responsible for complete practical production of film and television projects from idea and script development through production processes to completed product. Seminars cover raising finance, budgeting, script selection, company law, contracts, insurance and copyright. Assessment by submission of evidence of production experience and interview

P Design for Film and Television

Course based on all aspects of 3-dimensional production design in film and television including history, aesthetics and techniques. Inter-related with film and television direction and production courses. Assessment by submission of practical work and interview

Animation Course
Faculty of Communication
Kensington Gore
London SW7 2EU
Tel: 071 584 5020 x 343
Fax: 071 225 1487

P MA in Animation

Two-year full-time course. Some possibility of part-time courses. Course work divided into 10% theoretical and 90% practical

Royal Holloway University of London

Department of Drama and Theatre Studies
Egham Hill
Egham
Surrey TW20 0EX
Tel: 0784 434455
Fax: 0784 431018

BA (Hons) Drama and Theatre Studies

Special options in television: a two-year course for second and third year students. Principally a practical course concerned with the creation of meaning in video and television forms. Techniques of

Television: all students take a course in basic audio-visual literacy. A comparison is made between Theatre Arts and Television Arts in the area of texts and their translation into productions. History of Film: a two-year course for all second and third years

BA (Hons) Media Arts

Modular degree offering an opportunity for studying the media with a specific emphasis on the Arts. Students combine analytic study with practical production of a range of televised and filmed material including all forms of drama, documentaries, arts educational programmes and animation. Students gain experience in producing, directing, scriptwriting and researching

MA Drama and Theatre Studies

Special option in television: a one-year course which constitutes one third of the degree. The students explore the televisual medium through practical projects designed to provide audio-visual vocabularies. Finally, they are expected to translate an extract of a play, short story or poem into an audio-visual form or devise an original short narrative or non-narrative piece

St Helens College

School of Arts, Media and Design
Brook Street
St Helens
Merseyside WA10 1PZ
Tel: 0744 33766 x221

B/TEC National Diploma in Media

A two-year full-time course aiming to provide a foundation in basic skills relevant to many areas of the media industry and the opportunity, through option selection, to examine one or more sectors in detail: television, film and video; sound and radio; print and publishing; audio-visual exhibition

P B/TEC HND in Design (Multi Discipline)

A two-year full-time course offering pathways in TV/Video, Audio, Graphic Design, 3D craft, 3D spatial design

BA (Hons) Media and Cultural Studies

It is possible to study the first year of this course as part of the integrated credit scheme at St Helens College and years 2 and 3 at Liverpool John Moores University. Media and Cultural Studies is one of the academic areas offering modules within the Integrated Credit Scheme. The ICS offers a full range of academic awards. Students study mass media and communications including areas such as television news, documentary, drama, film, journalism and photojournalism. The other theme in the degree is the study of popular culture, including both cultural practices and cultural texts

University College Salford

Centre for Media, Performance and Communications
Adelphi
Peru Street
Salford
Manchester M3 6EQ
Tel: 061 834 6633
Fax: 061 834 3327

P BA (Hons) Television and Radio

BA (Hons) Media and Performance

BA (Hons) Media, Language and Business

B/TEC HND in Media Production

B/TEC HND in Media Performance

B/TEC National Diploma in Media and Communications

MA Television Features and Documentary Production (in association with Granada TV)

MSc Media Business and Legal Affairs

Visiting Professor: David Plowright
Professional Patrons: Ken Russell, Ben Kingsley, Robert Powell, Gareth Morgan, George Martin CBE, Jack Rosenthal, Brian Redhead, Stuart Prebble, Ray Fitzwalter, Leslie Woodhead OBE
All courses are two-thirds practical production/performance based. The Granada Education Awards are available to students

Sandwell College

School of Electronics
Woden Road Campus
Woden Road
Wednesbury
West Midlands
WS10 0PE
Tel: 021 556 6000

P B/TEC National Diploma in Electronics and Television Studio Operations

A two-year, full-time course for those possessing artistic flair combined with an aptitude for electronics, who are seeking a career in television, broadcasting and its associated industries. The course consists of the following components: vision and sound principles, microelectronic systems, computer graphics, transmission principles, radio and television systems, programme production principles, communications and media studies, electrical and electronic principles, electronics, mathematics, European studies, language

University of Sheffield

Department of English Literature
Shearwood Mount
Shearwood Road
Sheffield S10 2TD
Tel: 0742 768555 x6043/6276

BA (Hons) English Literature

Students may study one or two Special Subjects in Film in their second or third years

MA Theatre and Film

One-year course on elements of both theatre and film studies. Work on all topics is assessed at the conclusion of the course

Sheffield Hallam University

Section of Communication Studies, Film and Media
36 Collegiate Crescent
Sheffield S10 2BP
Tel: 0742 720911

BA (Hons) Communication Studies

Course covers all aspects of communications, one area being Mass Communication. Option course in TV Fictions in Year 3. Some practical work

MA/PgD/Certificate in Communication Studies

Part-time course to gain certificate in 3 terms, Diploma in 6 terms, MA in 8 terms. Aims to develop theoretical understandings and analytical skills in relation to the processes and practices of communication in modern society. Students attend for two sessions of 2+ hours each week

School of Cultural Studies
Psalter Lane
Sheffield S11 8UZ
Tel: 0742 532601/720911
Film and Media Studies Programme

BA (Hons) Film Studies

BA (Hons) Media Studies

The Film and Media Studies Programme consists of two degree routes. The courses provide opportunities for the study of film and a range of media (including television, radio and journalism) from a variety of perspectives including historical development, social, political and economic contexts, and the artistic and aesthetic dimensions of film and media. The courses also provide a grounding in basic media production skills with units in film, video etc and scriptwriting in all years

BA (Hons) History of Art, Design and Film

Film studies is a major component of this course. Year 1: introduction to film analysis and history. Year 2: special study on Hollywood. Year 3:

critical and theoretical studies in Art, Design and Film and Contemporary Film Theory and Practice. No practical component

MA Film Studies
Two-year part-time course; two evenings per week, plus dissertation to be written over two terms in a third year. Main areas of study: Problems of Method; The Classical Narrative Tradition; British Cinema 1927-45; British Independent Cinema 1966-84. No practical component

P BA (Hons) Fine Art (Combined and Media Arts)
After initial work with a range of media, students can specialise in film and/ or video. Film productions range from short 8mm films to 16mm documentaries or widescreen features, to small 35mm productions

Northern Media School
School of Cultural Studies
5 Brown Street
Sheffield S1 2BS
Tel: 0742 753511
Fax: 0742 756818

P PG Diploma/MA Film & Television Production: Fiction Documentary/Non-fiction
We run highly targeted vocational one-year film and video courses in both Fiction and Documentary/ Factual film and video. These are designed specifically for those with substantial experience in film and video or a related field, and students produce work to full broadcast standard. Specialisms: Production and Direction; lighting camera and sound; film and video post-production; scriptwriting for film, TV and radio (fiction); acting for film, TV and radio (fiction); research (documentary); unit management (documentary)

The Business School, South Bank University

(in collaboration with South Thames College)
2-20 Walworth Road
London SE1
Tel: 071 277 1091
Fax: 071 252 6971

P BSc (Hons) Media and Society
Three-year course. Combines courses about the role of media with practical experience of television, audio, print and photographic production. Each year is divided into two semesters, and within that time a student must complete 8 units. At every level students do academic and practical work simultaneously. Year 1: Image Manipulation and the Mass Media in Britain; Year 2: Ways of Seeing and the Mass Media in the International Context; Year 3: Practical Implementation of Critical Work

The South Manchester College

School of Art and Design
Arden Centre
Sale Road
Northenden
Manchester M23 0DD
Tel: 061 998 5511 x165

P B/TEC/NVQ Level 3 in Audio Visual Design
Multi-disciplinary course working between video, film animation, photography, graphics, sound and tape/slide. Assessment is continuous based on practical projects linked to theoretical studies

South Thames College

Department of Design and Media
Wandsworth High Street
London SW18 2PP
Tel: 081 870 2241
Fax: 081 874 6163

P B/TEC Higher National Certificate in Design (Communication) – Television Production
Two-year part-time course. BKSTS approved. All students experience every aspect of making both portable single camera (location) and multi-camera (studio) television programmes, starting with discussion of a brief with a 'client' and submitting a programme proposal, through the implementation of the programme production to the submission of the finished product. In Year 1 every student produces and directs one studio programme and in Year 2 one single camera programme, plus a final production in a form chosen by the student. In addition to the practical work there are lectures, tutorials and visits to production companies

The University of Southampton

School of Education
Faculty of Educational Studies
Southampton
Hampshire SO9 5NH
Tel: 0703 593387
Fax: 0703 593556

Postgraduate Certificate in Education
This one-year initial training course for secondary/6th form teachers offers specialist work in Media Studies as an integral part of English Drama and Media Studies

Certificate and Diploma in Advanced Educational Studies – Media Education
Certificate is one year course involving 60 hours of contact time; the Diploma is taken over two years, with 120 hours of contact time. Both include a range of media courses. The Certificate is also available as a distance learning package, involving 240 hours of independent study

MA (Ed) Media Education
The MA in Education is run on a modular basis as a full- or part-time taught course. The course as a whole requires the completion of 12 15-hour units and a supervised dissertation. Included are television studies, media education, video in education, response studies and others

MPhil and PhD
Research degrees in any area of Media Education, Media Studies, Educational Broadcasting and Educational Technology are available

School of Modern Languages
Southampton SO9 5NH
Tel: 0703 592256/592389
Fax: 0703 593288

MA Culture and Society in Contemporary Europe
A core course of weekly lectures and seminars examines a series of issues in contemporary European culture and society. Accompanied by an option course chosen from three topics including Contemporary European Cinema

Staffordshire University

School of Arts
Department of History of Art and Design
College Road
Stoke on Trent ST4 2DE
Tel: 0782 744531
Fax: 0782 746113

BA (Hons) History of Art and Design
An introductory course in film studies is an optional module at level 1. During levels 2 and 3 a number of optional modules are also offered which include classical Hollywood cinema; New German cinema; representations and responses to Empire; European cinema in the 1920s; Czech cinema; and film comedy. The level 3 dissertation of 8,000 words may deal exclusively with film

BA (Hons) Film, Television and Radio Studies
An academic course with some practical components. Students take 12 modules in each year. Level 1 modules include broadcasting history; European cinema in the 1920s; media technology; writing for radio. Level 2 modules include alternative practices in film and broadcasting; gender in film and television; music and the audio visual media; script project; production project. Level 3 modules include African cinema; British broadcast

drama; contemporary American cinema; post-war west European cinema; the radio feature; surrealist cinema

University of Stirling

Stirling FK9 4LA
Tel: 0786 467520
Fax: 0786 451335

BA (Hons) in Film and Media Studies (Single and Joint Honours)
Four-year degree in which students follow courses in the theory and analysis of all the principal media. All students take courses in the theories of mass communication and in cultural theories, as well as problems of textual analysis and then select from a range of options, including practical courses in the problems of news reporting in radio and TV and in TV documentary. As a joint honours degree Film and Media Studies can be combined with a variety of other subjects

BA General Degree
Students can build a component of their degree in film and media studies ranging from as much as eight units (approximately 50% of their degree) if they take a major in the subject, down to as little as three if they wish merely to complete a Part 1 major. For the most part students follow the same units as do Film and Media Studies Honours students

MSc/Diploma in Media Management
One-year full-time programme consisting of two taught semesters (Sept-May) followed by a dissertation (May-Aug). Internationally oriented and comparative in approach, the course offers media practitioners a wider analytical perspective on the key issues affecting their work and offers graduates a rigorous foundation for a career in the media industry. Areas covered include media policy and regulation, media economics, management and marketing, analytical methods and case studies and advanced media theory

MLitt and PhD
Applications are encouraged for research in a number of areas of film and media studies including: national and cultural identity, screen interpretation, reception study, sociology of journalism, comparative media analysis

Suffolk College

Faculty of Creative Studies
Rope Walk
Ipswich
Suffolk IP4 1LT
Tel: 0473 255885
Fax: 0473 230054

P B/TEC HND in Design Communication
A two-year course with options in film/TV graphics, animation and art direction. Students complete a period of work experience with employers in film and TV companies. Facilities include two colour TV studios, post-production facilities for film and video, and a film animation unit. After the two years students can enter the third year BA (Hons) Art and Design, which is part of the Suffolk Modular Degree programme

B/TEC National Diploma in Media
A two-year full time course which provides students with a broad knowledge of media activities and working practices, command of written and spoken English, interviewing and presentation skills and familiarity with desk top publishing, sound recording and video production. Students choose specialist options from: print editing, origination and production, recording and production for sound, or writing and production for film and TV

The University of Sunderland

School of Arts, Design and Communications
Forster Building
Chester Road
Sunderland SR1 3RL
Tel: 091 515 2161
Fax: 091 515 2178

BA (Hons) Communication Studies
Study of linguistics, psychology and sociology in relation to inter-personal communications and mass communication. The course is primarily academic, but includes practical study of radio, video and computing. Options include: Perspectives on Visual Communications, The Languages of Film and Representations of Women in Painting and Film

BA (Hons) Media Studies
Comprises study of social, historical and artistic aspects of the mass media and popular culture together with development of practical skills in media arts. Public community radio station, Wear FM, is based on campus, and provides practical experience. TV studio, dark rooms and computer systems also in use

MA in Cultural and Textual Studies
One-year full-time or two-year part-time MA. Postgraduate courses are constructed from a wide range of modules, two of which are compulsory. These compulsory modules provide students with a flexible theoretical foundation, and a multi-media and comparative study of verbal and visual forms of cultural communication, representing both 'high' and 'popular' culture. Students are then asked to choose three other modules, and to write a dissertation which allows them to specialise in film studies if they wish

School of Arts, Design and Communications
Ashburne House
Backhouse Park
Ryhope Road
Sunderland SR2 7EF
Tel: 091 515 2113/36
Fax: 091 515 2132

BA (Hons) Creative Arts Studies
Embraces a variety of combinations of dance, drama, music and the visual arts. Students learn through practical and critical modes, developing knowledge and understanding of common and distinctive aspects of the creative arts. At least 2 art forms are studied

University of Sussex

School of Cultural and Community Studies
Arts Building, Falmer
Brighton BN1 9QN
Tel: 0273 678019
Fax: 0273 678466

BA Media Studies
The degree course in Media Studies enables students to develop a critical understanding of the press, cinema, radio and television and of the particular character of media communications. The media are studied in their historical development, as social and economic institutions, as technologies and techniques of communication, and as interlocking with other social circuits for the relay of meanings and values. The Major in Media Studies is taught in two Schools of Studies – Cultural and Community Studies (CCS) and European Studies (EURO): different School Courses accompany it according to the School. The course in EURO also involves study of a modern European language and an additional year abroad in Europe

BA English with Media Studies

BA Music and Media Studies
A three-year full-time degree course which includes analysis of television, film and the press, together with some opportunity to be involved in practical television, video and radio production

MA in Media Studies
The MA comprises a two-term core course in media

theory and research on which students study the conceptual, methodological and policy related issues emerging from the study of the media. In addition, students choose, in each of the first two terms, an optional course from: the image in consumer society; media technology and everyday life; Hollywood: industry and imaginary; media, state and nation; theories of representation: memories of the Holocaust; homosexuality, film and TV

Educational Development Building
Institute of Education
University of Sussex
Brighton BN1 9RG
Tel: 0273 606755
Fax: 0273 678466

MA Language, the Arts and Education
Full-time and two-year part-time course, for both art-makers and for teachers in schools, FE and HE. Though work on film/TV forms only a small part of the taught seminar courses, students can specialise in the film/ TV area for all written and practical work

Swansea Institute of Higher Education

Townhill Road
Swansea SA2 0UT
Tel: 0792 203482
Fax: 0792 208683

BA (Hons) Art and Media Studies
Three-year degree. Includes a substantial amount of practical work, of which video and tape-slide form a major element. The Modern English Studies option includes Film and TV Studies (no practical component)

BA (Hons) Humanities
Three-year degree with options. Modern English studies option includes film and TV studies (no practical element)

BEd Primary
This course includes a Literature and Media Studies main subject option

Thames Valley University, London

(formerly Polytechnic of West London)
Department of Humanities
St Mary's Road
Ealing
London W5 5RF
Tel: 081 579 5000

BA (Hons) Humanities
Students take 16 units, of which 10 may be in media studies, including radio production, video production and computer videographics

MA Cultural Studies
Part-time taught evening course of six units plus dissertation. Topics include film and television, popular culture. No practical component

Trinity and All Saints

(A College of the University of Leeds)
Brownberrie Lane
Horsforth
Leeds LS18 5HD
Tel: 0532 584341
Fax: 0532 581148

BA (Hons) Public Media
Three-year combined honours course, of which half is devoted to professional studies in public media and half in academic studies from another area. Film and TV studies is a major component within the course, which includes some practical work

University of Ulster at Belfast

Faculty of Art and Design
York Street
Belfast BT15 1ED
Tel: 0232 328515
Fax: 0232 321048

BA (Hons) Fine Art
BA (Hons) Design
BA (Hons) Combined Studies in Art and Design
B/TEC HND in Design Communication
Minor component units in theoretical and some practical elements of film, video and media studies as part of the core studies of all BA courses. Combined Studies students undertake a greater Media Studies input. Fine Art students may specialise in Fine Art video as part of their final studio work. Design students may take video production as part of their graphic design studio work. Design Communication students all take video production project work in Year 1 and as a major option in Year 2

P BA (Hons) Visual Communication
This new course has practical and theoretical film/video/media studies available to all its students and a specialist video degree pathway called Screen Based Imaging. Fine Art students may specialise in Fine Art video in Years 2 and 3. Other courses take what they need from the modules available across the Faculty

University of Ulster at Coleraine

Co Londonderry
Northern Ireland
BT52 1SA
Tel: 0265 44141

BA (Hons) Media Studies
Three-year course integrating theoretical, critical and practical approaches to film, TV, photography, radio and the press. Important practical component

MA in Media Studies
A two-year part-time course combining advanced study of the mass media with media practice. There are also specialist options dealing with media education and cultural policy. MA is awarded 40% on coursework and exams, 60% on dissertation (which may incorporate production element)

MPhil and DPhil
Students are accepted for MPhil and DPhil by thesis. Particular expertise is offered in the area of the media and Ireland, although supervision is provided in most areas of Media Studies

University of Wales, College of Cardiff

PO Box 908
French Section
EUROS
Cardiff CF1 3YQ
Tel: 0222 874000

BA French
Study of French cinema included as part of optional courses. Small practical component

BA German
Study of contemporary German cinema forms part of both compulsory and optional courses

University of Warwick

Joint School of Film and Literature
Faculty of Arts
Coventry CV4 7AL
Tel: 0203 523523

BA Joint Degree in Film and Literature
Four courses offered each year, two in film and two in literature. Mainly film studies but some TV included. No practical component

BA French or Italian with Film Studies
This degree puts a particular emphasis on film within and alongside its studies of French or Italian language, literature and society. No practical component

Various Degrees
Options in film studies can be taken as part of undergraduate degrees in other departments. No practical component

MA in Film and Television Studies
Taught courses on Textual Analysis, Methods in Film History, Modernity and Innovation, and Issues of Representation

MA, MPhil and PhD
Students are accepted for research degrees

University of Westminster

School of Communication
18-22 Riding House Street
London W1P 7PD
Tel: 071 486 5811

P BA (Hons) Film, Video and Photographic Arts
Modular degree with two pathways: Film and Television, and Photography and

Multimedia. Film and TV students combine theoretical study with practical productions. The Film and Television Pathway is BECTU-accredited. The principal aim of the Film and Television pathway is to familiarise students with the main critical concepts and practices which have shaped the development of international film and television culture, and to develop understanding of and practical abilities in the creative film and television process. It is expected that in Year 3 students will be able to sustain independent and creative work in areas of both theory and practice

BA (Hons) Media Studies

This degree studies the social context in which the institutions of mass communications operate, including film and television, and teaches the practice of print and broadcasting journalism and video production. On levels 2 and 3 students choose one of the following pathways: radio, journalism or video production. The course gives equal emphasis to theory/criticism and practice. The video pathway is accredited by BECTU

Linked MA and Postgraduate Diploma in Film and Television Studies

Advanced level part-time course (evenings and study weekends) concerned with theoretical aspects of film and TV. Modular credit and accumulation scheme, with exemption for work previously done. Postgraduate Diploma normally awarded after two years (70 credits), MA after three years (120 credits). Modules offered: Authorship, Structuralism, Realism and Anti-Realism, the Film and TV Audience, Problems of Method, Hollywood, Psychoanalysis, Third World Cinema, Issues in British Film Culture, Public Service Broadcasting, TV Genres and Gender, the Documentary Tradition, British TV Drama, Soviet Cinema, Production Studies. No practical component

MPhil and PhD Film and Television Studies (CNAA)

Research degrees in film and television history, theory and criticism. Applicants should have the Postgraduate Diploma and the MA in Film and Television Studies or equivalent qualifications and be able to submit a detailed research proposal

Short Courses in Film and Television

A range of introductory and specialist courses in film and TV skills, and in theory

Centre for Communication and Information Studies
235 High Holborn
London WC1V 7DN
Tel: 071 911 5157
Fax: 071 911 5156

MA in Communication

A one-year full-time course consisting of six modules taught over two semesters plus an independently researched dissertation on aspects of the mass media or telecommunications

MPhil and PhD research degrees in Communication and Information studies

West Surrey College of Art and Design

Department of Fine Art and Audio-Visual Studies
Falkner Road
The Hart
Farnham
Surrey GU9 7DS
Tel: 0252 722441

P BA (Hons) Photography

BA (Hons) Film and Video

BA (Hons) Animation

The approach in each course is essentially practical, structured to encourage a direct and fundamental appraisal of photography, film, video and animation through practice and by theoretical study. 70% practical, 30% theoretical. Courses are BECTU accredited

BA (Hons) Media Studies

A range of theoretical approaches to the mass media are examined. Emphasis is placed on the critical application of such theories to the actual production and consumption of media, primarily visual, culture. Units on professional practice, the European context of media production, and the learning of a modern European language prepare students for a career in the media industry

Weymouth College

Cranford Avenue
Weymouth
Dorset DT4 7LQ
Tel: 0305 208856

P B/TEC National Diploma in Media

Two-year full-time course designed as a solid foundation in a range of media skills but which allows for some specialisation in either television and video or sound and radio

Wimbledon School of Art

Merton Hall Road
London SW19 3QA
Tel: 081 540 0231
Fax: 081 543 1750

P BA (Hons) Fine Art

Students enrol in either Painting or Sculpture. Some Painting students study film and/or video

University of Wolverhampton

School of Humanities and Social Sciences
Castle View
Dudley
West Midlands DY1 3HR
Tel: 0902 323400
Fax: 0902 323379

Modular Degree and Diploma Scheme

The programmes (Dip HE, two-year full-time and BA/BA (Hons) three-year full-time), offer a range of subjects which include critical and historical work in Film, TV and the Media. Students select programmes to include subjects on a Major/Minor or Joint basis from the following: Media and Communication, Theatre Studies, Art and Design History, History, French. These may be combined with a wide range of other subjects

DISTRIBUTORS (NON-THEATRICAL)

Companies here control UK rights for non-theatrical distribution (for domestic and group viewing in schools, hospitals, airlines and so on). For an extensive list of titles available non-theatrically with relevant distributors' addresses, see the 'British National Film & Video Catalogue', available for reference from BFI Library Services and major public reference libraries. Other sources of film and video are listed under Archives and Film Libraries (p74) and Workshops (p316)

ABC Films
via Glenbuck Films

Academy Television
104 Kirkstall Road
Leeds LS3 1JS
Tel: 0532 461528
Fax: 0532 429522
Pamela Cook
Maria Pickersgill
Sue Yeadon
Distributor for many ITV companies, including Yorkshire, Thames, Tyne Tees and Channel 4. Has educational and 'Healthwatch' catalogues, and further industry catalogue, providing training packages for companies

Aegis Healthcare
via Training Services

Air India
Publicity Dept
17-18 New Bond Street
London W1Y 0BD
Tel: 071 493 4050
Fax: 071 629 0515

Albany Video Distribution
Battersea Studios
Television Centre
Thackeray Road
London SW8 3TW
Tel: 071 498 6811
Fax: 071 498 2104
Val Martin
Education videos

Amber Films
5 Side
Newcastle upon Tyne
NE1 3JE
Tel: 091 232 2000
Fax: 091 230 3217

Artificial Eye Film Co
via Glenbuck Films

Arts Council of Great Britain
via Concord Video and Film Council

Audience Planners
4 Beadles Lane
Oxted
Surrey RH8 9JJ
Tel: 0883 717194
Fax: 0883 714480

Australia Rail, Australia Tourist Commission
and
Austrian Tourist Office
via Audience Planners

BBC Training Videos
Woodlands
80 Wood Lane
London W12 0TT
Tel: 081 576 2361
Fax: 081 576 2867

BFI Film & Video Distribution
(now incorporating Glenbuck Films)
21 Stephen Street
London W1P 1PL
Tel: 071 255 1444
Fax: 071 580 5830
Sylvia Marshall
General catalogue available via BFI Publications on 071 636 3289. Subject supplements available on request from above or from BFI Publications

BFI Production
via BFI Film & Video Distribution

Hugh Baddeley Productions
via Viewtech Film and Video

Banking Information Service
via Multilink Film Library

Barclays Bank Film Library
via Multilink Film Library and Training Services

Bermuda Tourism
via Audience Planners

Big Bear Records
PO Box 944
Birmingham B16 8UT
Tel: 021 454 7020/8100
Fax: 021 454 9996

Black Audio Film Collective
7-12 Greenland Street
Camden
London NW1 0ND
Tel: 071 267 0846
Fax: 071 267 0845
Lina Gopaul
Avril Johnson
David Lawson
Black independent films (see Distributors (theatrical) for titles)

Blue Dolphin Films
via Glenbuck Films

Boulton Hawker Films
Hadleigh
near Ipswich
Suffolk IP7 5BG
Tel: 0473 822235
Fax: 0473 824519
Educational films and videos, specialising in health education, biology, and social welfare

Brent Walker Films
via Glenbuck Films

British Coal Enterprise
via Training Services

British Gas Video Library
Poplar Hall
Little Tey Road
Feering
Colchester
Essex CO5 9RP
Tel: 0376 573292

British Home Entertainment
via Glenbuck Films

British Telecom Film Library
via Training Services and Education Distribution Service

British Transport Films
via FAME (see under Archives & Film Libraries)

British Universities Film and Video Council
55 Greek Street
London W1V 5LR
Tel: 071 734 3687
Fax: 071 287 3914
Videocassettes and videodiscs for sale direct from above address. Hire via Concord Video and Film Council

Bryanston Films
via Filmbank

Bulgarian Tourist Office
via Audience Planners

John Burder Films
7 Saltcoats Road
London W4 1AR
Tel: 081 995 0547
Fax: 081 995 3376
Training and safety programmes

CBS Broadcast
via Glenbuck Films

CCD Product & Design
via Training Services

CFL Vision
PO Box 35
Wetherby
Yorks LS23 7EX
Tel: 0937 541010
Fax: 0937 541083

CTVC Video
Hillside Studios
Merry Hill Road
Bushey
Watford WD2 1DR
Tel: 081 950 4426
Fax: 081 950 1437
Ann Harvey
Christian, moral and social programmes

Caledonian MacBrayne
via Audience Planners

Canada House Film and Video Library
Canada House
Trafalgar Square
London SW1Y 5BJ
Tel: 071 258 6405
Fax: 071 258 6322
Maggie Warwick
Features, animation, wildlife and documentaries from Canada on free loan to film societies, educational institutions, etc

Castle Target
via Glenbuck Films

Castrol Video and Film Library
Athena Avenue
Swindon
Wiltshire SN2 6EQ
Tel: 0793 693402
Fax: 0793 511479
Motorsport films

Cayman Islands Tourist Office
via Audience Planners

Central Independent Television
Video Resource Unit
Broad Street
Birmingham B1 2JP
Tel: 021 643 9898
Dee Stone

Central Office of Information
via CFL Vision

Channel Four International
60 Charlotte Street
London W1P 2AX
Tel: 071 927 8541
Fax: 071 580 2622
Stephen Mowbray
Also via Glenbuck Films

Children's Film and Television Foundation
via Glenbuck Films. For further details, see under Organisations

Cinema Action
27 Winchester Road
London NW3 3NR
Tel/Fax: 071 722 5781
Features and documentaries 'provoking the bourgeoisie'

Cinenova (Women's Film and Video Distribution)
113 Roman Road
London E2 0HU
Tel: 081 981 6828
Fax: 081 983 4441
Promotion and distribution of films and videos by women spanning ninety years of filmmaking from around the world

Columbia TriStar Films (UK)
via Filmbank

Concord Video and Film Council
201 Felixstowe Road
Ipswich
Suffolk IP3 9BJ
Tel: 0473 715754/726012
Videos and films for hire/ sale on domestic and international social issues – counselling, development, education, the arts, race and gender issues, disabilities, etc – for training and discussion

Connaught Training
(formerly Gower)
Gower House
Croft Road
Aldershot
Hants GU11 3HR
Tel: 0252 331551
Fax: 0252 344405
Customer Service Dept
Training videos, looseleaf activities and management games

Connoisseur Films and **Contemporary Films**
via Glenbuck Films

Coronet/MTI International
via Viewtech Film and Video

DS Information Systems (National Audio Visual Library)
Arts Building
Normal College
Siliwen Road
Bangor
Gwynedd LL57 2DZ
Tel: 0248 370144
Fax: 0248 351415
B Mullett
Educational audio visual aids consisting of videotapes, 16mm films, slides and overhead projector transparencies available for hire or purchase

Danish Embassy
55 Sloane Street
London SW1X 9SR
Tel: 071 333 0200
Fax: 071 333 0270

Danish Tourist Board
via Audience Planners

Darvill Associates
280 Chartridge Lane
Chesham
Bucks HP5 2SG
Tel: 0494 783643
Fax: 0494 784873
Also available via Glenbuck Films

Derann Film Services
99 High Street
Dudley
W Midlands DY1 1QP
Tel: 0384 233191
Fax: 0384 456488
8mm package movie distributors, and bulk video duplicators

The Walt Disney Co
via Filmbank

Walt Disney Educational Productions
via Viewtech Film and Video

Duke of Edinburgh Awards
via Glenbuck Films

Dutch Embassy Films
via DS Information Systems

Educational and Television Films
247a Upper Street
London N1 1RU

Tel: 071 226 2298
Fax: 071 226 8016
Documentary films from USSR and Eastern Europe. Archive film library

Educational Media Film & Video
235 Imperial Drive
Rayners Lane
Harrow
Middx HA2 7HE
Tel: 081 868 1908/1915
Fax: 081 868 1991
Lynda Morrell
Distributors of British educational, health (including Nurse Education), safety and business/training programmes. Also represent many overseas producers. Free catalogue available on request

Education Distribution Service
Unit 2
Drywall House Estate
Castle Road
Sittingbourne
Kent ME10 3RL
Tel: 0795 427614
Fax: 0795 474871

Electric Pictures
via Glenbuck Films and BFI Film & Video Distribution

Electricity Association Video Library
30 Millbank
London SW1P 4RD
Tel: 071 344 5827
Fax: 071 344 5800

Entertainment Films
via Filmbank

Essential (16mm) Films
via Concord Video and Film Council

Esso Videos
via Esso Information Service
PO Box 695
Sudbury
Suffolk CO10 6YM
Tel: 0787 370272
Fax: 0787 880866

Euro-London Films
via Glenbuck Films

Excel Training
via Training Services

Filmbank Distributors
Grayton House
498-504 Fulham Road
London SW6 5NH
Tel: 071 386 9909/5411
Fax: 071 381 2405
Handles 16mm and video on behalf of major, and some other, UK distributors

Film Booking Offices
211 The Chambers
Chelsea Harbour
London SW10 0XF
Tel: 071 734 5298 / 071 437 1572
Fax: 071 352 4182
Margaret Atlas
Distributors and booking agents for film societies and universities

Films of Scotland
via SCET Training Resources

FinnImage
via Darvill Associates

Finnish Embassy
via Audience Planners

First Independent Films
via Glenbuck Films

First Training
via Training Services

Ford Film and Video Library
Audio Visual Services
Ford Motor Company
Room 1/455
Eagle Way
Brentwood
Essex CM13 3BW
Tel: 0277 252766
Fax: 0277 252896
Elizabeth Pelling

GTO
and
Gala Film Library
via Glenbuck Films

Gateway Films
via Viewtech Film and Video

German National Tourist Office
via Audience Planners

bfi **Glenbuck Films**
(now incorporated in BFI Film & Video Distribution)
21 Stephen Street
London W1P 1PL
Tel: 071 957 8938
Fax: 071 580 5830
Handles non-theatrical 16mm, 35mm and video

Sheila Graber Animation
50 Meldon Avenue
South Shields
Tyne and Wear
NE34 0EL
Tel/Fax: 091 455 4985
Over 70 animated shorts available – 16mm, video and computer interactive

Granada Television Film Library
via Concord Video and Film Council

Greek National Tourist Office
via Audience Planners

HandMade Films
via Glenbuck Films

City of Heidelberg
via Audience Planners

IAC (Institute of Amateur Cinematographers)
24c West Street
Epsom
Surrey KY18 7RJ
Tel: 0372 739672

Imperial War Museum
Department of Film (Loans)
Lambeth Road
London SE1 6HZ
Tel: 071 416 5000
Fax: 071 416 5379
Documentaries, newsreels and propaganda films from the Museum's film archive

India Government Tourist Office
via Audience Planners

Institute of Contemporary Arts
and
Intercontinental Films
via Glenbuck Films

Jamaica Tourist Board
and
Japan Tourist Office
via Audience Planners

Robert Kingston Films
via Glenbuck Films

Leeds Animation Workshop
(A Women's Collective)
45 Bayswater Row
Leeds LS8 5LF
Tel: 0532 484997
Producers and distributors of animated films on social issues

London Film Makers' Co-op
42 Gloucester Avenue
London NW1 8JD
Tel: 071 586 4806
Fax: 071 483 0068
Experimental/art-based films: 2,000 classic and recent titles for hire from 1920s to current work, new catalogue available

London Video Access (LVA)
3rd Floor
5-7 Buck Street
London NW1 8NJ
Tel: 071 284 4588
Fax: 071 267 6078
Britain's national centre for video and new media art, housing an extensive collection of video art. Work dating from the 1970s to the present

Longman Training
Longman House
Burnt Mill
Harlow
Essex CM20 2JE
Tel: 0279 623927
Fax: 0279 623795
Amanda Alexander
Producer of video-based training for health and safety (Millbank) and skills development. Also supplier of technology-based training

Luxembourg National Tourist Office
via Audience Planners

MTV Finland
via Darvill Associates

Macau Tourist Office
via Audience Planners

Mainline Pictures
via Glenbuck Films and BFI Film & Video Distribution

Malaysian Tourist Office
via Audience Planners

Mayfair Entertainments (UK)
and
Medusa Communications
via Glenbuck Films

Melrose Film Productions
16 Bromells Road
Clapham Common
London SW4 0BL
Tel: 071 627 8404

Multilink Film Library
5 The Square
Vicarage Farm Road
Peterborough PE1 5TS
Tel: 0733 67622
Distributors of films/videos to the education sector

Muppet Meeting Films™
via Video Arts (©Jim Henson Productions Inc)

National Film and Television School
Beaconsfield Studios
Beaconsfield
Bucks HP9 1LG
Tel: 0494 671234
Fax: 0494 674042

Netherlands Information Service
and
Netherlands PD Films
via Darvill Associates

Norwegian Embassy Films
via DS Information Systems

Oasis (UK) Films
via Filmbank and Glenbuck Films

Open University Educational Enterprises
12 Cofferidge Close
Stony Stratford
Milton Keynes
MK11 1BY
Tel: 0908 261662
Fax: 0908 261001
Diana Ruault

Out on a Limb
Battersea Studios
Television Centre
Thackeray Road
London SW8 3TW
Tel: 071 498 9643
Fax: 071 498 2104
Films and videos made by or of particular interest to lesbians and gay men

Pacific International Enterprises
via Glenbuck Films

Pathé Cannon
via Filmbank

Edward Patterson Associates
Treetops
Cannongate Road
Hythe
Kent CT21 5PT
Tel/Fax: 0303 264195
Health, safety and education video programming

Portuguese National Tourist Office
via Audience Planners

Post Office Video and Film Library and Education Service
PO Box 145
Sittingbourne
Kent ME10 1NH
Tel: 0795 426465
Fax: 0795 474871
Includes many video programmes and supporting educational material including curriculum guidelines

The Production Gallery
6 Carsons Drive
Great Cornard
Sudbury
Suffolk CO10 0NE
Tel/Fax: 0787 880364
Angela Bryant
Educational videos for home use produced by its chief executive ('Make Your Mark' series)

Promotions Sound & Vision
via Training Services

RoSPA
Film Library
Head Office

Cannon House
Priory Queensway
Birmingham B4 6BS
Tel: 021 200 2461
Fax: 021 200 1254
Safety films

RSPCA
Causeway
Horsham
West Sussex RH12 1HG
Tel: 0403 264181
Fax: 0403 241048
New catalogue available

Radio Netherlands Television
and
Radio Sweden International
via Darvill Associates

Rank Film Library
via Filmbank and Viewtech Film and Video

Retake Film and Video Collective
19 Liddell Road
London NW6 2EW
Tel: 071 328 4676

Royal College of Art
Department of Film and Television
Kensington Gore
London SW7 2EU
Tel: 071 584 5020 x412
Fax: 071 589 0178

SCET Training Resources
74 Victoria Crescent Road
Dowanhill
Glasgow G12 9JN
Tel: 041 334 9314
Fax: 041 334 6519
Educational, training and general interest titles

Scottish Tourist Board Films
via SCET Training Resources

Shell Video Library
Unit A2
Faraday Road
Newbury
Berks RG13 2AD
Tel: 0635 551156

Southbrook Film Productions
via Glenbuck Films

South West Arts
Bradninch Place
Gandy Street
Exeter EX4 3LS
Tel: 0392 218188
Fax: 0392 413554

Steel Bank Film Co-op
Brown Street
Sheffield S1 2BS
Tel: 0742 721235
Fax: 0742 795225
TV documentaries, drama features, arts programmes

Supreme Films
via Glenbuck Films

Swedish Embassy (Cultural Dept)
via Darvill Associates and Glenbuck Films

Swiss National Tourist Office/ Swiss Federal Railways
Swiss Centre
Swiss Court
London W1V 8EE
Tel: 071 734 1921
Fax: 071 437 4577

TTT PlayBack Communications
via Video Arts

TV Choice
80-81 St Martin's Lane
London WC2N 4AA
Tel: 071 379 0873
Fax: 071 379 0263

Team Video Productions
Canalot
222 Kensal Road
London W10 5BN
Tel: 081 960 5536

Television History Centre
42 Queen Square
London WC1N 3AJ
Tel: 071 405 6627
Fax: 071 242 1426
Programmes for hire or purchase about work, health, women, community action, particularly suitable for educational discussion groups 16 plus
See also under Production Companies

Texaco Film Library
Public Affairs & Advertising Department
Texaco
1 West Ferry Circus
London E14 4HA
Tel: 071 719 3000
Fax: 071 719 5175
Neil van Coevorden

Thames Television Video Sales
via Academy Television

Touchstone Pictures
via Filmbank

Tourism Victoria/ Tasmania
via Audience Planners

Training Services
Brooklands House
29 Hythegate
Werrington
Peterborough PE4 7ZP
Tel: 0733 327337
Fax: 0733 575537
Christine Tipton

Transatlantic Films
17 Girdlers Road
London W14 0PS
Tel: 071 727 0132
Fax: 071 603 5049
Richard Banks

Twentieth Century Fox
via Filmbank

Twinray
via Glenbuck Films

UIP (UK)
via Filmbank

United States Travel and Tourism Administration
via Audience Planners

Vera Productions
30-38 Dock Street
Leeds LS10 1JF
Tel: 0532 428646
Fax: 0532 426937
Alison Garthwaite
Catherine Mitchell

Video Arts
Dumbarton House
68 Oxford Street
London W1N 9LA
Tel: 071 637 7288
Fax: 071 580 8103
Distributes the John Cleese training films; the full range of Playback videos; *Take It from the Top* – the David Frost interviews; *In Search of Excellence* and other films from the Nathan/Tyler Business Video Library. Video Arts also distributes a selection of meeting breaks from Playback; Mediamix and the Muppet Meeting Films

Video Communicators Pty
via Training Services

Viewtech Film and Video
161 Winchester Road
Brislington
Bristol BS4 3NJ
Tel: 0272 773422/717030
Fax: 0272 724292
Also via Glenbuck Films

Virgin Films
and
Visual Programme Systems
via Glenbuck Films

WFA Media & Cultural Centre
9 Lucy Street
Manchester M15 4BX
Tel: 061 848 9782/5
Fax: 061 848 9783
Fiona Johnson

Warner Bros Films
via Filmbank

Washington DC Convention Bureau
via Audience Planners

Weintraub
via Filmbank

Welsh Arts Council
Film, Video & TV Dept.
Museum Place
Cardiff CF1 3NX
Tel: 0222 394711
Fax: 0222 221447

West Derbyshire Tourist Office
via Audience Planners

Westbourne Film Distribution
1st Floor
17 Westbourne Park Road
London W2 5PX
Tel: 071 221 1998
Fax: 071 833 2605
Classic children's films
The Singing Ringing Tree
The Tinderbox

The University of Westminster
School of Communications
18-22 Riding House Street
London W1P 7PD
Tel: 071 911 5000 x2726

Workcare
and
York MDM
via Training Services

DISTRIBUTORS (THEATRICAL)

These are companies which acquire the UK rights to films for distribution to cinemas and, in many cases, also for sale to network TV, satellite, cable and video media. Listed is a selection of features certificated by the censor for those companies after April 1992, and/or some past releases or re-releases available during this period

Albany Video Distribution
Battersea Studios
Television Centre
Thackeray Road
London SW8 3TW
Tel: 071 498 6811
Fax: 071 498 2104
Films and video art

All American Leisure Group
6 Woodland Way
Petts Wood
Kent BR5 1ND
Tel: 0689 871535
Fax: 0689 871519

Apollo Film Distributors
14 Ensbury Park Road
Bournemouth BH9 2SJ
Tel: 0202 520962

Arrow Film Distributors
18 Watford Road
Radlett
Herts WD7 8LE
Tel: 0923 858306
Fax: 0923 859673
Distributors of new films
Europa Europa
Hellraiser III
Madame Bovary
Mistress
Sofie
Storyville

Artificial Eye Film Co
211 Camden High Street
London NW1 7BT
Tel: 071 267 6036/
482 3981
Fax: 071 267 6499
Blue
Un Coeur en Hiver
IP5
L.627
The Quince Tree Sun
Savage Nights
Tango
A Winter's Tale

Arts Council of Great Britain
See under Organisations

bfi BFI Film & Video Distribution
21 Stephen Street
London W1P 1PL
Tel: 071 255 1444
Fax: 071 580 5830
Features, including
Daughters of the Dust
Knife in the Water
Sure Fire
Shorts, including
A is for Autism
First Night
Heart Songs
Secret Joy of Falling Angels
Tale of the Fox

bfi BFI Production
29 Rathbone Street
London W1P 1AG
Tel: 071 636 5587
Fax: 071 580 9456
Sales and UK distribution of British independent features and shorts
Anchoress
Blue Black Permanent
Distant Voices, Still Lives
Elenya
Fellow Traveller
Psychotherapy
Wittgenstein
Young Soul Rebels

Black Audio Film Collective
7-12 Greenland Street
Camden
London NW1 0ND
Tel: 071 267 0846
Fax: 071 267 0845
Black independent films
Handsworth Songs
Mysteries of July
Seven Songs for Malcolm X
Testament
A Touch of the Tar Brush
Twilight City
Who Needs a Heart
See also under Distributors (Non-Theatrical)

Blue Dolphin Films
15-17 Old Compton Street
London W1V 6JR
Tel: 071 439 9511
Fax: 071 287 0370
The Butcher's Wife
Cool World
End of the Golden Weather
Hearts of Darkness
Naked Tango
Night of the Living Dead
The Two Jakes

Bordeaux Films International
22 Soho Square
London W1V 5FJ
Tel: 081 959 8556
See under Production Companies for list of films

BratPack Entertainment
Canalot Studios
222 Kensal Road
London W10 5BN
Tel: 081 969 7609
Fax: 081 969 2284
Distributors and producers of children's TV and video
Fingerprint Farm
Little Boy
Puppydog Tales
Puss in Boots
Ugly Duckling

Buena Vista International (UK)
Beaumont House
Kensington Village
Avonmore Road
London W14 8TS
Tel: 071 605 2890
Fax: 071 605 2827
The Adventures of Huck Finn
Aladdin
Aristocats
The Lion King
Sister Act 2
Stakeout 2
The 3 Musketeers
Tim Burton's The Nightmare before Christmas

John Burder Films
7 Saltcoats Road
London W4 1AR
Tel: 081 995 0547
Fax: 081 995 3376
Broadcast TV programmes
See also under Distributors (Non-Theatrical)

Cavalcade Films
Regent House
235-241 Regent Street
London W1R 8JU
Tel: 071 734 3147
Fax: 071 734 2403

Chain Production
11 Hornton Street
London W8 7NP
Tel: 071 937 1981
Fax: 071 376 0556
Specialist in Italian films: library of 1,000 titles available for UK exploitation. Releasing on video *Quiet Days in Clichy*; 'Sword and Sandals' Epics on Channel 4

Cinenova (Women's Film and Video Distribution)
113 Roman Road
London E2 0HU
Tel: 081 981 6828
Fax: 081 983 4441
Promotion and distribution of women's film and video
Privilege
Reservaat
Shoot for the Contents
The Third Woman
See also under Distributors (Non-Theatrical)

Columbia TriStar Films (UK)
19-23 Wells Street
London W1P 3FP
Tel: 071 580 2090
Fax: 071 436 0323
Feature releases from the Columbia and TriStar companies and Orion Pictures
Bitter Moon
Bram Stoker's Dracula
A Few Good Men
Husbands and Wives
A League of Their Own
Shadows and Fog
Single White Female
Thunderheart

Contemporary Films
24 Southwood Lawn Road
Highgate
London N6 5SF
Tel: 081 340 5715
Fax: 081 348 1238

Electric Pictures
15 Percy Street
London W1P 9FD
Tel: 071 636 1231
Fax: 071 636 1675
The Baby of Mâcon
Bodies Rest & Motion
Indochine
Leon the Pig Farmer
Mean Streets
Orlando
The Story of Qiu Ju
Tous les matins du monde

Elephant Entertainments
Theatre One
Ford Street
Coventry CV1 5FN
Tel: 0203 226490
Fax: 0203 258971

English Film Co
6 Woodland Way
Petts Wood
Kent BR5 1ND
Tel: 0689 871535
Fax: 0689 871519

Entertainment Film Distributors
27 Soho Square
London W1V 5FL
Tel: 071 439 1606
Fax: 071 734 2483
Boxing Helena
Damage
Much Ado About Nothing
Peter's Friends
Piano
Super Mario Bros
Surf Warriors
The Thief and the Cobbler

Feature Film Company
68-70 Wardour Street
London W1V 3HP
Tel: 071 734 2266
Fax: 071 494 0309
Big Wednesday
Slacker
Soft Top, Hard Shoulder
The Trial

Film and Video Umbrella
6a Orde Hall Street
London WC1N 3JW
Tel: 071 831 7753

Fax: 071 831 7746
Promoting experimental film and electronic arts
Art & Science
The Body in Extremis
Computer World
Naked City – recent film and video from New York
Seeing in the Dark – new work by Bill Viola
This Side of the Channel – a UK electronic image Retrospective
To Camera – three programmes of video and performance
What You See is What You Get – media constructions of political identity

Film Booking Offices
211 The Chambers
Chelsea Harbour
London SW10 0XF
Tel: 071 734 5298/071 437 1572
Fax: 071 352 4182

First Independent
69 New Oxford Street
London WC1A 1DG
Tel: 071 528 7767
Fax: 071 528 7770
Deep Cover
Honeymoon in Vegas
The Lawnmower Man
Mr Saturday Night
Naked
Nostradamus
Night and the City
Raining Stones

Gala Films
26 Danbury Street
Islington
London N1 8JU
Tel: 071 226 5085
Fax: 071 226 5897
The Accompanyist
Cup Final
The Double Life of Véronique
The Man in My Life
Mensonge
Mon Père, Ce Héros
The Old Lady who Walked in the Sea
Olivier, Olivier

bfi **Glenbuck Films**
British Film Institute
21 Stephen Street
London W1P 1PL
Tel: 081 957 8938
Fax: 081 580 5830

The Samuel Goldwyn Company
St George's House
14-17 Wells Street
London W1P 3FP
Tel: 071 436 5105
Fax: 071 580 6520
Golden Gate
Mr Wonderful
Much Ado About Nothing
Peter's Friends
The Program

Guild Film Distribution
Kent House
14-17 Market Place
Great Titchfield Street
London W1N 8AR
Tel: 071 323 5151
Fax: 071 631 3568
Chaplin
Cliffhanger
1492 – Conquest of Paradise
Hoffa
Malcolm X
Murder in the First
The Real McCoy
Stargate

HandMade Films (Distributors)
26 Cadogan Square
London SW1X 0JP
Tel: 071 584 8345
Fax: 071 584 7338
Eight projects currently in development; three for release in 1994, two to be shot in the US and one to be shot in the UK

Hemdale Film Distribution
21 Albion Street
London W2 2AS
Tel: 071 724 1010
Fax: 071 724 9168
John Smallcombe
Blood Red
The Boost
Chattahoochee
Criminal Law
Miracle Mile
Staying Together
Vampire's Kiss
War Party

ICA Projects
12 Carlton House Terrace
London SW1Y 5AH
Tel: 071 930 0493
Fax: 071 873 0051
Benny's Video
A Brighter Summer Day
Paris is Burning
Tetsuo II: Body Hammer
Triple Bogey on a Par 5 Hole
Vacas

MGM/UA see **United International Pictures (UK)**

Mainline Pictures
37 Museum Street
London WC1A 1LP
Tel: 071 242 5523
Fax: 071 430 0170
Chain of Desire
The Premonition
Ruby in Paradise
The Wedding Banquet

Mayfair Entertainment UK
9 St Martin's Court
London WC2N 4AJ
Tel: 071 895 0328
Fax: 071 895 0329
Après l'amour
Baraka
Belle Epoque
Daens
The Fencing Master
House of Angels
Mediterraneo
The Mystery of Edwin Drood

Medusa Communications
Regal Chambers
51 Bancroft
Hitchin
Herts SG5 1LL
Tel: 0462 421818
Fax: 0462 420393
See also under Video Labels

Metro Tartan
79 Wardour Street
London W1V 3TH
Tel: 071 734 8508/9
Fax: 071 287 2112
Bound and Gagged
The Cement Garden
Hardboiled
Jamón Jamón
Léolo
Man Bites Dog
One False Move
Who's the Man

Miracle Communications
69 New Oxford Street
London WC1A 1DG
Tel: 071 528 7767
Fax: 071 528 7772

New Realm Entertainments
2nd Floor
80-82 Wardour Street
London W1V 3LF
Tel: 071 437 9143
Fax: 0372 469816

Oasis Films
3rd Floor
155-157 Oxford Street
London W1R 1TB
Tel: 071 734 7477
Fax: 071 734 7470
A Bout de Souffle
The Lunatic
Manhunter
Speaking Parts
True Love
Venus Peter
Wings of Desire
Yaaba

Orbit Films
7-11 Kensington High Street
London W8 5NP
Tel: 071 221 5548
Fax: 071 727 0515
The Golden Years of Television: vintage product from the first decade of American TV, including features and serials

Out on a Limb
Battersea Studios
Television Centre
Thackeray Road
London SW8 3TW
Tel: 071 498 9643
Fax: 071 498 2104
Films and videos made by or of particular interest to lesbians and gay men
Being At Home With Claude
Damned If You Don't
Female Misbehaviour
Forbidden Love
My Father is Coming
No Skin Off My Ass
Seduction: The Cruel Woman
Virgin Machine

Paramount see **United International Pictures (UK)**

Poseidon Film Distributors
Hammer House
113 Wardour Street
London W1V 3TD
Tel: 071 734 4441
Fax: 071 437 0638
Autism
Dyslexia
Lysistrata

Rank Film Distributors
127 Wardour Street
London W1V 4AD
Tel: 071 437 9020
Fax: 071 434 3689
Candyman
Kalifornia
Posse: The Revenge of Jessie Lee
Red Rock West
Reservoir Dogs
Romeo is Bleeding
Strictly Ballroom
Young Americans

Squirrel Films Distribution
119 Rotherhithe Street
London SE16 4NF
Tel: 071 231 2209
Fax: 071 231 2119
Specialising in films for children
As You Like It
La Chasse aux Papillons
Une Epoque Formidable
Little Dorrit
The Little Gang
Sherlock Jr
Tales of Beatrix Potter
Le Tartuffe

Supreme Film Distributors
Premier House
77 Oxford Street
London W1R 1RB
Tel: 071 437 4415
Fax: 071 734 0924

TKO Communications
PO Box 130
Hove
East Sussex BN3 6QU
Tel: 0273 550088
Fax: 0273 540969
Adventures of Scaramouche
Catch Me a Spy
Diamond Mercenaries
Gallavants
The Mark of Zorro

Twentieth Century Fox Film Co
20th Century House
31-32 Soho Square
London W1V 6AP
Tel: 071 437 7766
Fax: 071 434 2170
Beverly Hillbillies
Ghost in the Machine
The Good Son
Hot Shots! Part Deux
Mrs Doubtfire
Once Upon a Forest
Rising Sun
Teenage Mutant Ninja Turtles III

UA (United Artists)
see **United International Pictures (UK)**

United International Pictures (UK)
Mortimer House
37-41 Mortimer Street
London W1A 2JL
Tel: 071 636 1655
Fax: 071 636 4118
(Accounts/Sales)
071 323 0121 (Publicity)
Releases product from Paramount, Universal, and MGM/UA
Beethoven
Far and Away
Housesitter
Jurassic Park
Patriot Games
Scent of a Woman
Sliver
Son of the Pink Panther

Universal
see **United International Pictures (UK)**

Warner Bros Distributors
135 Wardour Street
London W1V 4AP
Tel: 071 734 8400
Fax: 071 437 5521
Feature releases from Warner Bros, New Regency and Morgan Creek Productions
Dave
Demolition Man
Dennis
Free Willy
The Fugitive
Made in America
A Perfect World
The Secret Garden

Westbourne Film Distribution
First Floor
17 Westbourne Park Road
London W2 5PX
Tel: 071 221 1998
Fax: 071 833 2605
Classic children's films
The Singing Ringing Tree
The Tinderbox

Winstone Film Distributors
80-82 Wardour Street
London W1V 3LF
Tel: 071 439 4525
Fax: 071 437 0584
Sub-distributors for Electric, Oasis, Medusa, Goldwyn, Out on a Limb and Metro Tartan (latter three restricted)
Being At Home With Claude
Leon the Pig Farmer
One False Move (commercial cinemas only)
Orlando
Romper Stomper
Tous les matins du monde
Waterdance

FACILITIES

AFM Lighting
5a Oakwood Business Park
1-5 Standard Road
London NW10 6EX
Tel: 081 961 1935
Fax: 081 961 8595
Lighting equipment hire

Abbey Road Studios
3 Abbey Road
London NW8 9AY
Tel: 071 286 1161
Fax: 071 289 7527
Four studios; music to picture; film sound transfer facilities; audio post-production; audio sweetening for video and TV; Sonic Solutions computer sound enhancement system; 35mm projection
Residential accommodation, restaurant and bar

Advision Studios
1 Montague Place
Kemptown
Brighton BN2 1JE
Tel: 0273 677375
Fax: 0273 672597
Digital/analogue 24/48-track studio; pre-production studio; wide range of outboard gear; fully residential.
State-of-the-art mobile studio for location recording, post-production and audio for video

After Image Facilities
32 Acre Lane
London SW2 5SG
Tel: 071 737 7300
Fax: 071 326 1850
Full broadcast sound stage – Studio A (1,680 sq ft, black, chromakey blue, white cyc) and insert studio (730 sq ft hard cyc). Multiformat on-line post production. Special effects – Ultimatte/blue screen

Air Studios Lyndhurst
Lyndhurst Hall
Lyndhurst Road
Hampstead
London NW3 5NG
Tel: 071 794 0660
Fax: 071 794 8518
Neve VRP 72ch console, flying faders, LCRS Monitors, 4,000 sq ft studio, four booths. 72ch Neve/Focusrite, GML Automation, 1,500 sq ft studio. 72ch SSL 8000G console with Ultimation, LCRS Monitors. 48ch AMS Logic 2 digital console, LCRS Monitors. All formats multitrack transfer bay. TV dubbing suite, 20ch Logic 2, 16 output Audiofile plus Exabyte

Angel Recording Studios
311 Upper Street
London N1 2TU
Tel: 071 354 2525
Fax: 071 226 9624
2 x 100-musician studio complex with mixing to 35mm and 16mm film
Customised Neve desks

Anvil Film and Recording Group
Denham Studios
North Orbital Road
Denham
Uxbridge
Middx UB9 5HH
Tel: 0895 833522
Fax: 0895 835006
35/16mm film and video production; studio re-recording, ADR, post-sync FX recording, transfers, foreign version dubbing; cutting rooms, neg cutting, off-line editing

Avolites
184 Park Avenue
London NW10 7XL
Tel: 081 965 8522
Fax: 081 965 0290
Manufacture and sale of dimming systems, memory and manual lighting control consoles. Also complete range of distribution hardware

BBRK
Ealing Studios
Ealing Green
Ealing
London W5 5EP
Tel: 081 567 6655
Fax: 081 758 8579
Art direction and construction, building services, prop hire, lighting and studios (see also entry for Ealing Studios under Studios)

BUFVC
55 Greek Street
London W1V 5LR
Tel: 071 734 3687
Fax: 071 287 3914
16mm cutting room and viewing facilities
Betacam 2 machine edit facility for low cost assembly work/off-line

Jim Bambrick and Associates
10 Frith Street
London W1V 5TZ
Tel: 071 434 2351
Fax: 071 734 6362
16mm, 35mm cutting rooms. Avid non-linear editing suite and 3 machine Edit Master off-line video edit suite

Barcud
Cibyn
Caernarfon
Gwynedd LL55 2BD
Tel: 0286 671671
Fax: 0286 671679
Video formats: 1"C, Beta SP, D2
OB Unit 1: up to 7 cameras 4VTR
OB Unit 2: up to 10 cameras 6VTR, DVE, Graphics Betacam units
Studio 1: 6,500 sq ft studio with audience seating and comprehensive lighting rig
Studio 2: 1,500 sq ft studio with vision/lighting control gallery and sound gallery
3 Edit Suites; 2 Graphics Suites one with Harriet
DVE: 3 channels Charisma, 2 channels Cleo
2 Sound Post-production suites with Audiofile and Screen Sound; BT lines

CTS Studios
The Music Centre
Engineers Way
Wembley
Middlesex HA9 0DR
Tel: 081 903 4611
Fax: 081 903 7130
Largest of 4 studios holds 130 musicians with three alternatives between 10 and 40
Synchronised film projection available with Telecine or video facilities for recording music to picture
Digital or analog available
Digital mastering
Restaurant, car park

Canalot Production Studios
222 Kensal Road
London W10 5BN
Tel: 081 960 6985/8580
Fax: 081 968 6020
Media business complex

housing over 70 companies, involved in TV, film, video and music production

Capital FX
21A Kingly Court
London W1R 5LE
Tel: 071 439 1982
Fax: 071 734 0950
Graphics, sub-titling, opticals and special effects

Capital Group Studios
13 Wandsworth Plain
London SW18 1ET
Tel: 081 874 0131
Fax: 081 871 9737
Central London: 3,000 and 2,000 sq ft fully equipped broadcast standard television studios. Comprehensive post-production facilities, including two multi-format on-line edit suites. (D3/D2/1"/Beta SP). Graphics Harriet suite. Multi-track sound dubbing (Dolby SR/A) to picture including DAT. Augan OMX Hard Disk Editing. Commentary booth. BT lines. Telecine. Canteen. Private car park. All support facilities

Carlton Broadcast Facilities
87 St John's Wood Terrace
London NW8 6PY
Tel: 071 722 8111
Fax: 071 483 4264
OBs: Multi-camera and multi-VTR vehicles
Post Production: 3 suites, 1 SP component, 2 multi format with 1", D2, D3, Abekas A64, A72, Aston and colour caption camera
Studios: 2 fully equipped television studios (1 in St John's Wood, 1 in Piccadilly Circus), 1-5 cameras, multi-format VTRs, BT lines, audience seating
Audio: SSL Screensound digital audio editing and mixing system

Charter Broadcast
47 Theobald Street
Borehamwood
Herts WD6 4RY
Tel: 081 905 1213
Fax: 081 905 1424
Broadcast equipment hire company with comprehensive range of facilities including cameras, camcorders, lenses, VTRs, mixers, matrices, DVE's, character generators, communications, audio equipment, radio camera and radio links, all of whch can be hired individually. Can provide turnkey operations for short or long term events anywhere. All systems designed for rapid installation and flexibility

Chromacolour
16 Grangemills
Weir Road
London SW12 0NE
Tel: 081 675 8422
Fax: 081 675 8499
Animation supplies and equipment

Chrysalis Mobiles
3 Chrysalis Way
Langley Bridge
Eastwood
Nottingham NG16 3RY
Tel: 0773 718111
Fax: 0773 716004
6 x OB units, PAL and component. Also component edit suite with A53 DVE and Aston 4

Chrysalis Television Facilities
Hawley Crescent
Camden
London NW1 8NP
Tel: 071 284 7900
Fax: 071 482 0690
Five edit suites, Avid, Edit Master; Quantel Paintbox, Caption cameras; Telecine 4:2:2 secondary colour correction; standards conversion; duplication; D1, D2, D3, NTSC/PAL, Digital Betacam, Betacam SP, 1", BVU, U-Matic, VHS, Quad MII, Hi 8; up-links, down-links; two studios; transmissions; 24 hour cover

Cine Image Film Opticals
16A Newman Street
London W1P 3HD
Tel: 071 637 9321
Fax: 071 637 0082
Film opticals, titles and effects on 35 and 16mm; film rostrum

Cine-Europe
7 Silver Road
Wood Lane
London W12 7SG
Tel: 081 743 6762
Fax: 081 749 3501
16mm, Super 16 cameras, lenses and grip equipment hire

Cine-Lingual Sound Studios
27-29 Berwick Street
London W1V 3RF
Tel: 071 437 0136
Fax: 071 439 2012
3 sound studios, 16/35mm computerised ADR; Foley recording; Dolby stereo mixing; sound transfers; cutting rooms

Cinebuild
Studio House
Rita Road
London SW8 1JU
Tel: 071 582 8750
Fax: 071 793 0467
Special effects: rain, snow, fog, mist, smoke, fire, explosions; lighting and equipment hire
Studio: 200 sq metres

Cinecontact
175 Wardour Street
London W1V 3AB
Tel: 071 434 1745
Fax: 071 494 0405
1 x VHS off-line edit suite. ARRI SRII camera and DAT sound kit for hire. Office space available

Cinequip Lighting Co
Units 6-8 Orchard Street
Industrial Estate
Salford
Manchester M6 6FL
Tel: 061 736 8034
Fax: 061 745 8023
Lighting equipment hire

Cinevideo
Broadcast Television Equipment Hire
7 Silver Road
White City Industrial Park, Wood Lane
London W12 7SG
Tel: 081 743 3839
Fax: 081 743 8417
Video formats: Beta SP, D1, D2, D3. Cameras: Ikegami HK355, HL57, HLV55, Sony BVP370, BVP70isp, BVP90. Full range of microwave links/radio cameras. PAL/NTSC

Clark Television Production
Cavendish House
128-134 Cleveland Street
London W1P 5DN
Tel: 071 388 7700
Fax: 071 388 3366
Editing: 2 component on-line suites (Sony BVW75, 2 x Sony BVW65, Grass Valley 100 CV Vision mixer, Aston Cap gen, Sony 900 Edit controller) + commentary; graphic facilities; video crews; production offices; tape library facility; 600 sq ft 2 cam studio

Colour Film & Video Services Group
10 Wadsworth Road
Perivale
Greenford
Middx UB6 7JX
Tel: 081 998 2731
Fax: 081 997 8738
Videotape to film transfer specialists, direct from broadcast video to 35mm and 16mm negative; Telecine mastering and tape dubbing all formats; Betacam SP component edit suite and 'Alphabet' video assembly from A+B cut neg; 16mm sound dubbing studios; full Super 16mm facilities inc Telecine wet gate; bulk cassette duplication; full film laboratory services

Complete Video
Slingsby Place
London WC2E 9AB
Tel: 071 379 7739
Fax: 071 497 9305
Telecom lines
Video formats: 1"C, D1, D2, BVU, U-Matic, SP Betacam
Editing: Sony BVE 9000, Grass Valley 200 Vision Mixer, Harry, Abekas A64, Aston 3
Vision effects: Grass Valley DVE, ADO 100, Quantel Mirage, Encore, Paintbox, Abekas A60, Symbolics 3-D Computer Graphics System, Sony System G 3D Digital Special FX System
Sound: SSL 32 channel and DDA 16 channel consoles, voiceover and sound library
Telecine: 35mm/16mm 4:2:2 telecine, Steadifilm, Colourist colour corrector, pin registration gate

Corinthian and Synchro-Sonics
5 Richmond Mews

Richmond Buildings
London W1V 5AG
Tel: 071 734 3325
Fax: 071 437 3502
16mm cutting rooms; sound transfer; video transfer; equipment hire; commentary to picture studio; digital track laying and mixing to 16mm or video; digital sound fx and music libraries

Crow Film and TV Services
12 Wendell Road
London W12 9RT
Tel: 081 749 6071
Fax: 081 740 0795
Video formats: Betacam SP, D2, D3, 1" and BVU
Edit 1: Sony 9000, Grass Valley 200 Vision Mixer, 2-channel Charisma/Cleo, Aston Caption Character Generator, Sony 1/4" Play-in with time code, Rostrum Camera
Edit 2: 900 Edit Controller, Grass Valley 1800 Vision Mixer, Abekas A51, Aston 3, 1/4" Play-in, Rostrum Camera
Off-line: Edit Master, Auto conforming, hi/lo-band suite, 2 x VHS editing suites

Crystal Film and Video
50 Church Road
London NW10 9PY
Tel: 081 965 0769
Fax: 081 965 7975
Aatons, Arriflex, Nagras, radio mics, lights and transport; Sony Beta SP; studio 50' x 30'; crews

Cygnet
The Studios
Communication Business Centre
14 Blenheim Road
High Wycombe
Bucks HP12 3RS
Tel: 0494 450541
Fax: 0494 462154
Full production facilities for 16mm and video

DBA Television
21 Ormeau Avenue
Belfast BT2 8HD
Tel: 0232 231197
Fax: 0232 333302
Crew hire and 16mm edit facilities, sound transfers; Aaton, Steenbeck

Dateline Productions
79 Dean Street
London W1V 5HA
Tel: 071 437 4510
Fax: 071 287 1072
16mm, 35mm film editing, off-line editing, negative cutting

De Lane Lea Sound Centre
75 Dean Street
London W1V 5HA
Tel: 071 439 1721
Fax: 071 437 0913
2 high speed 16/35mm Dolby stereo dubbing theatres with Dolby SR; high speed ADR and FX theatre (16/35mm and NTSC/PAL video); Synclavier digital FX suite; digital sound FX suite with audition room inc video; sound rushes and transfers; video transfers to VHS and U-Matic; 13x35mm cutting rooms. See also under Studios

Delta Sound Services
Shepperton Studios Centre
Squires Bridge Road
Shepperton
Middx TW17 0QD
Tel: 0932 562045
Fax: 0932 568989
16mm, 35mm and video dubbing theatre; post-sync and footsteps; effects work; in-house sound transfers

Denman Productions
60 Mallard Place
Strawberry Vale
Twickenham TW1 4SR
Tel: 081 891 3461
Fax: 081 891 6413
Video and film production, ENG crews and equipment, including Denmount Alti-Cam 100' high remote camera system

Despite TV
113 Roman Road
London E2 0HU
Tel: 081 983 4278
Hi-band kit plus lights. 3 machine series 9 lo-/hi-/SP edit suite with 4A controller, Amiga 2000, 6 channel audio mixer

Digital Sound House
14 Livonia Street
London W1V 3PH
Tel: 071 434 2928/437 7105
Fax: 071 287 9110
Sound transfer; 16/35mm 1/4" DAT; FX library; FX/voiceover booth; cutting rooms

Diverse Production
6 Gorleston Street
London W14 8SX
Tel: 071 603 4567
Fax: 071 603 2148
Beta SP component edit suite; Beta SP/D3 to D3 composite edit suite (1" VTRs available); 2 channels A53 with warp; Flashfile library store; Aston Motif, Aston 3; 3 paint systems; 2 cameras (1 caption, 1 rostrum); small studio; 2 SVHS off-line edit suites; 1 lo-band off-line edit suite

Document Films
8-12 Broadwick Street
London W1V 1FH
Tel: 071 437 4526
Film cutting rooms; 16mm Aaton crews, 16mm, 35mm sound transfer bay, mono and stereo; production offices

Dolby Laboratories
Wootton Bassett
Wilts SN4 8QJ
Tel: 0793 842100
Fax: 0793 842101
Cinema processors for replay of Dolby Stereo Digital, Dolby Stereo SR and Dolby Stereo encoded soundtracks; audio noise reduction equipment

Dubbs
25-26 Poland Street
London W1V 3DB
Tel: 071 629 0055
Fax: 071 287 8796
Videotape duplication
Standards conversion
DAT Audio layback

Edinburgh Film and Video Productions
Edinburgh Film and TV Studios
Nine Mile Burn by Penicuik
Midlothian EH26 9LT
Tel: 0968 672131
Fax: 0968 672685
Stage: 50 sq metres; 16/Super 16/35mm cutting rooms; 16mm, 35mm transfer facilities; preview theatre; sound transfer; edge numbering; lighting grip equipment hire; scenery workshops

Edinburgh Film Workshop Trust
29 Albany Street
Edinburgh EH1 3QN
Tel: 031 557 5242
Fax: 031 557 3852
Facilities include lo-band edit suite, rostrum camera; VHS off-line suite; film cutting room (16mm)

The Edit Works
Units 1-6, 2nd Floor
Chelsea Garden Market
Chelsea Harbour
London SW10 0XE
Tel: 071 352 5244
Fax: 071 376 8645
Video formats: 1"C, D2, D3, SP Betacam
Editing: Component – Sony 9100, Grass Valley 200 vision mixer
Composite – Sony 9100, Grass Valley 300 vision mixer; off-line: Sony 5000, 4 x U-Matic
Vision effects: ADO100, Abekas A72
Sound: voiceover booth available to all suites
Random access editing

Edric Audiovisual Hire
34-36 Oak End Way
Gerrards Cross
Bucks SL9 8BR
Tel: 0753 884646
Fax: 0753 887163
Audiovisual and video production facilities

Elstree Light & Power
Elstree Studios
Shenley Road
Borehamwood
Herts WD6 1JG
Tel: 081 207 5188/081 953 1600
TV silent generators; BAC & CEE17 distribution to BS 5550. HMI, MSR & tungsten heads; grips and rigging equipment; transport; crew; design and production services

Essential Pictures
Canalot Production Studios
222 Kensal Road
London W10 5BN
Tel: 081 969 7017
Fax: 081 960 8201
Studio: 32' x 22'
Broadcast standard 3 camera TV studio, with satellite links, 24 channel lighting, sound proofed and air-conditioned, gallery and dressing room
Non-linear editing: Avid Media Composer

Off-line: U-Matic edit master suites; SVHS & VHS off-line suites
On-line: Edit 1: "Composium" Digital suite with 2 channels DVE; Beta SP; Digital Beta SP; D2, D3, D5; Abekas A60 x 2; Paintbox & Graphics
Edit 2: multiformat suite; Autoconform Cox T16; ADO 2000; Beta SP; 1"
Edit 3: 2 machine cuts only Beta SP suite
Subtitling: translations, voice-overing and subtitling with Screen Subtitling computer equipment. Language transfer post-production and management advice
Satellite conferencing and transmissions, Satellite and Cable Channel management and cassette duplication

Eye Film and Television
The Guildhall
Church Street
Eye
Suffolk IP23 7BD
Tel: 0379 870083
Fax: 0379 870987
Betacam SP shoot and edit facilities with associated production services

Faction Films
28-29 Great Sutton Street
London EC1V 0DU
Tel: 071 608 0654/3
Fax: 071 608 2157
Non-linear editing. 6 plate 16mm Steenbeck edit suite; sound transfer; VHS edit suite with 6 channel mixer; U-Matic and VHS viewing and transfer; production office space; Nagra 4.2 and redhead lighting kit. Spanish/English translation service

Fantasy Factory Video
42 Theobalds Road
London WC1X 8NW
Tel: 071 405 6862
Video formats: U-Matic, hi-band SP, hi-band and lo-band, Hi 8, video 8
Editing: 3 machine hi-band SP and lo-band with listing, automated vision mixer, EDIS DVE, with full timecode system using VITC and LTC and Quanta Cap Gen
2 machine BVU SP/lo-band with For-A Cap Gen, 6-channel audio mixer; training courses in video editing on the above suites. Specialise in problem solving, eg refurbishing old tapes, subtitling, timecode transfers, interformat copying, stills offscreen, computer to video etc

Film Work Group
Top Floor
Chelsea Reach
79-89 Lots Road
London SW10 0RN
Tel: 071 352 0538
Fax: 071 351 6479
Video and film post-production facilities and graphic design. 3 machine hi-band SP with effects, 2 machine lo-band, transfer facilities, videographics and 6-plate Steenbeck

FinePoint Broadcast
Hill House
Furze Hill
Kingswood
Surrey KT20 6EZ
Tel: 0737 370033
Fax: 0737 373633
Broadcast facilities hire in PAL and NTSC; VTRs in Digital Betacam, Beta SP, D2, D3, 1" and other formats. Sony BVP-90 cameras; Abekas A51 & A53; Charisma; Canon 55:1 lenses; Eve vision mixers etc

The Frame Store
33 Great Pulteney Street
London W1R 3DE
Tel: 071 439 1267
Fax: 071 439 0129
Full service digital post-production facility. New Henry suite, two Harry suites with V-series Paintbox, Encore and Kaleidoscope; two digital edit suites with Kadenza vision mixers and Kaleidoscope; Avid 4000 Media Composer; Classic Paintbox; 6 DVTRs; Ultimatte; 2 RTDs; A60; A64; Delta 1; 3 machine off-line; Beta Editing; IMC computer controlled video rostrum camera with Sony M7 CCD Camera; Ursa Telecine with Pogle Colour Corrector, Matchbox Frame Store, Russell Square secondary colour corrector and Pin-up; Softimage 3D animation; T-morph; Painterley Effects; copying and playout facilities

Mike Fraser
225 Goldhawk Road
London W12 8ER
Tel: 081 749 6911
Fax: 081 743 3144
Neg cutting, rubber numbering, computer logging, post production supervision through OSC/R

Frontline Television Services
44 Earlham Street
London WC2H 9LA
Tel: 071 836 0411
Fax: 071 379 5210
Component Broadcast Editing and Multi-Format Composite suite, both with Grass Valley 200 vision mixer, Sony 9000 edit controller, Abekas A53D, Aston 4/A72 Graphics generators. Computerised video rostrum camera, tape duplication, Broadcast standards conversion via ADAC and telecine

GBS Film Lighting
169 Talgarth Road
London W14 9DA
Tel: 081 748 0316
Fax: 081 563 0679
Lighting equipment hire

Gaul Bryers (GB)
Hammersley House
5-8 Warwick Street
London W1R 5RA
Tel: 071 439 1449
Fax: 071 439 1339
Post-production company specialising in Quantel Flash Harry and Henry video manipulation

General Screen Enterprises
Highbridge Estate
Oxford Road
Uxbridge
Middx UB8 1LX
Tel: 0895 231931
Fax: 0895 235335
Studio: 100 sq metres
16mm, 35mm opticals including matting, aerial image work, titling; editing, trailers, promos, special effects, graphics, VistaVision; computerised rostrum animation motion control; video suite; preview theatre

Goldcrest Post Production Facilities
36/44 Brewer Street
London W1R 3HP
Tel: 071 439 4177
Fax: 071 437 6411
Dubbing theatre with SSL 5000 console, Dolby A & SR, film and video projection; high speed ADR, effects recording, built-in Foley surfaces and extensive props; Synclavier 9600 16 track direct to disk; AMS Audiofile suite with Yamaha digital desk; sound transfer bays all film and video formats with Dolby A & SR; 41 cutting rooms (35/16mm); 14 production offices; Rank Cintel MkIIIC enhanced 4:2:2, Pogle and secondary colour correction, all film formats including Super 16mm; Video formats 1", Beta SP, U-Matic, VHS and D2; ADAC standards conversion; off-line editing 3 machine U-Matic with Paltex edit controller

Grip House Facilities and Studios
5-11 Taunton Road
Metropolitan Centre
Greenford
Middx UB6 8UQ
Tel: 081 578 2382
Fax: 081 578 1536
Grip equipment and studio hire
Also: Grip House North
Unit E20 Eleventh Ave
Team Valley Trading Estate
Gateshead NE11 0JY
Tel: 091 491 1220
Fax: 091 491 1221
Grip equipment hire only

Hall Place Studios
4 Hall Place
Leeds LS9 8JD
Tel: 0532 405553
16mm/U-Matic/VHS production units, lighting, cutting rooms, lo-band and SVHS edit suites, rostrum camera, film/video studio, 16-track sound studio with SMPTE video dubbing, 4-track 16mm dubbing, sound transfer, sound effects library. See also under Workshops for information on training courses

Hammonds Audio Visual and Video Services
Presentation Division
60-64a Queens Road
Watford
Herts WD1 2LA
Tel: 0923 239733
Fax: 0923 221134
ENG crews; BVU, Pro S SVHS, Hi 8, Professional editing, multiformat. DVE, separate full audio-recording studio and video studio facilities. SVHS off-line; duplication and STDS conversion via AVS systems

Headline Video Facilities
3 Nimrod Way
Elgar Road
Reading
Berks RG2 0EB
Tel: 0734 751555
Fax: 0734 861482
Video formats: 1", Betacam SP, BVU SP
Two fully component multi-format broadcast edit suites with 2 channels DVE. 2 Paintboxes, Harriet, DGS 3.2 3D system. Duplication and standards conversion

Hillside Studios
Merry Hill Road
Bushey
Herts WD2 1DR
Tel: 081 950 7919
Fax: 081 421 8085
Production and post-production facilities
Betacam, 1"C, D3 and Betacam SP plus component shooting
Two studios: 1,500 sq ft – drive in access and 384 sq ft. On-line and off-line editing suites – composite and component. Audio pre-production and post-production studios. Audience seating for 100, set design, construction, 3 conference rooms and licensed restaurant

Humphries Video Services
Unit 2, The Willow Business Centre
17 Willow Lane
Mitcham
Surrey CR4 4NX
Tel: 081 648 6111
Fax: 081 648 5261
Evershed House
71 Chiltern Street
London W1M 1HT
Tel: 071 636 3636
Videocassette duplication, standards conversion, mastering, dubbing facilities; full packaging and distribution service

ITN
200 Gray's Inn Road
London WC1X 8XZ
Tel: 071 430 4330
Fax: 071 430 4434
Studio for live or recording with satellite link-up facilities, 2,000 sq ft – audience seating available; video dubbing and transfer, all formats; standards conversion; IDF graphic design service; Flash Harry/ Paintbox dry hire/ training; sound dubbing suites; tape recycling

IVPTV
16A York Place
Edinburgh EH1 3EP
Tel: 031 558 1888
Fax: 031 557 5465
Edit 1: Two Ampex 1" VTRs, Sony 9000 edit controller, Grass Valley 300 switcher, Kaleidoscope with Kurl and Wipe, Dubner character generator, Abekas A64 Digital Disk Recorder, two Beta SP studio players, DAT Audio with T/c
Edit 2: Sony 910 edit controller, JVC KM-3000 component mixer, three Beta SP studio players
Off-line edit suite; Matisse Paint and 3-D; Symbolics XL1200 3-D Animator; video studio
Cameras: Ampex CVC 50 (2), Ampex CVC 7

Interact Sound
160 Barlby Road
London W10 6BS
Tel: 081 960 3115
Fax: 081 964 3022
16mm/35mm Film dubbing, (12 track Dolby Stereo, SR & A); sound transfer and digital sound edit suites

International Broadcast Facilities
12 Neal's Yard
London WC2H 9DP
Tel: 071 497 1515
Fax: 071 379 8562
D2, D3, 1" PAL & NTSC, Beta SP PAL & NTSC, 1"B, BVU SP, U-Matic SVHS, cassette duplication, Hi 8 broadcast standards conversions

André Jacquemin Recording
68a Delancey Street
London NW1 7RY
Tel: 071 485 3733
Fax: 071 284 1020
Digital hard disk recording & 24 track analogue recording studio for post-production. Computer memory on mixing desk and direct to film mixing facilities including 35/16mm transfer work, large sound effects and music library

Terry Jones PostProductions
The Hat Factory
16-18 Hollen Street
London W1V 3AD
Tel: 071 434 1173
Fax: 071 494 1893
35mm post production, plus Lightworks non-linear editing and hi-band computerised off-line facilities

Lane End Productions
63 Riding House Street
London W1P 7PP
Tel: 071 637 2794
Fax: 071 580 0135
Video formats: 1"C, Betacam SP, BVU, U-Matic, VHS
Vision effects: Grass Valley mixer, colour camera, Aston 3, Abekas A53D, off-line editing
Transfer and standards conversion, most systems

Lee Lighting
Wycombe Road
Wembley
Middx HA0 1QD
Tel: 081 900 2949 (hire)
Fax: 081 903 3012
Tel: 081 900 2900 (accounts)
Fax: 081 902 5500
Film and TV lighting equipment rental

Light House Media Centre
The Chubb Buildings
Fryer Street
Wolverhampton WV1 1HT
Tel: 0902 716044/55
Fax: 0902 717143
3 Machine U-Matic edit suite with computerised controller (BVE 900 & BVE 600); Betacam/U-Matic Eng kits, also animation and chroma keying

Lighthouse Film and Video
Brighton Media Production Centre
11 Jew Street
Brighton BN1 1UT
Tel: 0273 202044
Fax: 0273 748833
Hi 8 production kits
Video editing: 3 machine hi-band U-Matic and 2 machine lo-band U-Matic, Panasonic MX-50 vision mixer DVE & caption camera, Fostex 8 track mixer. 16mm film: Arriflex BL, Nagra III, O'Connor tripod, 4 plate Steenbeck and pic sync.
Lights: 8 x 800w, 2k kit and pepper spot
Multimedia Apple Mac Quadra 950 graphics and animation workstations
Dry hire, crews and training, small studio and production desks

London Fields Film and Video
10 Martello Street
London E8 3PE
Tel: 071 241 2997
Computer graphics; video editing; 16mm editing

London Film Makers' Co-op
42 Gloucester Avenue
London NW1 8JD
Tel: 071 722 1728
Fax: 071 483 0068
Houses a wide range of 16mm and Super 8 production equipment and facilities including b/w printing and processing (service or DIY), optical printer, rostrum camera, Steenbecks (both 16mm and Super 8), sound transfer facilities

London Video Access (LVA)
5-7 Buck Street
London NW1 8NJ
Tel: 071 284 4323
Fax: 071 267 6078
3 machine hi-band SP mastering (lo-band/hi-band SP source) suite; off-line suites (VHS, lo-band, Hi 8); computer graphics and animation; viewing; duplication; production equipment hire; exhibition equipment hire

M2 Facilities Group
The Forum
74-80 Camden Street

London NW1 0EG
Tel: 071 387 5001
Fax: 071 387 5025
Component and digital editing, graphics and sound post-production

MAC Sound Hire
1-2 Attenburys Park
Park Road
Altrincham
Cheshire WA14 5QE
Tel: 061 969 8311
Fax: 061 962 9423
Hire of professional sound equipment

The Machine Room
76 Old Compton Street
London W1V 5PA
Tel: 071 734 3433
Fax: 071 287 3773
Film & Video transfers, nitrate handling, PAL/NTSC/SECAM, full serial-digital routing
Film to tape transfer: Rank Cintel MKIII Digiscan & 4:2:2 Wet Gate Telecine 625 or 525, Super 35, 35mm (inc full aperture gate), Super 16, 16mm and Super 8. Pogle grading system, Vari-speed 16-30fps, XYZoom, Pan/Scan, secondary colour correction, direct film transfer to NTSC, grain reduction. Separate magnetic & optical sound follower + Dolby. ¼" Nagra, sound track relaying, thermal stills picture print out + time code, "digital restoration process" for archive sound tracks, ultrasonic film cleaning, also service for 9.5mm and 8mm film
Video formats: D1, D2, D3, 1", Betacam SP, MII, 2" Quad, BVU SP, BVU, Hi 8, U-Matic, SVHS, VHS
Standards conversion: PAL-NTSC-SECAM. Vistek Vector with VMC. D1-625 to D1-525 transfers. D2, D3, 1", Betacam SP, U-Matic, SVHS, VHS
Other services include: editing – D1, Betacam SP, 1"; Avid non-linear off-line, Paintbox, Harry, Harriette & 3D graphics; sound studio and voice overs; slide transfers

Magnetic Image Production Facilities
6 Grand Union Centre
West Row
London W10 5AX
Tel: 081 960 7337
Fax: 081 968 1378
On-line video editing using Integra, multi-format component digital processing system. Standards conversions for all countries and video duplication. Beta SP shooting also available

Mayflower Sound Studios
3 Audley Square
Mayfair
London W1Y 5DR
Tel: 071 493 0016
Fax: 071 355 4071
Complete foreign version service, any language or film/video format; voice over, dubbing/lip sync; Automated Dialogue Replacement (ADR); Digital sound effects and music library

Media Arts
Town Hall Studios
Regent Circus
Swindon SN1 1QF
Tel: 0793 493454
Fax: 0793 490420
Video cameras: F10s, KY1900s, M3, M7
Video editing: VHS 2-machine, Series 5 2/3-machine, 3-machine lo-/hi-/SP and effects
Sound studio and effects; interview studio; 8mm/16mm cutting rooms; B/w and colour photography; Lighting: Reds and 2000W; dry hire, crews, training

Mersey Film and Video
Bluecoat Chambers
School Lane
Liverpool L1 3BX
Tel: 051 708 5259
Fax: 051 707 0048
2/3 Machine lo-band, Hi 8 and VHS editing; lo-band SVHS production kits; lo-band and VHS exhibition equipment; Amiga 2000 computer graphics; lighting kits, microphone kits

Metropolis Video
8-10 Neal's Yard
London WC2H 9DP
Tel: 071 240 8423
Fax: 071 379 6880
Off-line editing: 4 suites
1 x 3 machine Editmaster computerised lo-band giving 8"CMX Disc for autoconform; VITC read from off-line edit
2 x 2 machine lo-band
1 x 2 machine VHS
Video duplication: all formats, large or small runs. Overnight Betacam rushes service. Rushes transferred with BITC, VITC overnight for off-line next day

MetroVideo
The Old Bacon Factory
57-59 Great Suffolk Street
London SE1 0BS
Tel: 071 928 2088
Fax: 071 261 0685
Metro Mansions
6-7 Great Chapel Street
London W1V 3AG
Tel: 071 439 3494
Fax: 071 437 3782
Video formats: Betacam SP, D1, D2, D3, MII, BVU SP, VHS, SVHS, 1", lo-band, hi-band, Digital Betacam
Cameras: BVW 300/400/507, PVW 537, Hi 8 EVW 537. Panasonic F10/F15 CCD, DXC-M7, DXC3000
ADAC standards conversion PAL/NTSC, 1", D2, D3, Betacam SP or M2, BVU SP, Hi 8
Videowalls, Prowalls, video projectors, large screen monitors, data display

The Mill
40/41 Great Marlborough Street
London W1V 1DA
Tel: 071 287 4041
Fax: 071 287 8393
Disk-based digital editing Harry, Harriet, Ursa
Telecine with DCP tape-to-tape grading, AVR5 Avid, System G, morphing and Softimage 3D, IMC rostrum and digital animation rig

Mister Lighting
2 Dukes Road
Western Avenue
London W3 0SL
Tel: 081 993 9911
Fax: 081 993 9533
Lighting equipment and studio hire

Molinare
34 Fouberts Place
London W1V 2BH
Tel: 071 439 2244
Fax: 071 734 6813
Video formats: Digital Betacam, D1, D2, D3, 1", Beta SP, BVU, U-Matic, VHS. NTSC: 1", Beta SP, U-Matic & VHS
Editing: 1 x D1 serial digital suite, 2 x component multi-format, 2 x composite multi-format DVEs: 2 x A57, 4 x A53, 4 x ADO, Encore. Storage: 2 x A66, A64. Caption Generators: Aston Motif, A72, Aston Caption, Aston 3
Graphics: Harry with V7 Paintbox, Encore and D1. Harriet with V7 Paintbox, D1 and Beta SP. 3D graphics with Silicon Graphics and Softimage
Telecine: Rank Cintel 111 with 4.2.2 digital links, Pogle and DCP controller and secondary colour grading, 35mm, 16mm, S16mm
Audio: 2 x 24 track and Audiofile studios, track-laying studio with Dawn, voice record studios, transfer room, sound FX libraries
Duplication, standards conversion, Matrix camera, BT landlines, satellite downlink

Morgan Broadcast
4.16 Wembley Commercial Centre
East Lane
Wembley
Middx HA9 7XD
Tel: 081 908 6377
Fax: 081 908 4211
Large screen video projection specialists

Motion Control Studio
CNN House
19-22 Rathbone Place
London W1P 1DF
Tel: 071 436 5544
Fax: 071 580 5673
Studio with Mark Roberts overhead motion control rig

The Moving Picture Company
25 Noel Street
London W1V 3RD
Tel: 071 434 3100
Fax: 071 437 3951/734 9150
Video formats: D1, D2, 1"C, MII, Beta SP, Betacam, hi-/lo-band, SVHS
Cameras: Sony BVP 330 portable and Sony DXC 3000 CCD
Editing: four edit suites (three fully digital), using

CMX editors. Henry suite
Vision effects: ADO, Abekas A53-D, A64, A84
Telecine: two Rank Cinetel URSAs, for 16mm or 35mm film, each with Register Pin and Steadi-guide gates, open gate, digital noise reduction. Matchbox, Russell Square secondary colour grading
Graphics: 3 x Paintbox/Harrys, with Encore HUD and A53D; 3 x Alias 3-D computer animation systems, with 4-D 240 renderers; Aston 3 and 4 character generators
Studio: 47' x 30' x 13' L eye
Tape to film transfers (Filmtel®)
Video rostrum studio
Cutting rooms for 16mm/35mm and off-line editing suite

Northern Light
39-41 Assembly Street
Leith
Edinburgh EH6 7RG
Tel: 031 553 2383
Lighting equipment hire

The OBE Partnership
16 Kingly Street
London W1R 5LD
Tel: 071 734 3028
Fax: 071 734 2830
Film Editors

Oasis Television
76 Wardour Street
London W1V 3LF
Tel: 071 434 4133
Fax: 071 494 2843
4 large on-line edit suites, composite or component: D3, D2, 1"C, Beta SP
3 graphics suites: Acrobat plus Matador for 3D and 2D animation, Matisse paint system
2 Lightworks non-linear off-line suites
High quality dubbing and duplication

Omnititles
37 Ripplevale Grove
London N1 1HS
Tel: 071 607 9047
Fax: 071 704 9594
Spotting and subtitling services for film, TV, video, satellite and cable. Subtitling in most world languages

Oxford Film and Video Makers
The Stables
North Place
Headington
Oxford OX3 9HY
Tel: 0865 741682
Fax: 0865 742901
Cameras: Sony DXC-325, Panasonic F10, Arriflex 16mm and Super 8
Recorders: Sony 8800SP (with T/c), Sony 4800
Editing: Sony lo-band U-Matic, 16mm Steenbecks

PMPP Facilities
69 Dean Street
London W1V 5HB
Tel: 071 437 0979
Fax: 071 434 0386
On-line: Multi-format component and composite suites; D3, D2, 1", BETA SP and BVU SP with Charisma DVE, Aston 3 and/or A72
Off-line: 3 x Avid non-linear systems; BVU SP, lo-band and VHS with Shotlister; and 3 machine computerised lo-band with effects
Computer Graphics: Acrobat 3D animation on Indigo Silicon Graphics, Matisse 2D paint system + Abekas A65 digital disk recorder
Sound Dubbing: Audiofile digital recording and dubbing to picture or 24 track; voice over recording to picture, DAT or ¼"; music recording and MIDI programming; A-DAT digital multi-track recording
Pack-shot/chroma key studio
Hi-fi stereo duplication bank and standard conversions facilities

The Palace
8 Poland Street
London W1V 3DG
Tel: 071 439 8241
Fax: 071 287 1741
Two multiformat composite on-line edit suites with D3, 1" and Betacam SP formats
Digital effects: 3 channels of ADO 3000 with Infinity and Digimatte

Panavision UK
Wycombe Road
Wembley
Middx HA0 1QN
Tel: 081 903 7933
Fax: 081 902 3273
Services many television, commercial and feature film productions

Picardy Television
Picardy House
4 Picardy Place
Edinburgh EH1 3JT
Tel: 031 558 1551
Fax: 031 558 1555
Facilities include: dry/crewed camera hire; multi format editing including Betacam SP component, D3, DVE and graphics; full broadcast standard studio for single/multi camera shoots and casting; EVS video paint system with 2 and 3D animation, Parallax Acrobat 3-D modeller

Picture Post Productions
13 Manette Street
London W1V 5LB
Tel: 071 439 1661
Fax: 071 494 1661
35/16mm film editing; off-line editing and Avid

Pinewood Studios
Iver, Bucks SL0 0NH
Tel: 0753 656301
Fax: 0753 656844
16/35mm dubbing and ADR. Two large high-speed stereo dubbing theatres with automated consoles; small general purpose recording theatre; large ADR and sound effects theatre; preview theatre: 115 seats, 70/35/16mm, all formats stereo sound; four-bay sound transfer area; mono/stereo sound negative transfer; 60 full service cutting rooms

Prominent Facilities
68a Delancey Street
London NW1 7RY
Tel: 071 284 0242
Fax: 071 284 1020
Cutting rooms; sound transfers; edit suites; production offices; preview theatre

Q Studios
Queniborough Industrial Estate
1487 Melton Road
Queniborough
Leicester LE7 8FP
Tel: 0533 608813
Fax: 0533 608329
Video formats: Betacam SP, BVU, 1"
Component editing with Charisma DVE, off-line edit, 24 track sound, original music production, computer graphics; two drive-in studios (1,350 and 754 sq ft), black and chromakey drapes, computer controlled lighting. Full production services available including crews, set construction, on-line and off-line editing

Rank Video Services
Phoenix Park
Great West Road
Brentford
Middx TW8 9PL
Tel: 081 568 4311
Fax: 081 847 4032
10,500 realtime slaves, all hi-fi capable and 20 Hi-speed Sony Sprinters; specialist corporate duplication department including standards conversion

Red Post Production
Hammersley House
4-8 Warwick Street
London W1R 5RA
Tel: 071 439 1449
Fax: 071 439 1339
Dry hire post-production facility house with Quantel Henry and Flash Harry machines. Full technical and professional backup for independent operators and other post-production houses

Redapple
214 Epsom Road
Merrow
Guildford
Surrey GU1 2RA
Tel: 0483 455044
Fax: 0483 455022
Video formats: Beta SP, NTSC/PAL
Film format: 16mm
Cameras: Sony BVP50's, Sony BVP400's, ENG/EFP units
Film: 16mm Arriflex unit
Transport: 5 estate cars, pressurised twin engine aircraft
Two lighting vehicles

Reuters Television
66-67 Newman Street
London W1P 3LA
Tel: 071 436 5692
Fax: 071 580 9676
Three-camera broadcast studio with Paintbox, Newsmatte, Aston and autoscript. Single-camera interview studio with Newsmatte; 3 machine

edit with 2-channel DVE, Abekas A34, Beta SP, 1", BVU formats; 2-machine Beta SP component editing; Voice-over booth; V-series Paintbox, Aston Wallet and caption generator, rostrum camera; 525 BVU; AVS standards converter; Hi 8, SVHS formats; BT circuits, dedicated satellite pathways to Brightstar and VisEurope. Specialists in news and current affairs; corporate and commercial post-production

Reuters Television
40 Cumberland Avenue
London NW10 7EH
Tel: 081 965 7733
Fax: 081 965 0620
Post-production services include: telecine with Da Vinci colour grading; interview studios, multi format edit suites: D3/D2 1"C, Betacam; two Betacam component edit suites; computer graphics Quantel Paintbox; audio liftoff/layback – DAT, ¼", 16mm, 35mm; standards conversion: ACE, Vistek with motion control & Quantel; duplication: D2, D3, 1"C, 1"B, 2" Quad, Betacam SP, MII, BVU, U-Matic, SVHS, VHS, Hi 8, Video 8 formats; computerised tape handling; satellite transmissions; international shipping. Free West End pick up and delivery service; open 24 hours

Richmond Film Services
The Old School
Park Lane
Richmond
Surrey TW9 2RA
Tel: 081 940 6077
Fax: 081 948 8326
Sound equipment available for hire, sales of tape and batteries, and UK agent for Ursta recordists' trolleys and Denecke timecode equipment

Rockall Data Services
The Rockall Centre
320 Western Road
London SW19 2QA
Tel: 081 640 6626
Fax: 081 640 1297
Safe storage of documents, film, video and audio material

Rostrum Cameras
11 Charlotte Mews
off Tottenham Street
London W1P 1LN
Tel: 071 637 0535
Fax: 071 323 3892
16/35mm Rostrum computerised cameras

Rushes
66 Old Compton Street
London W1V 5PA
Tel: 071 437 8676
Fax: 071 734 2519
Post production: digital, analogue editing; Flash Harry, Harriet, 3-D animation; Motion Control Studio; CIS compositing; URSA telecine; Nicam playouts; Lightworks

SVC Television
142 Wardour Street
London W1V 3AU
Tel: 071 734 1600
Fax: 071 437 1854
Video Post Production/ Digital Editing/Telecine/ Computer Graphics/ Harry/Motion Control Rig

Salon Post-Productions
13-14 Archer Street
London W1V 7HG
Tel: 071 437 0516
Fax: 071 437 6197
35/16mm Steenbecks and editing equipment hire; cutting rooms; 35/16mm Steenbeck, telecine, U-Matic and VHS edit suites

Sammy's – Samuelson Film Service London
21 Derby Road
Metropolitan Centre
Greenford
Middx UB6 8UJ
Tel: 081 578 7887
Fax: 081 578 2733
Cameras: Panavision, Moviecam, Arriflex
Lenses: Canon, Cooke, Nikon, Leitz, Zeiss, Hasselblad
Video assist, sound, editing, stock, consumables and transport 24hrs

Michael Samuelson Lighting
Pinewood Studios
Iver Heath
Bucks SL0 0NH
Tel: 0753 631133
Fax: 0753 630485
Milford Place
Lennox Road
Leeds LS4 2BL
Tel: 0532 310770
Fax: 0532 310383
Unit K, Llantrisant Business Park
Llantrisant
Mid Glamorgan CF7 8LF
Tel: 0443 227777
Fax: 0443 223656
Block 12, Unit 3, Cambuslang Investment Park
Clydesmill Drive
Cambuslang
Glasgow G32 8RS
Tel: 041 641 3000
Fax: 041 641 0333
Units 7/8
Piccadilly Trading Estate
Great Ancoats Street
Manchester M1 2NP
Tel: 061 272 8462
Fax: 061 273 8729
Meridian Studios
Television Centre
Northam
Southampton SO2 0TA
Tel: 0703 222555
Fax: 0703 335050
Hire of film and television lighting equipment and generators. Six UK depots. Largest range of MSR discharge equipment in Europe including the powerful SUNPAR range from France

Sheffield Independent Film
5 Brown Street
Sheffield S1 2BS
Tel: 0742 720304
Fax: 0742 795225
Aaton XTR "Plus" with CCD video assist, Arriflex BL, 6-plate Steenbeck and Picsyncs. Nagra IS, Revox/B77, SQN mixer, SVHS edit suite, 2 machine and 3 machine edit with Type 9, Type 5, Hi 8, BVU 950, and digital effects. SP U-Matic cameras and Portapaks, lighting equipment and 1,200' studio

Shepperton Studios
Studios Road
Shepperton
Middx TW17 0QD
Tel: 0932 562611
Fax: 0932 568989
Cutting rooms; 16mm, 35mm viewing theatres

Signal Vision
Parkgate Industrial Estate
Knutsford
Cheshire WA16 8DX
Tel: 0565 755678
Fax: 0565 634164
2 edit suites (D2/1"/ Betacam SP); Paintbox computer graphics; 1,600 sq ft studio; VHS duplication; Standards conversion

Soho Images
8-14 Meard Street
London W1V 3HR
Tel: 071 437 0831
Fax: 071 734 9471
Rank Cintel 4:2:2 telecines for transfer of 35mm, 16mm and Super 16mm to all VTR formats, with wetgate available for 16mm and Super 16mm
All laboratory processing and printing with video rushes service. Broadcast standards conversions PAL-NTSC-SECAM via ADAC, cassette to cassette via AVS 6500 as well as duplication from single/bulk quantities

Spitfire Television
19 Hatton Street
London NW8 8PR
Tel: 071 724 7544
Fax: 071 724 2058
Presentation studio with two cameras and chromakey cyc, control room, fully soundproofed, air conditioned
Two 100% component edit suites with GVG200 and GVG110 vision mixers
16 x Beta SP machines, plus 1", D1, D3, BVU, U-Matic – Mavigraph stills from video
Avid off-line 2500 top of the line digital non-linear off-line editor with 6 gigabytes of storage
Harry, Paintbox and Vertigo 3D animation

Brian Stevens Animated Films
11 Charlotte Mews
off Tottenham Street
London W1P 1LN
Tel: 071 637 0535
Fax: 071 323 3892
Studio specialising in graphic, technical and cartoon animation

Studio Sound
84-88 Wardour Street
London W1V 3LF
Tel: 071 734 0263
Fax: 071 434 9990
Film and video recording, dubbing and transfer facilities, "Screensound" digital audio system

TSI Video
10 Grape Street
London WC2H 8DY
Tel: 071 379 3435
Fax: 071 379 4589
Video formats: 1" x 9, Betacam SP x 9, plus BVU, D2
Editing: 3 suites – Sony edit controllers in component and composite with any combination of above, Grass Valley vision mixer, 4 channels of Charisma DVE with key channels and CLEO, caption camera, Aston Motif character generators
Computer graphics: Quantel VE series Paintbox and Harriet, digital library store
Sound: Q Lock/Eclipse synchronisers, 24 track dubbing and voiceover recording with Opus Digital Audio post production. Four BT lines (vision and sound), BT control lines (2 in, 2 out), colour caption cameras

TV Media Services
420 Sauchiehall Street
Glasgow G2 3JD
Tel: 041 331 1993
Fax: 041 331 2821
Film and editing on Betacam SP and BVUSP

TVi
Film House
142 Wardour Street
London W1V 3AU
Tel: 071 434 2141
Fax: 071 439 3984
Post production/Telecine/Sound/Copying and Standards Conversion
Extensive post-production, telecine and copying services to programme makers, distributors and broadcasters. Facilities include multiformat digital and analogue editing, telecine with wetgate including UNITAB, and digital and component dubbing or standards conversion. All services are available with all major formats of VTR including D1, D2 and D3

TVP Videodubbing
2 Golden Square
London W1R 3AD
Tel: 071 439 7138
Fax: 071 494 1907
On-line editing with A53, ADO, A64, AVS floating point, 3-D character generator; off-line editing with Editmaster; telecine transfers: 35mm, 16mm, Super 8mm, digital vision processor to conceal blemishes and neg sparkle during transfer; landlines to Telecom Tower for line feeds and commercial play-outs; dubbing and duplication: D1, D2, D3, 1", Betacam SP, Hi 8, BVU, U-Matic, VHS and Betamax
Standards conversions: D1, D2, 1", Betacam SP, and all cassette formats

Tattooist International
Westgate House
149 Roman Way
London N7 8XH
Tel: 071 700 3555
Fax: 071 700 4445
16mm cutting room, Super 16 and stereo options, lo-band U-Matic off-line, Aaton camera hire specialists, Steadicam, time lapse equipment, production offices

Team Television
The Exchange Buildings
Mount Stuart Square
Cardiff CF1 6EA
Tel: 0222 484230
Fax: 0222 494210
Edit 1 Multiformat: 1"C, Beta SP, 2 Channel Charisma, Quantel DLS; Edit 2: fully component Beta SP; Telecine 16mm/35mm, Quantel V series Paintbox with caption camera; duplicating

Tele-Cine
Video House
48 Charlotte Street
London W1P 1LX
Tel: 071 916 3711
Fax: 071 916 3700/01
Multiformat editing, transfer and standards conversion; digital audio post-production
Telecines: FDL90 suite with Pogle controller, FDL60 suite with Da Vinci; all digital and analogue VTR formats; BT land lines

Third Eye Productions
Unit 210 Canalot Studios
222 Kensal Road
London W10 5BN
Tel: 081 969 8211
Fax: 081 960 8790
Fully equipped 16mm cutting room and SVHS off-line edit suite

Tiny Epic Video Co
37 Dean Street
London W1V 5AP
Tel: 071 437 2854
18 suites of off-line editing 24 hours a day, 7 days a week. 10 x Sony 5 series U-Matic (and Shotlister); 2 x Panasonic 6500 VHS (and Shotlister); 4 x Panasonic 7500 SVHS (and Shotlister); 1 x 3 machine U-Matic with GVG100 (with vision mixer and Editmaster controller); 1 x Sony 9000 series lo-/hi-band/hi-band SP (and Shotlister). Dubbing: all formats including Hi 8 and DAT. Music and sound effects; EDL generation, EDL translation; autoconforming

Twickenham Film Studios
St Margaret's
Twickenham
Middlesex TW1 2AW
Tel: 081 892 4477
Fax: 081 891 0168
Two dubbing theatres, ADR effects theatre, 41 cutting rooms, Dolby installation

VMTV
1st Floor
34 Fouberts Place
London W1V 2BH
Tel: 071 439 4536
Fax: 071 437 0952
OBs: Five units with 2-12 cameras, 1" or Beta SP record format, full complement ancillary equipment, plus new digital truck
Studios: Two West End broadcast studios
Dry hire: Betacam SP and 16mm equipment with/without crews

VTR
64 Dean Street
London W1V 5HG
Tel: 071 437 0026
Fax: 071 439 9427
2 x Rank Cintel MkIIIC enhanced 4:2:2 telecines with Pogle DCP grading – DCP mastergrading system. 2 x Kadenza digital edit suites based on 2 x D1s A66 and A64 disks in each with Kaleidoscope DVE, A72 character generators and ¼" or DAT playback
3-D graphics – Silicon Graphics Crimson with Softimage and T-morph
Quantel Harry with Kaleidoscope DVE; Harriet with V-Series Paintbox. Quantel Henry with Max option

The Video Duplicating Co
VDC House
South Way
Wembley
Middx HA9 0EH
Tel: 081 903 3345
Fax: 081 900 1427
Comprehensive video services in all formats, tape to tape, bulk cassette duplication

Vector Television
Battersea Road
Heaton Mersey
Stockport
Cheshire SK4 3EA
Tel: 061 442 7887
Fax: 061 443 1325
3 on-line edit suites, 2 multiple source, D1, D3 1"C, Betacam SP or BVU SP composite suites and 1, 3 machine Beta SP component suite. All suites access 3 channels of ADO 2000 or A53-D digital effects. Abekas A72 or Aston 3 Character Generators, and CCD Caption Cameras
Harry, with Encore HUD Paintbox, Clip Management and Colour Caption Camera on-line.
Symbolics 3D computer animation system
Audio post-production centered around a digital Yamaha DMC 1000, AMS Audiofile digital editor and a full range of outboard equipment
Duplication multi standard PAL, NTSC, SECAM to and from most formats. 120 stereo high grade VHS recorders
2 broadcast studios. Sound proof drive-in scene dock doors, 80 lanterns controlled by Gemini 2, 2 dressing rooms, make-up, laundry, 3 production offices and green room, complete with curved cyclorama, twin track with blue black tabs

Video Film & Grip Company
Unit 1, I-Mex House
6 Wadsworth Road
Perivale
Middx UB6 5BB
Tel: 081 566 9110
Fax: 081 997 8011
Unit 9, Orchard Street
Industrial Estate
Salford
Manchester M6 6FL
Tel: 061 745 8146
Fax: 061 745 8161
Cardiff Studios
Culverhouse Cross
Cardiff CF5 6XT
Tel: 0222 599777
Fax: 0222 597957
Suppliers of 35mm camera equipment for TV commercials etc, 16mm camera equipment for documentaries, Beta SP video equipment for broadcast, and extensive range of cranes, dollies and ancillary grip equipment

The Video Lab
Back West Crescent
St Annes on Sea
Lancs FY8 1SU
Tel: 0253 725499/712011
Fax: 0253 713094
Cintel Telecine 9.5/8/ Super 8/16/35mm, slides and stills
Video formats: 2", 1"C, BVU, U-Matic, Beta SP
Cameras: Sony
Duplication, standards conversion
Specialists in transfer from discontinued videotape formats.
Library of holiday videos (Travelogue), corporate and TV production, TV and cinema commercial production

Video Time
22-24 Greek Street
London W1V 5LG
Tel: 071 439 1211
Fax: 071 439 7336
One stop facilities with 16 different formats including D1, D2 PAL/ NTSC & D3. Standards conversion, Telecine 4:2:2 16/35mm PAL/NTSC/ SECAM. Audio layback. Specialists in CAV/CLV disc cutting, disc mastering and CRV discs

Videola (UK)
171 Wardour Street
London W1V 3TA
Tel: 071 437 5413
Fax: 071 734 5295
Video formats: 1", U-Matic, Beta SP
Camera: JVC KY35
Editing: 3 machine Beta SP
Computer rostrum camera; 3D computer graphic workstation with Paintbox image processing

Videolondon Soundstudios
16-18 Ramillies Street
London W1V 1DL
Tel: 071 734 4811
Fax: 071 494 2553
5 sophisticated sound recording studios, 3 with overhead TV projection systems. 16mm, 35mm and video post-synch recording and mixing. Two NED digital audio suites with three further NEDs and one AudioFile assignable to any of the studios. All sound facilities for film or video post-production including 1" PAL and Betacam SP with Lightworks editing non-linear system

Videoscope
Ty-Cattwg Cottage
Llancarfan
Barry
South Glam CF6 9AG
Tel: 0446 710963
Fax: 0446 710023
Video formats: hi-band U-Matic, Betacam, 1"
Cameras: Sony 3000
Timecode transfer, 3-machine, hi-band editing, SP editing; copying bank

Warwick Dubbing Theatre
WFS (Film Holdings)
151-153 Wardour Street
London W1V 3TB
Tel: 071 437 5532
Sound recording and mixing to video and film; sound transfer, magnetic stereo/mono optical; ADR post sync; FV dubbing; edge numbering

West One Television
10 Bateman Street
London W1V 5TT
Tel: 071 437 5533
Fax: 071 287 8621
West One West
186 Campden Hill Road
London W8 7TH
Tel: 071 221 8221
5 multi format on-line suites, 1 component suite; 9 channels of ADO; Quanta Delta & Aston 3; D3, D2, 1" & 1" PCM, Betacam SP, BVU & lo-band, Hi 8, Video 8, SVHS & VHS

Windmill Lane Pictures
4 Windmill Lane
Dublin 2
Ireland
Tel: 010 353 1 6713444
Fax: 010 353 1 6718413
Film, video, news, graphics and production facilities

Wiseman
27-35 Lexington Street
London W1R 3HQ
Tel: 071 439 8901
Fax: 071 437 2481
Edit 1: Abekas A84, A64, A60, A72, A57, caption camera, 2 x D1 DVTR, 2 x Betacam SP, CMX controller
Edit 2: GVG 200CV, A72, ADO, caption camera, 2 x 1" VPR3, 2 x Betacam SP, 1 x D2 DVTR, ACE controller
Edit 3: GVG 200CV, A72, ADO, caption camera, 3 x Betacam SP, 2 x 1" VPR3, 1 x D2 DVTR, ACE controller
Off-line: Lightworks non-linear + 2 machine U-Matic
Telecine: Rank Cintel 4:2:2 XYZoom, Pogle, Matchbox, Varispeed, Stedigate, digital grain reducer, 16mm and Super 16mm wetgate, Digislate, Aaton and Arri timecode readers
Harriet: with VE series Paintbox, Caption camera and Sony colour video printer, D1 DVTR
Harry: Long play Harry with VE series Paintbox and Encore HUD, D1 DVTR, caption camera, clip management
Rostrum: IMC computer controlled camera
3D: Softimage with T-morph package
Audio: Lexicon Opus digital audio suite, v/o booth, CD and effects libraries
Duplication: to and from D1, D2, D3, 1"C, Betacam SP, 2" Quad, most cassette formats. Nagra-T and DAT
Standards conversion: to and from PAL, NTSC, SECAM via ADAC and AVS6500

Wolff Productions
6a Noel Street
London W1V 3RB
Tel: 071 439 1838/734 4286
35mm/16mm rostrum camera work; animation production

World Wide Sound
21-25 St Anne's Court
London W1V 3AW
Tel: 071 434 1121
Fax: 071 734 0619
16mm, 35mm, digital and Dolby recording track laying facilities specialising in post sync foreign dubbing

Worldwide Television News Corporation
The Interchange
Oval Road
Camden Lock
London NW1
Tel: 071 410 5200
Fax: 071 413 8302/8303/ 8327
BVU editing (PAL and NTSC); multi-machine editing with digital effects and colour captioning; Betacam record/replay; 1"C editing; digital standards conversion; PAL/SECAM transcoding; duplication; local and international feeds, studio facilities; Matisse graphics

FESTIVALS

Listed below by country of origin are some international film, TV and video festivals with contact addresses and brief synopses

AUSTRALIA

Australian International Video Festival (Oct)
PO Box 661
Glebe NSW 2037
Tel: (61) 2 552 4220
Fax: (61) 2 552 4229
Competitive (honourable awards only). Video art, computer animation, reportage, video dance, music video, installations and special forums

Melbourne International Film Festival (June)
PO Box 296
Fitzroy 3065
Victoria
Tel: (61) 3 417 2011
Fax: (61) 3 417 3804
Short film competition includes special interest in films dealing with science, architecture and films for youth (5-18)

Sydney Film Festival (June)
PO Box 25
Glebe NSW 2037
Tel: (61) 2 660 3844
Fax: (61) 2 692 8793
Non-competitive for feature films, documentaries and shorts not previously shown in Australia

AUSTRIA

Viennale – Vienna International Film Festival (Oct)
Stiftgasse 6
1070 Vienna
Tel: (43) 1 526 5947
Fax: (43) 1 934172
Non-competitive for features and documentaries

BELGIUM

Art Movie (Feb)
1104 Kortrijkse Steenweg
9051 Ghent
Tel: (32) 92 21 89 46
Fax: (32) 92 21 90 74
International festival of films about art

Brussels International Film Festival (Jan)
Chaussée de Louvain 30
1030 Brussels
Tel: (32) 2 218 10 55
Fax: (32) 2 218 66 27
Non-competitive sections include a Euro-Panorama, and special focus on Nordic Cinema. Also Belgian focus. Competitive for short films from Belgium; also special programmes of international shorts

Brussels International Festival of Fantasy, Thriller and Science Fiction Films (March)
144 avenue de la Reine
1210 Brussels
Tel: (32) 2 242 17 13
Fax: (32) 2 216 21 69
Competitive for features and shorts (less than 20 mins)

International Flanders Film Festival (Oct)
1104 Kortrijksesteenweg
9051 Ghent
Tel: (32) 9 221 8946
Fax: (32) 9 221 9074
Competitive, with official selection on 'The impact of music on film', for films over 60 mins. Deadline for entry forms mid August

BRAZIL

Banco Nacional International Film Festival (Sept)
Rua Voluntários da Pátria 88
CEP 22270-010
Rio de Janeiro RJ
Tel: (55) 21 285 8505
Fax: (55) 21 286 4029
Non-competitive, promoting films that would not otherwise get to Brazilian screens

São Paulo International Film Festival (Oct)
Al. Lorena 937, Cj. 303
01424-0001 São Paulo SP
Tel: (55) 11 883 5137
Fax: (55) 11 853 7936
Non-competitive for features/shorts/documentary/animation and experimental films which must have been produced during 2 years preceding the festival

BULGARIA

International Festival of Comedy Films (May odd years)
House of Humour and Satire
PO Box 104
5300 Gabrovo
Tel: (359) 66 2 7229
Fax: (359) 66 2 9300
Competitive; full-length and short films

BURKINA FASO

Panafrican Film and Television Festival of Ouagadougou
(Feb odd years)
Secrétariat Général Permanent du FESPACO
01 BP 2505
Ouagadougou 01
Tel: (226) 30 75 38
Fax: (226) 31 25 09
Competitive, featuring African filmmakers whose work must have been produced during the three years preceding the festival and not shown before at FESPACO

CANADA

The Atlantic Film Festival (Sept-Oct)
2015 Gottingen Street
Halifax
Nova Scotia B3K 3B1
Tel: (1) 902 422 3451
Fax: (1) 902 422 4006
Competitive for international, Canadian and particularly Atlantic Canadian film and video production. Also showcases, including Scottish Perspectives, a Children's International Film and Television Festival, and The Future of Television

Banff Television Festival (June)

PO Box 1020
Banff
Alberta T0L 0C0
Tel: (1) 403 762 3060
Fax: (1) 403 762 5357
Competitive for films made for TV, including features, drama specials, limited series, continuing series, documentaries, children's programmes and comedy which were broadcast for the first time in the previous year

International Festival of New Cinema and Video (Oct)
3726 Boulevard Saint-Laurent
Montreal
Quebec H2X 2V8
Tel: (1) 514 843 4725
Fax: (1) 514 843 4631
Non-competitive for innovative films produced during previous two years which have not been screened in Canada

Montreal World Film Festival (+ Market) (Aug)
1455 de Maisonneuve Blvd West
Montreal
Quebec H3G IM8
Tel: (1) 514 848 3883
Fax: (1) 514 848 3886
Official competition and themed sections outside competition

Ottawa International Animation Festival (Sept-Oct even years)
2 Daly Avenue
Ottawa
Ontario K1N 6E2
Tel: (1) 613 232 6727
Fax: (1) 613 232 63153

Toronto International Film Festival of Festivals (Sept)
70 Carlton Street
Toronto
Ontario M5B 1L7
Tel: (1) 416 967 7371
Fax: (1) 416 967 9477
Non-competitive for feature films and shorts not previously shown in Canada. Also includes some American premieres, retrospectives and national cinema programmes. Films must have been completed within the year prior to the festival to be eligible

Vancouver International Film Festival (Oct)
Suite 410
1008 Homer Street
Vancouver
British Columbia
V6B 2X1
Tel: (1) 604 685 0260
Fax: (1) 604 688 8221
Third largest festival in North America, with special emphasis on East Asian and Canadian cinema. Also nonfiction features, British and European cinema and 'The Screenwriter's Art'. Submission deadline end July

CROATIA

Zagreb World Festival of Animated Films (June even years)
Kneza Mislava 18
POB 438
41000 Zagreb
Tel: (38) 41 41 01 28/34/31
Fax: (38) 41 44 30 22
Competitive for animated films (up to 30 mins). Categories: films from 30 secs-5 mins, 5-30 mins, debut film. Films must have been completed in two years prior to festival and not have been awarded prizes at Annecy

CUBA

International Festival of Latin American Cinema (Dec)
Calle 25
1155 Vedado (e/10 y 12)
Havana 4
Tel: (53) 7 34 169
Fax: (53) 7 33 30 32
Competitive for films produced in or about America. Market for features, documentaries, animation

CZECH REPUBLIC

GOLDEN PRAGUE International TV Festival (June)
Czech Television
Na Hrebenech II
147 41 Prague 4
Tel: (42) 2 6927234
Fax: (42) 2 6927202
Competitive for TV music programmes in two categories: dramatic music programmes or concert works and other types of music programmes. Applications must be submitted by 5 March, and videos by 5 April

Karlovy Vary International Film Festival (July)
Ministry of Culture of the Czech Republic
Valdstejnská 10
118 11 Prague 1
Tel: (42) 2 513 23 38
Fax: (42) 2 53 70 55
Feature films in competition; Panorama, retrospectives, market

Prague International Film Festival (Oct-Nov)
PIFF/Space films
Karlovo Námestí 19
120 00 Prague 2
Tel: (42) 2 204820/ 204687/204823
Fax: (42) 2 202723
Non-competitive for features not previously shown in Czech Republic or former Czechoslovakia that would not otherwise get to Czech screens

DENMARK

Balticum Film and TV Festival (May)
c/o National Film Board of Denmark
Vestergade 27
1456 Copenhagen K
Tel: (45) 33 13 26 86
Fax: (45) 33 13 02 03
Non-competitive for short films and documentaries from the countries around the Baltic Sea

International Odense Film Festival (July-Aug)
Slotsgade 5
5000 Odense C
Tel: (45) 66 13 13 72 x4294
Fax: (45) 65 91 43 18
Competitive for fairy-tale and experimental-imaginative films. Deadline for entries 1 May

EGYPT

Cairo International Film Festival (Nov-Dec)
17 Kasr El Nil Street
Cairo
Tel: (20) 2 392 3562/392 3962/393 3832
Fax: (20) 2 393 8979
Competitive for feature films, plus a Film, TV and Video market

Cairo International Film Festival for Children (Sept)
17 Kasr El Nil Street
Cairo
Tel: (20) 2 392 3562/392 3962/393 3832
Fax: (20) 2 393 8979
Competitive for children's films: features, shorts, documentaries, educative, cartoons, TV films and programmes for children up to 14 years

FINLAND

Midnight Sun Film Festival (June)
Jäämerentie 9
99600 Sodankylä
Tel: (358) 693 21313/ 21008
Fax: (358) 693 28646
Non-competitive for feature films, held in Finnish Lapland

Tampere International Short Film Festival (March)
PO Box 305
33101 Tampere
Tel: (358) 31 2130034
Fax: (358) 31 2230121
Competitive for short films, max. 35 mins. Categories for animated, fiction and documentary short films, released on or after 1 Jan 1993. Videos accepted for selection only. 10-15 large retrospectives and tributes of short films from all over the world

FRANCE

Annecy International Festival of Animation (+ Market) (June)
JICA/MIFA
BP 399
74013 Annecy Cedex
Tel: (33) 50 57 41 72
Fax: (33) 50 67 81 95

Competitive for animated short films, feature-length films, TV films, commercials, produced in the previous 26 months

Avoriaz International Fantasy Film Festival (Jan)
33 avenue MacMahon
75017 Paris
Tel: (33) 1 42 67 71 40
Fax: (33) 1 46 22 88 51
Competitive for science fiction, horror, supernatural and fantasy feature films, which have not been commercially shown in France or participated in festivals in Europe

Cannes International Film Festival (May)
71 rue du Faubourg St Honoré
75008 Paris
Tel: (33) 1 42 66 92 20
Fax: (33) 1 42 66 68 85
Competitive section for feature films and shorts (up to 20 mins) produced in the previous year, which have not screened outside country of origin nor been entered in other competitive festivals, plus non-competitive section: Un Certain Regard
Other non-competitive events:
Directors Fortnight (Quinzaine des Réalisateurs) and Programme of French Cinema (Cinémas en France)
215 rue du Faubourg St Honoré
75008 Paris
Tel: (33) 1 45 61 01 66
Fax: (33) 1 40 74 07 96
Critic's Week (Semaine de la Critique)
90 rue d'Amsterdam
75009 Paris
Tel: (33) 1 40 16 98 30/ (33) 1 45 74 53 53

Cinéma du Réel (International Festival of Visual Anthropology) (March)
Bureau du Festival
Cinéma du Réel
Bibliothèque Publique d'Information
19 rue Beaubourg
75197 Paris Cedex 04
Tel: (33) 1 44 78 45 16/ 44 23
Fax: (33) 1 44 78 12 24
Documentaries only (film or video). Competitive – must not have been released commercially or been awarded a prize at an international festival in France. Must have been made in the year prior to the Festival

Cognac International Film Festival of the Thriller (March-April even years)
33 avenue MacMahon
75017 Paris
Tel: (33) 1 42 67 71 40
Fax: (33) 1 46 22 88 51
Competitive for thriller films, which have not been commercially shown in France or participated in festivals in Europe

Deauville European Festival of American Film (Sept)
33 avenue MacMahon
75017 Paris
Tel: (33) 1 42 67 71 40
Fax: (33) 1 46 22 88 51
Non-competitive for American feature films, not yet released in Europe (except UK), or shown in other French film festivals

FIFREC (International Film and Student Directors Festival) (April)
FIFREC
BP 7144
30913 Nîmes Cedex
Tel: (33) 66 84 47 40
Fax: (33) 72 02 20 36
Official film school selections (3 per school) and open selection for directors from film schools, either students or recent graduates. Categories include fiction, documentaries and animation. Also best film school award. Films to be under 40 mins

Festival des Trois Continents (Nov)
BP 3306
44033 Nantes Cedex 01
Tel: (33) 40 69 09 73/40 69 74 14
Fax: (33) 40 73 55 22
Films from Africa/Asia/ Latin and Black America. Competitive section, tributes to directors and actors, panoramas

Festival du Film Britannique de Dinard (Sept)
47 boulevard Féart
35800 Dinard
Tel: (33) 99 88 19 04
Fax: (33) 99 46 67 15
Competitive – tribute meeting between French and English producers

Festival International de Films de Femmes (March)
Maison des Arts
Place Salvador Allende
94000 Créteil
Tel: (33) 1 49 80 38 98
Fax: (33) 1 43 99 04 10
Competitive for feature films, documentaries, shorts, retrospectives directed by women and produced in the previous 23 months and not previously shown in France

French-American Film Workshop (July)
10 Montée de la Tour
30400 Villeneuve-les-Avignon
Tel: (33) 90 25 93 23
Fax: (33) 90 25 93 24
For independent film-makers, offering the 'Kodak Tournage Award' to one French and one American film-maker to enable them to make another film

MIPCOM (Oct)
179 avenue Victor Hugo
75116 Paris
Tel: (33) 1 44 34 4444
Fax: (33) 1 44 34 4400
International film and programme market for TV, video, cable and satellite

MIP-TV (April)
179 avenue Victor Hugo
75116 Paris
Tel: (33) 1 44 34 4444
Fax: (33) 1 44 34 4400
International Television programme market

Montbéliard International Video and TV Festival (June even years)
Centre International de Création Vidéo
Montbéliard Belfort
BP5
25310 Herimoncourt
Tel: (33) 81 30 90 30
Fax: (33) 81 30 95 25
Competitive for documentaries, news, fiction, art, animation, music, computer graphics produced during 18 months preceding festival

GERMANY

Berlin International Film Festival (Feb)
Internationale Filmfestspiele Berlin
Budapester Strasse 50
1000 Berlin 30
Tel: (49) 30 254 890
Fax: (49) 30 254 89249
Competitive for feature films and shorts (up to 15 mins), plus a separate competition for children's films – feature length and shorts – produced in the previous year and not entered for other festivals. Also has non-competitive programme consisting of forum of young cinema, Panorama, film market and New German films

Feminale Women's Film Festival (May even years)
Feminale eV
Luxemburger Strasse 72
5000 Cologne 1
Tel: (49) 221 416066
Fax: (49) 221 417568
Non-competitive for films by women directors only, made in last 2 years, all genres, formats, lengths. Retrospectives, special programmes

Filmfest Hamburg (Aug-Sept)
Friedensallee 7
2000 Hamburg 50
Tel: (49) 40 39826 283
Fax: (49) 40 390 4040
Non-competitive, international features and shorts for cinema release (fiction, documentaries), presentation of one film country/ continent, premieres of Hamburg-funded films, and other activities

Internationales Leipziger Festival für Dokumentar- und Animationsfilm (Nov-Dec)
Dokfilmwoche GmbH

Elsterstrasse 22-24
04709 Leipzig
Tel/Fax: (37) 41 294660
Competition, special programmes, film and video market, international jury and awards

International Film Festival Mannheim (Nov)
Collini-Center, Galerie
68161 Mannheim
Tel: (49) 621 10 29 43
Fax: (49) 621 29 15 64
The idea of Mannheim is to feature a single, concentrated competition programme which is dedicated to the slogan 'International Authors' Cinema – New Independents and Art Films'. Features and documentaries by new and established directors eligible

Munich Film Festival (June-July)
Internationale Münchner Filmwochen
Kaiserstrasse 39
8000 Munich 40
Tel: (49) 89 38 19 04 0
Fax: (49) 89 38 19 04 26
Non-competitive for feature films, shorts and documentaries which have not previously been shown in Germany

Nordic Film Days Lübeck (Nov)
Postfach 2132
23539 Lübeck
Tel: (49) 451 122 4105
Fax: (49) 451 122 4106
Festival of Scandinavian and Baltic films

Oberhausen International Short Film Festival (April)
Christian-Steger Str 10
4200 Oberhausen 1
Tel: (49) 208 825 2652
Fax: (49) 208 852 591
Competitive for documentaries, animation, experimental and short features (up to 35 mins), student films, and video productions produced in the previous 16 months; national section and side programmes; international symposia on new developments in the media field

Prix Europa (Sept-Oct)
Sender Freies Berlin
Masurenallee 8-14
1000 Berlin 19
Tel: (49) 30 3031 1610
Fax: (49) 30 3031 1619
Competitive for fiction, non-fiction, series/serials in television. Open to all TV stations and TV producers in Europe. 6 awards of 6,250 ECU

Prix Futura Berlin
International Radio and TV Contest (March-April odd years)
Sender Freies Berlin
Masurenallee 8-14
1000 Berlin 19
Tel: (49) 30 3031 1610
Fax: (49) 30 3031 1619
Competitive for documentary and drama both on radio and TV. One entry per category in TV, 2 per category in radio for day competition. Evening competition has similar categories, but is for young people and independent producers. One entry per category per organisation

PRIX JEUNESSE International (May-June even years)
Bayerischer Rundfunk
Rundfunkplatz 1
8000 Munich 2
Tel: (49) 89 5900 2058
Fax: (49) 89 5900 3053
Competitive for children's and youth TV programmes (age groups up to 7, 7-12 and 12-17), in fiction and non-fiction, produced in the previous two years. (In odd years: seminars in children's and youth TV)

Internationales Trickfilm Festival Stuttgart (March even years)
Stuttgarter Trickfilmtage
Teckstrasse 56
(Kulturpark Berg)
7000 Stuttgart 1
Tel: (49) 2 62 26 99
Fax: (49) 2 62 49 80
Competitive for animated short films of an artistic and experimental nature, which have been produced in the previous two years and not exceeding 35 mins

Internationales Filmwochenende Würzburg (Jan)
Gosbertsteige 2
97082 Würzburg
Tel: (49) 931 414 098
Fax: (49) 931 416 279
Competitive for recent European and international productions

HONG KONG

Hong Kong International Film Festival (March-April)
Level 7, Admin Building
Hong Kong Cultural Centre
10 Salisbury Road
Tsimshatsui
Kowloon
Hong Kong
Tel: (852) 734 2903
Fax: (852) 366 5206
Non-competitive for feature films, documentaries and invited short films, which have been produced in the previous two years. Also local short film competition

HUNGARY

Agria Filmszemle (Aug)
Postafiok 18
3301 Eger
Tel: (36) 36 10 553
Fax: (36) 36 10 553
Non-competitive for Hungarian feature films and shorts

INDIA

Bombay International Film Festival for Documentary, Short and Animation Films
(Feb-March even years)
Films Division
Ministry of Information & Broadcasting
Government of India
24-Dr G Deshmukh Marg
Bombay 400 026
Tel: (91) 22 3861461
Fax: (91) 22 3861421
Competitive for fiction, non-fiction and animation, plus international jury award and information section. Films to have been produced between Jan 1990 and Nov 1992

International Film Festival of India (+ Market) (Jan)
Directorate of Film Festivals
Fourth Floor
Lok Nayak Bhavan
Khan Market
New Delhi 110 003
Tel: (91) 11 615953/697167
Fax: (91) 11 694920
Non-competitive, held in different Indian cities by rotation, including New Delhi, Bangalore, Bombay, Calcutta, Hyderabad, and Trivandrum. 1994 festival to be held in Calcutta

IRELAND

Cork Film Festival
(Oct)
Hatfield House
15 Tobin Street
Cork
Tel: (353) 21 271711
Fax: (353) 21 275945
Non-competitive for features, documentaries and short films. Competitive for European short films (up to 30 mins) and films in black and white, produced in the previous two years

Dublin Film Festival (Feb-March)
1 Suffolk Street
Dublin 2
Tel: (353) 1 6792937
Fax: (353) 1 6792939
Non-competitive, screening over 150 films from 42 countries in the 1993 festival. Fims of every category welcomed for submission

ISRAEL

Jerusalem Film Festival (July)
PO Box 8561
Wolfson Gardens
Hebron Road
91083 Jerusalem
Tel: (972) 2 724 131
Fax: (972) 2 733 076
Non-competitive panorama, recent international cinema: features, documentaries, animation, shorts, video, television. Competitive Israeli section: features, documentaries, shorts; retrospectives, tributes and restorations

ITALY

Da Sodoma a Hollywood (April)
Turin Lesbian and Gay

Film Festival
Associazione Culturale L'Altra Comunicazione
Via T Tasso 11
10122 Turin
Tel: (39) 11 436 6855
Fax: (39) 11 521 3737
Specialist lesbian/gay themed festival. Competitive for features, shorts and documentaries. Also retrospectives and special showcases for both cinema and television work

Festival dei Popoli – International Review of Social Documentary Films (Nov-Dec)
Via de'Castellani 8
50122 Florence
Tel: (39) 55 29 43 53
Fax: (39) 55 21 36 98
Competitive and non-competitive sections for documentaries on sociological, historical, political, anthropological subjects as well as music, art and cinema, produced during the year preceding the festival. The films for the competitive section should not have been screened in Italy before

Giffoni Film Festival (July-Aug)
Piazza Umberto I
84095 Giffoni Valle Piana
Tel: (39) 89 868 544
Fax: (39) 89 866 111
Competitive for full-length fiction, animated full-length, medium-length and shorts for children 6-12, 12-14 and 12-18 years. Entries must have been produced within 2 years preceding the festival

MIFED (Oct)
Largo Domodossola 1
20145 Milan
Tel: (39) 2 480 12912
Fax: (39) 2 499 77020
International cinema and television market

Mystery & Noir Film Festival (Nov-Dec)
Via dei Coronari 44
00186 Rome
Tel: (39) 6 683 3844
Fax: (39) 6 686 7902
Competitive for thrillers between 30-180 mins length, which have been produced in the previous year and not released in Italy. Festival now takes place at Courmayeur

Pesaro Film Festival (Mostra Internazionale del Nuovo Cinema) (June)
Via Villafranca 20
00185 Rome
Tel: (39) 6 445 6643
Fax: (39) 6 491163
Non-competitive. Particularly concerned with the work of new directors and emergent cinemas, with innovation at every level. In recent seasons the festival has been devoted to a specific country or culture

Pordenone Silent Film Days (Le Giornate del Cinema Muto) (Oct)
c/o La Cineteca del Friuli
Via Osoppo 26
33014 Gemona
Tel: (39) 432 98 04 58
Fax: (39) 432 97 05 42
Non-competitive silent film festival. Annual award for restoration and preservation of the silent film heritage

Prix Italia (Sept)
RAI Radiotelevisione Italiana
Via del Babuino 9
00187 Rome
Tel: (39) 6 312 782
Fax: (39) 6 322 5270
Competitive for television and radio productions from national broadcasting organisations. In the three categories (arts and music, drama, documentaries) each broadcasting organisation may submit: Radio – maximum 4 entries; Television – in case of 1 channel max. 2 entries; in case of more than 1 channel max. 3 entries

Taormina International Film Festival (July)
Palazzo Firenze
Via Pirandello 31
98039 Taormina
Sicily
Tel: (39) 6 325 1387
Fax: (39) 6 325 2756
Competitive for directors of first and second feature films. Emphasis on new directors and cinema from developing countries

Turin International Festival of Young Cinema (Nov)
Piazza San Carlo 161
10123 Turin
Tel: (39) 11 5623309
Fax: (39) 11 5629796
Competitive sections for feature and short films. Italian Space section (videos and films) open solely to Italian work. All works must be completed during 13 previous months, with no prior release in Italy

Venice Film Festival (Sept)
Mostra Internazionale d'Arte Cinematografica
La Biennale di Venezia
Ca' Giustinian
San Marco
30124 Venice
Tel: (39) 41 521 8711
Fax: (39) 41 522 7539
Non-specialised competitive festival of cinematographic art for feature films. Categories: competition, documentary and short section, retrospective. Requirements: non-participation at other international festivals, and/or screenings outside country of origin. Submission before 30 June

JAPAN

International Animation Festival Hiroshima (Aug)
4-17 Kako-machi
Naka-ku
Hiroshima 730
Tel: (81) 82 245 0245
Fax: (81) 82 245 0246
The festival programme consists of competition, panorama, retrospective, homage, tributes etc

Tokyo International Film Festival (+ Market) (Sept-Oct)
Organising Committee
Asano Building No 3
2-14-19 Ginza, Chuo-Ku
Tokyo 104
Tel: (81) 3 3563 6305
Fax: (81) 3 3563 6310
Competitive. Young cinema section for films by young or new directors; best of Asian films section, and Nippon Cinema now: masterpieces by contemporary Japanese directors

Tokyo Video Festival (Nov)
c/o Victor Co of Japan
1-7-1 Shinbashi
Victor Bldg, Minato-ku
Tokyo 105
Tel: (81) 3 3289 2815
Fax: (81) 3 3289 2819
Competitive for videos; compositions on any theme and in any style accepted, whether previously screened or not

MALTA

Golden Knight International Amateur Film & Video Festival (Nov)
PO Box 450
Valletta CMR,01
Tel: (356) 222345/236173
Fax: (356) 225047
Three classes: amateur, student, professional – not exceeding 30 minutes

MARTINIQUE

Images Caraïbes (Caribbean Film and Video Festival)
(June even years)
77 route de la Folie
97200 Fort-de-France
Tel: (596) 70 23 81
Fax: (596) 63 23 91
Competitive for all film and video makers native to the Caribbean Islands – features, shorts and documentary

THE NETHERLANDS

Dutch Film Days (Sept)
Stichting Nederlandse Filmdagen
Hoogt 4-10
3512 GW Utrecht
Tel: (31) 30 322684
Fax: (31) 30 313200
Annual screening of all new Dutch features, shorts, documentaries and animations. Retrospectives, seminars, talks shows, lectures, Golden Calf awards

International Documentary Filmfestival Amsterdam (Dec)
Kleine-Gartman-plantsoen 10
1017 RR Amsterdam
Tel: (31) 20 6273329

Fax: (31) 20 6385388
Competitive for documentaries of any length, 35mm or 16mm, produced in 15 months prior to the festival; retrospectives; Joris Ivens award; seminars and workshops

International Film Festival Rotterdam
(Jan-Feb)
PO Box 21696
3001 AR Rotterdam
Tel: (31) 10 411 8080
Fax: (31) 10 413 5132
Non-competitive, comprising 200 features, documentaries, shorts. Main programme presents international premiers and a selection of the last year's festivals. Several sidebars and retrospectives. Cinemart: co-production market for films in progress. Deadline for entries 1 December

NEW ZEALAND

Wellington Film Festival (July)
PO Box 9544
Te Aro
Wellington
Tel: (64) 4 385 0162
Fax: (64) 4 801 7304
Non-competitive for feature and short films. By invitation only

NORWAY

International Norwegian Film Festival (Aug)
PO Box 145
5501 Haugesund
Tel: (47) 52 73 43 00
Fax: (47) 52 73 44 20
Non-competitive film festival

POLAND

International Short Film Festival in Kraków (May-June)
Apollo Film
ul. Pychowicka 7
30-364 Kraków
Tel: (48) 12 67 13 55
Fax: (48) 12 67 15 52
Competitive for short films (up to 30 mins), including documentaries, fiction, animation, popular science and experimental subjects, produced in the previous 15 months and not awarded prizes in other international festivals

PORTUGAL

Cinanima (International Animated Film Festival) (Nov)
Apartado 43
4501 Espinho Codex
Tel: (351) 2 721 621/724 611
Fax: (351) 2 726 015
Competitive for features, advertising, children, youth, experimental, first work and didactic films. Also includes work by student directors. Entries must have been completed in the two years preceding the festival

Fantasporto – Oporto International Film Festival (Feb)
Rua da Constituição 311
4200 Porto
Tel: (351) 2 4108990/1/2
Fax: (351) 2 4108210
Competitive section for feature films and shorts, particularly fantasy and science fiction films. FIAPF accredited, includes New Directors week (non-official competition), and retrospective section dedicated to British cinema. Also programme of Portuguese cinema

Festival Internacional de Cinema da Figueira da Foz (Sept)
Apartado de Correios 5407
1709 Lisbon Codex
Tel: (351) 1 346 9556
Fax: (351) 1 342 0890
Competitive for fiction and documentary films, films for children, shorts and video. Some cash prizes. Also retrospective of Portuguese cinema. Entries must have been produced during 20 months preceding Festival

Festival Internacional de Cinema de Troia
(June)
Troia
2902 Setúbal Codex
Tel: (351) 65 44121/44124
Fax: (351) 65 44123
Three categories: Official Section, First Films, Man and His Environment, also Information section. The official section is devoted to films coming from those countries which have a limited production (less than 21 features per year). Films must not have been screened previously in Portugal and must have been produced during 24 months preceding the festival. Also film market and several retrospectives in the Information section

PUERTO RICO

Puerto Rico International Film Festival (Nov)
70 Mayagüez Street
Ste. B-1
Hato Rey PR 00918
Tel: (809) 764 7044
Fax: (809) 753 5367
Non-competitive international event with emphasis on Latin-American, Spanish features and special section on women directors

RUSSIA

International Film Festival of Festivals
(June)
10 Kamennoostrovsky Avenue
St Petersburg 197101
Tel: (7) 812 238 5811
Fax: (7) 812 238 5276
Non-competitive, aimed at promoting films from all over the world that meet the highest artistic criteria, and the distribution of non-commercial cinema

Moscow International Film Festival (July odd years)
Interfest
General Management of International Film Festivals
10 Khokhlovsky per.
Moscow 109028
Tel: (7) 095 227 8924
Fax: (7) 095 227 0107
Competitive for feature films produced in the 2 years prior to the festival and not shown in competition in other international festivals. Also includes out of competition screenings and retrospectives

SERBIA

Belgrade International Film Festival (Jan-Feb)
Sava Centar
Milentija Popovica 9
11070 Novi Beograd
Tel: (38) 11 222 49 61
Fax: (38) 11 222 11 56
Non-competitive for features reflecting high aesthetic and artistic values and contemporary trends

SINGAPORE

International Film Festival (April)
168 Kim Seng Road
Singapore 0923
Tel: (65) 738 7567
Fax: (65) 738 7578
Specialised competitive festival for Best Asian Film. Non-competitive includes panorama of international film. 8mm, 16mm, 35mm and video are accepted. Films must not have been shown commercially in Singapore

SLOVAKIA

Forum – International Festival of First Feature Films, Bratislava (Nov-Dec)
Festival Forum
Grösslingova 32
811 09 Bratislava
Tel: (42) 7 361 232
Fax: (42) 7 363 461
Competitive for first features, produced or first run from October 1993 to September 1994 of minimum duration 50 mins. Other programme categories: Forum Special, Retrospectives, Film School Profile, New Slovak and Czech Films

SPAIN

Bilbao International Festival of Documentary and Short Films (Nov-Dec)
Colón de Larreátegui 37
4º drcha.
48009 Bilbao
Apdo. Postal 579
Tel: (34) 4 24 8698/7860
Fax: (34) 4 24 5624
Competitive for animation, fiction and documentary

International Film Festival of Gijón (July)
Paseo de Begoña 24 entlo
33205 Gijón (Asturias)
Tel: (34) 85 34 37 39
Fax: (34) 85 35 41 52
Competitive for features and shorts made for young people. Must have been produced during 18 months preceding the festival and not awarded a prize at any other major international film festival

Huesca International Short Film Festival (June)
C/Villahermosa, 2. 1º
22001 Huesca
Tel: (34) 74 22 70 58
Fax: (34) 74 24 66 00
Competitive for short films (up to 30 mins) on any theme except tourism and promotion

Imagfic – Madrid International Film Festival (April)
Gran Via 62-8
28013 Madrid
Tel: (34) 1 541 3721/5545
Fax: (34) 1 542 5495
Competitive, promoting 'Cinema of the Imagination', expressed in a wide variety of styles (eg SF, horror, thriller and mystery films)

San Sebastian International Film Festival (Sept)
PO Box 397
20080 San Sebastian
Tel: (34) 43 481 212
Fax: (34) 43 481 218
Competitive for feature films produced in the previous year and not released in Spain or shown in any other festivals. Non-competitive for Zabaltegi/Open Zone. Also retrospective sections

Sitges International Fantasy Film Festival (Oct)
Diputacion 279
08007 Barcelona
Tel: (34) 3 488 1038
Fax: (34) 3 487 4192
Official section – competitive for fantasy and horror films. Also shorts, informative section, retrospective, premieres. Seven chances section, showing films of new talents within the cinema world

Mostra de Valencia/Cinema del Mediterrani (Oct)
Pza del Arzobispo 2 bajo
46003 Valencia
Tel: (34) 6 392 1506
Fax: (34) 6 391 5156
Competitive official section. Informative section, special events section, 'mostra' for children, and International Congress of Film Music

Valladolid International Film Festival (Oct)
Calle Angustias 1
PO Box 646
47003 Valladolid
Tel: (34) 83 30 57 00/77/88
Fax: (34) 83 30 98 35
Competitive for 35mm features and shorts, plus documentaries, entries not to have been shown previously in Spain. Also film school tributes, retrospectives and selection of new Spanish productions

SWEDEN

Gothenburg Film Festival (Feb)
Box 7079
402 32 Gothenburg
Tel: (46) 31 41 05 46
Fax: (46) 31 41 00 63
Non-competitive for features, documentaries and shorts not released in Sweden

Stockholm International Film Festival (Nov)
PO Box 7673
10395 Stockholm
Tel: (46) 8 20 05 50
Fax: (46) 8 20 05 90
Competitive for innovative current feature films, survey of European cinema, focus on American independents and retrospective. Around 100 features have their Swedish premiere during the festival. FIAPF accredited

Uppsala International Short Film Festival (Oct)
Box 1746
751 47 Uppsala
Tel: (46) 18 12 00 25
Fax: (46) 18 12 13 50
Competitive for shorts (up to 60 mins), including fiction, animation, documentaries, children's and young people's films. 35mm and 16mm only

SWITZERLAND

Festival de Films de Fribourg (Jan-Feb)
Rue de Locarno 8
1700 Fribourg
Tel: (41) 37 22 22 32
Fax: (41) 37 22 79 50
Films from Africa, Asia and Latin America

Golden Rose of Montreux TV Festival (April)
PO Box 234
1211 Geneva 8
Tel: (41) 22 708 99 11
Fax: (41) 22 781 52 49
Competitive for TV productions (24-60 mins) of light entertainment, music and variety, first broadcast in the previous 14 months

International Video Week (Nov odd years)
5 rue du Temple
1201 Geneva
Tel: (41) 22 732 20 60
Fax: (41) 22 738 42 15
Competitive for original work displaying an individual approach and made during two years before festival

Locarno International Film Festival (+ Market) (Aug)
Via della Posta 6, CP 465
6600 Locarno
Tel: (41) 93 31 02 32
Fax: (41) 93 31 74 65
Competitive for fiction by young directors. French subtitles required

International Film and Videofestival of Lucerne – VIPER (Oct)
PO Box 4929
6002 Lucerne
Tel: (41) 41 51 7407
Fax: (41) 41 52 8020
Non-competitive for experimental films and videos, plus retrospective, special programs and "Swiss Videoworkshop" (retrospective program of current Swiss video)

Nyon International Documentary Film Festival (Oct)
PO Box 98
1260 Nyon
Tel: (41) 22 361 60 60
Fax: (41) 22 361 70 71
Competitive. Includes retrospectives and informative screenings

Vevey International Comedy Film Festival (July)
La Grenette
Grand Place 29
1800 Vevey
Tel: (41) 21 921 2292
Fax: (41) 21 921 1065
Competitive for long, medium and short films (no video), plus 'hommage' and retrospective. Films must not have been shown in Switzerland or won a prize at another IFFPA festival

TUNISIA

International Film Festival of Carthage (Oct-Nov even years)
The JCC Managing Committee
PO Box 1029-1045
Tunis RP
Tel: (216) 1 260 323
Official competition open to African and Arab short and full-length films. Entries must have been made within two years before festival and not have been awarded first prize at any previous international festival in an African or Arab country. Also has an information section, a

childhood and youth film section and an international film market

TURKEY

Istanbul International Film Festival (April)

Istanbul Foundation for Culture and Arts
Yildiz Kültür ve Sanat Merkezi
Besiktas 80700
Istanbul
Tel: (90) 1 258 32 12
Fax: (90) 1 261 88 23
Two competitive sections, international and national. The International Competition for feature films on art (literature, theatre, cinema, music, dance and plastic arts) is judged by an international jury and the 'Golden Tulip Award' is presented as the Grand Prix. Entry by invitation

UNITED KINGDOM

Birmingham International Film and Television Festival (Oct)

c/o Central Independent Television
Central House
Broad Street
Birmingham B1 2JP
Tel: 021 616 4213
Fax: 021 616 4392
Non-competitive for features and shorts, plus retrospective and tribute programmes. The Festival hosts conferences debating topical issues in film and television production

Black Sunday – The British Genre Film Festival (bi-annual)

51 Thatch Leach Lane
Whitefield
Manchester M25 6EN
Tel/Fax: 061 766 2566
Non-competitive for horror, thriller, fantasy, science-fiction and film noir genres produced in the previous year. First choice festival for UK premieres of many of the above genre films. Special guests and retrospective programmes

Brighton Festival Media Programme (May)

Duke of York's Cinema
Preston Circus
Brighton BN1 4AA
Tel: 0273 602503
Non-competitive thematic film festival with seminars/discussions with visiting directors and other professionals, screening retrospectives, previews, new releases and films directly from production companies abroad. Special interest in political/cultural issues

The British Short Film Festival (Oct)

Room 313, BBC TV
Threshold House
65-69 Shepherds Bush Green
London W12 7RJ
Tel: 081 743 8000 x62222/62052
Fax: 081 740 8540
Competitive for short film and video (up to 40 mins), all categories. Thematic and specialised programmes, seminars, workshops and special events. Prizes awarded for drama, documentary, best British and International

Cambridge Film Festival (July)

Arts Cinema
8 Market Passage
Cambridge CB2 3PF
Tel: 0223 462666
Fax: 0223 462555
Non-competitive for feature films; some selected from other festivals, original choices, short retrospectives and revived classics

Cinemagic – International Film Festival for Young People (Dec)

Northern Ireland Film Council
7 Lower Crescent
Belfast BT7 1NR
Tel: 0232 232444
Fax: 0232 239918
Competitive for international feature films aimed at 7-15 year olds. Also includes film workshops, talks, young film critic of the year competition and a regional campaign for the children's jury

Edinburgh Fringe Film & Video Festival (Dec)

29 Albany Street
Edinburgh EH1 3QN
Tel: 031 556 2044
Fax: 031 557 3852
Competitive for low-budget/independent/innovative works from Britain and abroad. All submissions welcome

Edinburgh International Film Festival (Aug)

Filmhouse
88 Lothian Road
Edinburgh EH3 9BZ
Tel: 031 228 4051
Fax: 031 229 5501
Competitive for best: new British animation, British feature, student film, and first time feature produced in previous two years (except Britain, produced in previous year). Programme strands include retrospectives, documentaries, features and shorts, special events and lectures

Edinburgh International Television Festival (Aug)

2nd Floor
24 Neal Street
London WC2H 9PS
Tel: 071 379 4519
Fax: 071 836 0702
Conference discussing current issues in television, accompanied by screenings of television programmes grouped according to the themes/topics under discussion

Green Screen (Nov)

45 Shelton Street
London WC2H 9JH
Tel: 071 379 7930
Fax: 071 379 7197
Non-competitive selection of environmental films, question and answer sessions following every film showing, with well known environmentalists, media personnel and celebrities with environmental clout taking part

IVCA Awards (Feb)

International Visual Communications Association
Bolsover House
5-6 Clipstone Street
London W1P 7EB
Tel: 071 580 0962
Fax: 071 436 2606
Competitive for industrial/training films and videos, covering all aspects of the manufacturing and commercial world, plus categories for non-broadcast, educational, environmental, leisure and communications subjects. Programme, Special and Production (Craft) Awards, and CBI Effectiveness Award. Closing date for entries November

International Animation Festival (May)

11 Stephen Mews
London W1A 0AX
Tel: 071 255 1444
Fax: 071 255 2315
Non-competitive, showcasing the best of international and British animation, plus historical retrospectives, thematic programmes, workshops and panel discussions

International Documentary Festival (March)

The Workstation
15 Paternoster Row
Sheffield S1 2BX
Tel: 0742 796511
Fax: 0742 796522
Non-competitive festival dedicated to excellence in documentary film, both historical and contemporary. Themed festival screenings by invitation only, including Cinema Verite – USA and Under Fire, tribute to camera crew and directors filming in combat conditions from WW2 to present. Also professional delegate screening and seminar series

International Festival of Film and TV in the Celtic Countries (Scotland, Wales, Ireland, Brittany – March-April peripatetic)

The Library
Farraline Park
Inverness IV1 1LS
Tel: 0463 226189
Competitive for films

whose subject matter has particular relevance to the Celtic nations

Leeds International Film Festival (Oct)
19 Wellington Street
Leeds LS1 4DG
Tel: 0532 478389
Fax: 0532 426761
Non-competitive for feature films, documentaries and shorts, plus thematic retrospective programme. Lectures, seminars and exhibitions

London International Film Festival (Nov)
National Film Theatre
South Bank
London SE1 8XT
Tel: 071 815 1322/1323
Fax: 071 633 0786
Non-competitive for feature films, shorts and video, by invitation only, which have not previously been screened in Great Britain. Films are selected from other festivals, plus original choices. Audience award, sponsored by Gold Bier, of £10,000 to most popular British feature film

London Jewish Film Festival (Oct)
National Film Theatre
South Bank
London SE1 8XT
Tel: 071 815 1322/1323
Fax: 071 633 0786
Non-competitive for film and video made by Jewish directors and/or concerned with issues relating to Jewish identity and other issues. Some entries travel to regional film theatres as part of a national tour in October/November

London Latin American Film Festival (Sept)
Metro Pictures
79 Wardour Street
London W1V 3TH
Tel: 071 434 3357
Fax: 071 287 2112
Non-competitive, bringing to London a line up of contemporary films from Latin American and surveying currents and trends

London Lesbian and Gay Film Festival (March)
National Film Theatre
South Bank
London SE1 8XT
Tel: 071 815 1322/1323
Fax: 071 633 0786
Non-competitive for film and videos of special interest to lesbian and gay audiences. Some entries travel to regional film theatres as part of a national tour from April to June. Entries must be UK premieres

Raindance Film Festival and Script Competition (Oct)
6 Chelsea Wharf
15 Lots Road
London SW10 0QJ
Tel: 071 351 7748
Fax: 071 376 5116
Competitive for features with budgets under £1 million and under £100,000, shorts, music videos, documentaries, scripts. Prize of £5,000 for best script. Awards for best British feature, best foreign feature in English, best foreign feature in another language. Deadline Sept 1, submission in all formats

Shots in the Dark – Mystery Festival (May-June)
Broadway Media Centre
14 Broad Street
Nottingham NG1 3AL
Tel: 0602 526600
Fax: 0602 526622
Non-competitive for all types of mysteries and thrillers. Includes previews and premieres of major Hollywood thrillers, retrospectives, TV events and special guests

Southampton Film Festival (Sept)
City Arts
Civic Centre
Southampton SO9 4XF
Tel: 0703 832457
Fax: 0703 231384
Non-competitive for feature films and shorts. Archive/retro section, 'Guardian' interview, premieres and previews, video and animation. SFF is an umbrella film exhibition event

Tyneside International Film Festival (Oct)
Tyneside Cinema
10-12 Pilgrim Street
Newcastle upon Tyne
NE1 6QG
Tel: 091 232 8289
Fax: 091 221 0535
Non-competitive for feature films and shorts, by invitation only. Special seasons, presentations and on-stage interviews, plus retrospective programmes

Video Positive (April-May odd years)
International Biennale of Video and Electronic Media Art
Moviola
Bluecoat Chambers
Liverpool L1 3BX
Tel: 051 709 2663
Fax: 051 707 2150
Non-competitive for video and electronic media art produced world-wide in the two years preceding the festival. Includes community and education programme, screenings, workshops and seminars. Some commissions available

Welsh International Film Festival, Aberystwyth (Nov)
c/o Premiere Cymru
Wales Cyf
Unit 8c
Cefn Llan
Aberystwyth
Dyfed SY23 2AH
Tel: 0970 617995
Fax: 0970 617942
Non-competitive for international feature films and shorts, together with films from Wales in Welsh and English. Also short retrospectives, workshops and seminars. D M Davies Award (£5,000) presented to the best short film submitted by a young film maker from Wales

Wildscreen: International Wildlife and Environment Film and Television Festival (Oct even years)
15 Whiteladies Road
Bristol BS8 1PB
Tel: 0272 733082/742163
Fax: 0272 239416
Competitive: Golden Panda awards include Conservation, Revelation, Newcomer, Outstanding Achievement and Photography. Eligible productions completed after 1 January 1992 and not entered in Wildscreen 92. Festival includes screenings, video kiosks, discussions

USA

AFI Los Angeles Film Festival (June)
2021 N Western Avenue
Los Angeles CA 90027
Tel: (1) 213 856 7707
Fax: (1) 213 462 4049
Non-competitive, FIAPF accredited. Features, documentaries, shorts by invitation

AFI National Video Festival (Feb)
2021 N Western Avenue
Los Angeles CA 90027
Tel: (1) 213 856 7707
Fax: (1) 213 462 4049
Screenings in Los Angeles, Washington. Accepts: ¾" U-Matic, NTSC/PAL/SECAM (No Beta, no 1")

American Film Market (Feb-March)
12424 Wilshire Blvd
Suite 600
Los Angeles CA 90025
Tel: (1) 310 447 1555
Fax: (1) 310 447 1666
Annual market for international film, TV and video

Asian American International Film Festival (July)
c/o Asian CineVision
32 East Broadway, 4th Floor
New York, NY 10002
Tel: (1) 212 925 8685
Fax: (1) 212 925 8157
Non-competitive, all categories and lengths. No video-to-film transfers accepted as entries. Films must be produced, directed and/or written by artists of Asian heritage

Chicago International Children's Film Festival (Oct)

Facets Multimedia
1517 West Fullerton Avenue
Chicago IL 60614
Tel: (1) 312 281 9075
Fax: (1) 312 929 5437
Competitive for entertainment films, videotapes and television programmes for children

Chicago International Film Festival (Oct)
415 North Dearborn
Chicago IL 60610
Tel: (1) 312 644 3400
Fax: (1) 312 644 0784
Competitive for feature films, shorts, animation, TV productions, student films and commercials

Cleveland International Film Festival (April)
6200 SOM Center Road #C20
Cleveland OH 44139
Tel: (1) 216 349 0270
Fax: (1) 216 349 0210
Non-competitive for feature, narrative, documentary, animation and experimental films

Denver International Film Festival (Oct)
999 Eighteenth Street
Suite 1820
Denver CO 80202
Tel: (1) 303 298 8223
Fax: (1) 303 298 0209
Non-competitive. New international features, tributes to film artists, independent features, documentaries, shorts, animation, experimental works and children's films

Hawaii International Film Festival (Nov)
1777 East/West Road
Oahu
Honolulu HI 96848
Tel: (1) 808 944 7007
Fax: (1) 808 949 5578

Houston International Film and Video Festival – Worldfest-Houston (+ Market) (April)
PO Box 56566
Houston TX 77256-6566
Tel: (1) 713 965 9955
Fax: (1) 713 965 9960
Competitive for features, shorts, documentary, TV production and TV commercials. Independent and major studios, experimental and video with inclusive film market. New Worldfest Discovery Programme automatically enters all winners and finalist in the top 200 festivals worldwide. 200 page programme book available. Fest produces a 120 min VHS winners tape with clips of all major winners

Miami Film Festival (Feb)
Film Society of Miami
444 Brickell Avenue
Suite 229
Miami FL 33131
Tel: (1) 305 377 3456
Fax: (1) 305 577 9768
Non-competitive film festival

National Educational Film and Video Festival (Dec)
655 Thirteenth Street
Oakland CA 94612
Tel: (1) 415 465 6885
Competitive for educational media. Festival Week events, which include a Media Market for distributors and producers, seminars on funding and marketing and interactive technology, public screenings and award events take place in May

New York Film Festival (Sept-Oct)
Film Society of Lincoln Center
70 Lincoln Center Plaza
4th Floor
New York NY 10023
Tel: (1) 212 875 5610
Fax: (1) 212 875 5636
Non-competitive for feature films, shorts (up to 30 mins), including drama, documentary, animation and experimental films. Films must have been produced one year prior to the festival and must be New York premieres

PHILAFILM – The Philadelphia International Film Festival (July)
121 North Broad Street
Suite 618
Philadelphia PA 19107
Tel: (1) 215 977 2831
Fax: (1) 215 977 2856
A competition and market (sales, rentals), designed to showcase the works of Minority and Independent film and videomakers from around the world. Entry form required for participation. Film and video entries accepted. Categories are: features, shorts, documentaries, animation, experimental and student

San Francisco International Film Festival (April-May)
1521 Eddy Street
San Francisco CA 94115-4102
Tel: (1) 415 567 4641
Fax: (1) 415 921 5032
Feature films, by invitation, shown non-competitively. Shorts, documentaries, animation, experimental works and TV productions eligible for Golden Gate Awards competition section

San Francisco International Lesbian and Gay Film Festival (June)
346 Ninth Street
San Francisco CA 94103
Tel: (1) 415 703 8650
Fax: (1) 415 861 1404
Largest lesbian/gay film fest in the world. Features, documentary, short film and video. Entry deadline 1 March

Seattle International Film Festival (May-June)
801 East Pine
Seattle WA 98122
Tel: (1) 206 324 9996
Fax: (1) 206 324 9998
Jury prize for best first feature. Other audience-voted awards. Submissions accepted 1 Jan to 15 March

Sundance Film Festival (Jan)
PO Box 16450
Salt Lake City UT 84116
Tel: (1) 801 328 3456
Fax: (1) 801 575 5175
Competitive for American independent dramatic and documentary feature films produced no earlier than 15 Oct 1992. Also presents a number of international and American premieres and short films, as well as sidebars, special retrospectives and seminars

US International Film & Video Festival (June)
841 North Addison Avenue
Elmhurst IL 60126-1291
Tel: (1) 708 834 7773
Fax: (1) 708 834 5565
International awards competition for Sponsored, Business, Television and Industrial productions produced or released in the 18 months preceding the annual 1 March entry deadline. Formerly the US Industrial Film and Video Festival, founded 1968

URUGUAY

International Children's Film Festival (July)
Cinemateca Uruguaya
Carnelli 1311
Casilla de Correo 1170
11200 Montevideo
Tel: (598) 2 48 24 60
Fax: (598) 2 49 45 72
Competitive for fiction, documentaries and animation for children

International Festival of Documentary and Experimental Films (Sept)
Cinemateca Uruguaya
Carnelli 1311
Casilla de Correo 1170
11200 Montevideo
Tel: (598) 2 48 24 60
Fax: (598) 2 49 45 72
Competitive

International Film Festival of Uruguay (March-April)
Cinemateca Uruguaya
Carnelli 1311
Casilla de Correo 1170
11200 Montevideo
Tel: (598) 2 48 24 60
Fax: (598) 2 49 45 72
Competitive for fiction and Latin American videos

FILM SOCIETIES

Listed below are UK film societies which are open to the public (marked OP after the society name), those based in educational establishments (ST), private companies and organisations (CL), and some corporate societies (CP). Societies providing disabled access to their venues are marked DA – always contact the organiser beforehand to confirm details. Addresses are grouped in broad geographical areas, along with the regional officers who can offer specific local information. There is a constant turnover of society officers, so if you are not certain whom to contact or your enquiry goes astray, you should contact the Film Society Unit at the BFI

BFFS CONSTITUENT GROUPS

The Film Society Unit exists to service the British Federation of Film Societies.
The BFFS is divided into Constituent Groups which usually follow the borders of the Regional Arts Boards, but sometimes include more than one RAB area

Eastern
Bedfordshire, Cambridgeshire, Essex, Hertfordshire, Lincolnshire, Norfolk, Suffolk

London
32 London Boroughs and the City of London

Midlands
Derbyshire (excluding High Peak District), Leicestershire, Northamptonshire, Nottinghamshire, Hereford and Worcester, Shropshire, Staffordshire, Warwickshire, Metropolitan districts of Birmingham, Coventry, Dudley, Sandwell, Solihull, Walsall, Wolverhampton

North West
Cheshire, High Peak district of Derbyshire, Lancashire, Metropolitan districts of Bolton, Bury, Knowsley, City of Liverpool, Manchester, Oldham, Rochdale, St Helens, Salford, Sefton, Stockport, Tameside, Trafford, Wigan, Wirral, Northern Ireland

Northern
Cleveland, Cumbria, Durham, Northumberland, Metropolitan districts of Gateshead, Newcastle, North Tyneside, South Tyneside, Sunderland

Scotland

South East
Kent, Surrey, East Sussex, West Sussex

South West
Avon, Channel Islands, Cornwall, Devon, Dorset (except districts of Bournemouth, Christchurch and Poole), Gloucestershire, Somerset

Southern
Berkshire, Buckinghamshire, Hampshire, Isle of Wight, Oxfordshire, Wiltshire, Districts of Bournemouth, Christchurch, Poole

Wales

Yorkshire
Humberside, North Yorkshire, Metropolitan districts of Barnsley, Bradford, Calderdale, Doncaster, Kirklees, Leeds, Rotherham, Sheffield, Wakefield

EASTERN

Eastern Group BFFS
Mr Gerry Dobson
Kennel Cottage
Burton
Nr Lincoln
Lincs

Bancroft School Film Society ST
Daniel Moy
Secretary
50 Monkhams Avenue
Woodford Green
Essex

Bedford Film Society OP
Marchant Robin
17 Cherwell Road
Bedford

Berkhamsted Film Society OP DA
Dr C J S Davies
Seasons
Garden Field Lane
Berkhamsted
Herts HP4 2NN

Braintree District Arts Council CP DA
Mr I Williams
7 Rosemary Avenue
Braintree
Essex CM7 7SZ

British Telecom Film Society CL
Mr A P Martin

Research Dept RT52
Rm 40B/MLB4
Martlesham Heath
Ipswich
Suffolk IP5 7RE

Bury St Edmunds Film Society OP DA
Mr D I Smith
Rectory Cottage
Drinkstone
Bury St Edmunds
Suffolk IP30 9SP

Cambridge Union Film Society ST
Chairman Film Committee
Cambridge Union Society
Bridge Street
Cambridge
CB2 1UB

Chelmsford Film Club OP DA
Mr Lawrence Islip
11 Sunningdale Road
Chelmsford
Essex CM1 2NH

Circle Foundation Trust Co Ltd CP DA
Mrs Sherley Hunt
156 Keith Road
Barking
Essex IG11 7TY

Epping Film Society OP DA
Mr A R Carr
58 Centre Drive
Epping
Essex CM16 4JE

University of Essex Film Society ST
Elizabeth Havard
Students' Union Building
Wivenhoe Park
Colchester CO4 3SQ

Eye Theatre CP DA
Artistic Director
Broad Street
Eye
Suffolk IP23 7AF

Great Yarmouth Film Society OP
Mr E C Hunt
21 Park Lane
Norwich
Norfolk NR2 3EE

Hatfield Polytechnic Film Society ST
David Cowan
Wall Hall Campus
Aldenham
Watford
Herts WD2 8AZ

Ipswich Film Society OP
Mr T Cloke
4 Burlington Road
Ipswich
Suffolk IP1 2EU

Kings Lynn Centre for the Arts OP
St Georges Guildhall Ltd
27 King Street
Kings Lynn
Norfolk PE30 1HA

Leighton Buzzard Library and Arts Centre OP
Mr Stuart Antrobus
Lake Street
Leighton Buzzard
Beds LU7 8RX

Letchworth Film Society OP DA
Mr Sean Boughton
29 Norton Road
Letchworth
Herts SG6 1AA

Lincoln Film Society OP
Mr M Bingham
27 Breedon Drive
Lincoln
Lincs LN1 3XA

Long Road Sixth Form College Film Society ST DA
Ms Julie Lindsay
Long Road
Cambridge CB2 2PX

Lowestoft Film Society OP DA
Mr Ken Jarmin
228 Denmark Road
Lowestoft
Suffolk

Old Town Hall Film Society OP
Jackie Alexander
Old Town Hall Arts Centre
High Street
Hemel Hempstead
Herts HP1 3AE

Peterborough Film Society OP
Mr A J Bunch
196 Lincoln Road
Peterborough
Cambs PE1 2NQ

Playhouse Co-op Film Society (Harlow) OP
Mrs S Herbert
72 Broadfields
Harlow
Essex CM20 3PT

St Felix School Film Society ST DA
Mr Paul Wilson
Librarian
St Felix School
Southwold
Suffolk IP18 6SD

Saint John's College Film Society ST
Paul Moxon
St John's College
Cambridge CB2 1TP

Stamford Schools' Film Society ST
Dr J P Slater
Stamford School
St Paul's Street
Stamford
Lincs PE9 2BS

UEASU Film Society ST DA
Mr N Rayns
Entertainments Officer
University Plain
Norwich
Norfolk NR4 7TJ

Welwyn Garden City Film Society OP DA
Mr Michael Massey
3 Walden Place
Welwyn Garden City
Herts AL8 7PG

Westcliff High School for Boys Film Society ST
Alexander Marlow Mann
Kenilwern Gardens
Westcliff on Sea
Essex SS1 0BD

LONDON

James Allen Girls Film Society ST
Mrs M Lovick, Secretary
East Dulwich Grove
East Dulwich
London SE22 8TE

Tom Allen Arts Centre OP DA
Claire White
Film Club
Grove Crescent Road
Stratford
London E15 1BJ

ARC Film Society CL
Pamela Strangman
Room 1140, General Services
American Embassy
24 Grosvenor Square
London W1A 1AE

Australian Film Society OP
Mr S Hughes
'Eagle', 33 Delius Way
Stanford-le-Hope
Essex SS17 8RG

Avant-Garde Film Society OP DA
Mr C White
9 Elmbridge Drive
Ruislip
Middlesex HA4 7XD

BBC Film Club CL
Ms Trudi Cowper
Room E.265
BBC Enterprises
80 Wood Lane
London W12 0TT

Barclays Bank Film Society CL DA
The Secretary
PO Box 256
Fleetway House (1st Floor)
25 Farringdon Street
London EC4A 4LP

Bikkhon Film Society OP DA
Mujibur Rahman Osmani
34 Broadhurst House
Joseph Street
London E3 4HY

The Biograph Film Society OP
Ms Carol Swords
Pimlico Arts and Media
St James the Less School
Moreton Street
London SW1V 2PT

Broomhill Film Society CP DA
A Castro
55 Canadian Avenue
Catford
London SE6 3AX

Brunel Film Society ST DA
The President
Brunel University
Uxbridge
Middlesex UB8 3PH

Chiswick Film Society OP DA
Mr A V Downend
Hounslow Library
Treaty Centre
Hounslow TW3 1ES

The Elgin Abseiling Film Club OP
c/o Richard Guard, BMC
89.5 Worship Street
London EC2A 2BE

Gothique Film Society OP DA
Mr R James
75 Burns Avenue
Feltham
Middlesex TW14 9LX

University of Greenwich Film Society ST
Andrew Winter
Secretary
127 Shooters Hill Road
Blackheath
London

Holborn Film Society OP DA
Mrs Noel Mcleod
48 Witley Court
Coram Street
London WC1N 1HD

ICRF Film Club CL
Ms Marie Fleetwood
PO Box 123
Tissue Antigen Lab.
Lincoln's Inn Fields
London WC2A 2PX

Imperial College Union Film Society ST DA
Ian Nichol
5 Sterling Place
South Ealing
London W5 4RA

Institut Français Film Society OP
The Secretary
(Cinema Dept)
17 Queensberry Place
London SW7 2DT

John Lewis Partnership Film Society CL DA
Mr P Allen
Social Secretary
8th Floor
171 Victoria Street
London SW1E 5NN

Kingston University Film Society ST
Alison Hardy
72 Norman Hall
Birkenhead Avenue
Kingston-upon-Thames
Surrey KT2 6RR

Lensbury Film Society OP
Mrs A Catto
Shell Centre
Room Y1085, York Road
Waterloo
London SE1 7NA

Mullard House Film Society CL
Miss L S Denny
Mullard House
Torrington Place
London WC1E 7HD

NPL Film Society CL
Mr R Townsend
National Physical Laboratory
Queens Road
Teddington
Middx TW11 0LW

PCL Student Union Film Society ST
Secretary
104-108 Bolsover Street
London

PNL Film Society ST
Ms Dena Blakeman
73 Warner Road
Camberwell
London SE5 9NE

Pull It Cinema OP
Herve Nahon
38-46 James Town Road
Camden Town
London NW1 7BY

RCA Film Society ST
Magali Moreau
Royal College of Art
Kensington Gore
London SW7 2EU

Richmond Film Society OP
Celia Woods
29 Arlington Road
Teddington
Middx TW11 8NL

Scandinavian Film Society OP
Mrs Françoise Cowie
111 Old Brompton Road
London SW7 3LE

South Bank Poly Film Society ST
Anjun Qaiyum
16 Pollard Road
Whetstone
London N20 0UB

South London Film Society OP
Dr M Essex-Lopresti
14 Oakwood Park Road
Southgate
London N14 6QG

John Stanley Media Management CL
John Stanley
Unit 2 Mill House Farm
North Elmham
Dereham
Norfolk NR20 5HN

The Travelling Cinema OP
Herve Nahon
89 Victoria Road
London NW6 6TD

UCL Film Society ST
Mr R Graves
University College London
25 Gordon Street
London WC1A 0AH

UWCC Film Society ST DA
Miss Tonya Creswell
20 Garrick's Island
Hampton
Middlesex TW17 2EW

Waltham Forest (Libs) Film Society OP
Mrs V Bates
William Morris Gallery
Lloyd Park
Forest Road
Walthamstow
London E17 4PP

Woolwich and District Co-op Film Society OP
Mr P Graham
10 Harden Court
Tamar Street
Charlton
London SE7 8DQ

MIDLANDS

Midland Group BFFS
Dr Paul Collins
Beech Haven
Cobden Street
Stourbridge
West Midlands

Bablake School Film Society ST
Mr J R Lawrence
Coventry School – Bablake
Coundon Road
Coventry CV1 4AU

Bishops Castle Film Society OP
Ms J Parker
4 Lavender Bank
Bishops Castle
Shropshire SY9 5BD

Bromsgrove Film Society OP DA
Mr Chris Page
80 New Road
Bromsgrove
Worcs B60 2LA

Central Television SSC Film Society CL DA
Mr G Lee
Central House
Broad Street
Birmingham B1 2JP

The Forum Cinema CP
Tony Whitehead
Lings Forum
Weston Favell Centre
Northampton NN3 4JR

University of Keele Film Society ST
Mrs D Steele
Accounts Office
Students Union
Keele
Staffs ST5 5BJ

Kinver Film Society OP DA
Mr S L Downes
141 Northway
Sedgley, Dudley
West Midlands DY3 3PY

Loughborough Students Union Film Society ST
Student Union Building
Ashby Road
Loughborough
Leics LE11 3EA

Ludlow and District Film Society OP DA
Graeme Sawyer
3 Upper Linney
Ludlow
Shropshire

Malvern Film Society OP
Mr George Wells
42 North Malvern Road
Malvern
Worcs WR14 4LT

New Kettering Film Society OP
Mr Meredith
Art Department
Tresham Institute
Rockingham Road
Kettering
Northants

Nottingham Polytechnic SU Film Society ST DA
Laura M W Smith
73 Birkin Avenue
Hyson Green
Nottingham NG7 5AW

Oundle School Senior Film Society ST
Mr David Sharp

North Street
Oundle
Peterborough
Northants PE8 4AL

Shrewsbury Film Society OP DA
Ms B Mason
Pulley Lodge
Lower Pulley Lane
Bayston Hill
Shrewsbury
Shropshire SY3 0DW

Solihull Film Society OP DA
Mario Bryanston
34 Silhill Hall Road
Solihull
W Midlands B91 1JU

Stafford Film Society OP DA
Jerry McPherson
Orchard View
Off Mill Lane
Acton Gate
Staffs ST17 0RA

Stourbridge Film Society OP DA
Mrs M J Keightley
1A Pargeter Street
Stourbridge
W Midlands DY8 1AU

Tile Hill College Film Society OP
Mick Wheeler
Communications Unit
Tile Hill College of FE
Tile Hill Lane
Coventry CV4 9SU

Vale of Catmose Film Society OP DA
Mr Peter Green
Vale of Catmose College
Oakham
Rutland LE15 6NJ

University of Warwick Film Society ST DA
The Secretary
Students Union
University of Warwick
Coventry CV4 7AL

Weston Coyney and Caverswall Film Society OP DA
Mr R S Johnson
86 School Lane
Caverswall
Stoke-on-Trent
ST11 9EN

NORTH WEST

North West Group BFFS
Mr Alan Payne
18 Cecil Street
Lytham St Annes
Lancs FY8 5NN

Birkenhead Library Film Society OP
Mr H G Mortimer
Music Dept
Borough Road
Birkenhead
Merseyside L41 2XB

Chester Film Society OP
Mr Dick Richards
11a Oakfield Road
Chester
Cheshire CH1 5AG

Chorley Film Society OP
Mr R Hubbard
174 Water Street
Chorley
Lancs PR1 1EX

Citadel Arts Centre OP
Paul Hogan/Robert Cave
Waterloo Street
St Helens WA10 1PX

Deeside Film Society OP DA
Mr Ramsey Hewson
44 Albion Street
Wallasey
Merseyside L45 9JG

Ellesmere Port Library Film Society OP DA
Mr J G Fisher
Ellesmere Port Library
Elles Port, Civic Way
Chester L65 0BG

Forum Film Society OP DA
Mrs M Holleran
Central Library
Wythenshawe
Manchester M22 5RT

Foyle Film Club OP
Mr Martin Bradley
7-8 Magazine Street
Londonderry BT48 6HJ

Frightnite Horror Film Society OP
Mr Stephen Faragher
35 Hilberry Avenue
Tuebrook
Liverpool L13 7ES

Frodsham Film Society OP
Mr M F Donovan
58 The Willows
Frodsham
Cheshire WA6 7QS

Heswall Film Society OP DA
Mr Alvin Sant
18 Fairlawn Court
Bidston Road
Birkenhead L43 6UX

The Knowsley Film Society ST
J Corner
c/o Knowsley Community College
Rupert Road
Roby
Merseyside L36 9TD

University of Lancaster Film Society ST
The President
Lowsdale College
University of Lancaster
Bailrigg
Lancs LA1 4GT

Lytham St Annes Film Society OP DA
Mr A Payne
18 Cecil Street
Lytham St Annes
Lancs FY8 5NN

Manchester and Salford Film Society OP DA
Mr H T Ainsworth
64 Egerton Road
Fallowfield
Manchester M14 6RA

Manchester University Film Society ST DA
Hon Secretary
Union Building
Oxford Road
Manchester M13 9PR

Merseyside Film Institute OP
Mr G Donaldson
45 Bluecoat Chambers
School Lane
Liverpool L1 3BX

Preston Film Society OP DA
Mr M Lockwood
14 Croftgate
Highgate Park, Fulwood
Preston
Lancs PR2 4LS

Runcorn Library Film Society OP DA
Ms S Davies
Runcorn Library
Shopping City
Runcorn
Cheshire WA7 2PF

The Society of Fantastic Films OP
Mr H Nadler
5 South Mesnefield Road
Salford
Lancs M7 0QP

Southport Film Guild Film Society OP
Steve Arnold
18 Alexander Close
Burscough
Ormskirk
Lancs LA0 5SR

Turnpike Film Society OP
Wendy Heaton
c/o Leigh Library
Civic Square
Leigh WN7 1EB

UMIST Union Film Society ST
Hon Secretary
PO Box 88
Sackville Street
Manchester M60 1QD

University of Ulster Film Society ST DA
Mrs J Rushton
c/o Estates Dept
Cromore Road
Coleraine
N. Ireland BT52 1SA

Workers' Film Association Film Society OP
F Johnson
WFA Ltd
9 Lucy Street
Old Trafford
Hulme
Manchester M15 4BX

NORTHERN

Northern Group BFFS
Peter Swan
48 Brackenway
Albany Village
Washington
Tyne & Wear NE37 1AP

201 Film Society (Durham) ST
Mr D Boffey
Van Mildert College
University of Durham
Durham DH1 3LH

The Arts Centre, Darlington CP DA
Mrs Diann Allenby
Arts Assistant

Vane Terrace
Darlington
Co Durham DL3 7AX

Bede Film Society ST
The President
College of St Hild & St Bede
Durham University
Durham DH1 1SZ

Centre Film Club OP DA
Mrs S D Travers
64 Corporation Road
Redcar
Cleveland TS10 1PB

Cleveland Film Group OP
Mr Steven D Moses
45 Oxford Road
Linthorpe
Middlesbrough
Cleveland TS5 5DY

Durham University Film Unit ST DA
Nick Southgate
St Aidan's College
Windham Hill
Durham DH1 3LJ

Film Club at the Maltings OP
Charlotte Hobson
c/o The Maltings
East Street
Berwick Upon Tweed
Northumberland
TD15 1AJ

Film Club at the Roxy OP
Gwyneth Walker
13 Conishead House
Priory Road
Ulverston
Cumbria LA12 9QQ

Hartlepool Film Society OP
Mr A Gowing
6 Warkworth Drive
Hartlepool
Cleveland TS26 0EW

Newcastle Polytechnic (SU) Film Society ST DA
Mrs M Bennett
Union Building
2 Sandyford Road
Newcastle-upon-Tyne
NE1 8SB

Penrith Film Club OP DA
Mr D Simpson
Ravensworth
Skelton
Penrith
Cumbria CA11 9SQ

SCOTLAND

Scottish Group BFFS
Ronald Currie
15 Charlotte Street
Ayr KA7 1DZ

A.U. Film Society ST
Mr Douglas Gibbs
Cuthuli House
50/52 College Bounds
Aberdeen AB2 3DS

Arbroath High Film Society ST DA
Miss Jane Baird
Arbroath High
Keptie Road
Arbroath
Tayside DD11 3EN

Ayr & Craigie Film Society OP DA
Mr R J Currie
15 Charlotte Street
Ayr KA7 1DZ

Bank of Scotland Film Society CL DA
Mr H Boyd
Tax Department
PO Box 41
101 George Street
Edinburgh EH2 3JH

The Barony Film Society OP DA
G Harrower
68 Grange Terrace
Bo'ness
West Lothian EH51 4LP

Berwickshire High School ST DA
Eric Sykes
Berwickshire High School
Duns
Berwickshire TD11 3QQ

Broughton High School Junior Film Society ST DA
Mr L Timson
Broughton High School
Carrington Road
Edinburgh EH4 1EG

Callander Film Society OP
Mr D N Skelsey
Benmore House
19 Bridgend
Callander
Perthshire FK17 8AG

Crieff Film Society OP
Mr C Lacaille
Boghaugh
South Crieff Road
Comrie
Perthshire PH6 2HF

Dead By Dawn CP DA
Adele Hartley
11/1 New Arthur Place
The Pleasance
Edinburgh Eh8 9TH

Duncan of Jordanstone Film Society ST
Mr Alan Woods
Duncan of Jordanstone College of Art
Perth Road
Dundee DD1 4LP

East Kilbride Film Society OP
Harry Winslow
21 Loch Laxford
East Kilbride
Strathclyde G74 2DL

Eastwood Film Society OP DA
Mrs J I Marchant
11 Beechlands Drive
Clarkston
Glasgow G76 7XA

Edinburgh Film Guild OP DA
Ms Helene Telford
Secretary
Filmhouse
88 Lothian Road
Edinburgh EH3 9BZ

Edinburgh University Film Society ST DA
Societies' Centre
60 The Pleasance
Edinburgh EH8 9TJ

Electric Shadows ST
Mr P Mukherjee
Glasgow University Film Club
5 Park Quadrant
Glasgow G3 6BS

The Findhorn Foundation Film Society CP DA
James Donovan
The Universal Hall and Arts Centre
The Park
Forres
Morayshire IV36 0TZ

Glasgow Polytechnic Film Society ST
Sally Gummitt
Glasgow Polytechnic
Cowcaddens Road
Glasgow G4 0BA

Haldane Film Society OP DA
Mr T G Crocket
62 Cardross Road
Dumbarton
Dunbartonshire G82

Linlithgow Film Society OP
Jenny Gilford
81 Belsyde Court
Linlithgow
West Lothian EH49 7RL

Lloyds Bowmaker Film Club CL
Helen Watson
Finance House
Orchard Brae
Edinburgh EH4 1PF

The Not Altogether Normal Film Society OP DA
Mr Kenneth Burns
28 Dochart Drive
Coatbridge
Strathclyde ML5 2PF

Paisley Arts Centre Film Society OP DA
Paul Hogan
New Street
Paisley
Renfrewshire PA1 1EZ

Robert Burns Centre – Film Theatre OP DA
Kenneth Eggo
Dumfries Museum
The Observatory
Dumfries DG2 7SW

Scottish Office Film Society CL
H MacKenzie
10 Ormelie Terrace
Joppa
Edinburgh EH15 2EX

Shetland Film Club OP
Mr S Hubbard
Secretary
Nethaburn
Wester Quarff
Shetland ZE2 9EZ

Standard Life Film Society CL
Mr P Steven
7 Tanfield
Canonmills
Edinbrugh EH3 5JS

University of Stirling Film

Circle **ST**
Paul Weaver
Film/Media Department
Stirling FK9 4LA

Strathallan School Film Society **ST**
Morag Rogers
Strathallan School
Forgandenny
Perth PH2 9EG

Trinity Academy Film Society **ST DA**
Mr T Ablett
c/o Trinity Academy
Craighall Avenue
Edinburgh EH6 4RT

Tweeddale Film Club **OP DA**
Mrs Jeanette Carlyle
Top Floor
23 Marchmont Road
Edinburgh EH9 1HY

West Kilbride Film Club **OP DA**
Mrs E Rhodes
3 Cubrieshaw Drive
West Kilbride
Ayrshire KA23 9DU

SOUTH EAST

South East Group BFFS
Tim Ffrench-Lynch
32 Wyndham Road
Chatham
Kent ME4 6QS

Aquila Film Society **CL DA**
Mr M A Lever
ATC Block 4, DRA
Golf Road
Bromley
Kent BR1 2JB

Arundel Festival Film Society **OP**
Mr D A Edginton
1 Tower House Gardens
Arundel
West Sussex BN18 9BH

Charterhouse Film Society **OP**
Christopher O'Neill
Brooke Hall
Charterhouse
Godalming
Surrey GU7 2DX

Chichester City Film Society **OP DA**
Mr R Gibson
Westlands, Main Road
Hunston
Chichester
West Sussex PO20 6AL

Cranbrook Film Society **OP**
Mrs C Williams
St Helens
Moor Hill
Hawkhurst
Kent TN18 4NY

Cranleigh Film Society **OP DA**
Mr H B Hemingway
9 Hitherwood
Cranleigh
Surrey GU6 8BN

Ditchling Film Society **OP**
Mr G Hinckley
11 The Fieldway
Lewes Road
Ditchling
Hassocks
West Sussex BN6 8UA

Dover Film Society **OP**
Mr D Antony Pratt
19 Bramley Avenue
Canterbury
Kent CT1 3XW

Eastbourne Film Society **OP DA**
Miss B Wilson
2 Chalk Farm Close
Willingdon
Eastbourne
East Sussex BN20 9HY

Farnham Film Society at the Maltings **OP**
Mrs P Woodroffe
c/o The Maltings
Bridge Square
Farnham
Surrey GU9 7QR

Faversham Film Society **OP**
Mrs V Cackett
15 South Road
Faversham
Kent ME13 7LR

Frame 25 **ST DA**
James Rennie, President
21 Somerset Road
Canterbury
Kent CT1 1RH

Hastings Arts Film Society **OP**
Jim McCulloch
Great Gable
Maple Walk, Cooden
Bexhill on Sea
East Sussex

Hastings College Film Society **ST**
Helen Dessent
Department of Art & Design
Hastings College of Art & Technology
Archery Road
St Leonards on Sea
E Sussex TN38 0HX

Horsham Film Society **OP DA**
Mr Norman Chapman
Farthings
King James Lane
Henfield
Sussex BN5 9ER

Intimate Cinema Film Society **OP**
Mr A Henk
10 Aston Way
Epsom
Surrey KT18 5LZ

Lancing College Film Society **ST**
Dr S Cornford, Common Room
Lancing College
Lancing
Sussex BN15 0RW

Lewes Film Guild **OP DA**
Ms Mary Burke
6 Friars Walk
Lewes
East Sussex BN7 2LE

Maidstone Film Society **OP**
Moira Hancock
2 Brockenhurst Avenue
Maidstone
Kent ME15 7ED

Medway Film Society **OP**
Caroline Reed
55 Maidstone Road
Rochester
Kent

Oscar Film Unit **ST**
Penny Evans, Secretary
University of Surrey
Guildford
Surrey GU2 5XH

Platform Kino **OP DA**
Helen Greenfield
Platform Theatre
Burrell Road
Haywards Heath
West Sussex RH16 1TN

Slough Co-operative Film Society **OP DA**
Dr Jo Hughes
1 Vanstone Cottages
Bagshot Road
Englefield Green
Egham
Surrey TW20 0RS

Stables Film Society **OP**
Mr Fred Nash
c/o The Stables Theatre
32 Vale Road
Silverhill
St Leonards on Sea
East Sussex TN37 6PS

Steyning Film Society **OP**
Mrs V Whitaker
103 High Street
Steyning BN44 3RE

The Studio Film Society **OP DA**
Mr Malcolm Allen
28 Beckenham Road
Beckenham BR3 4LS

Tunbridge Wells Film Society **OP DA**
Peter Warner
Flat 3, 44 Lime Hill Road
Tunbridge Wells
Kent TN1 1LL

Walton and Weybridge Film Society **OP**
Joan Westbrook
28 Eastwick Road
Walton on Thames
Surrey KT12 5AD

West Hoathly Film Society **OP DA**
Mrs W Cole
2 Fern Cottage
Sandy Lane
West Hoathly
W Sussex RG19 4QQ

West Kent College Film Society **ST DA**
Mr D B Davies
West Kent College of FE
Brook Street
Tonbridge
Kent TN9 2PN

Woking's New Cinema Club **OP DA**
Mr A Rozelaar
67 Lansdown Close
St Johns
Woking
Surrey GU21 1TG

SOUTH WEST

South West Group BFFS
Mr Brian Clay

The Garden Flat
71 Springfield Road
Cotham
Bristol BS6 5SW

Bath Film Society OP
Chris Baker
6 Orange Grove
Bath
Avon BA1 1LP

Bath Schools' Film Society ST
Secretary
47 Bobbin Lane
Westwood
Bradford on Avon
Wilts BA15 2DL

Bath University Film Society ST
BUFS Secretary
Students Union
University of Bath
Claverton Down
Bath
Avon BA2 7AY

Blandford Forum Film Society OP DA
J E England
6 Kings Road
Blandford Forum
Dorset DT11 7LD

The Blundells Sixth Form Film Club ST DA
Steve Goodwin
8 Alstone Road
Tiverton
Devon EX16 4JL

Bournemouth and Poole Film Society OP
Mrs C Stevenson
15 Milestone Road
Oakdale
Poole
Dorset BH15 3DR

Bradford on Avon Film Society OP
Debbie Slater
16 Trowbridge Road
Bradford on Avon
Wiltshire BA15 1EP

Bridport Film Society OP DA
Mrs M Wood
Greenways
9 Bowhayes
Bridport
Dorset DT6 4EB

Bristol Student Films ST DA
The Chairman
University of Bristol
Students Union
Queens Road
Clifton
Bristol BS8 1LN

Cheltenham Film Society OP DA
Mrs G Sage
35 Bookway Road
Charlton Kings
Cheltenham
Glos GL53 8HF

Cheltenham Ladies College Film Society ST DA
Miss Amanda Boyle
Bayshill Road
Cheltenham
Glos GL50 3EP

Cinematheque OP DA
Ms Nina Gilman
42 Bowden Road
Templecombe
Somerset BA8 0LF

Cinsoc Exeter University ST
The President
Devonshire House
Stocker Road
Exeter
Devon EX4 4PZ

Dartington Arts Theatre OP DA
The Arts Manager
The Gallery
Dartington Hall
Totnes
Devon TQ9 6DE

Dorchester Film Society OP DA
Ann Evans
62 Casterbridge Road
Dorchester
Dorset DT1 2AG

Exeter Film Society OP
Ms H James
16 Pavilion Place
Exeter
Devon EX2 4HR

Falmouth Film OP DA
Antonio Villalon
Falmouth Arts Centre
Church Street
Falmouth
Cornwall

Falmouth School of Art/Design ST DA
Mr W Flint
Student Union Film Club
Woodlane
Falmouth TR11 4RA

Gloucester Film Society OP DA
Mr C Toomey
8 Garden Way
Longlevens
Gloucester GL2 9UL

Holsworthy Film Society OP
Mel Landells
East Down
Clawton
Holsworthy
Devon EX22 6QF

Honiton Film Club OP
Lucy Ellson
c/o King Rollo Films
Dolphin Court
High Street
Honiton
Devon

Jersey Film Society OP DA
Mr John Christensen
Oak Cottage
Old Road, Gorey Village
Jersey
Channel Isles JE3 9EX

Kingsbridge Theatre and Cinema CP DA
William Stanton
138 Church Street
Kingsbridge
Devon TQ7 1DB

Lyme Regis Film Society OP DA
Mrs P Nod
Treasurer
Coombe Street
Lyme Regis
Dorset

Mendip Film Society OP
D J Brain
Orchardleigh
Bristol Road
West Harptree
Bristol

The Octagon Film Society OP
Mr Clifford Edwards
Okehampton College
Mill Road
Okehampton
Devon EX20 1PW

PSW (Exmouth) Film & Video Society ST
Ms E M Purdie
Students Union
Poly of South West
Douglas Avenue
Exmouth
Devon

Reels on Wheels OP
Alison Cameron
Community Resource Centre
Milford Park
Milford Road
Yeovil BA21 4QD

Shaftesbury Arts Centre Film Society OP DA
Mr P Schilling
Sheepwash Cottage
Burton, Mere
Warminster
Wilts BA12 6BR

Sherborne School Film Society ST DA
Mr A Swift
Abbey Road
Sherborne
Dorset DT9 3AP

Stroud and District Film Society OP DA
Tim Mugford
Manor Farm
Besbury Common
Minchinhampton
Stroud
Glos

Trowbridge College Film Society ST
Ms Antoinette Midgley
Dept of General & Social Studies
Trowbridge College
College Road
Trowbridge
Wilts BA14 0ES

SOUTHERN

Southern Group BFFS
Mr Dudley Smithers
1 Vanstone Cottages
Bagshot Road
Englefield Green
Egham
Surrey TW20 0RS

Abingdon College & District Film Society ST DA
Mr M Bloom
Abingdon College of FE
Northcourt Road
Abingdon
Oxon 0X14 1NN

Amersham & Chesham Film Society OP
A W Burrows
Hon Treasurer
73 Lye Green Road
Chesham
Bucks HP5 3NB

Ashcroft Arts Centre Film Society OP DA
The Secretary
Osborn Road
Fareham
Hants PO16 7DX

Aylesbury Vale Film Society OP DA
Mr A Smart
Brook Farm, Brooke End
Weston Turville
Bucks HP22 5RQ

Barton Peveril College 6th Form Film Society ST
Mr T C Meaker
Cedar Road
Eastleigh
Hants SO5 5ZA

Bracknell Film Society OP DA
Mr Roger C Birtchnell
14 Trumbull Road
Bracknell
Berks RG12 2EN

Chertsey Film Society OP DA
Mr H Lawes
29 Sayes Court
Addlestone
Surrey KT15 1NA

Eton College Film Society ST
Andrew Robinson
Bawldins End
Eton College
Windsor
Berks SL4 6DB

Harwell Film Society CL DA
Ms J Allan
AEA Technology,
Building 424
Harwell Laboratory
Didcot
Oxon OX11 0RA

Havant College Film Society ST
Mr P Turner
New Road
Havant
Hants PO9 1QL

Havant Film Society OP DA
Mrs P Stallworthy
c/o Havant Arts Centre
East Street
Havant
Hants PO9 1BS

Henley-on-Thames Film Society OP DA
Mr P Whitaker
10 St Andrews Road
Henley-on-Thames
Oxon RG9 1HP

Marlborough College Senior Film Society ST DA
Mr C Joseph
Marlborough College
Marlborough
Wilts SN8 1PA

Newbury Film Society OP DA
Stuart R Durrant
41 Jubilee Road
Newbury
Berks RG14 7NN

Open Film Society ST DA
Mr David Reed
Faculty of Technology
The Open University
Walton Hall
Milton Keynes
Bucks MK7 6AA

Radley College Film Society ST
Mr C R Barker
Radley College
Abingdon
Oxon OX14 2HR

Rewley House Film Theatre Club OP DA
Mr R T Rowley
Director
1 Wellington Square
Oxford OX1 2JA

St Anne's Film Society ST DA
Erica Maran
St Anne's College
Oxford OX2 6HS

Southampton Film Theatre – The Phoenix OP DA
Dr Peter Street
24 The Parkway
Bassett
Southampton SO2 3PQ

Swindon Film Society OP
Peter Robson
4 Church End
Purton
Swindon SN5 9EB

Union Films ST DA
Southampton University
Students' Union
Highfield
Southampton SO9 5NH

West End Centre (Aldershot) Film Society OP
Ms J Bowden
West End Centre
Queens Road
Aldershot
Hants GU11 3JD

Winchester College Film Society ST
Mr P J M Roberts
Winchester College
Winchester
Hants SO23 9NA

Winchester Film Society OP DA
Ms Ann Thomas
24 Bereweeke Road
Winchester
Hants SO22 6AN

Windsor Arts Centre Film Society OP
Mr C Brooker
St Leonards Road
Windsor
Berks SL4 3DB

WALES

Welsh Group BFFS
Mrs Lyn Jones
15 Bellevue Road
West Cross
Swansea SA3 5QA

Abergavenny Film Society OP DA
FAO Mr A Hutchinson
Wern-Y-Cwm
Llandewi Skirrid
Abergaveny
Gwent NP7 8AW

Congress Film Club (CFC) OP DA
David Giles
4 Fields Road
Oakfield
Cwmbran
Gwent NP44 3EF

Haverfordwest Film Society OP DA
Mrs J Evans
25 Greenhill Crescent
Merlins Bridge
Haverfordwest
Dyfed SA61 1LX

Maindy Film Club OP
Mr Neal Hammond
Workmens Hall
Church Road
Ton Pentre
Mid Glam CF41 7EH

Phoenix Film Club OP DA
J M Ounsted
30 Chrischurch Road
Newport
Gwent NP9 7SP

Presteigne Film Society OP DA
Mr R Scadding
Llugw Farm
Llanbister Road
Llandrindod Wells
Powys

Swansea Film Society OP
Dave Phillips
Taliesin Arts Centre
University College of Swansea
Singleton
Swansea SA2 8PZ

Theatr Mwldan Film Society OP DA
Nicholas Carey
Coedwynog
Velindre
Crymych SA41 3XW

University College of North Wales Film Society ST
Tony Brooks
16 Farrar Road
Bangor
Gwynedd LL57 1LJ

Valley Pictures OP DA
Mr Dallas Stone
Centre House
Cefn Community Centre
Cefn Coed
Merthyr Tydfil CF48 2NA

YORKSHIRE

Yorkshire Group BFFS
Mr Richard Fort
8 Bradley Grove
Silsden
Keighley
West Yorks BD20 9LX

Ampleforth Film Society ST DA
Rev S P Wright, MA OSB
Junior House
Ampleforth College
York YO6 4EN

BIHE Film Society OP
Russell Law
9 Carnoustle Close
Swinton
Mexborough
South Yorks

University of Bradford Union Film Society ST
The Secretary
Richmond Road
Bradford
West Yorks BD7 1DP

Halifax Playhouse Film Club OP DA
Mr N Riley-Gledhill
Treasurer
253 Skircoat Green Road
Halifax
West Yorks HX2 7QL

Harrogate Film Society OP
Mr P Caunt
19 Keats Walk
Harrogate
North Yorks HG1 3LN

Hebden Bridge Film Society OP
Diane Stead
Mytholm House
Mytholm
Hebden Bridge
West Yorks HX7 6DS

Ilkley Film Society OP DA
Mr R J Fort
8 Bradley Grove
Silsden
Keighley
West Yorks BD20 9LX

Lynchpin Film Society ST DA
Doj Graham
2 Sunnybank Court
Sunnybank
Denby Dale
West Yorks HD8 8TJ

Scarborough Film Society OP
Mr A E Davison
29 Peasholm Drive
Scarborough
North Yorks Y012 7NA

Sheffield University SU Film Unit ST DA
The Chair
Student Union
Sheffield University
Western Bank
Sheffield S10 2TG

Judith Ann Simpson CP
Rose Cottage
Carperby
Leyburn
North Yorks DL8 4DA

Wakefield Film Society OP
Charles Rose
Secretary
17 Oxford Road
Dewbury
West Yorks

York University Film Society ST DA
Ms Sarah Vick
Students' Union
Goodricke College
Heslington
York Y01 5DD

FUNDING

The list below is representative of the schemes available at any current time, but not definitive since the volatile nature of funding, both public and private, means that schemes emerge and fall by the wayside unpredictably. These funding schemes cover development, distribution, exhibition etc as well as production. The funds available fall into three main categories: direct grants, production finance and reimbursable loans. Where possible approximate closing dates are given, however it is advisable to check directly with the institution. In almost all cases these schemes are not open to students

Access for Disabled People to Arts Premises Today (ADAPT)
The ADAPT Trust
Cameron House
Abbey Park Place
Dunfermline
Fife KY12 7PZ
Tel: 0383 623166
Fax: 0383 622149
Hon. Director: Geoffrey Lord OBE
ADAPT (Northern Ireland)
c/o Northern Ireland Council on Disability
2 Annadale Avenue
Belfast BT7 3JR
Tel: 0232 491011
Fax: 0232 491627
Contact: Judith Jordan
Charitable trusts providing advice and funding to primary arts venues in the UK including cinemas which are themselves registered charities. Challenge funding of up to £25,000 may be made to arts venues who are trying to become fully accessible to disabled people. All work has to be carried out to British Standards. ADAPT also administers the British Gas ADAPT Awards (qv) which recognise and reward examples of best practice in access to arts venues for disabled people. Rolling scheme; no closing date

Arts Council of Great Britain
Department of Film, Video and Broadcasting
14 Great Peter Street
London SW1P 3NQ
Tel: 071 333 0100
Fax: 071 973 6581
The Arts Council supports the production of film and video within two broad strands: documentaries on arts subjects and artists' film and video. Funding is not provided on an ad hoc basis, but rather through particular schemes with specific deadlines. For an outline of all schemes, send a stamped, addressed envelope marked 'Leaflet' to the above address

Arts Documentaries
Professionally made programmes for broadcast by independent production companies. Any arts activity eligible for Arts Council support is within the terms of reference, plus related subjects such as crafts, popular culture

Dance for the Camera (with BBC2)
15 minute professional programmes made collaboratively by choreographers and directors. Annual deadline

Sound on Film (with BBC2)
30 minute professional programmes made collaboratively by composers and directors. Annual deadline

Synchro (in association with Carlton Television)
Five minute productions on black arts subjects for broadcast with £10,000 budget

Black Arts Video Project
Non-broadcast productions on black arts subjects. Two levels – for experienced makers (up to £8,000) and beginners (£5,000)

Artists' Film and Video Committee
Large and Small Awards
For film and video artists whose work is innovative, experimental and derives from a fine art practice. Budget range £2,000-£9,000. Annual deadline, usually September

Arts Council/Channel Four Experimenta
For large scale experimental work for television by film and video artists, up to £25,000. Annual deadline, usually January

Arts Council/Channel Four Animation Awards
For innovative animated work for television, up to £20,000. Annual deadline, usually January

One Minute Television
With BBC2's *The Late Show*. Sixty-second film/video artworks for television. Annual deadline, usually September

BBC Bristol Television Features
Whiteladies Road

Bristol BS8 2LR
Tel: 0272 742494
Fax: 0272 237934
10 x 10 Scheme for New Directors
Producer: Colin Rose
Produces 10 ten-minute films per annum. It is an initiative to encourage and develop new and innovative film making talent in all genres through the provision of modest production finance combined with practical guidance. Now in its seventh series, the scheme is open to any director with no previous credit on network TV, including film school students
Animation
Producer: Colin Rose
All work for adult audiences. No children's animation. Single short films bought-in after completion or occasionally pre-purchased. Single animated films of 30 mins or longer, or series of 10 minute films commiss-ioned from established practitioners. Projects should generally be appropriate for internat-ional co-production

BFI Cinema Services and Development Division

21 Stephen Street
London W1P 1PL
Tel: 071 255 1444
Fax: 071 436 7950
Head of Division: Irene Whitehead
Three Departments: Exhibition; Distribution; Funding.
Exhibition Department administers a wide range of services including programme advice and booking, publicity and documentation to the regional film theatre network. Officers also consult and advise the Funding Unit on issues of funding for regional exhi-bition clients and projects
Distribution Depart-ment (now incorporating Glenbuck Films) prom-otes the best of historical and contemporary cinema to a wide range of theatric and non-theatric users. We also make available a range of specialist titles on video sell-through
Funding Unit administers grants to the Regional Arts Boards, Wales Film Council and London Film and Video Development Agency (qv) in support of clients and schemes including production, exhibition, training and archive work. Also administers: direct grants to BFI revenue clients (mainly RFTs); the Regional Exhibition Project Fund which offers one-off and short-term funding to applicants from the cultural film exhibition sector; and the Develop-ment Budget which operates on incentive funding rules, mainly by invitation, and fund projects including the development of new cinemas, production and training resource centres. The Funding Unit prod-uces an annual 'Guide to Funding for Low Budget Film and Video Produc-tion', available on request

BFI Production

29 Rathbone Street
London W1P 1AG
Tel: 071 636 5587
Fax: 071 780 9456
Head of Production: Ben Gibson
Three areas of production finance:
Low budget features
Application on a script or treatment basis. Unsolicited manuscripts and general applications are responded to within 4-6 weeks. The Production Board, a collection of industry representatives, meets every two months to consider shortlisted applications. Features are not generally fully finan-ced by the BFI, every feature project taken on will involve a fund-raising element. The BFI offers a wide range of production relationships and holds legal and financial control once a project is taken on. Two to three features produced in any one year
New Directors Scheme
Executive Producer: Kate Ogborn
For film and video makers who are in the early stages of their careers or for people changing careers. Aims to produce five productions a year with a budget ceiling of £30,000, all productions to be made under Equity and BECTU agreements. Advertised annually in November; submissions accepted in January with final selection made by May
Production Projects Fund
Director: Steve Brookes
Offers grant support to innovative, low budget film and video production in Scotland, Wales, London and English regions. The Fund emphasises development and is unlikely to fully fund projects. Applicants are encouraged to seek other funders (public sector or industry). Open for applications for development, completion and production (up to £30,000). (At time of writing Production Projects is set up for once yearly application. A rolling format of 3 times a year is planned, details from the Director)

British Council

11 Portland Place
London W1N 4EJ
Tel: 071 389 3065
Fax: 071 389 3041
Contacts: Satwant Gill, Kevin Franklin
Does not provide direct funds to filmmakers but can assist in the coordination and shipping of films to festivals, and in some cases can provide funds for the filmmaker to attend when invited

British Gas ADAPT Awards

Cameron House
Abbey Park Place
Dunfermline
Fife KY12 7PZ
Tel: 0383 623166
Fax: 0383 622149
Contact: Gillian Dinsmore
Operated by ADAPT (qv) to recognise and reward the best practice in making arts venues accessible to disabled people. Prizes of £2,500 in each of seven categories, with a prize of £5,000 for the best venue overall, the money to be spent on further improvements in accessibility

British Screen Finance

14-17 Wells Mews
London W1P 3FL
Tel: 071 323 9080
Fax: 071 323 0092
Contact: Annette Caulkin
Invests in British films or films made under co-production treaties with other countries. Scripts should be submitted with full background information to Annette Caulkin. All scripts are read. Scripts that are part of production package are preferred, and the project must have commercial potential as a theatrical release. British Screen's contribution rarely exceeds £500,000

Channel 4/ MOMI Animators

Professional Residencies scheme
Museum of the Moving Image
South Bank
London SE1 8XT
Tel 071 815 1376
Contact: Animation Coordinator
Four Professional Residencies are awarded to young or first time animators. A fee of £2,500 plus a budget of up to £1,350 towards materials. At the end of residency at MOMI, project will be considered for commission by Channel 4. (Likely deadline end of August 1994)

The Fulbright Commission

Fulbright House
62 Doughty Street
London WC1N 2LS
Tel: 071 404 6880
Fax: 071 404 6834
Programme Director: Catherine Boyle
Fulbright-T.E.B. Clarke Fellowship in Screenwriting
An annual fellowship for a British screenwriter to spend nine months in the United States. The award covers round-trip travel plus a grant of £18,000
Fulbright Graduate Student Awards

Open to British citizens wishing to undertake a minimum of nine months postgraduate study in the United States. An upper second or first class degree is required. Awards cover round-trip travel and maintenance costs. A number of awards covering travel only are also available

Glasgow Film Fund

Scottish Film Production Fund
74 Victoria Crescent Road
Glasgow G12 9JN
Tel: 041 337 2526
Fax: 041 337 2562
Contact: Ivan Mactaggart
Production investment for feature films made in Glasgow or by Glasgow's production sector. The Scottish Film Production Fund administers the Glasgow Film Fund and its board meets regularly to consider applications. Application forms, dates of meetings and deadlines from SFPF office

The London Production Fund

2nd Floor
25 Gosfield Street
London W1P 7HB
Tel: 071 637 3588
Fax: 071 637 3578
Maggie Ellis
Felicity Oppé
The London Film and Video Development Agency, Carlton Television, Channel 4 and the BFI have established this fund to support the production of independent and innovative film and video projects. A total of £200,000 is currently available

Development Awards
Support of up to £3,000 each to assist in the development of scripts, storyboards, project packages, pilots etc

Project and completion awards
offer support up to £15,000 each for production or part-production costs. Awards will be made on the basis of written proposal and applicants' previous work. The Fund is interested in supporting as diverse a range of films and videos as possible

The Nicholl Fellowships in Screenwriting

Academy of Motion Picture Arts and Sciences
8949 Wilshire Boulevard
Beverly Hills
CA 90211
USA
Tel: (1) 310 247 3059

Annual screen writing fellowship awards
Up to five fellowships of US$25,000 each to new screenwriters. Eligible are writers in English who have not earned money writing for commercial film or television. Collaborations and adaptations are not eligible. A completed entry includes a feature film screenplay approx 100-130 pages long, an application form and a US$25 entry fee. Send self-addressed envelope for rules and application form. Entries must be postmarked by 1 May 1994

Northern Ireland Film Council

7 Lower Crescent
Belfast BT7 1NR
Tel: 0232 232444
Fax: 0232 239918
Contact: Geraldine Wilkins

Production Fund
A total of £50,000 available to offer support for development and production of projects of artistic and cultural relevance to Northern Ireland, and of an original and creative nature. Awards are between £500 and £10,000. Small bursaries are available for independent student projects. Deadline end of September

Partners in Europe

The Prince's Trust
8 Bedford Row
London WC1R 4BA
Contacts: Anne Engel, Raphaëlle Sadler

Go and See Grants
Awards (£500 max) to help young people explore collaborative projects with partners in European countries. Applicants must be under 26 and out of full-time education

European Pépinières
On behalf of Eurocréation in France, coordinates the Pépinières Programme in the UK, a competition offering artists between the ages of 20 and 30 residencies in a number of European cities spanning a range of disciplines

The Richard Mills Travel Fellowship
In association with the Gulbenkian Foundation and the Peter S Cadbury Trust, offers 3 grants of £1,000 for people working in community arts in the areas of housing, minority arts, special needs, or arts for young people, especially the unemployed. The Fellowships are applicable to people under 35

Scottish Film Council

Dowanhill
74 Victoria Crescent Road
Glasgow G12 9JN
Tel: 041 334 4445
Fax: 041 334 8132
Director: David Bruce
Deputy Director: Erica King

First Reels
Annual production awards scheme run in collaboration with Scottish Television. Two levels of award – £500 and £2,000 – available for new or inexperienced film and video makers. Capital fund available for non-revenue recurring projects, eg within regional film theatre network, workshop sector etc. This fund will be allocated to new development attracting 50% of costs from other sources

Scottish Film Production Fund

74 Victoria Crescent Road
Glasgow G12 9JN
Tel: 041 337 2526
Fax: 041 337 2562
Contact: Ivan Mactaggart
SFPF fosters and develops film and video production in Scotland. The SFPF meets six times a year to consider applications primarily for development of narrative fiction films. All productions must have particular connection with and relevance to Scotland. Total resources for script and production support this financial year are £230,000

REGIONAL ARTS BOARDS

Eastern Arts Board

Cherry Hinton Hall
Cherry Hinton Road
Cambridge CB1 4DW
Tel: 0223 215355
Fax: 0223 248075
Cinema and Broadcasting Officer: Martin Ayres

Low Budget Production Fund
Development up to £500 for research, script development etc. Project funding up to £5,000 (sole funding and co-production). Completion and distribution up to £5,000 also available

First Take
In conjunction with Anglia Television. Commissions for screening by the regional ITV company, projects by new producers/directors/writers. Anglia Screen Guide available

Cinema and Broadcasting Initiatives, Festival, Publishing, Exchanges and Fellowships and Training Funds
Support for development projects, events and feasibility studies

Write Lines
Film, video and TV script reading service for aspiring writers

Film and video database
For organisations and practitioners in region. Application forms and information available from Helen Dixon, Cinema and Broadcasting Assistant

East Midlands Arts Board

Mountfields House
Forest Road
Loughborough
Leics LE11 3HU
Tel: 0509 218292
Fax: 0509 262214
Contacts: Jeff Baggott, Caroline Pick
Script development up to

£1,000; production bursaries up to £500; limited production grants; biennial awards of £10,000. Small awards made for exhibition, group and individual training and distribution. Details on application available on request

London Film and Video Development Agency

2nd Floor
25 Gosfield Street
London W1P 7HB
Tel: 071 637 3577
Fax: 071 637 3578
Chief Executive: Steve McIntyre

Project Grants
Programme of support for training projects, workshops etc announced annually

Exhibition
Deficit guarantees available for Film Festivals

London Production Fund (qv)
Funding available for project development, as a contribution towards production costs, and for completion of projects. Details of all the above available on request

North West Arts Board

12 Harter Street
Manchester M1 6HY
Tel: 061 228 3062
Fax: 061 236 5361
Contact: Jackie Morrissey, Film and Video Officer

Film and Video General Projects
Offers financial support to a range of projects which will strengthen the practice and provision of film and video in the region. The total budget available is £17,000. The limit on individual awards is £3,000. Any organisation or group resident in the North West Arts Board region is eligible to apply (excluding existing revenue clients). Applications are considered throughout the year. Application forms and guidelines available on request

Film and Video Training Projects
Offers financial assistance to encourage training projects which will contribute to the long-term development of film and video activity in the NWAB region. The total budget available is £17,000. The limit on individual awards is £3,000. Any organisation or groups resident in the NWAB region is eligible to apply (excluding existing revenue clients). Applications are considered throughout the year. Application forms and guidelines available on request

Film and Video Production
Offers financial assistance to groups and individuals in the region towards film and video production and development projects. The total budget available is £30,000. The limit on individual production awards is £3,000; development awards £500. Guidelines, deadlines and application forms available on request

Northern Arts Board

9-10 Osborne Terrace
Jesmond
Newcastle-upon-Tyne
NE2 1NZ
Tel: 091 281 6334
Fax: 091 281 3276
Northern Arts has established a Media Investment Fund in order to encourage and support film and video projects within the Northern Arts region. All activities supported by the fund must: be of benefit to the region; contribute to the development of media in the region; use the region's skills and facilities where possible. Applications can be made to the fund for:

Script development
Up to £3,000 (if taken up by a commercial company grant is paid back in full by the first day of principal shoot)

Pilot projects
Up to £2,000: short tapes which give the style and feel of a production in order to attract further funding

Production
The full amount will be considered for short experimental productions up to £3,000 or productions up to £10,000. Part funding up to £10,000 will be given to productions over £10,000 or completion monies for post-production on work not funded by Northern Arts

Time Limited Development Projects
Rotation funding of projects on a two, sometimes three year basis

Broadcasting Development Fund
£11,000 available to fund imaginative partnership projects between arts organisations, or individual artists working on joint commissions with broadcasting agencies in the region

Capital
The fund will consider applications from non-profit distribution organisations for capital support but not more than 50% of the total cost. The fund is normally available twice yearly, closing dates in February and September Full details of all the above on application

South-East Arts Board

10 Mount Ephraim
Tunbridge Wells
Kent TN4 8AS
Tel: 0892 515210
Fax: 0892 549383
Contact: Tim Cornish

Exhibition Subsidy
Grants of up to £2,000 are awarded to venues in the region whose policy is educative. Full details on application

Production Grants
Grants for beginners of up to £500 awarded. Other production money for 1993/94 is already committed to broadcast co-productions. Full details on application

South West Arts

Bradninch Place
Gandy Street
Exeter EX4 3LS
Tel: 0392 218188
Fax: 0392 413554
Three categories of annual production awards:

Small Awards
for individuals. Materials only basis. Up to £1,000

Intermediate Awards
for individuals or "one-off" group projects. Materials only basis. Up to £3,000

Major/Group Awards
which contribute to the production programmes of film and video workshops, resources and production co-operatives in the region. Normally up to £4,000, but in exceptional circumstances circumstances larger awards may be made. Occasional "one-off" major awards are made for collaborations with regionally based TV based ITV or BBC companies; these are widely advertised. Financial support is offered for exhibition of independent 'art-house', historic, experimental and community films and videos

Southern Arts Board

13 St Clement Street
Winchester
Hants SO23 9DQ
Tel: 0962 855099
Fax: 0962 861186
Workshop production grants up to £500; individual film and video production grants up to £3,000. One grant of up to £10,000 will also be available. Annual David Altshul Award of £1,000 for creative excellence in film and video within the region (students also eligible). A script appraisal service is available, entitled "Write Reactions". An Exhibition Fund is also available towards the costs of programme development, educational events, marketing and training. A Media Education Fund provides support for projects, residencies, programme of speakers to promote Media Education in the statutory and non-statutory sectors. Full details on all the above on application

West Midlands Arts Board

82 Granville Street
Birmingham B1 2LH

Tel: 021 631 3121
The Birmingham/West Midlands Film and Video Production Fund
The fund ia a joint initiative by Birmingham City Council, West Midlands Arts and Channel 4 Television. The fund offers three categories of Awards – Production Awards, Initial Awards and Production development awards
Production Awards
For 15 minute programmes with a budget of up to £15,000 and can include salaries. Application deadline March 94. It is anticipated that up to 5 awards will be made each year
Initial Awards
For 1 to 7 minute programmes with a budget of up to £5,000 and are for materials only. Application deadline March 94. It is anticipated that up to 5 awards will be made each year
Production Development Awards
are for production development proposals with a budget in the range of £500 to £2,000. The application deadline is autumn 1993. It is anticipated that 5 awards will be made in 1993/4
Recipients of awards have access to production resources and the opportunity to have their work broadcast through the First Cut initiative with Central Television and Channel 4.
All awards are open to anyone living or working in the West Midlands region. For application details please contact the Film, Video and Television production co-ordinator at WMA

Yorkshire and Humberside Arts Board
21 Bond Street
Dewsbury
West Yorks WF13 1AX
Tel: 0924 455555
Fax: 0924 466522
Contact: Tony Dixon
YHA offers two schemes:
Film Producton scheme
For individuals, the Film Production Scheme is for the development, production and distribution of short films and tapes up to 10 mins
Community Media scheme
For groups, the Community Media scheme provides awards of £500 for training in production skills

EUROPEAN AND PAN-EUROPEAN SOURCES

EURIMAGES
Council of Europe
Palais de l'Europe
67075 Strasbourg
France
Tel: (33) 88 41 26 40
Fax: (33) 88 41 27 60
Contact: Executive Secretary
Provides financial support for feature-length fiction films, creative documentaries and distribution. The largest levels of funding are available for feature films (up to £0.5m per film) made by at least 3 member country partners

European Co-production Association
c/o ZDF Enterprises GmbH
6500 Mainz/Hechtsheim
Germany
Tel: (49) 6131 991 321-3
Fax: (49) 6131 991 324
Contact: Martin Pieper
A consortium of European public service TV networks for the co-production of TV fiction series. Can offer complete finance. Development funding is also possible. Proposals should consist of full treatment, financial plan and details of proposed co-production partners. Projects are proposed directly to Secretariat or to member national broadcasters (Channel 4 in UK)

European Co-production Fund
c/o British Screen Finance
14-17 Wells Mews
London W1P 3FL
Tel: 071 323 9080
Fax: 071 323 0092
The Fund's aim is to enable UK producers to collaborate in the making of films which the European market demonstrably wishes to see made but which could not be made without its involvement. The ECF offers commercial loans, up to 30% of the total budget, for full length feature films intended for theatrical release. Producers who are citizens or residents of an EC member state and who have companies incorporated in the EC may apply. The film must be a co-production involving at least two companies, with no link of common ownership, established in two separate EC states and must be a "relevant" film under the terms of the 1985 Films Act

Film Fonds Hamburg
Friedensallee 14-16
2000 Hamburg 50
Germany
Tel: (49) 40 390 5883
Fax: (49) 40 390 4424
Contacts: Eva Hubert, Michael Eckelt
Producers of cinema films can apply for a subsidy of up to 2 million German marks – amounting to at most 30% of the overall production costs of the finished film. Foreign producers can also apply for this support, whether for German co-productions or entirely foreign productions. Financial support provided by the Film Fonds can be used in combination with other private or public funding, including that of TV networks

First Film Foundation – Film Europe
Canalot Studios
222 Kensal Road
London W10 5BN
Tel: 081 969 5195
Coordinator: Angeli Macfarlane
The First Film Foundation operates a development fund for its pan-European feature film programme Film Europe. Sponsored by Kodak it helps new writers and directors through critical stages in the development of films by employing a 'godfather' system where new directors are advised by senior producers and directors

The MEDIA 95 Programme
13 projects (from a total of 19) dealing with various aspects of the film and television industries. Further information on these and the other MEDIA 95 projects can be obtained from Louise Casey, European Information Officer, at the BFI. See also their entries under Organ-isations (Europe)

BABEL (Broadcasting Across the Barriers of European Language)
c/o European Broadcasting Union
Case Postale 67
1218 Grand Saconnex
Geneva
Switzerland
Tel: (41) 22 717 21 11
Fax: (41) 22 798 58 97
Chairman: Philippe Bélingard
Coordinator: Frank Naef
Promotes multi-lingual approaches to post-production and distribution of European audio-visual productions. Non-reimbursable grants of up to 50% of post-production budget. Priority given to completed productions in less widely spoken languages

DOCUMENTARY
(Project Development and Promotion Packaging)
Skindergade 29a
1159 Copenhagen K
Denmark
Tel: (45) 33 15 00 99
Fax: (45) 33 15 76 76
Contact: Thomas Stenderup
Loans are available to independent producers for development or

promotion packaging of creative documentaries. Projects are allocated points according to current priorities and projects with sufficient points may receive a loan, with additional selection if too many projects apply

EFDO (European Film Distribution Office)

Friedensallee 14-16
2000 Hamburg 50
Germany
Tel: (49) 40 390 9025
Fax: (49) 40 390 6249
It assists the theatrical distribution of low/mid budget European feature films by providing conditionally repayable, interest-free loans to European distributors from no less than 3 different countries

EVE (Espace Vidéo Européen)

c/o Irish Film Institute
6 Eustace Street
Dublin 2
Republic of Ireland
Tel: (353) 1 679 5744
Fax: (353) 1 679 9657
Chief Executive:
John Dick
Loan Scheme Manager:
Norma Cairns
EVE's main purpose is to increase the supply of European product on video, by offering conditionally repayable loans to European video publishers up to a 40% ceiling as follows: ECU 25,000 for feature films, ECU 15,000 for documentaries/classics, ECU 30,000 for a series of documentaries

Euro Media Garanties

66 rue Pierre Charron
75008 Paris
France
Tel: (33) 1 43 59 88 03
Fax: (33) 1 45 63 85 58
Sylvie Depondt
Offers guarantees of bank loans through a fund to financial operators involved in European film and audiovisual productions. Projects to involve at least three member countries of the Council of Europe. In principle, up to 70% of the loan finance could be guaranteed, depending on the nature of the production and the total guarantee fund available

Europa Cinemas

10 rue Auber
75009 Paris
France
Tel: (33) 1 40 17 07 74
Fax: (33) 1 40 17 06 47
Claude-Eric Poiroux
Sylvie Peyre
This project is intended for cinema exhibitors who already actively favour European films, and is to provide them with technical and financial support so they can develop their programming, promotion and in-house activities. Exhibitor will have to finance at least 50% of the cost of these activities

European Film Academy

Katharinenstrasse 8
1000 Berlin 31
Germany
Tel: (49) 30 893 4132
Fax: (49) 30 893 4134
Secretary General: Aina Bellis
The EFA promotes meetings between European film professionals, organises masterclasses, symposia, screenings, produces publications, and organises the European Film Awards. It carries out its projects in close co-operation with co-production partners at the project location, and can contribute up to 50% of the project financing

European Script Fund

39c Highbury Place
London N5 1QP
Tel: 071 226 9903
Fax: 071 354 2706
Director General: Bo Christensen
Assists the development of projects that are of European interest, through loans reimbursable on production. Producers, writers, directors, companies should request an application form with guidelines from the above address

GRECO (Groupement Européen pour la Circulation des Oeuvres)

Bahnhofstrasse 33
85774 Unterföhring b. München
Germany
Tel: (49) 89 950 83 290
Fax: (49) 89 950 83 292
Co-ordinator: Maritta von Uechtritz
GRECO promotes the circulation of high quality TV fiction. Independent producers of TV fiction who own distribution rights to work are eligible. Their project must have the support of at least 3 broadcasters in 3 different languages, and they may apply for a maximum of 12.5% of its budget. Loans must be reimbursed from the first returns

MAP-TV (Memory – Archives – Programmes TV)

c/o France 3
Place de Bordeaux
67005 Strasbourg Cédex
France
Tel: (33) 88 56 68 46
Fax: (33) 88 56 68 49
Contact: J J Lemoine
Its aim is to enhance the value of the European audiovisual archives, particularly by helping set up co-productions of archive based creative programmes. Three partners from at least two different countries should be involved. Loans can be offered up to 7.5% of the estimated programme budget, with the applicant and partners giving an equivalent amount during the development phase

Media Business School

Torregalindo 10, 4th floor
28016 Madrid
Spain
Tel: (34) 1 359 02 47
Fax: (34) 1 345 76 06
General Manager:
Fernando Labrada
The MBS is the training, research and development arm of the MEDIA programme of the EC. It operates through the establishment of training and development structures, the organisation of seminar cycles and the publication of reports. The MBS can contribute up to 50% of the funding of approved projects

Media Investment Club

4 Avenue de l'Europe
94366 Bry-sur-Marne Cédex
France
Tel: (33) 1 49 83 32 72/ 49 83 28 63
Fax: (33) 1 49 83 25 82
Secretary General:
Patrick Madelin
The Club (whose members include industrial companies, communications groups and financial organisations) acts as co-producer for audio-visual productions in pioneering areas of new technology, through reimbursable loans. Financial investment negotiated on a case by case basis

Media Salles

Piazza Luigi di Savoia 24
20124 Milan
Italy
Tel: (39) 2 669 02 41
Fax: (39) 2 669 15 74
Secretary General:
Elisabetta Brunella
Founded to carry out initiatives for cinema exhibitors within the fields of promotion, information and training

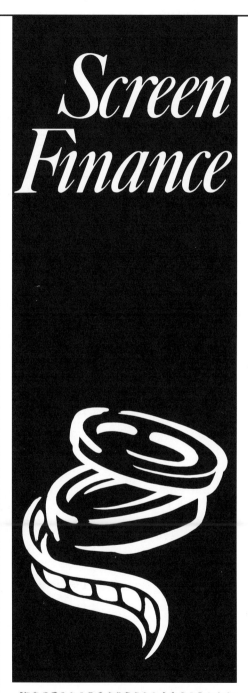

INTERNATIONAL SALES

These companies acquire the rights to audiovisual product for sale to foreign distributors in all media (see also Distributors (Non-Theatrical) and (Theatrical) pp140-149)

Action Time
Wrendal House
2 Whitworth Street West
Manchester M1 5WX
Tel: 061 236 8999
Fax: 061 236 8845
Keri Lewis Brown
Specialises in international format sales of game shows and light entertainment. Through the Action Group, the international consortium of independent production companies, the format *Love at First Sight* has been seen in ten different versions, in Europe, Russia and the USA

All American Leisure Group UK
6 Woodland Way
Petts Wood
Kent BR5 1ND
Tel: 0689 871535
Fax: 0689 871519

Allied Arts International
The Forum
74-80 Camden Street
London NW1 0JL
Tel: 071 383 4258
Fax: 071 383 7174
John Kelleher
James Wills
Anne McGrath
Television distributors of opera, ballet, dance, music specials and documentary programmes for producers NVC Arts and Allied Entertainments

Allied Vision
The Glassworks
3-4 Ashland Place
London W1M 3JH
Tel: 071 224 1992
Fax: 071 224 0111
Peter McRae
Catherine Peak

Arts Council of Great Britain
14 Great Peter Street
London SW1P 3NQ
Tel: 071 973 6454
Fax: 071 973 6581
Richard Gooderick
Arts Council Films is the in-house distributor of the Arts Council financed programmes. It also specialises in the development funding and distribution of innovative, high quality broadcast programmes by working closely with independent programme makers and international broadcasters. See also under Organisations

August Entertainment
10 Arminger Road
London W12 7BB
Tel: 081 742 9099
Fax: 081 742 9311
Eleanor Powell
Danica Harms
International sales agent for independent producers. Films include *The Lawnmower Man II: Mindfire, True Romance, Only the Strong, Another 9 1/2 Weeks, Nostradamus*

Australian Film Commission
2nd Floor
Victory House
99-101 Regent Street
London W1R 7HB
Tel: 071 734 9383
Fax: 071 434 0170
Pressanna Vasudevan

BBC Enterprises
Woodlands
80 Wood Lane
London W12 0TT
Tel: 081 743 5588/
576 2000
Fax: 081 746 0310
Commercial exploitation and export of BBC product, including books, audio tapes and programmes edited as videograms for consumer and educational markets. Also responsible for BBC television programme sales, co-productions and BBC magazines

bfi BFI Production
29 Rathbone Street
London W1P 1AG
Tel: 071 636 5587
Fax: 071 580 9456
Sue Bruce-Smith
Sales and distribution of mainly BFI Production films *Anchoress, Psychotherapy, Wittgenstein, Distant Voices, Still Lives, Young Soul Rebels*

Jane Balfour Films
Burghley House
35 Fortess Road
London NW5 1AD
Tel: 071 267 5392
Fax: 071 267 4241
Jane Balfour
Mary Barlow
Sarah Banbury
Distribution agent for Channel 4 and independent producers, handling drama, documentaries and specialised feature films

The Box Office
3 Market Mews
London W1Y 7HH
Tel: 071 499 3968
Fax: 071 491 0008
Paul Shields
International film and television consultancy

British Home Entertainment
5 Broadwater Road
Walton-on-Thames
Surrey KT12 5DB
Tel: 0932 228832
Fax: 0932 247759
Clive Williamson
Video distribution/TV marketing. *An Evening with the Royal Ballet, Othello, The Mikado, The Soldier's Tale, Uncle Vanya, Gulliver's Travels, King and Country, The Hollow Crown*

CBC International Sales
43-51 Great Titchfield Street
London W1P 8DD
Tel: 071 580 0336
Fax: 071 323 5658
Susan Hewitt
Yvonne Body
Véronique Vergès
The marketing division of Canadian Broadcasting Corporation and Société Radio-Canada

CBS Broadcast International
1 Red Place
London W1Y 3RE
Tel: 071 355 4422

Fax: 071 355 4429
Sonja Mendes
Anne Hirsch
Wide range of US TV product

CTVC
Hillside Studios
Merry Hill Road
Bushey
Watford
Herts WD2 1DR
Tel: 081 950 4426
Fax: 081 950 1437
Peter Davies
Documentaries, children's programmes, sports coverage and documentaries, music, drama and animation programmes – all with bias towards positive human values

Castle Target International
A29 Barwell Business Park
Leatherhead Road
Chessington
Surrey KT9 2NY
Tel: 081 974 1021
Fax: 081 974 2674
Terry Shand
Buddy's Song, The Monk, That Summer of White Roses, Conspiracy

Central Television Enterprises
Hesketh House
43-45 Portman Square
London W1H 9FG
Tel: 071 486 6688
Fax: 071 486 1707
Anthony Utley
Evi Nicopoulos
Louise Sexton
Sale of all Central TV-produced films and TV programmes. Also representing Carlton Television, HTV and Meridian Broadcasting

Channel 4 International
60 Charlotte Street
London W1P 2AX
Tel: 071 631 4444
Fax: 071 580 2622
Colin Leventhal
Bill Stephens
Frances Berwick
Trading subsidiary of Channel Four Television dealing with the sales of films and programmes commissioned by Channel Four and related activities such as the licensing of books, records and videos

Chatsworth Television Distributors
97-99 Dean Street
London W1V 5RA
Tel: 071 734 4302
Fax: 071 437 3301
Halina Stratton
Genevieve Dexter
Extensive library of documentary and special interest films. Also Chatsworth-produced light entertainment, drama and adventure series

CiBy Sales
10 Stephen Mews
London W1P 1PP
Tel: 071 333 8877
Fax: 071 333 8878
Wendy Palmer
Fiona Mitchell
Perrine Teze
Established in 1992, CiBy Sales is responsible for the international multi-media exploitation of films produced by French production company CiBy 2000 and other independent producers. Titles include: *Little Buddha, The Hour of the Pig, Kika, The Flemish Board, The Glass Shield, L'Ombre du Doute, Tombés du Ciel (Lost in Transit)*

Cine Electra
National House
60-66 Wardour Street
London W1V 3HP
Tel: 071 287 1123
Fax: 071 722 4251
Julia Kennedy
The company distributes a diverse slate of films internationally. Titles include: *Magnificat, Baby of Mâcon, Prospero's Books, The Ring with the Crowned Eagle, Moving, Walk Me Home, Utz, Dismissed from Life, All That Really Matters.* Also documentaries *Beatrice Wood: Mama of Dada* and *The Eternal Tramp*, about Charlie Chaplin. New productions will include: *The Circle of the White Rose, Hamlet in America, Polish Death* and *Pushkin*

Colstar International
11 Wythburn Place
London W1H 5WL
Tel: 071 437 5725
Fax: 071 706 1704
Distributors of documentaries, series, drama shorts, feature-length tele-drama worldwide. Library includes *The Open Door on Photography* series, *Blockade, Klaus Fuchs, Stefan Zweig, J.K., Australian Panorama, Journeys Across Australia, Ben Cropp's Natural History World* series, *Rhythm, The Fox, Underwater Adventures*

Columbia TriStar International Television
19 Wells Street
London W1P 3FP
Tel: 071 637 8444
Fax: 071 528 8849
Nicholas Bingham
Patrice van de Walle
Marck O'Connell
European TV production and international distribution of Columbia's and TriStar's feature films and TV product

CORI Distribution Group
19 Albemarle Street
London W1X 3HA
Tel: 071 493 7920
Fax: 071 493 8088
Marie Hoy
Bob Jenkins
Involved in international sales and co-production funding, with offices in London and Los Angeles. Recently acquired titles include *Diamond Fleece*

Darvill Associates
280 Chartridge Lane
Chesham
Bucks HP5 2SG
Tel: 0494 783643
Fax: 0494 784873
Television programme suppliers for FinnImage, MTV Finland, Radio Netherlands Television, Radio Sweden International, Netherlands Information Service, Dutch Film Archives

The Walt Disney Company
Beaumont House
Kensington Village
Avonmore Road
London W14 8TS
Tel: 071 605 2400
Fax: 071 605 2593
Etienne de Villiers
Ed Borgerding
Worldwide television distribution arm of a major US production company

English Film Co (Exports)
6 Woodland Way
Petts Wood
Kent BR5 1ND
Tel: 0689 871535
Fax: 0689 871519

Film Booking Offices
211 The Chambers
Chelsea Harbour
London SW10 0XF
Tel: 071 734 5298/071 437 1572
Fax: 071 352 4182
Brian Sammes

Film Four International
60 Charlotte Street
London W1P 2AX
Tel: 071 631 4444
Fax: 071 580 2622
Bill Stephens
Heather Playford-Denman
Film sales arm of Channel Four, set up in 1984 to sell feature films which it finances or part-finances. Recent titles include *Naked, Raining Stones, Bad Behaviour, Bhaji on the Beach, Shopping, The Getaway* and *Wild West*

Goldcrest Films and Television
65/66 Dean Street
London W1V 5HD
Tel: 071 437 8696
Fax: 071 437 4448
Thierry Wase-Bailey
Major feature film production, sales and finance company. Recent films include *All Dogs Go to Heaven, Black Rainbow, Rock-A-Doodle, The Harvest, Me and Veronica* and *Painted Heart*

The Samuel Goldwyn Co
St George's House
14-17 Wells Street
London W1P 3FP
Tel: 071 436 5105
Fax: 071 580 6520
Diana Hawkins
Gary Phillips
Kate Robinson
Caroline Henshaw
Offices in Los Angeles, London, New York. Acquisition, sales, distribution and

marketing of films and television product worldwide. Recent film titles include *Much Ado About Nothing, Mr Wonderful, Golden Gate, The Program, Peter's Friends.* Television product includes: *The American Gladiators, Why Didn't I Think of That?, Gamepro*, The Goldwyn Classics Library and the Rogers and Hammerstein Library

Grampian Television
Queen's Cross
Aberdeen AB9 2XJ
Tel: 0224 646464
Fax: 0224 635127
Michael J McLintock
North Scotland ITV station producing a wide range of product including documentaries, sport, children's, religion, as well as daily news and current aggairs. Titles include: *A Prince Among Islands* which follows Prince Charles on a visit to the tiny island of Berneray; *A Year in Spain* featuring interviews with King Juan Carlos and children's animation *James the Cat*. Through ITEL, Grampian are seeking partners for a range of projects including Gaelic language programmes

Granada LWT International
The London Television Centre
Upper Ground
London SE1 9LT
Tel: 071 737 8381
Fax: 071 928 8476
Sydney Perry
Nadine Nohr
International programme sales and distribution for Granada Television and London Weekend Television. Leading titles include *Prime Suspect, Agatha Christie's Poirot, The Jewel in the Crown* and *Upstairs, Downstairs*

HIT Entertainment
The Pump House
13-16 Jacob's Well Mews
London W1H 5PD
Tel: 071 224 1717
Fax: 071 224 1719
Peter Orton
Sophie Turner Laing
Jane Smith
Distributors of children's, family and light entertainment programming including *Basket Fever, The Ed Sullivan Show, Marlin Bay, End of Golden Weather, Sex on the Reef, Kea – Mountain Parrot*, TVNZ Library – SPP and NHU

Hemdale
21 Albion Street
London W2 2AS
Tel: 071 724 1010
Fax: 071 724 9168
John Smallcombe
UK sales office of US production company. Titles include *Terminator, Platoon, The Last Emperor* and *Return of the Living Dead*

ITC Entertainment Group
24 Nutford Place
London W1H 5YN
Tel: 071 262 3262
Fax: 071 724 0160
Lynden Parry
Distributors of *Sam and Me, Robin Hood Trilogy, UFO Café, Touch and Die, Super Space Theatre, Heritage Collection I and II, ITC's Excellent Adventures, Thunderbirds, Stingray, Doppelganger, Trouble Bound*

ITEL
48 Leicester Square
London WC2H 7FB
Tel: 071 491 1441
Fax: 071 493 7677
Andrew Macbean
Distribution and production development company owned by Anglia Television and Home Box Office. Represents Anglia Television Entertainment, Survival, National Geographic Television and Programming from Home Box Office and Roadshow, Coote and Carroll

J & M Entertainment
2 Dorset Square
London NW1 6PU
Tel: 071 723 6544
Fax: 071 724 7541
Julia Palau
Michael Ryan
Peter Rogers
Anthony Miller
Linda Deacy
Specialise in sales of all media, distribution and marketing of independent feature films. Recent films include: *The Road to Wellville, Princess Caraboo, Sugar Hill, What's Eating Gilbert Grape? Saint of Fort Washington, House of Angels*

Link Entertainment
7 Baron's Gate
33-35 Rothschild Road
Chiswick
London W4 5HT
Tel: 081 995 5080
Fax: 081 747 9452
Claire Derry
David Hamilton
Jo Kavanagh
Specialists in children's programmes for worldwide distribution and character licensing. New properties include: *GFI, Eye of the Storm, Creature Comforts, What-a-Mess, Family Ness, Spider!, Magic Roundabout, Barney* and many classic children's programmes

London Films
Kent House
14-17 Market Place
Great Titchfield Street
London W1N 8AR
Tel: 071 323 5251
Fax: 071 436 2834
Andrew Luff
Natural Lies: 3 x 1 hour thriller series; *Lady Chatterley's Lover*: 4 x 1 hour; *The Second Imperative*: 6 x 1 hour documentary; *An Ungentlemanly Act*: 119 mins, BAFTA-winning TV movie

London Television Service
Hercules House
Hercules Road
London SE1 7DU
Tel: 071 261 8592
Fax: 071 928 5037
Jackie Huxley
LTS is a specialist production and distribution organisation that handles the promotion and marketing of British documentary programmes worldwide to television, cable, satellite and non-broadcast outlets. The flagship science and technology series *Perspective* has sold to television in over 90 countries

Lumiere Pictures
167-169 Wardour Street
London W1V 3TA
Tel: 071 439 1790
Fax: 071 734 1509
Chris Cary
Martin Bigham
James Graham
Sales of library, foreign sales, feature film production

MCA TV
1 Hamilton Mews
London W1V 9FF
Tel: 071 491 4666
Fax: 071 493 4702
Roger Cordjohn
Penny Craig
UK operation for the major US corporation which owns Universal Pictures

MCEG Virgin Vision see **VVL**

MGM/UA Television see **Turner International**

Majestic Films and Television International
PO Box 13
Gloucester Mansions
Cambridge Circus
London WC2H 8XD
Tel: 071 836 8630
Fax: 071 836 5819
Guy East
Organises finance, sales, distribution and marketing of feature films and television productions throughout the world. Recent titles include *Airborne, Camilla, The Telegraphist, Rapa Nui, The Fencing Master, The Man Without a Face, Damage, Into The West*

Manifesto Film Sales
Third Floor
10 Livonia Street
London W1V 3PH
Tel: 071 439 2424
Fax: 071 437 9964
Aline Perry
David Livingstone
Recent titles include: *Kalifornia, Dream Lover, The Ballad of Little Jo, Young Americans, Romeo*

is Bleeding, Posse, A Home of Our Own, The Hudsucker Proxy

NBD Television
Unit 2
105 Lancaster Road
London W11 1QF
Tel: 071 243 3646
Fax: 071 243 3656
Nicky Davies Williams
Maro Korkou
Company specialising in music and light entertainment. Clients include Channel Four, Warner Bros Records, Sony Music International, Channel X, Celador and MPL

National Film Board of Canada
1 Grosvenor Square
London W1X 0AB
Tel: 071 258 6480
Fax: 071 258 6532
Jane Taylor
European sales office for documentary, drama and animation productions from Canada's National Film Board

Orbit Films
7-11 Kensington High Street
London W8 5NP
Tel: 071 221 5548
Fax: 071 727 0515
Chris Ranger
Gordon Pilkington
Specialises in vintage product from the first decade of American TV: *The Golden Years of Television* and contemporary documentaries, children's programming. 65 x 30 mins *Series Noires* for Super Channel

Paramount Television
49 Charles Street
London W1X 7PA
Tel: 071 629 1150
Fax: 071 491 2086
Patrick Stambaugh

Perfect Features
14 Cromford Road
London SW18 1NX
Tel: 081 877 9563
Fax: 081 877 0690
Grace Carley
Financing and sales of low-budget cult-type movies, including *Deadline* (Anders Palm), *Meet the Feebles* (1989), *Brain Dead* (1992) and *Heavenly Creatures* (1993), all from Peter Jackson

Photoplay Productions
21 Princess Road
London NW1 8JR
Tel: 071 722 2500
Fax: 071 722 6662
Kevin Brownlow
David Gill
Patrick Stanbury
European dealer for the Blackhawk 16mm library of silent and early sound films

Picture Music International
EMI House
20 Manchester Square
London W1A 1ES
Tel: 071 486 4488
Fax: 071 465 0748/9
Dawn M Stevenson
Caroline Dare
Luisa Diana-Kuramapu
Freddie Mercury *The Great Pretender*, Sarah Chang *The Young Virtuoso*, Kyung-Wha Chung *Beethoven Violin Concerto in D Major*, Montreux Jazz Festival – 2 x 1 hour specials, available as separate concerts, The Nicholas Brothers' *We Sing and We Dance*, Pet Shop Boys *Performance*, Quireboys *Live*, Robert Palmer *At the Albert Hall*, Frank Sinatra *Sinatra*, Roxette *Live in Sydney*

Playpont Films
1-2 Ramillies Street
London W1V 1DF
Tel: 071 734 7792
Fax: 071 734 9288
Don Getz
Ellen Trost
International sales representatives for feature films and TV series. Titles include *Who Do I Gotta Kill?, Enemy* and *Man Eaters*

Richard Price Television Associates (RPTA)
Seymour Mews House
Seymour Mews
Wigmore Street
London W1H 9PE
Tel: 071 935 9000
Fax: 071 935 1992
Richard Price
RPTA distributes for over 150 producers

RM Associates
46 Great Marlborough Street
London W1V 1DB
Tel: 071 439 2637
Fax: 071 439 2316
Sally Fairhead
In addition to handling the exclusive distribution of programmes produced/ co-produced by Reiner Moritz's company RM Arts, RM Associates works closely with numerous broadcasters and independent producers to bring together a comprehensive catalogue of music and arts programming

Rank Film Distributors
127 Wardour Street
London W1V 4AD
Tel: 071 437 9020
Fax: 071 434 3689
Nicole Mackey
A library of 500 feature films plus TV series. Also 200 hours of colour programming from the Children's Film and Television Foundation. Recent product includes *Fried Green Tomatoes at the Whistle Stop Café* and *Just Like a Woman*

Red Rooster Film and Television Entertainment
29 Floral Street
London WC2E 9DP
Tel: 071 379 7727
Fax: 071 379 5756
Linda James
Feature film production and producers and distributors of quality television fiction and feature films: *Body and Soul, The Life and Times of Henry Pratt, The Gift, The Diamond Brothers – South by Southeast, Kersplat!, Just Ask for Diamond, Coming Up Roses, Joni Jones*

S4C Enterprises
Parc Ty Glas
Llanishen
Cardiff
CF4 5DU
Tel: 0222 747444
Fax: 0222 754444
Christopher Grace
Teleri Roberts
Edith Hughes

Distributing programmes commissioned by S4C from independent producers and from HTV Cymru/Wales – animation, drama, documentaries

Reuters Television
(formerly Visnews)
40 Cumberland Avenue
London NW10 7EH
Tel: 081 965 7733
Fax: 081 965 0620
Distribution of international TV news and sports material to clients around the world

Safir Films
49 Littleton Road
Harrow
Middx HA1 3SY
Tel: 081 423 0763
Fax: 081 423 7963
Lawrence Safir
Holds rights to a number of Australian, US and British pictures, including Sam Spiegel's *Betrayal*, and the Romulus Classics comprising more than 30 titles such as *The African Queen*, *Moulin Rouge*, *Room at the Top* and *Beat the Devil*

The Sales Company
62 Shaftesbury Avenue
London W1V 7AA
Tel: 071 434 9061
Fax: 071 494 3293
Carole Myer
Alison Thompson
Penny Rigby
The Sales Company is owned by British Screen, BBC Enterprises and Zenith Productions and handles foreign sales for their films for all rights. Recent films include: *The Crying Game*, *Orlando*, *Friends*, *Great Moments in Aviation* and *The Secret Rapture*. Also occasionally handles product from American Playhouse; *Ethan Frome* and *Shimmer*, and has worked with Allarts and New Zealand producers Bridget Ikin and John Maynard

Scottish Television Enterprises
Cowcaddens
Glasgow G2 3PR
Tel: 041 332 9999
Fax: 041 332 6982
Anita Cox
Alistair Moffat
Jeff Henry
Sales of programmes from Scottish Television, including *Doctor Finlay*, *Taggart*, *Crime Story*, *Captain Zed & the Zee Zone*, *What's Up Doc*, *Fun House*

Screen Ventures
49 Goodge Street
London W1P 1FB
Tel: 071 580 7448
Fax: 071 631 1265
Dominic Saville
Christopher Mould
Specialise in international TV and video licensing of music specials with artists such as John Lennon, Jimi Hendrix, Cher, Annie Lennox, Santana and Janis Joplin. Worldwide television sales agents for BMG Video International, The Jimi Hendrix Estate and The Woodstock Summer Project

Smart Egg Pictures
62 Brompton Road
London SW3 1BW
Tel: 071 581 1841
Fax: 071 581 8998
Tom Sjoberg
Independent foreign sales company. Titles include *Spaced Invaders*, *Cameron's Closet*, *Dinosaurs*, *Montenegro*, *The Coca-Cola Kid* and *Fatal Inheritance*

State Screen Distributions
Rowan House
9-31 Victoria Road
Park Royal
London NW10 6DP
Tel: 081 961 1717
Fax: 081 961 6454
Andrew Johnson
Simon Johnson
Sales company. Titles include *Tale of a Vampire*, *White Angel*, and package of five gothic horror films with Christopher Lee and Donald Pleasance

TCB Releasing
Stone House
Rudge
Frome
Somerset BA11 2QQ
Tel: 0373 830769
Fax: 0373 831028
Angus Trowbridge
Sales of jazz and blues music programmes to broadcast television and the home-video media (extracts, single programmes, series): *Jazz Legends* series (26 x 1 hr episodes), *Mingus Sextet in Oslo* concert, *Monk in Oslo* concert, *Bill Evans in Oslo* concert, *BBC Jazz 625* series (20 x half-hour episodes), *Blues Legends* (8 x 1hr episodes)

D L Taffner (UK)
10 Bedford Square
London WC1B 3RA
Tel: 071 631 1184
Fax: 071 636 4571
Specialising in entertainment programming; *Talkabout* (ITV game show), *As Time Goes By* (BBC sit-com), *The Saint* (LWT drama series), *Love on a Branch Line* (4 x 1hr mini-series for BBC). Also operates a joint venture with the Theatre of Comedy at the Shaftesbury Theatre. The parent company is a well-known producer and distributor based in New York, Los Angeles and Sydney

Talbot Television
57 Jamestown Road
London NW1 7DB
Tel: 071 284 0880
Fax: 071 916 5511
David Champtaloup
Tony Gruner
London arm of NY-based Fremantle Int. Produces and distributes game shows and light entertainment

Thames Television International
Teddington Studios
Teddington Lock
Middlesex TW11 9NT
Tel: 081 614 2800
Fax: 081 943 0344
Mike Phillips
Roger Miron
UK's largest independent production company. Represents Thames TV, Euston Films and Cosgrove Hall Productions for programme sales, co-productions, the non-theatrical and home video markets, publishing and merchandising

Trans World International
TWI House
23 Eyot Gardens
London W6 9TN
Tel: 081 846 8070
Fax: 081 746 5334
Eric Drossart
Buzz Hornett
Chris Guinness
TV and video arm of Mark McCormack's International Management Group, specialising in sports and arts programming – from live coverage and event highlights to made-for-TV programming and documentaries

Turner International
CNN House
19 Rathbone Place
London W1P 1DF
Tel: 071 637 6900
Fax: 071 637 6925
Howard Karshan
US production and distribution company. Distributor of MGM, pre-1950 Warner Bros features and Turner series

Twentieth Century Fox Television
31-32 Soho Square
London W1V 6AP
Tel: 071 437 7766
Fax: 071 439 1806/434 2170
Steve Cornish
Sales of all Twentieth Century Fox product to TV worldwide

VATV
60-62 Margaret Street
London W1N 7FJ
Tel: 071 636 9421
Fax: 071 436 7426
Jane Lighting
VATV is an international distribution company operating internationally in sales and co-productions. The Company represents over 100 independent companies, Channel Four Television, ITN, TV3 Spain and independently produced programmes for the BBC. The company has a sister company, Harlequin Film and Television, which is involved in development of drama

VCI Programme Sales
Strand VCI House
36-38 Caxton Way

Watford
Herts WD1 8UF
Tel: 0923 255558
Fax: 0923 817969
Paul Hembury
Karen Chillery
A wholly owned subsidiary of the Video Collection International, responsible for all overseas activities. Distributes a wide variety of product including music, sport, children's, fitness, documentary, educational, special interest and features. Has a joint venture partnership with VATV and ITN and distributes its product for home video internationally

VVL
(formerly MCEG Virgin Vision)
Atlantic House
1 Rockley Road
London W14 0DL
Tel: 081 740 5500
Fax: 081 967 1360/1
Bill Tennant
Helen Parker
International video sell-through and TV sales; *Diana – a Model Princess, Diana – a Portrait, Kama Sutra, Beatles 1st US Tour*, plus a library of music and comedy specials, sports videos and feature films

Viacom International
17-29 Hawley Crescent
London NW1 8EF
Tel: 071 284 7844
Fax: 071 284 7845
Peter Press
UK-based distribution operation for the US independent company. Current product includes *Roseanne* (sixth year), *Matlock* (eighth year), *The Cosby Show, Flying Blind, Perry Mason Movie Specials, Dick Van Dyke Mystery Movies, A Different World, Key West, Jake and the Fatman, Father Dowling, Superboy, Superforce.* Plus an extensive library of mini-series, children's adventure and animation, theatrical and made-for-TV movies

Vine International Pictures
8-12 Broadwick Street
London W1V 3FH
Tel: 071 437 1181
Fax: 071 494 0634
Marie Vine
Dee Emerson
Barry Gill
Sale of feature films such as *Erik the Viking, Mouche, Hammer of the Gods, The Prince of Jutland, Lost in the City of Light, Younger and Younger, Two Deaths, One Nation Invisible, Stringers*

Visnews see **Reuters Television**

Warner Bros International Television
135 Wardour Street
London W1V 4AP
Tel: 071 494 3710
Fax: 071 287 9086
Mr R Milnes
Mr D Peebler
Mrs D Brett
TV sales, marketing and distribution. Includes Lorimar Telepictures product. A division of Warner Bros Distributors, A Time Warner Entertainment Company LP

Worldwide Television News Corporation (WTN)
The Interchange
Oval Road
Camden Lock
London NW1
Tel: 071 410 5200
Fax: 071 413 8327 (Lib)
Gerry O'Reilly
Rex Jenkins
International TV news, features, sport, entertainment, documentary programmes, *Earthfile* (environmental series), *Healthfile*, weather, archive resources. Camera crews in major global locations, plus in-house broadcasting and production facilities

Yorkshire-Tyne Tees Enterprises
32 Bedford Row
London WC1R 4HE
Tel: 071 242 1666
Fax: 071 831 7260
Susan Crawley
Ann Gillham
International sales division of Yorkshire-Tyne Tees TV

LABORATORIES

Bucks Motion Picture Laboratories
714 Banbury Avenue
Slough
Berks SL1 4LH
Tel: 0753 576611
Fax: 0753 691762
West End pick up and delivery at:
Paramount House
162-170 Wardour Street
London W1
Comprehensive lab services in 35mm, Super 16mm and 16mm, starting Sunday night. West End rushes pick up until 11pm. Also day bath. Chromakopy: 35mm low-cost overnight colour reversal dubbing prints Photogard: European coating centre for negative and print treatment Chromascan: 35mm and 16mm video to film transfer

Colour Film Services Group
10 Wadsworth Road
Perivale
Greenford
Middx UB6 7JX
Tel: 081 998 2731
Fax: 081 997 8738
Full 35mm, 16mm and Super 16mm 24-hour laboratory services, handling all aspects of film work from feature films and TV programming to industrial shorts and commercials. In-house sound transfer and telecine mastering. Tape to film transfer to 35mm and 16mm. Bulk cassette duplication

Colour-Technique
Cinematograph Film Laboratories
Finch Cottage
Finch Lane, Knotty Green
Beaconsfield
Bucks HP9 2TL
Tel: 0494 672757
Specialists in 8mm, Super 8mm and 9.5mm blown up to 16mm with liquid gate printing. Stretch printing 16 fps & 18 fps to 24.32.48 fps. 16mm to 16mm optical printing from shrunk 16mm films with liquid gate printing. B&W dupe negs, colour internegs, colour reversal copies. Super 8mm copies from Super 8mm, standard 8mm, 16mm, 9.5mm

Film and Photo Design
13 Colville Road
South Acton Industrial Estate
London W3 8BL
Tel: 081 992 0037
Fax: 081 993 2409
Leading European lab for 16/35mm colour & b/w reversal dupes. Specialists in nitrate preservation. Full lab facilities

Filmatic Laboratories/ Filmatic Television
16 Colville Road
London W11 2BS
Tel: 071 221 6081
Fax: 071 229 2718
Complete Super 16 and 16mm film processing laboratory and sound transfer service with full video post production facility including Digital Wet Gate Telecines, D3, 1", Betacam SP and other video formats. On-line editing, duplication and standards conversion. Sync sound and A+B roll negative to tape transfer, Electronic Film Conforming (EFC) the system that produces the higest quality video masters from any original source, with frame accurate editing from film, non-linear disc or off-line video edit

The Film Clinic
8-14 Meard Street
London W1V 3HR
Tel: 071 734 9235/6
Fax: 071 734 9471
Scratch treatment, reconditioning and restoration of 16/35mm film. Archive specialists

Henderson Film Laboratories
18-20 St Dunstan's Road
South Norwood
London SE25 6EU
Tel: 081 653 2255
Fax: 081 653 9773
Full b/w laboratory service in 35mm and 16mm including b/w reversal processing in 16mm and Super 8. Blow-up to 16mm from 9.5mm and Std 8mm. Specialists in the handling of archive material, especially shrunken and nitrate film

London Film Makers' Co-operative
42 Gloucester Avenue
London NW1 8JD
Tel: 071 722 1728
Fax: 071 483 0068
16mm b/w printing and processing

Metrocolor London
91-95 Gillespie Road
London N5 1LS
Tel: 071 226 4422
Fax: 071 359 2353
Full 16mm, Super 16mm and 35mm processing services, handling a range from 16mm short films through pop promos, commercials, BBC and ITV programmes to feature films, video mastering, sound transfer and stereo-optical camera

Rank Film Laboratories Group
North Orbital Road
Denham
Uxbridge
Middx UB9 5HQ
Tel: 0895 832323
Fax: 0895 833617
Principal laboratories at Denham in the UK, Deluxe in Hollywood and Film House in Toronto, with a satellite laboratory in Leeds. Full optical facilities available from General Screen Enterprises at Uxbridge. Experienced sales and servicing personnel able to provide a complete worldwide film processing service

Soho Images
8-14 Meard Street
London W1V 3HR
Tel: 071 437 0831
Fax: 071 734 9471
Soho Laboratories offer day and night printing and processing of 16mm (including Super 16mm) and 35mm colour or b/w film

Technicolor
Bath Road
West Drayton
Middx UB7 0DB
Tel: 081 759 5432
Fax: 081 759 6270
24-hour laboratory service, adjacent to Heathrow Airport. Modern high speed plant caters for all formats: 16mm, 35mm, 70mm. Laboratories in Rome, Hollywood and New York

LEGISLATION

This section of the Handbook has a twofold purpose, first to provide a short summary of the principal instruments of legislation which relate to the film, television and video industries in the United Kingdom and in the European Community, and second to provide a brief history of this legislation in the UK. The relevant main Acts of Parliament which are currently in force are separated into three categories – Broadcasting and Cinema, Finance, and Copyright. Each of these sections contains a short summary of the legislation. EC legislation and a brief historical summary follow

BROADCASTING AND CINEMA

Broadcasting Act 1990

The Broadcasting Act 1990 established a new framework for the regulation of independent television and radio services, and for satellite television and cable television. Under the Act, the Independent Broadcasting Authority (IBA) and the Cable Authority were dissolved and replaced by the Independent Television Commission. The Radio Authority was established in respect of independent radio services. The Broadcasting Standards Council was made a statutory body and the Act also contains provisions relating to the Broadcasting Complaints Commission. Besides reorganising independent broadcasting, the Act provided for the formation of a separate company with responsibility for effecting the technical arrangements relating to independent television broadcasting – National Transcommunications Limited – as a first step towards the privatisation of the former IBA's transmission functions.

The Broadcasting Act 1990 repealed the Broadcasting Act 1981 and the Cable and Broadcasting Act 1984, amended the Wireless Telegraphy Act 1949, the Wireless Telegraphy Act 1967, the Marine [&c] Broadcasting (Offences) Act 1967 and the Copyright, Designs and Patents Act 1988.

The Broadcasting Act 1990 requires the British Broadcasting Corporation, all Channel 3 Licensees, the Channel Four Television Corporation, S4C (the Welsh Fourth Channel Authority) and the future Channel 5 Licensee to procure that not less than 25% of the total amount of time allocated by those services to broadcasting "qualifying programming" is allocated to the broadcasting of a range and diversity of "independent productions". The expression "qualifying programming" and "independent productions" are defined in the Broadcasting (Independent Productions) Order 1991.

Cinemas Act 1985

The Cinemas Act 1985 consolidated the Cinematographic Acts 1909 to 1952, the Cinematographic (Amendment) Act 1982 and related enactments. The Act deals with the exhibition of films and contains provisions for the grant, renewal and transfer of licences for film exhibition. There are special provisions for Greater London.

The Cinemas Act specifies the conditions of Sunday opening, and provides for exempted exhibition in private dwelling houses, and for non-commercial shows and in premises used only occasionally.

Video Recordings Act 1984

The Video Recordings Act 1984 controls the distribution of video recordings with the aim of restricting the depiction or stimulation of human sexual activity, gross violence, human genital organs or urinary or excretory functions. A system of classification and labelling is prescribed. The supply of recordings without a classification certificate

The information for this section has been kindly provided and presented by Michael Henry of solicitors Nicholson Graham & Jones. We gratefully acknowledge their continuing support

or the supply of classified recordings to persons under a certain age or in certain premises or in breach of labelling regulations is prohibited subject to certain exemptions.

Classification certificates are issued by the British Board of Film Classification. It is an offence to supply or offer to supply, or to have in possession for the purposes of supplying, an unclassified video recording. Supplying recordings in breach of classification, supplying certain classified recordings otherwise than in licensed sex shops, supplying recordings in breach of labelling requirements and supplying recordings with false indications as to classification are all offences under the Act. The Video Recordings Act provides for powers of entry, search and seizure and for the forfeiture of video recordings by the court.

Telecommunications Act 1984

The Telecommunications Act 1984 prohibits the running of a telecommunications system within the United Kingdom subject to certain exceptions which include the running of a telecommunication system in certain circumstances by a broadcasting authority. A broadcasting authority means a person who is licensed under the Wireless Telegraphy Act 1949 (see below) to broadcast programmes for general reception. Telecommunications systems include, among other things, any system for the conveyance of speech, music, other sounds and visual images by electric, magnetic, electro-magnetic electro-chemical or electro-chemical or electro-mechanical energy.

Wireless Telegraphy Acts 1967 and 1949

The 1967 Act provides for the Secretary of State to obtain information as to the sale and hire of television receiving sets. The Act allows the Secretary of State to prohibit the manufacture or importation of certain wireless telegraphy apparatus and to control the installation of such apparatus in vehicles.

The 1949 Act provides for the licensing of wireless telegraphy and defines "wireless telegraphy" as the sending of electro-magnetic energy over paths not provided by a material substance constructed or arranged for that purpose. The requirements to hold a licence under the Wireless Telegraphy Act 1949 or the Telecommunications Act 1984 are separate from the television and radio broadcast licensing provisions and cable programme source licensing provisions contained in the Broadcasting Act 1990.

Marine [&c] Broadcasting (Offences) Act 1967

The making of broadcasts by wireless telegraphy (as defined in the Wireless Telegraphy Act 1949) intended for general reception from ships, aircraft and certain marine structures is prohibited under this Act.

The Cinematograph Films (Animals) Act 1937

The Cinematograph Films (Animals) Act 1937 provides for the prevention of exhibiting or distributing films in which suffering may have been caused to animals.

Celluloid and Cinematograph Film Act 1922

This Act contains provisions which are aimed at the prevention of fire in premises where raw celluloid or cinematograph film is stored or used. Silver nitrate film which was in universal use until the 1950s and was still used in some parts of the world (notably the former USSR) until the 1970s is highly inflammable and becomes unstable with age. The purpose of the legislation was to protect members of the public from fire risks.

FINANCE

The Finance Act 1990, Capital Allowances Act 1990 and Finance (No 2) Act 1992

Section 80 and Schedule 12 to the Finance Act 1990 deals with the tax issues relating to the reorganisation of independent broadcasting provided for in the Broadcasting Act 1990.

Section 68 of the Capital Allowances Act 1990 replaces Section 72 of the Finance Act 1982 providing for certain expenditure in the production of a film, tape or disc to be treated as expenditure of a revenue nature.

Sections 41-43 of the Finance (No 2) Act 1992 amend the tax regime to provide accelerated relief for pre-production costs incurred after 10 March 1992 and production expenditure on films completed after that date. Section 69 of the Act makes certain consequential amendments to Section 68 of the Capital Allowances Act 1990.

Films Act 1985

The Films Act 1985 dissolved the British Film Fund Agency, ending the Eady levy system established in 1951. The Act also abolished the Cinematograph Film Council and dissolved the National Film Finance Corporation, transferring its assets to British Screen Finance Limited. The Act repealed the Films Acts 1960 – 1980 and also repealed certain provisions of the Finance Acts 1982 and 1984 and substituted new provisions for determining whether or not a film was "British" film eligible for capital allowances.

National Film Finance Corporation Act 1981

The National Film Finance Corporation Act 1981 repealed the Cinematograph Film Production (Special Loans) Acts of 1949 and 1954 and made provisions in relation to the National Film Finance Corporation which has since been dissolved by the Films Act 1985. The National Film Finance Corporation Act 1981 is, however, still on the statute book.

Film Levy Finance Act 1981

Although the British Film Fund Agency was dissolved by the British Film Fund Agency (Dissolution) Order 1988, SI 1988/37, the Film Levy Act itself is still in place.

COPYRIGHT

Copyright, Designs and Patents Act 1988

This Act is the primary piece of legislation relating to copyright in the United Kingdom. The Act provides copyright protection for original literary dramatic musical and artistic works, for films, sound recordings, broadcasts and cable programmes, and for typographical arrangements of published editions.

The Act repeals the Copyright Act 1956 which in turn repealed the Copyright Act 1911, but the transitional provisions of the Copyright, Designs and Patents Act 1988 apply certain provisions of the earlier legislation for the purpose of determining ownership of copyright, type of protection and certain other matters. Because the term of copyright for original literary dramatic and/or musical works is the life of the author plus 50 years, the earlier legislation will continue to be relevant until well into the next century.

The Act provides a period of copyright protection for films and sound recordings which expires 50 years from the end of the calendar year in which the film or sound recording is made, or if it is shown or played in public or broadcast or included in a cable programme service, 50 years from the end of the calendar year in which this occurred.

The Act introduced three new moral rights into United Kingdom legislation. In addition to the right not to have a work falsely attributed to him or her, an author (of a literary dramatic musical or artistic work) or director (of a film) has the right to be identified in relation to their work, and the right not to permit their work to suffer derogatory treatment. A derogatory treatment is any addition, deletion, alteration or adaptation of a work which amounts to a distortion or mutilation of the work or is otherwise prejudicial to the honour or reputation of the author or director. A person who commissions films or photographs for private and domestic purposes enjoys a new right of privacy established by the Act.

Another new development is the creation of a statutory civil right for performers, giving them the right not to have recordings of their performances used without their consent. United Kingdom copyright legislation was amended following a decision in Rickless -v- United Artists Corporation – a case which was brought by the estate of Peter Sellars and involved *The Trail of the Pink Panther*. The legislation is retrospective and protects performances given 50 years ago, not just in the United Kingdom, but in any country if the performers were "qualifying persons" within the meaning of the relevant Act. The performances which are covered include not only dramatic and musical performances, but readings of literary works, variety programmes and even mime.

Numerous other provisions are contained in the Copyright, Designs and Patents Act including sections which deal with the fraudulent reception of programmes, the manufacture and sale of devices designed to circumvent copy-protection, and patent and design law.

EUROPEAN COMMUNITY LEGISLATION

Directive 89/552 – on television without frontiers

The objective of the Directive is to eliminate the barriers which divide Europe with a view to permitting and assuring the transition from national programme markets to a common programme production and distribution Market. It also aims to establish conditions of fair competition without prejudice to the public interest role which falls to be discharged by television broadcasting services in the EC.

The laws of all Member States relating to television broadcasting and cable operations contain disparaties which may impede the free movement of broadcasts within the EC and may distort competition. All such restrictions are required to be abolished.

Member States are free to specify detailed criteria relating to language etc. Additionally, Member States are permitted to lay down different conditions relating to the insertion of advertising in programmes within the limits set out in the Directive. Member States are required to provide where practicable that broadcasters reserve a proportion of their transmission time to European works created by independent producers. The amount of advertising is not to exceed 15% of daily transmission time and the support advertising within a given one hour period shall not exceed 20%.

Directive 92/100 – on rental rights

Authors or performers have, pursuant to the Directive, an unwaiveable right to receive equitable remuneration. Member States are required to provide a right for performers in relation to the fixation of their performances, a right for phonogram and film producers in relation to their phonograms and first fixations of their films and a right for broadcasters in relation to the fixation of broadcasts and their broadcast and cable transmissions. Member States must also provide a "reproduction right" giving performers, phonogram producers, film producers and broadcasting organisations the right to authorise or prohibit the direct or indirect reproduction of their copyright works. The Directive also requires Member States to provide for performers, film producers, phonogram producers and broadcasting organisations to have exclusive rights to make available their work by sale or otherwise – known as the "distribution right".

Proposal for the Directive on the co-ordination of rules relating to copyright and neighbouring rights applicable to satellite transmission and cable re-transmission

The proposals offer a definition which specifies when the act of communication of a programme takes place in order to avoid the cumulative application of several national laws to one single act of broadcasting. The proposals require Member States to provide that the author of a copyright work will have the exclusive right to authorise or prohibit communication of the work to the public by satellite.

Proposal for a Directive harmonising the term of protection of copyright and certain related rights

The proposal is that the term of copyright should be harmonised throughout the Community as ending 70 years after the death of the author or 70 years after the work is lawfully made available to the public. The term for related rights is proposed to be the period of 50 years from the event which starts the term running. In order to avoid differences in the term of protection, the proposals suggest that when a term begins to run in one Member State it should begin to run throughout the Community.

The Directive will apply to all works which are protected by at least one Member State from 1 July 1994 as a result of the application of national provisions of copyright and related rights.

LEGISLATIVE HISTORY

CINEMA

Legislation for the cinema industry in the United Kingdom goes back to 1909, when the Cinematograph Act was passed providing for the licensing of exhibition premises, and safety of audiences. The emphasis on safety has been maintained through the years in other enactments such as the Celluloid and Cinematograph Film Act 1922, Cinematograph Act 1952 and the Fire Precautions Act 1971, the two latter having been consolidated in the Cinemas Act 1985.

The Cinematograph Films (Animals Act) 1937 was passed to prevent the exhibition and distribution of films in which suffering may have been caused to animals. The Cinematograph (Amendment) Act 1982 applied certain licensing requirements to pornographic cinema clubs. Excluded from licensing were the activities of bona fide film societies and "demonstrations" such as those used in shops, as well as exhibitions intended to provide information, education or instruction. Requirements for licensing were consolidated in the Cinemas Act 1985.

The Sunday Entertainments Act 1932 as amended by the Sunday Cinema Act 1972 and the Cinemas Act 1985 regulated the opening and use of cinema premises on Sundays. The Sunday Entertainments Act 1932 also established a Sunday Cinematograph Fund for "encouraging the use and development of cinematograph as a means of entertainment and instruction". This was how the British Film Institute was originally funded.

Statutory controls were imposed by the Cinematographs Films Act 1927 in other areas of the film industry, such as the booking of films, quotas for the distribution and renting of British films and the registration of films exhibited to the public. This Act was modified by the Cinematograph Films Acts of 1938 and 1948 and the Film Acts 1960, 1966, 1970 and 1980 which were repealed by the Films Act 1985.

The financing of the British film industry has long been the subject of specific legislation. The National Film Finance Corporation was established by the Cinematograph Film Production (Special Loans) Act 1949. The Cinematograph Film Production (Special Loans) Act 1952 gave the National Film Finance Corporation the power to borrow from sources other than the Board of Trade. Other legislation dealing with film finance were the Cinematograph Film Production (Special Loans) Act 1954 and the Films Acts 1970 and 1980. The Cinematograph Films Council was established by the Cinematograph Films Act 1948, but like the National Film Finance Corporation, the Council was abolished by the Films Act 1985.

The Cinematograph Films Act 1957 established the British Film Fund Agency and put on a statutory footing the formerly voluntary levy on exhibitors known as the "Eady levy". Eady money was to be paid to the British Film Fund Agency, which in turn was responsible for making payments to British film makers, the Children's Film Foundation, the National Film Finance Corporation, the British Film Institute and towards training film makers. The Film Levy Finance Act 1981 consolidated the provisions relating to the Agency and the exhibitors' levy. The Agency was wound up in 1988 pursuant to a statutory order made under the Films Act 1985.

The British Film Institute used to obtain its funding from grants made by the Privy Council out of the Cinematograph Fund established under the Sunday Entertainments Act 1932 and also from the proceeds of subscriptions, sales and rentals of films. The British Film Institute Act 1949 allows for grants of money from Parliament to be made to the British Film Institute as the Lord President of the Privy Council thinks fit.

BROADCASTING

The BBC first started as the British Broadcasting Company (representing the interests of some radio manufacturers) and was licensed in 1923 by the Postmaster General under the Wireless Telegraphy Act 1904 before being established by Royal Charter. The company was involved in television development from 1929 and in 1935 was licensed to provide a public television service.

The Independent Television Authority was established under the Television Act 1954 to provide additional television broadcasting services. Its existence was continued under the Television Act 1964 and under the Independent Broadcasting Act 1973, although its name had been changed to the Independent Broadcasting Authority by the Sound Broadcasting Act 1972 (which also permitted it to provide local sound broadcasting services).

The Broadcasting Act 1981 amended and consolidated certain provisions contained in previous legislation including the removal of the prohibition on certain specified people from broadcasting opinions expressed in proceedings of Parliament or local authorities, the extension of the IBA's functions to the provision of programmes for Channel 4 and the establishment of the Broadcasting Complaints Commission.

Cable programme services and satellite broadcasts were the subject of the Cable and Broadcasting Act 1984. This Act and the Broadcasting Act 1981 were repealed and consolidated by the Broadcasting Act 1990 which implemented proposals in the Government's White Paper "Broadcasting in the 1990's: Competition Choice and Quality" (Cm 517, November 1988). Earlier recommendations on the reform of the broadcasting industry had been made in the Report of the Committee on Financing the BBC (the Peacock Report) (Cmnd 9824, July 1986) and the Third Report of the Home Affairs Committee's inquiry into the Future of Broadcasting (HC Paper 262, Session 1987-88, June 1988).

LIBRARIES

This new section provides a directory of libraries and archives which have collections of books, periodicals and papers covering film and television. It includes the libraries of colleges and universities with graduate and post-graduate degree courses in the media. Most of these collections are intended for student and teaching staff use: permission for access should always be sought from the Librarian in charge

The BFI's own library is very extensive and attracts many users, often more than it is able to seat, and some of them travelling long distances. If you are interested in studying and reading about film or TV, the following libraries may provide a resource closer to home. It is hoped to extend and revise this section in future, so amendments and additions would be welcome

BATH

Bath University Library
Claverton Down
Bath
Avon BA2 7AY
Tel: 0225 826084
Fax: 0225 826229
Contact: The University Librarian

BIRMINGHAM

Birmingham Library Services
Subject Information Services
Reference Library
Chamberlain Square
Birmingham B3 3HQ
Tel: 021 235 4511
Fax: 021 233 4458
Contact: Director of Head of Arts Services

Birmingham University Library
Edgbaston
Birmingham B15 2TT
Tel: 021 414 5816
Fax: 021 471 4691
Contact: The Librarian

Central Independent Television
Broad Street
Birmingham B1 2JP
Tel: 021 643 9898
Contact: The Librarian

University of Central England in Birmingham
Information Services
Perry Barr
Birmingham B42 2SU
Tel: 021 331 5300
Fax: 021 331 6543
Contact: Dean of Information Services

BRADFORD

Bradford and Ilkley Community College
Great Horton Road
Bradford BD7 1AY
Tel: 0272 753026
Contact: The Librarian

BRIGHTON

Sussex University Library
Falmer
Brighton
East Sussex BN1 9QL
Tel: 0273 678163
Fax: 0273 678441
Contact: Information Services

BRISTOL

Avon County Council
Community Leisure Department
Central Library
Reference Library
College Green
Bristol BS1 5TL
Tel: 0272 276121
Fax: 0272 226775

University of Bristol
University Library
Tyndall Avenue
Bristol BS8 1TJ
Tel: 0272 30394
Fax: 0272 255334
Contact: The University Librarian

University of Bristol Theatre Collection
29 Park Road
Bristol BS1 5LT
Tel: 0272 303215
Fax: 0272 732657
Contact: The Keeper

West of England University at Bristol
Art & Design Library
Clanage Road
Bower Ashton
Bristol BS3 2JU
Tel: 0272 660222 x4750
Fax: 0272 763946
Contact: The Site Librarian

CANTERBURY

Canterbury College Library
New Dover Road
Canterbury
Kent CT1 3AJ
Tel: 0227 766081
Fax: 0227 762940
Contact: The Learning Resources Manager

Christ Church College Library
North Holmes Road
Canterbury
Kent CT1 1QU
Tel: 0227 767700
Fax: 0227 470442
Contact: The Librarian

University of Kent at Canterbury

Templeman Library
Canterbury
Kent CT2 7NU
Tel: 0227 764000
Fax: 0227 459025
Contact: The Librarian

CARLISLE

Cumbria College of Art and Design Library
Brampton Road
Carlisle
Cumbria CA3 9AY
Tel: 0228 25333 x206
Contact: The Librarian

CHISLEHURST

Ravensbourne College of Design & Communication Library
Walden Road
Chislehurst
Kent BR7 5SN
Tel: 081 468 7071
Fax: 081 295 1070
Contact: The Librarian

COLCHESTER

University of Essex
Albert Sloman Library
Wivenhoe Park
Colchester
Essex CO4 3SQ
Tel: 0206 873333
Contact: The Librarian

COLERAINE

University of Ulster Library
Coleraine
Northern Ireland
BT52 1SA
Tel: 0265 44141
Fax: 0265 40902

COVENTRY

Coventry University, Art and Design Library
Gosford Street
Coventry CV1 5RZ
Tel: 0203 838538
Fax: 0203 838686
Contact: The Librarian

Warwick University Library
Central Library
University of Warwick
Coventry CV4 7AL
Tel: 0203 523523
Fax: 0203 524211
Contact: Head of Reader Services

DERBY

Derby University Library
Kedleston Rd
Derby DE3 1GB
Tel: 0332 47181
Fax: 0332 294861
Contact: The Librarian

DOUGLAS

Douglas Public Library
Ridgeway Street
Douglas
Isle of Man
Tel: 0624 623021
Fax: 0624 662792
Contact: The Borough Librarian

DUNDEE

Duncan of Jordanstone College of Art Library
13 Perth Road
Dundee DD1 4HT
Tel: 0382 23261
Fax: 0382 27304
Contact: The College Librarian

EGHAM

Royal Holloway University of London
Egham Hill
Egham
Surrey TW20 OEX
Tel: 0784 434455
Fax: 0784 437520
Contact: The Librarian

EXETER

Exeter University Library
Stocker Road
Exeter
Devon EX4 4PT
Tel: 0392 263263
Contact: The Librarian

GLASGOW

Glasgow City Libraries
Mitchell Library
North Street
Glasgow G3 7DN
Tel: 041 221 7030
Fax: 041 204 4824

Glasgow Metropolitan University Library
Cowcaddens Road
Glasgow G4 0BA
Tel: 041 331 3000
Fax: 041 331 3005
Contact: The Reference Librarian

Scottish Council for Educational Technology
Dowanhill
74 Victoria Crescent Road
Glasgow G12 9JN
Tel: 041 334 9314
Fax: 041 334 6519
Contact: Resources & Information Officer

Scottish Film Council
Dowanhill
74 Victoria Crescent Road
Glasgow G12 9JN
Tel: 041 334 4445
Fax: 041 334 8132
Contact: Press Officer

University of Glasgow
The Library
Glasgow G12 8QQ
Tel: 041 339 8855
Contact: The Librarian

University of Strathclyde
The Andersonian Library
McCance Building
16 Richmond Street
Glasgow
Contact: The University Librarian

GRAVESEND

Voice of the Listener and Viewer
10 King's Drive
Gravesend
Kent DA12 5BQ
Tel: 0474 352835
Contact: The Information Officer

HUDDERSFIELD

University of Huddersfield Library
Queensgate
Huddersfield HD1 3DH
Tel: 0484 422288
Fax: 0484 517987
Contact: Head of Library Services

HULL

Hull University, Brynmor James Library
Cottingham Road
Hull HU6 7RX
Tel: 0482 46311
Fax: 0482 466205
Contact: The Librarian

Humberside University Library Services
Cottingham Road
Hull HU6 7RT
Tel: 0482 440550
Fax: 0482 449627
Contact: Head of Library Services

KINGSTON UPON THAMES

Heritage Centre
Museum & Art Gallery
Wheatfield Way
Kingston Upon Thames
Surrey KT1 2PS
Tel: 081 546 5386
Contact: The Local History Officer

Kingston University Library Services
Learning Resources Department
Penrhyn Road
Kingston Upon Thames
Surrey KT1 2EE
Tel: 081 547 2000
Fax: 081 547 7111
Contact: Head of Learning Resources

LEEDS

Leeds Metropolitan University Library
Calverley Street
Leeds
West Yorks
LS1 3HE
Tel: 0532 832600
Fax: 0532 833123
Contact: The Librarian

Trinity and All Saints College Library
Brownberrie Lane
Horsforth
Leeds
West Yorks
LS18 5HD
Tel: 0532 584341
Fax: 0532 581148
Contact: The Librarian

LEICESTER

Centre for Mass Communication Research
104 Regent Road
Leicester LE1 7LT
Tel: 0533 523863
Fax: 0533 523874
Contact: The Director

De Montfort University Library
PO Box 143
Leicester LE1 9BH
Tel: 0533 551551
Fax: 0533 550307
Contact: The Librarian

Leicester University Library
Box 248
University Road
Leicester LE1 9QD
Tel: 0533 522042
Fax: 0533 522066
Contact: The Librarian

LIVERPOOL

Liverpool City Libraries
William Brown Street
Liverpool L3 8EW
Tel: 051 255 5429
Fax: 051 207 1342

Liverpool John Moores University
Library Services
Trueman Buildings
15-21 Webster Street
Liverpool L3 2ET
Tel: 051 207 3581
Fax: 051 709 0172
Contact: Director of Library Services

LONDON

Barbican Library
Barbican Centre
London EC2Y 8DS
Tel: 071 638 0569
Fax: 071 638 2249
Contact: The Librarian

British Kinematograph Sound and Television Society
549 Victoria House
Vernon Place
London WC1B 4DJ
Tel: 071 242 8400
Fax: 071 405 3560
Contact: The Secretary

Camberwell College of Arts Library
Peckham Road
London SE5 8UF
Tel: 071 703 0987
Fax: 071 703 3689
Contact: The Librarian

Camden Public Libraries
Swiss Cottage Library
88 Avenue Road
London NW3 3HA
Tel: 071 860 6527

Centre for the Study of Communications and Culture
221 Goldhurst Terrace
London NW6 3EP
Tel: 071 328 2868
Fax: 071 372 1193
Contact: The Director

Cinema Advertising Association
127 Wardour Street
London W1V 4AD
Tel: 071 439 9531
Fax: 071 439 2395
Contact: The Secretary

College of North East London Library
High Road
Tottenham
London N15 4RU
Tel: 081 802 3111
Fax: 081 442 3091
Contact: The Librarian

East London University Library
Department of Art & Design
89 Greengate Street
London E13 0BG
Tel: 081 590 7722 x 3434
Fax: 081 849 3694
Contact: Site Librarian

Goldsmiths' College Library
New Cross
London SE14 6NW
Tel: 081 692 7171
Fax: 081 469 0516
Contact: The Librarian

Guildhall University Library Services
Calcutta House
Old Castle Street
London E1 7NT
Tel: 071 320 1000
Fax: 071 320 1117
Contact: Head of Library Services

Harrow College Libraries
Northwick Park
Harrow HA1 3TP
Tel: 071 911 5000
Fax: 081 864 6664
Contact: Site Librarian

Independent Television Commission Library
33 Foley Street
London W1P 7LP
Tel: 071 255 3000
Fax: 071 366 7800
Contact: The Librarian

Institute of Education Library (London)
20 Bedford Way
London WC1H OAL
Tel: 071 580 1122
Fax: 071 612 6126
Contact: The Librarian

International Institute of Communications
Library & Information Service
Tavistock House South
Tavistock Square
London WC1H 9LF
Tel: 071 388 0671
Fax: 071 380 0623
Contact: Information & Library Manager

London Borough of Barnet Libraries
Hendon Library
The Burroughs
Hendon
London NW4 4BE
Tel: 081 202 5625
Fax: 081 202 8520

London College of Printing & Distributive Trades
Department of Learning Resources
Elephant & Castle
London SE1 6SB
Tel: 071 735 9100
Fax: 071 587 5297
Contact: Head of Learning Resources

London Institute Central St Martins Library
Southampton Row
London WC1B 4AP
Tel: 071 753 9090
Fax: 071 243 0240
Contact: The Librarian

Middlesex University Library
Bounds Green Road
London N11 2NQ
Tel: 081 368 1299 x7328
Contact: The University Librarian

North London University
Computing, Library & Media Services
Holloway Road
London N7 8DB
Tel: 071 607 2789
Fax: 071 700 4272
Contact: Head of Library. & Media Services

Producers Alliance for Cinema and Television
Gordon House
Greencoat Place
London SW10 1PH
Tel: 071 233 6000
Fax: 071 233 8935
Contact: The Information Officer

Royal Television Society, Library and Archive
Holborn Hall
100 Gray's Inn Road
London WC1X 8AL
Tel: 071 430 1000
Fax: 071 430 0924
Contact: The Archivist

Thames Valley University Library & Information
(Ealing Campus)
St Mary's Road
Ealing
London W5 5RF
Tel: 081 579 5000
Fax: 081 566 5248
Contact: Head of Library & Information

University of Westminster Library
18/22 Riding House Street
London W1P 7PD
Tel: 071 911 5000
Fax: 071 911 5127
Contact: Site Librarian

MANCHESTER

Manchester Arts Library
Central Library
St Peters Square
Manchester M2 5PD
Tel: 061 234 1974
Fax: 061 234 1963

Contact: The Arts Librarian

Manchester Metropolitan University Library
All Saints Building
Grosvenor Square
Oxford Road
Manchester M15 6BH
Tel: 061 247 6104
Fax: 061 236 7383
Contact: The University Librarian

North West Film Archive
Manchester Metropolitan University
Minshull House
47-49 Chorlton Street
Manchester M1 3EU
Tel: 061 247 3097/8
Fax: 061 236 5319
Contact: The Curator

MORPETH

Northumberland County Library
The Willows
Morpeth
Northumberland
NE61 1TA
Tel: 0670 518802
Fax: 0670 518012
Contact: The County Librarian

NEWCASTLE UPON TYNE

Centre for Urban & Regional Development Studies
The University
Claremont Bridge
Newcastle Upon Tyne
Tyne & Wear NE1 4DG
Tel: 091 222 6000 x8016
Fax: 091 232 9259
Contact: The Director

University of Northumbria at Newcastle Library
Ellison Place
Newcastle Upon Tyne
Tyne & Wear NE1 8ST
Tel: 091 232 6002 x4125
Contact: The Librarian

NORWICH

University of East Anglia
University Library
Norwich NR4 7TJ
Tel: 0603 56161
Fax: 0603 58553
Contact: The Librarian

NOTTINGHAM

Nottingham Trent University Library
Burton Street
Nottingham NG1 4BU
Tel: 0602 418418
Fax: 0602 484266
Contact: The Librarian

Nottingham University Library
University Park
Nottingham NG7 2RD
Tel: 0602 484848
Fax: 0602 420825
Contact: The Librarian/ Keeper

PLYMOUTH

College of St Mark and St John Library
Derriford Road
Plymouth
Devon PL6 8BH
Tel: 0752 777188
Fax: 0752 711620
Contact: Head of Learning Resources

Plymouth College of Art and Design Library
Tavistock Place
Plymouth
Devon PL4 8AT
Tel: 0752 85984
Fax: 0752 385977
Contact: The College Librarian

PONTYPRIDD

Glamorgan University
Learning Resources Centre
Pontypridd
Mid Glam CF37 1DL
Tel: 0443 480480
Fax: 0443 480558
Contact: The Chief Librarian

POOLE

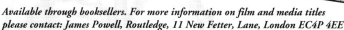

Bournemouth University Library
North Road
Parkstone
Poole
Dorset BH14 OLS
Contact: The Chief Librarian

PORTSMOUTH

Highbury College of Technology Library
Cosham
Portsmouth PO6 2SA
Tel: 0705 383131 x213
Contact: The Librarian

Portsmouth University Library
Frewen Library
Cambridge Road
Portsmouth
Hants PO1 2ST
Tel: 0705 827681
Contact: The University Librarian

READING

Reading University Bulmershe Library
Woodlands Avenue
Reading
Berks RG6 1HY
Tel: 0734 318652
Fax: 0734 352080
Contact: The Librarian

ROCHDALE

Rochdale Metropolitan Borough Libraries
Central Library
Esplanade
Rochdale
Lancs OL16 1AQ
Tel: 0706 864914
Fax: 0706 594475

SALFORD

University College Salford Library
Frederick Road
Salford
Greater Manchester
M6 6PU
Tel: 061 736 6541 x330
Fax: 061 745 8386
Contact: The College Librarian

SHEFFIELD

Sheffield Hallam University Library
Psalter Lane Site
Sheffield
South Yorks S11 8UZ
Tel: 0742 532721
Fax: 0742 532717
Contact: Site Librarian

Sheffield Libraries & Information Services
Art and Social Sciences Section
Central Library
Surrey Street
Sheffield
South Yorks S1 1XZ
Tel: 0742 734711/2
Fax: 0742 735009
Contact: The Librarian

STIRLING

University of Stirling Library
Stirling FK9 4LA
Tel: 0786 67520
Fax: 0786 51335

STOKE ON TRENT

Staffordshire University Library and Information Service
College Road
Stoke on Trent
Staffordshire ST4 2DE
Tel: 0782 744531
Fax: 0782 744035
Contact: The Librarian

SUNDERLAND

Sunderland University Library
Langham Tower
Ryhope Road
Sunderland SR2 7EE
Tel: 091 515 2000
Fax: 091 515 2423
Contact: The Librarian

SWANSEA

Swansea Institute of Higher Education Library
Townhill Road
Swansea
West Glam SA2 0UT
Tel: 0792 203482
Fax: 0792 298017
Contact: The Librarian

TEDDINGTON

Cinema Theatre Association
44 Harrowdene Gardens
Teddington
Middlesex TW11 0DJ
Tel: 081 977 2608
Contact: The Secretary

UXBRIDGE

Brunel University Library
Uxbridge
Middlesex UB8 3PH
Tel: 0898 274000
Fax: 0895 232806
Contact: The Librarian

WAKEFIELD

Bretton Hall College
Library and Learning Resources
Bretton Hall
West Bretton
Wakefield WF4 4LG
Tel: 0924 830261
Fax: 0924 830521
Contact: Director of Learning Resources

WARRINGTON

North Cheshire College Library
Warrington North Campus
Winwick Road
Warrington
Cheshire WA2 8QA
Tel: 0925 814343 x422
Contact: The College Librarian

WELLINGBOROUGH

Tresham Institute of Further and Higher Education Library
Church Street
Wellingborough
Northants NN8 4PD
Tel: 0933 224165
Contact: The Librarian

WINCHESTER

King Alfred's College Library
Sparkford Road
Winchester
Hampshire SO22 4NR
Tel: 0962 841515 x229
Fax: 0962 842280
Contact: The Librarian

WOLVERHAMPTON

Light House Cinema
Media Reference Library
The Chubb Buildings
Fryer Street
Wolverhampton
West Midlands WV1 1HT
Tel: 0902 716044
Contact: The Librarian

Wolverhampton Libraries and Information Services
Central Library
Snow Hill
Wolverhampton
West Midlands WV1 3AX
Tel: 0902 312025
Fax: 0902 714579

YORK

College of Ripon and York St John Library
Lord Mayors Walk
York YO3 7EX
Tel: 0904 656771
Contact: The Librarian

Educational Television Association
The King's Manor
Exhibition Square
York YO1 2EP
Tel: 0904 433929
Contact: The Administrator

ORGANISATIONS

Listed below are the main trade/government organisations and bodies relevant to the film and television industry. A separate list of the Regional Arts Boards is included at the end of this section

ABC (Association of Business Communicators)
3 Whitehall Court
Whitehall
London SW1A 2EL
Tel/Fax: 071 925 1331
Contact: Pida Ripley MA AKC
Trade association of professionals providing the highest standards of audio visual/video equipment/services

AMPS (Association of Motion Picture Sound)
28 Knox Street
London W1H 1FS
Tel: 071 402 5429
Contact: Brian Hickin
AMPS was formed in 1989 to promote and encourage science, technology and creative application of all aspects of motion picture sound recording and reproduction, and to seek to promote and enhance the status of those therein engaged

APRS – The Professional Recording Association
2 Windsor Square
Silver Street
Reading RG1 2TH
Tel: 0734 756218
Fax: 0734 756216
Represents the interests of the professional sound recording industry, including radio, TV and video studios and companies providing equipment and services in the field. It runs the international APRS Exhibition held at Olympia, London each year

Advertising Association
Abford House
15 Wilton Road
London SW1V 1NJ
Tel: 071 828 2771 (business)
Tel: 071 828 4831 (general)
Fax: 071 931 0376
Contact: Information Officer
A federation of 26 trade associations and professional bodies representing advertisers, agencies, the advertising media and support services. It is the central organisation for the UK advertising business, on British and European legislative proposals and other issues of common concern, both at national and international levels, and as such campaigns actively to maintain the freedom to advertise and to improve public attitudes to advertising. It publishes UK and European statistics on advertising expenditure, instigates research on advertising issues and organises seminars and courses for people in the communications business. Its Information Centre is one of the country's leading sources for advertising and associated subjects

Advertising Film and Videotape Producers' Association (AFVPA)
26 Noel Street
London W1V 3RD
Tel: 071 434 2651
Fax: 071 434 9002
Contact: Cecilia Garnett
The Association represents most producers of TV commercials. It negotiates with recognised trade unions, with the advertisers and agencies and also supplies a range of member services

Amalgamated Engineering and Electrical Union (AEEU)
Hayes Court
West Common Road
Bromley BR2 7AU
Tel: 081 462 7755
Fax: 081 462 4959
A trade union representing – among others – people employed in film and TV lighting/electrical/electronic work

Arts & Entertainment Training Council (AETC)
3 St Peter's Buildings
York Street
Leeds LS9 8AJ
Tel: 0532 448845
Fax: 0532 344014
Project Director: Rick Welton
An Industry Training Organisation, developing National and Scottish Vocational Qualifications for many occupations in music, dance, drama, visual arts and writing. It is responsible for strategic action to improve the quality, availability and effectiveness of vocational training within its industrial sector

Arts Council of Great Britain
Film, Video and Broadcasting
14 Great Peter Street
London SW1P 3NQ
Tel: 071 973 6443
Fax: 071 973 6581
Contact: Rodney Wilson
The Arts Council is funded by the Department of National Heritage to encourage and support the arts. One of the means of achieving its objectives is the financing of documentary films on the arts intended for broad public use, particularly television and education. As an extension of its support for the visual arts, funds are available for the production, distribution and exhibition of artists' film and video

Arts Council of Northern Ireland
185 Stranmillis Road
Belfast BT9 5DU
Tel: 0232 381591
Fax: 0232 661715

Director: Brian Ferran
See entry for Northern Ireland Film Council for Northern Irish activities in this area

Association for Media Education (AME)
Faculty of Education
Bretton Hall College
West Bretton
Wakefield
West Yorks WF4 4LG
Tel: 0924 830261
Fax: 0924 830521
Contact: Jeannette Ayton
The Association aims to promote media education at all levels; stimulate links with and between existing media education networks and provide a forum for the dissemination of effective ideas and practice. AME is open to anyone involved or interested in media education. It seeks to involve teachers and lecturers across all age phases as well as media professionals and cultural workers

Association for Media, Film and Television Studies in Higher and Further Education (AMFIT)
Centre for Extra-Mural Studies
Birkbeck College
University of London
26 Russell Square
London WC1B 5DQ
Tel: 071 631 6639
Fax: 071 631 6688
Secretary: Mary Wood
Chair: Sylvia Harvey
Tel: 0742 532656
Provides a professional forum for teachers and researchers in Media, Film and Television Studies in both further and higher education. Its Executive Committee is drawn from the college, polytechnic and university sectors. Organise an Annual Conference, seek to facilitate the exchange of information among members and liaise with various national bodies including 'sister' organisations: AME, NAHEFV, BUFVC and ACS

Association of Professional Composers (APC)
34 Hanway Street
London W1P 9DE
Tel: 071 436 0919
Fax: 071 436 1913
Contact: Rosemary Dixson
APC represents composers from all sides of the profession – concert music, film, television, radio, theatre, electronic media, library music, jazz and so on. Its aims are to further the collective interests of its members and to inform and advise them on professional and artistic matters

Audio Visual Association
46 Manor View
London N3 2SR
Tel: 081 349 2429
Contact: Sandy Boyle
Chairman: Terry Bowles
Tel: 081 398 7674
The Audio Visual Association is now a Special Interest Group of the British Institute of Professional Photography

Australian Film Commission (AFC)
European Marketing Branch
2nd Floor, Victory House
99-101 Regent Street
London W1
Tel: 071 734 9383
Fax: 071 434 0170
Contact: Pressana Vasudevan
The AFC is a statutory authority established in 1975 to assist the development, production and distribution of Australian films. The European marketing branch services producers and buyers, advises on co-productions and financing, and promotes the industry at markets and through festivals

BAFTA (British Academy of Film and Television Arts)
195 Piccadilly
London W1V 9LG
Tel: 071 734 0022
Fax: 071 734 1792
BAFTA was formed in 1946 by Britain's most eminent filmmakers as a non-profit making company. It aims to advance the art and technique of film and television and encourage experiment and research. Membership is available to those working actively within the film and/or television industries and who have worked for not less than three years in the two industries. BAFTA has facilities for screenings and discussion meetings, and makes representations to parliamentary committees. Its awards to the industries (Craft Awards and Production and Performance Awards) are annual televised events. The Academy has branches in Manchester, Glasgow, Cardiff and Los Angeles. See also under Awards and Preview Theatres

BARB (Broadcasters' Audience Research Board)
5th Floor, North Wing
Glenthorne House
Hammersmith Grove
London W6 0ND
Tel: 081 741 9110
Fax: 081 741 1943
Succeeding the Joint Industries' Committee on Television Audience Research (JICTAR), BARB commissions audience research on behalf of the BBC and ITV

BECTU (Broadcasting Entertainment Cinematograph and Theatre Union)
111 Wardour Street
London W1V 4AY
Tel: 071 437 8506
Fax: 071 437 8268
General Secretary: D A Hearn
Deputy General Secretary: R Lockett
BECTU is the UK trade union for workers in film, broadcasting and the arts. Formed in 1991 by the merger of the ACTT and BETA, the union is 42,000 strong and represents permanently employed and freelance staff in television, radio, film, cinema, theatre and entertainment. BECTU provides a comprehensive industrial relations service based on agreements with the BBC, ITV companies, Channel 4, PACT, AFVPA and MFVPA, Odeon, MGM, Apollo, Society of Film Distributors, National Screen Services, independent exhibitors and the BFI itself. Outside film and television, the union has agreements with the national producing theatres and with the Theatrical Management Association, the Society of West End Theatres and others

BKSTS (British Kinematograph Sound and Television Society)
M6-14 Victoria House
Vernon Place
London WC1B 4DF
Tel: 071 242 8400
Fax: 071 405 3560
Administration Officer: Suzie Brewer
Training Officer: Anne Fenton
Formed in 1931, the BKSTS is the technical society for film, television and associated industries. A wide range of training courses and seminars are organised with special rates for members. The society produces many publications including a monthly journal 'Image Technology' and a quarterly 'Cinema Technology' both free to members. Corporate members must have sufficient qualifications and experience, however student and associate grades are also available. Biennial conference has become a platform for new products and developments from all over the world

BREMA (British Radio and Electronic Equipment Manufacturers' Association)
Landseer House
19 Charing Cross Road
London WC2H 0ES
Tel: 071 930 3206
Fax: 071 839 4613
Trade association for British consumer electronics industry

BUFVC (British Universities Film and Video Council)

55 Greek Street
London W1V 5LR
Tel: 071 734 3687
Fax: 071 287 3914
Contact: Murray Weston
The BUFVC is an organisation, funded via the Open University, with members in many institutions of higher education. It provides a number of services to support the production and use of film, television and other audiovisual materials for teaching and research. It operates a comprehensive Information Service, produces a regular magazine 'Viewfinder', catalogues and other publications, such as the 'Researchers' Guide to British Film and Television Collections' and the 'BUFVC Handbook for Film and Television in Education', organises conferences and seminars and distributes specialised film and video material. It runs a preview and editing facility for film (16mm) and video (Betacam and other formats). Researchers in history and film/programme researchers come to the Council's offices to use the Slade Film History Register, with its information on British newsreels. BUFVC's Off-air recording back-up service records all television programmes from the four UK terrestrial television channels between 9am and 1.30am each day. The recordings are held for at least two months to allow educational establishments to request copies if they have failed to record the material locally under ERA licence

BVA (British Videogram Association)

22 Poland Street
London W1V 3DD
Tel: 071 437 5722
Fax: 071 437 0477
The BVA represents the interests – with particular regard to copyright – of British producers and distributors of pre-recorded videocassettes and videodiscs

British Academy of Songwriters, Composers and Authors (BASCA)

34 Hanway Street
London W1P 9DE
Tel: 071 436 2261
Fax: 071 436 1913
Represents its members interests within the music industry. It issues standard contracts between publisher and songwriter. Founded and administers the annual Ivor Novello Awards

British Amateur Television Club (BATC)

Grenehurst
Pinewood Road
High Wycombe
Bucks HP12 4DD
Computer BBS: 0933 413396
Non-profit making organisation run entirely by volunteers. BATC publish a quarterly technical publication 'CQTV' which is only available via subscription £9 per annum. CQTV is all about TV hardware brought down to a practical home construction level with circuits for all aspects of Television and Satellite Television. The circuits are backed by an extensive PCB service. Examples are simple fade to black, electronic testcard, sync generators and TV production Switchers

British Board of Film Classification (BBFC)

3 Soho Square
London W1V 5DE
Tel: 071 439 7961
Fax: 071 287 0141
The 1909 Cinematograph Films Act required public cinemas to be licensed by their local authority. Originally this was a safety precaution against fire risk but was soon interpreted by the local authorities as a way of censoring cinema owners' choice of films. In 1912, the British Board of Film Classification was established by the film industry to seek to impose a conformity of viewpoint: films cannot be shown in public in Britain unless they have the BBFC's certificate or the relevant local authorisation. The Board finances itself by charging a fee for the films it views. When viewing a film, the Board attempts to judge whether a film is liable to break the law, for example by depraving and corrupting a significant proportion of its likely audience. It then assesses whether there is material greatly and gratuitously offensive to a large number of people. The Board seeks to reflect contemporary public attitudes. There are no written rules but films are considered in the light of the above criteria, previous decisions and the examiners' personal judgement. It is the policy of the Board not to censor anything on political grounds. Five film categories came into effect in 1982, with the introduction of a '12' category in August 1989:

Universal: Suitable for all

Parental Guidance: Some scenes may be unsuitable for young children

Passed only for persons of 12 years and over

Passed only for persons of 15 years and over

Passed only for persons of 18 years and over

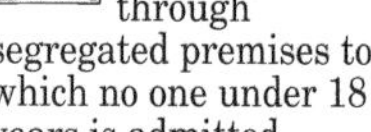
For Restricted Distribution only, through segregated premises to which no one under 18 years is admitted

The final decision, however, still lies with the local authority. In 1986 the GLC ceased to be the licensing authority for London cinemas, and these powers devolved to the Borough Councils. Sometimes films are passed by the BBFC and then banned by local authorities (*Straw Dogs, Caligula*). Others may have their categories altered (*Monty Python's Life of Brian, 9 1/2 Weeks*). Current newsreels are exempt from censorship. In 1985 the BBFC was designated by the Home Secretary as the authority responsible for classifying video works under the Video Recordings Act 1984. The film categories listed above are also the basis for video classification

British Broadcasting Corporation (BBC)

Portland Place
London W1A 1AA
Tel: 071 580 4468
The BBC provides its radio and TV services under the auspices of the Department of National Heritage, which deals with legislative and constitutional aspects of broadcasting. See also under Television Companies

British Copyright Council

29-33 Berners Street
London W1P 4AA
Provides liaison between societies which represent the interest of those who own copyright in literature, music, drama and works of art, making representation to Government on behalf of its member societies

The British Council

10 Spring Gardens
London SW1A 2BN
Contacts: John Cartwright, Rosemary Hood
11 Portland Place
London W1N 4EJ
Tel: 071 389 3065
Fax: 071 389 3041
As part of its work of promoting understanding of Britain in other countries, the British Council purchases film and television material for showing by its offices in around 100 countries. It also selects films for British film weeks and film festivals overseas. The British Council has a Film, TV and Video Advisory Committee chaired by David Puttnam CBE. The British Council receives funds from the

Foreign and Commonwealth Office and from the Overseas Development Administration

British Equity
Guild House
Upper St Martin's Lane
London WC2H 9EG
Tel: 071 379 6000
Fax: 071 379 7001
General Secretary: Ian McGarry
Equity was formed in 1930 by professional performers to achieve solutions to the problems of casual employment and short-term engagements. Equity has 45,000 members, and represents performers (other than musicians), stage managers, stage directors, stage designers and choreographers in all spheres of work in the entertainment industry. It negotiates agreements on behalf of its members with producers' associations and other employers. In some fields of work only artists with previous professional experience are normally eligible for work. Membership of Equity is treated as evidence of professional experience under these agreements. It publishes 'Equity Journal' five times a year

bfi British Federation of Film Societies (BFFS)
British Film Institute
21 Stephen Street
London W1P 1PL
Tel: 071 255 1444
Fax: 071 255 2315
The BFFS exists to promote the work of some 300 film societies in the UK. In 1982 the BFI set up the Film Society Unit to service the BFFS. See also pp170-179

British Film Commission
70 Baker Street
London W1M 1DJ
Tel: 071 224 5000
Fax: 071 224 1013
The British Film Commission has been established by Government to promote the UK as an international production centre and to encourage the use of British locations, services, facilities and personnel. It provides a computerised information service at no charge to enquirers and is a permanent source of information on all matters likely to impact overseas producers contemplating production in the UK

bfi British Film Institute (BFI)
21 Stephen Street
London W1P 1PL
Tel: 071 255 1444
Fax: 071 436 7950
Founded in 1933, the BFI was incorporated by Royal Charter in 1983; its aim is to encourage the development of the art of film and TV. It is funded largely by a grant from the Department of National Heritage. The BFI is involved in almost every aspect of film and television in the United Kingdom, through the Regional Film Theatre network including the National Film Theatre, a Distribution library, the preservation work of the National Film and Television Archive, and a Production arm which makes both feature-length and short low-budget films. The BFI also publishes books and the monthly magazine 'Sight and Sound' and acts as a centre for original research. The BFI Library and Stills, Posters and Designs Collection are unparalleled sources for the documentation of film and television history; highlights of these collections are on display in the prize-winning Museum of the Moving Image where the development of film and television is displayed from its earliest beginnings. For a full description of BFI activities, see pp6-14

British Institute of Professional Photography
Fox Talbot House
Amwell End
Ware
Hertfordshire SG12 9HN
Tel: 0920 464011
Fax: 0920 487056
Company Secretary: Alex Mair
The qualifying body for professional photography and photographic processing. Members represent specialisations in the fields of photography, both stills and moving images

British Screen Advisory Council
93 Wardour Street
London W1V 3TE
Tel: 071 413 8009
Fax: 071 734 5122
Contact: Fiona Clarke-Hackston
The BSAC is a non-statutory advisory body set up to replace the statutory-based Cinematograph Films Council and the non-statutory Interim Action Committee which were respectively abolished and wound up on the passing of the Films Act 1985. The Council is a broadly based industry body embracing all aspects of the audio-visual industry, including film, television and video, meeting every month under the Chairmanship of Lord Attenborough to consider a number of industry questions

British Screen Development (BSD)
(formerly The National Film Development Fund – NFDF)
14-17 Wells Mews
London W1P 3FL
Tel: 071 323 9080
Fax: 071 323 0092
Head of Development: Tessa Ross
BSD was set up as the NFDF in 1976 to make loans for the development of British cinema feature films. Funded originally from the Eady Levy, it has helped to develop such films as *Defence of the Realm*, *Dance with a Stranger*, *A Room with a View*, *Tree of Hands*, *Joyriders*, *A Very British Coup* and *Soursweet*. Under the 1985 Films Act, the fund received £350,000 annually from the Department of Trade and Industry for the development of scripts. BSD continues to receive an approximately similar level of funding but is now part of British Screen Finance (the semi-privatised successor of the NFFC). It has, however, a separate administrator and panel of independent consultants

British Screen Finance
14-17 Wells Mews
London W1P 3FL
Tel: 071 323 9080
Fax: 071 323 0092
Since January 1986, British Screen, a private company aided by Government grant, has taken over the role and the business of the National Film Finance Corporation which was dissolved following the Films Act 1985. The Department of National Heritage has committed support until March 1996. British Screen exists primarily to support new talent in commercially viable productions which might find difficulty in attracting mainstream commercial funding. Between 1986 and 1992 it supported 77 productions, and hopes to support a further 10 in 1993. Through British Screen Development it also runs a programme of 11-minute short films for first time writers, directors and producers

British Tape Industry Association
Carolyn House
22-26 Dingwall Road
Croydon CR0 9XF
Tel: 081 681 1680
Trade association for the manufacturers of audio and videotape

Broadcasting Complaints Commission (BCC)
Grosvenor Gardens House
35-37 Grosvenor Gardens
London SW1W 0BS
Tel: 071 630 1966
Fax: 071 828 7316
Secretary: Richard Hewlett
A statutory body set up by the Home Secretary under the Broadcasting

Act 1981 (and now operating under the 1990 Act) to consider complaints of unjust or unfair treatment or unwarranted infringement of privacy in television and radio programmes broadcast by the BBC, Independent Television, Channel 4 or Independent Radio as well as in programmes included in a licensed cable or satellite service

Broadcasting Press Guild

c/o Richard Last
The Ridge
Tiverton
Woking
Surrey GU22 7EQ
Tel/Fax: 0483 764895
Rosalie Horner
3 Dundonald Road
London NW10 3HP
Tel: 081 969 2608
An association of journalists who write about TV and radio in national, regional and trade press. Membership by invitation. Monthly lunches with leading industry figures as guests. Annual Television and Radio Awards

Broadcasting Research Unit

VLV Librarian
101 King's Drive
Gravesend
Kent DA12 5BQ
Tel: 0474 352835
The Broadcasting Research Unit was an independent Trust researching all aspects of broadcasting, development and technologies, operating from 1980-1991. Its publications and research are available from the above address

Broadcasting Standards Council

5-8 The Sanctuary
London SW1P 3JS
Tel: 071 233 0544
Fax: 071 233 0397
Chair: Lady Howe
Deputy Chair: Dame Jocelyn Barrow OBE
Director: Colin Shaw
The Broadcasting Standards Council monitors the portrayal of violence, of sex and matters of taste and decency (such as bad language or the treatment of disasters), in television or radio programmes or broadcast advertisements. The Council publishes a Code of Practice, carries out research and deals with complaints about these matters. The Council may also make complaints of its own. The BSC is a statutory body under the Broadcasting Act 1990

CFL Vision

PO Box 35
Wetherby
Yorkshire LS23 7EX
Tel: 0937 541010
Fax: 0937 541083
CFL Vision began in 1927 as part of the Imperial Institute and is reputedly the oldest non-theatrical film library in the world. It is part of the COI and is the UK distributor for their audiovisual productions as well as for a large number of programmes acquired from both public and private sectors. Over 300 titles, mostly on video, are available for loan or purchase by schools, film societies and by industry

The Cable Television Association

5th Floor
Artillery House
Artillery Row
London SW1P 1RT
Tel: 071 222 2900
Fax: 071 799 1471
Represents the interests of cable operators, installers, programme providers and equipment suppliers. For further information on cable, see under Cable and Satellite

Campaign for Press and Broadcasting Freedom

96 Dalston Lane
London E8 1NG
Tel: 071 923 3671
Fax: 071 923 3672
A broad-based membership organisation campaigning for more diverse, accessible and accountable media in Britain, backed by the trade union movement. Established in 1979, it now incorporates the Campaign Against Racism in the Media (CARM), the Television Users Group (TUG) and is developing regional structures. Specialist groups deal with specific issues (sexuality, censorship, disability, media racism etc). The CPBF mail order catalogue is regularly updated and includes books on all aspects of the media from broadcasting policy to sexism; video titles include *Making News*, *Wapping Lies*, *Mother Ireland*, *The Irish Question* and the Open Door films *It Ain't Half Racist, Mum*, *Why Their News is Bad News*; its bi-monthly journal 'Free Press' examines current ethical, industrial and political developments in media policy and practice. CPBF acts as a parliamentary lobby group on censorship and media reform

Celtic Film and Television Association

The Library
Farraline Park
Inverness IV1 1LS
Tel: 0463 226189
Fax: 0463 237001
Development of film, TV and video production relevant to the languages of the Celtic nations and regions. Organises an annual competitive festival/conference, itinerant Scotland/Ireland/Wales/Brittany in March/April

Central England Screen Commission

Waterside House
46 Gas Street
Birmingham B1 2JT
Tel: 021 643 9309
Fax: 021 643 9061
Contact: Kim Langford
Directory promoting talent and facilities in the region; database of media services; film commissioners; media business training; production fund for first time film makers; copyright registration scheme; information and advice service; media events planning/conferences/seminars; media association

Central Office of Information (COI)

Films and Television Division
Hercules Road
London SE1 7DU
Tel: 071 261 8500
Fax: 071 928 5037
Contact: Malcolm Nisbet
COI Films and Television Division is responsible for government filmmaking on informational themes as well as the projection of Britain overseas. The COI organises the production of a wide range of documentary films, television programmes, video programmes and audiovisual presentations including videodisc production. It uses staff producers and draws on the film and video industry for production facilities. It provides help to visiting overseas television teams

Centre for the Study of Communication and Culture

221 Goldhurst Terrace
London NW6 3EP
Tel: 071 328 2868
Fax: 071 372 1193
A Jesuit-founded centre which promotes inter-disciplinary applied research on the problems of modern communication. Particular attention is paid to issues affecting the Third World and to the field of religious communication

Children's Film and Television Foundation (CFTF)

Elstree Studios
Borehamwood
Herts WD6 1JG
Tel: 081 953 0844
Fax: 081 207 0860
In 1944 Lord Rank founded the Children's Entertainment Film Division to make films specifically for children. In 1951 this resulted in the setting up of the Children's Film Foundation (now CFTF), a non-profit making organisation which, up to 1981, was funded by an annual grant from the BFFA (Eady money). The CFTF no longer makes films from its own

resources but, for suitable children's/family cinema/ television projects, is prepared to consider financing script development for eventual production by commercial companies. Films from the Foundation's library are available for hiring at nominal charge in 35mm, 16mm and video format from Glenbuck Films, with overseas sales handled by Rank Film Distributors (see under Distributors and International Sales)

Church of England Communications Unit

Church House
Great Smith Street
London SW1P 3NZ
Tel: 071 222 9011 x356/7
Fax: 071 222 6672
(Out of office hours: 071 222 9233)
Contact: Rev Patrick Forbes
Responsible for liaison between the Church of England and the broadcasting and film industries. Advises the C of E on all matters relating to broadcasting

Cinema Advertising Association (CAA)

127 Wardour Street
London W1V 4AD
Tel: 071 439 9531
Fax: 071 439 2395
Contact: Paul Butler
The Cinema Advertising Association is a trade association of cinema advertising contractors operating in the UK and Eire. First established as a separate organisation in 1953 as the Screen Advertising Association, its main purpose is to promote, monitor and maintain standards of cinema advertising exhibition including the pre-vetting of commercials. It also commissions and conducts research into cinema as an advertising medium and is a prime sponsor of the CAVIAR annual surveys

Cinema and Television Benevolent Fund (CTBF)

22 Golden Square
London W1R 3PA
Tel: 071 437 6567
Fax: 071 437 7186
The CTBF is the trade fund operating in the UK for retired and serving employees (actors and actresses have their own Funds) who have worked for three or more years 'in any capacity, in the cinema, film or independent television industries'. The CTBF offers caring help, support and financial assistance, irrespective of age, and the Fund's home in Wokingham, Berkshire offers full convalescent facilities

Cinema and Television Veterans

166 The Rocks Road
East Malling
Kent ME19 6AX
Tel: 0732 843291
An association open to all persons employed in the film or television industries in their distribution, exhibition, or any of their production departments for at least thirty years

Cinema Exhibitors' Association (CEA)

22 Golden Square
London W1R 3PA
Tel: 071 734 9551
Fax: 071 734 6147
The first branch of the industry to organise itself was the cinema owners, who formed the CEA in 1912 and, following the merger with the Association of Independent Cinemas (AIC), is the only association representing cinema exhibition. CEA members account for the vast majority of all UK commercial cinemas, including independents, Regional Film Theatres and those cinemas in local authority ownership. The Association represents members' interests both within the industry, and to Government – European, national and local. It has been closely involved with all recent and proposed legislation affecting exhibition coming from both the UK Government and the European Commission

Cinema Theatre Association

40 Winchester Street
London SW1V 4NF
Tel: 071 834 0549
Contact: Richard Gray
The Cinema Theatre Association was formed in 1967 to promote interest in Britain's cinema building legacy, in particular the magnificent movie palaces of the 1920s and 1930s. It is the only major organisation committed to cinema preservation in the UK. It campaigns for the protection of architecturally important cinemas and runs a comprehensive archive. The CTA publishes a bi-monthly bulletin and the magazine 'Picture House'

Comataidh Telebhisein Gàidhlig (Gaelic Television Committee)

4 Harbour View
Cromwell Street Quay
Stornoway
Isle of Lewis PA87 2DF
Tel: 0851 705550
Fax: 0851 706432
Statutory body grant funding Gaelic television programmes primarily for reception in Scotland, financing research and training of persons employed or to be employed and other purposes connected with or relating to the making of such programmes. It will consider co-production and co-financing, particularly with other European minority language groups

Commonwealth Broadcasting Association

BBC White City
201 Wood Lane
London W12 7TS
Tel: 081 752 5022
Fax: 081 752 5139
Secretary-General: Stuart Revill
An association of 58 national broadcasting organisations in 51 Commonwealth countries

Composers' Guild of Great Britain

34 Hanway Street
London W1P 9DE
Tel: 071 436 0007
Fax: 071 436 1913
The Guild represents composers of serious music, covering the stylistic spectrum from jazz to electronics. Although its main function is to safeguard and assist the professional interests of its members, it also provides information for those wishing to commission music and will put performers or societies in touch with composers

Confederation of Entertainment Unions (CEU) see **Federation of Entertainment Unions (FEU)**

Critics' Circle

Film Section
7 Roehampton Lane
London SW15 5LS
Tel: 081 878 1187
Fax: 081 878 8727
Chairman: George Perry
Vice-Chairman: Christopher Tookey
Honorary Secretary: John Marriott
Honorary Treasurer: Peter Cargin
The film section of the Critics' Circle brings together most national and regional critics for meetings, functions and the presentation of annual awards

Cyngor Ffilm Cymru (The Wales Film Council)

Screen Centre
Ty Oldfield
Llantrisant Road
Llandaff
Cardiff CF5 2PU
Tel: 0222 578633
Fax: 0222 578654
Chairman: R Gerallt Jones
Chief Exec.: Mike Sweet
Exec. Director: John Hefin
An organisation which seeks to promote and develop the culture of the moving image in Wales. It supports and manages Wales' National Film Archive and is involved in establishing long term initiatives related to the development of Wales' film and television culture. It aims to encour-

age the development of the art of film in Wales; to foster study and appreciation of films for the cinema; to encourage the best use of television towards these ends; and to establish a National Film School of Wales

Deaf Broadcasting Council (DBC)
70 Blacketts Wood Drive
Chorleywood
Herts WD3 5QQ
Contact: Mrs R Myers
An umbrella consumer group working as a link between hearing impaired people and TV broadcasters – aiming for increased access to TV programmes

Defence Press and Broadcasting Committee
Room 2235
Ministry of Defence
Main Building
Whitehall
London SW1A 2HB
Tel: 071 218 2206
Secretary: Rear Admiral David Pulvertaft
The Committee is made up of senior officials from the Ministry of Defence, the Home Office and the Foreign & Commonwealth Office and representatives of the media. It issues guidance, in the form of D Notices, on the publication of information which it regards as sensitive for reasons of national security

Department for Education (DFE)
Sanctuary Buildings
Great Smith Street
London SW1P 3BT
Tel: 071 925 5000
Fax: 071 925 6973
The DFE is responsible for policies for education in England and the Government's relations with universities in England, Scotland and Wales

Department of National Heritage – Media Division (Films)
2-4 Cockspur Street
London SW1Y 5DH
Fax: 071 211 6460
Contacts: for MEDIA and Eurimages: Kevin Saldanha
Tel: 071 211 6435
For BSF and ECPF: Geraldine Offord
Tel: 071 211 6429
For Co-Productions: Chris Atkins
Tel: 071 211 6443
The Department of National Heritage is responsible for Government policy on films and Government funding for British Screen Finance and the European Co-Production Fund (administered by British Screen Finance). It is also responsible for the Government contribution to the MEDIA programme and Eurimages and administers the UK's co-production agreements

Designers and Art Directors Association of the United Kingdom
Graphite Square
85 Vauxhall Walk
London SE11 5HJ
Tel: 071 582 6487
Fax: 071 582 7784
A professional association, registered as a charity, which publishes an annual of the best of British and international design, advertising, television commercials and videos, and organises travelling exhibitions. Membership details are available on request

Directors' Guild of Great Britain
1st Floor
Suffolk House
1-8 Whitfield Place
London W1P 5SF
Tel: 071 383 3858
Fax: 071 383 5173
Represents interests and concerns of directors in all media

Edinburgh and Lothian Screen Industries Office
Filmhouse
88 Lothian Road
Edinburgh EH3 9BZ
Tel: 031 228 5960
Fax: 031 228 5967
Contact: George Carlaw
The Film Commission for the City of Edinburgh and the coastline, countryside and counties of Lothian. Advice on locations, crews and facilities and local authority liaison. A free service provided by the City of Edinburgh and Lothian Regional Council, to encourage film, video and television production in the area

Educational Policy and Services, BBC
BBC White City
201 Wood Lane
London W12 7TS
Tel: 081 752 5252
Contact: Lucia Jones
EPS supports the work of BBC Education radio and television production departments. It services the Educational Broadcasting Council representing professional users

Educational Television Association
The King's Manor
Exhibition Square
York YO1 2EP
Tel/Fax: 0904 433929
Contact: Josie Key
An umbrella organisation of institutions and individuals using TV and other media for education and training. Award scheme (video competitions) and conference held annually. Membership enquiries welcome

FOCAL (Federation of Commercial Audio Visual Libraries)
PO Box 422
Harrow
Middx HA1 3YN
Tel: 081 423 5853
Fax: 081 423 5853
Administrator: Anne Johnson
An international, non-profit making professional trade association representing commercial film/audiovisual libraries and interested individuals. Among other activities, it organises regular meetings, maximises copyright information, and produces a directory of libraries

The Federation Against Copyright Theft (FACT)
7 Victory Business Centre
Worton Road
Isleworth
Middlesex TW7 6ER
Tel: 081 568 6646
Fax: 081 560 6364
An organisation founded in 1982 by the legitimate film and video industry, dedicated to stamping out copyright piracy in the UK

Federation of Broadcasting Unions (FBU) see Federation of Entertainment Unions (FEU)

Federation of Entertainment Unions (FEU)
79 Redhill Wood
New Ash Green
Longfield
Kent DA3 8QP
Fax: 0474 874277
Secretary: John Morton OBE
The Federation comprises British Actors' Equity Association, Broadcasting Entertainment Cinematograph and Theatre Union, Film Artistes' Association, Musicians' Union, National Union of Journalists and Writers' Guild of Great Britain. It has two standing committees covering Film and Electronic Media and Live Entertainment. It provides liaison and co-ordination between the constituent unions and makes joint representations on agreed matters

Feminist Library and Information Centre (formerly WRRC)
5 Westminster Bridge Road
London SE1 7XW
Tel: 071 928 7789
Has a large collection of fiction and non-fiction including books, pamphlets, papers etc. It also keeps an index of research by and on women and women's issues and information on women's studies courses. It holds a wide selection of journals and newsletters from all over the world and publishes its own newsletter. Open Tuesday (11.00-20.00) and Saturday and Sunday (14.00-17.00)

Film Artistes' Association (FAA)

61 Marloes Road
London W8 6LE
Tel: 071 937 4567
Fax: 071 937 0790
Contact: George Avory
The FAA represents extras, doubles, stand-ins and small part artistes. Under an agreement with PACT, it supplies all background artistes in the major film studios and within a 40 mile radius of Charing Cross on all locations

Film Education
41-42 Berners Street
London W1P 3AA
Tel: 071 637 9932/9935
Fax: 071 637 9996
Contact: Ian Wall
Film Education is a film industry sponsored body. Its aims are to promote the use of film across the school curriculum and to further the use of cinemas by schools. To this end it publishes a variety of teaching materials – including study guides on individual films – and organises visits, lectures and seminars

First Film Foundation
Canalot Studios
222 Kensal Road
London W10 5BN
Tel: 081 969 5195
Fax: 081 960 6302
Contact: Deborah Burton
Set up to work with first time filmmakers in film and TV

German Film Board
4 Lowndes Court
Carnaby Street
London W1V 1PP
Tel: 071 437 2047
Fax: 071 437 2048
Contact: Dina Lom
UK representative of the German Film Board, the government industry organisation, and the German Film Export Union, concerned with distribution and to a growing extent co-production

Guild of British Animation
26 Noel Street
London W1V 3RD
Tel: 071 434 2651
Fax: 071 434 9002
Contact: Cecilia Garnett
Represents interests of producers of animated films. The AFVPA acts as secretariat for this association

Guild of British Camera Technicians
5-11 Taunton Road
Metropolitan Centre
Greenford
Middlesex UB6 8UQ
Tel: 081 578 9243
Fax: 081 575 5972
Contact: Penny Burnham
Editors, 'Eyepiece': Charles Hewitt and Kerry Burrows
Advertising Consultant: Ron Bowyer
The Guild exists to further the professional interests of technicians working with motion picture cameras. Membership is restricted to those whose work brings them into direct contact with motion picture cameras and who can demonstrate competence in their particular field of work. They must also be members of the appropriate union. By setting certain minimum standards of skill for membership, the Guild seeks to encourage its members, especially newer entrants, to strive to improve their art. Through its publication, 'Eyepiece', The Magazine of Moving Images, disseminates information about both creative and technical developments, past and present, in the motion picture industry

Guild of British Film Editors
c/o Alfred E Cox
Travair
Spurlands End Road
Great Kingshill
High Wycombe
Bucks HP15 6HY
Tel: 0494 712313
Fax: 02406 3563
To ensure that the true value of film and sound editing is recognised as an important part of the creative and artistic aspects of film production

Guild of Television Cameramen
1 Churchill Road
Whitchurch
Tavistock
Devon PL19 9BU
Tel/Fax: 0822 614405
Contact: Sheila Lewis
The Guild was formed in 1972 'to ensure and preserve the professional status of the television cameramen and to establish, uphold and advance the standards of qualification and competence of cameramen'. The Guild is not a union and seeks to avoid political involvement

IAC (Institute of Amateur Cinematographers)
24c West Street
Epsom
Surrey KT18 7RJ
Tel: 0372 739672
Encouraging amateurs interested in the art of making moving pictures and supporting them with a variety of services

ITV Network Centre
200 Gray's Inn Road
London WC1X 8HF
Tel: 071 843 8000
Fax: 071 843 8158
Chief Executive: Andrew Quinn
Network Director: Marcus Plantin
A body wholly owned by the ITV companies which independently undertakes the commissioning and scheduling of those television programmes which are shown across the ITV network. It also provides a range of services to the ITV companies where a common approach is required

IVCA (International Visual Communications Association)
Bolsover House
5-6 Clipstone Street
London W1P 7EB
Tel: 071 580 0962
Fax: 071 436 2606
Chief Executive: Bill McQuillan
IVCA is the professional association representing the interests of the users and suppliers of visual communications. In particular it pursues the interests of the producers, commissioners and manfacturers involved in the non-broadcast and independent facilities industries. It represents all sizes of company and freelance individuals, offering information and advice services, publications, a professional network, special interest groups, a magazine and a variety of events including the UK's Film and Video Communications Festival

Imperial War Museum
Department of Film
Lambeth Road
London SE1 6HZ
Tel: 071 416 5000
Fax: 071 416 5379
See entry under Archives and Film Libraries

Incorporated Society of British Advertisers (ISBA)
44 Hertford Street
London W1Y 8AE
Tel: 071 499 7502
Fax: 071 629 5355
Contact: Deborah Morris
The ISBA was founded in 1900 as an association for advertisers, both regional and national. Subscriptions are based on advertisers' expenditure and the main objective is the protection and advancement of the advertising interests of member firms. This involves organised representation, co-operation, action and exchange of information and experience, together with conferences, workshops and publications. ISBA offer a communications consultancy service for members on questions as varied as assessment of TV commercial production quotes to formulation of advertising agency agreements

Incorporated Society of Musicians (ISM)
10 Stratford Place
London W1N 9AE
Tel: 071 629 4413
Fax: 071 408 1538
Chief Executive: Neil Hoyle
A professional association for all musicians: teachers, performers and composers. The ISM produces various publications, including the monthly 'Music Journal', and gives advice

to members on all professional issues

Independent Film Distributors' Association (IFDA)
10a Stephen Mews
London W1P 0AX
Tel: 071 957 8957
Fax: 071 957 8968
Contact: Sid Brooks
IFDA was formed in 1973, and its members are mainly specialised film distributors who deal in both 16mm and 35mm from 'art' to 'popular music' films. They supply to many users including schools, hospitals, prisons, hotels etc

Independent Television Commission (ITC)
33 Foley Street
London W1P 7LB
Tel: 071 255 3000
Fax: 071 306 7800
The ITC operates under the Broadcasting Act 1990. It is the controlling body for Channels 3 (ITV), 4 and the proposed Channel 5, cable, satellite and 'additional services'. The ITC will license a variety of services and regulate these through its various codes on programme content, advertising sponsorship and technical standards

Institute of Practitioners in Advertising (IPA)
44 Belgrave Square
London SW1X 8QS
Tel: 071 235 7020
Fax: 071 245 9904
The IPA is the representative body for UK advertising agencies. It represents the collective views of its member agencies in negotiations with Government departments, the media and industry and consumer organisations

International Association of Broadcasting Manufacturers (IABM)
4-B High Street
Burnham
Slough SL1 7JH
Tel: 0628 667633
Fax: 0628 665882
Administrator: Alan Hirst
IABM aims to foster the interests of manufacturers of broadcast equipment from all countries. Areas of interest include liaison with broadcasters, standardisation and exhibitions. All companies active in the field of broadcast equipment manufacturing are welcome to join

International Federation of the Phonographic Industry (IFPI)
IFPI Secretariat
54 Regent Street
London W1R 5PJ
Tel: 071 434 3521
Fax: 071 439 9166
President: Sir John Morgan
An international association of 1018 members in 71 countries, representing the copyright interests of the sound recording and music video industries

International Institute of Communications
Tavistock House South
Tavistock Square
London WC1H 9LF
Tel: 071 388 0671
Fax: 071 380 0623
Contact: Carol Joy
The IIC promotes the open debate of issues in the communications field worldwide, in the interest of human and social advancement. Its current interests cover legal and policy, economic and public interest issues. It does this via its bi-monthly journal 'Intermedia'; through its unique international communications library, the annual conference and sponsored seminars and research forums. Papers and reports are published regularly

Liverpool Film Office
Central Libraries
William Brown Street
Liverpool L3 8EW
Tel: 051 225 5446
Fax: 051 207 1342
Film Commissioner: Helen Bingham
Locations Officer: Lynn Saunders
Provides a free film liaison service, and assistance to all productions intending to use locations, resources, services and skills in the Merseyside area. Undertakes research and location scouting, liaises with local agencies and the community. Offers access to the best range of locations in the UK through its extensive locations library. Members of AFCI, EFCOM network and the British Film Commission

London Screenwriters Workshop
84 Wardour Street
London W1V 3LF
Tel: 071 434 0942/081 551 5570
Fax: 081 550 7537
Contact: Ray Frensham
Promotes contact between screenwriters and producers, agents, development executives and other film and TV professionals through a wide range of seminars. Practical workshops provide training in all aspects of the screenwriting process. Membership is open to anyone interested in writing for film and TV, and to anyone in these and related media

MEDIA (Media: Economic Development and Investment Agency)
Stonehills
Shields Road
Gateshead
Tyne & Wear NE10 0HW
Tel: 091 438 4044
Fax: 091 438 5508
An initiative taken by North East Media Development Trust to develop the audio visual industry in the North of England. The Trust has established an audio visual training centre, a media park offering sheltered work space and access to equipment to media practitioners, and a facilities centre providing leading edge technology. The Trust has also taken the initiative to establish the North Screen Commission and the Northern Media Forum, a sector working group representing audio visual interests throughout the Northern Region

Mechanical-Copyright Protection Society (MCPS)
Elgar House
41 Streatham High Road
London SW16 1ER
Tel: 081 769 4400
Fax: 081 769 8792
Contact: General Licensing Department
MCPS is an organisation of music publishers and composers, which issues licences for the recording of its members' copyright musical works in all areas of television, film and video production. Free advice and further information is available on request

Mental Health Media Council
380 Harrow Road
London W9 2HU
Tel: 071 286 2346
Contact: Sylvia Hines
An independent charity founded in 1965, MHMC provides information, advice and consultancy on film/video use and production relevant to health, mental health, physical disability, learning difficulties and most aspects of social welfare. Resource lists, quarterly magazine 'Mediawise'. Also regular screenings and occasional video production

Music Film and Video Producers' Association (MFVPA)
26 Noel Street
London W1V 3RD
Tel: 071 434 2651
Fax: 071 434 9002
Contact: Cecilia Garnett
The MFVPA was formed in 1985 to represent the interests of pop/music promo production companies. It negotiates agreements with bodies such as the BPI and BECTU on behalf of its members. Secretariat

support is run through AFVPA

Musicians' Union (MU)
60-62 Clapham Road
London SW9 0JJ
Tel: 071 582 5566
Fax: 071 582 9805
Contact: Don Smith
The MU represents the interests of performing musicians in all areas

Music Publishers' Association
3rd Floor
Strandgate
18/20 York Buildings
London WC2N 6JU
Tel: 071 839 7779
Fax: 071 839 7776
The only trade association representing UK music publishers. List of members available at £4.50

National Association for Higher Education in Film and Video (NAHEFV)
c/o London International Film School
24 Shelton Street
London WC2H 9HP
Tel: 071 836 9642/240 0168
Fax: 071 497 3718
Contact: Martin Amstell
The Association's main aims are to act as a forum for debate on all aspects of film, video and TV education and to foster links with industry, the professions and Government bodies. It was established in 1983 to represent all courses in the UK which offer a major practical study in film, video or TV at the higher educational level. Some 35 courses are currently in membership

National Campaign for the Arts
Francis House
Francis Street
London SW1P 1DE
Tel: 071 828 4448
Fax: 071 828 5504
Director: Jennifer Edwards
Administrator: Stephanie McKennell
Campaigns & Information Officer: Chris Butcher
The NCA specialises in lobbying, campaigning (eg running "Vote Arts" events at election time and members seminars and conferences), research and information. It provides up-to-the-minute facts and figures for politicians, journalists and any other interested parties. The NCA is independent of any political party or government agency and is funded solely by membership subscriptions and donations from arts organisations and individuals

National Council for Educational Technology (NCET)
Sir William Lyons Road
Science Park
University of Warwick
Coventry CV4 7EZ
Tel: 0203 416994
Fax: 0203 411418
The National Council for Educational Technology is a registered charity funded by the Department for Education to be the national focus of expertise in educational technology. NCET develops and promotes the use of technology in every area of education and training

National Film and Television School
Beaconsfield Studios
Station Road
Beaconsfield
Bucks HP9 1LG
Tel: 0494 671234
Fax: 0494 674042
Director: Henning Camre
The National Film and Television School provides advanced training and retraining in all major disciplines to professional standards. Graduates are entitled to BECTU membership on gaining employment. It is an autonomous non-profit making organisation funded by the Department of National Heritage and the film and television industries. See also under Courses

National Film Trustee Company (NFTC)

14-17 Wells Mews
London W1P 3FL
Tel: 071 323 9080
Fax: 071 323 0092
Contact: Alun Tyers
An independent revenue collection and disbursement service for producers and financiers. The NFTC has been in business since 1971. It is a subsidiary of British Screen Finance

National Union of Journalists
314 Grays Inn Road
London WC1X 8DP
Tel: 071 278 7916
Fax: 071 837 8143
National Broadcasting Organiser: John Fray
NUJ represents all journalists working in broadcasting in the areas of news, sport, current affairs and features. It has agreements with all the major broadcasting companies and the BBC. It also has agreements with the main broadcasting agencies, WTN, Reuters Television and PACT, with approximately 5,000 members in broadcasting

National Viewers' and Listeners' Association (NVALA)
Ardleigh
Colchester
Essex CO7 7RH
Tel: 0206 230123
Contact: Mary Whitehouse
General Sec: John Beyer
Concerned with moral standards in the media, particularly the role of TV in the creation of social and cultural values

Networking
c/o Vera Productions
30-38 Dock Street
Leeds LS10 1JF
Tel: 0532 428646
Fax: 0532 451238
Contact: Alison Garthwaite
International organisation for women involved in film, video or television. Members receive a newsletter with articles, events, letters and reviews; entry in the Networking index; individual advice and help; a campaigning voice

Network of Workshops (NoW)
c/o Video in Pilton
30 Ferry Road Avenue
West Pilton
Edinburgh EH4 4BA
Tel: 031 343 1151
Fax: 031 343 2820
Contact: Joel Venet
A membership organisation which is open to all independent collective film and video groups who are committed to the cultural aims stated in the BECTU workshop declaration

New Producers Alliance (NPA)
c/o Impact Pictures
1st Floor, The Car Park
2 Lexington Street
London W1P 3HS
Tel: 071 437 3622
Fax: 071 437 3614
Administrator: Andrew Curtis
Established in 1993 by a group of young producers building upon their shared desire to make commercial films for an international audience, NPA is an independent networking organisation. It provides members with access to an information network encompassing not only new producers but also new writers, directors, financial and legal advice and assistance and other associated activities. NPA holds regular meetings and discussions, and membership is available to both individuals and corporate bodies, with fees set accordingly

Northern Ireland Film Council
7 Lower Crescent
Belfast BT7 1NR
Tel: 0232 324140
Fax: 0232 239918
Contact: Geraldine Wilkins
The Northern Ireland Film Council exists to promote the interests of the film and television industry in Northern Ireland and to develop a wider appreciation of and access to film and television culture in the community. The NIFC is engaged in fostering media education, exhibition (including Cinemagic, the international film festival for young people), production (through its newly established Production Fund), training, and archive

Northern Screen Commission (NSC)
Stonehills
Shields Road
Gateshead
Tyne & Wear NE10 0HW
Tel: 091 469 1000
Fax: 091 469 7000
Contact: Paul Mingard
Serving the international production community, NSC makes available the vast resources on offer in the North. It provides a one-stop shop for assistance with all aspects of film and TV production

Office of Fair Trading
Field House
15-25 Bream's Buildings
London EC4A 1PR
Tel: 071 242 2858
Fax: 071 269 8800
The Director General of Fair Trading has an interest in the film industry following the report by the Monopolies and Mergers Commission in 1983 on the supply of films for exhibition in cinemas, and the subsequent Films (Exclusivity Agreements) Order of 1989. Under the Broadcasting Act 1990, he also has two roles in relation to the television industry. In his report published in December 1992 he assessed the Channel 3 networking arrangment for competition and from 1 January 1993 he started to monitor the BBC's progress towards a requirement to source 25% of its programming from independent producers

PACT (Producers Alliance for Cinema and Television)
Gordon House
Greencoat Place
London SW1P 1PH
Tel: 071 233 6000
Fax: 071 233 8935
Chief Executive: John Woodward
Membership Officer: Martin Hart
PACT exists to serve the feature film and independent television production sector. Currently representing 1,400 companies, PACT is the UK contact point for co-production, co-finance partners and distributors. Membership services include a dedicated industrial relations unit, legal documentation and back-up, a varied calendar of events, courses and business advice, representation at international film and television markets, a comprehensive research programme, publication of a monthly newsletter 'Fact', an annual members' directory, and a number of specialist guidebooks, affiliation with European and international producers' organisations, plus extensive information and production advice. PACT works for participants in the industry at every level and operates a members' regional network throughout the UK with divisional offices in Scotland and the North. PACT lobbies actively with broadcasters, financiers and governments to ensure that the producer's voice is heard and understood in Britain and Europe on all matters affecting the film and television industry

Performing Right Society (PRS)
29-33 Berners Street
London W1P 4AA
Tel: 071 580 5544
Fax: 071 631 4138
PRS is a non-profit making association of composers, authors and publishers of musical works. It collects and distributes royalties for the use, in public performances, broadcasts and cable programmes, of its members' copyright music and has links with other performing right societies throughout the world. Explanatory literature and/or a film explaining the Society's operations is available from the Public Affairs Department

Phonographic Performance
Ganton House
14-22 Ganton Street
London W1V ILB
Tel: 071 437 0311
Fax: 071 734 2986
Formed by the British recording industry for the collection and distribution of revenue in respect of the UK public performance and broadcasting of sound recordings

Radio, Electrical and Television Retailers' Association (RETRA)
Retra House
St John's Terrace
1 Ampthill Street
Bedford MK42 9EY
Tel: 0234 269110
Fax: 0234 269609
Contact: Sonia Kurpita
Founded in 1942, the Association represents the interests of electronic retailers to all those who make decisions likely to affect the selling and servicing of electrical and electronic products

Reel Women
London Women's Centre
Wesley House
4 Wild Court
London WC2B 5AU
Tel: 071 404 7097
Contacts: Jini Rawlings, Joan Beveridge
A networking organisation for all women in film, video and television. It places particular emphasis on the creative interaction between women from the broadcast, non-broadcast and independent sectors and higher education, aiming to provide a forum for debate around issues affecting women in all areas of production and training, as well as around broader concerns about the representation and position of women in the industry and on screen. Seminars, screenings and workshops are held as well as regular 'nights out'

Royal Photographic Society
Milsom Street
Bath
Avon BA1 1DN
Tel: 0225 462841
Fax: 0225 448688
A learned society founded for the promotion and enjoyment of all aspects of photography. Contains a specialist Film and Video Group, secretary Tony Briselden, with a regular journal, meetings and the opportunity to submit productions for the George Sewell Award and the Hugh Baddeley Award; and an Audio-Visual group, secretary Richard Brown, FRPS, offering an extensive programme of events, seminars and demonstrations, and the bi-monthly magazine 'AV News'. Membership open to both amateur and professional photographers

Royal Television Society
Holborn Hall
100 Gray's Inn Road
London WC1X 8AL
Tel: 071 430 1000
Fax: 071 430 0924
Executive Director: Michael Bunce
Deputy Executive Director: Claire Price
The RTS, founded in 1927, has over 3,000 members in the UK and overseas, half of which are serviced by the Society's 15 regional centres. The Society aims to bring together all the disciplines of television by providing a forum for debate on the technical, cultural and social implications of the medium. This is achieved through the many lectures, conferences, symposia and training courses organised each year. The RTS publishes a monthly journal 'Television' as well as monographs, career broadsheets and a number of topical papers relating to Society events. The RTS Television Journalism Awards are presented every year in February and the Programme Awards in May. There are also Commercials, Design and Educational Television Awards. See also under Awards

Scottish Arts Council
12 Manor Place
Edinburgh EH3 7DD
Tel: 031 226 6051
Fax: 031 225 9833
Director: Seona Reid
See entry for Scottish Film Council for Scottish activities in this area

Scottish Broadcast & Film Training
74 Victoria Crescent Road
Glasgow G12 9JN
Tel: 041 334 2826
Fax: 041 334 8132
Contact: John McVay
A new industry led partnership responsible for the organisation and coordination of high quality training based on the current structural, technological and market needs of the industry. SBFT wil identify training needs in all sectors of the industry, evaluate, monitor and coordinate all aspects of professional training and qualifications in Scotland, and organise the provision of training

Scottish Film Council
Dowanhill
74 Victoria Crescent Road
Glasgow G12 9JN
Tel: 041 334 4445
Fax: 041 334 8132
Director: David Bruce
Deputy Director: Erika King
The Scottish Film Council is the national body with a remit to promote all aspects of moving image culture throughout Scotland. It aims to make viewing films and film making accessible throughout the community, to establish media education as an educational entitlement and to encourage the development of Scotland's film and television industries. SFC also houses the Scottish Film Archive

Scottish Film Production Fund
74 Victoria Crescent Road
Glasgow G12 9JN
Tel: 041 337 2526
Fax: 041 337 2562
Contact: Ivan Mactaggart
The Fund was set up in 1982 to foster and promote film production in Scotland. The board meets six times a year to consider applications for finance for projects which must have a particular connection with and relevance to Scotland. SFPF also administers the Glasgow Film Fund. The SFPF annual budget for development and production now stands at £230,000

Scottish Screen Locations
Filmhouse
88 Lothian Road
Edinburgh EH3 9BZ
Tel: 031 229 1213
Fax: 031 229 1070
Commissioner: Lee Leckie
Scotland's film commission offering free help and advice with locations, permissions, contacts, accommodation, local transport, facilities, crews and extras to all film and video makers considering shooting anywhere throughout the country

The Shape Network
1 Thorpe Close
London W10 5XL
Tel: 081 960 9248
Fax: 081 968 1674
Chair: Maggie Woolley
A federation of ten independent regional arts organisations which provide access and opportunity for people who are usually excluded from the arts: disabled, deaf and mentally ill people, elderly people. people with learning difficulties, homeless people etc. They run projects, events, festivals and ticket schemes, and offer training courses. Details of regional services from the above address

SKILLSET – The Industry Training Organisation for Broadcast, Film and Video
60 Charlotte Street
London W1P 2AX
Tel: 071 927 8585/8457
Fax: 071 436 4483
Director: Dinah Caine
S/NVQ Project Director:

Kate O'Connor
Founded and managed by the key employers and unions within the industry, SKILLSET operates at a strategic level providing relevant labour market and training information encouraging higher levels of investment in training, and developing and implementing occupational standards and the National and Scottish Vocation Qualifications based upon them. It seeks to influence national and international education and training policies to the industry's best advantage, strives to create greater and equal access to training opportunities and career development and assists in developing a healthier and safer workforce. SKILLSET is a UK-wide organisation

Society of Authors' Broadcasting Committee
84 Drayton Gardens
London SW10 9SB
Tel: 071 373 6642
Fax: 071 373 5768
Contact: Gareth Shannon
Specialities: Radio, television and film scriptwriters

Society of Cable Television Engineers (SCTE)
Fulton House Business Centre
Fulton Road
Wembley Park
Middlesex HA9 0TF
Tel: 081 902 8998
Fax: 081 903 8719
Contact: Mrs Beverley K Allgood MSAE
Aims to raise the standard of cable TV engineering to the highest technical level and to elevate and improve the status and efficiency of those engaged in cable TV engineering

Society of Film Distributors (SFD)
22 Golden Square
London W1R 3PA
Tel: 071 437 4383
Fax: 071 734 0912
General Secretary: D C Hunt
SFD was founded in 1915 and membership includes all the major distribution companies and several independent companies. It promotes and protects its members' interests and co-operates with all other film organisations and Government agencies where distribution interests are involved

Society of Television Lighting Directors
4 The Orchard
Aberthin
Cowbridge
South Glam CF7 7HU
Contact: Mike Baker
The Society provides a forum for the exchange of ideas in all aspects of the TV profession including techniques and equipment. Meetings are organised throughout the UK and abroad. Technical information and news of members' activities are published in the Society's magazine. The Society has no union or political affiliations

Sovexportfilm
38 Wolseley Road
London N8 8RP
Tel: 081 341 6945
Fax: 081 348 1390
Contact: Sergei Kuzmenko
Exports Russian films to different countries and imports films to Russia. Provides facilities to foreign companies wishing to film in Russia. Co-production information for producers

Telefilm Canada
22 Kingly Court
London W1R 5LE
Tel: 071 437 8308
Fax: 071 734 8586
Director: Robert Linnell
Canadian government organisation financing film and television productions. The London office advises on co-productions between Canada and the UK

Variety Club of Great Britain
32 Welbeck Street
London W1M 7PG
Tel: 071 935 4466
Fax: 071 487 4174
Charity dedicated to helping disabled and disadvantaged children throughout Great Britain

Voice of the Listener & Viewer
101 King's Drive
Gravesend
Kent DA12 5BQ
Tel: 0474 352835
An independent non-profit making association working to ensure high standards in broadcasting. Membership is open to all concerned for the future quality and range of British radio and television

The Wales Film Council see Cyngor Ffilm Cymru

Welsh Arts Council
Holst House
9 Museum Place
Cardiff CF1 3NX
Tel: 0222 394711
Fax: 0222 221447
Director: Emyr Jenkins
See entry for Cyngor Ffilm Cymru for details of Welsh activities in this area

Wider Television Access (WTVA)
c/o Flashbacks
6 Silver Place
London W1R 3LJ
A pressure group and publisher of 'Primetime' magazine, seeking to stimulate interest in old UK and US TV programmes and promote greater use of TV archives

Women in Film and Television (UK)
Garden Studios
11-15 Betterton Street
London WC2H 9BP
Tel: 071 379 0344
Fax: 071 379 1625
Chairwoman: Brenda Reid
Administration: Janet Fielding, Vivienne Quesnel
A membership organisation for women with a minimum of three years experience in the film and television industry. It is closely modelled on and affiliated to the American groups of the same name. Its aims are to provide information and career support for members, offer an educational forum for all media professionals, promote and safeguard the interests of women and champion and recognise women's achievements and contributions to the industry

Writers' Guild of Great Britain
430 Edgware Road
London W2 1EH
Tel: 071 723 8074
Fax: 071 706 2413
The Writers' Guild is the recognised TUC-affiliated trade union for writers working in film, television, radio, theatre and publishing. It has negotiated industrial agreements in all the areas mentioned above. These agreements set the minimum rates and conditions for each field of writing

REGIONAL ARTS BOARDS

For more details of RAB activities, see under Funding

Regional Arts Bureau
5 City Road
Winchester SO23 8SD
Tel: 0962 851063
Fax: 0962 852033
Executive Officer: Christopher Gordon
Liaison, lobbying and support for Regional Arts Boards

East Midlands Arts Board
Mountfields House
Forest Road
Loughborough
Leicestershire LE11 3HU
Tel: 0509 218292
Fax: 0509 262214
Chief Executive: John Buston
Arts Officers (Film, TV & Video): Caroline Pick, Jeff Baggott
Derbyshire (excluding High Peak District), Leicestershire, Northamptonshire, Nottinghamshire

Eastern Arts Board
Cherry Hinton Hall
Cherry Hinton Road
Cambridge CB1 4DW

Tel: 0223 215355
Fax: 0223 248075
Chief Executive: Jeremy Newton
Cinema & Broadcasting Officer: Martin Ayres
Bedfordshire, Essex, Cambridgeshire, Hertfordshire, Lincolnshire, Norfolk and Suffolk

London Arts Board

Elme House
133 Long Acre
London WC2E 9AF
Tel: 071 240 1313
Fax: 071 240 4580
The LAB is not responsible for film and video. All enquiries should be directed to the London Film and Video Development Agency

London Film and Video Development Agency (LFVDA)

2nd Floor
25 Gosfield Street
London W1P 7HB
Tel: 071 637 3577
Fax: 071 637 3578
Chief Executive: Steve McIntyre
The area of the 32 London Boroughs and the City of London

North West Arts Board

12 Harter Street
Manchester M1 6HY
Tel: 061 228 3062
Fax: 061 236 5361
Chief Executive: Brian Matcham
Film & Video Officer: Jacqueline Morrissey
Arts development organisation for the north west

Northern Arts Board

9-10 Osborne Terrace
Jesmond
Newcastle upon Tyne
NE2 1NZ
Tel: 091 281 6334
Fax: 091 281 3276
Chief Executive: Peter Hewitt
Head of Published & Broadcast Arts: John Bradshaw
Cleveland, Cumbria, Durham, Northumberland, Tyne and Wear

South-East Arts Board

10 Mount Ephraim
Tunbridge Wells
Kent TN4 8AS
Tel: 0892 515210
Fax: 0892 549383
Chief Executive: Chris Cooper
Media & Published Arts Manager: Tim Cornish
East Sussex, Kent, Surrey and West Sussex

South West Arts

Bradninch Place
Gandy Street
Exeter EX4 3LS
Tel: 0392 218188
Fax: 0392 413554
Chief Executive: Christopher Bates
Film & TV Officer: Judith Higginbottom
Avon, Cornwall, Devon, Dorset (except Bournemouth, Christchurch and Poole DCs), Gloucestershire and Somerset

Southern Arts Board

13 St Clement Street
Winchester
Hampshire SO23 9DQ
Tel: 0962 855099
Executive Director: Sue Robertson
Film, Video & Broadcasting Officer: Karen Fitzsimmons
Berkshire, Buckinghamshire, East Dorset, Hampshire, Isle of Wight, Oxfordshire and Wiltshire

West Midlands Arts Board

82 Granville Street
Birmingham B1 2LH
Tel: 021 631 3121
Fax: 021 643 7239
Chief Executive: Mick Elliott
Head of Broadcast & Published Media: Andy Stamp
Hereford and Worcester, Shropshire, Staffordshire, Warwickshire, West Midlands

Yorkshire & Humberside Arts Board

21 Bond Street
Dewsbury
West Yorks WF13 1AX
Tel: 0924 455555
Fax: 0924 466522
Executive Director: Roger Lancaster
Film & Photography Officer: Richard Taylor
Humberside and North, South, West Yorkshire

ORGANISATIONS (EUROPE)

There follows a list of some of the main pan-European film and television organisations, the various MEDIA projects instigated by the European Commission, and entries for each of the UK's eleven partner countries of the EC

PAN-EUROPEAN ORGANISATIONS

ACE – Ateliers du Cinéma Européen (European Film Studio)

68 rue de Rivoli
75004 Paris
France
Tel: (33) 1 44 61 88 30
Fax: (33) 1 44 61 88 40
Director: Colin Young
ACE is a joint project of the Media Business School (qv under MEDIA projects) and of the Club of European Producers. It has been established to work with producers during the development stafes of their projects, guiding them in a way that maximises their chances of reaching the largest possible target audience

AGICOA (Association de Gestion internationale collective des oeuvres audiovisuelles)

26 rue de St-Jean
1203 Geneva
Switzerland
Tel: (41) 22 340 32 00
Fax: (41) 22 340 34 32
Contacts: Rodolphe Egli, Luigi Cattaneo
AGICOA ensures the protection of the rights of producers worldwide when their works are retransmitted by cable. By entering their works in the AGICOA Registers, producers can claim royalties collected for them

Association Internationale de la Distribution par Câble (AID)

Boulevard Anspach 1
Box 28
1000 Brussels
Belgium
Tel: (32) 2 211 94 49
Fax: (32) 2 211 99 07
Contact: M de Sutter
International Alliance of Cable Distribution Organisations in the different European countries. It defends the interests of the different member countries

Audiovisual EUREKA

Permanent Secretariat
Avenue des Arts 44
1040 Brussels
Tel: (32) 2 511 06 40
Fax: (32) 2 512 91 66
A programme which aims to stimulate the European audiovisual market by favouring the establishment of a network of partners around concrete projects which concern all spheres of the audiovisual sector. The promotion and support of labelled projects is a priority, as well as providing an active network of services, relations, information and exchanges

Bureau de Liaison Européen du Cinéma

c/o Fédération Internationale des Associations de Distributeurs de Films (FIAD)
43 boulevard Malesherbes
75008 Paris
France
Tel: (33) 1 42 66 05 32
Fax: (33) 1 42 66 96 92
Contact: Gilbert Grégoire
Umbrella grouping of cinema trade organisations in order to promote the cinema industry, including CICCE, FEITIS, FIAD, FIAPF and FIPFA (qv)

Centre for Cultural Research

Am Hofgarten 17
5300 Bonn 1
Germany
Tel: (49) 228 211058
Fax: (49) 228 217493
Jägerstrasse 51
1080 Berlin
Germany;
c/o IKM
Karlsplatz 2
1010 Vienna
Austria
Contact: Prof A J Wiesand
Research, documentation, advisory tasks in all fields of the arts and media, especially with 'European' perspectives.
Participation in arts and media management courses at university level. Produces publications

Centre Internationale de Liaison des Ecoles de Cinéma et de Télévision (CILECT)

rue Thérésienne 8
1000 Brussels
Belgium
Tel: (32) 2 511 98 39
Fax: (32) 2 511 02 79
Contact: Henry Verhasselt
CILECT is a Non-Governmental Association, Status B, recognised by UNESCO, is represented in 47 countries in the five continents and has a membership of 87 institutions. Its aim is to promote co-operation among higher teaching and research institutes and among their staff and students, to raise standards of teaching and to improve the education of future creative film and television programme makers and scholars throughout the world

Comité des Industries Cinématographiques et Audiovisuelles des Communautés Européennes et de l'Europe Extracommunautaire (CICCE)

5 rue du Cirque
75008 Paris
France
Tel: (33) 1 42 25 70 63
Fax: (33) 1 42 25 94 27
Contact: Pascal Rogard
European committee of film and audiovisual industry associations, including producers, distributors and technical industries. It represents the industry to European governmental bodies, advises them on audiovisual policy and how to implement it

Coordination of European Independent Producers (CEPI)

59 rue de Châteaudun
75009 Paris
France
Tel: (33) 1 44 53 03 03
Fax: (33) 1 49 95 99 80
Contact: Alain Modot
Network of the European associations of TV producers

Culturelink/IRMO

Institute for Development and International Relations
Ul. Lj. Farkasa Vukotinovica 2
PO Box 303
41000 Zagreb
Croatia
Tel: (38) 41 454 522
Fax: (38) 41 444 059
Contact: Martina Mencer Salluzzo
Culturelink is a worldwide network for research and co-operation in cultural development. Areas of research/ activities: cultural development, cultural policies, cultural identities, cultural co-operation, mass media and communications (media policies in Europe and Croatia, audio-visual co-operation between Eastern and Western Europe, cultural impact of media policies). Documentation, database, bulletin (quarterly)

Department of National Heritage

Media Division (Films)
4th Floor
2/4 Cockspur Street
London SW1Y 5DH
Tel: 071 211 6000
Fax: 071 211 6210
Contacts:
For MEDIA, Eurimages, Audiovisual EUREKA and the British Film Commission: Kevin Saldanha
Tel: 071 211 6435
For the BFI, National Film and Television School, British Screen Finance, European Co-production Fund: Geraldine Offord
Tel: 071 211 6429
For International Co-Productions: Diana Brown
Tel: 071 211 6433
The Department of National Heritage is responsible for government policy on films. It contributes to the MEDIA programme, pays for the UK's annual subscription to Eurimages and contributes to the Audiovisual EUREKA programme. The Department administers the UK's Co-production agreements and provides funding for the BFI, British Screen Finance, the European Co-production Fund (administered by British Screen Finance), the National Film and Television School and the British Film Commission

EGAKU (European Committee of Trade Unions in Arts, Mass Media and Entertainment)

IPC
Blvd Charlemagne 1
PO Box 5
1041 Brussels
Belgium
Tel: (32) 2 238 09 51
Fax: (32) 2 230 0076
Contact: Jim Wilson
Addresses the concerns of unions whose members are engaged in the arts and all types of entertainment. It circulates information on wages and working conditions, maintains relations with other concerned international bodies, and reinforces its affiliated unions' activities at an international level

EUREKA Programme

Department of Trade and Industry
2nd Floor, Red Core
151 Buckingham Palace Road
London SW1W 9SS
Fax: 071 931 7194
Contacts:
For Advanced Broadcasting Technology: Brian Aldous
Tel: 071 215 1737
For UK EUREKA Office: Nick Kaspar
Tel: 071 215 1617
A co-operation mechanism which makes information available to industry and encourages collaborative projects for the development of advanced TV and radio broadcasting technologies

EUTELSAT (European Telecommunications Satellite Organisation)

Tour Maine-Montparnasse
33 avenue du Maine
75755 Paris Cedex 15
France
Tel: (33) 1 45 38 47 47
Fax: (33) 1 45 38 37 00
Contact: Vanessa O'Connor
EUTELSAT operates a satellite system for intra-European communications of all sorts. Traffic carried includes TV and Radio channels, programme exchanges, satellite newsgathering, telephony and business communications. The satellite's footprints cover the entire European continent and Mediterranean basin

Eurimages

Council of Europe
Palais de l'Europe
Avenue de l'Europe
67075 Strasbourg
France
Tel: (33) 88 41 26 40
Fax: (33) 88 41 27 60
Contact: Executive Secretary
Founded in 1988 by a group of Council of Europe member states. Its objective is to stimulate film and audiovisual production by partly financing the co-production and distribution of European cinematographic and audiovisual works. Eurimages now includes 23 member states

Eurocréation Media

3 rue Debelleyme
75003 Paris
France
Tel: (33) 1 44 59 27 06
Fax: (33) 1 40 29 92 46
Contact: Anne-Marie Autissier
Eric Naulleau
Tristan Mattelart
Eurocréation Media develops consultation and expertise in the field of European audiovisual and cinema (research, support for the organisation and conception of European events, training activities)

European Broadcasting Union (EBU)

Ancienne Route 17a
PO Box 67
1218 Grand-Saconnex
Geneva
Switzerland
Tel: (41) 22 717 2111
Fax: (41) 22 798 5897
Contact: Michael Type
The EBU is a professional association of national broadcasters with 114 members in 79 countries. Principal activities: daily exchanges of news, sports and cultural programmes for TV (Eurovision) and radio (Euroradio); Eurosport and Euronews TV channels; technical studies and legal action in the international broadcasting sphere

European Co-production Association

c/o ZDF Enterprises GmbH
6500 Mainz/Hechtsheim
Germany
Tel: (49) 6131 991 321-3
Fax: (49) 6131 991 324
Contact: Martin Pieper
A consortium of European public service TV networks for the co-production of TV fiction series. Can offer complete finance or development funding. Projects are proposed directly to

Secretariat or to member national broadcasters (Channel 4 in UK)

European Co-production Fund (ECF)

c/o British Screen Finance
14-17 Wells Mews
London W1P 3FL
Tel: 071 323 9080
Fax: 071 323 0092
The £5m ECF, provided over the years 1991-93, is available for investment in feature films made by European co-producers and for investment in European film development work. British Screen Finance is responsible for disbursing the Fund to producers in the form of loans on commercial terms. The Fund aims to improve the opportunity for UK producers to co-produce with EC partners

European Film Awards see European Film Academy (MEDIA)

The European Institute for the Media (EIM)

Kaistrasse 13
40221 Düsseldorf
Germany
Tel: (49) 211 90 10 40
Fax: (49) 211 90 10 456
Contact: Prof Dr Peter-Berndt Lange
A forum for research and documentation in the field of media in Europe. Its activities include: research into the media in Europe with a political, economic and juridical orientation; the organisation of conferences and seminars like the Annual European Forum for Television and Film; the management of a European satellite Educational Channel, Channel E; East-West Cooperation Programme; the development of an advanced studies programme for students and media managers

FIAD (Fédération Internationale des Associations de Distributeurs de Films)

43 boulevard Malesherbes
75008 Paris
France
Tel: (33) 1 42 66 05 32
Fax: (33) 1 42 66 96 92
Contacts: Gilbert Grégoire, Antoine Virenque
Represents the interests of film distributors

FIAF (International Federation of Film Archives)

rue Franz Merjay 190
1180 Brussels
Belgium
Tel: (32) 2 343 06 91
Fax: (32) 2 343 76 22
Contact: Mrs B van der Elst
For further information about FIAF, see under Archives and Film Libraries on p74

FIAPF (Fédération Internationale des Associations de Producteurs de Films)

33 avenue des Champs-Elysées
75008 Paris
France
Tel: (33) 1 42 25 62 14
Fax: (33) 1 42 56 16 52
Contact: André Chaubeau
An international level gathering of national associations of film producers (23 member countries). It represents the general interests of film producers in worldwide forums (WIPO, UNESCO, GATT) and with European authorities (EC, Council of Europe, Audiovisual EUREKA). It lobbies for better international legal protection of film and audiovisual producers

FIAT (International Federation of Television Archives)

Sten Frykholm
Sveriges Television SVT
105 10 Stockholm
Sweden
Tel: (46) 87845760
Fax: (46) 86631232
For further information about FIAT, see under Archives and Film Libraries on p74

Fédération Européenne des Industries Techniques de l'Image et du Son (FEITIS)

50 Avenue Marceau
75008 Paris
France
Tel: (33) 1 47 23 75 76
Fax: (33) 1 47 23 70 47
Contact: Jean Fleurent-Didier
A federation of European professional organisations representing those working in film and video services and facilities in all audio-visual and cinematographic markets

Fédération Internationale des Producteurs de Films Indépendants (FIPFI)

50 avenue Marceau
75008 Paris
France
Tel: (33) 1 47 23 70 30
Fax: (33) 1 47 20 78 17
Contact: René Thévenet
Federation of independent film producers, currently with members in 21 countries. It is open to all independent producers, either individual or groups, provided they are legally registered as such. FIPFI aims to promote the distribution of independent films, to increase possibilities for co-production, to share information between member countries and seeks to defend freedom of expression

Institut de Formation et d'Enseignement pour les Métiers de l'Image et du Son (FEMIS)

2 rue de la Manutention
75016 Paris
France
Tel: (33) 1 47 20 71 94
Fax: (33) 1 40 70 17 03
High level technical training in the audio-visual field for French applicants and those from outside France with a working knowledge of French. Organises regular student exchanges with other European film schools

Institut de Journalisme Robert Schuman – European Media Studies

rue de l'Association 32-34
1000 Brussels
Belgium
Tel: (32) 2 217 2355
Fax: (32) 2 219 5764
Contact: Anne de Decker
Post-graduate training in journalism. Drawing students from all over Europe, it offers a 9-month intensive training in journalism for press, radio and television. A residential college, it is based on three principles: Professional, European and Christian

International Federation of Actors (FIA)

Guild House
Upper St Martin's Lane
London WC2H 9EG
Tel: 071 379 0900
Fax: 071 379 8260
Contact: Michael Crosby
Trade union federation founded in 1952 and embracing 60 performers' trade unions in 44 countries. It organises solidarity action when member unions are in dispute, researches and analyses problems affecting the rights and working conditions of film, television and theatre actors as well as singers, dancers, variety and circus artistes. It represents members in the international arena on issues such as cultural policy and copyright and publishes twice-yearly news-sheet 'FOCUS' and occasional women's bulletin 'FEMINA'. Has observer status with UNESCO, WIPO and ILO

The Prince's Trust Partners in Europe

8 Bedford Row
London WC1R 4BA
Contact: Anne Engel
Offer "Go and See" grants (max £500) towards partnership projects in Europe to people under 26 (See also entry in Funding)

URTI (Université Radiophonique et Télévisuelle Internationale)
Permanent Secretariat
116 Avenue du Président-Kennedy
75786 Paris Cedex 16
France
Tel: (33) 1 42 30 23 61
Fax: (33) 1 40 50 89 99
Around 50 radio and television organisations are gathered under the banner of URTI to exchange and broadcast several hundred cultural programes a year

MEDIA PROJECTS

MEDIA Programme
Commission of the European Communities
Directorate General Audiovisual, Information, Communication, Culture
120 Rue de Trèves
1040 Brussels
Belgium
Tel: (32) 2 299 9436
Fax: (32) 2 299 92 14
Head of Programme: Holde Lhoest
MEDIA is the media programme of the European Community. It consists of projects supporting various aspects of the film and television industries. Enquires about the projects from the UK should be directed to the UK Media Desk

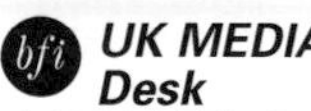

UK MEDIA Desk
c/o British Film Institute
21 Stephen Street
London W1P 1PL
Tel: 071 255 1444
Fax: 071 436 7950
Contact: Louise Casey
The MEDIA desk at the BFI provides written and oral information on Community audiovisual policy, particularly on the MEDIA '95 programme, Audiovisual EUREKA and Eurimages to professionals operating in the field of film, video and television

MEDIA Antenna Scotland
c/o Scottish Film Council
74 Victoria Crescent Road
Glasgow G12 9JN
Tel: 041 334 4445
Fax: 041 334 8132
Contact: Margaret O'Connor
A source of information and advice about the opportunities available to the Scottish screen community offered by the various MEDIA schemes

MEDIA Antenna Wales
c/o Screen Wales
Screen Centre
Llandaff
Cardiff CF5 2PU
Tel: 0222 578370
Fax: 0222 578654
Contact: Robin Hughes
Information about MEDIA opportunities for the Welsh screen community

BABEL (Broadcasting Across the Barriers of European Language)
c/o European Broadcasting Union
Ancienne Route 17a
PO Box 67
1218 Grand-Saconnex
Geneva
Switzerland
Tel: (41) 22 717 2111
Fax: (41) 22 798 5897
Contact: Christian Clausen
BABEL was set up to provide financial support for mainly European multilingual audiovisual production. It is aimed at assisting dubbing and subtitling, the development of new post-production techniques (eg multilingual news) and professional training in this sphere

CARTOON (European Association of Animation Film)
Blvd Lambermont 418
1030 Brussels
Belgium
Tel: (32) 2 245 1200
Fax: (32) 2 245 4689
Contacts: Corinne Jenart, Marc Vandeweyer
Provides financial assistance for development, studio grouping and training. A programme promotion and project financing support mechanism exists through CARTOON FORUM, CARTOON CATALOGUE and CARTOON database

DOCUMENTARY
Project Development and Promotion Packaging
Skindergade 29 A
1159 Copenhagen K
Denmark
Tel: (45) 33 15 00 99
Fax: (45) 33 15 76 76
Awards development and promotion loans for European creative documentaries

EAVE (European Audiovisual Entrepreneurs)
Rue de la Presse 14
1000 Brussels
Belgium
Tel: (32) 2 219 09 20
Fax: (32) 2 223 00 34
Contact: Raymond Ravar
Over the last three years EAVE has provided the only top-level professional training in development and co-production of European film and television projects. EAVE's objectives are to develop genuine European co-productions, to create a pan-European network for producers and to disseminate its expertise as widely as possible

EFDO (European Film Distribution Office)
Friedensallee 14-16
2000 Hamburg 50
Germany
Tel: (49) 40 390 90 25
Fax: (49) 40 390 62 49
Contact: Ute Schneider
It assists the theatrical distribution of low/mid budget European feature films by providing conditionally re-payable interest-free loans to European distributors from at least 3 different countries

EVE (Espace Vidéo Européen)
c/o Irish Film Institute
6 Eustace Street
Dublin 2
Ireland
Tel: (353) 1 679 5744
Fax: (353) 1 679 9657
Contacts: John Dick, Norma Cairns
Co-ordinated by the Irish Film Institute and the Médiathèque de la Communauté française de Belgique, EVE is a loan funbding mechanism for the video publication of European feature films, documentaries, animation and 'classics'

EURO AIM
210 Avenue Winston Churchill
1180 Brussels
Belgium
Tel: (32) 2 346 1500
Fax: (32) 2 346 3842
Contact: Nicholas Steil
It provides European producers and distributors with a range of services (databases, consultancies) and marketing activities (MIP-TV/MIPCOM/screenings/co-production market) to assist the promotion, marketing and distribution of European independent production

Euro Media Garanties
66 rue Pierre Charron
75008 Paris
France
Tel: (33) 1 43 59 88 03
Fax: (33) 1 45 63 85 58
Contact: Georges Prost
MEDIA/EUREKA project. The company offers to share the risks with financial operators involved in European film and audiovisual productions by guaranteeing their bank loans through a public and private guarantee fund

Europa Cinemas
22 Rue du Pont Neuf
75001 Paris
France
Tel: (33) 1 42 33 35 16
Fax: (33) 1 42 36 30 39
Contact: Claude-Eric Poiroux
This project encourages screenings and promotion of European films in a network of cinemas in key European cities

European Film Academy (EFA)
Katharinenstrasse 8
1000 Berlin 31

Germany
Tel: (49) 30 893 4132
Fax: (49) 30 893 4134
Contacts: Aina Bellis, Marion Döring
The EFA was founded in November 1991 to promote European Cinema worldwide and to strengthen its commercial and artistic position, to improve the knowledge and awareness of European cinema and to pass on the substantial experience of the Academy members to the younger generation of film professionals. The EFA (90 members, President: Ingmar Bergman, Chairman: Wim Wenders) organises Masterschools for young professionals, symposia, film screenings for the general public, and promotions tours for European films. At its foundation it took over the responsibility for the European Film Awards (Felix)

European Script Fund

39c Highbury Place
London N5 1QP
Tel: 071 226 9903
Fax: 071 354 2706
Contact: Bo Christensen
Provides development loans for film and television fiction with European appeal. Producers, writers, directors should request an application form with guildelines from the above address. Script funding is awarded to companies developing a range of projects for international audiences

European Scriptwriting and Film Analysis Certificate

Université Libre de Bruxelles
Faculty of Philosophy and Letters
ELICIT – CP/188
Av F D Roosevelt, 50
1050 Brussels
Belgium
Tel: (32) 2 650 42 39/40
Fax: (32) 2 650 24 50
Contacts: Dominique Nasta, Patricia Boeyen
Two year European Programme (MEDIA pilot initiative). Aims to provide academic training in scriptwriting, film criticism, teaching, film-club animation, research. Scriptwriting workshops dealing with many genres (adaptations, originals, TV series) and weekend script doctoring seminars. Links with EC and non EC countries. Admission conditions: candidates need a degree or proven involvement in screenwriting, film-analysis or film-making

GRECO (Groupement Européen pour la Circulation des Oeuvres)

Bahnhofstr. 33
85774 Unterföhring b. München
Germany
Tel: (49) 89 950 83 290
Fax: (49) 89 950 83 292
Managing Director: Robert Strasser
Coordinator: Maritta von Uechtritz
GRECO's objectives are to promote the distribution of European television fiction (TV movies and series), to strengthen the position of European television fiction producers, and to make television fiction available to a wider European television audience

LUMIERE Project

Rua Bernardo Lima 35-5º
1000 Lisbon
Portugal
Tel: (351) 1 57 08 25/09 65/08 97
Fax: (351) 1 57 06 67
Contact: José Manuel Costa, Vera Herold
The LUMIERE Project Association is concerned with the rescue and survival of the European film heritage. Launched by the leading European film archives, its objective is the permanent preservation of films whose survival is in danger, in order to make them accessible and give them new life. It also funds training in this sphere

MAP-TV (Memories-Archives-Programmes TV)

c/o France 3
1 Place de Bordeaux
67005 Strasbourg
France
Tel: (33) 88 56 68 46/47/48
Fax: (33) 88 56 68 49
Contact: Alison Hindhaugh, Jean-Jacques Lemoine
A professional association of broadcasters, producers and audio-visual archive organisations. It pools resources and expertise to support the knowledge, production and broadcast of European archive-based television works, awarding loans for their development

Media Business School

Torregalindo 10, 4º
28016 Madrid
Spain
Tel: (34) 1 359 0247/0036
Fax: (34) 1 345 7606
Contacts: Fernando Labrada, Antonio Saura, Jesús Hernández
A research, training and development centre addressing the structural problems facing the European audiovisual industry. Operates as an umbrella for various training initiatives, and organises seminar cycles and the publication of reports. Major projects include ACE (Ateliers du Cinéma Européen), a studio-style organisation which assists aspiring film-makers and PILOTS, which provides training for long-running television fiction series

Media Investment Club

4 avenue de l'Europe
94366 Bry-sur-Marne Cedex
France
Tel: (33) 1 49 83 28 63
Fax: (33) 1 49 83 25 82
Contacts: Patrick Madelin, Véronique Damien, Martine Colavossi, Lorraine Le Tac
A MEDIA/EUREKA project. Unites European businesses with financial institutions to fund projects made in or using new technologies. It supports production of audiovisual programmes using advanced technology; training of individuals in advanced audiovisual techniques

Media Salles

Piazza Luigi di Savoia 24
20124 Milan
Italy
Tel: (39) 2 669 84405
Fax: (39) 2 669 1574
Contact: Elisabetta Brunella
Media Salles is aimed at supporting cinema exhibition in Europe. Its lines of activity are promotion (advertising campaigns, services to cinemas, support for the "showcases" of European films); information on the economic trends in the sector; training for the enhancement of exhibitors' business skills

SCALE (Small Countries Improve Their Audiovisual Level in Europe)

Rua S Pedro de Alcântara 45-2º
1200 Lisbon
Portugal
Tel: (351) 1 347 8644/ 3923
Fax: (351) 1 347 8643
Contact: Artur Castro Neves
SCALE is established to support the audiovisual industries of the smaller countries of the European Communities in particular in the context of the growth of the audiovisual industry in Europe

SOURCES (Stimulating Outstanding Resources for Creative European Screenwriting)

Jan Luykenstraat 92
1071 CT Amsterdam
The Netherlands
Tel: (31) 20 672 0801
Fax: (31) 20 672 0399
Contact: Dick Willemsen
Organises workshops and other activities that stimulate and improve the craft of screenwriting in Europe

BELGIUM

BRTN
Auguste Reyerslaan 52
1043 Brussels
Tel: (32) 2 741 3111
Fax: (32) 2 734 9351
Contact: TV: Jan Ceuleers
Radio: Piet Van Roe
Public television and radio station serving Dutch speaking Flemish community in Belgium

Cinémathèque Royale de Belgique/Royal Film Archive
Rue Ravenstein 23
1000 Brussels
Tel: (32) 2 507 83 70
Fax: (32) 2 513 12 72
Contact: Gabrielle Claes
Film preservation. The collection can be consulted on the Archive's premises for research purposes. Edit the Belgian film annual

Commission du Film
Communauté Française de Belgique
Ministère de la Culture et des Affaires Sociales
Direction de l'Audiovisuel
Boulevard Léopold II 44
1080 Brussels
Tel: (32) 2 413 23 11
Fax: (32) 2 413 20 68
Contact: Serge Meurant
Gives official recognition to Belgian films; decides whether a film has sufficient Belgian input to qualify as Belgian

Commission de sélection de films
Ministère de la Culture et des Affaires Sociales
Direction de l'Audiovisuel
Boulevard Léopold II 40
1080 Brussels
Tel: (32) 2 413 22 42
Fax: (32) 2 413 20 68
Contacts: Christiane Dano, Serge Meurant
Assistance given to the production of short and long features, as well as other audiovisual production by independent producers

La Direction de l'Audiovisuel
Espace 27 Septembre
Boulevard Léopold II 44
1080 Brussels
Tel: (32) 2 413 22 21
Fax: (32) 2 413 20 68
Contact: Paule Caraël
Draws up regulations concerning the audiovisual industries; gives funding to film and TV; promotes audiovisual culture, especially in Francophone countries

Film Museum
Baron Horta Street 9
1000 Brussels
Tel: (32) 2 507 83 70
Fax: (32) 2 513 12 72
Contact: Gabrielle Claes
Permanent exhibition of the pre-history of cinema. 5 screenings per day – 3 sound, 2 silent. Organises 2 mini-festivals a year: l'Age d'Or Prize and prizes for the distribution of quality films in Belgium

Radio-Télévision Belge de la Communauté française (RTBF)
Blvd Auguste Reyers 52
1044 Brussels
Tel: (32) 2 737 21 11
Fax: (32) 2 737 26 30
Contact: Robert Stephane
Public broadcaster responsible for French language services

UPPT (Union professionnelle des producteurs de programmes de télévision)
21 rue Rasson
1040 Brussels
Tel: (32) 2 736 54 37
Fax: (32) 2 736 52 39
Contact: Pierre Levie
Trade association for TV producers

DENMARK

Danmarks Radio (DR)
Morkhojvej 170
2860 Soborg
Tel: (45) 35 20 30 40
Fax: (45) 35 20 39 39
Contact: Bo Lynnerup
Public service television and radio network

DFI (Danish Film Institute)
Store Søndervoldstraede 4
1419 Copenhagen K
Tel: (45) 31 57 65 00
Fax: (45) 31 57 67 00
Contact: Henrik Bering Liisberg
An autonomous self-governing institution under the auspices of the Ministry of Cultural Affairs, financed through the state budget. It offers support and funding to Danish feature films, import of international features, distribution and exhibition. Promotes and sells Danish films abroad, and finances two community access workshops

Det Danske Filmmuseum
Store Søndervoldstraede 4
1419 Copenhagen K
Tel: (45) 31 57 65 00
Fax: (45) 31 57 67 00
Contact: Ib Monty
The Film Museum, founded in 1941, is one of the world's oldest film archives. It has a collection of 15,000 titles from almost every genre and country, and has daily screenings. There is also an extensive library of books and pamphlets, periodicals, clippings, posters and stills

Filmarbejder-foreningen
Kongens Nytorv 21
Baghuset 3.sal
1050 Copenhagen K
Tel: (45) 33 14 33 55
Fax: (45) 33 14 33 03
Contact: Charlotte Bach
Trade union which organises film, video and television workers, and maintains the professional, social, economic and artistic interests of its members. Negotiates collective agreements for feature films, documentaries, commercials, negotiating contracts, copyright and authors' rights. Also protection of Danish film production

Producenterne
Kronprinsensgade 9B
1114 Copenhagen K
Tel: (45) 33 14 03 11
Fax: (45) 33 14 03 65
Contact: Niels Yde
The Danish Producers' Association of Film, TV, Video and AV

Statens Filmcentral
Vestergade 27
1456 Copenhagen K
Tel: (45) 33 13 26 86
Fax: (45) 33 13 02 03
Statens Filmcentral is the National Film Board of Denmark, created in 1939. It is regulated by the Ministry of Culture and produces, purchases and rents out shorts and documentaries on 16mm and video to educational institutions and libraries

FRANCE

Les Archives du Film du Centre National de la Cinématographie
7 bis rue Alexandre Turpault
78390 Bois d'Arcy
Tel: (33) 1 30 14 80 00
Fax: (33) 1 34 60 52 25
Contact: Michelle Aubert
Officially set up in 1969, it has collected over 131,000 films from 1893 to the present. The Archive is responsible for conserving and preserving nitrate films, including those from the Cinémathèque Française, the Cinémathèque de Toulouse and regional archives. An accelerated nitrate preservation programme was adopted by the Ministry of Culture in 1991 which has mandated the archive to copy all French nitrate productions by 2005

CNC (Le Centre National de la Cinématographie)
12 rue de Lübeck
75784 Paris Cedex 16
Tel: (33) 1 44 34 34 40
Fax: (33) 1 47 55 04 91
Contact: Dominique Wallon
A government institution, under the auspices of the Ministry of Culture. Its areas of concern are: the economics of cinema and the audiovisual industries; film regulation; the promotion of the cinema industries and the protection of cinema heritage. Offers financial assistance in all aspects of French cinema (production, exhibition, distribution etc)

La Cinémathèque Française

29 rue du Colisée
75008 Paris
Tel: (33) 1 45 53 21 86
Fax: (33) 1 42 56 08 55/ 47 04 79 34
Contacts: Jean Saint-Geours, Dominique Païni
Founded in 1936 by Henri Langlois, Georges Franju and Jean Mitry to save, conserve and show films. Now houses a cinema museum, screening theatres, library and stills and posters library

France 2
22 Avenue Montaigne
75387 Paris Cedex 07
Tel: (33) 1 44 21 42 42
Fax: (33) 1 44 21 51 45
Contact: George Vanberschmitt
France's main public service terrestrial television channel

Fédération de la Production Cinématographique Française
5 rue du Cirque
75008 Paris
Tel: (33) 1 42 25 70 63
Fax: (33) 1 42 25 94 27
Contacts: Alain Poiré, Pascal Rogard
National federation of French cinema production

Fédération Nationale des Distributeurs de Films
43 boulevard Malesherbes
75008 Paris
Tel: (33) 1 42 66 05 32
Fax: (33) 1 42 66 96 92
Contact: G Grégoire
National federation of film distributors

Institut National de l'Audiovisuel (INA)
4 avenue de l'Europe
94366 Bry-sur-Marne Cedex
Tel: (33) 1 49 83 21 12
Fax: (33) 1 49 83 31 95
Contact: Rémi Amar
Television and radio archive; research into new technology; research and publications about broadcasting; production of over 130 first works for television and 15 major series and collections. INA initiates major documentaries and cultural series involving partners from Europe and the rest of the world

National Federation of Technical Industries for Film and Television (FITCA)
50 avenue Marceau
75008 Paris
Tel: (33) 1 47 23 75 76
Fax: (33) 1 47 23 70 47
Contact: Jean Fleurent-Didier
A federation of technical trade associations which acts as intermediary between its members and their market. Maintains a database on all technical aspects of production, and helps French and European companies find suitable partners for research and development or commercial ventures

TF1
1 Quai du Point du Jour
92656 Boulogne
Tel: (33) 1 41 41 12 34
Fax: (33) 1 41 41 29 10
Contact: Jean-Pierre Morel
Privatised national television channel

GERMANY

ARD (Arbeitsgemeinschaft der öffentlich-rechtlichen Rundfunkanstalten der Bundesrepublik Deutschland)
Programme directorate of Deutsches Fernsehen
Arnulfstrasse 42
Postfach 20 06 22
8000 Munich 2
Tel: (49) 89 5900 01
Fax: (49) 89 5900 3249
Director: Dr Günter Struve
One of the two public service broadcasters in Germany, consisting of 13 independent broadcasting corporations

BVDFP (Bundesverband Deutscher Fernsehproduzenten)
Widenmayerstrasse 32
8000 Munich 22
Tel: (49) 89 22 35 35
Fax: (49) 89 228 55 62
Contact: Councillor Dr Johannes Kreile
Trade association for independent television producers

Bundesministerium des Innern (Federal Ministry of the Interior)
Postfach 170290
5300 Bonn 1
Tel: (49) 228 681 5566/ 5569
Fax: (49) 228 681 4665
Contacts: Detlef Flotho, Rainer Novak
Awards prizes, grants funds for the production and distribution of German feature films, short films, films for children and young people and documentaries. Promotes film institutes, festivals and specific events. Supervisory body of national archives for national film production

Deutsches Filmmuseum
Schaumainkai 41
60596 Frankfurt/Main
Tel: (49) 69 21 23 33 69
Fax: (49) 69 21 23 78 81
Contact: Walter Schobert
Incorporates the Komunales Kino, the municipally administered cinémathèque. Permanent and temporary exhibitions. It also has a film archive; equipment, documentation, stills, posters and designs, music and sound collections; a library and a videothèque

Deutsches Institut für Filmkunde
Schaumainkai 41
60596 Frankfurt/Main
Tel: (49) 69 617 045
Fax: (49) 69 620 060
Contact: Gerd Albrecht
The German Institute for Film Studies is a non-profit making organisation and its remit includes amassing culturally significant films and publications and documents about film; to catalogue them and make them available for study and research. It also supports and puts on screenings of scientific, cultural and art films

FFA (Filmförderungsanstalt)
Budapester Strasse 41
10787 Berlin
Tel: (49) 30 25 40 90 0
Fax: (49) 30 262 89 76
Contact: Kirsten Niehuus
Federal Film Fund of Germany, subsidising national projects in film production and the film industry generally. Based on the FFG (Law for German film funding), its tasks are to promote the quality of German films and to improve the economic structures of the film industry. The FFA subsidises script development, the production of features, documentaries and short films for the cinema. Other tasks include assistance for distribution, modernisation of cinemas, continuing education for film professionals etc

FSK (Freiwillige Selbstkontrolle der Filmwirtschaft)
Kreuzberger Ring 56
6200 Wiesbaden-Erbenheim
Tel: (49) 611 77 891 0
Fax: (49) 611 77 891 39
Film industry voluntary self-regulatory body

Film Fonds Hamburg
Friedensallee 14-16
2000 Hamburg 50
Tel: (49) 40 390 5883
Fax: (49) 40 390 4424
Contacts: Eva Hubert, Michael Eckelt
Facility aimed at promoting full-length 35mm theatrical film productions. It provides advice on film financing and on shooting in Hamburg. In conjunction with other film and media institutions, the Film Fonds is also responsible for the organisation of the co-production conference ECCO. It also provides subsidy and financial support (see Funding). Other regional offices around Germany offer similar facilities

Focus Germany
Senatsverwaltung für Kulturelle Angelegenheiten

Location Berlin
Europa-Center
10789 Berlin
Tel: (49) 30 2123 3339
Fax: (49) 30 2123 3288
Focus Germany has four offices in various parts of Germany: Hamburg, Berlin, Potsdam and Düsseldorf. It offers information and contacts on development, co-production, locations and subsidies

ZDF (Zweites Deutsches Fernsehen)

ZDF-Strasse
PO Box 4040
6500 Mainz 1
Tel: (49) 61 31 70-1
Fax: (49) 61 31 702 157
Contact: Prof. Dieter Stolte
Germany's largest single public service broadcaster

GREECE

ERT SA (Greek Radio Television)

Messoghion 402
153 42 Aghia Paraskevi
Athens
Tel: (30) 1 639 0772
Fax: (30) 1 639 0652
Contact: Evi Demiri
National public TV and radio broadcaster, for information, education and entertainment

Greek Film Centre

10 Panepistimiou Avenue
10671 Athens
Tel: (30) 1 361 7633/363 4586
Fax: (30) 1 361 4336
Contact: Voula Georgakakou
Governmental organisation under the auspices of the Ministry of Culture. Grants subsidies for production and promotion

Ministry of Culture

Cinema Department
14 Aristidou Street
Athens 10559
Tel: (30) 1 322 4737

IRELAND

An Chomhairle Ealáion/The Arts Council

70 Merrion Square
Dublin 2
Tel: (353) 1 611840
Fax: (353) 1 761302
Contact: Film Officer
Statutory body for the promotion of the arts. An Chomhairle Ealáion/The Arts Council funds the Irish Film Centre, Film Base, Federation of Irish Film Societies, Dublin and Cork Film Festivals etc. Also provides Ir£100,000 per annum for film and video awards

Bord Scannán na hÉireann/Irish Film Board

The Halls
Quay Street
Galway
Tel: (353) 91 61398
Fax: (353) 91 61405
Chief Executive: Rod Stoneman
Submissions Manager: James Flynn
Bord Scannán na hÉireann promotes the creative and commercial elements of Irish filmmaking and film culture for a home and international audience. Each year it supports a number of film projects in development and production by way of debt/equity. Normally two submission deadlines annually. Dates and application procedures available from the office

Film Censor's Office

16 Harcourt Terrace
Dublin 2
Tel: (353) 1 676 1985
Fax: (353) 1 676 1898
Contact: Sheamus Smith
The Official Film Censor is appointed by the Irish Government to consider and classify all feature films and videos distributed in Ireland

Film Institute of Ireland

Irish Film Centre
6 Eustace Street
Temple Bar
Dublin 2
Tel: (353) 1 679 5744
Fax: (353) 1 677 8755
Contacts: David Kavanagh, Mary Scally
The Film Institute promotes film culture through a wide range of activities in film exhibition and distribution, film/media education, various training programmes and the Irish Film Archive. Its premises, the Irish Film Centre in Temple Bar, are also home to Film Base, MEDIA Desk, The Junior Dublin Film Festival, The Federation of Irish Film Societies, Scriptcraft and Espace Vidéo Européen. The Building has conference facilities, a bar, a restaurant and a bookshop as well as two cinemas seating 260 and 115 respectively

RTE (Radio Telefis Eireann)

Donnybrook
Dublin 4
Tel: (353) 1 643 111
Fax: (353) 1 643 082
Contact: Joe Barry
Ireland's public service broadcaster

ITALY

ANICA (Associazione Nazionale Industrie Cinematografiche e Audiovisive)

Viale Regina Margherita 286
00198 Rome
Tel: (39) 6 884 1271
Fax: (39) 6 440 4128/884 8789
Contact: Gino de Dominicis
Trade association for TV and movie producers and distributors, representing technical industries (post-production companies/ dubbing/studios/labs); home video producers and distributors; TV and radio broadcasters

Cineteca Italiana

Via Palestro 16
20121 Milan
Tel: (39) 2 799 224
Contact: Gianni Comencini
Film archive, film museum

Centro Sperimentale di Cinematografia Cineteca Nazionale

Via Tuscolana 1524
00173 Rome
Tel: (39) 6 722 941
Fax: (39) 6 721 1619

Fininvest Television

Palazzo dei Cigni
20090 Segrate Milan
Tel: (39) 2 210 2
Fax: (39) 2 210 22939
Contact: Adriano Galliano
Major competitor to RAI, running television channels Canale 5, Italia Uno and Rete Quattro

Istituto Luce

Italnoleggio Cinematografico
Via Tuscolana 1055
00173 Rome
Tel: (39) 6 722 2492
Fax: (39) 6 722 2493
Contacts: Giuseppe Sangiorgi, Beppe Attene, Patrizia de Cesari
Created to spread culture and education through cinema. It invests in film, distributes films of cultural interest and holds Italy's largest archive

Museo Nazionale del Cinema

Palazzo Chiablese
Piazza San Giovanni 2
10122 Turin
Tel: (39) 11 436 1365/436 1148
Fax: (39) 11 521 2341
Contacts: Roberto Morano, Paolo Bertetto, Sergio Toffetti
The museum represents photography, pre-cinema and cinema history. Its collections include films, books and periodicals, posters, photographs and cinema ephemera

RAI (Radiotelevisione Italiana)

Viale Mazzini 14
00195 Rome
Tel: (39) 6 361 3608
Fax: (39) 6 323 1010
Contact: Gianni Pasquarelli
Italian state broadcaster

LUXEMBOURG

Cinémathèque Municipale – Ville de Luxembourg

Rue de la Chapelle 19
1325 Luxembourg
Tel: (352) 4796 2644
Fax: (352) 45 93 75
Contact: Fred Junck
Official Luxembourg film

archive. Holds 2 screenings daily per weekday, every year 'Live Cinema' performances – silent films with music. Member of FIAF

CLT Multi Media

45 Bld Pierre Frieden
1543 Luxembourg
Tel: (352) 42 1 42 2170
Fax: (352) 42 1 42 2760
Contact: Karin Schintgen
Radio, TV; production/distribution; press/publishing

THE NETHERLANDS

Ministry of Welfare, Health and Cultural Affairs (WVC)

PO Box 3009
2280 HK Rijswijk
Tel: (31) 70 340 6764/6150
Fax: (31) 70 340 5742
Contacts: Gamila Ylstra, Séamus Cassidy
The film department of the Ministry is responsible for the development and maintenance of Dutch film policy. Various different organisations for production, distribution, promotion and conservation of film are subsidised by this department

Nederlandse Omroepprogramma Stichting (NOS)

Postbus 26444
1202 JJ Hilversum
Tel: (31) 35 779 222
Fax: (31) 35 773 568
Contact: Louis Heinsman
Public corporation responsible for co-ordinating three-channel public television

Netherlands Filmmuseum

Vondelpark 3
1071 AA Amsterdam
Tel: (31) 20 589 1400
Fax: (31) 20 683 3401
Contact: Hoos Blotkamp
Film museum with three public screenings each day, permanent and temporary exhibitions, library, film-cafe and film distribution

Onafhankelijke Televisie Producenten (OTP)

Tielweg 6
PO Box 2174
2800 BH Gouda
Tel: (31) 1820 71422
Fax: (31) 1820 71533
Contact: Andries Overste
Trade association for independent television producers (currently thirteen members)

PORTUGAL

Cinemateca Portuguesa

Rua Barata Salgueiro 39
1200 Lisbon
Tel: (351) 1 54 62 79
Fax: (351) 1 352 3180
Contact: João Bénard da Costa, Ana Costa e Almeida, José Manuel Costa
National film archive, preserving, restoring and showing films. Includes a public documentation centre, a stills and posters archive and a small museum

IPC (Instituto Portugues de Cinema)

Rua S Pedro de Alcântara 45-1º
1200 Lisbon
Tel: (351) 1 346 66 34
Fax: (351) 1 347 27 77
Contact: Eduarda Ribeiro Rosa
Governmental organisation; supports production and exhibition and helps promotion and distribution of Portuguese films abroad. Negotiates national and international agreements connected with film

RTP (Radiotelevisão Portuguesa)

Avenida 5 de Outubro 197
1094 Lisbon Cedex
Tel: (351) 1 793 1774
Fax: (351) 1 793 1758
Contact: Maria Manuela Furtado
State-owned public television service, now also broadcasting to other countries by satellite

Secretariado Nacional para o Audiovisual (SNA)

Praga Francisco Sá
Garneiro 11-2º E
1000 Lisbon
Tel: (351) 1 848 4491/6095
Fax: (351) 1 808 170
Contact: Zita Searra
SNA has two aims: the definition of a coherent global audiovisual policy and a coordinated and integrated policy to increase the value of Portuguese culture and language

SPAIN

Academia de las Artes y de las Ciencias Cinematográficas de España

General Oraá 68
28006 Madrid
Tel: (34) 1 563 33 41
Fax: (34) 1 563 26 93
Contact: Antonio Giménez-Rico

Filmoteca Española

Carretera de la Dehesa de la Villa s/n
28040 Madrid
Tel: (34) 1 549 00 11
Fax: (34) 1 549 73 48
Spanish national archive recognised by FIAF, with a Library and a Stills Department

ICAA (Instituto de la Cinematografia y de las Artes Audiovisuales)

Ministerio de Cultura
Plaza del Rey Nº1
28071 Madrid
Tel: (34) 1 532 74 39
Fax: (34) 1 531 92 12
Contact: Juan Miguel Lamet Martinez
The promotion, protection and diffusion of cinema and audiovisual activities in production, distribution and exhibition. Gives financial support in these areas to Spanish companies. Also involved in the promotion of Spanish cinema and audiovisual arts, and their cultural communication between the different communities within Spain

RTVE (Radiotelevisión Española)

Apartado de Correos
Prado del Rey
28023 Madrid 1
Tel: (34) 1 346 4000
Fax: (34) 1 581 7125
National public service broadcaster

PR COMPANIES

These are companies which handle all aspects of promotion and publicity for film and video production companies and/or individual productions

The Associates
34 Clerkenwell Close
London EC1R 0AU
Tel: 071 608 2204
Fax: 071 250 1756
Amanda Evans

Tony Brainsby PR
16b Edith Grove
London SW10 0NL
Tel: 071 834 8341
Fax: 071 352 9451
Tony Brainsby

Byron Advertising, Marketing and PR
Byron House
Wallingford Road
Uxbridge
Middx UB8 2RW
Tel: 0895 252131
Fax: 0895 252137
Les Barnes

CJP Public Relations
29 Chippenham Mews
London W9 2AN
Tel: 071 266 0167
Fax: 071 266 0165
Carolyn Jardine

Cantor Wise Publicity
2 Reynolds Close
London NW11 7EA
Tel: 081 905 5250
Fax: 081 905 5383
Melanie Cantor

Jacquie Capri Enterprises
c/o Floreat Productions
46 St James's Place
London SW1A 1MS
Tel: 071 499 1996
Fax: 071 499 6727

Max Clifford Associates
109 New Bond Street
London W1Y 9AA
Tel: 071 408 2350
Fax: 071 409 2294
Max Clifford

Corbett and Keene
122 Wardour Street
London W1V 3LA
Tel: 071 494 3478
Fax: 071 734 2024
Ginger Corbett
Sara Keene

Dennis Davidson Associates
Royalty House
72-74 Dean Street
London W1V 5HB
Tel: 071 439 6391
Fax: 071 437 6358
Dennis Davidson
Dennis Michael

Edelman Public Relations Worldwide
Kingsgate House
536 Kings Road
London SW10 0TE
Tel: 071 835 1222
Fax: 071 351 7676
Rosemary Brooks

Clifford Elson (Publicity)
223 Regent Street
London W1R 7DB
Tel: 071 495 4012
Fax: 071 495 4175
Clifford Elson
Patricia Lake-Smith

FEREF Associates
14-17 Wells Mews
London W1A 1ET
Tel: 071 580 6546
Fax: 071 631 3156
Peter Andrews
Ken Paul
Robin Behling
David Kemp

Soren Fischer Associates
37 Ollgar Close
London W12 0NF
Tel: 081 740 9059/0202 393033
Fax: 0202 301516
Soren Fischer

Foresight Promotions
4 Albion Court
Galena Road
London W6 0QT
Tel: 081 748 3550
Fax: 081 741 8461
Tim Smith

Lynne Franks PR
327-329 Harrow Road
London W9 3RB
Tel: 071 724 6777
Fax: 071 724 8484
Julian Henry

Good Relations
59 Russell Square
London WC1B 4HJ
Tel: 071 631 3434
Fax: 071 631 1399
Jeffrey Lyes

Christiana Gruber
32 Anselm Road
London SW6 1LJ
Christiana Gruber

Ray Hodges Communications
Unit 6 Kings Grove
Maidenhead
Berks SL6 4DX
Tel: 0628 75171
Fax: 0628 781301
Maureen Ward

Sue Hyman Associates
70 Chalk Farm Road
London NW1 8AN
Tel: 071 485 8489/5842
Fax: 071 267 4715
Sue Hyman

JAC Publicity
Hammer House
113 Wardour Street
London W1V 3TD
Tel: 071 734 6965
Fax: 071 439 1400
Claire Forbes

Richard Laver Publicity
3 Troy Court
Kensington High Street
London W8 7RA
Tel: 071 937 7322
Fax: 071 937 8670
Richard Laver

Lay & Partners
Citybridge House
235-245 Goswell Road
London EC1V 7JD
Tel: 071 837 1475
Fax: 071 833 4615
Nick Oldham

Limelight Public Relations
9 Coptic Street
London WC1A 1NH
Tel: 071 436 6949
Fax: 071 323 6791
Fiona Lindsay
Linda Shanks

Mathieu Thomas
8 Westminster Palace Gardens
Artillery Row
London SW1P 1RL
Tel: 071 222 0833
Fax: 071 222 5784
Paul Mathieu
Amanda Slayton

Optimum Communications
38 Bedford Square
London WC1B 3EG
Tel: 071 436 6681
Fax: 071 436 1694
Nigel Passingham

Porter Frith Publicity & Marketing
26 Danbury Street
London N1 8JU
Tel: 071 359 3734
Fax: 071 226 5897
Sue Porter
Liz Frith

Premier Relations
1 Meadway
Leatherhead
Surrey KT22 0LZ
Tel: 0372 842446
Fax: 0372 843819
Victoria Franklin

Riley Associates
19 Cambridge Gate Mews
Regent's Park
London NW1 4ED
Tel: 071 486 1097
Fax: 071 734 5411
Tony Riley

Rogers & Cowan/PSA
43 King Street
Covent Garden
London WC2E 8RJ
Tel: 071 411 3000
Fax: 071 411 3020
Philip Symes

Stone Hallinan McDonald
100 Ebury Street
London SW1W 9QD
Tel: 071 730 9009
Fax: 071 730 7492
Charles McDonald

Judy Tarlo
125 Old Brompton Road
London SW7 3RP
Tel: 071 835 1000
Fax: 071 373 0265
A division of Media Relations

Peter Thompson Associates
134 Great Portland Street
London W1N 5PH
Tel: 071 436 5991/2
Fax: 071 436 0509
Peter Thompson
Amanda Malpass

Town House Publicity
45 Islington Park Street
London N1 1QB
Tel: 071 226 7450
Fax: 071 359 6026
Mary Fulton

Stella Wilson Publicity
130 Calabria Road
London N5 1HT
Tel: 071 354 5672
Fax: 071 354 2242
Stella Wilson

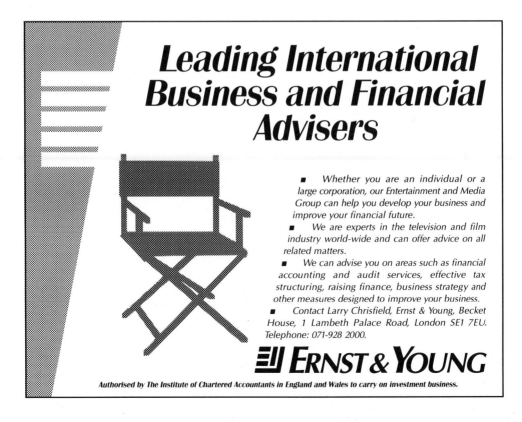

Winsor Beck Public Relations
Network House
29-39 Stirling Road
London W3 8DJ
Tel: 081 993 7506
Fax: 081 993 8276
Geri Winsor

PRESS CONTACTS

Below are magazine and newspaper critics and journalists who write about film, TV and video. Circulation figures may have altered since going to press. Also listed are the news and photo agencies which handle media news syndication, and TV and radio programmes concerned with the visual media

Animator (2pa)
Filmcraft Publications
13 Ringway Road
Park Street
St Albans AL2 2RE
Tel: 0727 872607
David Jefferson
Magazine for professional and non-professional animators
Lead time: 1 month
Circulation: 3,000

Arena (bi-monthly)
Third Floor, Block A
Exmouth House
Pine Street
London EC1R 0JL
Tel: 071 837 7270
Fax: 071 837 3906
Film/TV Editor: Peter Browne
Magazine for men covering general interest, film, literature, music and fashion
Lead time: 4 weeks
Circulation: 69,000

Ariel (weekly, Tues)
Room 5360
BBC White City
201 Wood Lane
London W12 7TS
Tel: 081 752 4762
Fax: 081 752 4768
Editor: Robin Reynolds
BBC staff magazine, with news as it relates to BBC staff
Lead time: Tuesday before publication
Circulation: 41,000

Art Monthly
Suite 17
26 Charing Cross Road
London WC2H 0DG
Tel/Fax: 071 240 0389
Patricia Bickers
Aimed at artists, art dealers, teachers, students, collectors, arts administrators, and all those interested in contemporary visual art
Lead time: 4 weeks
Circulation: 4,000

Artrage (monthly)
c/o MAAS
28 Shacklewell Lane
London E8 2EZ
Tel: 071 254 7295
Fax: 071 923 4465
Editor: Jacob Ross
Lifestyle, entertainments, listings magazine dealing with the arts
Lead time: 10th of preceding month
Circulation: 10,000

Asian Times
(weekly, Tues)
139-149 Fonthill Road
London N4 3HF
Tel: 071 281 1191
Fax: 071 263 9656
Editor: Arif Ali
Tabloid dealing with issues pertinent to community it serves
Press day: Thurs
Circulation: 17,500

The Big Issue
(weekly, Tues)
3-4 Albion Place
Galena Road
London W6 0LT
Tel: 081 741 8090
Fax: 081 741 2951
Editor: John Bird
Film: Davydd Chong
"Helping the homeless help themselves"
Lead time: Thurs, 2 weeks before
Circulation: 110,000

Bite (monthly)
423-425 Caledonian Road
London N7 9BQ
Tel: 071 607 7253
Fax: 071 700 6539
Film: Colette Maude
Monthly women's magazine, upbeat for the woman of today
Lead time: 6 weeks

Broadcast (weekly, Fri)
EMAP Media
33-39 Bowling Green Lane
Tel: 071 837 1212
Fax: 071 837 8326
Publisher: Jonathan Hallett
Editor: Peter Law
Broadcasting industry news magazine with coverage of TV, radio, cable and satellite, corporate production and international programming and distribution
Press day: Wed
Lead time: 2 weeks
Circulation: 10,400

The Business of Film (monthly)
24 Charlotte Street
London W1P 1HJ
Tel: 071 580 0141
Fax: 071 255 1264
Publisher/executive editor: Elspeth Tavares
Editor: Michael Goodridge
Aimed at film industry professionals – producers, distributors, exhibitors, investors, financiers
Lead time: 2 weeks

Capital Gay
(weekly, Fri)
Unit 58-60
49 Effra Road
London SW2 1BZ
Tel: 071 738 7010
Fax: 071 924 9174
Film/TV Editor: Nancy Lamont
Newspaper for lesbians and gay men in the South East combining news, features, arts and entertainment, what's on guide
Lead time: 1 week (Mon)
Circulation: 20,000

Caribbean Times incorporating African Times
(weekly, Tues)
139-149 Fonthill Road
London N4 3HF
Tel: 071 281 1191
Fax: 071 263 9656
Editor: Arif Ali
Tabloid dealing with issues pertinent to community it serves

Press day: Thurs
Circulation: 25,000

City Life (fortnightly)
164 Deansgate
Manchester M60 2RD
Tel: 061 839 1310
Fax: 061 839 1488
Editor: Mike Hill
Film Editor: Mike Barnett
What's on in and around Greater Manchester
Circulation: 15-18,000

Company (monthly)
National Magazine House
72 Broadwick Street
London W1V 2BP
Tel: 071 439 5372
Fax: 071 439 5117
Assistant editor: Sarah Kennedy
Glossy magazine for women aged 18-30
Lead time: 10 weeks
Circulation: 250,550

Cosmopolitan (monthly)
National Magazine House
72 Broadwick Street
London W1V 2BP
Tel: 071 439 7144
Fax: 071 439 5016
Film: Derek Malcolm
Arts/General: Vanessa Raphaely
For women aged 18-35
Lead time: 12 weeks
Circulation: 478,000

Creative Review (monthly)
50 Poland Street
London W1V 4AX
Tel: 071 439 4222
Fax: 071 734 6748
Editor: Lewis Blackwell
Deputy editor: Fay Sweet
Publisher: Annie Swift
Trade paper for creative people covering film, advertising and design. Film reviews, profiles and technical features
Lead time: 4 weeks
Circulation: 20,000

Daily Express
Ludgate House
72 London Road
London SE1 9UX
Tel: 071 928 8000
Fax: 071 922 7970
Showbusiness editor: David Wigg
Film critic: Rachel Simpson
Showbiz/TV writers: Louise Gannon, Paul Thompson
National daily newspaper
Circulation: 1,700,000

Daily Mail
Northcliffe House
2 Derry Street
London W8 5TT
Tel: 071 938 6000
Fax: 071 937 3745
Chief Showbusiness Writer: Baz Bamigboye
Showbusiness: Corinna Honan
Film: Christopher Tookey
TV: Peter Paterson
National daily newspaper
Circulation: 1,700,000

Daily Mirror
Holborn Circus
London EC1P 1DQ
Tel: 071 353 0246
TV: Simon London
National daily newspaper
Circulation: 3,570,000 incorporating The Daily Record (Scottish daily newspaper)

The Daily Star
Ludgate House
245 Blackfriars Road
London SE1 9UX
Tel: 071 928 8000
Fax: 071 922 7962
Film: Pat Codd
TV: Ollie Wilson
Video: Julia Westlake
National daily newspaper
Circulation: 766,002

Daily Telegraph
1 Canada Square
Canary Wharf
London E14 5DT
Tel: 071 538 5000
Fax: 071 538 6242
Arts: Nigel Reynolds
Film critic: Hugo Davenport
TV: Penny McDonald
National daily newspaper
Circulation: 1,039,000

The Economist (weekly, Thur)
25 St James's Street
London SW1A 1HG
Tel: 071 839 7000
Film/video/TV (cultural): Tony Thomas
Film/video/TV (business): John Heilemann
International coverage of major political, social and business developments with arts section
Press day: Wed
Circulation: 510,000

Elle (monthly)
20 Orange Street
London WC2H 7ED
Tel: 071 957 8383
Fax: 071 957 8400
Features researcher: Vicky Reid
Glossy magazine aimed at 18-35 year old working women
Lead time: 3 months
Circulation: 200,000

Empire (monthly)
Mappin House
4 Winsley Street
London W1N 4AR
Tel: 071 436 1515
Fax: 071 637 7031
Editor: Philip Thomas
Quality film monthly incorporating features, interviews and movie news as well as reviews of all new movies and videos
Lead time: 3 weeks
Circulation: 107,924

The European (weekly, Thurs)
Orbit House
5 New Fetter Lane
London EC4A 1AP
Tel: 071 822 2002
Fax: 071 377 4773
Arts editor: Sebastian O'Kelly
In-depth coverage of European news, politics and culture
Press day: Tues
Circulation: 167,457

Evening Standard (Mon-Fri)
Northcliffe House
2 Derry Street
London W8 5EE
Tel: 071 938 7531
Fax: 071 937 3193
Film: Alexander Walker
TV: Nicholas Hellen
London weekday evening newspaper
Circulation: 540,000

Everywoman (monthly)
34a Islington Green
London N1 8DU
Tel: 071 359 5496
Editor: Barbara Rogers
Arts editor: Barbara Norden
A current affairs magazine for women
Lead time: 6 weeks
Circulation: 15,000

FHM (monthly)
9-11 Curtain Road
London EC2A 3LT
Tel: 071 247 5447
Fax: 071 247 5892
Editor: Francis Cottam
Deputy Editor: Andrew Anthony
Fashion and features magazine for men
Lead time: 6 weeks
Circulation: 58,000

The Face (monthly)
Third Floor Block A
Exmouth House
Pine Street
London EC1R 0JL
Tel: 071 837 7270
Fax: 071 837 3906
Film/TV: Sheryl Garratt, Amy Raphael, Richard Benson
Visual-orientated youth culture magazine: emphasis on music, fashion and films
Lead time: 4 weeks
Circulation: 89,517

Fact (monthly)
Producers Alliance for Cinema and Television
Gordon House
Greencoat Place
London SW1P 1PH
Tel: 071 233 6000
Fax: 071 233 8935
Editor: John Murray
PACT members monthly

bfi **Film** (bi-monthly)
British Federation of Film Societies
Film Society Unit
BFI
21 Stephen Street
London W1P 1PL
Tel: 071 255 1444
Fax: 071 255 2315
Thematically based journal with information for Film Societies and other film exhibitors

Film Dope (irregular – 3 a year)
74 Julian Road
Nottingham NG2 5AN
Fax: 0602 822594
Derek Owen
Mainly an A-Z of international film personalities but also includes some long interviews
Circulation: 1,000

Film Review (monthly + 4 specials)
Visual Imagination
9 Blades Court
Deodar Road
London SW15 2NU
Tel: 081 875 1520
Fax: 081 875 1588
Reviews of films on cinema screen and video; star interviews and profiles; book reviews
Lead time: 1 month
Circulation: 50,000

Financial Times
1 Southwark Bridge
London SE1 9HL

Tel: 071 873 3000
Fax: 071 873 3076
Arts: J D F Jones
Film: Nigel Andrews
TV: Christopher Dunkley
National daily newspaper
Circulation: 290,134

Flicks (monthly)
2 Filmer Studios
75 Filmer Road
London SW6 7JF
Tel: 071 384 1818
Fax: 071 371 7573
Managing editor: Val Lyon
Magazine of the film industry, free to cinema goers throughout the country, or by subscription
Lead time: 6 weeks
Circulation: 423,383

Gay Times (monthly)
Ground Floor
Worldwide House
116-134 Bayham Street
London NW1 0BA
Tel: 071 482 2576
Fax: 071 284 0329
Film critics: Paul Burston, Rose Collis
TV: David Smith
Britain's leading Gay magazine. Regular film and television coverage
Lead time: 6 weeks
Circulation: 37,500

The Guardian
119 Farringdon Road
London EC1R 3ER
Tel: 071 278 2332
Fax: 071 837 2114
Arts: Ian Mayes
Film: Derek Malcolm
TV: Nancy Banks-Smith
Media editor: Georgina Henry
PR manager: Camilla Nicholls
Weekend Editor: Roger Alton
National daily newspaper
Circulation: 428,000

Harpers & Queen
(monthly)
National Magazine House
72 Broadwick Street
London W1V 2BP
Tel: 071 439 7144
Fax: 071 439 5506
Arts editor: Rupert Christiansen
Film critics: Andrew Motion, Hugo Williams
Glossy magazine for women
Lead time: 12 weeks
Circulation: 86,000

The Herald
195 Albion Street
Glasgow G1 1QP
Tel: 071 738 8000
Fax: 071 738 8159
Film critic: William Russell
TV editor: Ken Wright
Scottish daily newspaper
Circulation: 120,468

The Hollywood Reporter
(daily; weekly international, Tues)
23 Ridgmount Street
London WC1E 7AH
Tel: 071 323 6686
Fax: 071 323 2314/16
European bureau chief: Louise McElvogue
European news editor: Edwin Riddell
Showbusiness trade paper

i-D Magazine
(monthly)
5th Floor
44 Earlham Street
London WC2H 9LA
Tel: 071 240 3282
Fax: 071 240 3250
Film/TV: Matthew Collin
Youth/fashion magazine with film features
Lead time: 8 weeks
Circulation: 40,000

Illustrated London News (6 issues a year)
20 Upper Ground
London SE1 9PP
Tel: 071 928 2111
Fax: 071 620 1594
Editor: James Bishop
Film listings: George Perry
News, pictorial record and commentary, and a guide to coming events
Lead time: 8-10 weeks
Circulation: 53,970

In Camera (quarterly)
Kodak Ltd
Motion Picture and TV Imaging
PO Box 66
Hemel Hempstead
Herts HP1 1LU
Tel: 0442 61122
Fax: 0442 844458
Editor: Josephine Ober
Business editor: Lindsay Dack
Journal for motion picture industry, primarily for camera operators, but also for other technicians and anyone in the industry
Lead time: 4 weeks
Circulation: 21,000

The Independent
40 City Road
London EC1Y 2DB
Tel: 071 253 1222
Fax: 071 956 1894
Film: Sheila Johnston
TV: John Lyttle
National daily newspaper
Circulation: 372,152

The Independent on Sunday
40 City Road
London EC1Y 2DB
Tel: 071 253 1222
Fax: 071 956 1469 (features)
Film critic: Quentin Curtis
National Sunday newspaper
Lead time: 1-2 weeks
Circulation: 370,000

Interzone (monthly)
217 Preston Drive
Brighton BN1 6FL
Tel: 0273 504710
Film: Nick Lowe
TV: Wendy Bradley
Science-fiction magazine
Lead time: 8 weeks
Circulation: 10,000

Jazz Express
(monthly)
29 Romilly Street
London W1V 6HP
Tel: 071 437 6437
Fax: 071 434 1214
Film: Stephen Bourne
TV: Nicholas Meade
Music magazine with strong jazz bias, featuring other forms of culture, such as film and fashion
Lead time: 2 weeks
Circulation: 10,000

Jewish Chronicle
(weekly, Fri)
25 Furnival Street
London EC4A 1JT
Tel: 071 405 9252
Fax: 071 405 9040
Editor: Edward J Temko
Film critic: Pamela Melnikoff
Arts editor: David Sonin
Press day: Wed
Circulation: 50,000

The List
(fortnightly, Thur)
14 High Street
Edinburgh EH1 1TE
Tel: 031 558 1191
Fax: 031 557 8500
Editor: Robin Hodge
Film editor: Alan Morrison
TV: Tom Lappin
Glasgow and Edinburgh events guide
Lead time: 1 week
Circulation: 12,000

Mail on Sunday
Northcliffe House
2 Derry Street
London W8 5TS
Tel: 071 938 6000
Fax: 071 937 3745
Film critic: Tom Hutchinson
Media correspondent: Paul Nathanson
National Sunday newspaper
Press day: Fri/Sat
Circulation: 1,942,331

Marie Claire
(monthly)
2 Hatfields
London SE1 9PG
Tel: 071 261 5240
Fax: 071 261 5277
Film: Anthony Quinn
Women's magazine
Lead time: 3 months
Circulation: 310,000

Media Week
(weekly, Thur)
33-39 Bowling Green Lane
London EC1R 0DA
Tel: 071 837 1212
Fax: 071 837 3285
Editor: Richard Gold
Broadcast Editor: Steven Armstrong
News magazine aimed at the advertising and media industries
Press day: Wed
Circulation: 18,700

Melody Maker
(weekly, Tues)
King's Reach Tower
Stamford Street
London SE1 9LF
Tel: 071 261 5502
Fax: 071 261 6706
Film: Alan Jones, Simon Price
Pop/rock music newspaper
Press day: Fri
Circulation: 70,000

Midweek
(weekly, Thur)
7-9 Rathbone Street
London W1P 1AF
Tel: 071 636 6651
Fax: 071 872 0806
Film editor: Derek Malcolm
General interest male/female London living and arts oriented. 18-35 target age readership
Leadtime: 2 weeks
Circulation: 124,000

The Modern Review
(bi-monthly)
6 Hopgood Street
London W12 7JU
Tel: 081 749 0593/071 278 2994
Fax: 081 749 0593/071 278 4427
Film editor: Toby Young
TV: William Cook
Arts review
Lead time: 4 weeks
Circulation: 30,000

Morning Star
1-3 Ardleigh Road
London N1 4HS
Tel: 071 254 0033
Fax: 071 254 5950
Film: Jeff Sawtell
TV: Jeffrey James
The only national daily owned by its readers as a co-operative. Weekly film and TV reviews
Circulation: 28,000

Moving Pictures International
(weekly, Thur)
1 Richmond Mews
London W1V 5AG
Tel: 071 287 0070
Fax: 071 287 9637
Editor: Kirk Ellis
Worldwide coverage of television, film, video and cable
Press day: Wednesday
Circulation: 9,500

Ms London
(weekly, Mon)
7-9 Rathbone Street
London W1P 1AF
Tel: 071 636 6651
Fax: 071 872 0805
Free magazine with drama, video, film and general arts section
Press day: Fri
Circulation: 125,000

19 (monthly)
IPC Magazines
King's Reach Tower
London SE1 9LS
Tel: 071 261 6360
Fax: 071 261 7634
Film/Arts: Verity Watkins
Magazine for young women
Lead time: 12 weeks
Circulation: 200,000

New Musical Express (weekly, Wed)
25th Floor
King's Reach Tower
Stamford Street
London SE1 9LS
Tel: 071 261 5000
Fax: 071 261 5185
Film/TV: Gavin Martin
Rock music newspaper
Press day: Mon
Circulation: 121,001

New Scientist
(weekly, Sat, avail Thur)
King's Reach Tower
Stamford Street
London SE1 9LS
Tel: 071 261 5000
Fax: 071 261 6464
Editor: Alun Anderson
Audio-visual: Barry Fox
Contains articles and reports on the progress of science and technology in terms which the non-specialist can understand
Press day: Mon
Circulation: 103,000

The New Scriptwriter (bi-monthly)
111 Queens Crescent
London NW5 4EX
Tel: 071 485 5199
Tel/Fax: 071 482 4030
Editor: Randal Flynn
For people trying to break into business, with info on movie business, scriptwriting and directing. By subscription
Lead time: 3 weeks

News of the World
(weekly, Sun)
News International
1 Virginia Street
London E1 9XR
Tel: 071 782 4000
Editor: Pat Chapman
TV: Charles Catchpole
National Sunday newspaper
Press day: Sat
Circulation: 4,750,000

New Statesman and Society
(weekly, Fri)
Foundation House
Perseverance Works
38 Kingsland Road
London E2 8DQ
Tel: 071 739 3211
Fax: 071 739 9307
Editor: Steve Platt
Arts editor: Boyd Tonkin
Independent radical journal of investigation, revelation, politics and comment
Press day: Mon
Circulation: 26,000

Nine to Five
(weekly, Mon)
4-8 Pear Tree Street
London EC1V 3SB
Tel: 071 454 7800
Fax: 071 608 3035
Film/TV editor: John Symes
Free London magazine
Press day: Wed
Circulation: 125,000

The Observer
(weekly, Sun)
Chelsea Bridge House
Queenstown Road
London SW8 4NN
Tel: 071 627 0700/350 3546
Fax: 071 627 5570
Arts editor: Gillian Widdicombe
Film: Philip French
TV: John Naughton
National Sunday newspaper
Press day: Fri
Circulation: 532,521

Observer Magazine
(weekly, Sun)
Editor: Simon Kelner
Supplement to 'The Observer'

Options (monthly)
King's Reach Tower
Stamford Street
London SE1 9LS
Tel: 071 261 5000
Fax: 071 261 6023
Film: Brian Case
TV: Jane Phillimore
Magazine for women
Lead time: 12 weeks
Circulation: 150,000

The People
(weekly, Sun)
Holborn Circus
London EC1P 1DQ
Tel: 071 353 0246
Fax: 071 822 2193
National Sunday newspaper
Press day: Fri
Circulation: 2,096,000

Picture House
(irregular)
Cinema Theatre Association
5 Coopers Close
Burgess Hill
West Sussex RH15 8AN
Tel: 0444 246893
Documents past and present history of cinema buildings
Lead time: 8 weeks
Circulation, 2,000

The Pink Paper
(weekly, Thur)
77 City Garden Row
London N1 8EZ
Tel: 071 608 2566
Fax: 071 608 2544
Film/TV: James Cary Parkes
Britain's national lesbian and gay newspaper
Leadtime: 14 days
Circulation: 40,000

Premiere (monthly)
Mappin House
4 Winsley Street
London W1N 7AR
Tel: 071 436 1515
Fax: 071 580 6495
Associate editor: John Naughton
An up-market film monthly with an American bias, containing personality features, on the set reports, news and reviews
Leadtime: 2 months
Circulation: 45,000

Q (monthly)
1st Floor
Mappin House
4 Winsley Street
London W1N 7AR
Tel: 071 436 1515
Fax: 071 323 0680
Editor: Danny Kelly
Film/TV editor: John Naughton
Specialist music magazine for 18-45 year olds. Includes reviews of new albums, films and books
Lead time: 14 days
Circulation: 172,000

Radio Times
(weekly, Tues)
Woodlands
80 Wood Lane
London W12 0TT
Tel: 081 576 2000
Features Fax: 081 576 3160
Listings Fax: 081 576 3161/2
Film: Derek Winnert, Barry Norman
Features: Michelle Dickson
Listings: Roger Hughes
Weekly guide to all UK television, BBC Radio and satellite programmes
Circulation: 1,592,741

Scotland on Sunday
20 North Bridge
Edinburgh EH1 1YT
Tel: 031 243 3601
Fax: 031 220 2443
Film editor: Richard Mowe
Film critic: Allan Hunter
TV: Gerard Gilbert
Quality Scottish Sunday

newspaper with colour magazine
Lead time: 6 days
Circulation: 92,000

The Scotsman
20 North Bridge
Edinburgh EH1 1YT
Tel: 031 225 2468
Fax: 031 226 7420
Arts Editor: Allen Wright
Scottish daily newspaper

Screen (quarterly)
(incorporating Screen Education)
The John Logie Baird Centre
University of Glasgow
Glasgow G12 8QQ
Tel: 041 330 5035
Fax: 041 330 8010
Journal of essays on film and television studies

Screen Digest
(monthly)
37 Gower Street
London WC1E 6HH
Tel: 071 580 2842
Fax: 071 580 0060
Editorial chairman: John Chittock
Editor: David Fisher
Executive editor: Ben Keen
Assistant editor: Mark Smith
International industry news digest and research report covering film, TV, cable, satellite, video and other multimedia information. Has a centre page reference system every month on subjects like law, statistics or sales. Now also available on a computer data base via fax at 071 580 0060 under the name Screenfax
Lead time: 10 days

Screenfax (database)
Available on-line via Dialog, Predicasts, Profile or by fax: 071 580 0060. Provides customised print-outs on all screen media subjects with summaries of news developments, market research. See entry under Screen Digest

Screen Finance
(fortnightly)
FT Newsletters
30-31 Great Sutton Street
London EC1V 0DX
Tel: 071 490 8994
Fax: 071 490 1686
Editor: Neil McCartney
Detailed analysis and news coverage of the film and TV industries in the UK and Europe
Lead time: 1 week

Screen International
(weekly, Thur)
EMAP Media
33-39 Bowling Green Lane
London EC1R 0DA
Tel: 071 837 1212
Fax: 071 837 8326
Editor: Oscar Moore
International trade magazine for the film, TV, video, cable and satellite industries. Regular news, features, production information from around the world
Press day: Wed
Features lead time: 3 weeks
Circulation: 10,094

Shivers (bi-monthly)
Visual Imagination
9 Blades Court
Deodar Road
London SW15 2NU
Tel: 081 875 1520
Fax: 081 875 1588
Horror film reviews and features
Editor: Alan Jones
Lead time: 1 month
Circulation: 30,000

bfi **Sight and Sound** (monthly)
British Film Institute
21 Stephen Street
London W1P 1PL
Tel: 071 255 1444
Fax: 071 436 2327
Editor: Philip Dodd
Relaunched in May 1991, incorporating 'Monthly Film Bulletin'. Includes regular columns, feature articles, a book review section and review/synopsis/credits of every feature film theatrically released plus a brief listing of every video
Copy date: 15th of each month
Circulation: 30,000

South Wales Argus
Cardiff Road
Newport
Gwent NP9 1QW
Tel: 0633 810000
Fax: 0633 810195
Film critic: Adrian Ross
Features editor: Lesley Williams
Regional evening newspaper
Lead time: 2 weeks
Circulation: 39,500

The Spectator
(weekly, Thur)
56 Doughty Street
London WC1N 2LL
Tel: 071 405 1706
Fax: 071 242 0603
Arts editor: Jenny Naipaul
Film: Mark Amory
TV: Martyn Harris
Independent review of politics, current affairs, literature and the arts
Press day: Wed
Circulation: 43,500

Stage, Screen and Radio (10 issues a year)
111 Wardour Street
London W1
Tel: 071 437 8506
Fax: 071 437 8268
Editor: Janice Turner
Journal of the film, broadcasting, theatre and leisure union BECTU. Reporting and analysis of these industries and the union's activities plus coverage of technological developments
Lead time: 4 weeks
Circulation: 55,931

Starburst
(monthly + 4 specials)
Visual Imagination
9 Blades Court
Deodar Road
London SW15 2NU
Tel: 081 875 1520
Fax: 081 875 1588
Editor: Stephen Payne
Science fiction, fantasy and horror films, TV and video
Lead time: 1 month
Circulation 40,000

State: The Magazine of the Motion Picture
(bi-monthly)
51 Thatch Leach Lane
Whitefield
Manchester M25 6EN
Tel/Fax: 061 766 2566
Editor: David Bryan
Features Editor: Eddie Murphy
Reviews, profiles and information on the latest cinema and video releases. Also includes star interviews and other movie news all geared towards the film enthusiast
Lead time: 4 weeks
Circulation: 15,000

The Sun
PO Box 481
1 Virginia Street
London E1 9BD
Tel: 071 782 4000
Fax: 071 488 3253
Film critic: Peter Cox
TV: Garry Bushell
National daily newspaper
Circulation: 3,732,175

Sunday Express
Ludgate House
245 Blackfriars Road
London SE1 9UX
Tel: 071 928 8000
Fax: 071 620 1656
Film/Theatre: Clive Hirschhorn
National Sunday newspaper
Circulation: 1,692,487

Sunday Express Magazine
Ludgate House
245 Blackfriars Road
London SE1 9UX
Tel: 071 928 8000
Editor: Jean Carr
Features editor: Maria Trkulja
Supplement to 'Sunday Express' newspaper
Lead time: 6 weeks

Sunday Magazine
1 Virginia Street
London E1 9BD
Tel: 071 782 7000
Fax: 071 782 7474
Editor: Sue Carroll
Features editor: Jonathan Worsnop
Supplement to 'News of the World'
Lead time: 6 weeks

Sunday Mirror
33 Holborn Circus
London EC1P 1DQ
Tel: 071 353 0246
Fax: 071 822 3405
Film critic: Madeleine Harmsworth
TV: Keith Richmond
National Sunday newspaper
Circulation: 2,999,000

Sunday Telegraph
1 Canada Square
Canary Wharf
London E14 5DT
Tel: 071 538 5000
Fax: 071 538 1330
Arts: John McEwen
Film: Christopher Tookey
TV: A.N. Wilson
National Sunday newspaper
Circulation: 580,771

Sunday Times
News International
1 Virginia Street
London E1 9BD
Tel: 071 782 5000
Films editor: George Perry
Film critic: Iain Johnstone
TV reviews: Craig Brown
National Sunday newspaper
Press day: Fri
Circulation: 1,188,373

Sunday Times Magazine
News International
1 Virginia Street
London E1 9BD
Tel: 01 782 7000
Editor: Kate Carr
Films editor: George Perry
Supplement to 'Sunday Times'
Lead time: 6 weeks
Circulation: 1,310,000

TV Quick
(weekly, Mon)
25-27 Camden Road
London NW1 9LL
Tel: 071 284 0909
Film/TV editor: Adrian Turner
Mass market television magazine
Lead time: 3 weeks

TV Times
(weekly, Tues)
10th Floor
King's Reach Tower
Stamford Street
London SE1 9LS
Tel: 071 261 5000
Fax: 071 261 7777
Editor: Terry Pavey
Film editor: David Quinlan
Weekly magazine of listings and features serving viewers of independent TV, BBC TV, satellite and radio
Lead time: 6 weeks
Circulation: 1,113,997

TV Zone
(monthly + 4 specials)
Visual Imagination
9 Blades Court
Deodar Road
London SW15 2NU
Tel: 081 875 1520
Fax: 081 875 1588
Editor: Jan Vincent-Rudzki
Magazine of cult TV
Lead time: 1 month
Circulation: 35,000

Talking Pictures
(quarterly)
52a Lascotts Road
Wood Green
London N22 4JN
Tel: 081 881 7469
Editor: Nigel Watson
A serious look at mainstream cinema
Lead time: 2 months
Circulation: 500

Tatler (monthly)
Vogue House
1 Hanover Square
London W1R 0AD
Tel: 071 499 9080
Fax: 071 409 0451
Film/TV editor: Jessamy Calkin
Smart society magazine favouring profiles, fashion and the arts
Lead time: 12 weeks
Circulation: 73,000

The Teacher
(8 issues a year)
National Union of Teachers
Hamilton House
Mabledon Place
London WC1H 9BD
Tel: 071 388 6191
Fax: 071 387 8458
Editor: Mitch Howard
Circulation: 250,000 mailed direct to all NUT members and to educational institutions

Telegraph Weekend Magazine
Editor: Sarah Cameron
Supplement to Saturday edition of the 'Daily Telegraph'
Lead time: 6 weeks

Television
(8 issues a year)
Royal Television Society
Holborn Hill
100 Gray's Inn Road
London WC1X 8AL
Tel: 071 430 1000
Fax: 071 430 0924
Editor: Peter Fiddick
Deputy editor: Louise Bishop
Assistant editor: Barbara Cormie
Society's TV trade magazine
Lead time: 2 weeks
Circulation: 4,000

Television Today
(weekly, Thur)
47 Bermondsey Street
London SE1 3XT
Tel: 071 403 1818
Fax: 071 403 1418
Editor: Jeremy Jehu
Weekly trade paper constituting the middle section of 'The Stage'

Televisual (monthly)
50 Poland Street
London W1V 4AX
Tel: 071 439 4222
Fax: 071 287 0768
Editor: Mundy Ellis
Monthly business magazine for production professionals in the business of moving pictures
Circulation: 8,900

Time Out
(weekly, Tues)
Tower House
Southampton Street
London WC2E 7HD
Tel: 071 836 4411
Fax: 071 836 7118
Film: Geoff Andrew
Film listings: Wally Hammond
Films on TV: Tom Charity
TV: Alkarim Jivani
London listings magazine with cinema and TV sections
Listings lead time: 8 days
Features lead time: 1 week
Circulation: 99,177

The Times
News International
1 Virginia Street
London E1 9BD
Tel: 071 782 5000
Fax: 071 488 3242
Film/video critic: Geoff Brown
Film writer: David Robinson
Arts (TV): Richard Morrison
Saturday magazine editor: Nicholas Wapshott
National daily newspaper
Circulation: 380,000

The Times Educational Supplement
(weekly, Fri)
Priory House
St John's Lane
London EC1M 4BX
Tel: 071 253 3000
(from Jan 94) 071 782 5000
Fax: 071 608 1599
Arts: Heather Neill
Film critic: Robin Buss
Broadcasting: Sean Coughlan
Press day: Wed
Circulation: 130,000

The Times Educational Supplement Scotland
(weekly, Fri)
37 George Street
Edinburgh EH2 2HN
Tel: 031 220 1100
Fax: 031 220 1616
Editor: Willis Pickard
Press day: Wed

The Times Higher Educational Supplement
(weekly, Fri)
Admiral House
66-68 East Smithfield
London E1 9XW
Tel: 071 253 3000
Fax: 071 490 0827
Arts & Features: Gerard Kelly
Press day: Wed
Lead time for reviews: copy 10 days before publication
Circulation: 17,500

The Times Literary Supplement
(weekly, Fri)
Priory House
St John's Lane
London EC1M 4BX
Tel: 071 253 3000
Fax: 071 251 3424
Arts editor: Giles Foden
Press day: Tues
Circulation: 30,000

Today
News International
1 Virginia Street
London E1 9BS
Tel: 071 782 4600
Film: Sue Heal
TV: Pam Francis
Showbusiness editor: Ivan Waterman
National daily newspaper
Circulation: 545,000

Tribune (weekly, Fri)
308 Gray's Inn Road
London WC1X 8DY
Tel: 071 278 0911
Film/TV editor: Jeff Lovitt
Political and cultural weekly
Lead time: 10 days
Circulation: 10,000

Variety (weekly, Mon)
34-35 Newman Street
London W1P 3PD
Tel: 071 637 3663
Fax: 071 580 5559
European editor: Adam Dawtrey
International showbusiness newspaper
Press day: Fri

Vertigo (quarterly)
7-9 Earlham Street
London WC2H 9LL
Tel: 071 240 2350
Marc Karlin
Critical quarterly for filmmakers and audiences
Circulation: 3,000

Video Home Entertainment
(weekly, Sat)
Strandgate
18-20 York Buildings
London WC2 6JU
Tel: 071 839 7774
Fax: 071 839 4393
Editor: Sean King
Video trade publication for rental and retail
Lead time: Tuesday before publication
Circulation: 9,000

Viewfinder (3pa)
BUFVC
55 Greek Street
London W1V 5LR
Tel: 071 734 3687
Fax: 071 287 3914
Editor: Nick Wray
Periodical for people in higher education and research, includes articles on the production, study and use of film, TV and related media
Deadlines: 10th Jan, Apr, Oct
Circulation: 5,000

Vogue (monthly)
Vogue House
Hanover Square
London W1R 0AD
Tel: 071 499 9080
Fax: 071 493 1345
Editor: Alexandra Shulman
Features: Joanna Jeffreys, Eve MacSweeney
Glossy magazine for women
Lead time: 12 weeks

The Voice (weekly, Tues)
370 Coldharbour Lane
London SW9 8PL
Tel: 071 737 7377
Fax: 071 274 8994
Editor: Winsome Grace Cornish
Film: Deidre Forbes
TV: Winsome Hines
Britain's leading black newspaper with mainly 18-35 age group readership. Regular film, TV and video coverage
Press day: Fri
Circulation: 47,321

Western Mail
Thomson House
Cardiff CF1 1WR
Tel: 0222 583583
Fax: 0222 583652
Film: Mario Basini, Nicole Sochor
TV: Peter Jones
Daily newspaper
Circulation: 77,000

What's On in London (weekly, Tues)
178-186 Pentonville Road
London N1 9LB
Tel: 071 278 4393
Fax: 071 837 5838
Editor: Michael Darvell
London based weekly covering cinema, theatre, music, arts, books, entertainment and video
Press day: Mon
Lead time: 10 days
Circulation: 50,000

What's on TV
(weekly, Tues)
King's Reach Tower
Stamford Street
London SE1 9LS
Tel: 071 261 7769
Fax: 071 261 7739
Film/TV editor: Mike Hollingsworth
TV listings magazine
Lead time: 3 weeks
Circulation: 1,430,000

Yorkshire Post
Wellington Street
Leeds
West Yorkshire LS1 1RF
Tel: 0532 432701
Fax: 0532 443430
Regional daily morning newspaper
Deadline: 10.00 pm
Circulation: 94,000

Yorkshire on Sunday
PO Box 470
Drake Street
Bradford BD1 1JG
Tel: 0274 732244
Fax: 0274 726633
Showbusiness/Arts editor: Phil Penfold
Sunday regional newspaper

NEWS AND PHOTO AGENCIES

Associated Press
12 Norwich Street
London EC4A 1BP
Tel: 071 353 1515

Central Office of Information
Hercules Road
London SE1
Tel: 071 928 2345

Central Press Features
20 Spectrum House
32-34 Gordon House Road
London NW5 1LP
Tel: 071 284 1433
Fax: 071 284 4494
Film: Leo Zanelli
TV: Kay Shelley

Fleet Street News Agency
68 Exmouth Market
London EC1R 4RA
Tel: 071 278 5661
Fax: 071 278 8480

Knight-Ridder Financial News Agency
72-78 Fleet Street
London EC4Y 1HY
Tel: 071 353 4861
Fax: 071 583 5032

London News Service
68 Exmouth Market
London EC1R 4RA
Tel: 071 278 1223
Fax: 071 278 8480

Press Association
85 Fleet Street
London EC4P 4BE
Tel: 071 353 7440
Fax: 071 936 2364 (Photo), 071 936 2363 (News)

Reuters
85 Fleet Street
London EC4P 4AJ
Tel: 071 250 1122

United Press International
Meridian House
2 Greenwich View
Millharbour
London E14 9NN
Tel: 071 538 5310
Fax: 071 538 1051
Bureau Chief: Michael Collins

BBC TELEVISION

BBC
Television Centre
Wood Lane
London W12 7RJ
Tel: 081 743 8000
BBC1
Omnibus; Film '94
BBC2
Arena; The Late Show; Moviedrome
For further details contact:
Music & Arts Department
BBC Television
Tel: 081 895 6611

INDEPENDENT TELEVISION

Anglia Television
Anglia House
Norwich NR1 3JG
Tel: 0603 615151
Anglia News provides a dual news service covering the east and west of the region

Border Television
Television Centre
Carlisle CA1 3NT
Tel: 0228 25101
Lookaround

Carlton Television
101 St Martin's Lane
London WC2N 4AZ
Tel: 071 240 4000
Fax: 071 240 4171
The Beat, Big City, The Little Picture Show

Central Independent Television
Central House
Broad Street
Birmingham B1 2JP
Tel: 021 643 9898
East Midlands Television Centre
Nottingham NG7 2NA
Tel: 0602 863322
Unit 9, Windrush Court
Abingdon Business Park
Abingdon
Oxon OX14 1SA
Tel: 0235 554123
Central News (separate bulletins prepared for east, south and west); *Central Lobby; Central Weekend; First Night; It's a Living; Tuesday Special*

Channel Television
The Television Centre
La Pouquelaye
St Helier
Jersey
Channel Islands
Tel: 0534 68999
Fax: 0534 34414
Television Centre
St George's Place
St Peter Port
Guernsey
Channel Islands
Tel: 0481 723451

GMTV
London Television Centre
Upper Ground

London SE1 9LT
Tel: 071 827 7000
Fax: 071 827 7001

Grampian Television
Queen's Cross
Aberdeen AB9 2XJ
Tel: 0224 646464
North Tonight; Crossfire; Telefios; Fionnan-Feoir

Granada Television
Quay Street
Manchester M60 9EA
Tel: 061 832 7211
36 Golden Square
London W1R 4AH
Tel: 071 734 8080
Bridgegate House
5 Bridge Place
Lower Bridge Street
Chester CH1 1SA
Tel: 0244 313966
White Cross
Lancaster LA1 4XQ
Tel: 0524 60688
Albert Dock
Liverpool L3 4BA
Tel: 051 709 9393
Daisyfield Business Centre
Appleby Street
Blackburn BB1 3BL
Tel: 0254 690099
Granada Tonight, Celebration

HTV Wales
Television Centre
Culverhouse Cross
Cardiff CF5 6XJ
Tel: 0222 590590
Primetime; Get Going; 4+4; Playback; Weekend Ahead

HTV
Television Centre
Bath Road
Bristol BS4 3HG
Tel: 0272 778366
Press Officer: 0272 722214
Fax: 0272 722400
HTV News; The West This Week; HTV Newsweek

Independent Television News
200 Gray's Inn Road
London WC1X 8XZ
Tel: 071 833 3000

LWT
The London Television Centre
Upper Ground
London SE1 9LT
Tel: 071 620 1620
The South Bank Show; Aspel & Company; London Tonight

Meridian Broadcasting
TV Centre
Northam Road
Southampton SO2 0TA
Tel: 0703 222555
Fax: 0703 335050

Scottish Television
Cowcaddens
Glasgow G2 3PR
Tel: 041 332 9999
The Gateway
Edinburgh EH7 4AH
Tel: 031 557 4554
Chief Press Officer: Stephen McCrossan

Tyne Tees Television
The Television Centre
City Road
Newcastle upon Tyne
NE1 2AL
Tel: 091 261 0181
Fax: 091 261 2302

Ulster Television
Havelock House
Ormeau Road
Belfast BT7 1EB
Tel: 0232 328122
Fax: 0232 238484

Westcountry Television
Western Wood Way
Language Science Park
Plymouth PL7 5BG
Tel: 0752 333333
Fax: 0752 333444

Yorkshire Television
The Television Centre
Leeds LS3 1JS
Tel: 0532 438283
Fax: 0532 433655
Regional news programme: *Calendar*

Channel Four Television
60 Charlotte Street
London W1P 2AX
Tel: 071 631 4444
Fax: 071 323 0858
Channel 4 News c/o ITN; *Right to Reply*

S4C
Parc Ty Glas
Llanishen
Cardiff CF4 5DU
Tel: 0222 747444
Fax: 0222 754444
Head of Press and Public Relations: Manon Williams

BBC RADIO

BBC
Broadcasting House
London W1A 1AA
Tel: 071 580 4468
Fax: 071 636 2476
RADIO 1
Steve Wright, Simon Bates, Mark Goodier
RADIO 2
Cinema 2; Gloria Hunniford Show; Regional Arts Programmes; Saturday Arts Programme; Sunday Arts Programme
RADIO 3
Night Waves; Third Opinion
RADIO 4
Kaleidoscope
RADIO 5
Morning Edition; Get Set
WORLD SERVICE
Bush House
Strand
London WC2B 4PH
Tel: 071 257 2171
Fax: 071 240 3938
Meridian; On Screen

BBC LOCAL RADIO STATIONS

BBC Radio Bristol
PO Box 194
Bristol BS99 7QT
Tel: 0272 741111
Fax: 0272 238323
Morning West; Newshour

BBC CWR (Coventry & Warwickshire)
25 Warwick Road
Coventry CV1 2WR
Tel: 0203 559911
Fax: 0203 520080

BBC Radio Cambridgeshire
PO Box 96
Cambridge CB2 1LD
Tel: 0223 259696

BBC Radio Cleveland
PO Box 95FM
Broadcasting House
Newport Road
Middlesbrough TS1 5DG
Tel: 0642 225211

BBC Radio Cornwall
Phoenix Wharf
Truro TR1 1UA
Tel: 0872 75421
Fax: 0872 40679

Seen and Heard; Weekend Breakfast

BBC Radio Cumbria
Annetwell Street
Carlisle CA3 8BB
Tel: 0228 592444
Fax: 0228 511195
Open Air; Allan Smith; Roundabout

BBC Radio Derby
PO Box 269
Derby DE1 3HL
Tel: 0332 361111
Fax: 0332 290794
Sound and Vision

BBC Radio Devon
PO Box 100
Exeter EX4 4DB
Tel: 0392 215651
PO Box 5
Catherine Street
Plymouth PL1 2AD
Tel: 0752 260323
Devon Arts

BBC Essex
198 New London Road
Chelmsford
Essex CM2 9XB
Tel: 0245 262393
Fax: 0245 492983

BBC Radio Foyle
PO Box 927
8 Northland Road
Londonderry BT48 7NE
Tel: 0504 262244
Fax: 0504 260067

GLR (Greater London Radio)
35c Marylebone High Street
London W1A 4LG
Tel: 071 224 2424
Fax: 071 487 2908

BBC GMR
PO Box 95.1
Oxford Road
Manchester M60 1SD
Tel: 061 200 2000
Fax: 061 228 6110

BBC Radio Guernsey
Commerce House
Les Banques
St Peter Port
Guernsey
Tel: 0481 728977

BBC Hereford & Worcester
Hylton Road
Worcester WR2 5WW
Tel: 0905 748485
Fax: 0905 748006

BBC Radio Humberside

9 Chapel Street
Hull HU1 3NU
Tel: 0482 23232
Fax: 0482 226409

BBC Radio Jersey
Broadcasting House
Rouge Bouillon
St Helier
Jersey
Tel: 0534 70000
Fax: 0534 32569

BBC Radio Kent
Sun Pier
Chatham
Kent ME4 4EZ
Tel: 0634 830505
Soundtrack; Film Buff of the Year

BBC Radio Lancashire
Darwen Street
Blackburn
Lancs BB2 2EA
Tel: 0254 262411
Fax: 0254 680821
Weekday arts and entertainment spot *In Lancashire Tonight*

BBC Radio Leeds
Broadcasting House
Woodhouse Lane
Leeds LS2 9PN
Tel: 0532 442131
Fax: 0532 420652

BBC Radio Leicester
Epic House
Charles Street
Leicester LE1 3SH
Tel: 0533 516688
Fax: 0533 511463

BBC Radio Lincolnshire
PO Box 219
Newport
Lincoln LN1 3XY
Tel: 0522 511411
Fax: 0522 511058
What's On Diary; Gallery

BBC Radio Merseyside
55 Paradise Street
Liverpool L1 3BP
Tel: 051 708 5500
Fax: 051 637 1656

BBC Radio Newcastle
Broadcasting Centre
Fenham
Newcastle upon Tyne
NE99 1RN
Tel: 091 232 4141
Fax: 091 232 5082

BBC Radio Norfolk
Norfolk Tower
Surrey Street
Norwich NR1 3PA
Tel: 0603 617411
Fax: 0603 633692

BBC Radio Northampton
Broadcasting House
Abington Street
Northampton
Northants NN1 2BH
Tel: 0604 239100
Fax: 0604 230709

BBC Radio Nottingham
PO Box 222
Nottingham NG1 3NZ
Tel: 0602 415161
Fax: 0602 481482

BBC Radio Oxford
269 Banbury Road
Oxford OX2 7DW
Tel: 0865 311444
Fax: 0865 311996

BBC Radio Peterborough
PO Box 957
Peterborough PE1 1YT
Tel: 0733 312832
Fax: 0733 343768

BBC Radio Sheffield
Ashdell Grove
60 Westbourne Road
Sheffield S10 2QU
Tel: 0742 686185
Fax: 0742 664375

BBC Radio Solent
Broadcasting House
10 Havelock Road
Southampton SO1 0XR
Tel: 0703 631311
Fax: 0703 339648

BBC Somerset Sound
14-16 Paul Street
Taunton TA1 3PF
Tel: 0823 252437
Fax: 0823 332539

BBC Radio Stoke
Cheapside
Hanley
Stoke-on-Trent ST1 1JJ
Tel: 0782 208080
Fax: 0782 289115
The Afternoon Show

BBC Radio Surrey
Broadcasting House
University of Surrey
Guildford
Surrey GU2 5AP
Tel: 0483 306113
Fax: 0483 304952

BBC Radio Sussex
1 Marlborough Place
Brighton BN1 1TU
Tel: 0273 680231
Fax: 0273 601241

BBC Three Counties Radio
PO Box 3CR
Hastings Street
Luton
Bedfordshire LU1 5XL
Tel: 0582 441000
Fax: 0582 401467

BBC Radio WM
PO Box 206
Birmingham B5 7SD
Tel: 021 414 8484
Fax: 021 414 8817

BBC Wiltshire Sound
Broadcasting House
Prospect Place
Swindon SN1 3RN
Tel: 0793 513626
Fax: 0793 513650

INDEPENDENT NATIONAL RADIO

Classic FM
Academic House
24-28 Oval Road
London NW1 7DQ
Tel: 071 284 3000
Fax: 071 713 2630

Longwave Radio Atlantic 252
74 Newman Street
London W1P 3LA
Tel: 071 436 4012
Fax: 071 436 4015

Virgin 1215 AM
1 Golden Square
London W1R 4DJ
Tel: 071 434 1215
Fax: 071 434 1197

INDEPENDENT LOCAL RADIO

BRMB-FM
Radio House
Aston Road North
Birmingham B6 4BX
Tel: 021 359 4481
Fax: 021 359 1117

Beacon Radio
267 Tettenhall Road
Wolverhampton
WV6 0DQ
Tel: 0902 757211
Fax: 0902 745456

Breeze AM
PO Box 300
Southend-on-Sea
Essex SS1 1SY
Tel: 0702 333711
Fax: 0702 345224

CN.FM 103
PO Box 1000
The Vision Park
Chivers Way
Histon
Cambridge CB4 4WW
Tel: 0223 235255
Fax: 0223 235161

Capital Radio/ Capital Gold
Euston Tower
Euston Road
London NW1 3DR
Tel: 071 608 6080
Fax: 071 387 2345
The Way It Is; The David Jensen Show

Chiltern Radio
Chiltern Road
Dunstable LU6 1HQ
Tel: 0582 666001
Fax: 0582 661725

DevonAir Radio
35-37 St David's Hill
Exeter EX4 4DA
Tel: 0392 430703
Fax: 0392 411893

Downtown Radio
Newtownards BT23 4ES
Tel: 0247 815555
Fax: 0247 815252

Essex Radio
Radio House
Clifftown Road
Southend-on-Sea
SS1 1SX
Tel: 0702 333711

GWR
Lime Kiln Studios
Wootton Bassett
Swindon
Wilts SN4 7EX
Tel: 0793 853222
Station Director: Steve Orchard

Great North Radio
Swalwell
Newcastle upon Tyne
NE99 1BB
Tel: 091 496 0377
Fax: 091 488 8611

Great Yorkshire Radio
PO Box 777
Sheffield S6 1RH
Tel: 0742 852121
Fax: 0742 853159

Hallam FM
Radio House
900 Herries Road
Sheffield S6 1RH

Tel: 0742 853333
Fax: 0742 853159

Horizon Radio
Broadcast Centre
Crownhill
Milton Keynes MK8 0AB
Tel: 0908 269111
Fax: 0908 567203

IRN
200 Gray's Inn Road
London WC1X 3XZ
Tel: 071 430 4814
Fax: 071 430 4834

Invicta Radio
Radio House
John Wilson Business Park
Whitstable
Kent CT5 3QX
Tel: 0227 772004
Fax: 0227 771558

LBC Newstalk
72 Hammersmith Road
London W14 8YE
Tel: 071 603 2400
Fax: 071 371 1515

Leicester Sound FM
Granville House
Granville Road
Leicester LE1 7RW
Tel: 0533 551616
Fax: 0533 550869

London Talkback Radio
72 Hammersmith Road
London W14 8YE
Tel: 071 333 0003
Fax: 071 371 2456

Marcher Gold
The Studios
Mold Road
Gwersyllt
Wrexham
Clwyd LL1 4AF
Tel: 0978 752202
Fax: 0978 759701

MAX AM
PO Box 1548
Forth House
Forth Street
Edinburgh EH1 3LF
Tel: 031 556 9255
Fax: 031 558 3277

Mercia-FM
Hertford Place
Coventry CV1 3TT
Tel: 0203 633933
Fax: 0203 258206

Mid-Anglia Radio (Hereward Radio)
PO Box 225
Queensgate Centre
Peterborough PE1 1XJ
Tel: 0733 346225
Fax: 0733 896400

Moray Firth Radio
PO Box 271
Inverness IV3 6SF
Tel: 0463 224433
Fax: 0463 243224

Northsound Radio
45 King's Gate
Aberdeen AB2 6BL
Tel: 0224 631561
Fax: 0224 633282

Piccadilly Gold/ Piccadilly Key
127-131 The Piazza
Piccadilly Plaza
Manchester M1 4AW
Tel: 061 236 9913
Fax: 061 228 1503

Plymouth Sound
Earl's Acre
Alma Road
Plymouth PL3 4HX
Tel: 0752 225401
Fax: 0752 255962

The Pulse
PO Box 3000
Bradford
W Yorks BD1 5NE
Tel: 0274 731521
Fax: 0274 392031

Radio Aire FM/ Magic 828
PO Box 2000
Leeds LS3 1LR
Tel: 0532 452299
Fax: 0532 421830/343985

Radio Broadland
47-49 St Georges Plain
Colegate
Norwich NR3 1DB
Tel: 0603 630621
Fax: 0603 666353

Radio City
PO Box 1548
Liverpool L69 7DQ
Tel: 051 227 5100
Fax: 051 471 0330

Radio Clyde
Clydebank Business Park
Glasgow G81 2RX
Tel: 041 306 2345
Fax: 041 306 2300

Radio Forth RFM
PO Box 4000
Forth House
Forth Street
Edinburgh EH1 3LF
Tel: 031 556 9255
Fax: 031 558 3277

Radio Mercury/ County Sound
PO Box 964
Guildford GU1 4XX
Tel: 0483 451964
Fax: 0483 31612

Radio Tay
PO Box 123
Dundee DD1 9UF
Tel: 0382 200800
Fax: 0382 24549

Radio Wyvern
5-6 Barbourne Terrace
Worcester WR1 3JZ
Tel/Fax: 0905 612212

Red Dragon FM
West Canal Wharf
Cardiff CF1 5XJ
Tel: 0222 384041
Fax: 0222 373011

Red Rose Gold AM/ Red Rose Rock FM
PO Box 999
Preston PR1 1XR
Tel: 0772 556301
Fax: 0772 201917

SGR FM – Bury St Edmunds
PO Box 250
Bury St Edmunds
Suffolk
Tel: 0284 702622

SGR FM – Ipswich
PO Box 250
Ipswich
Suffolk
Tel: 0473 461000
Fax: 0473 741200

Severn Sound
Old Talbot House
67 Southgate Street
Gloucester GL1 2DQ
Tel: 0452 423791
Fax: 0452 529446

Signal Radio
Stoke-on-Trent ST4 2SR
Tel: 0782 747047
Fax: 0782 744110

South Coast Radio
Whittle Avenue
Segensworth West
Fareham
Hants PO15 5PA
Tel: 0489 589911
Fax: 0489 589453

Southern FM
PO Box 2000
Brighton BN41 2SS
Tel: 0273 430111
Fax: 0273 430098

Southern Radio
Radio House
PO Box 99
Fareham
Hants PO15 5TA
Tel: 0489 589911
Fax: 0489 589453

Swansea Sound
Victoria Road
Gowerton
Swansea SA4 3AB
Tel: 0792 893751
Fax: 0792 898841

2-Ten FM
PO Box 210
Reading RG3 5RZ
Tel: 0734 413131
Fax: 0734 431215

2CR FM
5-7 Southcote Road
Bournemouth BH1 3LR
Tel: 0202 294881
Fax: 0202 299314

TFM
Yale Crescent
Stockton-on-Tees
Cleveland TS17 6AA
Tel: 0642 615111
Fax: 0642 606300

Touch AM
PO Box 99
Cardiff CF1 5YJ
Tel: 0222 373011
Fax: 0222 384014

Trent FM/GEM AM
29-31 Castle Gate
Nottingham NG1 7AP
Tel: 0602 581731
Fax: 0602 588614

WABC
267 Tettenhall Road
Wolverhampton
WV6 0DQ
Tel: 0902 757211
Fax: 0902 745456

West Sound
Radio House
54A Holmston Road
Ayr KA7 3BE
Tel: 0292 283662
Fax: 0292 262607

Xtra-AM (Birmingham)
Radio House
Aston Road North
Birmingham B6 4BX
Tel: 021 359 4481
Fax: 021 359 1117

Xtra-AM (Coventry)
West End House
Hertford Place
Coventry CV1 3TT
Tel: 021 359 4481
Fax: 021 359 1117

PREVIEW THEATRES

BAFTA
195 Piccadilly
London W1V 9LG
Tel: 071 465 0277
Fax: 071 734 1009
Formats: Twin 16mm and Super 16mm double-head stereo, 35mm double-head Dolby stereo at all aspect ratios, U-Matic and VHS stereo. General Electric Talaria projector. Catering by Roux Restaurants
Seats: Princess Anne: 213, Run Run Shaw: 30, Function Room: up to 200

BFI
21 Stephen Street
London W1P 1PL
Tel: 071 255 1444
Fax: 071 436 7950
Formats: 35mm double-head/Dolby stereo optical, 16mm double-head/optical, Betacam, U-Matic hi/lo-band/triple standard, VHS triple standard, PAL S-VHS, video projection
Seats: 1 (film/video): 36, 2 (video): 12, 3 (film): 36

British Universities Film and Video Council (BUFVC)
55 Greek Street
London W1V 5LR
Tel: 071 734 3687
Fax: 071 287 3914
Formats: Viewing rooms equipped with 16mm double-head, Betacam, S-VHS, VHS, lo-band and hi-band U-Matic, Betamax, Phillips 1500
Seats: 15-20 max

CFS Conference Centre
22 Portman Close
London W1A 4BE
Tel: 071 486 2881
Fax: 071 486 4152
Formats: 16mm and 35mm film projection, video projection. Full bar and in-house catering
Seats: 110

Century Preview Theatres
31-32 Soho Square
London W1V 6AP
Tel: 071 437 7766
Fax: 071 434 2170
Formats: Century Theatre: 35mm Dolby optical and magnetic stereo, Dolby A & SR noise reduction, 2,000' double-head capacity, spotlights and microphone for conventions, new sound system ready for digital; Executive Theatre: Dolby A & SR stereo optical and magnetic 2,000' double-head capacity
Seats: Century: 61, Executive: 38

Chapter Cinema
Market Road
Canton
Cardiff CF5 1QE
Tel: 0222 396061
Fax: 0222 225901
Formats: 35mm optical, 16mm double-head, high quality video projection, U-Matic/VHS – all standards. 2 Channel infrared audio amplification/simultaneous translation system in both screens. Reception space, bars and restaurant
Seats: 1: 195, 2: 69

Columbia TriStar Films UK
19-23 Wells Street
London W1P 3FP
Tel: 071 580 2090
Fax: 071 436 0323
Formats: 16mm, 35mm double-head Dolby SR stereo and full video projection. Catering and reception facilities
Seats: 65

Crown Theatre
86 Wardour Street
London W1V 3LF
Tel: 071 437 2233
Fax: 071 434 9990
Formats: 16mm, 35mm double-head, Super 16mm, Betacam SP, U-Matic, Dolby stereo, large-screen video. In-house catering
Seats: 45

De Lane Lea Sound Centre
75 Dean Street
London W1V 5HA
Tel: 071 439 1721
Fax: 071 437 0913
Formats: 35mm and 16mm, Dolby stereo SR & A with double-head capacity. 3/4" hi- and lo-band video and VHS
Bar and catering available
Seats: 30

Edinburgh Film & TV Studios
Nine Mile Burn
Penicuik EH26 9LT
Tel: 0968 672131
Fax: 0968 672685
Formats: 16mm and 35mm double-head stereo, U-Matic, VHS
Seats: 100

Grip House Preview Theatre
5-11 Taunton Road
Metropolitan Centre
Greenford
Middx UB6 8UQ
Tel: 081 578 2382
Fax: 081 578 1536
Formats: 16mm and 35mm, optical and magnetic double-head projection
Seats: 40

ICA
12 Carlton House Terrace
London SW1Y 5AH
Tel: 071 930 0493
Fax: 071 873 0051
Formats: Cinema: 35mm com-opt, Dolby CP, 16mm com-opt, Barco large-screen video projection. VHS, NTSC, lo-band U-Matic. Cinematheque: 16mm com-opt, Super 8, large-screen video projection. VHS, NTSC, lo-band U-Matic. Nash function rooms available for receptions: up to 250 capacity. Cafe Bar available exclusively till noon
Seats: Cinema: 208, Cinematheque: 50

Imperial War Museum
(Corporate Hospitality)
Lambeth Road
London SE1 6HZ
Tel: 071 416 5394
Fax: 071 416 5374
Formats: 35mm and 16mm; Betacam, U-Matic, S-VHS and VHS
Catering: by arrangement
Seats 200

King's Lynn Arts Centre
27 King Street
King's Lynn
Norfolk PE30 1HA
Tel: 0553 774725
Formats: 16mm, 35mm
Seats: 349

The Metro
11 Rupert Street
London W1V 7FS
Tel: 071 287 3515
Fax: 071 287 2112
Formats: 16mm and 35mm. Two screens available from 10am-2pm
Seats: 1: 195, 2: 85

The Minema
45 Knightsbridge
London SW1X 7NL
Tel: 071 235 4225
Fax: 071 235 4330
Formats: 35mm and 16mm, full AV systems
Minema Café adjacent to cinema, seating 44
Seats: 68

Mr Young's
14 D'Arblay Street
London W1V 3FP
Tel: 071 437 1771
Tel/Fax: 071 734 4520
Formats: 16mm, Super 16mm, 35mm, Super 35mm, U-Matic, VHS, Betamax, Dolby stereo double-head optical and magnetic Dolby SR. Bar area, catering by request. Both theatres non-smoking
Seats: 1: 42, 2: 25

Pinewood Studios
Iver
Bucks SL0 0NH
Tel: 0753 656296
Fax: 0753 656844
Formats: 16mm, 35mm, 70mm, U-Matic
Seats: Five theatres with 12 to 115 seats

Preview 167
167-169 Wardour Street
London W1V 3TA
Tel: 071 413 0838
Fax: 071 734 1509
Formats: U-Matic, 35mm, Dolby stereo SR, VHS. Lift
Seats: 35-40

Prominent Facilities THX Preview Theatre
68a Delancey Street
London NW1 7RY
Tel: 071 284 0242
Fax: 071 284 1020
Formats: 35mm Dolby optical and magnetic, 2,000' double-head, rock 'n' roll. All aspect ratios, and Super 35, 24-25-30 fps, triple-track, interlock, Dolby A & SR, 16mm D/H married. Large screen video projection. Fully air conditioned, kitchen and reception area. Wheelchair access
Seats: 26

RSA
8 John Adam Street
London WC2N 6EZ
Tel: 071 930 5115
Fax: 071 321 0271
Formats: S-VHS, lo-band U-Matic, Video 8, other formats by arrangement, includes data projection facilities. Full catering available
Seats: 60

Rank Preview Theatre
127 Wardour Street
London W1V 4AD
Tel: 071 437 9020 x257
Fax: 071 434 3689
Formats: U-Matic, 16mm, 35mm double-head, Dolby Stereo SR, VHS, U-Matic, slides. Lift to theatre
Seats: 58

Richmond Filmhouse
3 Water Lane
Richmond
Surrey TW9 1TG
Tel: 081 332 0030
Fax: 081 332 0316
Formats: 35mm, Dolby Spectral Sound
Seats: 150

SCET Cinema
Dowanhill
74 Victoria Crescent Road
Glasgow G12 9JN
Tel: 041 334 9314
Fax: 041 334 6519
Formats: Video, 16mm, 35mm, double band. Level access for two wheelchairs. Bar and restaurant
Seats: 173

Shepperton Studios
Studios Road
Shepperton
Middx TW17 0QD
Tel: 0932 562611
Fax: 0932 568989
Formats: 35mm, 16mm, Video U-Matic, NTSC, PAL, Secam, VHS
Seats: 1 (35mm): 40, 2 (16mm): 20

Sherman Theatre
Senghennydd Road
Cardiff CF2 4YE
Tel: 0222 396844
Formats: 16mm, 35mm, Dolby stereo, U-Matic. Level access for two wheelchairs. Bar and restaurant
Seats: 474

Twickenham Film Studios
St Margaret's
Twickenham
Middx TW1 2AW
Tel: 081 892 4477
Fax: 081 891 0168
Formats: 16mm, 35mm
Seats: 31

Warner Bros Preview Theatre
135 Wardour Street
London W1V 3TD
Tel: 071 734 8400
Fax: 071 437 5521
Formats: 16mm, 35mm double-head, Dolby stereo. VHS/U-Matic video projection
Seats: 33

Watershed Media Centre
1 Canons Road
Bristol BS1 5TX
Tel: 0272 276444
Fax: 0272 213958
Formats: Super 8mm, 16mm double-head, 35mm, U-Matic, VHS
Seats: 1: 200, 2: 50

PRODUCTION COMPANIES

Listed below are UK companies currently active in financing and/or making audiovisual product for UK and international media markets. Film and video workshops (p316) are also active in this area. Not generally listed are the numerous companies making TV commercials, educational and other non-broadcast material

Aardman Animations
Gas Ferry Road
Bristol BS1 6UN
Tel: 0272 227227
Fax: 0272 227225
Peter Lord,
David Sproxton
Titles include *Adam*, dir Peter Lord, Academy Award nom. 1992; *Loves Me...*, dir Jeff Newitt; *Not Without My Handbag*, dir Boris Kossmehl; *The Wrong Trousers*, dir Nick Park. Aardman is committed to adult animation with the emphasis on character and movement

Acacia Productions
80 Weston Park
London N8 9TB
Tel: 081 341 9392
Fax: 081 341 4879
J Edward Milner,
Nikki Milner
Spirit of Trees (8 x 30 min) Channel 4; *Socotra: Island of Dragon's Blood* (20 min with WWF). In production: *Sustainable Forestry in Papua New Guinea* (with UKFSP)

Action Time
Wrendal House
2 Whitworth Street West
Manchester M1 5WX
Tel: 061 236 8999
Fax: 061 236 8845
Stephen Leahy, Trish Kinane
Entertainment programme devisors and producers in UK and Europe. Recent productions include *Lose A Million, Michael Ball*

Adventure Pictures
1 Blackbird Yard
Ravenscroft Street
London E2 7RP
Tel: 071 613 2233
Fax: 071 256 0842
David Batty, Sally Potter, Christopher Sheppard
Produced Sally Potter's *Orlando*, with other features in development. Also TV documentaries: *Death of a Runaway* (RTS award nomination 1992)

After Image
32 Acre Lane
London SW2 5SG
Tel: 071 737 7300
Fax: 071 326 1850
Jane Thorburn,
Mark Lucas
After Image is best known for the long-running arts series *Alter Image* featuring artists and performers. Recent productions: two TV operas called *Camera* and *Empress of Newfoundland*, *Les Ballets Africains*, 7 x *Dazzling Image* (2nd series) and *Jazz Package* for Channel 4

Agenda Television
TV Centre
St David's Square
Swansea SA1 3LG
Tel: 0792 470470
Fax: 0792 790586
Peter Elias Jones
Wales' largest independent production company. Nightly magazine programme *Heno* for S4C. Series: *Borderlands* (C4), *A Sense of Europe; Booze, Barbours, Bores and Brilliance; How Green Was My Valley* (all for BBC). Expanding into entertainment, drama, features

Alive Productions
37 Harwood Road
London SW6 4QP
Tel: 071 384 2243
Fax: 071 384 2026
TV programme production, currently *Star Test* and the *Star Chamber* for Channel 4

All American Leisure Group
6 Woodland Way
Petts Wood
Kent BR5 1ND
Tel: 0689 871535
Fax: 0689 871519

Allied Vision/Allied Film Productions
The Glassworks
3-4 Ashland Place
London W1M 3JH
Tel: 071 224 1992
Fax: 071 224 0111
Edward Simons,
Peter McRae
Completed *The Lawnmower Man* in 1991. Producing *Nostradamus, The Lawnmower Man II, Howling VII* and *The Mangler* in 1993

Alomo Productions
see **SelecTV**

Amy International Productions
2a Park Avenue
Wraysbury
Middx TW19 5ET
Tel: 0784 483131/483288
Fax: 0784 483812
Susan George,
Simon MacCorkindale
Odds End, Lucan, Dragon Under the Hill, The Liaison

Andor Films
8 Ilchester Place
London W14 8AA
Tel: 071 602 2382
Fax: 071 602 1047
Production of theatrical motion pictures

Anglia Television Entertainment
48 Leicester Square
London WC2H 7FB
Tel: 071 321 0101
Graeme McDonald,
Brenda Reid,
David FitzGerald
The Chief, Growing Rich, Framed, A Dangerous Man: Lawrence After Arabia, Frankie's House, A Fair and Easy Passage, Unnatural Causes, A Brief History of Time, The Josephine Baker Story, Riders, Far from Home, Polo, Thieftaker, Hans Christian Andersen,

Bodies and Crimes, Dancing in the Dark

Anglo/Fortunato Films
170 Popes Lane
London W5 4NJ
Tel: 081 840 4196
Fax: 081 840 0279
Luciano Celentino
Feature film production company

Animation City/AC Live
69 Wells Street
London W1P 3RB
Tel: 071 580 6160
Fax: 071 436 8934
Ammie Purcell
Company currently producing *Prince Cinders* (half hour animation), *Angry George Irons* (10 min animation), *Eric Carle* (5 x 7 min animations) commercials and title sequence for UK and European clients

Antelope
3 Fitzroy Square
London W1P 5AH
Tel: 071 387 4454
Fax: 071 388 9935
Peter Montagnon, Mick Csaky
Dramas and documentaries for broadcast TV in UK, USA, Europe and Japan. Past productions: *Testament, Fonteyn, Nureyev, Terror, The Midas Touch, Carols from Prague, Tina Modotti, Childhood, the Cosmic Joke, The Royal Collection, Royal Gardens, the Cuban Missile Crisis, A Diplomat in Japan, Very Jean Muir*. In production: *The Pier, Dudley Moore, Elisabeth Frink, Mao Zedong*. In development: *Carols from Winchester, Animal Minds*

Arena Films
Teddington Studios
Broom Road
Teddington
Middlesex TW11 9LN
Tel: 081 943 5274/5276
Fax: 081 943 1457
Specialising in European co-production. Produced: *Coup de Foudre*, 27 half-hour films for TV, for Telecip and Reteitalia. Also made *Vincent and Theo* released theatrically UK and USA, and for UK and US TV *Magic Moments*

Argo Productions
5 South Villas
Camden Square
London NW1 9BS
Tel: 071 485 9189
Fax: 071 485 6808
Robert Fleming
Broadcast documentaries. 1989 *Flying Squad* 8 x 30 min for Thames TV; 1991 *Gracewell* 1 x 75 min for Channel 4; 1992 *Murder Squad* 1 x 60 min and 6 x 30 min for Thames TV; 1993-4: *Scotland Yard* 1 x 60 min, 8 x 30 min

Ariel Productions
93 Wardour Street
London W1V 3TE
Tel: 071 494 2169
Fax: 071 494 2695
Otto Plaschkes
Produced *Shadey*, written by Snoo Wilson, directed by Philip Saville and starring Anthony Sher, for Film Four International. In development are *Changing Places*, scripted by Peter Nichols, *The Well* by Marc Zuber and *A Hero of our Time*, adapted by Derek Marlowe

Aspect Film and Television Production
36 Percy Street
London W1P 9FG
Tel: 071 636 5303
Fax: 071 436 0666
Mark Chapman
Producers of documentaries, comedies and drama

bfi BFI Production
29 Rathbone Street
London W1P 1AG
Tel: 071 636 5587
Fax: 071 580 9456
Ben Gibson
Division of the BFI which is the UK's national agency for cultural subsidy of innovative and experimental film, shorts, features and development

BJE
Home Farm
Church Hill
High Littleton
Bristol BS18 5HF
Tel: 0761 471055
Fax: 0761 472996
John King
Current productions include: *Dusk the Badger; The Elephant; Telly Addicts; Countryfile; Top Gear; Walk on the Wildside; A Year in Provence; Noel's Addicts*

BTS Television
1 Lostock Avenue
Poynton
Nr Stockport
Cheshire
Tel: 0625 850887
Corporate, broadcast and interactive video

Bandung
Block H
Carkers Lane
53-79 Highgate Road
London NW5 1TL
Tel: 071 482 5045
Fax: 071 284 0930
Tariq Ali
Recent productions include fourth series of *Rear Window*, Channel 4's international arts programme, and the BFI/Channel 4 film *Wittgenstein*, directed by Derek Jarman. Next production *Locke*, the third in the Philosophers Series for Channel 4

Barraclough Carey Productions
Cambridge House
Cambridge Grove
London W6 0LE
Tel: 081 741 4777
Fax: 081 741 7674
Jenny Barraclough, George Carey
Documentary, current affairs. Recent productions for Channel 4 include: *Gambler's Guide to Winning (Equinox), Murder in Mississippi, As It Happens, America on Trial (Secret History)*. For BBC: *Redemption Song, Moving Pictures, Biteback* (BBC's right-to-reply show), *Battlecries, Inside Story: Welcome to Hell*

Basilisk Communications
31 Percy Street
London W1P 9FG
Tel: 071 580 7222
Fax: 071 631 0572
James Mackay
Recent film and TV productions: *Man to Man*, dir John Maybury (BBC); *The Garden*, dir Derek Jarman (Channel 4); *The Gay Man's Guide to Safer Sex*, dir David Lewis (Terrence Higgins Trust); *Blue*, dir Derek Jarman

Peter Batty Productions
Claremont House
Renfrew Road
Kingston
Surrey KT2 7NT
Tel: 081 942 6304
Fax: 081 336 1661
Peter Batty
Recent Channel 4 productions include *Swastika Over British Soil, A Time for Remembrance, The Divided Union, Fonteyn and Nureyev, The Algerian War, Swindle* and *Il Poverello*. Previous independent productions include *The Story of Wine, Battle for Warsaw, Battle for Dien Bien Phu, Birth of the Bomb, Search for the Super, Battle for Cassino, Operation Barbarossa* and *Farouk: Last of the Pharaohs*

Beambright
Alton House
105 Howards Lane
London SW15 6NZ
Tel: 081 780 9838
Fax: 081 780 9875
Therese Pickard
Close My Eyes, written and directed by Stephen Poliakoff, produced by Therese Pickard for Film Four. *Century*, in association with the BBC, for theatrical release, also with Poliakoff and Pickard. Several features in development and a series for Carlton Television

Bedford Productions
2nd Floor
21 Cork Street
London W1X 1HB
Tel: 071 287 9928
Fax: 071 287 9870
Mike Dineen, Francis Megahy, Russ Kane, Richard Mervyn
TV, documentary, drama production, and business to business programming

Bevanfield Films
2a Duke Street
Manchester Square
London W1M 5AA
Tel: 071 487 4920
Fax: 071 487 5472
Mary Swindale
Continues to produce animated and live-action programmes for TV, video and cinematic release, and has expanded into the corporate sector. The most recent live-action feature film was *The*

Mystery of Edwin Drood released April 1993

Big Star in a Wee Picture
The Production Centre
5 Newton Terrace Lane
Glasgow G3 7PB
Tel: 041 204 3435
Fax: 041 204 2081
David Muir
Arts, entertainment, current affairs and features programming for UK broadcast. Recent credits include 16 x *Burning Books*; 4 x *Sin* with Bruce Morton, 5 x *The Glittering Haze* and *The Great Dictator* for Channel 4. 8 x *Axiom*, 2 x *EX-S* and *Rain* for BBC Scotland and 6 x *Talking Loud* for STV/Grampian

Bordeaux Films International
22 Soho Square
London W1V 5FJ
Tel: 081 959 8556
Recent projects include *Caravans, Double Jeopardy, Giselle, Guns and the Fury, Laura, Mr Wrong* and *The Witch*

British Lion
Pinewood Studios
Iver Heath
Bucks SL0 0NH
Tel: 0753 651700
Peter Snell
As Britannic Films, first project was the telemovie *Squaring the Circle*, co-financed with TVS and Metromedia Producers Associates. *Lady Jane* for Paramount Pictures and *Turtle Diary*, in assocition with United British Artists. *A Man for All Seasons* for Turner Network Television and *Treasure Island* also for TNT. Recent productions: *A Prayer for the Dying* for Samuel Goldwyn Company and *The Crucifer of Blood* for TNT. *Death Train* for USA Network and Yorkshire TV

Britt Allcroft Group
3 Grosvenor Square
Southampton SO1 2BE
Tel: 0703 331661
Fax: 0703 332206
Linda Rhodes
Recent works: *Thomas the Tank Engine and Friends*, 78 x 5 min episodes live action animation. *Shining Time Station*, award winning children's TV series, 40 half-hour episodes networked on the USA's PBS. One hour holiday special featuring Lloyd Bridges. *Magic Adventures of Mumfie* – 13 x 10 min episodes

Broadcast Communications (Corporate)
14 King Street
London WC2E 8HN
Tel: 071 240 6941
Fax: 071 379 5808
Michael Braham
Braham is currently executive producer of the Channel 4 *Business Programme* and *Business Daily*

Brook Productions
21-24 Bruges Place
Randolph Street
London NW1 0TF
Tel: 071 482 6111
Fax: 071 284 0626
Anne Lapping, Philip Whitehead, Udi Eichler
Channel 4: *A Week in Politics, Sunday Bloody Sunday, Fin de Siècle, In the Shadow of the Fatwa, The Golden Years.* Thames: *The Kennedys.* Current: *Dispatches, Sorry, Judas* (both Channel 4), *A Week in Politics*

Buena Vista Productions
Beaumont House
Kensington Village
Avonmore Road
London W14 8TS
Tel: 071 605 2550
Fax: 071 605 2597
David Simon
International TV production arm of The Walt Disney Studios

John Burder Films
7 Saltcoats Road
London W4 1AR
Tel: 081 995 0547
Fax: 081 995 3376
John Burder
Corporate and broadcast worldwide. Recent productions include: *The Common Sense Guides* (18 Safety Training Videos), productions for Thorn EMI and many other sponsors

Burrill Productions
19 Cranbury Road
London SW6 2NS
Tel: 071 736 8673
Fax: 071 731 3921
Petra Willoughby de Broke, Timothy Burrill
Burrill Productions co-produced *Return of the Musketeers, Valmont, The Lover, Bitter Moon* and *Sweet Killing*

Buxton Films
PO Box 1486
London SW1V 1PF
Tel/Fax: 071 931 9875
Jette Bonnevie
Development and production company for features, TV and video. Particularly interested in European co-productions

Cabochon Film Productions
16a Brechin Place
London SW7 4QA
Tel: 071 373 6453
Fax: 071 720 1302
Celestino Coronado
Films include: *The Lindsay Kemp Circus, Miroirs, Hamlet* (1978), *A Midsummer Night's Dream* (1985), *Smoking Mirror*. Cabochon Films is preparing a documentary on the life of the blind actor-dancer-singer *The Incredible Orlando* and is developing a feature film adaptation of Calderon's *Life is a Dream* set in modern Spain. The company welcomes commissions for commercials, promos, pop videos etc

Carnival (Films and Theatre)
12 Raddington Road
Ladbroke Grove
London W10 5TG
Tel: 081 968 1818
Fax: 081 968 0155
Brian Eastman
Films: *Shadowlands, Under Suspicion, Wilt, Whoops Apocalypse.* Current TV: *Anna Lee, All or Nothing at All, Agatha Christie's Poirot* (LWT), *Jeeves and Wooster* (Granada), *The Big Battalions* (Channel 4), *Head Over Heels* (Carlton)

Cartwn Cymru
Model House
Bull Ring
Llantrisant
Mid Glamorgan
Tel: 0443 222316
Fax: 0443 229242
Naomi Jones
Animation production. ITV Network: *Toucan 'Tecs*; BBC1/S4C: *Funnybones*; S4C/BBC Enterprises: *Turandot, the Animated Opera*

Ceddo Film/Video
63-65 Coburg Road
Wood Green
London N22 6UB
Tel: 081 889 7654
Fax: 081 889 4492
Imruh Bakari, Lazell Daley, Charles Donaldson
Film/video production and training. Productions include: *Street Warriors, We are the Elephant, The People's Account, Time and Judgement, Omega Rising, Flame of the Soul, Racism – A Response, Blue Notes and Exiled Voices*

Celador Productions
39 Long Acre
London WC2E 9JT
Tel: 071 240 8101
Fax: 071 836 1117
Paul Smith, Nic Phillips
TV: primarily entertainment programming for all broadcast channels. Includes game shows, variety, with selected situation comedy, drama and factual output

Celtic Films
1-2 Bromley Place
London W1P 5HB
Tel: 071 637 7651
Fax: 071 436 5387
Muir Sutherland
The Monk, Sharpe for Central Television

Chain Production
11 Hornton Street
London W8 7NP
Tel: 071 937 1981
Fax: 071 376 0556
Garwin Davison, Roberta Licurgo
Film sales/distribution/production specialist in Italian films; UK-Italian production co-ordinators

Channel X
Middlesex House
34/42 Cleveland Street
London W1P 5FB
Tel: 071 436 2200
Fax: 071 436 1475
Katie Lander
Channel 4: *Saturday Zoo, Sean's Show, Americana, Seriously Seeking Sid, Tonight with Jonathan Ross.* BBC2: *A Word in Your Era, The Smell of Reeves and Mortimer*

Charisma Films
14-15 Vernon Street
London W14 0RJ
Tel: 071 603 1164
Fax: 071 603 1175
James Atherton

Chatsworth Television
97-99 Dean Street
London W1V 5RA
Tel: 071 734 4302
Fax: 071 437 3301
Malcolm Heyworth
Sister company to Chatsworth distribution and merchandising companies. Producers of light entertainment and drama. Best known for the long running *Treasure Hunt* and *The Crystal Maze* for Channel 4. Drama projects in development for BBC: *The Colin Wallace Story* and *Poor Sisters*

Cheerleader Productions
62 Chiswick High Road
London W4 1SY
Tel: 081 995 7778
Fax: 081 995 7779
Charles Balchin
American Football, Sumo Wrestling, NHL Ice Hockey, Baseball, Equestrian Sport, Motor Sport, Tennis, Water Sport, Basketball, Darts, Speedway. Over 200 hours a year of network sport

Children's Film and Television Foundation
Elstree Studios
Borehamwood
Herts WD6 1JG
Tel: 081 953 0844
Fax: 081 207 0860
Stanley Taylor
How's Business produced by the CFTF and made by the Children's Film Unit; *My Friend Walter* (Portobello Pictures/ Thames Television and Wonderworks); *Harry's Mad* (Film & General Productions for Central Television, script development by CFTF); *The Borrowers* (Working Title Television/BBC Enterprises)

The Children's Film Unit
Suite 9
Hamilton House
66 Upper Richmond Road
London SW15
Tel: 081 871 2006
Fax: 081 871 2140
Brianna Perkins
A registered Educational Charity, the CFU makes low-budget films for TV and PR on subjects of concern to children and young people. Crews and actors are trained at regular weekly workshops in Putney. Work is in 16mm and video and membership is open to children from 8-16. Latest feature for Channel 4 *Emily's Ghost*

Childsplay Productions
8 Lonsdale Road
London NW6 6RD
Tel: 071 328 1429
Fax: 071 328 1416
Kim Burke
TV producers specialising in children's and family programming. Recent productions include a new film special of *Streetwise* for ITV; new six part ecological thriller *Eye of the Storm*. Currently developing sit-com for children *Pirates* and *Deux Chevaux*, 13-part drama set in France

Chrysalis Television Productions
The Chrysalis Building
Bramley Road
London W10 6SP
Tel: 071 221 2213
Fax: 071 221 6286
Tony Orsten
Specialising in news, sport, current affairs and entertainment; producers of *Italian Football, Indycar, ITV Snooker*

Cine Electra
National House
60-66 Wardour Street
London W1V 3HP
Tel: 071 287 1123
Fax: 071 722 4251
Julia Kennedy
The company specialises in European co-productions. Recent titles include: *The Baby of Mâcon* by Peter Greenaway, *The Ring with the Crowned Eagle* by Andrzej Wajda, *Utz* by George Sluizer, *Walk Me Home* by Timothy Neat. Kennedy is Executive Producer on Ben Kingsley's *The Circle of the White Rose* and producer on Armin Mueller-Stahl's *Hamlet in America*. Also forthcoming *Polish Death!* (working title) by Waldemar Krzystek and *Pushkin* by Tony Palmer

Cinema Verity
The Mill House
Millers Way
1a Shepherds Bush Road
London W6 7NA
Tel: 081 749 8485
Fax: 081 743 5062
Verity Lambert
Fifth series *May to December*. Second series *So Haunt Me*. *Comics* by Lynda La Plante for Channel 4

Clark Television Production
Cavendish House
128-134 Cleveland Street
London W1P 5DN
Tel: 071 388 7700
Fax: 071 388 3366
Selina Kay
Dispatches, The Black Bag, The Chrystal Rose Show, Headline, Class Action, Hard News, Opinions

Clement Le Frenais
see ***SelecTV***

Clio & Co
91 Mildmay Road
London N1 4PU
Tel: 071 249 2551
Rosalind Pearson, Suzanne Neild
Produce documentaries about women's history. Productions include *A Peace of Her Mind, Women Like Us* and *Women Like That* for Channel 4

Colstar International
11 Wythburn Place
London W1H 5WL
Tel: 071 437 5725
Fax: 071 706 1704
Producers and distributors of international documentary and drama programming for broadcast. Credits include *In Search of Wildlife, Defending Wildlife, The Wandering Company, Antarctic Challenge, Sport in Flight*. Co-productions include *A Movement of Thought, Acquaria*

The Comedy House
24 D'Arblay Street
London W1V 3FH
Tel: 071 437 4551
Fax: 071 439 1355
John Goldstone
Set up in 1990 to develop comedy films with British and American talent. Produced *Carry on Columbus* 1992, now in development with 3 theatrical movies

The Comic Strip
43a Berwick Street
London W1V 3RE
Tel: 071 439 9509
Fax: 071 734 2793
Lolli Kimpton, Nira Park

Compact Television
118 Cleveland Street
London W1P 5DN
Tel: 071 387 4045
Fax: 071 388 0408
Kent Walwin

Compass Film Productions
First Floor
175 Wardour Street
London W1V 3FB
Tel: 071 439 6456
Fax: 071 434 9256
Simon Heaven, Heather Simms
Documentaries: *Violent Lives* (4 x 1 hour Channel 4), *A Door to Understanding* and *Pat, Michael and David* (2 x half hour for Channel 4 *People First* series), *The Last Chance Hotel* (1 x half hour BBC Wales), *Cardboard Citizens* (1 x half hour for Channel 4 *Gimme Shelter* season) and *Behind the Mask* (1 x 40 min for BBC *40 Minutes*)

Contrast Films
311 Katherine Road
London E7 8PJ
Tel: 081 472 5001
Ruhul Amin
Produce documentaries and feature films. Productions include: *Purbo London* and for Channel 4: *Flame in my Heart, A Kind of English, Moviewallah*

Cosgrove Hall Productions
8 Albany Road
Chorlton-cum-Hardy
Manchester M21 1BL
Tel: 061 881 9211
Fax: 061 881 1720
Brian Cosgrove, Mark Hall
Award-winning animation subsidiary of Thames TV,

now an independent producer of cartoon and model animation. Creators of *Dangermouse*, *The Wind in the Willows*, *Count Duckula*, *The B.F.G.*, *Truckers*, *Noddy* and *Hell's Penguins*

Countrywide Films
Production Office
Television Centre
Northam
Southampton SO9 5HZ
Tel: 0703 230286/834139
Anthony Howard, Elisabeth Howard, Sheila Rogers
Cathedral for LWT, *Country Ways* for Meridian, *Country Faces* for BBC1, *Missa Luba* for Philips, *A Taste of the Country* for TVS

Creative Law
Media Legal
Burbank House
75 Clarendon Road
Sevenoaks
Kent TN13 1ET
Tel: 0732 460592
John Wheller
Production arm of Media Legal developing legal projects for film and TV

Crystalvision
Communications House
5 Factory Lane
Croydon CR9 3RA
Tel: 081 781 6444
Fax: 081 681 2340
Specialist sports programming together with children's programmes and drama. Produced 8 part series *The Complete Skier* for Channel 4, *World Invitation Club Basketball* for Screensport and *The Royal Dublin Horseshow* for American TV, several smaller OB's for ITV and satellite channels

DBA Television
21 Ormeau Avenue
Belfast BT2 8HD
Tel: 0232 231197
Fax: 0232 333302
David Barker
Northern Ireland's leading production company. Wide range of documentary programmes for Channel 4 and BBC. Recent credits: *New York Law* (BBC1 *Inside Story*); *Plain Tales from Northern Ireland* (6 x 30 min for BBC2); *Hobo* and *Drink Talking* (BBC) and *The Mass* (Channel 4). In production: 3 part series for BBC2 network

Dakota Films
6 Meard Street
London W1V 3HR
Tel: 071 287 4329
Fax: 071 287 2303

Distant Horizon
84-86 Regent Street
London W1R 5PF
Tel: 071 734 8690
Fax: 071 734 8691
Paul Janssen
Recent productions include *To the Death*, *Sarafina!*, *Chain of Desire*, *The Road to Mecca* and *Cry the Beloved Country*

Diverse Production
Gorleston Street
London W14 8XS
Tel: 071 603 4567
Fax: 071 603 2148
Philip Clarke, Rita Shamia
Company with commitment to innovative TV. Producers of *The Pulse*, *The Little Picture Show*, *Check Out*, *Europe Express*, *Singles*, *Winning*, *Computing for the Terrified* and a number of other broadcast series and single documentaries

Domino Films
8 Stockwell Terrace
London SW9 0QD
Tel: 071 582 0393
Fax: 071 582 0437
Joanna Mack, Harold Frayman
Well-established company producing wide range of factual programmes including the award-winning *Selling Murder*, *Secret World of Sex*, *Lost Children of the Empire* and *Heil Herbie*. Other productions include *Eve Strikes Back*, *Breadline Britain 1990s*, *Soviet Citizens* and *Out of Sight*

Double Exposure
Unit 22-23
63 Clerkenwell Road
London EC1M 5PS
Tel: 071 490 2499
Fax: 071 490 2556
Production and distribution of broadcast and educational documentaries in the UK and abroad

Dramatis Personae
19 Regency Street
London SW1P 4BY
Tel: 071 834 9300
Maria Aitken, Nathan Silver
TV series *Men of Parts: Inigo Jones, Christopher Wren, John Vanbrugh* in preparation. Company concerned primarily with self-generated features on artistic skills and human development having broad cultural or social interest

Driftwood Films
Old Church Hall
183a Petersham Road
Richmond
Surrey TW10 7AW
Tel: 081 332 6365
Fax: 081 332 6369
Malcolm Taylor
In development: *The Seven Senses*, *Manshadow*. Also comedy and drama corporate films

Edinburgh Film and Video Productions
Edinburgh Film and TV Studios
Nine Mile Burn
by Penicuik
Midlothian EH26 9LT
Tel: 0968 672131
Fax: 0968 672685
Robin Crichton
Major Scottish production company established in 1961. Latest production *Torch* – an international TV co-production drama

Elmgate Productions
Shepperton Studios
Studios Road
Shepperton
Middx TW17 0QD
Tel: 0932 562611
Fax: 0932 569918
Chris Burt, Sandra Frieze
Feature films, TV films and series, including *Van der Valk* series 1 and 2 and *A Question of Guilt*, a two hour film for the BBC

Endboard Productions
114a Poplar Road
Bearwood
Birmingham B66 4AP
Tel: 021 429 9779
Fax: 021 429 9008
Yugesh Walia, Sunandan Walia
Producers of TV programmes and information videos. In 1991/2 produced the second series (8 episodes) of *Kabaddi* for Channel 4. Also produced one half-hour documentary for Central TV's series *Encounter* for the ITV network. *A Very Dangerous Practise* for Channel 4's *Close to Home* series

Enigma Productions
Pinewood Studios
Pinewood Road
Iver
Bucks SL0 0NH
Tel: 0753 630555
Fax: 0753 630393
David Puttnam
Film and TV production

Equal Media
Wadenhoe Lodge
Wadenhoe
Oundle
Peterborough PE8 5SZ
Tel: 08015 268
Fax: 08015 417
Sarah Hobson
A production company working particularly with stories and filmmakers from Africa, Asia, Latin America and the Black diaspora. Recent productions include *Behind the Cocaine War* (Channel 4); *Another Form of Abuse* (FORWARD/DHSS); *Something Like a War* (Channel 4)

Mary Evans Productions
115 Goldhawk Road
London W12 8EJ
Tel: 081 740 5319/749 3877
Bray Studios
Down Place
Water Oakley
Windsor Road
Windsor
Berkshire SL4 5UG
Tel: 0628 22111
Fax: 0628 770381

Faction Films
28-29 Great Sutton Street
London EC1V 0DU
Tel: 071 608 0654/3
Fax: 071 608 2157
Sylvia Stevens, Dave Fox, Peter Daye, Grant Keir
Group of independent filmmakers. Titles include: *Irish News: British Stories*, *Year of the Beaver*, *Picturing Derry*, *Trouble the Calm*, *Provocation or Murder* (C4 *Dispatches*), *Mariscal* (BBC *Arena*), *Games People Play* (BBC2 series)

Fairwater Films
North Chambers
Castle Arcade
Cardiff CF1 2BX
Tel: 0222 640140
Fax: 0222 230482
Tony Barnes
Award winning animation and video producers. Recent work includes *Sid the Sexist* for Viz comic, *The Shoe People* for Storm Group. Many productions in development including *Things That Go Bump, Wrestling Rabbit, Cheese and Crackers* and *Transylvania Pet Shop*

Film Form Productions
64 Fitzjohn's Avenue
London NW3 5LT
Tel/Fax: 071 794 6967
Susi Oldroyd
Tony Harrild
Film/video production, drama and documentary for TV and video distribution. Full crewing, writers, producers and directors

Film Four International
60 Charlotte Street
London W1P 2AX
Tel: 071 631 4444
Fax: 071 580 2622
International film sales and distribution arm of Channel 4, often credited as a co-production partner for UK and international productions. Decisions on programming and finance relating to these productions are initiated by Film on Four, the film programming strand of Channel 4's drama department

FilmFair Animation
5 Dean Street
London W1V 5RN
Tel: 071 734 2826
Fax: 071 734 5064
Rob Dunbar
Producers of cartoon, model and special effects series and commercials. *The Wombles, Paddington Bear, Huxley Pig, Gingerbread Man, Astro Farm, The Dreamstone, Brown Bear's Wedding and White Bear's Secret* and *Treasure Island*

The Filmworks
65 Brackenbury Road
Hammersmith
London W6 0BG
Tel: 081 741 5631
Fax: 081 748 3198
Recent productions: *On the Trail of the Chinese Wildman, Struggle for the Pole – In the Footsteps of Scott, A Day in the Life of a Medical Officer, Antarctic Challenge* and *Anything's Possible.* Current animation series: *Captain Star – Inventing the Universe*

The First Film Company
38 Great Windmill Street
London W1V 7PA
Tel: 071 439 1640
Fax: 071 437 2062
Feature film, TV and commercial production. *Dance with a Stranger, Soursweet, The Commitments, The Railway Station Man.* Among projects in development: *Flying Hero Class* based on the novel by Thomas Keneally and *Django Reinhardt*, an original screenplay by Shelagh Delaney

Flamingo Pictures
47 Lonsdale Square
London N1 1EW
Tel: 071 607 9958
Christine Oestreicher

Flashback Productions
22 Kildare Terrace
London W2 5LX
Tel: 071 727 9904
Stephen Wegg-Prosser
Producers of *Flashback*, a 20-part series for Channel 4 which won a BFI Award and *The Games in Question, Fifties Features, Tales Out of School* and 60 programmes on *The March of Time.* Makers of documentaries for Channel 4, the BBC and overseas co-producers. Commmitted to public service broadcasting

Flashback Television
2/3 Cowcross Street
London EC1M 6DR
Tel: 071 490 8996
Fax: 071 490 5610
Taylor Downing
Producers of a wide range of factual programming for broadcast and non-broadcast. We specialise in historical documentaries, drama documentaries, arts documentaries and natural history programming. We have made many sports programmes and have excellent relations with the International Olympic Committee. Several projects in production and development

Focus Films
Rotunda Studios
Rear of 116-118 Finchley Road
London NW3 5HT
Tel: 071 435 9004
Fax: 071 431 3562
David Pupkewitz,
Marsha Levin,
Lisa Disler
Film and TV production. *Diary of a Sane Man* – experimental feature with assistance from Channel 4, *Crimetime* feature film, ESF development award; *Heritage Music* series in development; *How to be a Teenager* youth series in development. Various documentaries

Mark Forstater Productions
Unit 60
Pall Mall Deposit
124 Barlby Road
London W10 6BL
Tel: 081 964 1888
Fax: 081 960 9819
Mark Forstater Productions 1991: *Paper Marriage* directed by Krzysztof Lang, *The Touch* directed by Krzysztof Zanussi, *La Cuisine Polonaise* directed by Jacek Bromski. 1993 *Grushko* (BBC drama series), *Transcontinental*

Forum Television
11 Regent Street
Bristol BS8 4HW
Tel: 0272 741490
Fax: 0272 743629
David Parker
Co-operative making documentaries with emphasis on the South West. Offers film/video editing suites. Recent titles for BBC include: *Video Letters* and *Adultery* – a four-part series. For C4: *Neighbours* and *Britannia*, an animation. For HTV: *Secrets of the Moor*, 7 x 26 min films about Exmoor, *Hounded Harts, Professional Dreamer, Miniature Masterpieces, Taking the Strain, When You Ran Me Down* and *Battle on the Beach*

Fourth Wall Productions
1 Little Argyll Street
London W1R 5DB
Tel: 071 437 2222
Fax: 071 734 0663
Lino Ferrari
Bob Marsland
Broad based TV production company, including *The Frank Bough Interview* for Sky News, *A Day to Remember* for BBC2, *The Astrology Show* for Channel 4. Current productions include documentary series

Freeway Films
67 George Street
Edinburgh EH2 2JG
Tel: 031 225 3200
Fax: 031 225 3667
John McGrath
Drama for TV and cinema

Friday Productions
23a St Leonards Terrace
London SW3 4QG
Tel/Fax: 071 730 0608
Georgina Abrahams
Goggle Eyes, 4 x 40 min family comedy drama series based on Anne Fine's novel, adapted by Deborah Moggach, for BBC. *Harnessing Peacocks*, 1 x 120 min film based on Mary Wesley's novel, adapted by Andrew Davies for Meridian. Also *Mozart at Buckingham Palace* for Thames, 4 series of *Hudson and Halls* for BBC, *The December Rose* for BBC

Front Page Films
23 West Smithfield
London EC1A 9HY
Tel: 071 329 6866
Fax: 071 329 6844
Produced *The Mini Sagas*, six theatrical shorts which were released by UIP alongside *A Fish Called Wanda, Parenthood* and *The Naked Gun.* Owners of the Richmond Filmhouse. 1990 production *Get Back*, a feature with Paul McCartney directed by Richard Lester as well as two TV dramas for Channel 4. A number of feature films are currently in development/pre-production

Frontroom Films
Avonway
Naseby Road
London SE19 3JJ
Tel/Fax: 081 653 9343
Robert Smith
Adios writer Sue Townsend; *Cry for the Moon* writer Sharman Macdonald; *Captain Swing* writer James Whyllie, *Saxons* writer Andy Rashleigh, *The View* writer Judy Leather

Fugitive Features
Unit 1
14 William Road
London NW1 3EN
Tel: 071 383 4373
Fax: 071 383 5681
Makers of *The Krays* and *The Reflecting Skin*

Fulcrum Productions
254 Goswell Road
London EC1V 7EB
Tel: 071 253 0353
Fax: 071 490 0206
Christopher Hird
Involved in making investigative, financial and arts documentaries. Recent productions: four *Dispatches* for Channel 4 on business and social issues; *The Years that Rocked the Planet* and *Advent Calendar* for BBC2; *Greed and Glory* Channel 4 three part series on the City of London; *Homophobia in Hollywood* for Channel 4's *Out*, *Follow the Money* BBC2 four part business series

David Furnham Films
39 Hove Park Road
Hove
East Sussex BN3 6LH
Tel: 0273 559731
Interests in How-To video publishing, educational children's programming

Gainsborough (Film and TV) Productions
8 Queen Street
London W1X 7PH
Tel: 071 409 1925
Fax: 071 408 2042
John Hough
Made *Hazard of Hearts, The Lady and the Highwayman, A Ghost in Monte Carlo and Duel of Hearts*

Gallus Besom Productions
25 Greenside Place
Edinburgh EH1 3AA
Tel: 031 556 2429
Fax: 031 556 2430
Zad Rogers
Film and TV production

John Gau Productions
Burston House
1 Burston Road
London SW15 6AR
Tel: 081 788 8811
Fax: 081 789 0903
John Gau, Susan Gau
TV documentary production

Noel Gay Television
6th Floor
76 Oxford Street
London W1N 0AT
Tel: 071 412 0400
Fax: 071 412 0300
Charles Armitage
Recent productions: *The Happening* (series 1 & 2), *The Last Laugh, La Triviata, Up Yer News, Merlin, QD, Hysteria!, Pallas* (series 1 & 2), *Dave Allen, Once in a Lifetime, Frank Stubbs Promotes*. Associate companies: Grant Naylor Productions, Jelly Telly, Picture That, Nautilus, Rose Bay Film Productions

General Entertainment Investments
65-67 Ledbury Road
London W11 2AD
Tel: 071 221 3512
Fax: 071 792 9005
John Oakley
Feature film producers/ financiers. Recent work includes *Tropic of Ice*, Anglo-Finnish co-production, *Soweto*, African music feature, *Olympus Force*, Anglo-Greek co-production. Currently preparing *Extreme Remedies* and *Living Evidence*, Anglo-European productions

Global Features
49 Hornton Street
London W8 7NT
Tel/Fax: 071 937 1039
Documentary and drama-documentary programme makers, specialising in social and religious themes. Last credit *Shadow on the Cross*

Bob Godfrey Films
199 Kings Cross Road
London WC1X 9DB
Tel: 071 278 5711
Fax: 071 278 6809
Bob Godfrey, Mike Hayes
Prominent studio. Titles include: *Henry's Cat* (children); *Trio, Angel's Delight, Oracle* (commercials); *Revolution, Happy Birthday Switzerland, Wicked Willie, The Bunburys* (entertainment)

Goldcrest Films and Television
65/66 Dean Street
London W1V 5HD
Tel: 071 437 8696
Fax: 071 437 4448
John Quested, Joanna Deakin
Major feature film production, sales and finance company. Recent films include *All Dogs Go To Heaven, Black Rainbow, Rock-a-Doodle* and *Scorchers*

The Grade Company
8 Queen Street
Mayfair
London W1X 7PH
Tel: 071 409 1925
Fax: 071 408 2042
Lord Grade
Company recently completed production on fourth TV film based on Barbara Cartland novels and developing other potential film projects

Granada Film
36 Golden Square
London W1R 4AH
Tel: 071 734 8080
Fax: 071 494 6360
Steve Morrison, Pippa Cross, Janette Day
Feature film production. Actively developing quality films for the international market including *Prime Suspect, The Fifth Child* and *Jack and Sarah*

Grand Slam Sports
Durham House
Durham House Street
London WC2N 6HF
Tel: 071 839 4646
Fax: 071 839 8392
Ron Allison, Derek Brandon, Simon Reed, John Watts, Nick Sharrard
Productions: *World Wide Soccer 1990-92, BBC Snooker 1991-93, SIS Horse Racing, International Sports News* for the Channel 4 Daily 1988-92, *Summer Paralympics* 1992. Over 300 hours a year and over 50 sports covered since 1988

Grasshopper Productions
50 Peel Street
London W8 7PD
Tel: 071 229 1181
Fax: 071 229 2070
Joy Whitby
Productions to date: for children *Grasshopper Island, Emma and Grandpa* and *East of the Moon*, film series based on the Terry Jones Fairy Tales with music by Neil Innes; *The Angel and the Soldier Boy*, 25 min animation by Alison de Vere and *On Christmas Eve*, 25 min animation by Cosgrove Hall (both based on picture books by Peter Collington) and family telefilm *A Pattern of Roses*, based on the novel by KM Peyton

Greenpoint Films
5a Noel Street
London W1V 3RB
Tel: 071 437 6492
Fax: 071 437 0644
Ann Scott
A loose association of ten filmmakers: Simon Relph, Christopher Morahan, Ann Scott, Richard Eyre, Stephen Frears, Patrick Cassavetti, John Mackenzie, Mike Newell, David Hare and Christopher Hampton. Films include Eyre's *The Ploughman's Lunch* and *Laughterhouse*, Morahan's *In The Secret State*, Hare's *Wetherby* and *Paris by Night*, Giles Foster's *Tree of Hands*, Mike Bradwell's *Chains of Love*, Peter Barnes' *Nobody Here But Us Chickens* and *Bye Bye Columbus*, Mike Newell's *The Good Father* and *Enchanted April*. Latest production *The Secret Rapture*, script by David Hare, directed by Howard Davies

Griffin Productions
Balfour House

46-54 Great Titchfield Street
London W1P 7AE
Tel: 071 636 5066
Fax: 071 436 3232
Adam Clapham
Producing *The Doomsday Gun* for HBO, *Maria* for Lifetime and BBC, *Private Parts* for Yorkshire TV, *The Place of Lions* for STV and *Wenceslas* for The Family Channel

The Gruber Brothers
Shepperton Studios
Studios Road
Shepperton
Middx TW17 0QD
Tel: 0932 572274
Fax: 0932 572277
Richard Holmes, Stefan Schwartz
The Gruber Brothers completed *The Lake* in 1992 and went on to make *Soft Top, Hard Shoulder*

Reg Grundy Productions
1 Bargehouse Crescent
34 Upper Ground
London SE1 9PN
Tel: 071 928 8942
Fax: 071 928 8417
Shari Murphy
TV production company. Game/quiz shows, drama

The Half Way Production House
Units 1 & 2 Taylors Yard
67 Alderbrook Road
London
SW12 8AD
Tel: 081 673 7926
Fax: 081 675 7612
Georgina Hart, Emma Stewart

Hammer Film Productions
Elstree Studios
Borehamwood
Herts WD6 1JG
Tel: 081 953 1600
Fax: 081 905 1127
Roy Skeggs, Richelle Wilder
The company responsible for many classic British horror films. Current production schedule involves the development of 8 features for theatrical release and 3 projects for TV production

HandMade Films (Productions)
26 Cadogan Square
London SW1X 0JP
Tel: 071 584 8345
Fax: 071 584 7338
George Harrison, Denis O'Brien
Producers of *Monty Python's Life of Brian, The Long Good Friday, Time Bandits, Privates on Parade, The Missionary, A Private Function, Mona Lisa, Withnail and I, Five Corners, Bellman and True, Track 29, The Lonely Passion of Judith Hearne, The Raggedy Rawney, Powwow Highway, Nuns on the Run*. 8 projects currently in development; 3 for release in 1994, 2 to be shot in the US and 1 in the UK

Harcourt Films
58 Camden Square
London NW1 9XE
Tel: 071 267 0882
Fax: 071 267 1064
Jeremy Marre
Producer and director of documentaries. *The Grateful and the Dead* for *Arena* BBC/Arts Council/ PBS Network. *Ladyboys* 50 min with TVF for Channel 4. *Improvisation – On the Edge* 4 x 50 min for Channel 4 and RM Arts. *Enemies of Silence* and *The Left-Handed Man of Madagascar* for BBC's *Under the Sun*

Hartswood Films
Teddington Studios
Broom Road
Teddington
Middlesex TW11 9NT
Tel: 081 977 3252
Fax: 081 943 3696
Beryl Vertue, Elaine Cameron
Independent production company for film and TV, owned and run by Beryl Vertue. 1992 – 2 series of *Men Behaving Badly*. 1993 – 3 x 1 hr drama *A Woman's Guide to Adultery* for Carlton

Hat Trick Productions
10 Livonia Street
London W1V 3PH
Tel: 071 434 2451
Fax: 071 287 9791
Denise O'Donoghue, Jimmy Mulville, Geoffrey Perkins, Mary Bell
Specialising in comedy, current productions include: *Round the Bend* for *YTV, Whose Line Is It Anyway, Paul Merton – The Series, Drop the Dead Donkey, S & M, The Big One, Clive Anderson Talks Back* for Channel 4 and for the BBC new series of *The Harry Enfield Television Programme, Have I Got News For You, The Brain Drain*

Hawkshead
48 Bedford Square
London WC1B 3DP
Tel: 071 255 2551
Fax: 071 580 8101
Tom Barnicoat, Frances Whitaker, Angela Law, Jane Mitchell
Productions include: *Sunday Best* (GMTV), *Grass Roots* (Meridian), *John Berger* (BBC2/Arte), *New Directions* (Carlton), *Dorset Detours* (Meridian/ C4/HTV West), *Delia Smith's Summer Collection* (BBC2)

Hemdale Holdings
21 Albion Street
London W2 2AS
Tel: 071 724 1010
Fax: 071 724 9168
John Smallcombe
Produced *Terminator, Return of the Living Dead, Body Slam, River's Edge, Vampire's Kiss, Shag, Staying Together, Chattahoochee, Salvador, Platoon* and *The Last Emperor*

Jim Henson Productions
1b Downshire Hill
Hampstead
London NW3 1NR
Tel: 071 431 2818
Fax: 071 431 3737
Duncan Kenworthy, Martin Baker, Angus Fletcher
Producers of high quality children's/family entertainment for TV and feature films, usually with a puppetry or fantasy connection. Current productions include *Dinosaurs* (sitcom series), *Dog City* (animation series), *City Kids* (series), *Borgel* (special), *The Secret Life of Toys* (children's series). Recent productions include *A Muppet Christmas Carol* (feature film)

Hightimes Productions
5 Anglers Lane
Kentish Town
London NW5 3DG
Tel: 071 482 5202
Fax: 071 485 4254
Al Mitchell, Tony Humphreys
The company specialises in developing, packaging and producing light entertainment and comedy ideas for TV. It has recently expanded its activities to include drama and has a variety of projects at different stages of development. Hightimes packaged *Me and My Girl* (five series) for LWT and *The Zodiac Game* (two series) for Anglia. Produced thirteen episodes of *Guys N' Dolls*, licensed to BSB, and *Trouble in Mind*, a situation comedy for LWT

Holmes Associates
17 Rathbone Street
London W1P 1AF
Tel: 071 637 8251
Fax: 071 637 9024
Andrew Holmes, Diane Holmes, Alison Carter
Recent work: *The Cormorant,* Screen Two for BBC Wales; *John Gielgud Looks Back*, 64 min documentary for Channel 4; *The House of Bernarda Alba*, 100 min film for Channel 4/WNET/ AMAYA; *Signals*, Channel 4's weekly arts series; *Piece of Cake* and *Rock Steady*

Horntvedt Television
The Power House
Alpha Place
Flood Street
London SW3 5SZ
Tel: 071 376 7611
Fax: 071 351 2951
Kit Horntvedt, Howard Webster
Return of Wind Power, Racing Rock, Grosvenor Gardens Mentor for RICS

Hourglass Productions
4 The Heights
Charlton
London SE7 8JH
Tel: 081 858 6870
John Walsh
Documentary work includes Oscar-winning *Ray Harryhausen: Movement into Life* and *The Masque of Draperie in the Presence of Her Majesty the Queen.* Also various music promos.

Currently: production of theatrical motion pictures. First feature film due for cinema release towards the end of 1994

Michael Hurll Television
6 Brewer Street
London W1R 3SP
Tel: 071 465 0103
Fax: 071 287 4315
Susie Dark
Richard Digance (LWT), *BAFTA Advertising Awards* (Sky), *British Comedy Awards 1992* (LWT), *A Carlton New Year* (Carlton), *The Royal Television Society Hall of Fame* (Carlton), *Bob Downe Under* (LWT Night Network)

Hyndland Television
Kelvingrove House
54 Kelvingrove Street
Glasgow G3 7SA
Tel: 041 332 1005
Fax: 041 332 1009
David Kemp
Documentaries and journalism

ITM (Music) Productions
16 Raleigh Road
Southville
Bristol BS3 1QR
Tel: 0272 661116
Fax: 0272 720387
Peter Giles, Alex Galvin
Specialist music production company for film, TV and video

Iambic Productions
The Production House
147a St Michael's Hill
Bristol BS2 8DB
Tel: 0272 237222
Fax: 0272 238343
8 Warren Mews
London W1P 5DJ
Tel: 071 388 3323
Fax: 071 388 7121
Music, arts and drama TV productions for UK network and world TV. Regular producers of *South Bank Show* (LWT) and rock and classical music programmes for BBC and Channel 4

The Ideas Factory
Maxron House
Green Lane
Romiley
Stockport SK6 3JG
Tel: 061 406 6685
Fax: 061 406 6672
Martin Duffy
Producers of Channel 4's *Big 8 Wheelchair Basketball* sports series. Company has special interest in sports TV for the disabled

Illuminations
19-20 Rheidol Mews
Rheidol Terrace
London N1 8NU
Tel: 071 226 0266
Fax: 071 359 1151
John Wyver, Linda Zuck
Producers of cultural programmes for Channel 4, BBC Television and others. Recent projects include *Round IX* live from *Documenta* for Channel 4; *Antenna* on *Time Travel*; *Bookmark* on *Love Poetry*, *The Two Belles* for *Every Picture Tells a Story*, and *Painted Passions*, five programmes exploring Christ's Passion through art for BBC2. Several projects in development including a major documentary series about the beginnings of cinema

Illuminations Interactive
19-20 Rheidol Terrace
London N1 8NU
Tel: 071 226 0266
Fax: 071 359 1151
Terry Braun, John Wyver
Company developing and producing Interactive MultiMedia projects about the visual and performing arts. Productions include *Ways of Looking* for the Arts Council of Great Britain, *BRANCUSI* for the International Visual Arts Information Network and *The Horn* for the exhibition of musical instruments at the Horniman Museum in London

Illustra Communications
13-14 Bateman Street
London W1V 6EB
Tel: 071 437 9611
Fax: 071 734 7143
Douglas Kentish

Initial Film and Television
74 Black Lion Lane
Hammersmith
London W6 9BE
Tel: 081 741 4500
Fax: 081 741 9416
Malcolm Gerrie, Eric Fellner
Feature films include: *Sid and Nancy, Hidden Agenda, A Kiss Before Dying, Liebestraum, Wild West, The Hawk.* TV programmes include: *Time Will Tell, Madstock, Magic & Loss, U2 Zoo TV, Orchestra!, Concerto!* TV drama includes: *Wexford Trilogy, Frankie's House, Underbelly*

Insight Productions
Gidleigh Studio
Gidleigh
Chagford
Newton Abbot
Devon TQ13 8HP
Tel: 0647 432686
Fax: 0647 433141
Brian Skilton
Established in 1982, nearly 40 broadcast film credits; arts, entertainment, a 'Film on Four' *Playing Away*, environmental documentaries *Dartmoor the Threatened Wilderness, Taming the Flood* and *Camargue* and a documentary series *Flavio Titolo – Blind Sculptor* for HTV/Westcountry. In production: *Southern Lands* for Meridian, *Fragile Earth – New Forest* for Channel 4

International Broadcasting Trust (IBT)
2 Ferdinand Place
London NW1 8EE
Tel: 071 482 2847
Fax: 071 284 3374
Paddy Coulter
A consortium of 70 leading development agencies and environmental organisations, formed to make programmes about the Third World. Recent productions include *Bitter Harvest*, a drama for BBC2 Screenplay on aid and human rights in the Caribbean, *The Global Environment*, 10 part series for BBC Schools, *The Dispossessed*, a 4 part international series (with YTV) on refugees for Channel 4, and the *Ed Case Showcase* series (with Hawkshead) for BBC *Nature*

Interprom
7a Tythings Court
Minehead
Somerset TA24 5NT
Tel: 0643 706774
Fax: 0643 702698
Clive Woods
Brewhouse Jazz, 5 concerts taped in Taunton, Somerset and featuring top American jazz musicians

Island World Productions
12-14 Argyll Street
London W1V 1AB
Tel: 071 734 3536
Fax: 071 734 3585
Tony Garnett
Theatrical films and TV programmes

Kai Productions
1 Ravenslea Road
London SW12 8SA
Tel: 081 673 4550
Fax: 081 675 4760
Mike Wallington
Channel 4 productions: *Malltime* (1987), *Robotopia* (1989), *Homes on Wheels* (1992), *L.A. Requiem* (1993), *Kalashnikov & Co* (1993)

Kestrel Films
11 Landford Road
London SW15 1AQ
Tel: 081 788 6244
Bill Shapter

Kilroy Television Company
Teddington Studios
Teddington Lock
Teddington
Middlesex TW11 9NT
Tel: 081 943 3555
Fax: 081 943 3646
Clive Syddall
Produces nearly 100 hours of network TV a year, specialises in current affairs, documentary and other factual programming

King Rollo Films
Dolphin Court
High Street
Honiton
Devon EX14 8LS
Tel: 0404 45218
Fax: 0404 45328
Clive Juster
Producers and distributors of the animated series: *Mr Benn, King Rollo, Victor and Maria, Towser, Watt the Devil, The Adventures of Spot, The Adventures of Ric, Anytime Tales* and *Art*

Kohler
16 Marlborough Road
Richmond
Surrey TW10 6JR

Tel: 081 940 3967
Michael Kohler
Cabiri, The Experiencer

Koninck
175 Wardour Street
London W1V 3AB
Tel: 071 734 4943
Fax: 071 494 0405
Keith Griffiths, Janine Marmot, Susan Schulman
Producers of cultural documentaries, animation and fiction. Latest projects include *The Cardinal and the Corpse* by Chris Petit, *Temptation of Sainthood* by Simon Pummell, *Food* by Jan Svankmajer and *Abstract Cinema* by Keith Griffiths. In production: *London* by Patrick Keiller, *Faust* by Jan Svankmajer, *The Institute Benjamenta* by The Brothers Quay. Feature films in development: *Change of Heart, The Presence, To The North*

Landseer Film and Television Productions
140 Royal College Street
London NW1 0TA
Tel: 071 485 7333
Fax: 071 485 7573
Emma Craven
Documentary, drama, music and arts, children's and current affairs. Recent productions: *Not Pots* (Channel 4); *Kenneth MacMillan at 60* (BBC), *The Russians are Coming* (Channel 4), *Biosphere II* (Central), *Hakan Hardenberger* (LWT *South Bank Show*), *La Stupenda* (BBC *Omnibus*), *Winter Dreams* (BBC2), *Sunny Stories: Enid Blyton* (BBC *Arena*), *J.R.R.T.* (Tolkien Partnership)

Langham Productions
10 Abbeville Road
London SW4 9NJ
Tel/Fax: 081 675 3326
Michael Latham, Michael Johnstone
Productions include *Fighting Back* (BBC1), *Science Frontiers* (US Learning Channel), *Equinox* (Channel 4)

Helen Langridge Associates
75 Kenton Street
London WC1N 1NN
Tel: 071 833 2955
Fax: 071 837 2836
Helen Langridge
Feature development, TV, commercials and music videos

Brian Lapping Associates
21-24 Bruges Place
Randolph Street
London NW1 0TF
Tel: 071 482 5855
Fax: 071 284 0626
Producers of TV programming, including *Countdown to War* (Granada/ITV) with Ian McKellen as Hitler (Gold Medal, New York TV Festival), *The Second Russian Revolution* (BBC2) (RTS prize, Broadcasting Press Guild Prize, New York TV Festival Silver Medal), *Question Time* (BBC1), *Hypotheticals* (BBC2), *The Washington Version* (BBC2)

Large Door
41-45 Beak Street
London W1R 3LE
Tel: 071 439 1381
Fax: 071 439 0849
John Ellis, Karol-An Kirkman
Founded in 1982, specialising in documentaries on cinema and related topics. Currently developing the definitive *History of World Cinema* for the 1995 Centenary. Recent productions include *Those British Faces* (12 parts); *Brazil: Beyond Citizen Kane* (90 min); and *The Complicity of Women* (52 min). Many awards for series like *Visions* (1982-85) and *This Food Business* (1989)

Laurel Productions
116-118 Grafton Road
London NW5 4BA
Tel: 071 267 9399
Fax: 071 267 8799
Chris Oxley
Documentary, current affairs, arts, environmental, drama-docs, and other factual programmes. Recent productions include *Fragile Earth – The River Detectives; The Battle for Barts* (LWT); *Murder on Moss Side* (Channel 4 *Dispatches*)

Leda Serene
66 Crownstone Court
London SW2 1LT
Tel: 071 733 2861
Ingrid Lewis, Frances-Anne Solomon
Produced *I Is A Long-Memoried Woman* (Leda Serene/XOP Video 1990) which won a Gold Award at the International Film and TV Festival of New York. Produced *Reunion* (BBC2) 1993. Projects in development include *Shadowlands, The Womanists* and *What My Mother Told Me*, 40 min drama

Little Bird Co
91 Regent Street
London W1R 7TA
Tel: 071 434 1131
Fax: 071 434 1803
James Mitchell, Jonathan Cavendish, Alan Gavin
Feature films: *Joyriders, December Bride*, and *Into the West*. Television: *The Irish R.M., Troubles, The Lilac Bus, In the Border Country* and *The Brother*

Living Tape Productions
Ramillies House
1-2 Ramillies Street
London W1V 1DF
Tel: 071 439 6301
Fax: 071 437 0731
Nick Freethy, Stephen Bond
Producers of educational and documentary programmes for TV and video distribution. Currently completed major new TV series *Oceans of Wealth*

Euan Lloyd Productions
Pinewood Studios
Iver Heath
Bucks SL0 0NH
Tel: 0753 651700
Fax: 0753 656844
Euan Lloyd
Since 1968, Lloyd has made nine major action adventures including *The Wild Geese, Who Dares Wins* and *The Sea Wolves*. In development: *A Hole in One*

London Films
Kent House
14-17 Market Place
Great Titchfield Street
London W1N 6AR
Tel: 071 323 5251
Fax: 071 436 2834
Tom Donald, Wendy Oberman
Founded in 1932 by Alexander Korda. Many co-productions with the BBC, including *I, Claudius, Poldark* and *Testament of Youth*. Produced *The Country Girls* for Channel 4. In receipt of a direct drama commission from a US network for *Scarlet Pimpernel* and *Kim*. Renowned for productions of classics, most recently *Lady Chatterley*, directed by Ken Russell

Lusia Films
7-9 Earlham Street
London WC2 1HL
Tel: 071 240 2350
Fax: 071 497 0446
Marc Karlin
Karlin made *For Memory*, a BFI/BBC co-production, and a four-part series of documentaries on Nicaragua. Also a two-hour film *Utopias* for Channel 4 and a film on the last ten years of the Nicaraguan revolution. Forthcoming *Century's End* for Channel 4

Jo Lustig
PO Box 472
London SW7 4NL
Tel: 071 937 6614
Fax: 071 937 8680
Jo Lustig, Dee Lustig
Represents Mel Brooks and Managing Director of Brooksfilms (UK). Co-producer *84 Charing Cross Road* (Brooksfilms and Columbia), producer of TV documentaries: *Larkin* (Bookmark BBC-TV); *Maria Callas – Life and Art* (Channel 4); *The Unforgettable Nat 'King' Cole* (BBC TV); *John Cassavetes* (BBC TV); *Hollywood Babylon* (BBC *Arena*) and drama for BBC *The Last Romantics* with Ian Holm, directed by Jack Gold

Malachite Productions
East Kirkby House
Spilsby
Lincolnshire PE23 4BX
Tel: 0790 763538/071 487 5451
Fax: 0790 763409
Charles Mapleston, Nancy Thomas
Producers of people-based documentary programmes on music, design, painting, photography, arts, anthropology and environmental issues for

broadcast TV. Recent productions include: *I Close My Eyes..., John Clare's Journey, Buried Landscapes, Fiore – Sculpting Tuscany, Clarke's Penny Whistle* and *A Voyage with Nancy Blackett*

Malone Gill Productions
Canaletto House
39 Beak Street
London W1R 3LD
Tel: 071 287 3970
Fax: 071 287 8146
Georgina Denison
Currently making *Nature Perfected* for Channel 4/ NHK/ABC. Recent productions: *The Feast of Christmas* for Channel 4, *Nomads*, Channel 4/ ITEL, *The Buried Mirror: Reflections on Spain and the New World*, BBC2/ Discovery Channel

Manhattan Films
217 Brompton Road
London SW3 2EJ
Tel/Fax: 071 581 2408
Robert Paget
Directed and wrote *The Choice* in Switzerland. Preparing *Magic Days* to be shot in London. *Friendly Enemies* in development with US major

Mike Mansfield TV
5-7 Carnaby Street
London W1V 1PG
Tel: 071 494 3061
Fax: 071 494 3057
Hilary McLaren, Esq
Cue the Music 52 x 1 hour ITV; *Whale On..!* 50 x 1 hour LWT/ITV; *Animal Country* 14 x half hour ITV/Anglia; *Fanfare for a New World* 1 x 90 min S4C/Granada;*The Music Game* 10 x half hour HTV/Channel 4

Jo Manuel Productions
Suite 60
124-128 Barlby Road
London W10 8BL
Tel: 081 964 1888
Fax: 081 960 9819
Jo Manuel,
Tracey Seaward
Comedy pilot *London Funnies* for Showtime Networks Inc. Currently in pre-production on *Widow's Peak* £4m feature film to shoot in Ireland. Various sell-through videos for Pickwick

Maya Vision
43 New Oxford Street
London WC1A 1BH
Tel: 071 836 1113
Fax: 071 836 5169
Sally Thomas
1992/93 productions: *Barcelona* with Robert Hughes (*Omnibus*, BBC1), *Darshan* (*Travellers Tales*, Channel 4), *Do Families Need Fathers?* (*Critical Eye*, Channel 4), 5 items for *Out* (Channel 4), *Between A Rock and A Hard Place* (Experimenta/Arts Council/Channel 4), *Cold Jazz* (BFI New Directors). Currently producing several documentaries and developing a feature for the BFI

Medialab
Unit 8 Chelsea Wharf
15 Lots Road
London SW10 0QH
Tel: 071 351 5814
Fax: 071 351 7898
Geoff Foulkes
Commercials, music videos, documentaries. Producers of *MTV Live!* concert series and *Exposed Films* series of exposé documentaries

Meditel Productions
Bedford Chambers
The Piazza
Covent Garden
London WC2E 8HA
Tel: 071 836 9216
Fax: 071 240 3818
Joan Shenton
Provides medical, science-based and factual documentaries for TV. Made *AZT – Cause For Concern, The AIDS Catch* and *AIDS and Africa* (for Channel 4 *Dispatches*). *Impotence – One in Ten Men* (for Channel 4), and *HRT – Pause for Thought* (for Thames TV *This Week*). Currently developing drama

Mentorn Films
Mentorn House
140 Wardour Street
London W1V 3AV
Tel: 071 287 4545
Fax: 071 287 3728
Tom Gutteridge,
John Needham
Light entertainment, drama, arts and entertainment, lifestyle and children's programmes. *Challenge Anneka, Passport, Happy Families, Surprise Party, Billy's Finest Hour, Capital Woman, WideAngle, Swot or Wot, 1st Night* (with subsidiary Mentorn Midlands), *I Can Do That!* (with subsidiary Mentorn South), *First Reaction, Excellent, Entertainment UK, Hollywood Report*. Currently developing light entertainment/drama projects

Merchant Ivory Productions
46 Lexington Street
London W1P 3LH
Tel: 071 437 1200
Fax: 071 734 1579
Ismail Merchant, Paul Bradley
Producer Ismail Merchant and director James Ivory together made, among other films for theatrical and TV release, *Shakespeare Wallah, Heat and Dust, The Bostonians, A Room with a View, Maurice, Slaves of New York, Mr & Mrs Bridge, The Ballad of the Sad Cafe, Howards End, The Remains of the Day* and *In Custody*. Projects in development: *Jefferson in Paris* and *The Playmaker*

Mersey Television
Campus Manor
Childwall Abbey Road
Liverpool L16 0JP
Tel: 051 722 9122
Fax: 051 722 1969
Phil Redmond
Independent production company responsible for Channel 4 thrice-weekly drama series, *Brookside*. Mersey Music and Mersey Casting are subsidiary companies

Mersham Productions
41 Montpellier Walk
London SW7 1JH
Tel: 071 589 8829
Fax: 071 584 0024
Lord Brabourne
Lord Brabourne is a Fellow and a Governor of the BFI. Amongst other films, he has produced in conjunction with Richard Goodwin four films based on stories by Agatha Christie and *A Passage to India* directed by David Lean. During 1986, co-produced *Little Dorrit*. In 1988/9, co-produced the TV series *Leontyne*

Metrodome Films
40 Crawford Street
London W1H 2BB
Tel: 071 723 3494
Fax: 071 724 6411
Paul Brooks, Alan Martin
Formed in 1992 following Paul Brooks' success as executive producer of *Leon the Pig Farmer*. *Bedlam* and *Lock-in* financed for 1993, *The Line* due to shoot in 1994

Momentum Productions
20 Sewdley Street
London E5 0AX
Tel: 081 985 8823
Fax: 081 986 7217
Guy Meyer, Lisa Blundell
Trailers, promos and commercials. Producers of dance films and film documentaries *Taster* and *Yesterday's Shadows*

Moving Picture Productions
179 Wardour Street
London W1V 3FB
Tel: 071 434 3100
Fax: 071 734 9150
Lauren Campbell
Commercials production – UK, Europe, USA. Corporate and interactive communications

NFH
37 Ovington Square
London SW3 1LJ
Tel: 071 584 7561
Fax: 071 589 1863
Norma Heyman, Rachel Wood, Sonali Wijeyaratne
Recently completed: *Clothes In the Wardrobe* (BBC Screen Two) and *The Innocent* (German/ UK co-production, dir John Schlesinger). In pre-production: *My Sister In This House* (Channel 4/ British Screen) and *Mary Reilly* (Columbia TriStar, dir Stephen Frears)

NVC Arts
The Forum
74-80 Camden Street
London NW1 0JL
Tel: 071 388 3833
Fax: 071 383 5332
Shelagh Hughes
Produces recordings of live opera and dance from the world's leading international venues and

companies. Recent recordings include *La Traviata* from La Fenice, Venice, *Mlada* and *A Life for the Tsar* from the Bolshoi Opera and Kenneth MacMillan's *Winter Dreams* with The Royal Ballet

New Era Productions
23 West Smithfield
London EC1A 9HY
Tel: 071 236 5532
Fax: 071 236 5504
Marc Samuelson, Peter Samuelson, Rachel Cuperman
Tom and Viv directed by Brian Gilbert, written by Michael Hastings and Adrian Hodges from Hastings' Royal Court play

New Media
12 Oval Road
London NW1 7DH
Tel: 071 916 9999
Fax: 071 482 4957
Susi Barrett
Multimedia design and production company providing a comprehensive service for the production of LaserVision, CD ROM, CD ROM XA, DVI, CD-I and CDTV

Nirvana Films
81 Berwick Street
London W1V 3PF
Tel: 071 439 8113
Fax: 071 494 2006
Tim Dennison, Jim Groom
The production of feature films for the world market. One feature *Revenge of Billy the Kid* finished. In pre-production on *Zombie God Squad*

North South Productions
Woburn Buildings
1 Woburn Walk
London WC1H 0JJ
Tel: 071 388 0351
Fax: 071 388 2398
Film and video production company that specialises in programmes on environmental issues, world development, travel and other international themes. Productions include BBC series *Only One Earth*, Channel 4 series *Wild India, Stolen Childhood, How to Save the Earth* and many other documentaries and current affairs programmes for Channel 4

Nub Television
1st Floor
116 Grafton Road
London NW5 4BA
Tel: 071 485 7132
Fax: 071 284 0260
Michael Whiteley
Recent productions include *Dispatches* in Nigeria (Channel 4), Profile of Calipsonian Trinidad/UK, *Travellers' Tales* in Nigeria (Channel 4), 4 part series on Spain (Channel 4), *Talkin' Turkey* (Channel 4) Christmas programme

OG Films
Pinewood Studios
Pinewood Road
Iver Heath
Bucks SLO 0NH
Tel: 0753 651700
Fax: 0753 656844
Oliver Gamgee
Production, packaging, and distribution company for feature films and TV

Orbit Films
7/11 Kensington High Street
London W8 5NP
Tel: 071 221 5548
Fax: 071 727 0515
Gordon Pilkington
Currently producing independent shorts; comedy, music programmes for TV broadcast; documentaries, community programmes. *Serie Noire*, a hosted look at vintage classic TV for Super Channel

Orchid Productions
Garden Studios
11-15 Betterton Street
Covent Garden
London WC2H 9BP
Tel: 071 379 0344
Fax: 071 379 0801
Jo Kemp
Sovereign House
Sovereign Street
Pendleton
Manchester M6 3LY
Tel: 061 737 2816
Fax: 061 745 7248
Neil Molyneux
Pilot for half hour special with Phil Cool (Central TV). Network animation series *The Raggy Dolls* for Yorkshire TV. Also commercials

Orlando TV Productions
Up-the-Steps
Little Tew
Oxon OX7 4JB
Tel: 0608 83218
Fax: 0608 83364
Mike Tomlinson
TV documentaries. *Equinox* for Channel 4, *Nova* for WGBH-Boston, *Horizon* for BBC

Oxford Film Company
6 Erskine Road
London NW3 3AJ
Tel: 071 483 3637
Fax: 071 483 3567
Mark Bentley, Andy Paterson
Producers of feature films and TV including the BAFTA Award-winning series *Naked Hollywood* and *Naked Sport*. Feature films in production in 1993/94 include *Restoration* adapted by Rupert Walters from the Rose Tremain novel, directed by Michael Hoffman, and *Delirious*, an original screenplay by Frank Cottrell Boyce to be directed by Michael Winterbottom

Oxford Independent Video
Pegasus Theatre
Magdalen Road
Oxford OX4 1RE
Tel: 0865 250150
Maddie Shepherd
A specialist arts education producer, distributor and trainer. Works in collaboration with innovative artists and performers from across the world, selecting and commissioning a broad range of high quality work. OIV tapes are distributed across the UK and internationally

Oxford Scientific Films
Long Hanborough
Oxford OX8 8LL
Tel: 0993 881881
Fax: 0993 882808
10 Poland Street
London W1V 3DE
Tel: 071 494 0720
Fax: 071 287 9125
OSF specialises in natural history and environmental documentaries, commercials, corporate and medical videos, sports programmes. See also under Archives and Libraries and Specialised Goods and Services

PCP – The Producers Creative Partnership
Ramillies House
1-2 Ramillies Street
London W1V 1DF
Tel: 071 439 1966
Fax: 071 439 1977
Michael Darlow, Joan C Wilcox
Produces drama, music, arts, documentary and entertainment programmes for TV. Titles include *Beyond Belief – Religion on Trial*, 3 x 1 hour for Channel 4; *Chad Varah – the Good Samaritan*, 1 hour for Channel 4; *Decisions Decisions*, 6 x 30 min for Channel 4

Pacesetter Productions
New Barn House
Leith Hill Lane
Ockley
Surrey RH5 5PH
Tel: 0306 70433
Fax: 0306 881021
Adele Spencer
On-going feature, documentary, TV drama and sponsored production

Paladin Pictures
Teddington Studios
Broom Road
Teddington Lock
Teddington
Middlesex TW11 9NT
Tel: 081 740 1811
Fax: 081 740 7220
Clive Syddall
Popular quality documentary, drama and music and arts programming. Recent productions include: *The Vanishing Rembrandts, The Assassin* and *Great Railway Journeys of the World 2*, for BBC 2. In development: *Harry S* – 90 min special on Harry Truman; *Behind the Shades* – 90 min special on George Shearing; *Roots* – Journey in search of a homeland, 6-part series

Panoptic Productions
35 Heddon Street
London W1R 7LL

Tel: 071 287 3931
Fax: 071 287 1518
Michael Jones, Jean Newington
Producer of *Dispatches* (Hungary), *Sex on TV, Trial of Lady C (Sexual Intercourse Began in 1963)*, 3 programmes in Channel 4's *Banned* season, *Lost Lawrence, Sex and the Censors, A History of British Business Culture, The First Genocide, Saint Mugg* and *L.A. Divine*

Parallax Pictures
7 Denmark Street
London WC2H 8LS
Tel: 071 836 1478
Fax: 071 497 8062
Sally Hibbin
Film production. Recent films include Ken Loach's *Riff Raff* and *Raining Stones*, and Les Blair's *Bad Behaviour*

Paramount British Pictures
Paramount House
162-170 Wardour Street
London W1V 4AB
Tel: 071 287 6767
Fax: 071 734 0387
Danton Rissner

Paramount Revcom
46-54 Great Titchfield Street
London W1P 7AE
Tel: 071 636 5066
Fax: 071 436 3252
Michael Deakin
Drama, mini-series and TV movies. Co-produced Jeffrey Archer's *Not a Penny More, Not a Penny Less* with BBC for USA Network. Co-producing *The Doomsday Gun* with HBO

Paravision (UK)
114 The Chambers
Chelsea Harbour
London SW10 0XF
Tel: 071 351 7070
Fax: 071 352 3645
Nick Barton, Linda Agran
Paravision (UK) is the international production arm of Paravision International – the major French media group. The company is currently developing feature films, telemovies, drama series and documentaries

Partridge Films
The Television Centre
Bath Road
Bristol BS4 3HG
Tel: 0272 723777
Fax: 0272 719340
Michael Rosenberg, Carol O'Callaghan (Library)
Makers of wildlife documentaries and videos for TV and educational distribution. Extensive natural history stock shot library

Pelicula Films
7 Queen Margaret Road
Glasgow G20 6DP
Tel: 041 945 3333
Fax: 041 946 8345
Mike Alexander
1992-93: feature film *As An Eilean (From the Island)* in Gaelic and English for Channel 4, Grampian TV, Gaelic Television Committee; *Back to Africa*, documentary for Channel 4's *Travellers' Tales* series; *The Land*, music documentary with singer/songwriter Dougie McLean for BBC TV

Pennies from Heaven
83 Eastbourne Mews
London W2 6LQ
Tel: 071 402 0051/ 081 576 1197
Kenith Trodd
Kenith Trodd is a prolific producer of films for the BBC and others. Recent work includes *After Pilkington, The Singing Detective, She's Been Away, Old Flames, They Never Slept, For the Greater Good, Common Pursuit* and *Femme Fatale* all for the BBC. He also produced for PFH the features *Dreamchild* and *A Month in the Country*. Much of this work has been from screenplays by Dennis Potter, the company's other principal director

Penumbra Productions
21a Brondesbury Villas
London NW6 6AH
Tel: 071 328 4550
Fax: 071 328 3844
H O Nazareth, Eve Pomerance
Cinema and TV productions, specialising in the relationship between 'North and South'. 1991 *Repomen* for Channel 4's *Cutting Edge*; 1992 *China Rocks*; 1993 *Bombay and Jazz*. In development: two cinema features *Slave Brides* and *No Risk Involved*, and series on world music

Persistent Vision Productions
299 Ivydale Road
London SE15 3DZ
Tel: 071 639 5596/081 673 7924
John Stewart, Carol Lemon
In distribution: *Crash* and *The Gaol*. In pre-production: a feature *Virtual Death*. In development: *Revenge* and other thriller/horror features

Photoplay Productions
21 Princess Road
London NW1 8JR
Tel: 071 722 2500
Fax: 071 722 6662
Kevin Brownlow, David Gill, Patrick Stanbury
Originators of 'Thames Silents – Live Cinema' events. Producers of documentaries and TV versions of silent feature films. Specialist research and library services for early cinema. Production credits: *Hollywood, Unknown Chaplin, Keaton – A Hard Act to Follow, Harold Lloyd – The Third Genius*. TV restoration of Harold Lloyd features for Lloyd Estate and TTI. Channel 4 Silents/Live Cinema presentation of *The Four Horsemen of the Apocalypse*. With Camden Parkway cinema reviving a series of earlier Thames Silents. Recently completed: *D.W. Griffith – Father of Film*, a 3-part documentary for Channel 4, and embarking on series about silent film in Europe for BBC2

Picture Palace Films
53a Brewer Street
London W1R 3FD
Tel: 071 734 6630/439 9882
Fax: 071 734 8574
Malcolm Craddock, Alex Usborne
Recently completed *Sharpe's Rifles* and *Sharpe's Eagle* 2 x 2 hrs for Central set in the Peninsular War. Also *The Orchid House*, 4 x 1 hour drama series set in the Caribbean during 1918 and 1938 for Channel 4. In pre-production for *Sharpe II, Tales of a Hard City* 90 min documentary about low life in Sheffield, for Channel 4, Yorkshire TV and La Sept. Also *How to Speak Japanese* 103 min TV film with NHK. In development: *Scarlet Women* by Sandra Goldbacher and Tony Grisoni; *Little Napoleons* by Michael Abbensetts; *Love's Executioner* by Tim Willocks; *Poor Sisters* by Leslie Stewart; *Somebody to Love* by Julie Welch and Giles Foster

Picture Parade
106 Canalot Production Studios
222 Kensal Road
London W10 5BN
Tel: 081 964 1500
Fax: 081 964 4907
Claire Rawcliffe
In production: *The Hidden Navy*, 13 half hours on the history of the Royal Navy for the Discovery Channel Europe and NTV Entertainment. *Flanders and Swann Animations*, a series of short animations based on the animal songs of Michael Flanders and Donald Swann, animated by Maurice Pooley. *Mr Guitar*, 1 hour documentary for Channel 4 featuring Chet Atkins

Pictures of Women
Top Floor
56 Carysfort Road
London N16 9AD
Tel/Fax: 071 249 9632

Planet 24
Thames Quay
Norex Court
195 Marsh Wall
London E14 9SG
Tel: 071 712 9300
Fax: 071 712 9400
Charles Parsons
The Word, The Big Breakfast, Access All Areas

PolyGram Filmed Entertainment
30 Berkeley Square
London W1X 5HA
Tel: 071 493 8800
Fax: 071 499 2596

Portman Entertainment
Pinewood Studios
Iver Heath
Bucks SL0 0NH
Tel: 0753 630366
Fax: 0753 630332
Victor Glynn, Andrew Warren, Ian Warren, Chris Brown, Philip Hinchcliffe, Hilary Heath
Friday on my Mind, mini-series for the BBC, *Hostage*, feature film for Tyne Tees, *The Perfect Husband*, internationally co-produced feature, *Crimebroker*, for Ten Network Australia

Portobello Pictures
42 Tavistock Road
London W11 1AW
Tel: 071 379 5566
Fax: 071 379 5599
Eric Abraham
Specialise in feature film and TV drama. Completed programmes: John le Carré's *A Murder of Quality*; Roald Dahl's *Danny the Champion of the World* (feature); *My Friend Walter* (children's TV film); *Royal Ballet: Hobson's Choice*. In production: *The Life and Extraordinary Adventures of Private Ivan Chonkin* (feature). Projects in development: *The War Zone* (feature), *Darkness at Noon* (feature), *Ghosts* (feature), *Number the Stars* (feature), *St Tiggywinkles* (series)

Poseidon Productions
1st Floor
Hammer House
113 Wardour Street
London W1V 3TD
Tel: 071 734 4441/437 2520
Fax: 071 437 0638
Frixos Constantine
Productions include: *Autism – A World Apart* for Channel 4, *Lysistrata* a feature film co-production with the USSR, *Great Russian Writers,* a mini-series for Channel 4, a documentary on dyslexia for Channel 4 and *Russian Composers* for BBC Wales

Praxis Films
14 Manor Drive
Binbrook
Lincoln LN3 6BX
Tel: 0472 398547
Fax: 0472 398683
Tony Cook, John Goddard
Film and video production of documentaries, current affairs and educational programmes. Recent credits include series for Yorkshire Television and films for Channel 4's *Secret History, Dispatches, Cutting Edge* and *The World This Week* series. Extensive archive of sea, fishing, rural and regional material

Primetime Television
Seymour Mews House
Seymour Mews
Wigmore Street
London W1H 9PE
Tel: 071 935 9000
Fax: 071 935 1992
Richard Price, Ian Gordon, Nigel Whitehouse
Independent TV production/packaging company associated with distributors RPTA. Specialise in international co-productions. Recent projects include: *Porgy and Bess; Jose Carreras – A Life* (LWT); *CIA* (BBC/A&E/NRK); *Brain Sex* (Primedia/ Quality Time Television); *Peter Ustinov on the Orient Express* (Primedia); *First Circle* (Technisonor/Communications Claude Heroux/Primedia)

The Production Gallery
6 Carsons Drive
Great Cornard
Sudbury
Suffolk CO10 0NE
Tel: 0787 880364
Fax: 0787 312370
Angela Bryant
Children's classics/ educational video production and now partnering computer software companies in development of CD-I and CD-Rom programming

Productions Associates (UK)
Pinewood Studios
Iver Heath
Bucks SL0 0NH
Tel: 071 486 9921
Fax: 0753 656844

Prominent Features
68a Delancey Street
London NW1 7RY
Tel: 071 284 0242
Fax: 071 284 1004
Steve Abbott, Anne James
Company formed by Steve Abbott, John Cleese, Terry Gilliam, Eric Idle, Anne James, Terry Jones and Michael Palin to produce in-house features. Produced *The Adventures of Baron Munchausen, Erik The Viking, A Fish Called Wanda, American Friends* and *Splitting Heirs*

Prominent Television
68a Delancey Street
London NW1 7RY
Tel: 071 284 0242
Fax: 071 284 1004
Steve Abbott, Anne James
Company formed by Steve Abbott, John Cleese, Terry Gilliam, Eric Idle, Anne James, Terry Jones and Michael Palin to produce in-house TV programmes. Produced eight part travel documentary series *Pole to Pole*

RM Arts
46 Great Marlborough Street
London W1V 1DB
Tel: 071 439 2637
Fax: 071 439 2316
Reiner Moritz
RM Arts produces a broad range of music and arts programming and co-produces on an international basis with major broadcasters including BBC, LWT, Channel 4, ARD and ZDF in Germany, NOS-TV in Holland, Danmarks Radio, The French Société Européene de Programmes de Télévision (La Sept), SVT in Sweden and Thirteen/ WNET in America

RSPB Film and Video Unit
The Lodge
Sandy
Bedfordshire SG19 2DL
Tel: 0767 680551
Fax: 0767 692365
Producers of *Osprey, Kingfisher, Where Eagles Fly, Barn Owl, The Year of the Stork* and *Flying for Gold.* The unit also acts as an independent producer of environmental films and videos

Sarah Radclyffe Productions
1 Water Lane
Kentish Town Road
London NW1 8NZ
Tel: 071 911 6100
Fax: 071 911 6150
Dixie Linder
Sarah Radclyffe previously founded and was co-owner of Working Title Films and was responsible for, amongst others, *My Beautiful Laundrette, Wish You Were Here*, and *A World Apart*. Sarah Radclyffe Productions was formed in 1993 and productions to date are *Second Best*, dir Chris Menges and *Sirens*, dir John Duigan

Ragdoll Productions
11 Chapel Street
Stratford upon Avon
Warwickshire CV37 6ET
Tel: 0789 262772
Fax: 0789 262773
Anne Wood
Specialist children's TV producer of live action and animation. *Pob* for Channel 4, *Playbox* for Central, *Storytime* for BBC, *Magic Mirror* for ITV, *Boom!* for Channel 4, *Rosie & Jim* (series 1 & 2) for ITV, *Brum* for BBC, *Tots TV* for Central

Rodney Read
45 Richmond Road
Twickenham
Middlesex TW1 3AW
Tel: 081 891 2875
Fax: 081 744 9603
Rodney Read
Film and video production offering experience in factual and entertainment programming. Also provide a full range of back-up facilities for the feature and TV industries, including 'making of' documentaries, promotional programme inserts, sales promos, trailers and commercials. Active in production for UK cable

Recorded Picture Co
8-12 Broadwick Street
London W1V 1FH
Tel: 071 439 0607
Fax: 071 434 1192

Jeremy Thomas
Thomas produced Nagisa Oshima's *Merry Christmas, Mr Lawrence*, Stephen Frears' *The Hit*, Nicolas Roeg's *Insignificance*, *The Last Emperor* and *The Sheltering Sky* directed by Bernardo Bertolucci and *The Naked Lunch* directed by David Cronenberg. Most recently produced: *Little Buddha*, directed by Bernardo Bertolucci. Jeremy Thomas is Chairman of the BFI

Red Rooster Film & Television Entertainment
29 Floral Street
London WC2£ 9DB
Tel: 071 379 7727
Fax: 071 379 5756
Linda James, Stephen Bayly, Jenny Reeks, Jill Green
Company formed in 1982 by James and Bayly, producing quality TV drama and feature films. Produced 34 hours of film including TV movies and 2 features. Productions broadcast in 1992/93 include *Body and Soul* for Carlton and David Nobbs' *Life and Times of Henry Pratt* for Granada. Projects in development include *The Brilliant*, a long-running drama series for LWT and Charles Palliser's *The Quincunx* adapted by Anthony Horowitz

Redwing Film Company
1 Wedgwood Mews
12/13 Greek Street
London W1V 5LW
Tel: 071 734 6642
Fax: 071 734 9850
Film, TV and commercial production

Regent Productions
The Mews
6 Putney Common
Putney
London SW15 1HL
Tel: 081 789 5350
Fax: 081 789 5332
William G Stewart
Productions for 1993 include two new series of the Channel 4 quiz series *Fifteen-to-One* (125 programmes). Development deals include quiz shows, a seven-part drama series and a current affairs project

Renegade Films
13 Arbuthnot Road
London SE14 5LS
Tel: 071 639 1688
Fax: 071 277 5135
Robert Buckler, Amanda Mackenzie Stuart
Previous credits include *Pressure, The Last Place on Earth, Facts of Life*, currently packaging features *Brothers in Trouble* (producer/writer Robert Buckler, director Udayan Prasad), *The Bangers and Chips Explosion* (prods Robert Buckler, Amanda Mackenzie Stuart, writers Tony Robinson, Brough Girling). Other projects include TV maxi series, children's sitcom, animation

Replay
29 Leslie Road
Chobham
Woking
Surrey GU24 8LB
Tel/Fax: 0276 857040
Production of broadcast and corporate documentaries and drama – including 50 min programme on World Hovercraft Championships broadcast by ITV in 1992 and *Mourning*, a 15 min black comedy currently in post-production

Ritefilms
20 Bouverie Road West
Folkestone
Kent CT20 2SZ
Tel: 0303 252335
Mobile: 0860 614902
George Wright
Current affairs TV news gathering. Film production, documentary and corporate

Riverfront Pictures
Dock Cottages
Peartree Lane
Glamis Road
Wapping
London E1 9SR
Tel: 071 481 2939
Fax: 071 480 5520
Jeff Perks, Carole Crouch
Specialise in music, arts and drama-documentaries. Independent productions for Channel 4/BBC. Latest production: Channel 4 *Cutting Edge*

Roadshow Productions
c/o 6 Basil Mansions
Basil Street
London SW3 1AP
Tel: 071 584 0542
Fax: 071 584 1549
Kurt Unger,
Daniel Unger
Recent productions include feature film *Return from the River Kwai*

Roberts & Wykeham Films
7 Barb Mews
London W6 7PA
Tel: 071 602 4897
Fax: 071 602 3016
Sadie Wykeham,
Joel Wykeham,
Gwynne Roberts
Recent productions include: *The Road Back to Hell* (BBC *Everyman*), *Kurdistan: The Dream Betrayed* (C4 *Dispatches*). Also packaging and editing services: *The Late Late Show* (RTE) for Channel 4 1988-1993

Rose Bay Film Productions
6th Floor
76 Oxford Street
London W1N 0AT
Tel: 071 412 0400
Fax: 071 412 0300
Matthew Steiner, Simon Usiskin
Drama, features, documentary and entertainment

Sands Films
119 Rotherhithe Street
London SE16 4NF
Tel: 071 231 2209
Fax: 071 231 2119
Christine Edzard,
Richard Goodwin
The Fool, The Long Day Closes (for BFI), *A Dangerous Man* (for Anglia), *As You Like It*. In preparation: *My Sister in this House* and *Foreign Moon*

Saturn Films
31 Healey Street
London NW1 8SR
Tel: 071 284 4104
Fax: 071 284 4075
Terrence Francis,
Kamscilla Naidoo
An independent film company specialising primarily in documentaries exploring new perspectives on the international black community and creating innovative programme strands which adequately reflect today's multicultural society in Britain

Scala Productions
39-43 Brewer Street
London W1R 3FD
Tel: 071 734 7060
Fax: 071 437 3248
Nik Powell,
Stephen Woolley
Backbeat, The Crying Game

Scimitar Films
6-8 Sackville Street
London W1X 1DD
Tel: 071 603 7272
Fax: 071 602 9217
Michael Winner
Winner has produced and directed many films, including *Death Wish 3, Appointment with Death, A Chorus of Disapproval, Bullseye!* and *Dirty Weekend*

Scottish Television Enterprises
Cowcaddens
Glasgow G2 3PR
Tel: 041 332 9999
Fax: 041 332 6982
Alistair Moffat, Jeff Henry
Doctor Finlay (period drama series), *Taggart* (detective series), *Crime Story* (drama), *Captain Zed and the Zee Zone* (animation), *What's Up Doc* (children's live TV), *Fun House* (children's series/game show)

Screen Ventures
49 Goodge Street
London W1P 1FB
Tel: 071 580 7448
Fax: 071 631 1265
Christopher Mould,
Dominic Saville
Production company specialising in documentaries, current affairs and music production such as *Mojo Working*, a 13 part music series for Channel 4, *Genet*, a South Bank Show for LWT and *Heart of Gold*, a half hour documentary. Music specials include Muddy Waters, James Brown and John Lennon

SelecTV
6 Derby Street
London W1Y 7HD
Tel: 071 355 2868
Fax: 071 629 1604

M J Pilsworth
Incorporates Alomo, Clement Le Frenais and WitzEnd. *Lovejoy, Birds of a Feather, The New Statesman, Get Back, Love Hurts, Nightingales, So You Think You've Got Troubles, Wall of Silence, Full Stretch, Over the Rainbow, Laughing Gas, Pie in the Sky, Hecklers, Goodnight Sweetheart, Freddie and Max, The Old Boy Network*

Seventh Art Productions
20 Eaton Place
Brighton BN2 1EH
Tel: 0273 777678
Fax: 0273 323777
Amanda Wilkie
Factual programming both for the national networks and international broadcasters. Established ten years ago by filmmaker Phil Grabsky, with experience in all areas from raising finance to distribution. Titles include: *Spain – In the Shadow of the Sun* (4-part series for Channel 4/SVT/YLE), *Talkin' Turkey – The Alternative Christmas Lunch* (for Channel 4), *Blueprint for Democracy* (assoc. producers for Channel 4 *Dispatches*), *Nepal – Elections 1991* (for Sky News/Visnews), *The Great Commanders* (6-part series for Channel 4/A&E/Ambrose Video/SBS/Sovtelexport), *The Secret South* (3-part series for Meridian Broadcasting). Various projects in development with BBC/C3/C4 and international broadcasters

Shadowlands Productions
Twickenham Studios
St Margaret's
Twickenham TW1 2AW
Tel: 081 892 4477
Fax: 081 744 2766
Lord Attenborough, Terry Clegg, Brian Eastman, Diana Hawkins
Feature *Shadowlands* in production 1993

Shooting Star Film Productions
8 Queen Street
London W1X 7PH
Tel: 071 409 1925
Pinewood Studios
Iver Heath
Bucks SLO 0NH
Tel: 0753 651700
John Hough
Features, documentaries, TV drama. Films: *Biggles, Legend of Hell House, Dirty Mary Crazy Larry, American Gothic, Distant Scream*

Siriol Productions
Phoenix Buildings
3 Mount Stuart Square
Butetown
Cardiff CF1 6RW
Tel: 0222 488400
Fax: 0222 485962
Robin Lyons
Formerly Siriol Animation. Producers of high quality animation for TV and the cinema. Makers of *SuperTed, The Princess and the Goblin, Under Milk Wood, Santa and the Tooth Fairies, Santa's First Christmas* and*Tales of the Tooth Fairies*

Skreba
5a Noel Street
London W1V 3RB
Tel: 071 437 6492
Fax: 071 437 0644
Ann Skinner,
Simon Relph
Produced *Return of the Soldier* and *Secret Places*, directed by Zelda Barron. Other projects include *Bad Hats, A Profile of Arthur J Mason, Honour, Profit and Pleasure* and *The Gourmet*. Relph produced *Comrades* and *Camilla*, and co-produced Louis Malle's *Damage*. Skinner was executive producer on *Heavenly Pursuits* and produced *The Kitchen Toto, A Very British Coup, One Man's War, God on the Rocks* and *A Pin for the Butterfly*

Skyline Film and Television Productions
4 Picardy Place
Edinburgh EH1 3JT
Tel: 031 557 4580
Fax: 031 556 4377
126 Rusthall Avenue
London W4 1BS
Tel: 081 747 8444
Fax: 081 995 2117
Trevor Davies, Leslie Hills, Steve Clark-Hall,

Mairi Bett
Producers of Derek Jarman's *Edward II*, *Narrow Rooms* and *The Big Day* for Channel 4. Plus *Birds of Paradise* for BBC, *Scottish Women* and *Shadowing* for Scottish Television. Development, funding, and production association with Zenith and output deal for factual programmes with Scottish Television

Soho Communications
8 Percy Street
London W1P 9FB
Tel: 071 637 5825
Fax: 071 436 9740
Tony Coggans
Where Have All the Flowers Gone? 1 hour TV documentary, *Forbidden Planet* 1 x half hour TV documentary

Specific Films
25 Rathbone Street
London W1P 1AG
Tel: 071 580 7476
Fax: 071 494 2676
Michael Hamlyn
Formed in 1991 with PolyGram to produce comedy feature films structured around comedy committee of Mel Smith, Griff Rhys-Jones, Stephen Fry, Hugh Laurie, Richard Curtis, Dawn French, Jennifer Saunders, Peter Fincham and Michael Hamlyn. In pre-production: *Priscilla – Queen of the Desert*

Speedy Films
8 Royalty Mews
Dean Street
London W1V 5AW
Tel: 071 437 9313/494 4043
Fax: 071 434 0830
Irene Kotlarz
Animated shorts, commercials and titles. Currently in production *Abdultees* 11 min animated short for Channel 4

Spidercom Films
12 D'Arblay Street
London W1V 3FP
Tel: 071 287 5589/734 4743
Fax: 071 287 4743
Nick Burgess-Jones, William Green, Debbie Bourne
Documentaries: *Short Stories, Popham, Suddenly Last Summer.* Short films for MTV: *My Best Party, Ghana Fashion.* Pop promos and commercials. *Revengers Tragedy* in post production. Feature *The Painting* to be made 1994

Spitting Image Productions
17-19 Plumber's Row
Aldgate
London E1 1EQ
Tel: 071 375 1561
Fax: 071 375 2492
Joanna Beresford
Comedy-based production company specialising in international TV and film, commercials and corporate video, using puppets, live action, cell and stop-frame animation. Productions include 14 series of *Spitting Image* to June 1993, and co-production with the BBC *The Mary Whitehouse Experience* (2 series)

Stagescreen Productions
12 Upper St Martin's Lane
London WC2H 9DL
Tel: 071 497 2510
Fax: 071 497 2208
Jeffrey Taylor
Film, TV and theatre company whose work includes *A Handful of Dust, Death of a Son* (for BBC TV),*Where Angels Fear to Tread, Foreign Affairs* (for TNT)

State Screen Productions
Rowan House
9-31 Victoria Road
Park Royal
London NW10 6DP
Tel: 081 961 1717
Fax: 081 961 6454
Andrew Johnson, Simon Johnson
Feature film production. *The Tale of a Vampire* (1992). Current projects: *Fallen Angel, Black Wolf, Garden Man*

Stephens Kerr
8-12 Camden High Street
London NW1 0JH
Tel: 071 916 2124
Fax: 071 916 2125
Eleanor Stephens, Jean Kerr
Currently in production: *Talking about Sex* – for Channel 4 schools programming; a series on food and nutrition, also for Channel 4. Recent programming: *The Love Weekend, Food File II, Nights, Men Talk, Sex Talk, Love Talk,* all for Channel 4

Robert Stigwood Organisation
118-120 Wardour Street
London W1V 4BT
Tel: 071 437 2512
Fax: 071 437 3674
Robert Stigwood, David Land, David Herring
Theatre and film producer Stigwood is currently involved in the film of *Evita* and several other projects

Studio 9, The Video Producers
Monyhull Hall Road
Kings Norton
Birmingham B30 3QB
Tel: 021 444 4750
Gary Liszewski
New Directors Award winner. Produce drama, documentaries, promotional, entertainment and training films – broadcast and non-broadcast – from script to screen. Freelance crew and various equipment hire

Swanlind Communication
The Wharf
Bridge Street
Birmingham B1 2JR
Tel: 021 616 1701
Fax: 021 616 1520
Mike Davies, Peter Stack
Business TV, controlled communication. Programme production. Conference/event production and management. TV systems

TKO Communications
PO Box 130
Hove
East Sussex BN3 6QU
Tel: 0273 550088
Fax: 0273 540969
Jeffrey Kruger
A division of the Kruger Organisation, making music programmes for TV, satellite and video release worldwide as well as co-producing various series and full length feature films. Recent co-production with Central TV music division *21st Anniversary Tour of Glen Campbell* and *Johnny Cash – Live from Poland, Country Music Comes to Europe* series featuring major Nashville stars

TV Cartoons
39 Grafton Way
London W1P 5LA
Tel: 071 388 2222
Fax: 071 383 4192
John Coates, Claire Jennings, Norman Kauffman
TVC produced the Academy Award-nominated film *The Snowman*, and the feature *When The Wind Blows*, both adaptations from books by Raymond Briggs. Production was completed in May 1989 of *Granpa*, a half-hour television special for Channel 4 and TVS. Completed half hour special of Raymond Briggs' *Father Christmas* which was shown on Channel 4 Christmas 91/92. Currently in production with six half-hours called *The World of Peter Rabbit and Friends*, based on the books of Beatrix Potter

TV Choice
80-81 St Martin's Lane
London WC2N 4AA
Tel: 071 379 0873
Fax: 071 379 0263
Chris Barnard, Norman Thomas
Producer and distributor of dramas and documentaries about business, technology and finance TV Choice videos and learning packs are used in education and training in the UK and overseas. Co-producers feature film *Conspiracy* with new features in development

TVF
375 City Road
London EC1V 1NA
Tel: 071 837 3000
Fax: 071 833 2185
David Pounds
Production company specialising in factual output. Titles include *Dispatches, Without Walls, Equinox, Horizon.* 16 major awards for last eight programmes

D L Taffner UK
10 Bedford Square
London WC1B 3RA
Tel: 071 631 1184
Fax: 071 636 4571

Specialising in entertainment programming: *Talkabout*, ITV game show; *As Time Goes By*, BBC sitcom; *The Saint*, LWT drama series; *Love on a Branch Line*, 4 x 1 hour BBC mini-series. Also operate a joint venture with the Theatre of Comedy at the Shaftesbury Theatre. The parent company is a well known producer and distributor in New York, Los Angeles and Sydney

Talisman Films
5 Addison Place
London W11 4RJ
Tel: 071 603 7474
Fax: 071 602 7422
Alan Shallcross, Richard Jackson
Production of the whole range of drama for TV together with theatric features. Particularly committed to co-producing with continental European and North American partners. 1993: *The Rector's Wife*, 4 x 1 hour drama serial for Channel 4

TalkBack Productions
33 Percy Street
London W1P 9FG
Tel: 071 631 3940
Fax: 071 631 4273
Produced *Smith and Jones*, *Bernard and the Genie*, *Bonjour la Classe*, *Smith and Jones '92* (BBC1); *A Life in Pieces*, *Murder Most Horrid*, *The Day Today*, *Twelve Days of Christmas* (BBC2); *Tales from the Poop Deck* (Central); *De Mob* (Yorkshire)

Tartan Television
35 Little Russell Street
London WC1A 2HH
Tel: 071 323 3022
Fax: 071 323 4857
Norrie Maclaren, Christopher Mitchell
Producing for both TV and film

Richard Taylor Cartoon Films
76 Dukes Avenue
London N10 2QA
Tel: 081 444 7547
Fax: 081 444 7218
Richard Taylor, Catherine Taylor
Production of video teaching material for BBC English. Production of Channel 4 commission *The Mill*, directed and animated by Petra Freeman

Team Video Productions
Canalot
222 Kensal Road
London W10 5BN
Tel: 081 960 5536

Television History Workshop (THW)
42 Queen Square
London WC1N 3AJ
Tel: 071 405 6627
Fax: 071 242 1426
Sharon Goulds, Marilyn Wheatcroft, Greg Lanning
1992 productions include: *I Renounce War*, a documentary about conscientious objectors in the first and second world wars, part of BBC2's *War and Peace* season. *Learning to Fail*, a documentary for BBC2 about English attitudes to education

Teliesyn
Helwick House
19 David Street
Cardiff CF1 2EH
Tel: 0222 667556
Fax: 0222 667546
Carmel Gahan, Mary Simmonds, Colin Thomas, Angela Graham, Michele Ryan, Eiry Palfrey
Producers of *Hughesovska and the New Russia* documentary series for BBC/S4C. *Writing on the Line*, 4 x 1 hour drama documentary series for Channel 4. Currently producing *Wales Playhouse '93* for BBC Wales, a series of five short films bringing together new writers and new directors

Tempest Films
33 Brookfield
Highgate West Hill
London N6 6AT
Tel: 081 340 0877
Fax: 081 340 9309
Jacky Stoller, Paul Hines
Three two hour TV movies filmed in Canada, Germany and Ireland based on the books of Dick Francis. *Shrinks*, 7 hours for Euston Films. *Body and Soul*, 6 hours for Carlton TV. Currently 10 hours *Pie in the Sky* for SelecTV/BBC. In development *Grace*, 4 hours based on a book by Michael Stewart. Two drama series plus long running soap

Thin Man Films
9 Greek Street
London W1V 5LE
Tel: 071 734 7372
Fax: 071 287 5228
Simon Channing-Williams, Mike Leigh
A Sense of History Channel 4 1992; *Naked* FFI/First Independent 1993; *Untitled '94* in development

Third Eye Productions
Unit 210 Canalot Studios
222 Kensal Road
London W10 5BN
Tel: 081 969 8211
Fax: 081 960 8780
Alison Ramsey
TV productions covering the worlds of arts, music, ethnography and developing world culture

Tiger Aspect Productions
47 Dean Street
London W1V 5HL
Tel: 071 434 0672
Fax: 071 287 1448
Rowan Atkinson, Peter Bennett-Jones, Charles Brand, Mark Chapman, Paul Sommers
Mr Bean (Thames), *Just for Laughs 1993* (Channel 4), *Bill Hicks Live at the Dominion* (HBO/Channel 4), *Funny Business* (BBC/Showtime), *Root* (Central), *Coltrane in a Cadillac* (Meridian), *Great Railway Journey* (BBC), *Monkey Bay* (Channel 4)

Time and Light Productions
5 Darling Road
London SE4 1YQ
Tel/Fax: 081 692 0145
Roger Elsgood
Works with European agencies commissioning film and TV programmes featuring the work of artists and writers. Produced *Sea, See, C* with Henry Moore, *Time and Light* with John Berger, *Between the Dog and the Fox* with Marc Camille Chaimowicz and is currently making *La Musique Anglaise* for TV

Tiny Epic Video Co
37 Dean Street
London W1V 5AP
Tel: 071 437 2854
Fax: 071 434 0211
Roger Thomas

Topaz Productions
Manchester House
46 Wormholt Street
London W12 0LS
Tel: 081 749 2619
Fax: 081 749 0358
Malcolm Taylor, David Jason
Produced *The Poetry Book* and *The Adventures of Dai Mouse* independently in 1990 with sales to Channel 4 and ABC (Australia). In development: *After Milk Wood*, Dylan Thomas documentary and *Treasure Hunt*, Molly Keane film adaptation

Trans World International
TWI House
23 Eyot Gardens
London W6 9TR
Tel: 081 846 8070
Fax: 081 746 5334
Buzz Hornett, Bill Sinrich, Chris Guinness
TV and video sports production and rights representation branch of Mark McCormack's International Management Group. TWI represents the TV rights to many leading sports events including Wimbledon, British Open, US Open, World Championship of Golf and World Matchplay. Productions include the Men's ATP Tennis Tour, Volvo PGA Golf Tour, Test Cricket Series featuring England, Australia, India, Pakistan and the West Indies. Made-for-TV specials *Conquer the Arctic* and the *World's Strongest Man*. Also *High 5* and the international series *Sportraits*

Transatlantic Films
17 Girdlers Road
London W14 OPS
Tel: 071 727 0132
Fax: 071 603 5049
Revel Guest
Recent productions include a 10-part documentary series on the legacy of Ancient Greece in the modern world, *Greek Fire*; a 13-part

series, *In Search of Paradise*; a four-part series directed by Peter Greenaway, *Four American Composers*; *Placido – A Year in the Life of Placido Domingo*; and an eight-part series *The Horse in Sport* with Channel 4 and ABC Australia

Triple Vision

Euston House
81-103 Euston Street
London NW1 2ET
Tel: 071 388 5375
Fax: 071 387 7324
Penny Dedman,
Terry Flaxton
Film and TV production company. Documentary, drama, arts, pop promos

Twentieth Century Vixen

74b St James's Drive
London SW17 7RR
Tel/Fax: 081 682 0587
Tel: 071 727 8609
Claire Hunt,
Kim Longinotto
Film/video production and distribution, mainly social documentaries. Latest broadcast production *The Good Wife of Tokyo* (Channel 4) about Japanese women in a changing world. Next production about young women in a Japanese theatre group trying to become 'men' (BBC). Also tapes about special needs, women's issues and sexual abuse. Freelance work undertaken

Twenty Twenty Television

10 Stucley Place
London NW1 8NS
Tel: 071 284 2020
Fax: 071 284 1810
Claudia Milne,
Mike Whittaker
The company continues to produce programmes exclusively for broadcast TV, specialising in worldwide investigative journalism, current affairs, factually-based drama and science. Recent productions include *Storyline* series for Carlton current affairs/ documentary strand and *Maiden Voyages* travel series for Channel 4

Ty Gwyn Films

Y Ty Gwyn
Llanllyfni
Caernarfon
Gwynedd LL54 6DG
Tel: 0286 881235
Gareth Wynn Jones

Tyburn Productions

Pinewood Studios
Iver Heath
Bucks SL0 0NH
Tel: 0753 651700
Fax: 0753 656754
Kevin Francis,
Gillian Garrow
Long-established independent TV production company

UBA

32 Porchester Terrace
London W2 3TP
Tel: 071 402 6313
Fax: 071 724 5825
Peter Shaw
Production company for cinema and TV projects. Past productions include: *Turtle Diary* for the Samuel Goldwyn Company, *Castaway* for Cannon, *The Lonely Passion of Judith Hearne* for HandMade Films, *Taffin* for MGM, *Windprints* for MCEG Virgin Vision and *The Haunted Realm* drama documentary for Granada TV

Uden Associates

Chelsea Wharf
Lots Road
London SW10 0QJ
Tel: 071 351 1255
Fax: 071 376 3937
Fiona Reid, Patrick Uden, William Miller, Michael Proudfoot
Film and TV production company for broadcast through Channel 4, BBC and corporate clients

Unicorn Organisation

Pottery Lane Studios
34a Pottery Lane
Holland Park
London W11 4LZ
Tel: 071 229 5131
Fax: 071 229 4999
Michael Seligman,
Julian Roberts

Union Pictures

36 Marshall Street
London W1V 1LL
Tel: 071 287 5110
Fax: 071 287 3770
Brad Adams
Recent productions include: *Masterchef, Junior Masterchef, Harry, Dave Allen on ..., A Dog's Tale, Equinox, Family Fortunes*. In development: *Paparazzi, The Boro, Get Out of That, Magical Mind Magical Body*

Video Visuals

37 Harwood Road
London SW6 4QP
Tel: 071 731 0079
Fax: 071 384 2027
Currently produces *The Chart Show* for ITV

Videotel Productions

Ramillies House
1/2 Ramillies Street
London W1V 1DF
Tel: 071 439 6301
Fax: 071 437 0731
Nick Freethy,
Stephen Bond
Producers of educational and training packages for TV and video distribution

Visual Music

9 Williams Court
Trade Street
Cardiff CF1 5DQ
Tel: 0222 641511
Fax: 0222 668220
Pamela Hunt,
Kate Jones-Davies
Drama, documentaries, music, entertainment, reality. Past productions: *Gompa* (VATV), *In Living Memory* (BBC Wales), *Copswap* (HTV Wales), *Going Solo* (BBC2)

Viz

4 Bank Street
Inverkeithing
Fife KY11 1LR
Tel: 0383 412811
Fax: 0383 418103
Barbara Grigor,
Murray Grigor
Founded 1971. Most recent production *Blue Black Permanent*, dir Margaret Tait 1992. Also *The Fall and Rise of Mackintosh*, 1991; *The Why?s Man* – in pursuit of the question mark, with George Wyllie and Bill Paterson, 1990; *Irony Curtain* – art and politics between Russia and America, 1990; *The Great Wall of China* – Lovers at the Brink, 1989

WTTV

1 Water Lane
Kentish Town Road
London NW1 8NZ
Tel: 071 911 6100
Fax: 071 911 6150
Antony Root, Simon Wright, Grainne Marmion, Tim Bevan
1991: *Edward II*;1992: *Amnesty – The Big 30, Further Tales of the Riverbank, TV Squash, The Borrowers*; 1993: *Tales of the City, The Borrowers* (second series)

Wall To Wall Television

8-9 Spring Place
Kentish Town
London NW5 3ER
Tel: 071 485 7424
Fax: 071 267 5292
Alex Graham, Jane Root
Producers of drama, documentaries, factual and leisure programmes, including for ITV *A Statement of Affairs, The View, Big City*; for BBC *You Me and It, The Human Face*; for Channel 4 *Grow Your Greens, Eat Your Greens* with Sophie Grigson, *New Nightmares, For Love or Money* and *The Media Show*

The Walnut Partnership

Crown House
Armley Road
Leeds LS12 2EJ
Tel: 0532 456913
Fax: 0532 439614
Geoff Penn
Film and video production company

Warner Sisters

21 Russell Street
London WC2B 5HP
Tel: 071 836 0134
Fax: 071 836 6559
Lavinia Warner,
Jane Wellesley
Life's a Gas (Channel 4/ British Screen), *Rides* (Series 1 and 2 for BBC1). Development deals with CTE, Carlton, South Pacific Pictures

Waterloo Films

Silver House
31-35 Beak Street
London W1R 3LD
Tel: 071 494 4060
Fax: 071 287 6366
Dennis Woolf, Ray Davies
Producer of *Return to Waterloo*, a fantasy film for Channel 4 written and directed by Ray Davies of The Kinks, co-financed by Channel 4 and RCA Video Productions. Other projects in development

Watershed Television
11 Regent Street
Clifton
Bristol BS8 4HW
Tel: 0272 733833
Fax: 0272 733722
Film and video production. Broadcast, corporate, commercials

White City Films
79 Sutton Court Road
London W4 3EQ
Tel: 081 994 6795
Fax: 081 995 9379
Aubrey Singer
Current affairs and documentary productions

Michael White Productions
13 Duke Street
St James's
London SW1Y 6DB
Tel: 071 839 3971
Fax: 071 839 3836
Michael White
Trade product. Film and theatre producer. Recent films include *High Season, Eat the Rich, White Mischief, Nuns on the Run, The Pope Must Die, The Turn of the Screw*

David Wickes Productions
169 Queen's Gate
London SW7 5HE
Tel: 071 225 1382
Fax: 071 589 8847
David Wickes, Sue Davies
Wrote, directed and produced *Frankenstein* for Turner Pictures, starring Patrick Bergin, Randy Quaid and Sir John Mills

WitzEnd Productions
see ***SelecTV***

Woodfilm Productions
59 Campden Street
London W8 7EL
Tel: 071 243 8600
Elizabeth Wood
Producers of arts, features and TV drama; *The Pantomime Dame* for The Arts Council, *The Future of Things Past, Stairs, Go For It, Sophie* and *Say Hello to the Real Dr Snide* for Channel 4, *Nowhere To Go – But Up* for Carlton TV

Dennis Woolf Productions
Silver House
31-35 Beak Street
London W1R 3LD
Tel: 071 494 4060
Fax: 071 287 6366
Specialising in current affairs *Dispatches*, documentaries *Cutting Edge*, music *Epitaph: Charles Mingus,* and studio reconstructions of contemporary trials *The Court Report* series for Channel 4, *The Trial of Klaus Barbie* for the BBC

Workhouse Television
Granville House
St Peter Street
Winchester
Hants SO23 9AF
Tel: 0962 863449
Fax: 0962 841026
Carol Wade
Action – TVS, *Lifeschool* – BBC, *Select Business Programme, Equinox. Future Perfect, Wizadora, Leisure Programme, Southern Gold, Tale of 4 Cities* – Meridian. *Cookery Club* – Network/ Discovery

Working Title Films
1 Water Lane
Kentish Town Road
London NW1 8NZ
Tel: 071 911 6100
Fax: 071 911 6150/916 0669
922247 Alden Drive
Beverley Hills
California 90210
USA
Tel: (310) 777 1970
Fax: (310) 777 4698
Tim Bevan, Eric Fellner
Robin Hood (for 20th Century Fox), *London Kills Me, Map of the Human Heart, Bob Roberts, Romeo is Bleeding, Posse, The Young Americans, The Hudsucker Proxy, Four Weddings and a Funeral, Tales of the City* (for Working Title Television)

World Film Services
3rd Floor
12-14 Argyll Street
London W1V 1AB
Tel: 071 734 3536
Fax: 071 734 3585
John Heyman

World Wide Group
21-25 St Anne's Court
London W1V 3AW
Tel: 071 434 1121
Fax: 071 734 0619
Ray Townsend, Chris Courtenay Taylor
Catherine Cookson film series, *Finders Keepers, Kappatoo, Blue Skies* (for *Equinox*), *The Last Supper, The Last Soviet Citizen* (both for *Arena*)

Worldmark Productions
The Old Studio
18 Middle Row
London W10 5AT
Tel: 081 960 3251
Fax: 081 960 6150
Drummond Challis, David Wooster
Gold Rush – Official film of 1991 Rugby World Cup; *Great Danes* – official film of 1992 European Football Championships; *World Cup Spectacular* – 26 part TV series introducing 1994 World Cup. Plus corporate and commercials work

Year 2000 Film and Television Productions
3 Benson Road
Blackpool FY3 7HP
Tel: 0253 395403/824057
Michael Hammond
Film and TV producers

Yorkshire Film Co
Capital House
Sheepscar Court
Meanwood Road
Leeds LS7 2BB
Tel: 0532 441224
Fax: 0532 441220
Keith Hardy
Producers of satellite/ broadcast sports documentaries, news coverage, corporate and commercials in film and video

ZED
29 Heddon Street
London W1R 7LL
Tel: 071 494 3181
Fax: 071 434 1203
Sophie Balhetchet, Glenn Wilhide, Ruth Walsh
Completed productions include *Memento,* 8 part talk show hosted by Joan Bakewell, an adaptation of Mary Wesley's *The Camomile Lawn* written by Ken Taylor, directed by Sir Peter Hall. Two six-part drama series of *The Manageress* directed by Christopher King. Also *The Missing Reel* a drama documentary special written and directed by Christopher Rawlence

Zenith North
11th floor
Cale Cross House
156 Pilgrim Street
Newcastle upon Tyne
NE1 6SU
Tel: 091 261 0077
Fax: 091 222 0271
Ian Squires
Subsidiary of Zenith Productions. Producers of *Byker Grove* for BBC1; *Oasis* for Carlton Television; music specials for S4C; variety of productions for Tyne Tees Television

Zenith Productions
43-45 Dorset Street
London W1H 4AB
Tel: 071 224 2440
Fax: 071 224 3194
Scott Meek
Film and TV production company, subsidiary of Carlton Communications and Paramount Pictures. Productions include feature films *Trust, Simple Men, Just Like a Woman. Inspector Morse* for Central, *Shoot to Kill* for ITV, *Chimera* for Anglia, *Firm Friends* for Tyne Tees. Zenith Productions, Zenith North and Action Time comprise The Zenith Group

Zooid Pictures
72 Bickerton Road
London N19 5JS
Tel: 071 281 2407
Richard Philpott, Jasmine Nancholas
Producers of experimental and TV documentaries, recent productions include *The Flora Faddy Furry Dance Day* (10 min) and *Here in the Real World* (33 min). Also promos and campaign films, and operates 'The Art of Film' scheme, programming and promoting new British experimental cinema internationally (festivals, cinémathèques, TV etc). Specialist technical services to independent filmmakers

PRODUCTION STARTS

Below are listed British-made and/or financed features, USA productions based in Britain and some single television films running over 73 minutes which began production between January and December 1992

Alistair MacLean's Death Train
British Lion/Jadran Film/ USA Pictures/Yorkshire International Films
Location: Croatia, Slovenia
Producer: Peter Snell
Director/Screenwriter: David S Jackson
Director of Photography: Timothy Eaton
Editors: Eric Boyd-Perkins, Peter Musgrave
Cast: Pierce Brosnan, Patrick Stewart, Ted Levine, Alexandra Paul, Christoper Lee

bfi *Anchoress*
BFI/Corsan Film/ Ministry of the Flemish Community/BRTN/ASLK-CGER/Nationale Loterij-Loterie Nationale/Channel Four
Location: Leopoldsburg, Belgium
Executive in charge of production: Angela Topping
Producers: Paul Breuls, Ben Gibson
Associate Producers: Catherine Vandeleene, Judith Stanley-Smith
Director: Chris Newby
Screenwriters: Judith Stanley-Smith, Christine Watkins
Director of Photography: Michel Baudour
Editor: Brand Thumin
Cast: Natalie Morse, Eugene Bervoets, Toyah Willcox, Peter Postlethwaite, Christopher Eccleston

Anna Lee
LWT
Location: London
Executive Producer: Nick Elliott
Producer: Sue Birtwistle
Director: Colin Bucksey
Screenwriter: Andrew Davies, from the novel by Liza Cody
Director of Photography: Peter Sinclair
Editor: Jon Costelloe
Cast: Imogen Stubbs, Alan Howard, Michael Bryant, Barbara Leigh Hunt, Shirley Anne Field

As An Eilean (From the Island)
Pelicula Films/Gaelic Television Committee/ Channel Four
Location: Wester Ross, Glasgow
Executive Producer: Rod Stoneman
Producers: Douglas Eadie, Mike Alexander
Director: Mike Alexander
Screenwriter: Douglas Eadie, from the novels by Iain Crichton Smith
Director of Photography: Mark Littlewood
Editor: Fiona Macdonald
Cast: Ken Hutchinson, Tom Watson, Wilma Kennedy

The Baby of Mâcon
Allarts/UGC/Cine Electra/ Channel Four/Filmstiftung Nordrhein Westfalen
Location: Germany, Netherlands
Executive Producer: Denis Wigman
Producer: Kees Kasander
Co-Producer: Yves Marmion
Director/Screenwriter: Peter Greenaway
Director of Photography: Sacha Vierny
Editor: Chris Wyatt
Cast: Julia Ormond, Ralph Fiennes, Philip Stone, Jonathan Lacey, Don Henderson

Bad Behaviour
Parallax Pictures/Film on Four/British Screen
Location: North London
Executive Producer: Sally Hibbin

■ **Anchoress**

■ The Baby of Mâcon

Producer: Sarah Curtis
Director: Les Blair
Director of Photography: Witold Stok
Editor: Martin Walsh
Cast: Stephen Rea, Sinead Cusack, Philip Jackson, Phil Daniels

Being Human
Enigma Films/Warner Bros
Studio: Pinewood
Location: North of Scotland, Morocco, California, New York
Producers: David Puttnam, Robert F Colesberry
Associate Producer: Steve Norris
Director/Screenwriter: Bill Forsyth
Director of Photography: Michael Coulter
Editor: Mike Ellis
Cast: Robin Williams, John Turturro, Vincent D'Onofrio, Anna Galiena

Bhaji On The Beach
Umbi Films/Film Four International
Location: Blackpool/London
Producer: Nadine Marsh-Edwards
Director/Screenwriter: Gurinder Chadha
Director of Photography: John Kenway
Editor: Oral Ottley
Cast: Kim Vithana, Sarita Khajuria, Lalita Ahmed, Zohra Segal

■ Black and Blue

Black and Blue
BBC Screen One
Location: London, Liverpool
Executive Producer: Richard Broke
Producers: Ruth Caleb, G F Newman
Associate Producer: Simon Mills
Director: David Hayman
Screenwriter: G F Newman
Director of Photography: John Daly
Editor: Sue Wyatt
Cast: Christopher John Hall, Linus Roache, Martin Shaw, Iain Glen, Ray Winstone

bfi ***Blue Black Permanent***
Viz Permanent/Channel Four/BFI/Scottish Film Production Fund/Orkney Islands Council/City of Edinburgh District Council/Grampian Television/British Screen
Location: Edinburgh, Orkney
Executive in charge of production (BFI): Angela Topping
Executive Producers: Ben Gibson, Rod Stoneman, Kate Swan
Producer: Barbara Grigor
Director/Screenwriter: Margaret Tait
Director of Photography: Alex Scott
Editor: John MacDonnell
Cast: Celia Imrie, Gerda Stevenson, James Fleet, Jack Shepherd, Sean Scanlan

■ Blue Black Permanent

Blue Ice
Blue Ice Productions
Location: London
Executive Producer: Gary Levinsohn
Producers: Martin Bregman, Michael Caine, Louis Stroller
Associate Producer: Barney Reisz
Director: Russell Mulcahy
Screenwriter: Ron Hutchinson
Director of Photography: Dennis Crossan
Editor: Seth Flaum
Cast: Michael Caine, Sean Young, Ian Holm, Jack Shepherd, Alun Armstrong

Border Crossing
Trade Films/ZDF/Tyne Tees/Channel Four

■ Carry on Columbus

Location: Tyneside, Bremen, Stuttgart, Zwickau
Producers: Derek Stubbs, Stewart Mackinnon
Director: Stewart Mackinnon
Screenwriters: Michael Eaton, Stewart Mackinnon
Director of Photography: Lars Barthel
Editor: Ian Sutherland
Cast: Susanne Lothar, Paul Brennen, Adelheid Arndt, Gerhard Garbers, Hannelore Hoger

Carry on Columbus
Island World/Comedy House
Studio: Pinewood
Executive Producer: Peter Rogers
Producer: John Goldstone
Director: Gerald Thomas
Screenwriter: Dave Freeman
Director of Photography: Alan Jones
Editor: Chris Barnes
Cast: Jim Dale, Bernard Cribbins, Maureen Lipman, Peter Richardson, Alexei Sayle

The Cement Garden
Neue Constantin/ Laurentic Productions/ Torii Productions
Studio: Jacob Street
Location: Greenwich, Beckton
Executive Producers: Bernd Eichinger, Martin Moszkowicz
Producers: Bee Gilbert, Evie Variaveski
Director/Screenwriter: Andrew Birkin, from the novel by Ian McEwan
Director of Photography: Stephen Blackman
Editor: Toby Tremlett
Cast: Andrew Robertson, Charlotte Gainsborough, Alice Coulthard, Ned Birkin, Sinead Cusack

Century
BBC Films/Beambright
Executive Producers: Mark Shivas, Ruth Caleb
Producer: Therese Pickard
Director/Screenwriter: Stephen Poliakoff
Director of Photography: Witold Stok
Editor: Michael Parkinson
Cast: Charles Dance, Clive Owen, Miranda Richardson, Robert Stephens, Joan Hickson

■ Don't Leave Me This Way

The Clothes in the Wardrobe
BBC Films/NFH
Location: London, Egypt
Executive Producer: Mark Shivas
Producer: Norma Heyman
Director: Waris Hussein
Screenwriter: Martin Sherman, from the novel by Alice Thomas Ellis
Director of Photography: Rex Maidment
Editor: Ken Pearce
Cast: Jeanne Moreau, Joan Plowright, Lena Headey, David Threlfall

The Cormorant
Holmes Productions/BBC Wales/BBC Screen Two
Location: Cardiff, Snowdonia
Executive Producers: Andrew Holmes, Ruth Caleb
Producer: Ruth Kenley Letts
Director: Peter Markham
Screenwriter: Peter Ransley, from the novel by Stephen Gregory
Director of Photography: Ashley Rowe
Editor: Tim Kruydenburg
Cast: Ralph Fiennes, Helen Schlesinger, Buddug Morgan, Derek Hutchinson, Dyfan Roberts

Covington Cross
Reeves Entertainment/ Thames Television International/ Capital Cities/ABC
Location: Kent
Executive Producer/ Screenwriter: Gill Grant
Producer: Aida Young
Director: William Dear
Director of Photography: Alan Hume
Editor: Tariq Anwar
Cast: Nigel Terry, Cherie Lunghi, James Faulkner, Jonathan Firth, Ben Porter

Damage
NEF/Skreba/Le Studio Canal Plus/Channel Four/ European Co-Production Fund
Studio: Shepperton
Location: UK, France
Producer: Vincent Malle
Producer/Director: Louis Malle
Co-producer: Simon Relph
Screenwriter: David Hare, from the novel by Josephine Hart
Director of Photography: Peter Biziou
Editor: John Bloom
Cast: Jeremy Irons,

■ **Femme Fatale**

Juliette Binoche, Miranda Richardson, Rupert Graves, Ian Bannen

Dirty Weekend
Michael Winner Ltd
Location: London, Brighton
Executive Producer: Jim Beach
Producer/Director: Michael Winner
Screenwriters: Michael Winner, Helen Zahavi from the novel by Helen Zahavi
Director of Photography: Alan Jones
Editor: Chris Barnes
Cast: Lia Williams, Ian Richardson, David McCallum, Rufus Sewell, Miriam Kelly

Don't Leave Me This Way
First Choice/BBC TV
Location: London, Cambridge, Suffolk
Producers: Moira Williams, Charles Elton
Director: Stuart Orme
Screenwriter: Catherine Buchanan, from the novel by Joan Smith
Director of Photography: Jim Peters
Editor: Martin Walsh
Cast: Janet McTeer, Imelda Staunton, Rebecca Hall, Ian McNeice, Bill Nighy

Emily's Ghost
Children's Film Unit for Channel Four
Location: Suffolk
Producer: Brianna Perkins
Director: Colin Finbow
Crew: Children from the Children's Film Unit
Cast: Martin Jarvis, Rosalind Ayres, Anna Massey, Anna Jones, Ron Moody

Femme Fatale
BBC Screen Two/BBC Enterprises
Location: London, Devon
Producer: Kenith Trodd
Associate Producer: Julie Scott
Director: Udayan Prasad
Screenwriter: Simon Gray
Director of Photography: Graham Frake
Editor: Ken Pearce
Cast: Sophie Diaz, Simon Callow, Donald Pleasance, Colin Welland, Jacqueline Tong

Force of Duty
BBC Northern Ireland/BBC Screenplay/RTE Dublin
Location: Northern Ireland
Executive Producer: George Faber
Producer: Robert Cooper
Director: Pat O'Connor
Screenwriters: Bill Morrison, Chris Ryder
Director of Photography: Eric Gillespie
Editor: Declan Byrne
Cast: Donal McCann, Adrian Dunbar, Patrick Malahide, Ingrid Craigie, Paula McFettridge

Foreign Affairs
Stagescreen Productions/ Interscope Communications Inc/Turner Pictures
Location: UK
Executive Producers: Jeffrey Taylor, Ted Field
Producer: Patricia Clifford
Director: Jim O'Brien
Screenwriter: Chris Bryant, from the novel by Alison Lurie
Director of Photography: Michael Coulter
Editor: Susan Browdy
Cast: Joanne Woodward, Brian Dennehy, Eric Stoltz, Stephanie Beacham

■ **Force of Duty**

A Foreign Field
Fingertip Films/BBC Screen One
Executive Producer: Richard Broke
Production Executive for BBC: Chris Cameron
Producers: Martyn Auty, Steve Lanning
Director: Charles Sturridge
Screenwriter: Roy Clarke
Director of Photography: Richard Greatex
Editor: John Bloom
Cast: Alec Guinness, Lauren Bacall, Jeanne Moreau, Leo McKern, John Randolph

Friends
Film on Four/British Screen/Chrysalide/Rio SA/European Script Fund/Story Films
Location: Johannesburg
Producer: Judith Hunt
Director/Screenwriter: Elaine Proctor
Director of Photography: Dominique Chapuis
Editor: Tony Lawson
Cast: Kerry Fox, Michele Burgers, Dambisa Kente

Great Moments in Aviation
BBC Films/BBC Enterprises/Miramax
Studio: Pinewood
Producer: Philippa Giles
Director: Beeban Kidron
Screenwriter: Jeanette Winterson
Director of Photography: Remi Adefarasin
Editor: John Stothart
Cast: Rakie Ayola, John Hurt, Jonathan Pryce, Dorothy Tutin, Vanessa Redgrave

Harnessing Peacocks
Friday Productions/Meridian Broadcasting
Location: Hertfordshire, Devon
Producers: Georgina Abrahams, Betty Willingale
Director: James Cellan Jones
Screenwriter: Andrew Davies, from the novel by Mary Wesley
Director of Photography: David Feig
Editor: Tariq Anwar
Cast: John Mills, Peter Davidson, Serena Scott Thomas, Renee Asherson, Brenda Bruce

The Hawk
BBC Films/Initial/BBC Enterprises/Screen Partners
Location: Bristol
Executive Producers: Mark Shivas, Eric Fellner, Larry Kirstein, Kent Walwin
Producers: Ann Wingate, Eileen Quinn
Director: David Hayman
Screenwriter: Peter Ransley, from his novel
Director of Photography: Andrew Dunn
Editor: Justin Krish
Cast: Helen Mirren, George Costigan, Rosemary Leach, Owen Teale, Melanie Hill

Hedd Wyn
Pendefig Productions/S4C
Producer: Shan Davies
Director: Paul Turner
Screenwriter: Alan Llwyd
Director of Photography: Ray Orton
Editor: Chris Lawrence
Cast: Huw Garmon, Sue Roderick, Nia Dryhurst, Judith Humphreys, Emma Kelly

High Boot Benny
First City Features/Sandy Films
Location: Dunree, Co. Donegal
Executive Producers: David Kelly, Joe Comerford
Producer: David Kelly
Director/Screenwriter/Editor: Joe Comerford
Director of Photography: Donal Gilligan
Cast: Frances Tomelty, Alan Devlin, Marc O'Shea

Horse Opera
Initial Film and Television/Channel Four
Location: Arizona, UK
Executive Producer: Malcolm Gerrie
Producer: Debbie Mason
Associate Producer: Jenny King
Director: Bob Baldwin
Librettist: Jonathan Moore, based on an original play by Anne Cauldfield
Director of Photography: Ed Lachman
Editor: Collin Green
Cast: Phillip Guy-Bromley, Silas Carson, Gina Bellman, Siobhan McCarthy, Edward Tudor-Pole

■ The Innocent

■ Friends

■ The Hawk

The Hour of the Pig
BBC Films/Ciby 2000/ Hour of the Pig Productions/British Screen/European Co-Production Fund
Studio: Ealing
Location: France
Executive Producers: Michael Wearing, Yves Attal
Producer: David M Thompson
Director/Screenwriter: Leslie Megahey
Director of Photography: John Hooper
Editor: Isabelle Dedieu
Cast: Colin Firth, Ian Holm, Donald Pleasance, Harriet Walter, Amina Annabi

The Hudsucker Proxy
Silver Pictures/Working Title
Location: Wilmington, N Carolina
Executive Producers: Tim Bevan, Eric Fellner, Joel Silver
Producer: Ethan Coen
Director: Joel Coen
Screenwriters: Ethan and Joel Coen, Joel Silver
Director of Photography:

■ Hedd Wyn

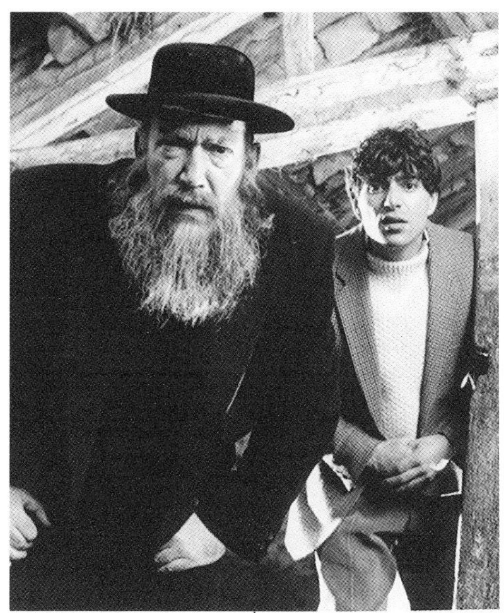

■ Leon the Pig Farmer

Roger Deakins
Editor: Thom Noble
Cast: Paul Newman, Jennifer Jason Leigh, Tim Robbins, Charles Durning, John Mahoney

The Hummingbird Tree
BBC Screen One/BBC Enterprises
Location: Trinidad
Executive Producer: Richard Broke
Producer: Gub Neal
Associate Producer: Ian Hopkins
Director: Noella Smith
Screenwriter: Jonathan Falla, from the novel by Ian McDonald
Director of Photography: Remi Adefarasin
Editor: Mark Day
Cast: Patrick Bergin, Susan Wooldridge, Tom Beasley, Marston Bloom

The Innocent
Island World/Norma Heyman/Chris Sievernich/ Wieland Schulz-Keil Production
Studio: DEFA Studios, Babelsberg
Location: Berlin
Producers: Norma Heyman, Chris Sievernich, Wieland Schulz-Keil
Director: John Schlesinger
Screenwriter: Ian McEwan, from his novel
Director of Photography: Dietrich Lohmann
Editor: Richard Marden
Cast: Anthony Hopkins, Isabella Rossellini, Campbell Scott

Leon the Pig Farmer
Leon the Pig Farmer plc
Location: London, Yorkshire
Executive Producers: Paul Brooks, David Altschuler, Howard Kitchner, Steven Margolis
Producers/Directors: Gary Sinyor, Vadim Jean
Associate Producer: Simon Scotland
Screenwriters: Gary Sinyor, Michael Normand
Director of Photography: Gordon Hickie
Editor: Ewa J Lind
Cast: Mark Frankel, Janet Suzman, Connie Booth, Brian Glover, Maryam d'Abo

Little Buddha
Ciby 2000/Recorded Picture Company
Location: Nepal, Bhutan, Seattle
Producer: Jeremy Thomas
Director: Bernardo Bertolucci
Screenwriters: Mark Peploe, Rudy Wurlitzer, from a story by Bernardo Bertolucci
Director of Photography: Vittorio Storaro
Editor: Pietro Scalia
Cast: Keanu Reeves, Chris

Isaak, Alex Weisendanger, Bridget Fonda

The Long Roads
BBC Screen Two/Freeway Films
Location: London, Skye, Liverpool, Glasgow
Executive Producers: John McGrath, Mark Shivas
Producer: Peter Kendal
Director: Tristram Powell
Screenwriter: John McGrath
Director of Photography: Steve Saunders
Editor: Roy Sharman
Cast: Edith MacArthur, Robert Urquhart, Anne Marie Timoney, John Buick, Paul Morrow

Love Lies Bleeding (Parole)
BBC Northern Ireland/BBC Screenplay/Telecip Paris
Location: Northern Ireland
Executive Producers: Pat Loughrey, Jacques Dercourt, George Faber
Producer: Robert Cooper
Director: Michael Winterbottom
Screenwriter: Ronan Bennett
Cast: Mark Rylance, Elizabeth Bourgine, Brendan Gleeson, Tony Doyle, John Kavanagh

Much Ado About Nothing
Renaissance Films/Samuel Goldwyn
Location: Tuscany
Producers: Kenneth Branagh, Stephen Evans, David Parfitt
Director: Kenneth Branagh
Screenwriter: Kenneth Branagh, from the play by William Shakespeare
Director of Photography: Roger Lanser
Editor: Andrew Marcus
Cast: Kenneth Branagh, Emma Thompson, Denzel Washington, Keanu Reeves, Michael Keaton

The Muppet Christmas Carol
Jim Henson Productions
Studio: Shepperton
Executive Producer: Frank Oz
Producer: Martin G Baker
Producer/Director: Brian Henson
Co-Producer/Screenwriter: Jerry Juhl, from the novel by Charles Dickens
Director of Photography: John Fenner
Editor: Michael Jablow
Cast: Michael Caine, Kermit the Frog, Miss Piggy, Gonzo the Great, Fozzie Bear

The Mystery of Edwin Drood
Bevanfield Films
Location: Rochester
Executive Producer: Mary Swindale
Producer: Keith Hayley
Associate Producer: Mark Crowdy
Director/Screenwriter: Timothy Forder, from the novel by Charles Dickens
Director of Photography: Martin McGrath
Editor: Susan Alhadeff
Cast: Robert Powell, Finty Williams, Jonathan Phillips, Nanette Newman

Naked
Film Four International/British Screen/Thin Man Films
Location: London
Producer: Simon Channing-Williams
Director/Screenwriter: Mike Leigh
Director of Photography: Dick Pope
Editor: John Gregory
Cast: David Thewlis, Lesley Sharp, Katrin Cartlidge, Greg Cruttwell, Claire Skinner

■ The Muppet Christmas Carol

Orlando
Adventure Pictures/British Screen/Rio SA/Mikado Films/Sigma Film/Lenfilm
Location: St Petersburg, London, Uzbekhistan
Producer: Christopher Sheppard
Co-Producers: Matthijs Van Heijningen, Jean Gontier, Luigi Musini, Roberto Cicutto, Vitaly Sobolev
Director: Sally Potter
Screenwriter: Sally Potter, from the novel by Virginia Woolf
Director of Photography: Alexei Rodionov
Editor: Hervé Schneid
Cast: Tilda Swinton, Charlotte Valandrey, Quentin Crisp, Heathcote Williams, John Wood

No Worries
Film Four International/British Screen/Palm Beach/Initial Film and Television/ Southern Star
Location: Gilgandra, Australia
Executive Producer: Kim Williams
Producers: David Elfick, Eric Fellner
Associate Producer: Nina Stevenson
Director: David Elfick
Screenwriter: David Holman
Director of Photography: Steve Windon
Editor: Louise Innes
Cast: Amy Terelinck, Geoff Morrell, Susan Lyons, Geraldine James, John Hargreaves

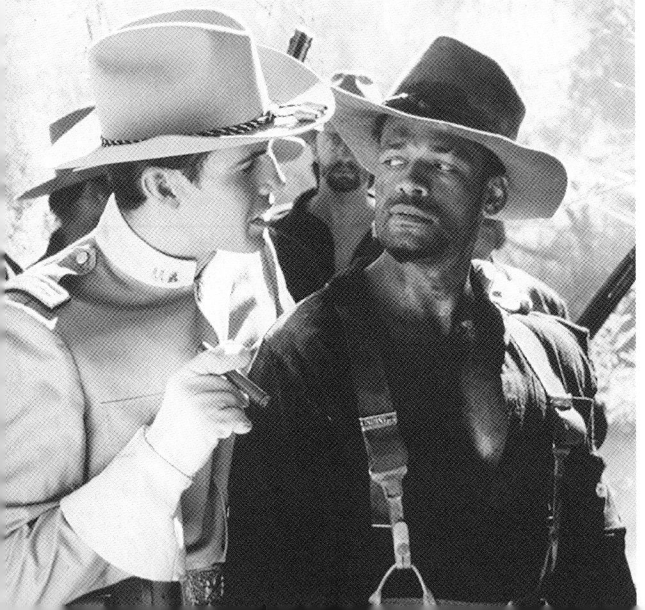

■ Posse

Peter's Friends
Renaissance Films
Location: London
Executive Producer: Stephen Evans
Producer/Director: Kenneth Branagh
Screenwriters: Martin Bergman, Rita Rudner
Director of Photography: Roger Lanser
Editor: Andrew Marcus
Cast: Kenneth Branagh, Alphonsia Emmanuel, Stephen Fry, Hugh Laurie, Emma Thompson

Posse
Polygram Filmed Entertainment/Working Title
Location: Tucson, Arizona
Executive Producers: Eric Fellner, Tim Bevan, Paul Webster, Bill Fishman
Producers: Jim Steele,

■ Orlando

Preston Holmes
Co-Producer: Jim Fishman
Director: Mario Van Peebles
Screenwriters: Sy Richardson, Dario Scardapane
Director of Photography: Peter Menzies
Editor: Mark Conte
Cast: Mario Van Peebles, Stephen Baldwin, Charles Lane, Tiny Lister Jr, Big Daddy Kane

Psychotherapy
BFI/TiMe/Skyline/NRW Filmstiftung/WDR/Martest Film AG
Location: Cologne, UK
Executive Producers: Ben Gibson, Wolfram Tichy
Executive in charge of production: Angela Topping
Producer: Steve Clark-Hall
Co-Producer: Michael Smeaton
Associate Producer: Beate Balser
Director/Screenwriter: Arthur Ellis
Director of Photography: Gil Taylor
Editor: Michael Bradsell
Cast: Trevor Eve, Steven Waddington, Marion Bailey, Ralph Brown

Raining Stones (The Estate)
Parallax Pictures/Film Four International
Location: Manchester
Producer: Sally Hibbin
Director: Ken Loach
Screenwriter: Jim Allen
Director of Photography: Barry Ackroyd
Editor: Jonathan Morris
Cast: Julie Brown, Bruce Jones, Tom Hickey, Ricky Tomlinson

The Remains of the Day
Merchant Ivory Productions
Location: West of England
Executive Producer: Harold Pinter
Producers: John Calley, Ismail Merchant, Mike Nichols
Director: James Ivory
Screenwriter: Ruth Prawer Jhabvala, from the novel by Kazuo Ishiguro
Director of Photography: Tony Pierce Roberts
Editor: Andrew Marcus
Cast: Anthony Hopkins, Emma Thompson, Christopher Reeve, James Fox

Romeo is Bleeding
Polygram Filmed Entertainment/Working Title/Hilary Henkin
Location: New York
Executive Producers: Tim Bevan, Eric Fellner
Producers: Hilary Henkin, Paul Webster
Screenwriter: Hilary Henkin
Director: Peter Medak
Director of Photography: Dariusz Wolski
Editor: Lee Percy
Cast: Gary Oldman, Lena Olin, Juliette Lewis, Annabella Sciorra, Roy Scheider

Running Late
Cinema Verity/Peter Bowles/BBC Screen One
Location: London
Executive Producer: Richard Broke
Producer: Verity Lambert
Associate Producer: Peter Bowles
Director: Udayan Prasad
Screenwriter: Simon Gray
Director of Photography: Jason Lehel
Editor: Barrie Vince
Cast: Peter Bowles, Roshan Seth, Renee Asherson, Adrian Rawlins, David Ryall

Seconds Out
BBC Screen One/BBC Enterprises
Location: London
Executive Producer: Richard Broke
Producer: Simon Passman
Director: Bruce McDonald
Screenwriter: Lynda La Plante
Director of Photography: Graham Frake
Editor: David Martin
Cast: Steven Waddington, Tom Bell, Colum Convey, Derek Newark, Clive Russell

The Secret Garden
Warner Bros/American Zoetrope
Studio: Pinewood
Location: Yorkshire
Executive Producers: Francis Ford Coppola, Fred Fuchs
Producers: Fred Roos, Tom Luddy
Director: Agnieszka Holland
Screenwriter: Caroline Thompson, from the novel by Frances Hodgson Burnett
Director of Photography: Roger Deakins
Editor: Isabelle Lorente
Cast: Maggie Smith, Heyden Prowse, Kate Maberley, Andrew Knott, Laura Crossley

The Secret Rapture
Greenpoint Films/Channel Four/British Screen
Location: Somerset/London
Producer: Simon Relph
Director: Howard Davies
Screenwriter: David Hare
Director of Photography: Ian Wilson
Editor: George Akers
Cast: Juliet Stevenson, Joanne Whalley-Kilmer, Penelope Wilton, Neil Pearson, Alan Howard

Sherlock Holmes – The Eligible Bachelor
Granada Television
Location: Manchester, Liverpool, Cheshire, Yorkshire, Herefordshire
Producer: June Wyndham Davies
Director: Peter Hammond
Screenwriter: T R Bowen, from the short story by Sir Arthur Conan Doyle
Director of Photography: David Odd
Editor: Paul Griffiths-Davies
Cast: Jeremy Brett, Edward Hardwicke, Rosalie Williams, Simon Williams, Paris Jefferson

Sherlock Holmes – The Sussex Vampyre
Granada Television
Location: Manchester, Cotswolds, Warwickshire
Executive Producer: Sally Head

■ Peter's Friends

Producer: June Wyndham Davies
Director: Tim Sullivan
Screenwriter: Jeremy Paul, from the novel by Sir Arthur Conan Doyle
Director of Photography: David Odd
Editor: Kim Horton
Cast: Jeremy Brett, Edward Hardwicke, Roy Marsden, Keith Barron, Elizabeth Spriggs

The Snapper
BBC Screen Two
Location: Dublin
Executive Producer: Mark Shivas
Producer: Lynda Myles
Associate Producer: Ian Hopkins
Director: Stephen Frears
Screenwriter: Roddy Doyle, from his novel
Director of Photography: Oliver Stapleton
Editor: Mick Audsley
Cast: Tina Kellegher, Colm Meaney, Eanna Macliam, Ciara Duffy, Peter Rowen

Soft Top, Hard Shoulder
Gruber Brothers Production
Location: London, Morecambe, Glasgow
Producer: Richard Holmes
Co-Producer: Georgina Masters
Director: Stefan Schwartz
Screenwriter: Peter Capaldi
Director of Photography: Henry Braham
Editor: Derek Trigg
Cast: Peter Capaldi, Elaine Collins, Frances Barber, Richard Wilson, Phyllis Logan

Son of the Pink Panther
MGM
Studio: Pinewood
Location: France, Jordan
Executive Producer: Nigel Wooll
Producer: Tony Adams
Director/Screenwriter: Blake Edwards
Director of Photography: Dick Bush
Editor: Robert Pergament
Cast: Roberto Benigni, Herbert Lom, Debrah Ferantino, Claudia Cardinale, Robert Davi

■ Wittgenstein

Splitting Heirs (Heirs and Graces)
Prominent Features
Location: London, Home Counties, Wiltshire, South of France
Executive Producer: Eric Idle
Producers: Simon Bosanquet, Redmond Morris
Director: Robert Young
Screenwriter: Eric Idle
Director of Photography: Tony Pierce Roberts
Editor: John Jympson
Cast: Rick Moranis, Eric Idle, Barbara Hershey, Catherine Zeta Jones, John Cleese

Tale of a Vampire
State Screen Productions
Location: London
Producer: Simon Johnson
Co-producer: Linda Kay
Director/Screenwriter/Editor: Shimako Sato
Director of Photography: Zubin Mistry

Cast: Julian Sands, Suzanna Hamilton, Kenneth Cranham, Ken Pritchard, Ian Rollison

The Trial
BBC Films/Europanda Entertainment BV
Location: Czechoslovakia
Executive producers: Kobi Jaeger, Reneiro Compostella, Mark Shivas
Producer: Louis Marks
Associate producer: Carolyn Montagu
Director: David Jones
Screenwriter: Harold Pinter, from the novel by Franz Kafka
Director of Photography: Phil Meheux
Editor: John Stothart
Cast: Kyle MacLachlan, Anthony Hopkins, Jason Robards, Juliet Stevenson, Polly Walker

Trust Me
BBC Screen One
Location: Bristol
Producer: Peter Goodchild

Associate Producers: Daphne Spink, Alison Gilby
Director: Tony Gow
Screenwriter: Tony Sarchet
Director of Photography: John Rhodes
Editor: John Jarvis
Cast: Alfred Molina, Ian Targett, Alphonsia Emmanuel

The Turn of the Screw
Michael White Productions/Lakedell/Cinemax
Studio: Shepperton
Location: Surrey
Executive Producer: Michael White, Pierre Spengler
Producer: Staffan Ahrenberg
Director: Rusty Lemorande
Screenwriter: Rusty Lemorande, from the novel by Henry James
Director of Photography: Witold Stok
Editor: Amina Mazani
Cast: Patsy Kensit, Stéphane Audran, Julian Sands, Clare Szekeres, Olivier Debray

An Ungentlemanly Act
Union Pictures/BBC TV
Studio: Ealing
Location: UK, Falkland Islands
Executive Producers: Michael Wearing, Franc Roddam
Producer: Bradley Adams
Associate Producer: Dave Edwards
Director/Screenwriter: Stuart Urban
Director of Photography: Peter Chapman
Editor: Howard Billingham
Cast: Ian Richardson, Rosemary Leach, Bob Peck, Ian McNeice, Hugh Ross

■ Soft Top, Hard Shoulder

PRODUCTION STARTS

Unnatural Causes
Anglia Films
Location: Norfolk
Executive in charge of production: David Fitzgerald
Producers: Brenda Reid, Hilary Bevan Jones
Director: John Davies
Screenwriter: Peter Buckman, from the novel by P D James
Director of Photography: Richard Crafter
Editor: Keith Judge
Cast: Roy Marsden, Simon Chandler, Keith Colley, Mel Martin, Bill Nighy

White Angel
Living Spirit Pictures
Location: London
Producer: Genevieve Jolliffe
Director: Chris Jones
Director of Photography: Chris Jones
Editor: John Holland
Cast: Harriet Robinson, Peter Firth, Don Henderson, Anne Catherine Arton, Harry Miller

The Wildlands
Hotspur/Archview/Creative Visions
Location: Kenya, Tanzania, Botswanaland, Zimbabwe
Executive Producer: Harry Percy
Producer: Gerald Green
Director/Screenwriter: Stewart Raffill
Director of Photography: Roger Olkowski
Editor: Peter Zinner
Cast: Jennifer McComb, Ashley Hamilton, Timothy Ackroyd, Harry Percy

bfi ***Wittgenstein***
Bandung/Channel Four/BFI/Uplink (Japan)
Studio: Theed Street
Executive Producers: Ben Gibson, Takashi Asai
Executive in charge of production: Eliza Mellor
Producer: Tariq Ali
Director: Derek Jarman
Associate Director: Ken Butler
Screenwriters: Terry Eagleton, Derek Jarman, Ken Butler

Director of Photography: James Welland
Editor: Budge Tremlett
Cast: Karl Johnson, Michael Gough, Tilda Swinton, John Quentin, Kevin Collins

The Young Americans
Polygram Filmed Entertainment/LIVE/Working Title/Trijbits Worrell Associates
Location: London
Executive Producer: Richard Gladstein

■ **The Turn of the Screw**

Producers: Paul Trijbits, Alison Owen
Director: Danny Cannon
Screenwriters: Danny Cannon, David Hilton
Director of Photography: Vernon Layton
Editor: Alex Mackie
Cast: Harvey Keitel, Viggo Mortensen, Iain Glen, Craig Kelly, Thandie Newton

bfi **– Produced/co-produced by the British Film Institute**

RELEASES

Listed here are films of 40 minutes and over, both British and foreign, which had their first theatrical release in the UK between January and December 1992. Entries quote the title, country of origin, director/s, leading players, distributor, release date (NB the production date may vary substantially from this), duration, gauge if other than 35mm, and the 'Sight and Sound' reference. A list of distributors' addresses and telephone numbers can be found on p146. Back issues of S&S are available for reference from BFI Library and Information Services

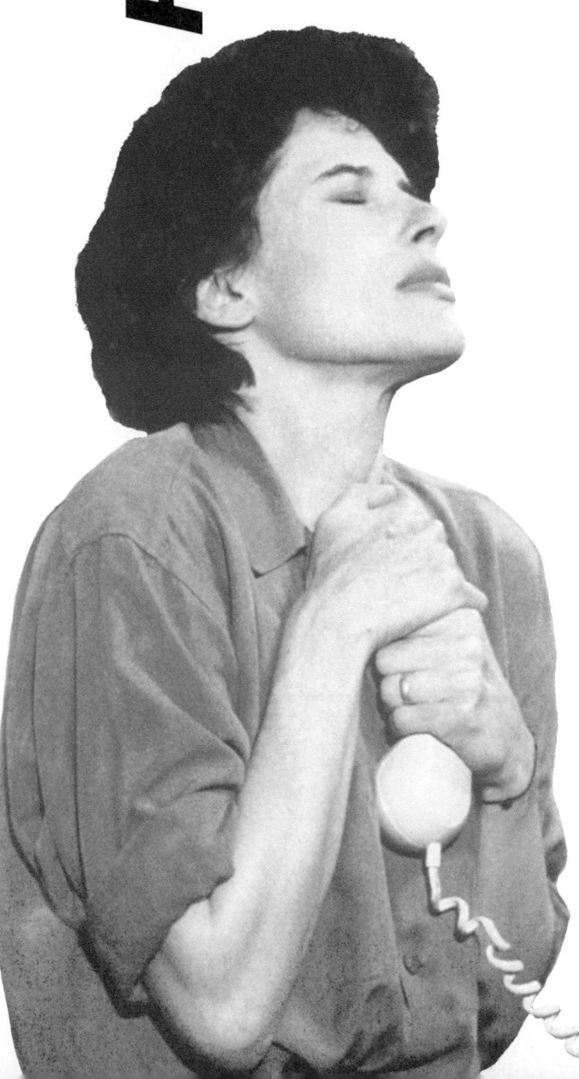

The Adjuster
(18) Canada Dir Atom Egoyan with Elias Koteas, Arsinée Khanjian, Maury Chaykin. Metro Pictures, 29 May 1992. 102 mins. S&S June 1992 p38

Afraid of the Dark
(18) UK/France Dir Mark Peploe with James Fox, Fanny Ardant, Paul McGann. Rank, 21 Feb 1992. 92 mins. S&S Apr 1992 p42

Alien³
(18) USA Dir David Fincher with Sigourney Weaver, Charles S Dutton, Charles Dance. 20th Century Fox, 21 Aug 1992. 115 mins. S&S Aug 1992 p46

L'Amant (The Lover)
(18) France/UK Dir Jean-Jacques Annaud with Jane March, Tony Leung, Frédérique Meininger. Guild, 19 June 1992. 115 mins. S&S July 1992 p38

Amantes (Lovers)
(18) Spain Dir Vicente Aranda with Victoria Abril, Jorge Sanz, Maribel Verdu. Mainline, 21 Aug 1992. 103 mins. Subtitles. S&S Oct 1992 p44

Les Amants du Pont-Neuf
(18) France Dir Léos Carax with Juliette Binoche, Denis Lavant, Klaus-Michael Gruber. Artificial Eye, 11 Sep 1992. 126 mins. Subtitles. S&S Sep 1992 p46

As You Like It
(U) UK Dir Christine Edzard with Cyril Cusack, James Fox, Don Henderson. Squirrel Films, 9 Oct 1992. 117 mins. S&S Oct 1992 p45

■ Afraid of the Dark

At Play in the Fields of the Lord
(15) USA Dir Hector Babenco with Tom Berenger, John Lithgow, Daryl Hannah. Entertainment, 10 Apr 1992. 186 mins. S&S Apr 1992 p43

Autobus see **_Aux yeux du monde_**

Aux yeux du monde (Autobus)
(15) France Dir Eric Rochant with Yvan Attal, Kristin Scott-Thomas, Marc Berman. Artificial Eye, 19 June 1992. 98 mins. Subtitles. S&S July 1992 p39

Barton Fink
(15) USA Dir Joel Coen with John Turturro, John Goodman, Judy Davis. Rank, 14 Feb 1992. 116 mins. S&S Feb 1992 p39

Basic Instinct
(18) USA Dir Paul Verhoeven with Michael Douglas, Sharon Stone, George Dzundza. Guild, 8 May 1992. 127 mins. S&S May 1992 p44

Batman Returns
(12) USA Dir Tim Burton with Michael Keaton, Danny DeVito, Michelle Pfeiffer. Warner Bros, 10 July 1992. 126 mins. S&S Aug 1992 p48

The Beast see **_La Bête_**

Beauty and the Beast
(U) USA Dir Gary Trousdale, Kirk Wise with the voices of Paige O'Hara, Robby Benson,

■ Beauty and the Beast

Richard White. Warner Bros, 9 Oct 1992. 84 mins. S&S Oct 1992 p45

Beethoven
(U) USA Dir Brian Levant with Charles Grodin, Bonnie Hunt, Dean Jones. UIP, 24 July 1992. 87 mins. S&S July 1992 p40

La Belle Noiseuse
(15) France Dir Jacques Rivette with Michel Piccoli, Jane Birkin, Emmanuelle Béart. Artificial Eye, 20 Mar 1992. 239 mins. Subtitles. S&S Apr 1992 p44

La Belle Noiseuse – Divertimento
(15) France Dir Jacques Rivette with Michel Piccoli, Jane Birkin, Emmanuelle Béart. Artificial Eye, 8 Apr 1992. 126 mins. Subtitles

The Best Intentions see ***Den Goda Viljan***

La Bête (The Beast)
(18) France Dir Walerian Borowczyk with Sirpa Lane, Lisbeth Hummel, Elisabeth Kahnson. ICA (exhib. only), 12 June 1992. 102 mins, uncut version. Subtitles. MFB Oct 1978 p194

■ Batman Returns

Betty Blue – Version Intégrale
(18) France Dir Jean-Jacques Beineix with Béatrice Dalle, Jean-Hughes Anglade, Consuelo de Havilland. 20th Century Fox, 21 Feb 1992. 183 mins. Subtitles. Original version MFB Oct 1986 p298

Bian Zou Bian Chang (Life on a String)
(no cert) China/UK/Germany Dir Chen Kaige with Liu Zhongyuan, Huang Lei, Xu Qing. ICA Projects, 31 Jan 1992. 103 mins. Subtitles. S&S Mar 1992 p36

Big Girls Don't Cry...They Get Even see ***Stepkids***

Bill & Ted's Bogus Journey
(PG) USA Dir Peter Hewitt with Alex Winter, Keanu Reeves, Jeff Miller. Columbia TriStar, 3 Jan 1992. 93 mins. S&S Jan 1992 p38

■ Beethoven

■ Bugsy

Billy Bathgate
(15) USA Dir Robert Benton with Dustin Hoffman, Nicole Kidman, Loren Dean. Warner Bros, 10 Jan 1992. 107 mins. S&S Jan 1992 p39

Bis ans Ende der Welt (Until the End of the World)
(15) Germany/France/Australia Dir Wim Wenders with Solveig Dommartin, William Hurt, Sam Neill. Entertainment, 24 Apr 1992. 158 mins. S&S May 1992 p44

■ Basic Instinct

Bitter Moon see ***Lunes de fiel***

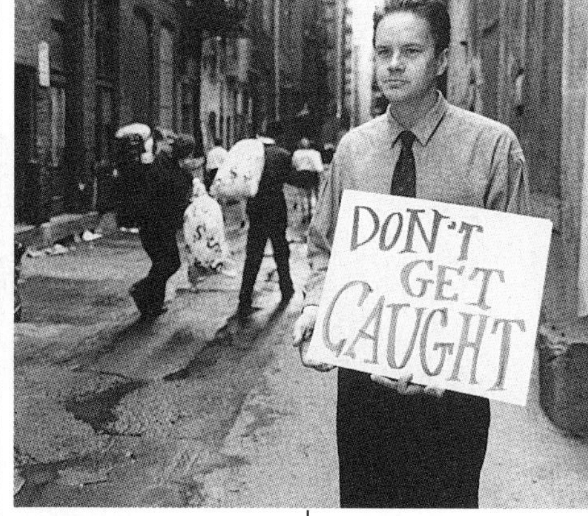

■ Bob Roberts

Black Robe
(15) Canada/Australia Dir Bruce Beresford with Lothaire Bluteau, Aden Young, Sandrine Holt. Entertainment, 31 Jan 1992. 100 mins. S&S Mar 1992 p37

Blade Runner – The Director's Cut
(15) USA Dir Ridley Scott with Harrison Ford, Rutger Hauer, Sean Young. Warner Bros, 27 Nov 1992. 117 mins. Original version MFB Nov 1982 p275

Blame it on the Bellboy
(12) UK Dir Mark Herman with Dudley Moore, Bryan Brown, Richard Griffiths. Warner Bros, 24 Jan 1992. 78 mins. S&S Mar 1992 p38

Blue Ice
(15) USA Dir Russell Mulcahy with Michael Caine, Sean Young, Ian Holm. Guild, 9 Oct 1992. 105 mins. S&S Dec 1992 p40

Bob Roberts
(15) USA Dir Tim Robbins with Tim Robbins, Giancarlo Esposito, Alan Rickman. Rank, 11 Sep 1992. 104 mins. S&S Sep 1992 p47

The Bodyguard
(15) USA Dir Mick Jackson with Kevin Costner, Whitney Houston, Gary Kemp. Warner Bros, 26 Dec 1992. 129 mins. S&S Jan 1993 p40

Boomerang
(15) USA Dir Reginald Hudlin with Eddie Murphy, Robin Givens, Halle Berry. UIP, 30 Oct 1992. 117 mins. S&S Nov 1992 p38

The Bridge
(12) UK Dir Sydney Macartney with Saskia

■ Christopher Columbus

Reeves, David O'Hara, Joss Ackland. Eclectic Films/Feature Film Co, 10 Jan 1992. 102 mins. S&S Jan 1992 p41

Buffy the Vampire Slayer
(12) USA Dir Fran Rubel Kuzui with Kristy Swanson, Donald Sutherland, Paul Reubens. 20th Century Fox, 23 Oct 1992. 94 mins. S&S Nov 1992 p39

Bugsy
(18) USA Dir Barry Levinson with Warren Beatty, Annette Bening, Harvey Keitel. Columbia TriStar, 20 Mar 1992. 136 mins. S&S Apr 1992 p45

The Butcher's Wife
(12) USA Dir Terry Hughes with Demi Moore, Jeff Daniels, George

■ City of Joy

Dzundza. Blue Dolphin, 3 July 1992. 105 mins. S&S Aug 1992 p49

California Man (US Encino Man)
(PG) USA Dir Les Mayfield with Sean Astin, Brendan Fraser, Pauly Shore. Warner Bros, 25 Sep 1992. 88 mins. S&S Oct 1992 p47

Cape Fear
(18) USA Dir Martin Scorsese with Robert De Niro, Nick Nolte, Jessica Lange. UIP, 6 Mar 1992. 128 mins. S&S Mar 1992 p39

Carry On Columbus
(PG) UK Dir Gerald Thomas with Jim Dale, Peter Richardson, Alexei Sayle. UIP, 2 Oct 1992. 91 mins. S&S Oct 1992 p48

Chaplin
(12) UK Dir Richard Attenborough with Robert Downey Jnr, Dan Aykroyd, Geraldine Chaplin. Guild, 18 Dec 1992. 145 mins. S&S Jan 1993 p42

Christopher Columbus: The Discovery
(PG) USA Dir John Glen with Marlon Brando, Tom Selleck, George Corraface. Rank, 11 Sep 1992. 121 mins. S&S Oct 1992 p48

City of Joy
(12) UK/France Dir Roland Joffé with Patrick Swayze, Om Puri, Pauline Collins. Warner Bros, 2 Oct 1992. 135 mins. S&S Oct 1992 p49

Cool World
(12) USA Dir Ralph Bakshi with Kim Basinger, Gabriel Byrne, Brad Pitt. Blue Dolphin, 18 Dec 1992. 102 mins. S&S Jan 1993 p45

■ Chaplin

Coupe de Ville
(12) USA Dir Joe Roth with Patrick Dempsey, Arye Gross, Daniel Stern. Warner Bros, 17 Jan 1992. 97 mins. S&S Mar 1992 p40

Cousin Bobby
(PG) USA Dir Jonathan Demme. Documentary. Electric Pictures, 4 Sep 1992. 69 mins. S&S Sep 1992 p48

Cross My Heart see ***La fracture du myocarde***

The Crying Game
(18) UK Dir Neil Jordan with Forest Whitaker, Miranda Richardson, Stephen Rea. Mayfair Entertainment, 30 Oct 1992. 112 mins. S&S Nov 1992 p40

The Cutting Edge
(PG) USA Dir Paul M Glaser with D B Sweeney, Moira Kelly, Roy Dotrice. UIP, 28 Aug 1992. 102 mins. S&S July 1992 p42

Dahong Denglong Gaogao Gua (Raise the Red Lantern)
(PG) Hong Kong Dir Zhang Yimou with Gong Li, Ma Jingwu, He Caifei. Mayfair Palace, 21 Feb 1992. 125 mins. Subtitles. S&S Feb 1992 p41

Dakota Road
(15) UK Dir Nick Ward with Charlotte Chatton, Jason Carter, Rachel Scott. Mayfair Entertainment, 17 July 1992. 89 mins. S&S Aug 1992 p50

The Dark Wind
(15) USA Dir Errol Morris with Lou Diamond Phillips, Gary Farmer, Fred Ward. Guild, 15 May 1992. 111 mins. S&S June 1992 p39

Daydream Believer
(15) Australia Dir Kathy Mueller with Miranda Otto, Martin Kemp, Anne Looby. Feature Film Co, 7 Aug 1992. 86 mins. S&S Aug 1992 p51

Death Becomes Her
(PG) USA Dir Robert Zemeckis with Meryl Streep, Bruce Willis, Goldie Hawn. UIP, 4 Dec 1992. 104 mins. S&S Dec 1992 p41

Death in Brunswick
(15) Australia Dir John Ruane with Sam Neill, Zoe Carides, John Clarke. Electric Pictures, 7 Feb 1992. 109 mins. S&S Feb 1992 p42

Deceived
(15) USA Dir Damian Harris with Goldie Hawn, John Heard, Ashley Peldon. Warner Bros, 3 Apr 1992. 108 mins. S&S Apr 1992 p47

■ Double X

■ The Crying Game

bfi ***Def By Temptation***
(18) USA Dir James Bond III with James Bond III, Kadeem Hardison, Bill Nunn. BFI, 22 May 1992. 95 mins. S&S July 1992 p42

Delicatessen
(15) France Dir Jean-Pierre Jeunet, Marc Caro with Dominique Pinon, Marie-Laure Dougnac, Jean-Claude Dreyfus. Electric Pictures, 3 Jan 1992. 99 mins. Subtitles. S&S Jan 1992 p41

The Doctor
(12) USA Dir Randa Haines with William Hurt, Christine Lahti, Elizabeth Perkins. Warner Bros, 10 Apr 1992. 123 mins. S&S Apr 1992 p48

Don't Move, Die and Rise Again see ***Zamri, Umri, Voskresni!***

Don't Tell Her It's Me
(12) USA Dir Malcolm Mowbray with Shelley Long, Steve Guttenberg, Jami Gertz. Rank, 17 Jan 1992. 102 mins. S&S June 1991 p41

Don't Tell Mom the Babysitter's Dead
(12) USA Dir Stephen Herek with Christina

Applegate, Joanna Cassidy, John Getz. First Independent, 22 May 1992. 105 mins. S&S June 1992 p40

Double Impact
(18) USA Dir Sheldon Lettich with Jean-Claude Van Damme, Geoffrey Lewis, Alan Scarfe. Columbia Tri-Star, 31 Jan 1992. 109 mins. S&S Mar 1992 p41

The Double Life of Véronique see ***La Double Vie de Véronique***

Dutch see ***Driving Me Crazy***

Electric Moon
(15) UK Dir Pradip Krishan with Roshan Seth, Naseeruddin Shah, Leela Naidu. Film Four/Winstone, 4 Dec 1992. 103 mins. Subtitles. S&S Dec 1992 p42

Elenya
(PG) UK Dir Steve Gough with Margaret John, Pascale Delafouge Jones, Seiriol Tomos. BFI, 11 Dec 1992. 82 mins. S&S Dec 1992 p43

■ Elenya

1492: Conquest of Paradise
(15) USA Dir Ridley Scott with Gérard Depardieu, Armand Assante, Sigourney Weaver. Guild, 23 Oct 1992. 155 mins. S&S Nov 1992 p41

Far and Away
(12) USA Dir Ron Howard with Tom Cruise, Nicole Kidman, Thomas Gibson. UIP, 31 July 1992. 140 mins. S&S Aug 1992 p52

■ (Below) Freddie as F.R.O.7.

■ Def by Temptation

La Double Vie de Véronique (The Double Life of Véronique)
(15) France Dir Krzysztof Kieslowski with Irène Jacob, Halina Gryglaszewska, Kalina Jedrusik. Gala, 28 Feb 1992. 98 mins. Subtitles. S&S Mar 1992 p42

Double X
(15) UK Dir Shani S Grewal with Simon Ward, William Katt, Norman Wisdom. Feature Film Co, 5 June 1992. 97 mins. S&S July 1992 p43

Driving Me Crazy (US Dutch)
(12) USA Dir Peter Faiman with Ed O'Neill, Ethan Randall, JoBeth Williams. 20th Century Fox, 24 Jan 1992. 107 mins. S&S Mar 1992 p44

Emily Brontë's Wuthering Heights
(U) USA Dir Peter Kosminsky with Juliette Binoche, Ralph Fiennes, Janet McTeer. UIP, 16 Oct 1992. 106 mins. S&S Oct 1992 p60

Encino Man see ***California Man***

Europa
(15) Denmark Dir Lars von Trier with Jean-Marc Barr, Barbara Sukowa, Udo Kier. Electric Pictures, 17 Apr 1992. 114 mins. S&S May 1992 p47

Europa, Europa
(15) France/Germany Dir Agnieszka Holland with Salomon Perel, Marco Hofschneider, René Hofschneider. Arrow, 15 May 1992. 112 mins. Subtitles. S&S May 1992 p48

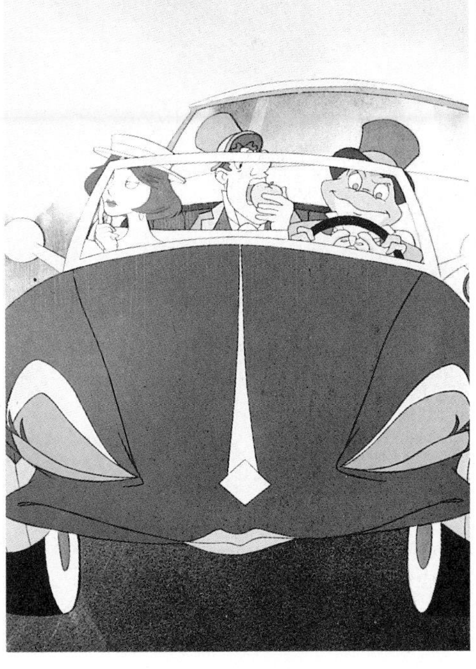

Father of the Bride (PG) USA Dir Charles Shyer with Steve Martin, Diane Keaton, Kimberly Williams. Warner Bros, 21 Feb 1992. 105 mins. S&S Mar 1992 p45

The Favour, the Watch and the Very Big Fish see ***Rue Saint-Sulpice***

Ferngully: The Last Rainforest (U) Australia Dir Bill Kroyer with the voices of Tim Curry, Samantha Mathis, Christian Slater. 20th Century Fox, 7 Aug 1992. 76 mins. S&S Aug 1992 p55

■ Gladiator

Final Analysis (15) USA Dir Phil Joanou with Richard Gere, Kim Basinger, Uma Thurman. Warner Bros, 10 Apr 1992. 124 mins. S&S June 1992 p41

The Five Heartbeats (15) USA Dir Robert Townsend with Robert Townsend, Michael Wright, Leon. 20th Century Fox, 5 June 1992. 121 mins. S&S July 1992 p44

Flaming Ears see ***Rote Ohren fetzen durch Asche***

For the Boys (15) USA Dir Mark Rydell with Bette Midler, James Caan, George Segal. 20th Century Fox, 7 Feb 1992. 145 mins. S&S Feb 1992 p44

La fracture du myocarde (Cross My Heart) (PG) France Dir Jacques Fansten with Sylvain Copans, Nicolas Parodi, Cécilia Rouaud. Mayfair Palace, 28 Feb 1992. 105 mins. Subtitles. S&S Apr 1992 p49

Frankie & Johnny (15) USA Dir Garry Marshall with Al Pacino, Michelle Pfeiffer, Hector Elizondo. UIP, 17 Jan 1992. 118 mins. S&S Dec 1991 p38

Freddie as F.R.O.7 (U) UK Dir Jon Acevski with the voices of Ben Kingsley, Jenny Agutter, Brian Blessed. Rank, 14 Aug 1992. 91 mins. S&S Aug 1992 p55

■ Grand Canyon

Freddy's Dead: The Final Nightmare (18) USA Dir Rachel Talalay with Robert Englund, Lisa Zane, Shon Greenblatt. Guild, 17 Jan 1992. 89 mins. S&S Feb 1992 p45

Freejack (15) USA Dir Geoff Murphy with Emilio Estevez, Mick Jagger, Rene Russo. Warner Bros, 27 Mar 1992. 109 mins. S&S May 1992 p48

Freud Flyttar Hemifran (Freud Leaving Home) (no cert) Sweden/Denmark Dir Susanne Bier with Gunilla Röör, Ghita Nørby, Palle Granditsky. NFT (exhib. only), 14 Oct 1992. 100 mins. Subtitles

Freud Leaving Home see ***Freud Flyttar Hemifran***

Fried Green Tomatoes at the Whistle Stop Café (12) USA Dir Jon Avnet with Mary Stuart Masterson, Mary Louise Parker, Kathy Bates. Rank, 13 Mar 1992. 130 mins. S&S Mar 1992 p46

Gas Food Lodging (15) USA Dir Allison Anders with Brooke Adams, Ione Skye, Fairuza Balk. Mainline, 2 Oct 1992. 101 mins. S&S Oct 1992 p50

Gladiator (15) USA Dir Rowdy Hetherington with James Marshall, Cuba Gooding Jnr, Brian Dennehy. Columbia TriStar, 26 June 1992. 102 mins. S&S July 1992 p45

Glengarry Glen Ross (15) USA Dir James Foley with Al Pacino, Jack Lemmon, Alec Baldwin. Rank, 30 Oct 1992. 100 mins. S&S Nov 1992 p43

Den Goda Viljan (The Best Intentions) (12) Sweden Dir Bille August with Samuel Fröler, Pernilla August, Max von Sydow. Artificial Eye, 3 July 1992. 181 mins. Subtitles. S&S July 1992 p46

Grand Canyon (15) USA Dir Lawrence Kasdan with Danny Glover, Kevin Kline, Steve Martin. 20th Century Fox, 1 May 1992. 134 mins. S&S May 1992 p50

The Hand that Rocks the Cradle (15) USA Dir Curtis

■ Hitler, ein Film aus Deutschland (Hitler, A Film From Germany)

Hanson with Annabella Sciorra, Rebecca De Mornay, Matt McCoy. Warner Bros, 24 Apr 1992. 110 mins. S&S May 1992 p51

Hear My Song
(15) UK Dir Peter Chelsom with Ned Beatty, Adrian Dunbar, Shirley Anne Field. Miramax, 13 Mar 1992. 105 mins. S&S Mar 1992 p47

Hello Hemingway
(no cert) Cuba Dir Fernando Pérez with Laura de la Uz, Raul Paz, Herminia Sanchez. Metro Pictures, 10 Jan 1992. 88 mins. Subtitles. S&S Mar 1992 p48

High Heels see ***Tacones Lejanos***

Une histoire inventée (An Imaginary Tale)
(no cert) Canada Dir André Forcier with Jean Lapointe, Louise Marleau, Marc Messier. Mayfair Palace, 21 Feb 1992. 100 mins. Subtitles. S&S May 1992 p52

■ Une histoire inventée (An Imaginary Tale)

Hitler, a Film from Germany see ***Hitler, ein Film aus Deutschland***

bfi ***Hitler, ein Film aus Deutschland (Hitler, a Film from Germany)***
(no cert) West Germany Dir Hans Jürgen Syberberg with Heinz Schubert, André Heller, Hellmuth Lange. BFI, 28 Aug 1992. Part 1: 96 mins. Part 2: 132 mins. Part 3: 97 mins. Part 4: 104 mins. Subtitles. S&S Sep 1992 p48

Home Alone 2: Lost in New York
(PG) USA Dir Chris Columbus with Macaulay Culkin, Joe Pesci, Daniel Stern. 20th Century Fox, 11 Dec 1992. 120 mins. S&S Jan 1993 p47

Homework see ***La Tarea***

Hook
(U) USA Dir Steven Spielberg with Dustin Hoffman, Robin Williams, Julia Roberts. Columbia TriStar, 10 Apr 1992. 141 mins. S&S Apr 1992 p50

■ Hook

Hors la vie
(15) France/Italy/Belgium Dir Maroun Bagdadi with Hippolyte Girardot, Rafic Ali Ahmad, Hussein Sbeity. Mainline, 31 Jan 1992. 97 mins. Subtitles. S&S Feb 1992 p46

The Hours and Times
(no cert) USA Dir Christopher Münch with David Angus, Ian Hart, Stephanie Pack. ICA Projects, 18 Sep 1992. 60 mins. S&S Oct 1992 p51

Housesitter
(PG) USA Dir Frank Oz with Steve Martin, Goldie Hawn, Dana Delany. UIP, 11 Sep 1992. 102 mins. S&S Sep 1992 p50

Howards End
(PG) UK Dir James Ivory with Anthony Hopkins, Vanessa Redgrave, Helena Bonham Carter. Mayfair Entertainment, 1 May 1992. 142 mins. S&S May 1992 p52

Husbands and Wives
(15) USA Dir Woody Allen with Woody Allen, Blythe Danner, Judy Davis. Columbia TriStar, 23 Oct 1992. 108 mins. S&S Nov 1992 p44

I Don't Kiss see ***J'embrasse pas***

bfi ***L'Ile au Trésor (Treasure Island)***
(no cert) France/USA Dir Raúl Ruiz with Melvil Poupaud, Martin Landau, Vic Tayback. BFI, 5 June 1992. 115 mins. S&S July 1992 p47

An Imaginary Tale see ***Une histoire inventée***

Immaculate Conception
(15) UK Dir Jamil Dehlavi with James Wilby, Melissa Leo, Shabana Azmi. Feature Film Co, 11 Sep 1992. 120 mins. S&S Sep 1992 p51

The Inner Circle see ***El Proiezionista***

Into the West
(PG) Eire Dir Mike Newell with Gabriel Byrne, Ellen Barkin, Ciarán Fitzgerald. Entertainment, 11 Dec 1992. 102 mins. S&S Jan 1993 p48

JFK
(15) USA Dir Oliver Stone with Kevin Costner, Gary Oldman, Sissy Spacek. Warner Bros, 24 Jan 1992. 189 mins. S&S Feb 1992 p48

Jacquot de Nantes
(PG) France Dir Agnès Varda with Philippe Maron, Edouard Joubeaud, Laurent Monnier. Gala, 8 May 1992. 118 mins. Subtitles. S&S Feb 1992 p47

J'embrasse pas (I Don't Kiss)
(18) France Dir André Téchiné with Philippe Noiret, Emmanuelle Béart, Manuel Blanc. Gala, 20 Mar 1992. 116 mins. Subtitles. S&S Apr 1992 p52

Jersey Girl
(15) USA Dir David Burton Morris with Jami Gertz, Dylan McDermott, Molly Price. Entertainment, 21 Aug 1992. 95 mins. S&S Sep 1992 p52

Johnny Suede
(15)USA/Switzerland/ France Dir Tom DiCillo with Brad Pitt, Richard Boes, Cheryl Costa.

■ **Jacquot de Nantes**

Artificial Eye, 12 June 1992. 97 mins. S&S July 1992 p48

Juice
(15) USA Dir Ernest R Dickerson with Omar Epps, Khalil Kain, Jermaine Hopkins. Electric Pictures, 28 Aug 1992. 91 mins. S&S Oct 1992 p52

Just Like a Woman
(15) UK Dir Christopher Monger with Julie Walters, Adrian Pasdar, Paul Freeman. Rank, 25 Sep 1992. 106 mins. S&S Sep 1992 p53

■ **Johnny Suede**

■ A League of Their Own

Kikuchi
(no cert) Japan Dir Kenchi Iwamoto with Jiro Yoshimura, Yasuhiro Oka, Misa Fukuma. ICA Projects, 10 Apr 1992. 68 mins. Subtitles. S&S May 1992 p53

Knight Moves
(18) USA/Germany Dir Carl Schenkel with Christopher Lambert, Diane Lane, Tom Skerritt. Columbia TriStar, 4 Sep 1992. 116 mins. S&S Oct 1992 p53

Kuffs
(15) USA Dir Bruce A Evans with Christian Slater, Milla Jovovich, Tony Goldwyn. Entertainment, 3 Apr 1992. 102 mins. S&S June 1992 p42

■ The Last of the Mohicans

Ladybugs
(PG) USA Dir Sidney J Furie with Rodney Dangerfield, Jonathan Brandis, Jackee. Warner Bros, 26 June 1992. 90 mins

The Last Boy Scout
(18) USA Dir Tony Scott with Bruce Willis, Damon Wayans, Chelsea Field. Warner Bros, 28 Feb 1992. 105 mins. S&S Mar 1992 p49

The Last of the Mohicans
(12) USA Dir Michael Mann with Daniel Day-Lewis, Madeleine Stowe, Russell Means. Warner Bros, 6 Nov 1992. 122 mins. S&S Nov 1992 p45

Late for Dinner
(PG) USA Dir W D Richter with Brian Wimmer, Peter Berg, Marcia Gay Harden. First Independent, 20 Mar 1992. 93 mins. S&S Apr 1992 p53

The Lawnmower Man
(15) UK/USA Dir Brett Leonard with Jeff Fahey, Pierce Brosnan, Jenny Wright. First Independent, 5 June 1992. 108 mins. S&S June 1992 p43

A League of Their Own
(PG) USA Dir Penny Marshall with Geena Davis, Tom Hanks, Lori Petty. Columbia TriStar, 18 Sep 1992. 128 mins. S&S Nov 1992 p44

Lethal Weapon 3
(15) USA Dir Richard Donner with Mel Gibson, Danny Glover, Joe Pesci. Warner Bros, 14 Aug 1992. 118 mins. S&S Aug 1992 p57

Liebestraum
(18) USA Dir Mike Figgis with Kevin Anderson, Pamela Gidley, Bill Pullman. UIP, 10 Jan 1992. 113 mins. S&S Jan 1992 p46

■ Lethal Weapon 3

■ Little Man Tate

Life on a String see ***Bian Zou Bian Chang***

Light Sleeper
(15) USA Dir Paul Schrader with Willem Dafoe, Susan Sarandon, Dana Delany. Guild, 13 Mar 1992. 103 mins. S&S Apr 1992 p54

Little Man Tate
(PG) USA Dir Jodie Foster with Jodie Foster, Dianne Wiest, Adam Hann-Byrd. Columbia TriStar, 17 Jan 1992. 99 mins. S&S Feb 1992 p51

The Long Day Closes
(12) UK Dir Terence Davies with Marjorie Yates, Leigh McCormack, Anthony Watson. Mayfair Palace, 22 May 1992. 85 mins. S&S June 1992 p44

The Lover see ***L'Amant***

Lovers see ***Amantes***

The Lunatic
(15) USA Dir Lol Creme with Julie T Wallace, Paul Campbell, Reggie Carter. Oasis, 14 Feb 1992. 94 mins. S&S June 1992 p45

Lunes de fiel (Bitter Moon)
(18) France/UK Dir Roman Polanski with Hugh Grant, Kristin Scott-Thomas, Emmanuelle Seigner. Columbia TriStar, 2 Oct 1992. 139 mins. S&S Oct 1992 p53

■ Life on a String (Bian Zou Bian Chang)

The Magic Riddle
(U) Australia Dir Yoram Gross with the voices of Robyn Moore, Keith Scott, Rod Hay. Rank, 10 Apr 1992. 94 mins. S&S June 1992 p45

The Mambo Kings
(15) USA Dir Arne Glimcher with Armand Assante, Antonio Banderas, Cathy Moriarty. Warner Bros, 29 May 1992. 104 mins. S&S June 1992 p46

The Man in the Moon
(PG) USA Dir Robert Mulligan with Sam Waterston, Tess Harper, Gail Strickland. UIP, 28 Feb 1992. 99 mins. S&S Mar 1992 p50

Marquis
(18) Belgium/France Dir Henri Xhonneux with Philippe Bizot, Bien de Moor, Gabrielle Van Damme. ICA Projects, 1 May 1992. 83 mins. Subtitles. S&S July 1992 p49

Masala
(18) Canada Dir Srinivas Krishna with Srinivas Krishna, Sakina Jaffrey, Zohra Segal. Metro Pictures, 7 Aug 1992. 106 mins. S&S Aug 1992 p58

■ Montalvo et l'enfant (Montalvo and the Child)

Medicine Man
(PG) USA Dir John McTiernan with Sean Connery, Lorraine Bracco, José Wilker. Guild, 29 May 1992. 105 mins. S&S June 1992 p47

Meet the Feebles
(18) New Zealand Dir Peter Jackson with the voices of Danny Mulheron, Donna Akersten, Stuart Devenie. Arrow, 10 Apr 1992. 97 mins. S&S May 1992 p55

Memoirs of an Invisible Man
(PG) USA Dir John Carpenter with Chevy Chase, Daryl Hannah, Sam Neill. Warner Bros, 15 May 1992. 99 mins. S&S June 1992 p48

Men of Respect
(18) USA Dir William Reilly with John Turturro, Katherine Borowitz, Dennis Farina. Columbia TriStar, 28 Feb 1992. 113 mins. S&S May 1992 p55

Merci la vie
(18) France Dir Bertrand Blier with Charlotte Gainsbourg, Anouk Grinberg, Gérard Depardieu. Artificial Eye, 10 Jan 1992. 118 mins. Subtitles. S&S Jan 1992 p49

Mississippi Masala
(15) USA Dir Mira Nair with Denzel Washington, Sarita Choudhury, Roshan Seth. Mayfair Palace, 17 Jan 1992. 113 mins. S&S Jan 1992 p50

Mobsters see ***Mobsters – The Evil Empire***

Mobsters – The Evil Empire (US Mobsters)
(18) USA Dir Michael Karbelnikoff with Christian Slater, Patrick Dempsey, Richard Grieco. UIP, 1 May 1992. 121 mins. S&S Mar 1992 p51

Mo' Money
(15) USA Dir Peter Macdonald with Damon Wayans, Stacey Dash, Joe Santos. Columbia TriStar, 18 Dec 1992. 90 mins. S&S Dec 1992 p44

The Monk
(15) UK/Spain Dir Paco Lara with Paul McGann, Sophie Ward, Isla Blair. Arrow, 28 Feb 1992. 106 mins. S&S Feb 1992 p52

■ Light Sleeper

Mon Père, ce héros
(PG) France Dir Gérard Lauzier with Gérard Depardieu, Marie Gillain, Patrick Mille. Gala, 30 Oct 1992. 104 mins. Subtitles. S&S Nov 1992 p47

Montalvo and the Child see ***Montalvo et l'enfant***

bfi ***Montalvo et l'enfant (Montalvo and the Child)***
(no cert) France Dir Claude Mourieras with Mathilde Altaraz, Christophe Delachaux, Robert Seyfried. BFI, 1 Nov 1992. 76 mins. S&S Nov 1992 p48

Moonrise
(no cert) New Zealand Dir David Blyth with Al Lewis, Justin Gocke, Milan Borich. NFT (exhib. only), 24 Oct 1992. 95 mins

The Muppet Christmas Carol
(U) USA Dir Brian Henson with Michael Caine, Kermit the Frog, Miss Piggy. Buena Vista, 18 Dec 1992. 86 mins. S&S Feb 1993 p51

My Cousin Vinny
(15) USA Dir Jonathan Lynn with Joe Pesci, Ralph Macchio, Marisa Tomei. 20th Century Fox, 17 July 1992. 119 mins. S&S July 1992 p50

My Father is Coming
(18) Germany/USA Dir Monika Treut with Alfred Edel, Shelley Kästner, Annie Sprinkle. Out on a Limb, 25 Sep 1992. 81 mins. S&S Nov 1992 p49

My Girl
(PG) USA Dir Howard Zieff with Dan Aykroyd, Jamie Lee Curtis, Macaulay Culkin. Columbia Tri-Star, 31 Jan 1992. 102 mins. S&S Feb 1992 p53

■ Mon père, ce héros

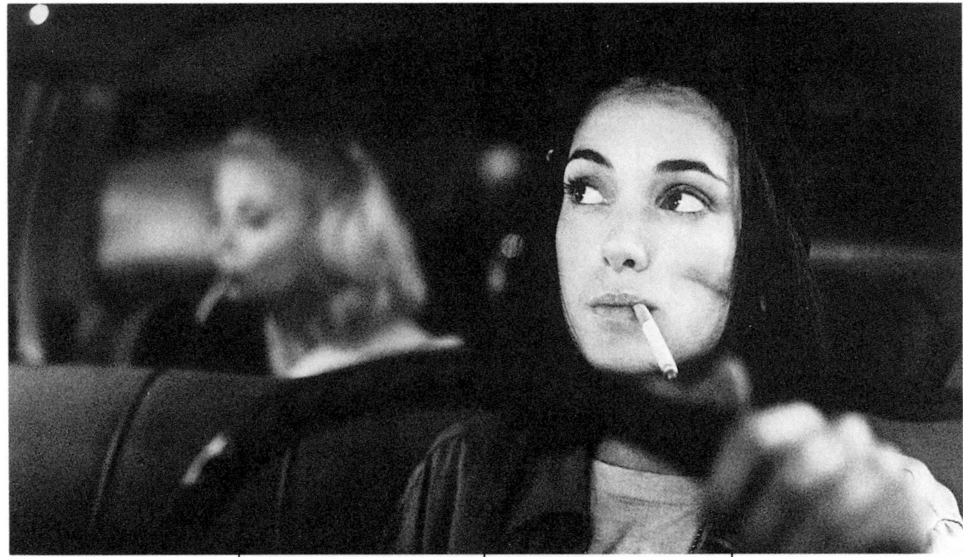

■ Night on Earth

My Own Private Idaho
(18) USA Dir Gus Van Sant with River Phoenix, Keanu Reeves, James Russo. Electric Pictures, 27 Mar 1992. 104 mins. S&S Apr 1992 p55

Naked Lunch
(18) UK/Canada Dir David Cronenberg with Peter Weller, Judy Davis, Ian Holm. First Independent, 24 Apr 1992. 115 mins. S&S May 1992 p56

Necessary Roughness
(12) USA Dir Stan Dragoti with Scott Bakula, Hector Elizondo, Robert Loggia. UIP, 27 Mar 1992. 108 mins. S&S Apr 1992 p56

The News Boys (US Newsies)
(PG) USA Dir Kenny Ortega with Christian Bale, Bill Pullman, Ann-Margret. Warner Bros, 14 Aug 1992. 121 mins. S&S Sep 1992 p53

■ The Player

Newsies see ***The News Boys***

Night on Earth
(15) USA Dir Jim Jarmusch with Winona Ryder, Gena Rowlands, Béatrice Dalle. Electric Pictures, 31 July 1992. 129 mins. Partly subtitled. S&S Aug 1992 p59

Noises Off
(12) USA Dir Peter Bogdanovich with Carol Burnett, Michael Caine, Denholm Elliott. Warner Bros, 24 July 1992. 104 mins. S&S Aug 1992 p60

Off and Running
(12) USA Dir Edward Bianchi with Cyndi Lauper, David Keith, Johnny Pinto. Rank, 12 June 1992. 90 mins. S&S Aug 1992 p60

Of Mice and Men
(PG) USA Dir Gary Sinise with John Malkovich, Gary Sinise, Ray Walston. UIP, 27 Nov 1992. 111 mins. S&S Jan 1993 p50

Once Upon a Crime
(PG) USA Dir Eugene Levy with John Candy, James Belushi, Cybill Shepherd. Entertainment, 6 Mar 1992. 94 mins. S&S Sep 1992 p55

Paradise
(12) USA Dir Mary Agnes Donoghue with Melanie Griffith, Don Johnson, Elijah Wood. Warner Bros, 19 June 1992. 111 mins. S&S July 1992 p51

Patriot Games
(15) USA Dir Philip Noyce with Harrison Ford, Anne Archer, Patrick Bergin. UIP, 25 Sep 1992. 117 mins. S&S Sep 1992 p56

Pepi, Luci, Bom... see ***Pepi, Luci, Bom y otras chicas del montón***

Pepi, Luci, Bom y otras chicas del montón (Pepi, Luci, Bom...)
(18) Spain Dir Pedro Almodóvar with Carmen Maura, Félix Rotaeta, Olvido "Alaska" Gara. Metro Pictures, 10 July 1992. 80 mins. Subtitles. S&S Aug 1992 p61

Peter's Friends
(15) UK Dir Kenneth Branagh with Hugh Laurie, Imelda Staunton, Stephen Fry. Entertainment, 13 Nov 1992. 101 mins. S&S Dec 1992 p45

The Playboys
(12) UK Dir Gillies MacKinnon with Albert Finney, Aidan Quinn, Robin Wright. Winstone/ Goldwyn, 5 June 1992. 109 mins. S&S June 1992 p50

The Player
(15) USA Dir Robert Altman with Tim Robbins, Greta Scacchi, Fred Ward. Guild, 26 June 1992. 124 mins. S&S July 1992 p52

The Pleasure Principle
(18) UK Dir David Cohen with Peter Firth, Lynsey Baxter, Haydn Gwynne. Mayfair Palace, 7 Feb 1992. 100 mins. S&S Feb 1992 p55

The Power of One
(12) USA Dir John G Avildsen with Stephen Dorff, John Gielgud, Armin Mueller-Stahl. Warner Bros, 4 Sep 1992. 127 mins. S&S Sep 1992 p57

Prague
(12) UK/France Dir Ian Sellar with Alan Cumming, Sandrine Bonnaire, Bruno Ganz. Winstone, 23 Oct 1992. 89 mins. S&S Nov 1992 p50

The Prince of Tides
(15) USA Dir Barbra Streisand with Nick Nolte, Barbra Streisand, Blythe Danner. Columbia TriStar, 21 Feb 1992. 132 mins. S&S Mar 1992 p52

The Princess and the Goblin
(PG) UK/Hungary Dir József Gémes with the voices of Joss Ackland, Claire Bloom, Roy Kinnear. Entertainment, 18 Dec 1992. 111 mins. S&S Jan 1993 p50

Problem Child 2
(PG) USA Dir Brian Levant with John Ritter, Michael Oliver, Jack Warden. UIP, 14 Feb 1992. 91 mins. S&S Mar 1992 p53

El Proiezionista (The Inner Circle)
(15) Italy Dir Andrei Konchalovsky with Tom Hulce, Lolita Davidovich, Bob Hoskins. Columbia TriStar, 3 July 1992. 137 mins. S&S June 1992 p50

Raise the Red Lantern
see ***Dahong Denglong Gaogao Gua***

Rapid Fire
(18) USA Dir Dwight H Little with Brandon Lee, Powers Boothe, Nick Mancuso. 20th Century Fox, 20 Nov 1992. 95 mins. S&S Nov 1992 p51

The Rapture
(18) USA Dir Michael Tolkin with Mimi Rogers, David Duchovny, Patrick Bauchau. Electric Pictures, 3 July 1992. 100 mins. S&S July 1992 p54

Rebecca's Daughters
(12) UK/Germany Dir Karl Francis with Peter O'Toole, Paul Rhys, Joely Richardson. Mayfair Palace, 24 Apr 1992. 97 mins. S&S May 1992 p57

Ricochet
(18) USA Dir Russell Mulcahy with Denzel Washington, John Lithgow, Ice T. First Independent, 24 Apr 1992. 102 mins. S&S May 1992 p58

Rote Ohren fetzen durch Asche (Flaming Ears)
(no cert) Austria Dir and with Angela Hans Scheirl, Ursula Purrer, Dietmar Schipeck. Cinenova, 6 Nov 1992. 84 mins. Subtitles

Ruby
(15) USA Dir John MacKenzie with Danny Aiello, Sherilyn Fenn, Frank Orsatti. Rank, 29 May 1992. 100 mins. S&S July 1992 p54

Rue Saint-Sulpice (The Favour, the Watch and the Very Big Fish)
(15) France/UK Dir Ben Lewin with Bob Hoskins, Jeff Goldblum, Natasha Richardson. Rank, 14 Feb 1992. 89 mins. S&S Feb 1992 p56

Rush
(18) USA Dir Lili Fini Zanuck with Jason Patric, Jennifer Jason Leigh, Sam Elliott. UIP, 5 June 1992. 120 mins. S&S Apr 1992 p58

Salmonberries
(12) Germany Dir Percy Adlon with k.d. lang, Rosel Zech, Chuck Connors. Electric Pictures, 10 Apr 1992. 95 mins. S&S Apr 1992 p59

Scorchers
(18) USA Dir David Beaird with Faye Dunaway, Denholm Elliott, James Earl Jones. Rank, 15 May 1992. 82 mins. S&S May 1992 p59

■ Scorchers

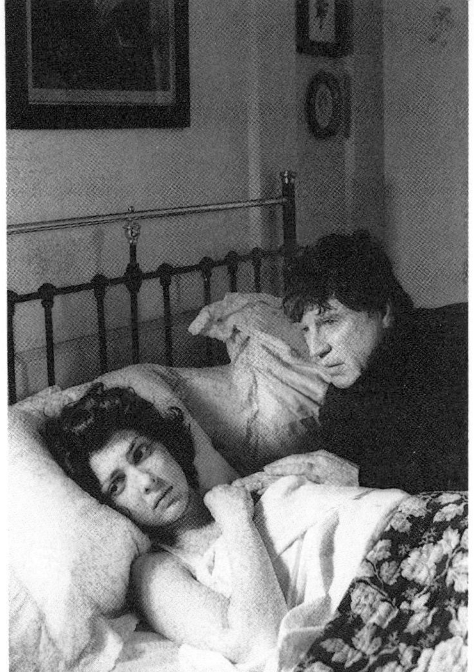

■ Secret Friends

Secret Friends
(15) UK Dir Dennis Potter with Alan Bates, Gina Bellman, Frances Barber. Feature Film Co, 25 Sep 1992. 97 mins. S&S Oct 1992 p54

Shining Through
(15) USA Dir David Seltzer with Michael Douglas, Melanie Griffith, Liam Neeson. 20th Century Fox, 20 Mar 1992. 132 mins. S&S Apr 1992 p60

Simple Men
(15) UK/USA Dir Hal Hartley with Robert Burke, William Sage, Karen Sillas. Metro Tartan, 6 Nov 1992. 105 mins. S&S Dec 1992 p47

Single White Female
(18) USA Dir Barbet Schroeder with Bridget Fonda, Jennifer Jason Leigh, Steven Weber. Columbia TriStar, 20 Nov 1992. 108 mins. S&S Nov 1992 p52

Sister Act
(PG) USA Dir Emile Ardolino with Whoopi Goldberg, Maggie Smith, Kathy Najimy. Buena Vista, 20 Nov 1992. 100 mins. S&S Dec 1992 p48

Slacker
(no cert) USA Dir Richard Linklater with Richard Linklater, Rudy Basquez, Jean Caffeine. Feature Film Co, 4 Dec 1992. 97 mins. S&S Dec 1992 p49

Sleepwalkers
(18) USA Dir Mick Garris with Brian Krause, Mädchen Amick, Alice Krige. Columbia TriStar, 3 July 1992. 89 mins. S&S Aug 1992 p62

Sneakers
(12) USA Dir Phil Alden Robinson with Robert Redford, Dan Aykroyd, Ben Kingsley. UIP, 13 Nov 1992. 125 mins. S&S Dec 1992 p50

Split Second
(18) UK Dir Tony Maylam with Rutger Hauer, Kim Cattrall, Neil Duncan. Entertainment, 5 June 1992. 90 mins. S&S July 1992 p56

Spotswood
(PG) Australia Dir Mark Joffe with Anthony Hopkins, Ben Mendelsohn, Toni Collette. Feature Film Co, 9 Oct 1992. 95 mins. S&S Jan 1993 p53

Star Trek VI: The Undiscovered Country
(PG) USA Dir Nicholas Meyer with William Shatner, Leonard Nimoy, DeForest Kelley. UIP, 14 Feb 1992. 110 mins. S&S Mar 1992 p54

Stepkids (US Big Girls Don't Cry... They Get Even)
(PG) USA Dir Joan Micklin Silver with Griffin Dunne, Dan Futterman, Patricia Kalember. Rank, 3 July 1992. 104 mins. S&S Aug 1992 p63

Stone Cold
(18) USA Dir Craig R Baxley with Brian Bosworth, Lance Henriksen, William Forsythe. Columbia TriStar, 19 June 1992. 92 mins. S&S Sep 1992 p58

Stop! Or My Mom Will Shoot
(PG) USA Dir Roger Spottiswoode with Sylvester Stallone, Estelle Getty, JoBeth Williams. UIP, 17 Apr 1992. 87 mins. S&S June 1992 p52

Straight Out of Brooklyn
(15) USA Dir Matty Rich with George T Odom, Ann D Sanders, Lawrence Gilliard Jnr. Artificial Eye, 4 Sep 1992. 83 mins. S&S Oct 1992 p55

Straight Talk
(PG) USA Dir Barnet Kellman with Dolly Parton, James Woods, Griffin Dunne. Warner Bros, 12 June 1992. 91 mins. S&S July 1992 p56

Strictly Ballroom
(PG) Australia Dir Baz Luhrmann with Paul Mercurio, Tara Morice, Bill Hunter. Rank, 16 Oct 1992. 94 mins. S&S Oct 1992 p56

Swoon
(18) USA Dir Tom Kalin with Daniel Schlachet, Craig Chester, Ron Vawter. Metro Pictures, 25 Sep 1992. 94 mins. S&S Sep 1992 p58

■ Strictly Ballroom

Tacones Lejanos (High Heels)
(18) Spain Dir Pedro Almodóvar with Victoria Abril, Marisa Paredes, Miguel Bosé. Rank, 27 Mar 1992. 114 mins. Subtitles. S&S Apr 1992 p61

Tale of a Vampire
(18) UK Dir Shimako Sato with Julian Sands, Suzanna Hamilton, Kenneth Cranham. State Screen, 20 Nov 1992. 100 mins. S&S Mar 1993 p51

La Tarea (Homework)
(18) Mexico Dir Jaime Humberto Hermosillo with Maria Rojo, José Alonso, Xanic Zepeda. Metro Pictures, 19 June 1992. 85 mins. Subtitles. S&S Aug 1992 p64

Tetsuo II: Bodyhammer
(18) Japan Dir Shinya Tsukamoto with Tomoroh Taguchi, Nobu Kanaoka, Shinya Tsukamoto. ICA Projects, 20 Nov 1992. 83 mins. Subtitles. S&S Dec 1992 p51

This Is My Life
(12) USA Dir Nora Ephron with Julie Kavner, Samantha Mathis, Gaby Hoffmann. 20th Century Fox, 4 Dec 1992. 94 mins. S&S Dec 1992 p52

■ Volere Volare

Thousand Pieces of Gold
(no cert) USA Dir Nancy Kelly with Rosalind Chao, Chris Cooper, Michael Paul Chan. NFT (exhib. only), 4 Dec 1992. 105 mins

Thunderheart
(15) USA Dir Michael Apted with Val Kilmer, Sam Shepard, Graham Greene. Columbia TriStar, 16 Oct 1992. 119 mins. S&S Oct 1992 p57

Till There Was You
(PG) Australia Dir John Seale with Mark Harmon, Deborah Unger, Jeroen Krabbé. Rank, 20 Mar 1992. 95 mins. S&S Apr 1992 p62

■ Unforgiven

Time Will Tell
(15) UK Dir Declan Lowney. Documentary. Theatrical Experience, 24 Apr 1992. 84 mins. S&S May 1992 p59

Traces of Red
(15) USA Dir Andy Wolk with James Belushi, Lorraine Bracco, Tony Goldwyn. Entertainment, 11 Dec 1992. 105 mins. S&S Feb 1993 p59

Treasure Island see ***L'Ile au Trésor***

Turtle Beach
(15) Australia Dir Stephen Wallace with Greta Scacchi, Joan Chen, Art Malik. Warner Bros, 5 June 1992. 88 mins. S&S July 1992 p57

Twin Peaks: Fire Walk with Me
(18) USA Dir David Lynch with Sheryl Lee, Ray Wise, Mädchen Amick. Guild, 20 Nov 1992. 134 mins. S&S Nov 1992 p53

Unforgiven
(15) USA Dir Clint Eastwood with Clint Eastwood, Gene Hackman, Morgan Freeman. Warner Bros, 18 Sep 1992. 131 mins. S&S Oct 1992 p58

Universal Soldier
(18) USA Dir Roland Emmerich with Jean-Claude Van Damme, Dolph Lundgren, Ally Walker. Guild, 24 July 1992. 103 mins. S&S Sep 1992 p59

Unlawful Entry
(18) USA Dir Jonathan Kaplan with Kurt Russell, Ray Liotta, Madeleine Stowe. 20th Century Fox, 30 Oct 1992. 111 mins. S&S Nov 1992 p54

Until the End of the World see ***Bis ans Ende der Welt***

Urga
(PG) France/USSR Dir Nikita Mikhalkov with Badema, Bayaertu, Vladimir Gostukhin. Mayfair Palace, 7 Feb 1992. 118 mins. Subtitles. S&S Apr 1992 p63

V.I. Warshawski
(15) USA Dir Jeff Kanew with Kathleen Turner, Jay O Sanders, Charles Durning. Warner Bros, 3 Jan 1992. 89 mins. S&S Jan 1992 p56

Van Gogh
(12) France Dir Maurice Pialat with Jacques Dutronc, Alexandra London, Bernard Le Coq. Artificial Eye, 8 May 1992. 159 mins. Subtitles. S&S May 1992 p60

■ Without You I'm Nothing

Volere Volare
(15) Italy Dir Maurizio Nichetti, Guido Manuli with Angela Finocchiaro, Maurizio Nichetti, Mariella Valentini. Metro Pictures, 8 May 1992. 96 mins. Subtitles. S&S May 1992 p61

Voyager
(15) Germany/France Dir Volker Schlöndorff with Sam Shepard, Julie Delpy, Barbara Sukowa. Mayfair Palace, 17 Apr 1992. 100 mins. S&S Feb 1992 p58

Waiting
(15) Australia Dir Jackie McKimmie with Noni Hazlehurst, Deborra-Lee Furness, Frank Whitten. Contemporary, 14 Aug 1992. 94 mins. S&S Aug 1992 p64

The Waterdance
(15) USA Dir Neal Jimenez, Michael Steinberg with Eric Stoltz, Wesley Snipes, William Forsythe. Samuel Goldwyn, 27 Nov 1992. 107 mins. S&S Dec 1992 p53

Waterland
(15) UK Dir Stephen Gyllenhaal with Jeremy Irons, Sinead Cusack, Ethan Hawke. Mayfair Entertainment, 21 Aug 1992. 95 mins. S&S Sep 1992 p60

Wayne's World
(PG) USA Dir Penelope Spheeris with Mike Myers, Dana Carvey, Rob Lowe. UIP, 22 May 1992. 95 mins. S&S June 1992 p52

■ Van Gogh

White Men Can't Jump
(15) USA Dir Ron Shelton with Wesley Snipes, Woody Harrelson, Rosie Perez. 20th Century Fox, 9 Oct 1992. 112 mins. S&S Oct 1992 p59

White Sands
(15) USA Dir Roger Donaldson with Willem Dafoe, Mary Elizabeth Mastrantonio, Mickey Rourke. Warner Bros, 4 Sep 1992. 101 mins. S&S Sep 1992 p62

Without You I'm Nothing
(18) USA Dir John Boskovich with Sandra Bernhard, John Doe, Steve Antin. Electric Pictures, 14 Aug 1992. 89 mins. S&S Sep 1992 p63

Year of the Gun
(15) USA Dir John Frankenheimer with Andrew McCarthy, Sharon Stone, Valeria Golino. First Independent, 10 Jan 1992. 111 mins. S&S Feb 1992 p59

Zamri, Umri, Voskresni! (Don't Move, Die and Rise Again)
(12) USSR Dir Vitaly Kanevsky with Dinara Drukarova, Pavel Nazarov, Elena Popova. Artificial Eye, 1 Oct 1992. 103 mins. Subtitles. S&S Dec 1992 p54

bfi – distributed by the British Film Institute

■ The Waterdance

A Paramount Communications Company

SPECIALISED GOODS AND SERVICES

Acricius
c/o Robin Browne BSC
1900 Hillwood Drive
Bloomfield Hills
Michigan 48304
USA
Tel: 0101 313 645 5298
Special effects cinematography. Specialist camera equipment

Agfa-Gevaert
Motion Picture Division
27 Great West Road
Brentford
Middlesex TW8 9AX
Tel: 081 231 4310
Fax: 081 231 4947
Manufacturers of the complete range of both colour and black and white films for the motion picture and television industries

Any Effects
64 Weir Road
London SW19 8UG
Tel: 081 944 0099
Fax: 081 944 6989
Will Kinder
Mechanical (front of camera) special effects
Pyrotechnics: simulated explosions, bullet hits
Fine models for close up camera work
Weather: rain, snow, fog, wind
Breakaways: Shatterglass, windows, bottles, glasses, collapsing furniture, walls, floors
Specialised engineering rigs and propmaking service

Barclays Bank
27 Soho Square
London W1A 4WA
Tel: 071 439 6851
Fax: 071 434 9035
Asmita Kapadia
Large business centre providing a comprehensive range of banking services to all aspects of the film and television industry

Boulton-Hawker Films
Hadleigh
Ipswich
Suffolk IP7 5BG
Tel: 0473 822235
Fax: 0473 824519
Time-lapse, cinemicrography and other specialised scientific filming techniques

Dolly Brook Casting Agency
52 Sandford Road
East Ham
London E6 3QS
Tel: 081 472 2561/470 1287
Fax: 081 552 0733
Russell Brook
Specialises in walk-ons, supporting artistes, extras and small parts for films, TV, commercials, modelling, photographic, voice-overs, pop-videos

Cabervans
Caberfeidh
Cloch Road
Gourock
Renfrewshire
PA19 1BA
Tel/Fax: 0475 38775
Trisha MacKenzie
Top quality motorhomes, caravans, wardrobe and make-up units, transport

Cool Million
Unit 16A
149 Roman Way
Islington
London N7 8XH
Tel: 071 609 9191
Fax: 071 609 0638
Dot O'Rourke
Promotional merchandising, sourcing of unusual items, launch parties and roadshows

Crews Employment Agency
111 Wardour Street
London W1V 4AY
Tel: 071 437 0721/0810/0350
Fax: 071 494 4644
Lynda Loakes
A BECTU licensed employment agency. Operating a computerised database, they are able to scan for freelance union members by grade, geographical location, foreign languages, specialist skills and experience. This is a free service to the film and television industry

De Wolfe Music
80-88 Wardour Street
London W1V 3LF
Tel: 071 439 8481
Fax: 071 437 2744
Warren De Wolfe
Alan Howe
World's largest production music library. Represent 20 composers for commissions, TV and film scores. Offices worldwide, sound FX department, 3 x 24-track recording studios all with music to picture facilities

Diverse Design
Gorleston Street
London W14 8XS
Tel: 071 603 4567
Fax: 071 603 2148
Steve Billinger
Full service design with in house facilities. Innovative programes include *Obsessions, Small Objects of Desire, Under the Sun, The View, Checkout '93, Europe Express, The Pulse*

Downes Presenters Agency
96 Broadway
Bexleyheath
Kent DA6 7DE
Tel: 081 304 0541
Fax: 081 301 5591
Wendy Downes
Agents representing presenters experienced in the fields of presentations, documentaries, commentaries, narrations, industrial videos, training films, voice-overs, conferences and commercials

EOS Electronics AV
EOS House
Weston Square
Barry CF6 7YF
Tel: 0446 741212
Fax: 0446 746120
Specialist manufacturers of video animation, video time lapsing and video archiving equipment. Products: Supertoon Low-Cost School Animation System, AC580 Low-Band Controller, BAC900 Broadcast Animation Controller, LCP3 Compact Disc, Listening Posts

ETH Screen Music
11A Forth Street
Edinburgh EH1 3LE
Tel: 031 557 2721
Harald Tobermann
Producer and publisher of original music for moving images. Complete creative team – composers, arrangers, musicians. All styles and genres

Eureka Location Management
51 Tonsley Hill

London SW18 1BW
Tel: 081 870 4569
Fax: 081 871 2158
Suzannah Holt
Finds and manages locations for film and television in Britain and abroad. Offices in London and Toronto

FTS Bonded
Aerodrome Way
Cranford Lane
Hounslow
Middlesex TW5 9QB
Tel: 081 897 7973
Fax: 081 897 7979
J C Mangan
A J Loader
Inventory management, technical facilities including film checking and tape duplication, storage and distribution

Film Finances
1-11 Hay Hill
Berkeley Square
London W1X 7LF
Tel: 071 629 6557
Fax: 071 491 7530
Graham Easton
David Wilder
James Shirras
Provide completion guarantees for the film and television industry

Film Location Finders
Victoria House
25 Victoria Street
Liverpool L1 6BD
Tel/Fax: 051 236 5640
K Dorgan
Locations library, location finding, period vehicles

The Film Stock Centre Blanx
70 Wardour Street
London W1V 3HP
Tel: 071 494 2244
Fax: 071 287 2040/494 2645
D John Ward
Approved distributor of film, video tape, magnetic recording stock, spacing and polaroid – all major brands

Harkness Screens and Hall Stage
The Gate Studios
Station Road
Borehamwood
Herts WD6 1DQ
Tel: 081 953 3611
Fax: 081 207 3657
Eddie Daniels
John Lewis
Projection screens and complete screen systems, fixed and portable, front or rear, flat, curved, flying, roller etc. Curtain tracks, festoons, cycloramas, raise and lower equipment, stage equipment, installation and maintenance

Hirearchy Classic and Contemporary Costume
45 Palmerston Road
Boscombe
Bournemouth
Dorset BH1 4HW
Tel: 0202 394465
Fax: 0202 309660
Specialise in twentieth century costume hire, including accessories, jewellery, militaria, textiles and luggage

Hothouse Models & Effects
Studios 1 & 2
Tenpenny Hill
Thorrington
Colchester
Essex CO7 8JD
Tel/Fax: 0206 252282
Large scale props and sets; working models; high detail close-ups, miniatures, creatures/ puppets, advertisements, conceptual design

Kodak
Motion Picture and Television Imaging
PO Box 66
Hemel Hempstead
Herts HP1 1JU
Tel: 0442 61122
Fax: 0442 844458
A Kennedy
Suppliers of the full range of Eastman colour negative and print films, including the new family of EXR colour negative films

Lip Service Casting
Unit 131 Canalot Studios
222 Kensal Road
London W10 5BN
Tel: 081 969 8535
Fax: 081 968 6911
Voiceover agency for actors, and voiceover

casting agency. Publishers of 'The Voice Analysis' – a breakdown of actors' vocal profiles

Media Education Agency
5A Queens Parade
Brownlow Road
London N11 2DN
Tel: 081 888 4620
David Lusted
Consultancy, lectures and teacher in-service education (INSET) in film, television and media studies. Contacts include academics, educationists, broadcasters, writers and actors

Moving Image Touring Exhibition Service (MITES)
Moviola
Bluecoat Chambers
Liverpool L1 3BX
Tel: 051 707 2881
Fax: 051 707 2150
Martin Wallace
Courses for gallery curators, technicians and exhibitors concerned with the commissioning and presentation of moving image art works. Also development, advice, consultation services and an extensive exhibition equipment resource

Nicholson Graham & Jones
25-31 Moorgate
London EC2R 6AR
Tel: 071 628 9151
Fax: 071 648 3102
Michael Henry
A City-based law firm and a founder member of the international Globalex network in the UK, USA, Europe and the Far East. The Media and Intellectual Property Group handles film and television production, financing and distribution, cable satellite and telecommunications work, book and newspaper publishing syndication, advertising, merchandising and sponsorship arrangements, sports law, music publishing, sub-publishing and administration arrangements, technology transfer arrangements, patent, trade mark, service mark and know-how arrangements, franchising, computer hardware and software and advises on a wide range of intellectual property copyright, moral rights and performers right issues

Oxford Scientific Films (OSF)
Long Hanborough
Oxford OX8 8LL
Tel: 0993 881881
Fax: 0993 882808
10 Poland Street
London W1V 3DE
Tel: 071 494 0720
Fax: 071 287 9125
Specialists in macro, micro, time-lapse, high-speed and snorkel optic photography for natural history programmes, commercials, corporate videos and videodiscs

Radcliffes Transport Services
3-9 Willow Lane
Willow Lane Industrial Estate
Mitcham
Surrey CR4 4NA
Tel: 081 687 2344
Fax: 081 687 0997
Ken Bull
Gary Burgess
Specialist transport specifically for the film and television industry, both nationally and internationally. Fleet ranges from transit vans to 40' air ride articulated vehicles with experienced staff

The Screen Company
182 High Street
Cottenham
Cambridge CB4 4RX
Tel: 0954 50139
Fax: 0954 52005
Pat Turner
Manufacture, supply and installation of all types of front and rear projection screens for video, slide, film and OHP

Security Archives
Saref House
135 Shepherdess Walk
London N1 7PZ
Tel: 071 253 0027
Fax: 071 490 5181
Giulia Carrannante
Records management services including secure storage for film, video and audio tape, 24hr collection and delivery, computerised management and tracking

Simon Olswang & Co
1 Great Cumberland Place
London W1H 7AL
Tel: 071 723 9393
Fax: 071 723 6992
Established in 1981, one of the country's leading firms of entertainment and media solicitors. The firm specialises in all aspects of film, television, multimedia and video production, distribution and finance, cable, satellite and other communications media, recording and other music industry contracts and sponsorship

Stanley Productions
42-48 Brunel Road
Acton
London W3 7XR
Tel: 081 749 2939
Fax: 081 749 2403
Terry Doyle
Distributors of video and audio equipment, video and audio tape, film stock, and accessories. Large equipment stocks held, and all main brands of video tape

Ten Tenths
106 Gifford Street
London N1 0DF
Tel: 071 607 4887
Fax: 071 609 8124
Props service specialising in vehicles (cars, bikes, boats and planes) ranging from 1901 to present day – veteran, vintage, classic, modern – with additional wardrobe facilities

Touche Ross & Co
Hill House
1 Little New Street
London EC4A 3TR
Tel: 071 936 3000
Fax: 071 583 8517/1198
Gavin Hamilton Deeley
Mark Attan
Robert Reed
Advisors to film, television and broadcasting organisations. Business plans and financial models for companies, tax planning and business advice for individuals, and information on legal and regulatory developments affecting the sector

STUDIOS

Bray Studios
Down Place
Water Oakley
Windsor Road
Windsor
Berks SL4 5UG
Tel: 0628 22111/2
Fax: 0628 770381
Beryl Earl
Carole Copeland
STAGES
1 (sound) 955 sq metres
2 (sound) 948 sq metres
3 (sound) 235 sq metres
4 (sound) 173 sq metres
FILMS/PROGRAMMES
Small Metal Jacket and *The Vampyr* for BBC
Anglo Saxon Attitudes for Euston Films

Chamberlain Film Studio
16-20 Wharfdale Road
London N1 9RY
Tel: 071 837 3855
Ted Chamberlain
STAGE
1 80 sq metres
Also construction facilities

De Lane Lea Dean Street Studio
75 Dean Street
London W1V 5HA
Tel: 071 439 1721
Fax: 071 437 0913
STAGE
1 86 sq metres
Cove U shape, Sync, lighting rig, TV rig, full TV lighting; 2 make-up rooms, 1 wardrobe, 1 production office, full fitted kitchen

Ealing Studios
Ealing Green
London W5 5EP
Tel: 081 758 8507
Fax: 081 758 8579
Carol Pedley
STAGES
2 (sound) 540 sq metres
3a (sound) 323 sq metres
3b (sound) 323 sq metres
(3a and 3b may be combined to create area of 640 sq metres)
4 (silent) 432 sq metres
5 (Theatre B – sound) 98 sq metres
Theatre A (sound) 32 sq metres
FILMS
Blue Ice
Hour of the Pig
Object of Beauty
TELEVISION
Albert Campion
Blackeyes
The Buddha of Suburbia
Chronicles of Narnia
Clarissa
Fortunes of War
Inspector Alleyn
Memento Mori
The Men's Room
Middlemarch
A Perfect Spy
Portrait of a Marriage
The Secret Agent
Shackleton
The Singing Detective
Love Hurts for Alomo Productions
The Volunteer for Arden Films

Halliford Studios
Manygate Lane
Shepperton
Middx TW17 9EG
Tel: 0932 226341
Fax: 0932 246336
STAGES
A 334 sq metres
B 223 sq metres

Holborn Studios
49/50 EagleWharf Road
London N1 7ED
Tel: 071 490 4099
Fax: 071 253 8120
Ivan Merrell
STAGES
4 233 sq metres
6 273 sq metres
7 247 sq metres
All coved. Also eight fashion studios, set building, E6 lab, b/w lab, KJP in house, canal-side restaurant and bar

Isleworth Studios
Studio Parade
484 London Road
Isleworth
Middx TW7 4DE
Tel: 081 568 3511
Fax: 081 568 4863
STAGES
A 292 sq metres
B 152 sq metres
C 152 sq metres
D 152 sq metres

Jacob Street Studios
9-19 Mill Street
London SE1 2DA
Tel: 071 232 1066
Fax: 071 252 0118

Pinewood Studios
Iver Heath
Bucks SL0 0NH
Tel: 0753 651700
Fax: 0753 656844
R Busby
STAGES
A 1,685 sq metres
B 827 sq metres
C 827 sq metres
D 1,685 sq metres
E 1,685 sq metres
F 700 sq metres
G 247 sq metres
H 300 sq metres
J 825 sq metres
K 825 sq metres
L 880 sq metres
M 880 sq metres
007 (silent) 4,225 sq metres
South Dock (silent) 1,548 sq metres
Large Process 454 sq metres
Small Process 226 sq metres
FILMS
Being Human
Carry on Columbus
Frankenstein – The True Story
Great Moments in Aviation
Little Buddha
Secret Garden
Son of the Pink Panther
TELEVISION
Diana – Her True Story
Head over Heels
Parallel 9
Sarah

Rotherhithe Studios
169 Rotherhithe Street
London SE16 1QU
Tel: 071 231 2209
Fax: 071 231 2119
O Stockman
STAGES
A Bullhead 800 sq metres
B Rotherhithe 177 sq metres
Pre-production workshops, construction and post-production facilities
FILMS
As You Like It
Foreign Moon
Hard Times
The Long Day Closes

Shepperton Studios
Studios Road
Shepperton
Middx TW17 0QD
Tel: 0932 562611
Fax: 0932 568989
Paul Olliver
STAGES
A 1,668 sq metres
B 1,115 sq metres
C 1,668 sq metres

D 1,115 sq metres
E 294 sq metres
F 294 sq metres
G 629 sq metres
H 2,660 sq metres
I 657 sq metres
J 284 sq metres
K 120 sq metres
L 604 sq metres
M 259 sq metres
T 261 sq metres
P 338 sq metres
FILMS/PROGRAMMES
Hamlet starring Mel Gibson, Glenn Close; director Franco Zeffirelli; producer Dyson Lovell
Robin Hood: Prince of Thieves starring Kevin Costner, Morgan Freeman; director Kevin Reynolds; producers John Watson, Michael Kagan
The Crying Game starring Miranda Richardson, Forest Whitaker, Stephen Rea, Jaye Davidson; director Neil Jordan; producer Stephen Woolley
Damage starring Jeremy Irons, Juliette Binoche, Miranda Richardson; director Louis Malle, producers Simon Relph, Vincent Malle
Chaplin starring Robert Downey Jnr; director Lord Attenborough; producers Lord Attenborough, Mario Kassar
A Muppet Christmas Carol starring Michael Caine; director Brian Henson; producer Martin Baker

Southbrook Studios

Southbrook Studios see entries for **Westway Studios** and **Isleworth Studios**

Teddington Studios

Broom Road
Teddington Lock
Middlesex TW11 9NT
Tel: 081 977 3252
Fax: 081 943 4050
Steve Gunn
STAGES
1 650 sq metres
2 353 sq metres
3 130 sq metres
PROGRAMMES
Have I Got News for You
Kilroy
Birds of a Feather
Paul Merton
Over the Rainbow

Theed Street Studios

12 Theed Street
London SE1 8ST
Tel: 071 928 1953
Fax: 071 928 1952
Bill Collom
STAGE
A 151 sq metres
FILMS/PROGRAMMES
Birthnight for BBC2
Gay Men's Guide Part 1 for Terrence Higgins Trust
Without Walls for Channel 4
Wittgenstein for Channel 4/BFI

Twickenham Film Studios

St Margaret's
Twickenham
Middx TW1 2AW
Tel: 081 892 4477
Fax: 081 891 0168
Jane Jenkins
STAGES
1 701 sq metres
2 186 sq metres
3 516 sq metres

Wembley Studios

10 Northfield Industrial Estate
Beresford Avenue
Wembley
Middlesex HA0 1RT
Tel: 081 903 4296
Fax: 081 900 1353
STAGES
Studio 290 sq metres
Cyc 193 sq metres
Power: 900 amps 3 phase
Production offices, dressing rooms, kitchen

Westway Studios

8 Olaf Street
London W11 4BE
Tel: 071 221 9041
Fax: 071 221 9399
STAGES
1 602 sq metres
2 475 sq metres
3 169 sq metres
4 261 sq metres

TELEVISION COMPANIES

Below are listed all British television companies, with a selection of their key personnel and programmes. The titles listed are a cross-section of productions initiated (but not necessarily broadcast) during 1992 and the first quarter of 1993. 'F' and 'V' indicate whether productions were shot on film or video. For details of feature films made for television, see Production Starts (p264)

ANGLIA
Television Limited

Anglia Television

Anglia House
Norwich NR1 3JG
Tel: 0603 615151
Chairman: Sir Peter Gibbings
Chief Executive: David McCall
Managing Director, Broadcasting Division: Philip Garner

The Chief
Production company: Anglia Films
Producer: Ruth Boswell
Director: Anthony Quinn
Writers: Jeffrey Caine, Ray Jenkins, Peter Jukes
Cast: Martin Shaw, Tim Pigott-Smith, Karen Archer
6 x 1 hour V
Outspoken Chief Constable John Stafford accepts a new post as head of Europol in Brussels leaving the top job of the Eastland force vacant. Martin Shaw as the charismatic Alan Cade, a deputy assistant commissioner in the Metropolitan Police, takes the helm

Riders
Production company: Anglia Films
Producer: Roger Gregory
Director: Gabrielle Beaumont
Writers: Terence Brady, Charlotte Bingham
Cast: Marcus Gilbert, Michael Praed, Caroline Harker, Stephanie Beacham, Anthony Valentine, John Standing, Arabella Tjye, Serena Gordon, Anthony Calf
2 x 2 hour F
Based on Jilly Cooper's best selling novel about raunchy exploits amid the show jumping fraternity

Other productions include:
Anglia Live
Anglia Tonight
Countrywide
Cross Question
First Take
Food Guide
Go Fishing
Help
Knightmare
Love Call
Lucky Ladders
Marquee
Package Pilgrims
Survival

Border Television

The Television Centre
Carlisle CA1 3NT
Tel: 0228 25101
Chairman: Melvyn Bragg
Managing Director: James Graham
Head of Production & Assistant Controller of Programmes: Neil Robinson

Business First
Producer: Ian Fisher
7 x 30 mins
A yearly competition for small businesses in the Border Television region

Forum
Producer: Paul Baird
10 x 60 mins
Local current affairs and community issues programme

7th Heaven
Producer: Ian Fisher
Director: Harry King
10 x 30 mins
Broad based arts programme covering venues, performances etc in the Border region

Union and the League
Producer: Jack Johnstone
10 x 30 mins
A monthly series which proves that rugby union and rugby league can be covered in one programme

CARLTON

Carlton Television

101 St Martin's Lane
London WC2N 4AZ
Tel: 071 240 4000
Fax: 071 240 4171
Chief Executive: Nigel Walmsley
Managing Director: Paul Jackson
Director, Drama and International Development: Jonathan Powell
Director, Corporate Affairs: Peter Ibbotson
Director, Sales: Martin Bowley
Controller, Social/Factual: Paul Corley
Controller, Entertainment: John Bishop
Controller, Regional Affairs: Colin Stanbridge
Controller, Operations and Engineering: Chris Hibbert
Controller, Programme Planning, Presentation: Tim Riordan
Controller, Presentation and Promotions: Tim Simmons
Head of Acquisitions: Jeff Ford

Head of Press and Publicity: Chris McLaughlin

The Big Story
Production company: Twenty Twenty Television
Executive producer: Claudia Milne
Editor: Simon Berthon
16 weekly episodes
Presenter: Dermot Murnaghan
Networked current affairs strand

Brighton Belles
Production company: Humphrey Barclay Productions
Producer: Humphrey Barclay
Director: James Cellan-Jones
Adapted by Christopher Skala from the original Golden Girls scripts
10 x 30 mins
Cast: Sheila Hancock, Wendy Craig, Sheila Gish, Jean Boht

Dave Allen
Production company: Noel Gay Television
Executive producer: Bill Cotton
Producer: Nick Symons
Director: Tom Poole
Writer: Ian Davidson
7 x 30 mins
Comedy series

Frank Stubbs Promotes
Production company: Noel Gay Television
Producer: Hilary Bevan Jones
Directors: Richard Standeven, Tom Cotter
Writer: Simon Nye
7 x 1 hour
Cast: Timothy Spall, Lesley Sharp, Trevor Cooper, Nick Reding, Daniella Westbrook
Timothy Spall stars as Frank Stubbs, one of Soho's more successful ticket touts, who wants to become a promoter too

The Good Sex Guide
Production company: Prospect Pictures
Series producer: Vicki Barrass
Directors: Mike Adams, Richard Trayler-Smith
Comedy writers: Lenny Barker and Vicky Stepney, Jim Pullin
Presenter: Margi Clarke
7 x 30 mins
Adult education series about sex, including sketches highlighting some of the funniest sexual situations

A Woman's Guide to Adultery
Production company: Hartswood Films
Producer: Beryl Vertue
Director: David Hayman
Writer: Frank Cottrell Boyce
Cast: Theresa Russell, Sean Bean, Amanda Donohoe, Adrian Dunbar
3 episodes
Based on the best-selling novel by Carol Clewlow. Rose disapproves of adultery: her three closest friends are all entangled with married men, and she can see that it is always the women who suffer the most. But when she meets Paul, the sexual attraction is too strong to resist

Other programmes include:
Big City
Body and Soul
Capital Woman
Comedy Playhouse
Fantastic Facts!
The Frost Programme
Head Over Heels
Michael Ball
Sport in Question
A Statement of Affairs
Storyline
Thoi Noi

CENTRAL

Central Independent Television
Central House
Broad Street
Birmingham B1 2JP
Tel: 021 643 9898
Fax: 021 616 1531
East Midlands Television Centre
Lenton Lane
Nottingham NG7 2NA
Tel: 0602 863322
Fax: 0602 43552
35-38 and 43-45 Portman Square
London W1H 9AH
Tel: 071 486 6688
Fax: 071 486 1132/1707
46 Charlotte Street
London W1P 1LX
Tel: 071 637 4602
Fax: 071 580 7780
Unit 9 Windrush Court
Abingdon Business Park
Abingdon
Oxon OX14 1SA
Tel: 0235 554123
Fax: 0235 524024
Chairman and Chief Executive: Leslie Hill
Director of Finance: Kazia Kantor
Director of Personnel: Alan Pankhurst
Managing Director, Central Broadcasting: Andy Allan
Regional Advisory Council: Jean Parker, Murray Thomson, Michael Green, Nigel Walmsley
Director of Legal Affairs/ Company Secretary: Colin Campbell
Managing Director, Central Productions: Mike Watts
Managing Director, C.T.E: Philip Jones
Director, Programme Planning: Dawn Airey
Controller, Press and Publicity: John Palmer
Controller of News: Laurie Upshon
Controller of Regional Programmes: Steve Clark
Controller of Sport: Gary Newbon
Controller, Young People's: Lewis Rudd
Controller, Features and Documentaries: Roger James
Controller, Drama and MD Central Films: Ted Childs
Controller, Light Entertainment: Richard Holloway
Controller, Comedy: Paul Spencer

Just a Gigolo
Production company: Central Productions for Central Television
Producer: Paul Spencer
Director: Martin Dennis
Writers: Carl Gorham, Michael Hatt, Amanda Swift
Camera: Ian Keown
Editor: John Hawkins
Cast: Tony Slattery, Rowena King, Paul Bigley
7 x 30 mins V
A comnprehensive school teacher loses his job and is pressured by his greedy brother into becoming a paid escort. His new profession brings in much needed cash, but complications arise when he falls head-over-heels in love

Lifeboat
Production company: Central Television in association with National Geographic Television
Producer/Director: Graham Johnston
Co-producer: Andrew Barker
Camera: Graham Johnston
Editor: Stephen Singleton
6 x 30 mins F & V
Lifeboat chronicles one year in the life of the RNLI service in the seaside resort of Salcombe. It features the high drama of dangerous sea rescues, the frustrations of false alarms, the courage and dedication of the 14 lifeboat crew members. It also reflects the ups and downs of their everyday lives in the busy holiday town

The Lodge
Production company: Central Productions and Richmond Films for Central Television
Producer: Sandra Hastie
Directors: Bill Ward, Lorne Magory, Sharon Miller, Geoff Hogg
Writer: Victor Gialanella
Camera: Christopher Clayton
Editors: Geoff Hogg, Richard Milward
Cast: Martina Lazzeri, Louisa Milwood Haigh, David Thwaites, Nancy Lodder, Debra Michaels
10 x 30 mins V
Growing up in a children's home – the heartache and the humour. The series follows seven youngsters and their friends as they get to grips with living in a children's home

Peak Practice
Production company: Central Films for Central Television

Producer: Tony Virgo
Directors: Gordon Flemying, Antonia Bird, Alan Grint, Chris Lovett
Writers: Lucy Gannon, Andy de la Tour, Tony Etchells
Camera: Chris Howard
Editors: Dave Blackmoor, Mike Mulliner
Cast: Kevin Whately, Amanda Burton, Simon Shepherd, Sylvia Syms
1 x 90 mins,
7 x 60 mins F
Dr Jack Kerruish has spent the past three years as a doctor in Africa before returning to England with ambitions to work in a country practice. When one of the partners leaves The Beeches surgery to join a rival new clinic in the village, the two remaining partners are left with a dilapidated practice and the need for a new partner. But is Dr Kerruish the answer to their prayers?

Sharpe
Production company: Central Films, produced by Celtic Films and Picture Palace for Central Television
Executive Producers: Ted Childs, Muir Sutherland
Producer: Malcolm Craddock
Directors: Laurence Moody, Nick Hamm
Writer: Eoghan Harris
Camera: Ivan Strasburg
Editors: Robin Sales
Cast: Sean Bean, Assumpta Serna, Brian Cox, David Troughton
2 x 120 mins F
Maverick officer Richard Sharpe has earned promotion through the ranks of Wellington's army by courage and daring – and is now singled out for dangerous missions behind enemy lines in the Peninsular wars

Other productions include:
The Blackheath Poisonings
Celebrity Squares
Cook Report
The Dreamstone
Family Fortunes
Harry's Mad
Press Gang
$64,000 Question
Soldier, Soldier
Spitting Image
Viewpoint
Woof

Channel Television
Television Centre
La Pouquelaye
St Helier
Jersey JE2 3ZD
Tel: 0534 68999
Fax: 0534 59446
Television Centre
St George's Place
St Peter Port
Guernsey
Tel: 0481 723451
Fax: 0481 710739
Chairman: Major J R Riley
Managing Director: John Henwood

Channel Report
Programme Editor: Paul Brown
News Editor: Martyn Farley
Presenters: Paul Brown, Sarah Montague, Karen Rankine
News magazine broadcast Monday to Friday jointly presented from Channel's Jersey and Guernsey news studios – also featuring live or taped inserts from the smaller islands Sark and Alderney

An Introduction to Golf Rules and Etiquette
Producer/director: Bob Evans
1 x 1 hour
Ryder Cup golfer Tommy Horton explains some of the rules and etiquette of golf to racing driver Derek Warwick, as they play a match at the Royal Jersey Golf Club

House Workout
Producer/director: Jane Bayer
1 x 1 hour
Joan Rider's technique of incorporating exercises into the daily chores of housework

Morning Worship
Producer: Jane Bayer
Director: Paul Brown
1 x 1 hour
Sunday service from Bethlehem Methodist Chapel, Jersey

Wildlife on the Menu
Co-producers: Tim Ringsdore, John Le Signe
1 x 30 mins
The killing of wild animals for bush meat in Ghana threatens several species. Viv Wilson has a plan to save some of them by farming endangered species of antelope

Programmes in development:
Bertie the Bat (second series)
Face the Hanglider
Faith Alive
Fantastic Flying Journey
In the Footsteps of the Saints
Island of Dreams
The Islander
Midnight Clear
The Morning After
Murder in the Family
Schools at Work
State of the Ark
Zoolysses

GMTV
London Television Centre
Upper Ground
London SE1 9TT
Tel: 071 827 7000
Fax: 071 827 7001
Chairman: Greg Dyke
Managing Director: Christopher Stoddart
Director of Programmes: Peter McHugh
Senior News Editor: Nigel Hancock
Editor: Liam Hamilton

Grampian Television
Queen's Cross
Aberdeen AB9 2XJ
Tel: 0224 646464
Fax: 0224 635127
Chairman: Sir Douglas Hardie CBE JP
Chief Executive: Donald H Waters CA
Director of Television: Robert L Christie
Director of Finance: Graham Good CA
Director of Programmes: George W Mitchell

The Art Sutter Show
Director: Alan Franchi
Presenter: Art Sutter
10 x 60 mins
The genial host presents a series of live music and chat programmes with a varied line-up of guests live on Friday nights

North Tonight
Editor: Alistair Gracie
Nightly x 30 mins
Monday to Friday at 6pm, news magazine programme covering top news stories from all over North Scotland, ITV's largest transmission area, using electronically-linked studio centres in Aberdeen, Dundee, Inverness and Stornoway plus mobile crews and freelance cameramen throughout the region

Telefios
Editor: Bob Kenyon
Presenter: Angela MacKinnon
Twice daily x 10 mins
Gaelic news magazine – produced in the heart of the Gaidhealtachd at Grampian's new studios in Stornoway – which places Gaeldom and Gaelic issues firmly in a national and international context

We the Jury
Executive producer: George Mitchell
Presenter: Anne MacKenzie
4 x 60 mins
A jury of 12 local people deliver their verdict along with that of the studio audience and viewers who phone in. Local radio stations co-operate with follow-up discussion programmes

Other programmes include:
Country Matters
Crossfire
Living and Growing
Put it in Writing
The Sunday Service
The Way It Was

World Mountain Bike Championships

Granada Television

Granada Television Centre
Quay Street
Manchester M60 9EA
Tel: 061 832 7211
Fax: 061 832 7211 x3405
36 Golden Square
London W1R 4AH
Tel: 071 734 8080
Granada News Centre
Albert Dock
Liverpool L3 4BA
Tel: 051 709 9393
Fax: 051 708 4243
Granada News Centre
Bridgegate House
5 Bridge Place
Lower Bridge Street
Chester CH1 1SA
Tel: 0244 313966
Fax: 0244 320599
Granada News Centre
White Cross
Lancaster LA1 4XQ
Tel: 0524 60688
Fax: 0524 67607
Granada News Centre
Daisyfield Business Centre
Appleby Street
Blackburn BB1 3BL
Tel: 0254 690099
Fax: 0254 699299
Chief Executive: Charles Allen
Managing Director Broadcasting: Steve Morrison
Commercial Director: Kate Stross
Director of Sales: Michael Desmond
General Manager: Brenda Smith
Head of Drama: Sally Head
Head of Entertainment, Arts and Childrens: Brian Park
Head of Factual Programmes: Dianne Nelmes
Head of Sport: Paul Doherty

Coronation Street
Producer: Carolyn Reynolds
Cont x 30 mins
The northern town of Weatherfield forms the backdrop to life in a working class street with each of its inhabitants interacting to create a drama rich in humour, pathos and human experience

Maigret
Producer: Paul Marcus
Directors: John Strickland, Nicholas Renton, Stuart Burge
Cast: Michael Gambon
1 x 90 mins, 5 x 60 mins F
Adaptations of six of Georges Simenon's novels featuring the intuitive, pipe-smoking Chief Inspector Maigret

Prime Suspect II
Producer: Paul Marcus
Director: John Strickland
Writer: Allan Cubitt
Cast: Helen Mirren, John Benfield, Jack Ellis, Craig Fairbrass, Andrew Tiernan
2 x 2 hour F
In the sequel to the award winning and acclaimed *Prime Suspect*, Helen Mirren returns to star as tough female detective DCI Jane Tennison

September Song
Producer: Gareth Morgan
Director: David Richards
Cast: Russ Abbot, Michael Williams
1 x 60 mins
6 x 30 mins V
A moving tale of friendship and new futures. Alone through the death of his wife, school teacher Abbot accompanies small-time comedian Williams for an end-of-the-pier summer season in Blackpool

World in Action
Executive producer: Charles Tremayne
Cont x 30 mins
Challenging and campaigning current affairs series. The last series included investigations into Breast Implants, Kerb Crawling, two reports from Los Angeles, and reports on Homelessness

You've Been Framed
Producer: Mark Gorton
Director: Jenny Dodd
7 x 30 mins V
More than 35,000 videos have been sent to Jeremy Beadle so far for the next series which features all new material

Other programmes include:
Cluedo
Jeeves and Wooster
Medics
Stars in their Eyes
Surgical Spirit
This Morning
Up The Garden Path
Watching

HTV

Television Centre
Cardiff CF5 6XJ
Tel: 0222 590590
Fax: 0222 597183
The Television Centre
Bath Road
Bristol BS4 3HG
Tel: 0272 778366
Fax: 0272 722400
69 New Oxford Street
London WC1A 1DG
Tel: 071 379 0406
Fax: 071 399 5495
Chairman: Louis Sherwood
Chief Executive: Charles Romaine
Group Director of Programmes: Huw Davies
Group Director of Finance: Chris Rowlands
Group Director of Resources and Personnel: Ted George
Controller, Factual and General Programmes (Wales): Menna Richards
Controller, News and Sport (Wales): Russell Lyne
Director of Programmes (West): Steve Matthews
Head of News and Current Affairs (West): Ken Rees

Programmes (Cardiff) include:
Arts Documentaries
4 x 4
Get Going
Judas and the Gimp
Primetime
The Really Helpful Programme
The Sherman Plays
A Slice of Life
Wales and Westminster
Wales at Six
Wales This Week
A Welsh Life
Programmes (Bristol) include:
Between Two Rivers
Garden Club
Good Health
HTV News
Late and Live
The Music Game
The Pig Attraction
Rubbish – King of the Jumble
Simply the Best
The West This Week
Wycliffe
You're The Boss

Independent Television News

200 Gray's Inn Road
London WC1X 8XZ
Tel: 071 833 3000
Chief Executive: David Gordon
Editor-in-chief: Stewart Purvis
Editor of ITN programmes on ITV: David Mannion
Editor of ITN programmes on Channel 4: Richard Tait
ITN is the news provider nominated by the Independent Television Commission to supply news programming for the ITV network. Subject to review, this licence is for a ten year period from 1993. ITN also provides news for Channel 4 and for the Independent Radio News (IRN) network. It is recognised as one of the world's leading news organisations whose programmes and reports are seen in every corner of the globe. In addition to its base in London, ITN has permanent news bureaux in Washington, Moscow, South Africa, the Middle East, Hong Kong and Brussels as well as at Westminster and several other locations around the UK

News at Ten
Channel 4 News
Early Evening News
Lunchtime News
Morning and Afternoon Bulletins
The Parliament Programme on Channel 4
The Big Breakfast News on Channel 4

5.30am Morning News
Into the Night
Weekend News and Sport
Radio News
ITN World News
Special Programmes
World News for Airlines
ITN Videos
Corporate Television Networks

LWT (Holdings) plc

The London Television Centre
Upper Ground
London SE1 9LT
Tel: 071 620 1620
Chairman: Sir Christopher Bland
Deputy Chairman: Brian Tesler CBE
Group Chief Executive: Greg Dyke
Managing Director, LWT Productions: Nick Elliott
Director of Corporate Affairs: Barry Cox
Controller of Arts: Melvyn Bragg
Controller of Drama: Sarah Wilson
Controller of Entertainment: John Kaye Cooper
Controller of Factual Programmes: Simon Shaps

London's Burning
Executive producer: Sarah Wilson
Producer: Paul Knight
10 x 60 mins F
The sixth series of the ratings hit which chronicles the life and times of Blue Watch at Blackwall Fire Station in London's East End

The South Bank Show
Editor: Melvyn Bragg
Executive Producer: David Thomas
Head of Arts: Nigel Wattis
2 x 120 mins, 22 x 60 mins; 5 independently produced F/V
The 17th season of TV's top arts show ranges from Stevie Wonder and John Lee Hooker to Willy Russell and Margaret Atwood, with a two hour special on guitarist John Williams

Walden
Executive producer: David Cox
Editor: John Wakefield
25 x 50 mins, normally live
The week's big one-to-one political interview which sets the agenda

You Bet!
Executive producer: John Kaye Cooper
Producer: Linda Beadle
14 x 1 hr plus 1 special
Matthew Kelly hosts the people show with unusual challengers benefiting celebrities' favourite charities

Other programmes include:
Anna Lee
Barrymore
Beadle's About
Blind Date
The London Programme

MERIDIAN

Meridian Broadcasting

TV Centre
Northam Road
Southampton SO2 0TA
Tel: 0703 222555
Fax: 0703 335050
48 Leicester Square
London WC2H 7LY
Tel: 071 839 2255
Fax: 071 925 0665
TV Centre, Vintners Park
Maidstone
Kent
Tel: 0622 684679
Fax: 0622 684632
1-3 Brookway
Hambridge Lane
Newbury
Berks RG14 5UZ
Tel: 0635 522322
Fax: 0635 522620
Chairman: Clive Hollick
Chief Executive: Roger Laughton
Deputy Chief Executive: Malcolm Wall
Director of Public Affairs: Simon Albury
Director of Regional Development: Keith Clement
Director of Finance: Peter Hickson
Deputy Director Resources and Head of Engineering: Peter Booth
Director of Factual Programmes: Richard Creasey
Controller of Children's and Daytime Programmes: Janie Grace
Controller of Finance: John Cresswell
Controller of Programming: Richard Platt
Controller of Regional Programmes and Community Affairs: Mary McAnally
Controller of Drama: Colin Rogers
Controller of News, Sport and Current Affairs: Jim Raven
Head of Comedy for Meridian (SelecTV): Tony Charles
Head of Arts for Meridian (Antelope): Mick Csaky

FreeScreen
Producer: David Smith
30 mins Mon-Fri
Television's answer to the classified ads

Meridian This Week
Editor: Trish Powell
Presenter: Mai Davies
20 mins weekly
Current Affairs programme which investigates matters close to the hearts of viewers in the south and south east

Meridian Tonight
Producers: Alison Black, Paul Erlam (West); Iain McBride, Mark Percy (South East); Nick Myers, Steve McDonnell (South)
Directors: Lynn Skilton, Alan Gowdry (South); Paul Coleman, Neil Stainsby (South East); Martin Atkin, James Gould (West)
Editors: Andy Cooper (South); Mark Southgate (South East), Robin Britton (West)
Presenters: Debbie Thrower, Fred Dinenage (South); Mai Davies, Andy Craig (West); Alison Holloway, Mike Debbens (South East)
30 mins Mon-Thurs, 60 mins Fri
Regional news programme at 6pm

The Pier
Production company: Antelope South
Directors: Derek Guthrie, Jill Marshall
Executive Producer: Mick Csaky
Producer: Sue Judd
Series Editor: Stephen Phillips
Presenter: Pete McCarthy
45 mins
Meridian's arts and entertaiments programme

Three Minutes
Producer/director: Tony Steyger
Editor: Gerard Melling
5 mins
Meridian's community access programme

Other productions include:
Networked:
The Challenge (working title)
In the Wild
Ruth Rendell: Vanity Dies Hard, The Strawberry Tree, Master of the Moor
TV Weekly
Under the Hammer
Wizadora (series II)
Regional:
Countryways
Grass Roots
Midweek Sports
Saturday Sport

SCOTTISH TELEVISION

Scottish Television

Cowcaddens
Glasgow G2 3PR
Tel: 041 332 9999
Fax: 041 332 6982
200 Gray's Inn Road
London WC1X 8XZ
Tel: 071 396 6000
Fax: 071 396 6116
The Gateway
Edinburgh EH7 4AH
Tel: 031 557 4554
Fax: 031 557 3791
Chairman: William Brown CBE
Managing Director: Gus Macdonald

Director of Programmes: Alistair Moffat
Director of Broadcasting: Eileen Gallagher
Head of Programmes – Scotland: David Scott

The Advocates
Executive producer: Robert Love
Legal drama set in Edinburgh

The Disney Club
Executive Producer: Sandy Ross
Sunday morning children's network entertainment

Doctor Finlay
Executive Producer: Robert Love

Taggart
Executive Producer: Robert Love
Glasgow detective series

Take the High Road
Producer: Frank Cox
Drama serial set on Loch Lomond

Wheel of Fortune
Executive producer: Sandy Ross
Popular network game show

Other programmes include:
Connery
Life Stories
The Munro Show
NB
Scotland's War
Scotland Today
Scotsport
Scottish Frontiers on Medicine
Scottish Women
Talking Pictures
Wilderness
Win, Lose or Draw

Tyne Tees Television
The Television Centre
City Road
Newcastle upon Tyne
NE1 2AL
Tel: 091 261 0181
Fax: 091 261 2302
Chairman: Sir Ralph Carr-Ellison TD
Deputy Chairman: R H Dickinson
Managing Director: John Calvert
Director of Broadcasting: Peter Moth
Director of Finance: Michael Ranson
Head of Group Engineering: John Nichol
Head of News and Current Affairs: Olwyn Hocking
Head of Education: Sheila Browne

Cross Wits
Production company: Tyne Tees Television
Producer: Christine Williams
Director: Andy Martin
Presenter: Tom O'Connor
55 x 30 mins
Tom O'Connor hosts the compulsive word game for crossword fanatics which also involves the viewer. Two crossword buffs partner similarly addicted celebrities to solve as many clues and keywords as they can

Gimme 5
Production company: Tyne Tees Television
Executive Producer: Lesley Oakden
Producer: Ken Scorfield
Director: Malcolm Dickinson
Presenters: Nobby the Sheep, Jenny Powell, Lewis MacLeod
14 x 120 mins
A brand new series of the live, bumper Saturday morning fun show serving up two hours of music, madness and mayhem; fun, facts and fashion; cartoons, computers and bags of competitions as Studio 5 is handed over to the nation's kids

The Man Who Cried
Production company: Festival films/World Wide International Television
Producer: Ray Marshall
Director: Michael Whyte
Writer: Stan Barstow
Director of Photography: Fred Tammes
Editor: Scott Thomas
Cast: Ciaran Hinds, Kate Buffery, Amanda Root, Daniel Massey, Gemma Craven
2 x 90 mins
Adapted for television from Catherine Cookson's best seller and set against the turbulent background of the Depression and WW2, the story centres on Abel Mason who comits bigamy in a desperate bid to provide a home and security for himself and his young son Dick

Other programmes include:
The Back Page
Dales Diary
Earthmovers
The Friday Documentary
Head to Head
Network North
Robson's People
Samson Darts Classic
Sign On
Tyne Tees Today
Tyne Tees Weekend
A Woman's Place

Ulster Television
Havelock House
Ormeau Road
Belfast BT7 1EB
Tel: 0232 328122
Fax: 0232 246695
Chairman: J B McGuckian
Managing Director: J D Smyth
General Manager: J McCann
Controller of Programming: A Bremner
Controller, Corporate Communications: M McCann
Commissioning Editor (Documentaries, Music): A Crockart
Head of News and Current Affairs: M Beattie

The Chieftains and Guests
A rich mixture featuring the internationally famous group, with guests Nanci Griffith and Roger Daltry

High Days and Holidays
A series of cookery programmes presented by popular cookery expert Jenny Bristow. She also featured in another big viewer-response series, *Kitchen Garden*

Kelly
Into its fourth successful season, this 90-minute weekly programme hosted by Gerry Kelly provides a varied mixture of music and chat with well-known faces from today and yesterday

Once Upon a Place
An out-and-about series of programmes exploring the history of many Ulster places, including Portavogie, Upper Lough Erne and the Waterside in Londonderry

Sailortown
Joint UTV/Central production for Carlton's Comedy Playhouse series. Comedy set in Belfast's dockland community

UTV Live at Six
Five days a week hour-long news and features programme. Includes a wide range of strands – environment, health, home, entertainments, pets, local communities, consumer affairs

Westcountry Television
Western Wood Way
Langage Science Park
Plymouth PL7 5BG
Tel: 0752 333333
Fax: 0752 333444
Chairman: Sir John Banham
Deputy Chairman: Frank Copplestone
Chief Executive: Stephen Redfarn
Managing Director: John Prescott Thomas
Finance Director: Mark Haskell
Commercial Director: Caroline McDevitt

Press and Publicity: Mark Clare
Controller of News and Current Affairs: Richard Myers
Controller of Features: Jane Clarke
Controller of Operations and Engineering: Sim Harris

Yorkshire Television

The Television Centre
Leeds LS3 1JS
Tel: 0532 438283
Fax: 0532 445107
Television House
32 Bedford Row
London WC1R 4HE
Tel: 071 242 1666
Fax: 071 405 8062
Chairman: Sir Derek Palmar
Group Chief Executive: Clive Leach
Director of Programmes: Grant McKee
Controller of Drama: Keith Richardson
Controller of Entertainment: David Reynolds
Head of Documentaries and Current Affairs: Chris Bryer
Head of Education, Children's and Religious Programmes: Chris Jelley
Controller of Local Programmes: Richard Gregory
Head of Sport: Robert Charles
Controller of Corporate Affairs: Geoff Brownlee

Emmerdale
Executive producer: Keith Richardson
Producer: Morag Bain
Story Editor: Keith Temple
Cast: Sheila Mercier, Frazer Hines, Clive Hornby, Richard Thorp, Stan Richards, Malandra Burrows, Christopher Chittell, Cy Chadwick, Glenda McKay, Craig McKay, Norman Bowler, Claire King, Madeleine Howard, Peter Amory, Matthew Vaughan, Kate Dove, Tony Pitts
Twice weekly serial which was first transmitted in 1972

First Tuesday
Executive producer: Grant McKee
Deputy Editor: Chris Bryer
Producers: Various
Directors: Various
Editors: Terry Warwick, Clive Trist, Barry Spink, David Aspinall
12 x 1 hour (monthly)
Yorkshire's award winning documentary programme which brings national and international issues to the screen. Recipient of an International Emmy, a BAFTA award and the Grand Award at the International Film and TV Festival of New York for its film *Four Hours in My Lai*

Heartbeat
Executive Producer: Keith Richardson
Producer: Stuart Doughty
Directors: Roger Cheveley, Tim Dowd, Ken Horn, Terry Iland, James Ormerod
Writers: Johnny Byrne, Brian Finch, Rob Gittins, Patrick Harbinson, David Lane, Alan Whiting, Barry Woodward
Cast: Nick Berry, Niamh Cusack, Derek Fowlds, Frank Middlemass, Bill Maynard
10 x 1 hour
PC Nick Rowan (Nick Berry) and his wife Dr Kate Rowan (Niamh Cusack) have travelled up from London to Aidensfield, a little village on the North Yorkshire moors to make a new life for themselves in this fast moving drama series

Jimmy's
Executive Producer: Grant McKee
Producer/Director: Irene Cockcroft
Camera: Russell Glavin
Editors: Steve Fairholme, Tim Dawson, Don MacMillan, Joan Waddington
24 x 30 mins
Set in Britain's largest hospital, it tells the everyday stories of joy and anguish, pain and sorrow of the staff and patients, and behind the scenes workers at St James's University Hospital in Leeds

A Touch of Frost
Executive producers: David Reynolds, Richard Bates
Producer: Don Leaver
Directors: Don Leaver, David Reynolds, Anthony Simmons
Associate Producer: Peter Lover
Cast: David Jason
3 x 2 hours
David Jason stars as Detective Inspector Jack Frost who may have "policeman" written on his passport but that is where the resemblance ends. He's sloppy, disorganised and disrespectful. He attracts trouble like a magnet and is barely tolerated by his superiors, but when the chips are down he's the one man that everyone wants on their side

Other programmes include:
Bad Influence
Countdown
Darling Buds of May
Days of Majesty
Demob
It's a Vet's Life
The New Statesman
Runaway Bay
Through the Keyhole
Whicker's World
The Wolves are Howling

4
CHANNEL FOUR TELEVISION

Channel Four Television

60 Charlotte Street
London W1P 2AX
Tel: 071 631 4444
Chairman: Sir Michael Bishop CBE
Chief Executive: Michael Grade
Director of Programmes: John Willis
Deputy Director of Programmes & Controller, Arts & Entertainment: Andrea Wonfor
Director of Programme Acquisition: Colin Leventhal
Director of Advertising Sales and Marketing: Stewart Butterfield
Controller, Factual Programmes: Peter Salmon
Head of Drama: David Aukin
Commissioning Editors: David Lloyd (Senior Commissioning Editor, News & Current Affairs); Alan Fountain (Senior Commissioning Editor, Independent Film and Video); Peter Ansorge (Deputy Head of Drama, Series and Serials); Karen Brown (Education); Seamus Cassidy (Entertainment); Farrukh Dhondy (Multicultural Programmes); Bill Hilary (Youth & Entertainment); Waldemar Januszczak (Arts & Music); Nick Fraser (Talks and Religion); Mike Miller (Sport); Peter Moore (Documentaries); Michael Attwell (Science, Business & Features)
Head of Purchased Programmes: Mairi Macdonald

A very wide range of diverse programming from this network UK station

S4C

S4C

Parc Ty Glas
Llanishen
Cardiff CF4 5DU
Tel: 0222 747444
Fax: 0222 754444
Chairman: Prys Edwards
Chief Executive: Geraint Stanley Jones
Programme Controller: Deryk Williams
Head of Co-productions: Darrel James
Director of Marketing: Christopher Grace

Christmas Stallion
Production company: Lluniau Lliw
Executive producers: Elizabeth Mathews, Dafydd Huw Williams

clap clap clap clap
NEL FOU
ODUCTIONS
take
JULY '92
TOR
4

Director: Peter Edwards
Writer: Paul Mathews
Cast: Daniel J Travanti, Lynette Davies, Meredith Edwards, Sian Maclean
1 x 96 mins F
Gwen loves and lives for the magnificent horses on her grandfather's farm: will his sudden death force her to give up the life she loves?

Elenya
Production company: Frankfurter Film Production/Ffilmiau Llifon/BFI/S4C
Executive Producers: Ben Gibson, Michael Smeaton, Dafydd Huw Williams
Director/Writer: Steve Gough
Cast: Sue Jones Davies, Klaus Behrendt, Pascale Delafouge Jones
1 x 90 mins F
An evocative, thoughtful perspective of a wartime schoolgirl's escape from reality through a friendship with a German soldier

Hedd Wyn
Production company: Pendefig
Executive producer: Dafydd Huw Williams
Producer/Director: Paul Turner
Writer: Alan Llwyd
Cast: Huw Garmon, Judith Humphries, Sue Roderick
1 x 110 mins F
A powerful reminder to society of the waste and horrors of war which also carries a strong message of love and hope

The Legend of Lochnagar
Production company: The Dave Edwards Studio/ S4C/BBC Scotland/BBC Wales/ABC Television (USA)
Executive Producer: Chris Grace
Producer: Dave Edwards
Directors: Chris Fenna, John Hefin
Writers: Jocelyn Stevenson, Pamela Hickey, Dennis McCoy
Cast: live action – HRH the Prince of Wales, animation voice over: Robbie Coltrane
1 x 30 mins F
A funny and gently moral tale based on the children's book written by HRH the Prince of Wales

Pirates and Treasure Islands
Production Company: Psychology News, with S4C, Gaelic Television Committee and the Discovery Channel
Executive Producers: Cenwyn Edwards, Tomi Landis
Producer: David Cohen
Directors: David Cohen, Jan Euden, Dafydd Williams
Writer: Rosemary Kingsland
Executive Co-Ordinator: Darrel James
13 x 30 mins F/13 x 30 mins F
Factual documentary. Palm trees and paradise, Treasure maps and murder. Doubloons and deceit. *Pirates* tells the history of piracy from Roman times to the present day. *Treasure Islands* recounts the mystery and legends of shipwrecks and buried treasure through the ages

The Sorceress: Dame Kiri Te Kanawa
Production company: Rhombus Media Inc/Nos Dutch TV
Producers: Niv Fichman, Piet Erkelens
Director: Barbara Willis Sweete
Cast: Dame Kiri Te Kanawa
An exciting and exotic performance fantasy combining operatic singing and spectacular dance

Other programmes include:
Animated Operas
Aria
Glan Hafren
Halen yn y Gwaed
Jeux sans Frontieres
Miri Morio
Pobl y Cwm
Pris y Farchnad
Ollie and the Bogle
Shakespeare II
Tydi Coleg yn Grêt

BBC TELEVISION

British Broadcasting Corporation
Television Centre
Wood Lane
London W12 7RJ
Tel: 081 743 8000
Broadcasting House
Portland Place
London W1A 1AA
Tel: 071 580 4468
Chairman: Marmaduke Hussey
Director-General: John Birt
Deputy Director-General: Bob Phillis
Managing Director, Network Television and Chairman BBC Enterprises: Will Wyatt
Managing Director, Regional Broadcasting: Ronald Neil
Assistant Managing Director, Network Television: Jane Drabble
Controller of BBC1: Alan Yentob
Controller of BBC2: Michael Jackson

BBC Midlands
BBC Broadcasting Centre
Pebble Mill Road
Birmingham B5 7SA
Tel: 021 414 8888

BBC North
New Broadcasting House
Oxford Road
Manchester M60 1SJ
Tel: 061 200 2020

BBC Northern Ireland
Broadcasting House
Ormeau Avenue
Belfast BT2 8HQ
Tel: 0232 244400

BBC Scotland
Broadcasting House
Queen Margaret Drive
Glasgow G12 8DG
Tel: 041 339 8844

BBC South
Broadcasting House
Whiteladies Road
Bristol BS8 2LR
Tel: 0272 732211

BBC Wales
Broadcasting House
Llandaff
Cardiff CF5 2YQ
Tel: 0222 564888

BBC TV Children's Programmes
Television Centre
Wood Lane
London W12 7RJ
Head: Anna Home
Tel: 081 743 8000

Blue Peter
Programme editor: Lewis Bronze
Presenters: John Leslie, Diane-Louise Jordan, Anthea Turner
Continuing x 25 mins F and live V
Blue Peter began on October 1958. The programme is named after the blue and white flag which is raised within 24 hours of a ship leaving harbour: the idea is that the programme is like a ship setting out on a voyage, having new adventures and discovering new things

Grange Hill
Producer: Christine Secombe
Script Editor: Leigh Jackson
Writers: Kevin Hood, Chris Ellis, Alison Fisher, Sarah Daniels, Diane Whitley, Ol Parker
20 x 25 mins V
Fictional characters face true-to-life situations at a large comprehensive school

Others programmes include:
Hart Beat
The Really Wild Show
Take Two

BBC Community Programme Unit
39 Wales Farm Road
North Acton
London W3 6XP
Tel: 081 743 8000
This Unit is responsible for programmes made by and with the general public, usually as a direct response to public request. A voice is given to those who feel that the media distorts or ignores their point of view, and so offers viewers new

perspectives on issues of social concern they would not expect to find aired elswhere on television. Currently the Unit's output is presented under the titles, *Open Space*, *Video Diaries*, *Inside Out*, *Teenage Diaries* and *Video Nation*

Inside Out
A series of occasional documentaries consisting of a pair of films exploring two sides of an institution. Covered so far: Swansea jail and an infantry battalion

Open Space
Contributors make their own programme on their chosen subjects with production help from the Unit but keeping full editorial control, or in 'partnership' with the Unit if they prefer. Alternatively members of the public can simply suggest programme ideas

Teenage Diaries
Development of video diaries made by under 18s

Video Diaries
A unique series of programmes giving people self-operated video cameras to record the unfolding events of their lives

Video Nation
Unique project involving 60 people recording their lives and the events that surround them. Footage will provide the basis for a wide range of programme

BBC TV Documentaries
Kensington House
Richmond Way
London W14 0AX
Tel: 081 895 6611
Head: Paul Hamann

40 Minutes
Series Editor: Paul Watson
26 x 40 mins F
A series of documentary films about the way we live now

Fine Cut
Series Editor: Andre Singer

Inside Story
Editor: Steve Hewlett

Rough Justice
Series producer: Charles Hunter
Presenter: John Ware

Taking Liberties
Presenter: John Ware

BBC TV Drama
Television Centre
Wood Lane
London W12 7RJ
Tel: 081 743 8000
Head of Drama Group, BBC Television: Charles Denton
Head of Films: Mark Shivas
Head of Drama Series and Serials: Michael Wearing
Head of Single Drama: George Faber

Screen One
Executive Producer, BBC1 Films: Richard Broke
An annual series of popular feature-length films for television on BBC1. Highlights from the 1993 season include *Wide-Eyed and Legless, Tender Loving Care, A Foreign Field, The Bullion Boys*

Screen Two
BBC Television's original feature-length film strand. Highlights of the 1994 season include *All Things Bright and Beautiful, Deadly Crack, Genghis Cohn, The Railway Station Man, The Reflecting Skin, Skallagrigg*

Series and Serials

Between the Lines
Executive Producer: Tony Garnett
Producer: Peter Norris
Creator: J C Wilsher
Cast: Neil Pearson, Tom Georgeson, Siobhan Redmond, Robin Lermitte
13 x 50 mins
Produced in association with Island World

Brighton Boy
Creator: Tony McHale
Producer: Barry Hanson
8 x 50 mins
A London Films Production

Casualty
BBC1
Producer: Michael Ferguson
Cast: Derek Thompson, Cathy Shipton, Clive Mantle, Patrick Robinson
23 x 50 mins

Grushko
BBC1
Producer: Nicky Lund
Writers: Philip Kerr, Robin Mukherjee
Cast: Brian Cox
3 x 50 mins
A Mark Forstater/ Telepool production

Harry
BBC1
Producer: Martin McKeand
Creator: Franc Roddam
Cast: Michael Elphick, Ian Bartholomew, Julie Graham, Tom Hollander
12 x 50 mins
A Union Pictures Production

The House of Eliott
BBC1
Producer: Jeremy Gwilt
Principal cast: Stella Gonet, Louise Lombard, Aden Gillett
10 x 50 mins

The Inspector Alleyn Mysteries
BBC1
Producer: George Gallaccio
Cast: Patrick Malahide, Belinda Lang, William Simons
3 x 98 mins

Love Hurts
BBC1
Producer: Irving Teitelbaum
Created by Laurence Marks and Maurice Gran
Cast: Adam Faith, Zoe Wanamaker
10 x 50 mins
An Alomo Production

Lovejoy
Producer: Jo Wright
Cast: Ian McShane, Caroline Langrishe, Dudley Sutton, Chris Jury, Diane Parish, Malcolm Tierney
13 x 50 mins
Produced in association with WitzEnd/McShane Productions

Pie in the Sky
BBC1
Producer: Jacky Stoller
Created by Andrew Payne
Cast: Richard Griffiths, Maggie Steed, Malcolm Sinclair, Bela Enahoro
10 x 50 mins
A Witzend Production

Rides
BBC1
Producer: Frances Heasman
Executive Producer: Lavinia Warner
Devised and written by Carole Hayman
Cast: Jill Baker, Caroline Blakiston, Louise Jameson, James Purefoy
A Warner Sisters Production

The Riff Raff Element
BBC1
Producer: Liz Trubridge
Created and written by Debbie Horsfield
Cast: Ronald Pickup, Celia Imrie, Nicholas Farrell, Richard Hope
6 x 50 mins

Westbeach
BBC1
Producer: Susi Hush
Created by Tony Marchant
Cast: Deborah Grant, Oliver Cotton, Ricco Ross, David Horovitch, Annie Lambert
An Alomo Production

The Buddha of Suburbia
BBC2
Producer: Kevin Loader
Director: Roger Michell
Scriptwriters: Hanif Kureishi, Roger Michell (author Hanif Kureishi)
Camera: John McGlashan
Editor: Kate Evans
Cast: Naveen Andrews, Roshan Seth, Susan Fleetwood, Steven Mackintosh
4 x 50 mins F

Calling the Shots
BBC1
Producer: David Snodin
Director: Ross Devenish
Scriptwriter: Laura

Lamson
Camera: Alec Curtis
Editor: Ian Farr
Cast: Lynn Redgrave, Jack Shepherd, James Purefoy, Adie Allen
3 x 50 mins F

Love and Reason
BBC2
Producer: Hilary Salmon
Director: Carol Wilks
Scriptwriter: Ron Rose
Camera: Peter Chapman
Editor: Paul Williams
Cast: Phyllis Logan, Kevin McNally, Barbara Marten
3 x 50 mins V

Scarlet and Black
BBC1
Producer: Rosalind Wolfes
Director: Ben Bolt
Scriptwriter: Stephen Lowe (author Stendhal)
Camera: John McGlashan
Editor: Frances Parker
Cast: Ewan McGregor, Alice Krige, Christopher Fulford, T P McKenna, Rachel Weisz, Stratford Johns
3 x 75 mins F

Stark
BBC2
Producer: Michael Wearing
Director: Nadia Tass
Scriptwriter: Ben Elton
Camera: David Parker
Editor: Ken Sallows
Cast: Ben Elton, Jacqueline McKenzie, Colin Friels, Derrick O'Connor
3 x 50 mins F

To Play the King
BBC1
Producer: Ken Riddington
Director: Paul Seed
Scriptwriter: Andrew Davies (author Michael Dobbs)
Camera: Ian Punter
Editor: Dave King
Cast: Ian Richardson, Michael Kitchen
4 x 50 mins F

Screenplay
BBC2
Titles from the 1993 series include: *Boswell and Johnson's Tour of the Western Isles, Black Daisies for the Bride, The Vision Thing, Love Lies Bleeding, Henri*

Other programmes include:
EastEnders
and the plays in the BBC2 Performance Season:
The Changeling, The Entertainer, Hedda Gabler, Suddenly Last Summer

BBC Education
BBC White City
201 Wood Lane
London W12 7TF
Tel: 081 752 5252

Birthrights
Executive Producer: Chris Lent
6 x 30 mins
Films depicting British culture and identity from a black perspective, made by young black producers from the independent sector

Blooming Bellamy
Producer: John Percival
Presenter: David Bellamy
5 x 30 mins
The popular environmentalist investigates the truth behind witches' potions and old wives' tales and discovers that more than a third of modern drugs in the high street pharmacy derive from plants

A Cook's Tour of France II
Producer: Clare Brigstocke
Presenter: Mireille Johnston
5 x 30 mins
A second series of the successful gastronomic journey through regional France, showing French provincial cooking at its best

Hidden Assets
Producer: Suzy Davies
2 x 30 mins
Two documentaries for Adult Learners Week that give hope to women wanting to work and help employers devise and implement female-friendly policies, even during a recession

Living Islam
Producers: Hugh Purcell, Paul Kriwaczek
Presenter: Akbar Ahmed
6 x 50 mins
A timely look at Islam, filmed throughout the Islamic world. The foundations of the faith and the influence of the three major Muslim empires of the 16th century are examined in terms of present day Islam and Western attitudes to it

Spain means Business
Producer: Terry Doyle
5 x 30 mins
A look at how business is conducted in the country that until recently was the fastest growing economy in Europe. Broadcast largely in Spanish, with English subtitles

The Training Hour
A strand addressing the educational and vocational needs of those in employment, those returning to work or requiring further training and those involved in training or adult education. Includes **Careering Ahead**, that looks at new developments in the field of training; **Making Time**, that offers advice on time-management; **Winning**, on the value of training for small businesses, and **Computing for the Terrified**, a series designed to dispel myths about mice and fear of floppy discs

Other programmes include:
Advice Shop
Bazaar
Business Matters
Education Specials
Family Affairs
Measure for Measure
See Hear!
Tales from the Map Room

BBC TV Features
Fourth Floor
White City
London W12 7TS
Tel: 081 752 5252
Head: Mark Thompson
Manager: Steve Wallis

Behind the Headlines
BBC2
Editor: Charles Miller
Daily discussion programme hosted by a regular team of presenters which provides intelligent conversation and debate on topical issues

Biteback
BBC1
Editor: Anne Burns
Presenter: Sue Lawley
Monthly right of reply programme
Made by Barraclough Carey

Crime Limited
BBC1
Editor: John Getgood
Weekly crime series

Crimewatch UK
BBC1
Editor: Liz Mills
Monthly crime series

Did You See...?
BBC2
Editor: Anne Tyerman
Weekly review of the week's television programmes

Fifth Column
BBC2
Editor: Anne Tyerman
Weekly comment programme in which individuals provide personal perspectives on a subject of current interest, often presenting underrepresented or alternative points of view

Film '93
Producer: Bruce Thompson
Presenter: Barry Norman

Food and Drink
BBC2
Editor: Peter Bazalgette
Made by Bazal Productions

Holiday
BBC1
Series Producer: Jane Lush

Primetime
BBC1
Editor: Jill Dawson
Weekly magazine programme aimed at the older viewer, presented by Roy Castle and Maggie Philbin

Saturday Night Clive
BBC2
Editor: Richard Drewett
Presenter: Clive James
Clive James attempts to make some sense of the universe of ever expanding media

That's Life!
BBC1
Editor: Bryher Scudamore
Weekly consumer programme presented by Esther Rantzen which mixes serious investigations with light and musical items

Watchdog
BBC1
Editor: Sarah Caplin
Weekly consumer programme presented by Lynn Faulds Wood and John Stapleton

BBC TV Light Entertainment
Television Centre
Wood Lane
London W12 7RJ
Tel: 081 743 8000
Head of Light Entertainment Group: David Liddiment

Comedy Programmes
Head: Martin Fisher

* denotes independent production

'Allo 'Allo
Producer/Director: John B Hobbs
Scriptwriters: Jeremy Lloyd, Paul Adam
Cast: Gorden Kaye, Carmen Silvera

As Time Goes By *
Producer: Philip Jones
Director: Sydney Lotterby
Scriptwriter: Bob Larbey
Cast: Judi Dench, Geoffrey Palmer

Birds of a Feather
Producer: Michael Pilsworth for Alomo Productions
Directors: Nic Phillips, Charlie Hanson, Sue Bysh
Scriptwriters: Laurence Marks, Maurice Gran and team
Cast: Pauline Quirke, Linda Robson, Lesley Joseph

Bonjour La Classe *
Executive Producer: Peter Fincham
Producer: Jamie Rix
Scriptwriters: Paul Smith, Terry Kyan
Cast: Nigel Planer

Brittas Empire
Producer/Director: Mike Stephens
Scriptwriters: Richard Fegen, Andrew Norris
Cast: Chris Barrie

Chef! *
Producer: Charlie Hanson
Director: John Birkin
Scriptwriter: Peter Tilbury
Cast: Lenny Henry

Comic Strip *
Executive Producers: Michael White, Peter Richardson
Producer: Lolli Kimpton
Directors: Keith Allen, Peter Richardson, Paul Bartel, Robbie Coltrane
Scriptwriters: various
Cast includes: Robbie Coltrane, Adrian Edmondson, Dawn French, Jennifer Saunders, Josie Lawrence

Every Silver Lining
Producer: Richard Boden
Director: Nick Bye
Scriptwriter: Simon Block
Cast: Frances de la Tour, Andrew Sachs

Get Back *
Producer: Bernard McKenna
Director: Graeme Harper
Scriptwriters: Laurence Marks and Maurice Gran, Gary Lawson and John Phelps
Cast: Ray Winstone, Larry Lamb, Carol Harrison, Jane Booker, John Bardon

Grace and Favour
Producer/Director: Mike Stephens
Scriptwriters: Jeremy Lloyd/David Croft
Cast: John Inman, Mollie Sugden, Wendy Richard, Frank Thornton, Nicholas Smith

In Sickness And In Health
Producer: Richard Boden
Scriptwriter: Johnny Speight
Cast: Warren Mitchell, Carmel McSharry, James Ellis

KYTV
Producer: Jamie Rix
Director: John Kilby
Scriptwriters: Angus Deayton, Geoffrey Perkins
Cast: Angus Deayton, Geoffrey Perkins, Helen Atkinson Wood, Michael Fenton Stevens, Philip Pope

Keeping Up Appearances
Producer/Director: Harold Snoad
Scriptwriter: Roy Clarke
Cast: Patricia Routledge

Last of the Summer Wine
Producer/Director: Alan J W Bell
Scriptwriter: Roy Clarke
Cast: Bill Owen, Peter Sallis, Brian Wilde

Luv
Producer/Director: Mike Stephens
Scriptwriter: Carla Lane
Cast: Michael Angelis, Sue Johnston

May to December *
Producer: Sharon Bloom for Cinema Verity
Director: John Kilby
Scriptwriter: Paul A Mendelson, Geoffrey Deane
Cast: Anton Rodgers, Lesley Dunlop

Mulberry
Producer/Director: John B Hobbs
Scriptwriters: John Esmonde, Bob Larbey
Cast: Karl Howman, Geraldine McEwan

On the Up
Producer/Director: Gareth Gwenlan
Scriptwriter: Bob Larbey
Cast: Dennis Waterman

One Foot in the Grave
Producer/Director: Susan Belbin
Scriptwriter: David Renwick
Cast: Richard Wilson, Annette Crosbie

Only Fools and Horses
Producer: Gareth Gwenlan
Director: Tony Dow
Scriptwriter: John Sullivan
Cast: David Jason, Nicholas Lyndhurst, Buster Merryfield

The Real McCoy
Producer: Bill Wilson
Director: Terry Jervis
Writers: Paul Henry, Kim Fuller, Leo Chester, A-Dziko Simba, Lynn Peters, Meera Syal and team
Cast: Curtis, Llewella Gideon, Collette Johnson, Robbie Gee, Leo Chester

Side By Side
Executive Producer: Martin Fisher
Producer/Director: Sue Bysh
Scriptwriter: Richard Ommaney
Cast: Louisa Rix, Gareth Hunt

Smith and Jones *
Executive Producer: Peter Fincham
Producer: Jon Plowman
Director: Chris Bould
Scriptwriter: Various
Cast: Mel Smith, Griff Rhys Jones

So Haunt Me *
Producer: Caroline Gold for Cinema Verity
Director: John Stroud
Scriptwriter: Paul A Mendelson
Cast: Miriam Karlin, Tessa Peake-Jones, George Costigan

2point4 children
Executive producer: Richard Boden
Writer: Andrew Marshall
Cast: Belinda Lang, Gary Olsen

Us Girls *
Producer/Director: David Askey
Scriptwriter: Lisselle Kayla
Cast: Nicola Blackman, Mona Hammond, Marlaine Gordon, Allister Bain

Waiting for God
Producer/Director: Gareth Gwenlan
Scriptwriter: Michael

Aitkens
Cast: Graham Crowden, Stephanie Cole

You Rang, M'Lord?
Producer/Director: David Croft
Scriptwriters: Jimmy Perry, David Croft
Cast: Paul Shane, Su Pollard, Jeffrey Holland

Variety Programmes

Absolutely Fabulous
Producer: Jon Plowman
Director: Bob Spears
Writer: Jennifer Saunders
Cast: Jennifer Saunders, Joanna Lumley, June Whitfield, Julia Sawalha, Jane Horrocks

Big Break
Producer: Jim Burrowes
Director: Nick Hurran
Host: Jim Davidson
Referee: John Virgo
12 x 30 mins

Bruce's Guest Night
Producer: Kevin Bishop
Associate Producer: Jon Beazley
Host: Bruce Forsyth
6 x 60 mins

The Generation Game
Producer: David Taylor
Director: John Gorman
Programme Associates: Wally Malston, Garry Chambers
Hosts: Bruce Forsyth, Rosemarie Ford
15 x 60 mins plus Christmas Special

Noel's House Party
Producer/Director: Michael Leggo
Script Associate: Charlie Adams
Assistant Producer: Tom Webber
Host: Noel Edmonds
16 x 50 mins

The Paul Daniels Magic Show
Producer/director: Geoff Miles
Host: Paul Daniels
9 x 45 mins
Magician Paul Daniels and speciality act guests

Wogan
Executive Producer: Peter Estall
Talk show hosted by Terry Wogan

BBC TV Music and Arts
Kensington House
Richmond Way
London W14 0AX
Tel: 081 743 1272
Acting Head: Kim Evans
Arts Features Editor: Keith Alexander
Head of Music Programmes: Avril MacRory

Arena
Editors: Anthony Wall, Nigel Finch

Bookmark
Editor: Roly Keating

The Late Show
Editor: Mike Poole
Editor, Late Show Productions: Janice Hadlow

Omnibus
Editor: Nigel Williams
Executive Producer: Roger Thompson

Young Musician of the Year
Executive producer: Kriss Rusmanis

BBC TV News and Current Affairs
Television Centre
Wood Lane
London W12 7RJ
Tel: 081 743 8000
Fax: 081 749 6972
Managing Director, News and Current Affairs: Tony Hall
Editor of news programmes: Peter Bell
Editor of weekly and special programmes: Samir Shah

Main news programmes: BBC1 1.00pm, 6.00pm, 9.00pm; hourly summaries
Breakfast News
7.00am – 9.00am
Newsnight BBC2
10.30pm

Other programmes include:
Assignment
Breakfast with Frost
Business Breakfast
The Money Programme
On The Record
Panorama
Public Eye
Question Time
(independently produced by Brian Lapping Associates)
Scrutiny
Westminster Live

BBC TV Programme Acquisition
Centre House
56 Wood Lane
London W12 7RJ
Tel: 081 743 8000
Head of Programme Acquisition: Alan Howden
Purchased Programmes Head: June Morrow
Selects and presents BBC TV's output of feature films and series on both channels

Business Unit
Business Manager: Felicity Irlam
Contact for commissioned material and acquisition of completed programmes, film material and sequences for all other programme departments

BBC TV Religious Programmes
New Broadcasting House
Oxford Road
Manchester M60 1SJ
Tel: 061 599 3600
Head: Ernie Rea

Everyman
Editor: John Blake
28 x 40 mins F
Reflective religious documentary series

Heart of the Matter
Commissioning Executive: John Blake
18 x 35 mins F
Independently produced by Roger Bolton Productions

One World
Producer: Peter Firstbrook
Reports on development issues

Songs of Praise
Editor: Helen Alexander
39 x 35 mins V
Community hymn-singing

This is the Day
Editor: Noel Vincent
34 x 30 mins live and V
Morning worship from a viewer's home, with the viewing audience itself making up the congregation

Other programmes include:
Articles of Faith
The Cry
Praise Be!
Specials for BBC2

BBC School Programmes (Television)
White City
201 Wood Lane
London W12 7TF
Tel: 081 752 5252
Head: Terry Marsh

Ghostwriter
A co-production with Children's Television Workshop, New York
This Brooklyn-based mystery-adventure series aims to encourage reluctant readers to see literacy and language as enjoyable and fun. The lead character is a ghost who can only communicate through reading and writing. Special guests include New York film maker Spike Lee. A complementary radio series offers further mysteries for children to solve

History File
Executive Producer: Len Brown
Producer: Liz Cleaver
30 x 20 mins
A virtual reality museum bringshistory to life in this RTS award-winning series. Hi-tech computer graphics re-create the eras of the Second World War, the Romans and the Industrial Revolution

Scene
Executive producer: Richard Langridge
Producer: Cas Lester
30 x 30 mins
The world's longest running youth drama strand celebrates its 25th anniversary this year, with a season of special commissions from leading

playwrights including Tom Stoppard, Willy Russell, John Godber and Jane Thornton. Classic 'Scene' dramas shown again for a teenage audience include early television screenplays from Alan Plater and Willy Russell

Seeing Through Science
Executive Producer: Len Brown
Producer: Edwina Vardey
In her first mission as a TV presenter, astronaut Helen Sharman looks at science in action for 11-14 year olds. From mountain bikes to meteorites and from lasers to lycra, Helen brings chemistry, astronomy, meteorology and ecology to life, taking a close look at the human side of science in the real world

Storytime
Executive Producer: Judy Whitfield
Producer: Liz Bennett
Marti Caine, Matthew Kelly and Kristian Schmid are among the celebrity storytellers who open the book on the world of words for 4 to 5 year-olds. Set in a magical house of books, the series includes songs, stories and activities for children to do after each programme

Other programmes include:
Le Café des Rêves
The Geography Programme
Landmarks
Lifeschool
Mad About Music
Short Circuit
TV6
Teaching Today
Watch
Words and Pictures
Zig Zag

BBC TV Science and Features
Kensington House
Richmond Way
London W14 0AX
Tel: 081 895 6611
Head: David Filkin
Manager: Maggie Bebbington

Antenna
BBC2
Editor: Caroline Van den Brul
6 x 30 mins
Documentaries exploring the issues and ideas thrown up by research through the eyes of scientists and their critics

Horizon
BBC2
Editor: Jana Bennett
24 x 50 mins
Single subject documentaries presenting science to the general public and analysing the implications of new discoveries

QED
BBC2
Editor: Susan Spindler
Documentary series on subjects which spring from the world of science, medicine and technology and engage the emotions through powerful human stories

Tomorrow's World
BBC1
Executive producer: Dana Purvis
Presenters: Judith Hann, Howard Stableford, Kate Bellingham, Carmen Pryce
Live studio-based programme which includes filmed items investigating and demonstrating the latest in science and technology

BBC TV Sport and Events
Kensington House
Richmond Way
London W14 0AX
Tel: 081 895 6611
Fax: 081 749 7886
Head: Jonathan Martin
Deputy Head: John Rowlinson
Head of Events Programmes: Philip Gilbert

Football
Editor: Brian Barwick
Executive Producer: John Shrewsbury
Producer: Vivien Kent
Presenter: Desmond Lynam

Grandstand
Editor: Dave Gordon
Producer: Martin Hopkins
Presenter: Steve Rider

One Man and His Dog
Producer: Ian Smith
Presenter: Phil Drabble

Royal Tournament
Producer/Director: Peter Hylton Cleaver

Sportsnight
Editor: Brian Barwick
Producer: Vivien Kent
Presenter: Desmond Lynam

BBC TV Youth and Entertainment Features
Centre House
56 Wood Lane
London W12 7RJ
Tel: 081 743 8000
New Broadcasting House
Oxford Road
Manchester M60 1SJ
Head: Janet Street-Porter

Def II
The twice weekly Youth Programmes strand combines innovative original programming (**Reportage**, **Rough Guide to the World**) with cult series such as American hit **Fresh Prince of Bel Air**

The Full Wax
Executive Producer: Janet Street-Porter
Producer: Ed Bye
Off-beat talk show featuring American comedienne Ruby Wax

Reportage
Series editor: Tony Moss
Fast moving current affairs series, focusing on youth issues in the UK and around the world

Rough Guide to the World
Series producer: Rachel Purnell
Presenters: Magenta de Vine, Rajan Datar
Electronic scrapbook of cities and countries giving inside information on how to survive there

Smash Hits Pollwinners Party
Producer: Sharon Ali
Director: Terry Jervis
Live broadcast from the hippest awards presentation party

Standing Room Only
Series Producer: Alan Hurndall
Presenter: Kevin Allen
Football fanzine show looking at football from the punters' point of view

Other programmes include:
Dance Energy
The Look
Living Soap
Masterchef
Mastermind
Rapido (Rapido Television)
Rough Guide to Careers
A Soap Opera – The Vampire
Sylvania Waters
The Travel Show

VIDEO LABELS

These companies acquire the UK rights to all forms of audiovisual product and arrange for its distribution on videodisc or cassette at a retail level (see also under Distributors). Listed is a selection of titles released on each label

Albany Video Distribution
Battersea Studios
Television Centre
Thackeray Road
London SW8 3TW
Tel: 071 498 6811
Fax: 071 498 1494
Coffee Coloured Children
Framed Youth
Jean Genet is Dead
Looking for Langston
Ostia
The Passion of Remembrance
Perfect Image
Territories
Two in Twenty

Artificial Eye
211 Camden High Street
London NW1 7BT
Tel: 071 267 6036/482 3981
Fax: 071 267 6499
Les Amants du Pont-Neuf
Close My Eyes
Cyrano de Bergerac
Les Enfants du Paradis
Johnny Suede
L.627
Merci la Vie
Straight Out of Brooklyn
A Strange Place to Meet
A Winter's Tale

BBC Video
Woodlands
80 Wood Lane
London W12 0TT
Tel: 081 576 2236
Fax: 081 743 0393
BlackAdder
The Borrowers
Dr Who
Match of the Day series
Noddy
One Foot in the Grave
Pingu
Pole to Pole
Red Dwarf
Steptoe and Son

Braveworld
Symal House
Edgware Road
London NW9 0HU
Tel: 081 905 9191
Fax: 081 205 8619
Amadeus
Babette's Feast
One Flew Over the Cuckoo's Nest
Pelle the Conqueror
The Running Man
Stay Tuned

Buena Vista Home Video
Beaumont House
Kensington Village
Avonmore Road
London W14 8TS
Tel: 071 605 2400
Distribute and market Walt Disney, Touchstone, Hollywood Pictures and Henson product on video

CIC UK
Glenthorne House
5-17 Hammersmith Grove
London W6 0ND
Tel: 081 846 9433
Fax: 081 741 9773
A Universal/Paramount Company
Beethoven
Boomerang
Death Becomes Her
Far and Away
Housesitter
Lorenzo's Oil
Patriot Games
The Public Eye
Scent of a Woman
Sneakers

Chart Information Network
8th Floor
Ludgate House
245 Blackfriars Road
London SE1 9UR
Tel: 071 334 7333
Fax: 071 921 5942
Supplies BVA members with detailed sales information on the sell-through video market. Markets and licenses the Official Retail Video Charts for broadcasting and publishing around the world

Columbia TriStar Home Video
4th Floor
Horatio House
77-85 Fulham Palace Road
London W6 8JA
Tel: 081 748 6000
Fax: 081 748 4546
The Addams Family
Boyz N the Hood
Double Impact
A Few Good Men
Hook
Mortal Thoughts
My Girl
The Prince of Tides
Shattered
The Silence of the Lambs

bfi Connoisseur Video
10a Stephen Mews
London W1P 0AX
Tel: 071 957 8957/8
Fax: 071 957 8968
A joint venture between the British Film Institute and Argos Films, France, with films covering five decades of world cinema. Titles include:
The Aardman Animation Collection
Céline and Julie Go Boating
The Charge of the Light Brigade
8 1/2
Mr Hulot's Holiday
La Règle du Jeu
Scorsese x 4
The Seven Samurai
Swoon
Wings of Desire

Curzon Video
9 St Martin's Court
London WC2N 4AJ
Tel: 071 895 0328
Fax: 071 895 0329
Au Revoir Les Enfants
The Ballad of the Sad Cafe
Howards End
The Long Day Closes
The Mad Monkey
Mediterraneo
The Mystery of Edwin Drood
Paris Trout
Urga
Voyager

Dangerous to Know
20 Offley Road
Kennington Oval
London SW9 0LS
Tel: 071 735 8330
Fax: 071 793 8488

Boys on Film vol 1: Love?
Dr Poof
50 Ways to Tell your Mother
Feed Them to the Cannibals
Jumping the Gun
Lesbian Leather Shorts
Lesbian Lykra Shorts
Pink Narcissus
Sluts and Goddesses Video Workshop
Two of Us

Walt Disney Co see **Buena Vista Home Video**

Electric Pictures Video
15 Percy Street
London W1P 9FD
Tel: 071 636 1785
Fax: 071 636 1675
Belle de Jour
Delicatessen
Diva
Henry, Portrait of a Serial Killer
Mean Streets
Orlando
Salmonberries
Toto the Hero
Tous les Matins du Monde
A Woman Under the Influence

Elephant Video
Theatre One
Ford Street
Coventry CV1 5FN
Tel: 0203 226490
Fax: 0203 258971
Video distribution of feature films

Entertainment in Video
27 Soho Square
London W1V 5FL
Tel: 071 439 1979
Fax: 071 734 2483
Best of the Best 2
The Crow
Damage
Into the West
Mr Nanny
Peter's Friends
Sniper
Super Mario Bros
Traces of Red
Wind

First Independent Films
69 New Oxford Street
London WC1A 1DG
Tel: 071 528 0221
Fax: 071 528 7771
City Slickers
Deep Cover
Frauds
Honeymoon in Vegas
Misery
Mom and Dad Save the World
Mr Saturday Night

FoxVideo
Twentieth Century House
31-32 Soho Square
London W1V 6AP
Tel: 071 753 8686
Fax: 071 734 3187
Beverley Hillbillies
The Good Son
Hot Shots Part Deux
Once Upon a Forest
Rising Sun
Toys
Unlawful Entry
Used People
The Vanishing

Guild Home Video
Crown House
2 Church Street
Walton-on-Thames
Surrey KT12 2QS
Tel: 081 546 3377
Fax: 081 546 4568
1492 – Conquest of Paradise
Basic Instinct
Freddy's Dead 5 in 3D
Jacob's Ladder
The Lover
Medicine Man
The Player
Universal Soldier
Terminator 2: Judgment Day
Twin Peaks: Fire Walk With Me

Hollywood Pictures see **Buena Vista Home Video**

ITC Home Video
24 Nutford Place
London W1H 5YN
Tel: 071 262 3262
Fax: 071 724 0160
Theatrical, rental, sell-through
Doppelganger
Fear of a Black Hat
Last of the Mohicans
Space 1999
Sapphire and Steel
This is Tom Jones
Timeslip
Tiswas
Trouble Bound

Imperial Entertainment (UK)
Main Drive
GEC Estate
East Lane
Wembley
Middx HA9 7FF
Tel: 081 904 0921
Fax: 081 904 4306/908 6785
UK distributor of feature films including Danielle Steele video titles

Island Visual Arts
22 St Peter's Square
London W6 9NW
Tel: 081 741 1511
Fax: 081 741 8781
Distributed by PolyGram Video

Jubilee Film and Video
Egret Mill
162 Old Street
Ashton-under-Lyne
Manchester
Lancashire OL6 7ST
Tel: 061 330 9555

London Weekend Television
London Television Centre
Upper Ground
London SE1 9LT
Tel: 071 620 1620
Fax: 071 928 8476
An Audience with Victoria Wood
Hale and Pace
Jeeves and Wooster
King Lear
London's Burning
Poirot
Prime Suspect 1 & 2
Sherlock Holmes
Upstairs Downstairs
Watching

MGM/UA Home Video
5th Floor
84-86 Regent Street
London W1R 5PF
Tel: 071 915 1717
Fax: 071 734 8410
Benny and Joon
Meteor Man
Midnight Sting
Of Mice and Men
Son of the Pink Panther
Untamed Heart

Mainline Pictures
37 Museum Street
London WC1A 1LP
Tel: 071 242 5523
Fax: 071 430 0170
Chain of Desire
Crazy Love
Let's Get Lost
Lovers
Metropolitan
The Music Teacher
The Premonition
Ruby in Paradise
The Wedding Banquet

Media Releasing Distributors
27 Soho Square
London W1V 5FL
Tel: 071 437 2341
Fax: 071 734 2483
Day of the Dead
Eddie and the Cruisers
Kentucky Fried Movie
Return of Captain Invincible
Distributed through Entertainment in Video (qv)

Medusa Communications
Medusa Pictures Video Division
Regal Chambers
51 Bancroft
Hitchin
Herts SG5 1LL
Tel: 0462 421818
Fax: 0462 420393
Maniac Cop 3
Mutronics the Movie
Nails
Rage of Honour
Rage of Honour 2
Revenge of Billy the Kid
Timescape

Odyssey Video
15 Dufours Place
London W1V 1FE
Tel: 071 437 8251
Fax: 071 734 6941
Cul-de-Sac
The First of the Few
Flying Deuces
A Killing in a Small Town
Repulsion
Ring of Bright Water
Scum
She Said No
To Catch a Killer
A Woman of Substance

Orbit Films
7/11 Kensington High Street
London W8 5NP
Tel: 071 221 5548
Fax: 071 727 0515
A range of screen classics and literary classics

Out on a Limb
Battersea Studios
Television Centre
Thackeray Road
London SW8 3TW
Tel: 071 498 9643
Fax: 071 498 2104
Absolutely Positive
Being at Home with Claude
Exiles of Love
Forbidden Love
Looking for Langston

My Father is Coming
No Skin Off My Ass
A Prayer Before Birth
Sex and the Sandinistas
Two in Twenty

Pathé Video see **MGM/UA Home Video**

Pickwick Group
Pickwick House
The Waterfront
Elstree
Herts WD6 3BS
Tel: 081 207 6207
Fax: 081 207 5789
Basic Yoga for Today
Cindy Crawford – Shape Your Body
Jasper Carrott – All Of The Best Bits
The Lovers' Guide 1, 2 and 3
Nursery Rhymes and Songs
Red Rum National Hero
The Tale of Peter Rabbit
The Tale of Tom Kitten and Jemima Puddle-Duck

Picture Music International
20 Manchester Square
London W1A 1ES
Tel: 071 486 4488
Fax: 071 465 0748
Roman Atkinson Live
Kate Bush: The Whole Story
Iron Maiden: The First Ten Years
The Original Karaoke
The John Lennon Video Collection
Pet Shop Boys: Videography
Pink Floyd: Delicate Sound of Thunder
Queen: Box of Flix
Cliff Richard: Access All Areas The Concert
Tina Turner: Simply The Best

PolyGram Video
PO Box 1425
Chancellors House
72 Chancellors Road
Hammersmith
London W6 9QB
Tel: 081 846 8515
Fax: 081 741 9781
Video catalogue includes music videos, feature films, sport, special interest and children's videos. New titles available through retail/ sell-through outlets include:
Basic Instinct
The Beano
Bon Jovi
Leslie Nielsen
Thunderbirds
Universal Soldier
Rental division titles include:
Brain Dead
The Crying Game
Dust Devil

PolyGram Video International
347-353 Chiswick High Road
London W4 4HS
Tel: 081 994 9199
Fax: 081 742 5577
A subsidiary of PolyGram International making programmes for video release with such bands as Dire Straits, Bon Jovi, Tears for Fears, Elton John, INXS, Wet Wet Wet. Also acquires product for children's videos eg *X-Men* and sports and fitness tapes

Quadrant Video
37a High Street
Carshalton
Surrey SM5 3BB
Tel: 081 669 1114
Fax: 081 669 8831
Sports video cassettes

SIG Video Gems
The Coach House
The Old Vicarage
10 Church Street
Rickmansworth
Herts WD3 1BS
Tel: 0923 710599
Fax: 0923 710549
Act of Betrayal
A Flat Stomach in 15 Days
L A Step
Making Love – The French Way
92 Grosvenor Street
Professionals
Ruth Rendell Mysteries
Secret Weapon

20.20 Vision Video UK
Horatio House
77-85 Fulham Palace Road
London W6 8JA
Tel: 081 748 4034
Fax: 081 748 4546
Last Action Hero
Robocop 3

TBD
Unit 1
Rosevale Business Park
Newcastle under Lyme
Staffs ST5 7QT
Tel: 0782 566566
Fax: 0782 565400
Exclusive distributors for Scimitar Entertainment, Screen Entertainment, Sportsworld and distributors of over 3,000 other titles

Tartan Video
79 Wardour Street
London W1V 3TH
Tel: 071 494 1400
Fax: 071 439 1922
An extensive and eclectic range of world cinema
Titles include:
The Adjuster
Cinema Paradiso
Grand Illusion
Honeymoon Killers
Jamón Jamón
Léolo
Man Bites Dog
Pandora's Box
Seventh Seal
Wild Strawberries

Telstar Video Entertainment
The Studio
5 King Edward Mews
Byfeld Gardens
London SW13 9HP
Tel: 081 846 9946
Fax: 081 741 5584
A sell-through video distributor of music, sport, special interest, comedy, children and film programmes.
Chelsea End of Season 1992/93
Chippendales
Fighting Fit with Rowdy Roddy Piper
Foster & Allen – Heartstrings
Kamasutra
A Lesson with Leadbetter – Golf Instructional Series
Liverpool End of Season 1991/92
Trivial Pursuit – The Music Master Video Version
When Irish Eyes Are Smiling

Thames Video
Thames International
Broom Road
Teddington Lock
Teddington
Middx TW11 9NT
Tel: 081 977 3252
Fax: 081 943 0344
The BFG
Minder
Mr Bean
Rainbow
Rumpole of the Bailey
Sooty
Tommy Cooper
Torvill & Dean
Wind in the Willows
World At War

Touchstone see **Buena Vista Home Video**

VCI (Video Collection International)
36 Caxton Way
Watford
Herts WD1 8UF
Tel: 0923 255558
Fax: 0923 816744
Cinema Club
In Bed with Madonna
Inspector Morse
Jane Fonda's New Workout
Mr Bean
Music Club
Rosie & Jim
Sport Gone Crazy
Sports Club
Thomas the Tank Engine

Visionary Communications
28-30 The Square
St Annes-on-Sea
Lancashire FY8 1RF
Tel: 0253 712453
Fax: 0253 712362
Angelic Conversation
Kenneth Anger's *Magick Lantern Cycle*
William Burroughs' *Thee Films*
Cyberpunk
Derek Jarman's *Time Zones* and *Shadow of the Sun*
Claus Maeck's *Decoder*
Reefer and the Model
Svankmajer's *Alice*

Warner Home Video
135 Wardour Street
London W1V 4AP
Tel: 071 494 3441
Fax: 071 494 3297
Warner Home Video markets product from Warner Bros, MGM, United Artists, Pathé, Cannon, HBO, Lumiere Pictures and Lorimar
Bladerunner – The Director's Cut
The Bodyguard
Forever Young
James Bond
Last of the Mohicans
Lethal Weapon 3
Sommersby
Tiny Toons
Under Siege
Unforgiven

WORKSHOPS

The film and video workshops listed below are generally non-profit-distributing and subsidised organisations. Some workshops are also active in making audiovisual product for UK and international media markets. Those workshops with an asterisk (*) after their name were BECTU-franchised in the period to 31 March 1993

A19 Film and Video
21 Foyle Street
Sunderland
SR1 1LE
Tel: 091 565 5709
Mick Catmull
Nick Oldham
Video production, distribution and exhibition. A19 makes films and videotapes which reflect the needs, concerns and aspirations of people on Wearside. Also offers production facilities, training and advice to schools, community groups and institutions

AVA (Audio Visual Arts)
7b Broad Street
The Lacemarket
Nottingham
NG1 3AJ
Tel: 0602 483684
Two woman independent video production company specialising in arts and education. Wide range of commissioned work for artists, museums, galleries and educational organisations, including *Video Showcase* series on contemporary craftspeople. Grant aided production of *Great Expectations / Wedding Album*, a video installation funded by East Midlands Arts. Co-productions, residencies, placements with schools, colleges, PH day centres and community groups. Co-ordinators/producers of *'91 Degrees Fine Art*. In development: *Artists' TV*

Abertawe Video Productions
F6-7-10, Burrows Chambers
East Burrows Road
Swansea SA1 1RQ
Tel: 0792 476441
Melvyn Williams
Community co-operative dedicated to increasing the use and understanding of video and photography amongst all sections of the local community and surrounding areas. VHS, lo-band, Hi 8, darkroom and sound facilities. Regular training courses, production groups and screenings (brochure and rate card available)

Amber Side Workshop*
5 Side
Newcastle upon Tyne
NE1 3JE
Tel: 091 232 2000
Fax: 091 230 3217
Murray Martin
Film/video production, distribution and exhibition. Most recent productions *The Writing in the Sand, Dream On.* The Workshops' National Archive is based at Amber. Large selection of Workshop production on VHS, a substantial amount of written material and a database. Access by appointment

Avid Productions
2nd Floor
127 Clarendon Park Road
Leicester
LE2 3AS
Tel: 0533 702585
Laura McGregor
Video production for statutory and voluntary sector organisations. Training, promo, education, health education, with back-up publications where needed. Training in video and b/w photography. Geared to needs of individual groups. Particular interests in gay, women only and special needs groups. Consultancy offered

BMTT (Black Media Training Trust)
Unit 4+6, 1 Sydney Street
Sheffield
S1 4RG
Tel: 0742 797898
Fax: 0742 781772
Angela Baugh
Rathin Roy
Carl Baker
BMTT is a media production and training resource which aims to support and encourage activity within all Asian, African and African Caribbean communities. It is currently developing a foundation course for black people in newspaper journalism, radio broadcasting and film and video production to be run in 1993

Bath Community Television (BCTV)
7 Barton Buildings
Bath
Avon
BA1 2JR
Tel: 0225 314480
Ray Brooking
Andrew Graham
Community video resource involved in equipment hire, productions and training. VHS and lo-band U-Matic shooting and editing equipment at reasonable rates. Popular programme of training courses includes 'Film Scriptwriting', 'Video Editing', 'Basic Camcorder Skills' and 'Directing Film and Video Drama'

Belfast Film Workshop
37 Queen Street
Belfast
BT1 6EA
Tel: 0232 233874
Fax: 0232 246657
Alastair Herron
Kate McManus
Film co-operative offering

film/video/animation production and exhibition. Offers both these facilities to others. Made *Acceptable Levels* (with Frontroom), *Thunder Without Rain*, various youth animation pieces, a series of videos on traditional music and a series on local photographers

Birmingham Centre for Media Arts
7 Frederick Street
Birmingham
B1 3HE
Tel: 021 233 4061
Marian Hall
Alan Morris
Offers photography, film and video and animation resources, and provides an introducation to computer-based technology. Replaces TURC Video and Wide Angle Video, Film, Photography

Black Audio Film Collective*
7-12 Greenland Street
Camden
London
NW1 0ND
Tel: 071 267 0846
Fax: 071 267 0845
Lina Gopaul
Avril Johnson
Film and video production and consultancy. Committed to the development of black independent cinema and television. Productions include *Handsworth Songs*, *Twilight City*, *Testament*, *Mysteries of July*, *A Touch of the Tar Brush*, *Who Needs a Heart* and *Seven Songs for Malcolm X*

Black Witch
Holmes Building
46 Wood Street
Liverpool
L1 4AH
Tel: 051 707 0539
Ann Carney
Barbara Phillips
Video production, workshops in video and photography, exhibition (*Just the Job*)

Cambridge Women's Resource Centre
Hooper Street
Cambridge
CB1 2NZ
Tel: 0223 321148
Mary Knox
Video classes for women include scriptwriting, basic camera techniques, lighting, production and editing using U-Matic equipment

Caravel Media Centre
The Great Barn Studios
Cippenham Lane
Slough
SL1 5AU
Tel: 0753 534828
Fax: 0753 571383
Nick See
Training, video production, distribution, exhibition and media education. Offers all these facilities to others. Runs national video courses for independent videomakers

The Children's Film Unit
Suite 9
Hamilton House
66 Upper Richmond Road
Putney
London SW15
Tel: 081 871 2006
Fax: 081 871 2140
Brianna Perkins
A registered educational charity, the CFU makes low-budget films for television and PR on subjects of concern to children and young people. Crews and actors are trained at regular weekly workshops in Putney. Work is in 16mm and video and membership is open to children from 8-16. Latest films for Channel 4 *Hard Road, Doombeach, Survivors, Emily's Ghost*. For the Samaritans *Time to Talk*. For the Children's Film and Television Foundation *How's Business*

Cinema Action
27 Winchester Road
London
NW3 3NR
Tel/Fax: 071 722 5781
Gustav Lamche
35mm and 16mm film, video, photo, computer graphics, multimedia production, distribution and exhibition. Cooperative work. Productions include *Rocking the Boat, So That You Can Live, The Miners' Film, People of Ireland, Film from the Clyde, Rocinante, Bearskin* and *Precious Lives*

City Eye Southampton
1st Floor
Northam Centre
Kent Street
Northam
Southampton
SO1 1SP
Tel: 0703 634177
Coordinator: Richard McLaughlin
Film and video equipment hire. Educational projects. Production and post-production services. Screenings. Community arts media development. Training courses all year in varied aspects of video, film, photography and radio. Committed to providing opportunities for disadvantaged/under-represented groups. 50% discount on all non-profit/educational work

Clapham-Battersea Film Workshop
78 Harbut Road
London
SW11 2RB
Offers a range of 16mm filmmaking courses. 16mm production facilities are available to those completing courses. Weekly screenings of experimental and avant-garde films and an annual short film festival. Equipment: Eclair ACL and Bolex cameras; Steenbecks and Pic-syncs, sound recorders, lighting kits, Xenon double band projector

Connections: Hammersmith and Fulham's Media Project
Palingswick House
241 King Street
London
W6 9LP
Tel: 081 741 1766
Jacqueline Davis
Community media project providing short term training in production, post-production and computer animation. Undertakes commissioned productions and training programmes. Editing facilities in SVHS, VHS, U-Matic and Betacam SP. All facilities are fully wheelchair accessible

Cornwall Video Resource
First Floor
Royal Circus Buildings
Back Lane West
Redruth
Cornwall
TR15 2BT
Tel: 0209 218288
Lee Berry
Film/video production, facilities, training and arts/community based projects. Open to individuals and groups. Facilities include three machine hi-band SP U-Matic edit suite and hi-band production equipment. Some 16mm and Super 8 film making facilities available on request. Undertake commissions on productions. Commercial work and hire. Special rates for unfunded and grant-aided work

Counter Image
3rd Floor
Fraser House
36 Charlotte Street
Manchester
M1 4FD
Tel: 061 228 3551
Janet Shaw
Independent media charity. Offers production facilities and co-production support to independent film and video makers and photographers. Provides a range of short training courses, facilities and a database of film related services, training and practitioners in the NW region. Productions include *Concrete Chariots, Take One Simple Test, Special Offer, Andrew's Story, Seen and Not Heard*

CREU COF (Ceredigion Media Association)
Blwch Post 86
Aberystwyth
Dyfed

SY23 1LN
Tel: 0970 624001
Fax: 0970 617157
Catrin M S Davies
Dafydd O'Connor
Media education for all ages and interests with specific reference to Welsh speakers and to rural themes and issues. Runs longer term projects

Cultural Partnerships

90 De Beauvoir Road
London
N1 4EN
Tel: 071 254 8217
Fax: 071 254 7541
Virginia Haworth
Lol Gellor
Arts, media and communications company. Offer various training courses covering video techniques at basic/intermediate/advanced level as well as digital sound training and computer graphics and computer animation. Courses are free. Make promotional/training videos. Commissioned by BBC Birthrights series. Studio facilities for dry/wet hire: fully air conditioned and purpose built, 800 sq ft multi-purpose studio, BVU SP 3 machine edit suite, BVE910 edit controller, DV5 vision mixer, SVHS off-line, dynamic tracking, stereo sound, multi media potential, Macintosh Quadra based animation and graphics. 16 track recording studio with midi and mac

DARTS

Bentley West End Youth and Community Centre
Kirkby Avenue
Bentley
Doncaster
DN5 9TF
Tel: 0302 786946
Elaine Hirst
Resources and film/video teaching skills available

Despite TV

113 Roman Road
London
E2 0HU
Tel: 081 983 4278
Video co-operative providing training through production for people living or working in Tower Hamlets, Hackney, Newham. Facilities for hire include hi-band SP editing and Amiga graphics. The co-op produces both local topic and single-issue magazine tapes which are available for hire, as well as documentary for Channel 4 *Battle of Trafalgar*, plus sub-commission *The Bailiff Cometh*

Edinburgh Film Workshop Trust*

29 Albany Street
Edinburgh
EH1 3QN
Tel: 031 557 5242
Fax: 031 557 3852
David Halliday
Cassandra McGrogan
Robin MacPherson
Edward O'Donnelly
Scotland's only franchised Workshop. Broadcast, non-broadcast and community integrated production. Facilities include lo-band and hi-band U-Matic production; VHS, lo-band and hi-band edit suites; Neilson Hordell 16mm Rostrum camera; 8mm and 16mm cameras; film cutting room. Women's unit. Projects 1992 include *Scottish Eye* (C4); *Focal Point* and *Gaelic Animation in Schools* (BBC); *Uamh 'n Oir* (C4)

Edinburgh Film Workshop Trust Animation Workshop

address as above
Edward O'Donnelly

Education on Screen Productions

64 All Saints Road
Kings Heath
Birmingham
Tel: 021 444 3147
Mike Kalemkerian
Neil Gammie
Video production involving young people developing scripts through drama workshops. Offers training and production projects to schools, colleges and businesses in the West Midlands area

Electronic Arts Video

30 Estate Buildings
Railway Street
Huddersfield
HD1 1JY
Tel: 0484 518174
Andrew Wicks
Sally Jones
Community-based video production, training and facility hire. Avid digital editing system, Apple Macintosh based multimedia presentation and traditional video. Training available in digital editing skills and basic multimedia presentations

Exeter and Devon Arts Centre – Film and Video Resource

Bradninch Place
Gandy Street
Exeter
EX4 3LS
Tel: 0392 219741
Mark Jeffs
Film and video training for all, facilities and equipment hire. Training provided for schools, clubs and community organisations. Advice and consultancy on training, equipment and production

bfi Faction Films

28-29 Great Sutton Street
London
EC1V 0DU
Tel: 071 608 0654/3
Fax: 071 608 2157
Sylvia Stevens
Dave Fox
Peter Day
Group of independent filmmakers. Production facilities for hire include 6-plate 16mm Steenbeck edit suite; sound transfer; VHS edit suite with 6 channel mixer; U-Matic and VHS viewing and transfer; production office space; Nagra 4.2; redhead lighting kit. Spanish/English translation services. Titles include *Irish News: British Stories*, *Year of the Beaver*, *Picturing Derry*, *Trouble the Calm*, *Provocation or Murder*, *Mariscal*, *Columbus*, *O!*, *Dream Huts*, *Games People Play* (4-part series on sport and nationalism)

Film Work Group

Top Floor
Chelsea Reach
79-89 Lots Road
London
SW10 0RN
Tel: 071 352 0538
Fax: 071 351 6479
Paddy Towell
Video and film post-production facilities and graphic design. Three machine hi-band SP with effects, two machine lo-band, transfer facilities, videographics and 6-plate Steenbeck. Plus computer and video short courses. Special rates for grant-aided and not-for-profit projects

Filmshed

9 Mill Lane
Harbledown
Canterbury
Kent
CT2 8NE
Tel: 0227 769415
Tim Reed
Open-access collective for the promotion and production of independent film. Film production and exhibition. Offers exhibition facilities to others; filmmakers on tour and regular screenings of political/workshop films

First Take Video

(formerly Community Productions Merseyside)
Merseyside Innovation Centre
131 Mount Pleasant
Liverpool
L3 5TF
Tel: 051 708 5767
Offers training and production services to the voluntary, arts, community and education sectors across the North West. Joint projects with other arts groups and special needs groups. Training courses, both basic and intermediate, for the public in video production and editing. Commissioned productions for local authorities

Fosse Community Studios

Fosse Neighbourhood Centre
Leicester City Council
Mantle Road

Leicester
LE3 5HG
Tel: 0533 515577
Fax: 0533 515145
Alan Wilson
Sue Wallin
Brian McDowell
Hasu Patel
Sean Wainwright
Christina Wigmore
An audio-visual resource providing training in all aspects of video production, computer graphics, video editing and 8-track sound recording. Run a regular programme of short video and audio courses and City & Guilds 770 certificate course. Have a wide range of video and audio equipment for hire at low cost including VHS/SVHS shooting kits, video/photography studio with full lighting rig, 3 machine lo-band, 2 machine VHS & SVHS, 3 machine SVHS and MII edit suites, 8-track recording studio, with midi, sampling, DAT facilities and fully equipped music rehearsal studio

Four Corners Film Workshop
113 Roman Road
London
E2 0HU
Tel: 081 981 4243 (courses)/081 981 6111 (equipment)
Suzy Ilbrey
James Van Der Pool
Holds film production courses in S8mm and 16mm and film theory classes. A full programme runs all year round. Provides subsidised film equipment for the low budget independent film maker. Has a 40 seat cinema, S8mm and 16mm production and post-production facilities

Fradharc Ur
11 Scotland Street
Stornoway
Isle of Lewis PA87
Tel: 0851 705766
The first Gaelic film and video workshop, offering VHS and hi-band editing and shooting facilities. Production and training in Gaelic for community groups. Productions include *Under the Surface*, *Na Deilbh Bheo*, *The Weaver*, *A Wedding to Remember* and *As an Fhearran*

Fylm Ha Gwydheo Falmouth (Falmouth Film and Video)
3 Mount Edgcumbe Terrace
Falmouth
Cornwall
TR11 2BS
Tel: 0326 313818
Lee Berry
Mainly a networking, facilitating and production vehicle for independent film and video makers, artists and arts and community based groups. Closely linked with Cornwall Video Resource through membership. Skills sharing but no formal training courses via Falmouth Film and Video. Assistance with fundraising, grant applications, advice etc. Independent productions include: *Polsow Hudol*, *Owth Obery Yn Bal Sten* and *Pedn-an-Laaz – Ny Dall Dhymmoy*

Glasgow Film and Video Workshop
35 Avenuepark Street
Glasgow
G20 8TS
Tel: 041 946 3008
Joan Johnston
Aimara Reques
Tom Gerhardt
GFVW is a training/ access resource for film and video makers in Scotland. We offer equipment hire at subsidised rates; training in all aspects of VHS, lo-band U-Matic, Super 8 and 16mm production; advice and support. We run production and community based projects and distribute and promote the exhibition of films and videos made through the workshop. Relocating January 1994

Y Gweithdy Fideo/ The Video Workshop*
Chapter Arts Centre
Market Road
Canton
Cardiff
CF5 1QE
Tel: 0222 342755
Fax: 0222 644479
Diana Bianchi
Terry Dimmick
Emyr Jenkins
Film/video production, distribution and exhibition in English and Welsh, plus broadcast programmes. Offers production facilities to others. Working with community and arts organisations and trades unions on social, political and cultural issues

HAFAD 1st Chance Project
(Hammersmith & Fulham Action for Disability)
Beaufort House
Lillie Road
London SW6
Tel: 071 603 7481
Heather Davis
Reg McLaughlin
Basic training in video mainly aimed at people with disabilities. VHS and SVHS cameras and wheelchair-accessible edit suite for hire. Remote control adaption for camera – can be operated by manual joystick or footplate

The Half Way Production House
Units 1 & 2 Taylors Yard
67 Alderbrook Road
London
SW12 8AD
Tel: 081 673 7926
Fax: 081 675 7612
Georgina Hart
Emma Stewart
Funded by Europe, grants from the DOE and various national charities, HWPH runs training programmes in 16mm film production lasting 4 months, for unemployed people aged 16-25 wanting to work in the media industries or apply to film school. During the programme trainees make a short live action film. Work placements are offered to ex-trainees on HWPH professional productions.

Offers 16mm equipment for hire at subsidised rates including two fully equipped cutting rooms, sound transfer, studio

Hall Place Studios

4 Hall Place
Leeds
LS9 8JD
Tel: 0532 405553
Jacqui Maurice
Ali Hussein
Anna Zaluczkowska
Facility and training centre offering film/video/ sound production facilities on site and for hire on sliding scale. Also offers programme of training and events, some for women or black peoples only, membership scheme, community video development programme, and in-service training for youth/community workers

Hull Community Artworks

Northumberland Avenue
Hull
HU2 0LN
Tel: 0482 226420
Tony Hales
Film/video production, distribution and exhibition. Offers production and exhibition facilities to others. Holds regular training workshops

Hull Time Based Arts

8 Posterngate
Hull
HU1 2JN
Tel: 0482 216446
Fax: 0482 218103
Mike Stubbs
Film/video production, exhibition and education. Also promotes, produces and commissions experimental film, video, performance and music. Equipment for hire includes video projector, U-Matic production facilities and desk-top editing facilities

Intermedia Film and Video

19 Heathcoat Street
Hockley
Nottingham
NG1 3AF
Tel/Fax: 0602 505434
Malcolm Leick
Graham Forde
Leiza McLeod
Offers training, facilities, production, information and advice. Training based on established short course programme in 16mm film, video and related areas together with industry re-training

Ipswich Media Project

202 Brunswick Road
Ipswich
Suffolk
IP4 4DB
Tel: 0473 250685
Darryl Tester
Super 8 film, VHS, SVHS equipment. Familiarisation training and media work. Group archive being developed

Island Arts

The Tiller Centre
Tiller Road
Millwall
London
E14 8PX
Tel: 071 987 7925
Fax: 071 538 3314
Peter Ellis
Claire Manwani
Herbert Musisi
Equipment and edit suite hire for individuals and groups. Courses throughout the year, production and workshop facilities

Jackdaw Media Educational Trust

96a Duke Street
Liverpool
L1 5AG
Tel: 051 709 5858
Fax: 051 709 0759
Laura Knight
Strinda Davies
Yvonne Eckersley
Nick Cox
The national animation resource based in the North West. Hands-on animation sessions available for schools, colleges, community groups, galleries and museums. Adaptable for all ages, abilities and needs. TV and other commercial production work accepted. EOS video animation system, 16mm rostrum camera and 6 plate Steenbeck available for hire

Jubilee Arts

84 High Street
West Bromwich
West Midlands
B70 6JW
Tel: 021 553 6862
Fax: 021 525 0640
Sarah Jennings
Sylvia King
Bev Harvey
Multi-media arts development based in the West Midlands, using video, sound, photography, computer technology. Working in partnership with voluntary and statutory bodies in the public sector

Lambeth Video

Unit F7
245a Coldharbour Lane
London
SW9 8RR
Tel: 071 737 5903
Paola Eliahoo
Lambeth Video is a part-funded workshop. Runs production-based training and hires out equipment (hi-band production kit, 3-machine editing). Runs South London Documentary Project which is open to women and black applicants. Offers production bursaries to four new directors each year and traineeships on large-scale productions. Write or telephone for application forms

Latin American Independent Film & Video Association (LAIFA)

Latin American House
Kingsgate Place
London
NW6 4TA
Tel: 071 372 6442
Georgina Ochoa
Joachim Bergamin
Offers Super 16mm film editing facilities. VHS off-line. 16mm shooting equipment (Arri BL, Nagra 4.2). Workshops and exhibitions

Leeds Animation Workshop*

45 Bayswater Row
Leeds
LS8 5LF
Tel: 0532 484997
Jane Bradshaw
A women's collective producing and distributing animated films on social issues. Offers production, distribution and training. Productions include: *Risky Business, Give Us a Smile, Crops and Robbers, Out to Lunch, A Matter of Interest* and *Alice in Wasteland*. Free catalogue available on request

Lighthouse Film & Video

Brighton Media Production Centre
11 Jew Street
Brighton
BN1 1UT
Tel: 0273 202044
Fax: 0273 748833
Jane Finnis
Caroline Freeman
A training and resource centre providing courses, facilities, exhibition and production services to the south-east. Hi 8, U-Matic and 16mm production and post production facilities; multimedia Apple Mac Quadra 950 graphics and animation workstations; production desks and facilities for independent producers

Line Out

138 Charles Street
Leicester
LE1 1VA
Tel: 0533 621265
Kofi Boafoj
Professional and small format video facilities specialising in Super 8 film, all available for hire. Also running short courses, workshops and media education programmes. A membership organisation providing advice, information and lobbying

London Deaf Access Project

25 Cockspur Street
London
SW1Y 5BN
Tel: 071 839 6917
071 839 6926 (minicom)
Fax: 071 839 6915
Coordinator: Lesley McGilp
Translates information from English into British Sign Language (BSL) for Britain's deaf community, encourages others to do likewise and provides a consultancy/monitoring service for this purpose.

Promotes the use of video amongst deaf people as an ideal medium for passing on information. Runs workshops and courses for deaf people in video production, taught by deaf people using BSL. Is developing a national deaf video resource centre. Offers hire to deaf people of lo-band U-Matic, VHS and SVHS equipment, including use of SVHS edit suite. Interested to liaise with any other video projects who feel they should use BSL to make their own material accessible to deaf people. Titles include: *School Leavers, Access to Women's Services, Powerful Stuff*

London Fields Film and Video

10 Martello Street
London
E8 3PE
Tel: 071 241 2997
Sophie Outram
James Swinson
Prue Waller
Film and video production and distribution. Also provide production facilities and support for others

London Film Makers' Co-op

42 Gloucester Avenue
London NW1
Tel: 071 722 1728
Administration & Distribution 071 586 4806
Cinema 071 586 8516
Courses 071 722 1728
Fax: 071 483 0068
Film workshop, distribution library and cinema enables filmmakers to control the production, distribution and exhibition of their films. Workshop runs regular practical and theoretical film courses. Distribution has 2,000 experimental films for hire, from 20s to current work. Cinema screenings twice weekly. Work with cultural aesthetic/political aims which differ from the industry

London Media Workshops

Administrative Office
101 King's Drive
Gravesend
Kent
DA12 5BQ
Tel: 0474 564676
Linda Forbes
Jocelyn Hay
Training agency specialising in short intensive courses in writing for radio, television, video and press, and in directing and producing television and video programmes. Regular one and two day courses in London, specially tailored in-house courses by commission. Mail order booklist. Top working tutors. Small numbers allow individual attention

London Screenwriters Workshop

84 Wardour Street
London
W1V 3LF
Tel: 071 434 0942/081 551 5570
Fax: 081 550 7537
Ray Frensham
Paul Gallagher
Screenwriting workshops range from discussion of short TV scripts and film treatments to the development of full-length screenplays and analysis of deep structure. A range of seminars bring screenwriters together with producers, agents, development executives and other film and television professionals

London Video Access (LVA)

3rd Floor
5-7 Buck Street
London
NW1 8NJ
Tel: 071 284 4323
Fax: 071 267 6078
Michael Maziere
Clive Robertson
LVA is Britain's national centre for video and new media art. Offers a complete range of services including production based training, facility hire (production and post-production), distribution and exhibition of video and new media art and film

London Women's Centre

Wesley House
4 Wild Court
London
WC2B 5AU
Tel: 071 831 6946
A women's resource providing facilities for women and women's organisations to hire with a sliding scale of charges. Facilities include lo-band U-Matic video filming and editing equipment and 16mm, lo-band and VHS playback facilities including screening space. All equipment for use on the premises only. Rooms available for hire range from the 'Theatre Space' with a PA and lighting rig (capacity 150), to a variety of seminar/ meeting rooms. The centre houses a cafe and sports facilities

Media Arts

Town Hall Studios
Regent Circus
Swindon
SN1 1QF
Tel: 0793 493451
Fax: 0793 490420
Carol Comley
Steve Chapman
Emma Valentine
Production, distribution, exhibition and training. Well-equipped studios in film, video, photography and sound. Small media library, viewing facilities, media events, archive. Productions include *Plant the Town Green, Today is a Good Day, When I Was a Girl, The Weaver's Wife, Groping in the Dark* and *Birth of the Age of Woman*

The Media Workshop

Peterborough Arts Centre
Media Department
Orton Goldhay
Peterborough
PE2 0JQ
Tel: 0733 237073
Clifton Stewart
Video and photography productions, workshops and exhibitions. Offers U-Matic and VHS production/edit facilities including 3 machine SVHS editing and filming equipment, dark room, gallery and studio space suitable for film performances. Committed to equal access for all sections of the community

Mersey Film & Video

Bluecoat Chambers
School Lane
Liverpool
L1 3BX
Tel: 051 708 5259
Fax: 051 707 0048
Production facilities for lo-band/Hi 8, lights, mics etc. Post production for lo band/VHS/Hi 8. Amiga 2000, genlock, digitiser. Workshops and training courses

Migrant Media

90 De Beauvoir Road
London
N1 4EN
Tel: 071 254 9701
Fax: 071 254 7541
Ken Fero
Nasser Bakhti
Filiz Aziz
Media production and training centre for migrants and refugeees. Main work focuses on Middle East communities. Networks with similar organisations in other European and Arab countries. Broadcast credits include: *Germany – The Other Story* (FR3), *After the Storm* (BBC), *Sweet France* (C4). In development: *Iraq – Silence and Resistance* (C4)

Moving Image Touring Exhibition Service (MITES)

Moviola
Bluecoat Chambers
Liverpool
L1 3BX
Tel: 051 709 2663
Fax: 051 707 2150
Eddie Berg
Courses for gallery curators, technicians and exhibitors conerned with the commissioning and presentation of moving image art works. Also development, advice, consultation services and an extensive exhibition equipment resource

Network

Prominent Studios
68a Delancey Street
London
NW1 7RY

Tel: 071 272 5192
Fax: 071 284 1020
Bob Doyle
The facilities of Prominent Studios, including all that is required for 35mm, 16mm or video production, are made available to members of the Network for their own projects. New members must either do a course at Prominent, or have had previous experience

Northern Visions*

4-8 Donegall Street Place
Belfast
BT1 2FN
Tel: 0232 245495
Fax: 0232 326608
Marilyn Hyndman
Co-operative providing video production, distribution and exhibition. Hi/lo-band recording, Betacam recording, computerised hi-band edit (3 machines) with digital effects, 16 track sound recording and small studio. Commercial work undertaken. Training sessions. Special rates for community and campaign groups. Productions include 1990 *Schizophrenic City*, *The Write Off*, 1991 *Travelling People*, 1992 *Between Ourselves, Songs, Satire and Some Sense,* 1993 *Unfinished Business*

The Old Dairy Studios

156b Haxby Road
York
YO3 7JN
Tel: 0904 641394
Rob Parker
Video production, distribution, 16-track recording studio with DAT, cassette duplication, darkroom equipped for disabled access. Courses in video production and editing, sound recording, radio journalism and production, music, rhythm, creative writing and photography

Oxford Film and Video Makers

The Stables
North Place
Headington
Oxford
OX3 9HY
Tel: 0865 741682
Fax: 0865 742901
We offer specialised courses to meet the particular needs of various groups, open access courses covering the entire production process in film and video, equipment hire, distribution and exhibition, and productions which give voice to people normally denied one, such as *A Very English Lesson*, *Take a Second Look*, *Futures on the Line* and *Journeys*

Oxford Independent Video

Pegasus Theatre
Magdalen Road
Oxford
OX4 1RE
Tel: 0865 250150
Maddie Shepherd
Specialist arts education producer, distributor and trainer. OIV works in collaboration with innovative artists and performers from across the world, carefully selecting and commissioning a broad range of high quality work. OIV tapes are distributed across the UK, Europe and internationally

Paxvision

The Albany
Douglas Way
London
SE8 4AG
Tel: 081 692 6322
Fax: 081 692 6322
Video project providing services, video facilities and training (beginners to advanced) mainly targeted at the local community, independent video and film makers and disadvantaged groups or individuals. Also collaborate with local community groups and artists in video production; undertake commissions on production and music scoring. Facilities include Betacam SP and SVHS production equipment, VHS edit suite and SVHS edit suite with Amiga 2000 computer, graphics and titling. All services available at community and commercial rates

Picture This Independent Film & Video

Kingsland House
Gas Lane
St Philips
Bristol
BS2 0QW
Tel: 0272 721002
Fax: 0272 721750
Shafeeq Vellani
Lulu Quinn
Lisa Drake
Film and video production and training workshop. Specialise in arts/social documentary and artists' film and video, includint time based media installations. Offer short courses and longer term training projects. Have Super 8mm, 16mm film and VHS, hi-band U-Matic production and post-production equipment for hire. Recent work includes *Darwish*, *Loot*, *Paper House*, *Out of the Cinema* and *Something not very concrete* (installation with Indigo Alliance)

Pimlico Arts & Media Centre

St James the Less
Moreton Street
London
SW1 2PT
Tel: 071 976 6133
Fax: 071 630 9517
Gail Knight
Juliet Mayne
Runs courses for unemployed people in video, photography and graphic design to give them a grounding in preparation for employment. In addition weekend and evening workshops, talks and facility hire are available to the public

Platform Films

13 Tankerton House
Tankerton Street
London
WC1H 8HP
Tel: 071 278 8394
Chris Reeves
Film/video production and distribution. Also Panasonic VHS Hi-Fi sound VHS edit suite available for dry hire. Special rates for non-commercial and student productions

Plymouth Arts Centre

38 Looe Street
Plymouth
PL4 0EB
Tel: 0752 660060

Real Time Video

Huntley & Palmer Building
2 Gas Works Road
Reading
RG1 3HR
Tel: 0734 585627
Jackie Shaw
Process-based community access video workshop. Video production, training and exhibition. Runs courses and workshops, organises screenings and projects and offers consultancy on community video

Red Flannel Films*

Maritime Offices
Woodland Terrace
Maesycoed
Pontypridd
Mid Glamorgan
Tel: 0443 401743/480564
Fax: 0443 485667
Red Flannel is a women's collective working on film and video production, distribution, exhibition, education, training, archive and video library. Productions for hire and purchase are *Mam* (16mm and video), *If We Were Asked* (video), *Special Delivery* (16mm and video), *Otherwise Engaged* and *Women Have No Country*. Facilities for hire include SVHS, VHS and 16mm editing, VHS and SVHS production equipment

Retake Film and Video Collective

19 Liddell Road
London
NW6 2EW
Tel: 071 328 4676
Fax: 071 372 1231
Film/video production, distribution and training. Facilities hire: 2 machine U-Matic suite, 16mm cutting room. Productions include two feature dramas, *Majdhar* and *Hotel London* and documentaries *Living in*

Danger, Environment of Dignity, Who Will Cast the First Stone?, Sanctuary Challenge and *Hidden Worlds*. Hire of 16mm/lo-band U-Matic editing

SHIFT (Sheffield Independent Film and Television)
5 Brown Street
Sheffield
S1 2BS
Tel: 0742 720304
Fax: 0742 795225
Ruth Schofield
Registered charity established by Sheffield Independent Film (qv) to provide access to and facilitate training in film and video for disadvantaged groups and individuals. SHIFT runs short 3-5 day courses for community groups and longer 3-month ESF funded courses for the long-term unemployed. Video production skills on the ESF courses are underpinned with business training skills and experience to assist people wishing to set up their own businesses

Sankofa Film and Video
Unit K
32-34 Gordon House Road
London
NW5 1LP
Tel: 071 485 0848
Fax: 071 485 2869
Maureen Blackwood
Robert Crusz
Nadine Marsh-Edwards
Film/video production and distribution. Offers production facilities to others, organises screenings and discussions. Productions include *The Passion of Remembrance, Perfect Image, Dreaming Rivers, Looking for Langston, Young Soul Rebels, Inbetween, A Family Called Abrew*

Second Sight
Zair Works
111 Bishop Street
Birmingham
B5 6JL
Tel: 021 622 4223 (productions)
021 622 5750 (training)
Fax: 021 622 1554 (fao Second Sight)
Glynis Powell
Anne Cullis
Video production company specialising in arts, social issues and training programmes. Showreel and tapelist available on request. Runs practical training courses for women from beginners to hi-band production. Provides an information resource on all aspects of AV media. Gives consultancies on training programme construction and production within socially sensitive arenas

Sheffield Film Co-op*
Brown Street
Sheffield
S1 2BS
Tel: 0742 727170
Chrissie Stansfield
Women's film and video production workshop reflecting women's views on a wide range of issues. Distribute work on film/tape including *Changing Our Lives, Women of Steel, Let Our Children Grow Tall!, Bringing It All Back Home, Diamonds in Brown Paper, Thank You, That's All I Knew* and *Running Gay*

Sheffield Independent Film
5 Brown Street
Sheffield
S1 2BS
Tel: 0742 720304
Fax: 0742 795225
Colin Pons
A resource base for independent film and videomakers in the Sheffield region. Regular training workshops; access to a range of film and video equipment; technical and administrative backup; and regular screenings of independent film and video

Signals, Essex Media Centre
21 St Peters Street
Colchester

CO1 1EW
Tel: 0206 560255
Caroline Norbury
Film/video resource for community. U-Matic, SVHS and VHS production and post-production, Super 8 and 16mm film. Services in training, media education, equipment hire and production

Siren Film and Video Co-op

6 Harris Street
Middlesbrough
Cleveland
TS1 5EF
Tel: 0642 221298
Dave Eadington
Wendy McEvoy
Film/video production, distribution and exhibition. Offers production facilities to others. Workers' co-operative producing both drama and documentary

Star Productions/ Studios

1 Cornthwaite Road
London
E5 0RS
Tel: 081 986 4470/5766
Fax: 081 533 6597
Raj Patel
Film/video production company working from an Asian perspective. Multi-lingual productions. Offers studio for hire, video editing suite, 16mm cutting room. Production and exhibition facilities. Output includes community documentaries, video films of stage plays, feature films and corporate videos on health issues

Steel Bank Film Co-op*

Brown Street
Sheffield
S1 2BS
Tel: 0742 721235
Fax: 0742 795225
Jessica York
Simon Reynell
Dinah Ward
Noemie Mendelle
Film/video production and distribution. Work includes documentaries, art programmes, campaign tapes and fiction films. Productions include *Winnie*, *Security*, *Clocks of the Midnight Hours*, *Great Noises that Fill the Air*, *For Your Own Good*, *Spinster*, *Crimestrike* and *Custom-Eyes*

Swingbridge Video

Norden House
41 Stowell Street
Newcastle upon Tyne
NE1 4YB
Tel: 091 232 3762
Hugh Kelly
Sarah McCarthy
A community video project making productions for broadcast and non-broadcast distribution, with and on behalf of community and campaign groups in the North East. Film and video production and distribution. Productions include: *Singing the Blues*, *Where Shall We Go?*, *An English Estate*, *Happy Hours*, *White Lies* and many others

33 Video

Luton Community Arts Trust
33-35 Guildford Street
Luton
Beds
LU1 2NQ
Tel: 0582 419584
Fax: 0582 459401
Dermot Byrne
Production and training

TURC Video see Birmingham Centre for Media Arts

Trade Films*

36 Bottle Bank
Gateshead
Tyne and Wear
NE8 2AR
Tel: 091 477 5532
Fax: 091 478 3681
Derek Stubbs
Liz Wild
Film, TV and video production and distribution – fiction, documentary and factual programmes. Hi-band U-Matic and 16mm post-production facilities available. Recent productions include *Border Crossing* (128 min drama for Channel Four, ZDF and Tyne Tees Television), *The Trap* (60 min documentary for Channel Four), *Health & Safety: The European Challenge* (four videotapes for the European Commission)

Trilith Video

Corner Cottage
Brickyard Lane
Bourton
Gillingham
Dorset
SP8 5PJ
Tel: 0747 840750/840727
Trevor Bailey
John Holman
Sue Holman
Specialises in rural video on community action, rural issues and the outlook and experience of country-born people. Produces own series of tapes, undertakes broadcast and tape commissions and gathers archive film in order to make it publicly available on video. Distributes own work nationally. Recent work includes TSW feature

Valley and Vale Community Arts

Blaengarw Workmen's Hall
Blaengarw Road
Blaengarw
Mid Glamorgan
GF32 8AW
Tel: 0656 871911
Fax: 0656 870507
The Holm View Centre
Skomer Road
Gibbonsdown
Barry
South Glamorgan
Tel: 0446 742289
Alex Bowen
Video production, distribution and exhibition. Open-access workshop offering training to community groups in VHS, lo-band U-Matic and hi-8 formats

Vera Productions

30-38 Dock Street
Leeds
LS10 1JF
Tel: 0532 428646
Fax: 0532 451238
Alison Garthwaite
Catherine Mitchell
Film/video production (broadcast/non-broadcast), training, exhibition and distribution. Teach women and mixed groups. Speak on representation of women in film and TV. Information resource and networking newsletter

Video Access Centre

29 Albany Street
Edinburgh
EH1 3QN
Tel: 031 557 8211
Stephen Flitton
Oscar Van Heek
A membership-based association which provides resources and training for individuals and community groups to work with video. Courses are short and at basic or specialist level. Has VHS production facilities, runs monthly newsletter and information service. In 1991-2 'enabled' 135 videos to be made, some of which were broadcast as part of 'First Reels' (two films off-lined and four on-lined at VAC)

Video in Pilton

30 Ferry Road Avenue
Edinburgh
EH4 4BA
Tel: 031 343 1151
Fax: 031 343 2820
Hugh Farrell
Joel Venet
Lorna Simpson
Training and production facilities in the local community; documentary and fiction for broadcast. Contact address for UK Network of Workshops (see Organisations)

WAVES (Women's Audio Visual Education Scheme)

London Women's Centre
Wesley House
4 Wild Court
London
WC2B 5AU
Tel: 071 430 1076
Project launched March 1991, designed to offer training for women in the area of audio and visual media culture. The overall aim is to promote the ability of women to both enter the industry and make their own work. It is planned to offer training through inter-related modular courses and to create links with existing educational providers. The educational and training

programme will also attempt to redress the inequalities of opportunity faced by specific groups of women, as well as ensuring that all courses are as accessible as possible, culturally and physically

WFA
Media and Cultural Centre
9 Lucy Street
Manchester
M15 4BX
Tel: 061 848 9785
Fax: 061 848 9783
Mark Johnson
Main areas of work include media access and training, including City and Guilds 770 National Certificate, with a full range of production, post-production and exhibition equipment and facilities for community, semi-professional and profess-ional standards. Video production unit (BECTU). Distribution and sale of 16mm films and videos, booking and advice service, video access library. Cultural work, mixed media events. Bookshop/outreach work

Welfare State International
The Ellers
Ulverston
Cumbria
LA12 0AA
Tel: 0229 581127
Fax: 0229 581232
David Haley
A consortium of artists, musicians, technicians and performers. Film/video production, distribution and exhibition. Output includes community feature films and work for television. Titles include: *Piranha Pond* (Border TV) – RTS Special Creativity Award; *Ulverston Town Map* (community video); *Community Celebration* – Multinational Course leading to Lantern Procession (video); *Lord Dynamite* (video of LIFT performance)

Western Eye Television
Easton Business Centre
Felix Road
Bristol
BS5 0HE
Tel: 0272 415854
Fax: 0272 415899
Steve Spencer
Jayne Cotton
Adrian Mack
Video production for business and voluntary sector. Health and technology specialists. Also produce sell-through programmes, eg *The Complete Teach Yourself Juggling Kit*

Wide Angle Video, Film, Photography
see ***Birmingham Centre for Media Arts***

Women's Media Resource Project
89a Kingsland High Street
London
E8 2PB
Tel: 071 254 6536
Training/workshops. Offers accredited training – City and Guilds in Sound Engineering. Workshops/summer schools in Sound Engineering, Sound for Video, Sound Technol-ogies. Hire of equipment and studio, send SAE for leaflet. Recording/video packages for theatre, dance, artists, bands

Wrexham Community Video
The Place in the Park
Bellevue Road
Wrexham
Clwyd
LL13 7NH
Tel: 0978 358522
Darryl Corner
Video production and distribution. Short courses in video and sound production as well as subsidised facilities hire to qualifying groups. WCV welcomes the participation, support and creative involvement of everyone looking to work in video in a community context

bfi – Groups receiving financial support from BFI Production Projects in the form of workshop or production funding between April 1992 and March 1993

LIST OF ABBREVIATIONS

ABC Association of Business Communicators
ABSA Association of Business Sponsorship of the Arts
ACE Ateliers du Cinéma Européen
ACGB Arts Council of Great Britain
AETC Arts and Entertainment Training Council
AFC Australian Film Commission
AFCI Association of Film Commissioners International
AFI American Film Institute/Australian Film Institute
AFRS Advertising Film Rights Society
AFVPA Advertising Film and Videotape Producers' Association
AGICOA Association de Gestion Internationale Collective des Oeuvres Audiovisuelles
AIC Association of Independent Cinemas
AID Alliance Internationale de la Distribution par câble
AME Association for Media Education
AMFIT Association for Media Film and Television Studies in Higher and Further Education
AMPAS Academy of Motion Picture Arts and Sciences (USA)
AMPS Association of Motion Picture Sound
APC Association of Professional Composers
BABA British Advertising Broadcast Awards
BABEL Broadcasting Across the Barriers of European Language
BAFTA British Academy of Film and Television Arts
BARB Broadcasters' Audience Research Board
BASCA British Academy of Songwriters, Composers and Authors
BATC British Amateur Television Club
BBC British Broadcasting Corporation
BBFC British Board of Film Classification
BCC Broadcasting Complaints Commission
BCS British Cable Services
BECTU Broadcasting Entertainment Cinematograph and Theatre Union
BFFS British Federation of Film Societies
BFI British Film Institute
BIEM Bureau Internationale des Sociétés gérant les Droits d'Enregistrement
BIPP British Institute of Professional Photography
BKSTS British Kinematograph Sound and Television Society
BNFVC British National Film and Video Catalogue
BPI British Phonographic Industry
BREMA British Radio and Electronic Equipment Manufacturers' Association
BSAC British Screen Advisory Council
BSC Broadcasting Standards Council
BSD British Screen Development
BSkyB British Sky Broadcasting
BUFVC British Universities Film and Video Council
BVA British Videogram Association
CAA Cinema Advertising Association
CAVIAR Cinema and Video Industry Audience Research
CD Compact Disc
CDI Compact Disc Interactive
CD-Rom Compact Disc – Read Only Memory
CEA Cinematograph Exhibitors' Association of Great Britain and Ireland
CEPI Co-ordination Européenne des Producteurs Indépendantes
CFTF Children's Film and Television Foundation
CFU Children's Film Unit
C4 Channel Four
CICCE Comité des Industries Cinématographiques et Audiovisuelles des Communautés Européennes et de l'Europe Extracommunautaire
CILECT Centre Internationale de Liaison des Ecoles de Cinéma et de Télévision
CNN Cable News Network
COI Central Office of Information
COMEX Consortium of Media Exhibitors
CPBF Campaign for Press and Broadcasting Freedom
CTA Cinema Theatre Association
CTBF Cinema and Television Benevolent Fund
DADA Designers and Art Directors' Association
DBC Deaf Broadcasting Council
DBS Direct Broadcasting by Satellite
DFE Department for Education
DGGB Directors' Guild of Great Britain
DNH Department of National Heritage
DTI Department of Trade and Industry
DVI Digital Video Interactive
EATC European Alliance for Television and Culture
EAVE European Audiovisual Entrepreneurs
EBU European Broadcasting Union
ECF European Co-production Fund
EEC European Economic Community
EETPU Electrical, Electronic, Telecommunications and Plumbing Union
EFA European Film Academy
EFCOM European Film Commissioners
EFDO European Film Distribution Office
EGAKU European Committee of Trade Unions in Arts, Mass Media and Entertainment
EIFF Edinburgh International Film Festival
EIM European Institute for the Media
EITF Edinburgh International Television Festival
EURO AIM European Organisation for Audiovisual Production
EUTELSAT European Telecommunications Satellite Organisation
EVE Espace Vidéo Européen

LIST OF ABBREVIATIONS

FAA Film Artistes' Association
FACT Federation Against Copyright Theft
FBU Federation of Broadcasting Unions
FEITIS Fédération Européenne des Industries Techniques de l'Image et du Son
FEMIS Institut de Formation et d'Enseignement pour les Métiers de l'Image et du Son
FEPACI Fédération Pan-Africain des Cinéastes
FESPACO Festivale Pan-Africain des Cinémas de Ouagadougou
FEU Federation of Entertainment Unions
FIA International Federation of Actors
FIAD Fédération Internationale des Associations de Distributeurs de Films
FIAF Fédération Internationale des Archives du Film
FIAPF International Federation of Film Producers Associations
FIAT Fédération Internationale des Archives de Télévision
FICC Fédération Internationale des Ciné-Clubs
FIPFI Fédération Internationale des Producteurs de Films Indépendants
FOCAL Federation of Commercial Audio-Visual Libraries
FSU Film Society Unit
FTVLCA Film and Television Lighting Contractors Association
FX Effects/special effects
GRECO Groupement Européen pour la Circulation des Oeuvres
HBO Home Box Office
HDTV High Definition Television
HTV Harlech Television
HVC Home Video Channel
IABM International Association of Broadcasting Manufacturers
IAC Institute of Amateur Cinematographers
ICA Institute of Contemporary Arts
IFDA Independent Film Distributors' Association
IFFS International Federation of Film Societies (aka FICC)
IFPI International Federation of Producers of Phonograms and Videograms
IFTA International Federation of Television Archives (aka FIAT)
IIC International Institute of Communications
ILR Independent Local Radio
INR Independent National Radio
IPA Institute of Practitioners in Advertising
ISBA Incorporated Society of British Advertising
ISM Incorporated Society of Musicians
ITC Independent Television Commission
ITN Independent Television News
ITSC International Television Studies Conference
ITV Independent Television
ITVA Independent Television Association
IVCA International Visual Communications Association
IVLA International Visual Literacy Association
LAB London Arts Board
LAIFA Latin American Independent Film/Video Association
LFF London Film Festival
LFMC London Film Makers' Co-op
LSW London Screen-writers' Workshop
LVA London Video Access
LWT London Weekend Television
MAP-TV Memories–Archives–Programmes TV
MBS Media Business School
MCPS Mechanical Copyright Protection Society
MEDIA Measures to Encourage the Development of the Industry of Audiovisual Production
MFB Monthly Film Bulletin
MFVPA Music, Film and Video Producers Association
MGM Metro Goldwyn Mayer
MHMC Mental Health Media Council
MIDEM Marché International du Disque et de l'Edition Musicale
MIFED Mercato Internazionale del TV, Film e del Documentario
MIPCOM Marché International des Films et des Programmes pour la TV, la Vidéo, le Câble et le Satellite
MIP-TV Marché International de Programmes de Télévision
MOMI Museum of the Moving Image
MPAA Motion Picture Association of America
MPEAA Motion Picture Export Association of America
MU Musicians' Union
NAHEFV National Association for Higher Education in Film and Video
NATPE National Association of Television Programme Executives (now formally NATPE International)
NAVAL National Audio Visual Aids Library
NCET National Council for Educational Technology
NCVQ National Council for Vocational Qualifications
NFDF National Film Development Fund
NFT National Film Theatre
NFTC National Film Trustee Company
NFTS National Film and Television School
NFTVA National Film and Television Archive
NHMF National Heritage Memorial Fund
NIFC Northern Ireland Film Council
NPA New Producers Alliance
NoW Network of Workshops
NSC Northern Screen Commission
NTSC National Television Standards Committee
NUJ National Union of Journalists
NUT National Union of Teachers
NVALA National Viewers' and Listeners' Association
PACT Producers Alliance for Cinema and Television
PAL Programmable Array Logic/Phase Alternation Line
PRS Performing Right Society
RAB Regional Arts Board
RETRA Radio, Electrical and Television Retailers' Association
RFT Regional Film Theatre
RTS Royal Television Society
S&S Sight and Sound
SCALE Small Countries Improve their Audio-visual Level in Europe
SCET Scottish Council for Educational Technology
SCFVL Scottish Central Film and Video Library
SCTE Society of Cable Television Engineers
SECAM Séquentiel couleur à mémoire
SFC Scottish Film Council
SFD Society of Film Distributors
SFX Special Effects
S4C Sianel Pedwar Cymru
SIFT Summary of Information on Film and Television
SMATV Satellite Master Antenna Television
TVRO Television receive-only
UA United Artists
UIP United International Pictures
UNESCO United Nations Educational, Scientific and Cultural Organisation
URTI Université Radiophonique et Télévisuelle Internationale
VCPS Video Copyright Protection Society
VCR Video Cassette Recorder
VHS Video Home System
VLV Voice of the Listener and Viewer
WGGB Writers' Guild of Great Britain
WTN Worldwide Television News
WTVA Wider Television Access
YTV Yorkshire Television

INDEX

C

N

O

P

Q

R

S

T

U

V

W

Y

Z

INDEX OF ADVERTISERS